PSYCHOLOGY

ITS PRINCIPLES AND APPLICATIONS

HARCOURT, BRACE & WORLD, INC.

New York
Chicago
San Francisco
Atlanta
Dallas

T. L. ENGLE

Indiana University–Fort Wayne

LOUIS SNELLGROVE

Lambuth College

PSYCHOLOGY

ITS PRINCIPLES AND APPLICATIONS

FIFTH EDITION

CREDITS

Charts and Graphs: p. 167, from *Readings for an Introduction to Psychology* ed. by Richard A. King. Copyright © 1966 by McGraw-Hill Book Company. Used by permission of McGraw-Hill Book Company; p. 179, redrawn from Fig. 1, "Emotional Development in Early Infancy" by Kathrine M. B. Bridges from *Child Development*, p. 340. Copyright 1932 by The Society for Research in Child Development, Inc.; p. 181, redrawn from Fig. 48, p. 273, based on Sidney Pressy's unpublished data, *The Psychology of Adolescent Development* by Raymond G. Kuhlen (Harper & Row, 1952); p. 190, redrawn from Fig. 1, p. 31, of *The Measurement and Appraisal of Adult Intelligence*, 4th ed. by David Wechsler, Williams & Wilkins, 1958; p. 191, from K. W. Schaie, "Rigidity-Flexibility and Intelligence: A Cross-Sectional Study of the Adult Life Span from 20–70," *Psycho. Monos.*, Vol. 72, No. 9, Whole No. 462. Copyright © 1958 by the American Psychological Association, and reproduced by permission.

Picture Credits: (KEY: t—top; b—bottom; l—left; r—right. B—Bettmann Archive; BS—Black Star; MG—Magnum Photos, Inc.; M—Monkmeyer Press Photo Service; PR—Photo Researchers, Inc.; RG—Rapho-Guillumette; WW—Wide World.) Unit I: p. xii (1) Edmund B. Gerard, *Life* ©, (r) *The New York Times;* 1, Ken Heyman; 4, Rogers, M; 6, Cornell University; 10, Harbrace; 12 (t) Schreiber, RG, (b) Esther Bubley; 13 (tl) Martin Iger for Neil Miller, (tr) M, (b) NASA; 22 (l) Edmund Engleman, (r) B; 27, WW; 31, Harbrace; 35 (tl) Eric Hosking, PR, (bl) Constance P. Warner, (r) William A. Garnett; 37, Harbrace. Unit II: p. 40 (l) Three Lions, (r) Susan McCartney, PR; 41, Esther Bubley; 43, Suzanne Szasz, PR; 45, Radio Times Hulton Picture Library; 51, Harbrace; 58, Yerkes Laboratory of Primate Biology; 62, courtesy Grolier, Inc; 63, courtesy Leigh Weiner, IBM; 66–67, Hess, Three Lions; 73, Army News Feature; 79 (t) Ken Heyman, (m) Jules Zalon, DPI, (b) Harbrace; 86, Rene Burri, MG; 97, Harbrace; 106, Wayne Miller, MG; 109, UPI; 114 (t) Sanforth Roth, RG, (b) David Hurn, MG; 115 (tl) UPI, (tr) Martha Swope, (b) Ernst Haas, MG; 118, Harbrace; 120, Harbrace; 124, De Wys. Unit III: pp. 134–35, Wayne Miller, MG; 139 (t) George Rodger, MG, (m) George Zimbel, M, (b) De Wys; 151, Harbrace; 154, Christa Armstrong, RG; 156, David Linton; 161, Harbrace; 169, Edmund B. Gerard, *Life* ©; 174 (l) Arline Strong, (r) Ken Heyman; 175 (l) Arline Strong, (r) Ken Heyman; 183, John Rees, BS; 184, Ken Heyman; 185, Hugh Rogers, M; 196, Robert Capa, MG; 196–97, Zimbel, M; 197 (tl) Friedman Abels, (r) Cartier-Bresson, MG; 200 Ann Zane Shanks, M; 216, Ursula Mahoney, M; 221, Wayne Miller, MG. Unit IV: 224 (l) Lynn Millar, RG, (r) courtesy Dr. J. H. Tjio; 225, Arnold, MG; 228, courtesy Dr. J. H. Tjio; 236 (l) Inger Abrahamsen, RG, (r) Harbrace; 238, John Launois, © 1967, Curtis Publishing Company; 243 (t) Harbrace, (b) Ruth Sondak, FPG; 244, reprinted with permission from the *Saturday Evening Post*, © 1961, Curtis Publishing Company; 259, NASA; 266, Cartier-Bresson, MG; 268, Howard Friedman, Pix, Inc.; 275, Eric L. Brown; 279, Archie Lieberman, BS; 286, Harbrace, courtesy of Optometric Center of New York; 292, Keystone Viewing Company; 296, Merrim, M; 302, Davis Pratt, RG; 305, DPI; 309, PR; p. 311, William Vandivert, April 1960, with permission from *Scientific American;* 312, Larry Fried, Pix, Inc. Unit V: p. 318 (l) Harbrace, (r) MG; 319, Harbrace; 323, Neil Miller; 324, Harbrace; 327, Ann Zane Shanks; 331, Harbrace; 332, Fred Lyon, RG; 339 (t) courtesy McGraw-Hill Text-Films, (m) Harbrace, (b) Harbrace Archives; 349, courtesy Fred R. Sponhulz, Regional Primate Research Center; 351, Hella Hammid, RG; 353, Wayne Miller, MG; 359, Sybil Shelton, M; 364, Cornell Capa, MG; 369, courtesy *Columbia College Today;* 376, © United Feature Syndicate, Inc., 1955; 378, Hawaii Visitors Bureau; 382, WW; 386, Elizabeth Wilcox; 391, Sybil Shackman, M; 397, Ken Heyman; 401, Harbrace; 409, Jerry Cooke; 413, David Linton; 416, Medical Audio-Visual Department, Walter Reed Army Institute of Research; 424, Guttman-Maclay Collection, The Bethlehem Royal Hospital and Maudsley Hospital, London; 426, Eve Arnold, MG; 434, Ken Heyman; 436, Harbrace Archives. Unit VI: p. 440 (l) Ken Heyman, (r) Harbrace; 441, Susan McCartney; 444, Ken Heyman; 450, Elinore Sarluy; 453, Ken Heyman; 454, Harbrace; 463, Ann Zane Shanks; 465, Esther Bubley; 466, Dennis Stock, MG; 468, Harbrace; 476, B; 478, Ken Heyman; 483, Harbrace, courtesy of Shipcraft Guild; 491, WW; 504, William Vandivert, November 1955, with permission from *Scientific American*. Unit VII: p. 508 (l) Esther Bubley, (r) Schlack, M; 509, Elizabeth Wilcox; 515, Harbrace; 521, Wayne Miller, MG; 528, Jay Maisel; 533, courtesy California Institute for Men; 535, Ken Heyman; 537, Ewing Galloway; 538, Paul Conklin, Pix, Inc., 551, Harbrace; 560 (l) Bruce Roberts, RG, (tr) Linda Moser, DPI; 560–61 (t) Linda Moser, DPI, (b) Robert W. Young, DPI; 561 (tl) courtesy E. I. duPont de Nemours & Co., Inc., (r) George W. Martin, DPI; 565, Shelton, M.

ISBN 0-15-374834-6

About the authors

Dr. T. L. Engle is a professor of psychology at the Fort Wayne regional campus of Indiana University. For more than thirty years he has been widely known for his contributions to high school psychology courses. Dr. Engle has taught psychology at the secondary school level and has instructed high school teachers in methods and other education courses. After earning a Master's Degree in Education from Northwestern University, Dr. Engle received his Ph.D. in Psychology at Indiana University, where he has been teaching since 1938.

Dr. Engle is the co-author of *Points for Decision: A Guide to Help Youth Solve Their Problems* and the author of the *Engle Psychology Test.* Having begun publishing in professional journals while he was teaching at the high school level, he has now had more than fifty articles published in educational and psychological journals, of which about half are in the field of high school psychology.

Dr. Engle has participated in the work of committees of the American Psychological Association for many years. He has served as chairman of the APA's "Committee on High School Psychology" and the "Committee on Psychology in Secondary Schools." In addition, Dr. Engle has read numerous papers on high school psychology at APA and other psychological conventions and meetings.

Dr. Louis Snellgrove is a professor of psychology at Lambuth College (Jackson, Tennessee). Previously he taught psychology and was chairman of the department at Union University. Dr. Snellgrove has long been interested in research in the field of education at the secondary school level. He has taught at the high school level and has been a full-time counselor to high school students. He received an Ed.D. from the University of Alabama in Secondary Education. For the past five years Dr. Snellgrove has systematically collected and disseminated more than 175 projects and activities for the teaching of psychology to over 1500 high schools, and the project is still under way.

In addition to publishing articles on psychology, Dr. Snellgrove is the co-author of a National Science Foundation publication on equipment for experimental psychology in high schools and colleges, and author of the recent book *Psychological Experiments and Demonstrations.* An active member of the American Psychological Association, he is a member of the "Committee on High School Psychology," has been chairman of the APA "Committee on Apparatus Assistance to High Schools and Colleges," and has presented a number of papers on high school psychology at APA conventions.

Foreword

As young people approach adulthood, they become increasingly interested in understanding their own behavior and learning how it relates to the behavior of others. And psychology is the area of study which contributes most directly to understanding such behavior. In psychology, students examine the behavior of human beings and lower animals in an attempt to better understand human behavior.

In addition to understanding the behavior of persons around you — in your family, school, and community, it is important, at a time when most areas of the world may be reached in a matter of hours, to comprehend the behavior of peoples with very diverse traditions and customs. The very survival of man depends upon an understanding of interpersonal relationships on a worldwide basis. Psychology is a science which helps to give the individual such an understanding.

Furthermore, in this age of emphasis on science, the science of psychology is becoming increasingly popular and useful. Other sciences may lay the foundation for projecting man into space, but it is psychology which studies his behavior in the limited confines of a space capsule. It is psychology which will study his behavior under the strange environmental conditions found on the moon and in other frontiers of space.

However, it is not necessary to justify a study of psychology merely in terms of personal and social adjustment, or in terms of practical scientific applications. Curiosity is the cornerstone of knowledge. High school students are curious about many things in their environment, but they are especially curious about human behavior. Such intellectual curiosity is worthy of encouragement for its own sake.

A study of psychology should provide an appreciation of the ways in which the general methods of science can be applied to problems of behavior. At the same time it should make clear that no science, including psychology, has absolute and final answers — that all answers of science are tentative and subject to revision with increased knowledge. As a consequence of his study of psychology, the student will be less likely to accept the sweeping claims and generalizations about behavior that are made by pseudo-scientists. Hopefully, he will learn to recognize that many of the motives he attributes to others are really reflections of his own needs and values. At the same time, he will approach the problems of his own society with increasing objectivity. As the student progresses in his study of psychology, he should emerge with an ever-increasing appreciation for the dignity, the importance, and the brotherhood of man.

In most courses, student reading goes beyond the textbook. Each chapter of this textbook, therefore, contains suggestions for further reading. References to the original research studies mentioned in the text may be found in the *Teacher's Manual and Objective Tests,* available to teachers. Because the study of psychology is greatly enriched by direct experiences with some experimental procedures, each chapter of the textbook also contains suggestions for activities and simple experiments. A more thorough treatment of experiments may be found in the *Record of Activities and Experiments,* recently revised, which supplements this text.

Psychological terms are defined (and, when necessary, pronunciation given) within the text discussion. In many cases, examples are given to make the meaning of the term more concrete. At the back of the book is a Glossary, so that the student who may need to refresh his memory can do so quickly. In addition, a list of new or unfamiliar terms used in the chapter is given at the end of each chapter. By reviewing these end-of-chapter terms, the student can gradually build up a vocabulary as he progresses through the text. For the student who is interested in the use of statistics in psychology, there is an Appendix containing terms and procedures.

Many people have contributed to the preparation of this book. The authors wish to acknowledge the assistance and encouragement received from their colleagues in two committees of the American Psychological Association: the Committee on High School Psychology, Division on the Teaching of Psychology, and the Committee on Psychology in Secondary Schools, operating under the Education and Training Board. Through the years since publication of the Fourth Edition, many letters offering suggestions have been received from high school teachers and students. Their assistance is hereby gratefully acknowledged.

T. L. Engle
Department of Psychology
Indiana University—Fort Wayne

Louis Snellgrove
Department of Psychology
Lambuth College

Contents

CONTENTS

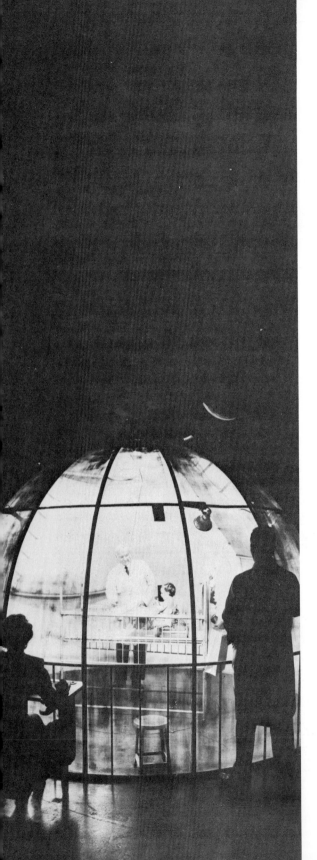

UNIT 1

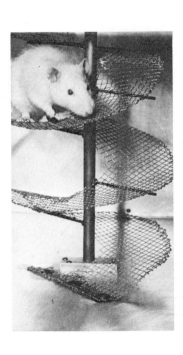

THE SCIENCE
OF PSYCHOLOGY

1

What is psychology?

Psychology is old as a study but young, vigorous, and growing as an organized science and profession. Since interest in what psychology studies — how people perceive and think and learn and why they behave as they do — is probably as old as mankind, psychology can be considered very old indeed. But psychology as an organized field of science, with laboratories, courses, teachers, textbooks, and reference works, and as a profession with standards for the training and ethical conduct of its members belongs almost entirely to the twentieth century.

Psychology has grown rapidly as a field for research, teaching, and application to immediate human problems. Advances in psychology often have worldwide effects. Great scientific work typically involves contributions from many lands, and modern psychology would not have grown up without the work of Russians, Austrians, Germans, Frenchmen, Englishmen, and others. Also, important work in psychology continues to go on in other nations of the world, notably Great Britain and Russia. Nevertheless, psychology is now identified with the United States. Especially since World War II, the United States has become the center for the theory and practice of psychology.

This book provides a survey of psychology that will be useful as part of the general education of an informed citizen and that might even be the first step toward a career in psychology. This opening chapter defines the science of psychology, shows its relationship to other sciences, and gives basic information about how and where psychologists work.

DEFINITION OF PSYCHOLOGY

Different books may give slightly varying definitions of psychology, but a generally acceptable definition is as follows: *psychology* is the science that studies the behavior of organisms. Three words in this definition — science, behavior, and organisms — require further examination.

Science. When we refer to psychology as a science, we mean that it is a systematic study. The work of any science is based on factual investigation, experiments, and other systematic means of collecting information, or data. It is not based on prejudiced opinion or unsupported judgment. The goal of all sciences is a better understanding of man and all the forces, conditions, and influences which make up his environment.

Scientists collect data by research, that is, by systematic, careful, first-hand observation of facts or events. (We call these observable facts or events *phenomena*.) Research usually involves description by measurement, reported in mathematical terms. But science does not stop when a set of facts has been described. The next step is to try to relate and explain what is described, to construct theories. A *theory* is simply a general principle, based on considerable data, proposed as an explanation for what is observed. It is a statement of relations among facts, supported by a comprehensive study of facts. Through research, scientists may be able to offer a well-grounded explanation of what has happened in the past and thus make it possible to predict what will happen in similar situations in the future. Long study of yellow fever, for example, led scientists to the theory that mosquitoes caused the disease and to the prediction that control of mosquitoes would cut down the disease.

It must be stressed that no science has all the facts on or all the answers to the problems it investigates. Science gives the best answers it can on the basis of the evidence it has. As investigation goes on, new facts are collected, and theories may have to be changed. Observations made with the help of artificial earth satellites led to revisions in our knowledge of the shape and dimensions of the earth. The most reliable reference sources and maps must be revised as new facts are established by science.

Behavior. Psychology has been defined as the science that studies behavior. In the sciences, common words are often used with technical meanings, and "behavior" is such a word. In psychology, *behavior* is defined as those activities of a human being or other organism that can be observed directly or by means of special instruments or techniques. Such activities as walking, running, and speaking are forms of behavior, but no more so than less easily observed forms. As an example, a person charged with a crime may appear calm, revealing no easily detectable behavior that suggests fear or guilt. With instruments, however, a psychologist may be able to measure such behavior because of telltale changes in the person's blood pressure, breathing, and pulse rate. Psychologists have techniques for studying and measuring many other kinds of behavior, such as learning, remembering, and reasoning.

Organisms. Psychologists use the word *organism* to refer to any living animal. Although psychologists are primarily interested in human beings, they often make studies of chimpanzees, rats, pigeons, and other animals.

The "mind" in psychology. Perhaps you are surprised that there is no mention of the "mind" in our definition of

The members of this crowd display some of the varied forms of behavior that psychologists analyze in systematic studies.

—is a part of the functioning of the entire organism, as you will see in the study of the nervous system later in the book. Nevertheless, such words as mind and mental are so common in our language that we cannot get away from them. It would take a very stilted teacher to announce to his class, "Bear in your organism that there will be an examination next Friday" rather than "Bear in mind that there will be an examination next Friday." Psychologists and physicians find it convenient to speak of mental health even though they do not assume that there is a mind whose health can be completely separated from the health of the whole person.

The word "mind" is an example of a *heuristic* (hyōō·ris'tik) concept, or a concept which is useful in understanding and explaining something but which has no physical counterpart or way of proving if the concept is true or false. Although the term "mind" is used occasionally in such fields as psychoanalysis, the word should be used cautiously, and is best left out of a definition of psychology.

THE PLACE OF PSYCHOLOGY AMONG THE SCIENCES

To understand the nature of psychology, it is helpful to consider how this science is related to other sciences. All sciences share certain methods and aims. They all grew out of philosophy. The ancient philosophers strove to understand the nature of man and the universe, and modern scientists (as well as philosophers) are still working toward this goal. In modern times so

psychology. At one time, it is true, psychology was described as the study of the mind. You may have heard or read discussions of the mind-body problem—the problem of the relation of mind, or that which is mental, to body, or that which is physical. This problem is based on the assumption that it is possible and profitable to consider mental behavior as separate from physical behavior.

Modern psychologists are not much concerned with a mind versus body problem. They do not regard mind and body as separate entities. Behavior that is called mental—for example, thinking

4

much knowledge has accumulated that scientists have found it necessary to concentrate on specialized areas. Thus, there are many sciences. Psychology draws upon the accumulated knowledge of several of these sciences and is drawn upon by them.

Since it would take volumes to trace all the relationships of psychology with other sciences, we shall consider only a few representative and important relations.

How is psychology related to chemistry and biology? Although it might seem that the research chemist in his laboratory is far from the field of psychology, there is a close relationship between behavior and body chemistry. Some forms of mental illness that were formerly spoken of as sickness of the mind can now be explained in terms of body chemistry. We are learning much about psychopharmacology — the study of the effects of drugs and poisons on psychological functions. Today the pharmaceutical houses are devoting much research effort to problems concerning the effects of certain drugs on the nervous system, such as the ataractic (tranquilizing) drugs.

Biology is another science which contributes to psychology. The relation of biology to psychology will be evident throughout this book — as, for example, in the study of emotions, which requires a knowledge of the activity of the glands and of parts of the brain.

How is psychology related to anthropology and sociology? The sciences of anthropology and sociology are closely allied to psychology. Cultural (or social) anthropology studies the culture — the way of life — of man. Although once focused on the behavior of nonliterate peoples, anthropology is becoming more and more concerned with the behavior of so-called civilized as well as so-called primitive peoples. Through his studies of widely divergent cultures, the anthropologist assists the psychologist in understanding the influences of environment upon the behavior of individuals.

Like cultural anthropology, sociology studies the behavior of human groups. Sociology is especially concerned with group life and social organization, chiefly in literate societies such as our own. Sociologists study such areas as growth and shifts of population, urban and rural living, voting trends, delinquency, and crime.

Data from all these studies contribute to understanding the behavior of the individual. In some areas — as in the study of families and other small groups — sociology is very close to the branch of psychology called social psychology. The distinction is that the psychologist focuses primarily on the individual, while the sociologist focuses primarily on the group.

To sum up the discussion of the place of psychology among the sciences, we may paraphrase a section from a report on the place of psychology in education: Psychologists (this report states) seek to provide a basic science of human thinking, learning, skills, motives, conduct, and so on, that will serve all the sciences of man — such as anthropology, sociology, government, and medicine — in

WHAT IS PSYCHOLOGY?

Psychology often benefits from studies conducted by other behavioral scientists, such as this anthropologist interviewing women in Nigeria.

much the same way that biology now serves the agricultural and medical sciences.

METHODS OF PSYCHOLOGICAL STUDY

Basically, the psychologist uses the same general methods of study as do scientists in all fields. Each science, however, uses a number of methods and techniques especially suited to the kind of phenomena that it is studying. Some of the special methods which psychologists use in their work will be described here.

What is natural observation? Before the development of psychology as a science, men observed and recorded examples of behavior. Even today psychologists use natural observation as a check on laboratory and other scientific work. We can learn something about

maternal behavior by observing mother monkeys with their young under uncontrolled conditions in the monkeys' natural state as well as under controlled conditions in a laboratory. We can learn something about how individuals adjust to social situations by observing them and their companions at informal social gatherings. We can learn about an individual's attitudes by listening to his conversation.

Natural observation quite often includes the use of tape recorders, motion pictures, photographs, and other permanent ways of recording data. Although natural observation gives a record of activities, it has the serious disadvantage of providing little or no information about why or how behavior occurs. Nevertheless, it does allow us to study organisms in their natural environment rather than in the artificial environment created by directed or laboratory observation.

What is directed observation? Directed observation (sometimes called experimental or laboratory observation) is a refinement of the uncontrolled observing of behavior that we all do. Psychologists, however, make observations under controlled conditions and according to a planned schedule. For example, they may plan to observe how children react to specific toys. All details, even though they seem trivial, are noted immediately either in shorthand, or by a tape recorder, a motion picture camera, or some other recording device.

What is the case-study method? Psychologists, social workers, and psychiatrists often use the case-study method as they attempt to help children and adults with problems of adjustment. These trained persons strive to get impartial and objective descriptions of the background forces that have probably influenced an individual's development. The case record includes information concerning family background, home life, neighborhood activities, school experience, health, and so on. This method is based on the idea that the more we know about an individual, the better we will be able to understand and to help him.

The case-study method is valuable and even indispensable in some psychological work. Nevertheless, it has certain limitations. For one thing, information often has to be obtained from parents, teachers, and other associates of the individual under study. These informants may unintentionally give partial and biased reports rather than the impartial and objective reports which psychologists need.

How are interviews used? In psychology, sociology, and other fields, interviews are widely used to obtain data. Your physician may have included an interview as part of his diagnostic technique when you went to see him. Your teachers and guidance counselor may have interviewed you. Certainly you have been interviewed if you have ever applied for a job. Public opinion researchers interview a sample of the population to gauge attitudes toward soaps, cigarettes, or other commercial products or to forecast voting trends. Psychologists use interviews for such purposes as compiling a case record on an individual or studying prejudices in groups.

The value of data from an interview depends upon how well the interviewer has been trained for his job. First of all, a good interviewer is careful to establish *rapport,* that is, an unconstrained and cooperative relationship with the interviewee. He knows in advance what questions he is going to ask and the general order in which he will ask them. Nevertheless, he keeps the interview flexible enough so that both parties can bring out topics not on the list of questions. The skilled interviewer can enrich the record by noting little hesitancies, tenseness, or topics the interviewee seems to try to avoid.

The entire interview may be tape-recorded so that the interviewer can play it back to himself for further consideration. He may call in other trained interviewers to hear and evaluate the entire recorded interview.

The interview method is widely used, but it is subject to serious limitations. One is the difficulty of eliminating the personal prejudices of the interviewer. Furthermore, it is often difficult to express the results of an interview in exact terms. A person may be recorded as "favorable" toward a group. But how favorable—100 percent? 50 percent? This sort of doubt rules out the precise measurement that is essential to all scientific work. As you will see in Chapter 6, however, interviews conducted by well-trained persons using modern techniques may yield scientifically valuable data.

What is the questionnaire method? In the latter part of the nineteenth and early part of the twentieth centuries, the questionnaire method was developed to provide greater accuracy in the study of human behavior. The method consists of sending a list of questions on a given subject to a selected group of individuals. Occasionally, the questions are asked directly in an interview. The questions do not constitute a test with right or wrong answers. Rather, they are designed to gather facts about the individual or to elicit his opinions. The answers to the questions can be treated statistically.

There are dangers in the use of the questionnaire method. Individuals answering a questionnaire may be inaccurate in their statements concerning their behavior. If he is asked very personal questions, the respondent may deliberately falsify his responses. Moreover, an investigator does not receive replies from 100 percent of those to whom he sends his questionnaire; frequently less than 50 percent reply. Those who do reply may not be a representative sample of the group under study. In spite of these limitations, however, a carefully formulated questionnaire sent to carefully selected groups may give valuable information concerning general trends in behavior.

How are tests and similar methods of measurement used? As you study psychology, you will find frequent references to tests and similar methods of measurement. Psychologists have devoted much time to developing tests of intellectual ability. They have also designed aptitude tests, which help predict what an individual is likely to be able to accomplish when and if he receives training in a given field. They have developed measuring devices that give clues to an individual's basic vocational interests. Psychologists have techniques for measuring attitudes toward social problems. They have developed techniques which enable one individual to rate other individuals on specified characteristics. In addition, psychologists have a number of techniques for measuring personality. During your school years you have taken many achievement tests designed to measure the extent to which you have mastered subject matter. If the tests were standardized ones, probably psychologists were involved in constructing them.

Tests and similar methods of measurement are valuable in psychology. They give more objective data than interviews and questionnaires. They give results that can be expressed in statistical terms, and often an individual's score can be compared with scores for large groups. Nevertheless, tests must be used with care. Some people think a psychologist can give them a few tests and then tell them exactly what college to attend, what job to take, and which girl to marry. There is no such magic in tests. Results must be interpreted by experts; and even with the best interpretation, test results do not give full and final answers to individual problems. Test results must always be used as a means to an end, never as an end in themselves, or the results are useless. Test results are only one aspect in studying the behavior of an organism.

What is the experimental method? You may think of experiments as activities carried out in laboratories containing dials, meters, rows and rows of bottles, glass tubing, and so on. Some experiments require such elaborate equipment, but many worthwhile experiments can be carried out in the classroom with the aid of simple apparatus. Method rather than apparatus determines the value of the work, although the accuracy of the equipment influences the accuracy of the ultimate results. The experimental method permits better control of conditions and provides for more accurate measurement than do other methods of study.

An experiment usually begins with the statement of a *hypothesis*, that is, a tentative assumption or proposition that is to be tested. One of the oldest ways of stating a hypothesis is the "If–then" method. For example, the following might be a hypothesis: *"If* students eat no lunch, *then* they will do less well in their afternoon classes than they would otherwise." In an experiment there must be two *variables,*

that is, conditions which can change in amount or quality. There is always an *independent variable,* which is the factor that produces the effects being examined in the experiment. This variable is manipulated and controlled by the experimenter in some systematic and predetermined manner. The independent variable is also usually the stimulus acting upon the organism in the experiment. A *stimulus* is any object, event, or situation which causes a response by the organism. Related to the independent variable is the *dependent variable,* the changed condition that is considered to be a consequence of, or to depend upon, the independent variable. The dependent variable in an experiment is generally the *response* of the organism, which is caused by the action of the stimulus. An illustration will clarify the use of variables in experiments.

What procedures are used in an experiment? Suppose that a psychologist wanted to conduct an experiment on the effect of a limited amount of sleep on students' examination grades. He might put forth the hypothesis, "If the sleep of students is limited the night before an exam, then their exam grades will be lower than they would be otherwise." So that he would know that lower grades were not caused by factors other than insufficient sleep—for example, by differences in age, sex, amount of study, or intellectual ability —he must control or eliminate the possibly influential variables other than insufficient sleep which might cause exam grades to be lower. One way of doing this is to match two groups of

This classroom experiment tests the effect of praise on performance. As he drops marbles into containers at random, the subject is given a word of praise if he unknowingly follows a certain pattern.

students carefully. For every student in one group, there would be a student of the same age, sex, and intellectual ability in the other group. Members of both groups would spend the same specified amount of time in study for the exam. In other words, the two groups would be made up of what might be called "psychological twins."

The psychologist might then instruct one group of students to get at least eight hours of sleep the night before the exam. To the other group, he might give instructions to get only four hours of sleep prior to the exam. The experiment would thus investigate the effect of a particular condition (a limited amount of sleep the night before an exam). Psychologists call the group in which the condition is present (in this case, the group which gets little sleep) the *experimental group*. The group in which the condition is not present is called the *control group*.

Since the amount of sleep is the factor being manipulated and is the stimulus acting upon the students, amount of sleep is the independent variable in the experiment. Examination grades are the dependent variable, since lower exam grades are, according to the hypothesis, a consequence of insufficient sleep and a response to the stimulus.

After giving the experimental and control groups identical examinations, the psychologist would study the grades and compare the performance of the two groups. If the students in the experimental group earned lower grades than did those in the control

THE SCIENCE OF PSYCHOLOGY

group, the psychologist's hypothesis would be supported.

The experimental method is basic to modern psychology. Much of this or any other psychology textbook is based on evidence produced by experiments, and many chapters of this book will refer to such evidence.

Throughout this book you will also find many words which are new to you. There will be other words, such as behavior, which are familiar but which have a different and specific definition in the study of psychology. Another such word is "subject." In psychology a *subject* is the organism, human or animal, participating in an experiment, whose responses constitute the dependent variable in the experiment.

Why do psychologists use animals in experiments?　Psychologists, though interested chiefly in human behavior, do much experimental work with animals. They may use rats, pigeons, chimpanzees, or almost any other animal as subjects for experimental work. The physical structure and to some extent the social behavior of such animals resemble that of man, so that work with animals leads the way toward scientific studies of human beings.

Animal behavior can be controlled to an extent that is not possible with human beings. A rat, for example, can be raised from birth in a cage, where a record can be kept of everything that happens to him. The rat can then be used in a learning experiment with the certainty that he has had no opportunity to learn except under the conditions of the experiment. Human beings, on the other hand, obviously have many ex-

periences that cannot be controlled or even recorded by an experimenter but that may influence experimental data. Another advantage of using animals as subjects is that many animals have relatively short life spans and reproduce at rapid rates. Thus, a psychologist can study the behavior of several generations — within a relatively short time. Furthermore, experiments involving brain or other surgery or involving the use of certain drugs can be performed with animals but not with man.

Although the psychologist studies animals in order to get clues to human behavior, he is careful to avoid *anthropomorphism,* that is, the attributing of human characteristics to other beings besides man. For example, we see a dog "begging" for a bone. When he barks, we may say that he "speaks" for the bone. When he buries the bone, we may be tempted to say that he thinks to himself, "I am not hungry now, so I shall bury it in this hole to keep the puppy next door from running off with it." Thinking in terms of words and sentences is a human characteristic, and there is no evidence that lower animals think in this way. We may be tempted to attribute language to the lower animal partly because we have been brought up on fairy stories suggesting that animals and even inanimate objects can talk. Although we can learn much about human behavior by observing the behavior of lower animals, it is inaccurate to attribute human characteristics to them.

One word of caution: The beginning student of psychology must not attempt experiments that involve injury or discomfort to an animal. Such work can

WHAT IS PSYCHOLOGY?

Methods of Psychological Study

There are many methods that psychologists can use to conduct research. Some of these methods are employed by other sciences, such as the interview method (right). Some of these methods have been developed primarily for psychological studies, such as play therapy, which is used to study the emotional conflicts of disturbed children (below). The technique that psychologists use most is the experimental method, which can be applied to studying the behavior of both animals and human beings. The procedures of the experimental method are useful for determining the behavior and motor responses of rats (page 13, above). The experimental method can also help psychologists study the physical responses of astronauts to weightlessness (page 13, below).

be done only under restricted conditions by a trained scientist, who can take the responsibility for judging that his project is for the eventual benefit of mankind. The American Psychological Association, a national professional organization for psychologists, has a Code of Ethics for the handling of animals under experimental conditions. This Code covers the living conditions of experimental animals and the ways in which such animals can and cannot be treated before, during, and after experiments. (Throughout this book you will find references to the APA. Actually there are two organizations with the same initials, the American Psychological Association and the American Psychiatric Association; but whenever "APA" appears in this book with no other explanation, it refers to the American Psychological Association.)

How do psychologists use experimental data? In designing, recording, and reporting experiments, psychologists make extensive use of mathematics. Advanced work in psychology requires the ability to understand mathematical procedures and to interpret statistics. Since the beginning student cannot be expected to understand all the mathematical terminology in research reports, this textbook will often summarize experiments rather than give statistical details.

When research is cited and one case is given to illustrate a point, students sometimes wonder, "What of it? One experiment with a small group of children or a litter of rats doesn't prove anything." That is true, but the experiment may illustrate basic principles and

provide useful research. There is not enough space in any one book to cite all the evidence supporting a principle. In addition, the results of one experiment often lead to the formation of new or different hypotheses and additional experiments.

If you want to learn how psychologists bring together, summarize, and evaluate experimental evidence, consult the *Psychological Bulletin,* a journal published by the American Psychological Association. In this journal specialists in specific areas of psychology summarize and make judgments about what has been written on their area. For example, you might find articles entitled "Teaching Machines: A Review" or "Physiological Effects of 'Hypnosis.'" These articles may be difficult to understand in detail because of technical language, but they will add to your appreciation of the scientific method in psychology. The *Psychological Bulletin* may be available in your school or public library.

The library can be a further help if you want to broaden your knowledge of research and theory. You may also wish to consult the "Suggestions for Further Reading" at the end of each chapter in this book.

If you do some supplemental reading in current journals, you may find reports of experimental data or theories that are not in agreement with what is said in the textbook. In such a case, the first step is to examine the source of the report. Sometimes the press describes as a "revolutionary discovery" what is really a hypothesis that has yet to be tested. If the report is from a truly scientific source, then fresh data and new ideas have emerged since this textbook went to press. The rapid progress of modern science is one factor that keeps the field of psychology exciting and challenging.

MAJOR FIELDS OF PSYCHOLOGICAL WORK

There are many areas for specialization in the broad field of psychology, as you will see in more detail when we study psychology as a vocation in Chapter 19. Here, though, we shall take a look at some major fields in which psychologists work.

Laboratory experimentation. The psychologists who work in a laboratory advance the scientific foundation upon which all psychology is based. As you know, psychologists often do experimental work with animals. But many experimental psychologists work directly with human subjects, especially children. They keep careful records of behavior under various conditions.

Assisting individuals. Some psychologists devote their time to assisting individuals with their personal problems. A psychologist tries to help individuals to help themselves—perhaps to plan their educational programs or to find the kind of job for which they are best fitted. Some psychologists assist persons who have personality disorders and who have difficulty adjusting to society. These psychologists may work in clinics, prisons, juvenile and other courts, mental hospitals, or their own offices.

Also working to help persons with personality disorders are psychiatrists (sī·kī′ə·trists). *Psychiatrists* are physicians who specialize in the prevention, diagnosis, and treatment of both mild and severe mental disorders.

Working with groups. Some psychologists try to understand how individuals influence groups and how groups influence individuals. Often working with sociologists, they study such social problems as the adaptation of immigrant groups to a new way of life. They also conduct public opinion polls.

Some psychologists work in industry, where they develop programs for selecting employees and for acquainting them with their jobs. They also work to improve employee morale. Advertising is a field in which some psychologists work; they may study buyer preferences and advertising appeal. Psychologists may also enter the field of human engineering. For example, such a psychologist may work with industrial design engineers to develop the kind of machine that would be most efficient for the workmen to operate. He may study such problems as what kind of highway signs can best be read by the motorist, and where such signs should be placed.

Working in schools. Obviously there is overlapping between this kind of psychological work and the kinds already mentioned. School psychologists advise students on educational and job plans. They help students with their personal problems. They try to improve relations among students, teachers, and parents and to help stu-

WHAT IS PSYCHOLOGY?

dents who are having difficulty with schoolwork. Psychologists often administer tests of various kinds in the schools, and, of course, they also teach and sometimes carry on research in schools, colleges, and universities.

What are some other areas in which psychologists work? There are many areas in which psychologists work, and in each of these areas there are additional types of specialists. The following is a list of the different divisions of the American Psychological Association, which will give you an idea of the diversity present in the field of psychology. (Since this list is growing, however, it would be advisable to consult the latest Directory of the APA for the most recent classification of divisions.)

Division of General Psychology
Division on the Teaching of
  Psychology
Division of Experimental
  Psychology
Division on Evaluation and
  Measurement
Division of Physiological and
  Comparative Psychology
Division on Developmental
  Psychology

Division of Personality and Social
  Psychology
Society for the Psychological
  Study of Social Issues
Division of Psychology and the
  Arts
Division of Clinical Psychology
Division of Consulting Psychology
Division of Industrial Psychology
Division of Educational
  Psychology
Division of School Psychologists
Division of Counseling
  Psychology
Division of Psychologists in Public
  Service
Division of Military Psychology
Division of Maturity and Old Age
Society of Engineering
  Psychologists
Division on Psychological Aspects
  of Disability
Division of Consumer Psychology
Division of Philosophical
  Psychology
Division for the Experimental
  Analysis of Behavior
Division of the History of
  Psychology
Division of Community
  Psychology
Division of Behavioral
  Pharmacology

Terms to Add to Your Vocabulary

anthropomorphism	independent variable	research
behavior	mind	response
control group	organism	science
dependent variable	phenomena	stimulus
experimental group	psychiatrist	subject
heuristic	psychology	theory
hypothesis	rapport	

THE SCIENCE OF PSYCHOLOGY

Suggestions for Activities

Remembering and even understanding what is said in each chapter of a textbook is not enough. The more personal experiences you can have with psychology, the broader your view and the better your understanding of the subject.

At the close of each chapter, there will be suggestions for activities. You may wish to conduct surveys, to make and use apparatus, to perform experiments. Probably there will not be time for all of you to carry out each suggestion. Perhaps committees can be designated to carry out certain activities and report their experiences to the whole class for discussion. If local conditions are such that you cannot carry out some of these activities, you may wish to suggest similar ones.

1. Ask several persons who have not studied psychology to complete some or all of the following sentences, and then compare their sentences. Keep all these materials and restudy them toward the end of the course. (1) Psychology is useful to people because . . . (2) Psychology is popular with many people because . . . (3) To me, common sense and psychology . . . (4) Some things psychologists tell us are . . . (5) In terms of ability to judge people, psychologists . . . (6) Psychologists ought to . . . (7) Psychologists know less about behavior than . . . (8) Psychology teaches you how to . . . (9) By studying psychology a person can . . . (10) Psychologists can predict behavior by . . . (11) Many psychologists are . . . (12) As scientists, psychologists are . . .

2. Check your school or public library to see if it has any psychological journals. The American Psychological Association publishes many journals, including *American Psychologist, Journal of Applied Psychology, Journal of Educational Psychology,* and *Journal of Experimental Psychology.* These are, how-ever, only a few of the journals published by the APA. There are more than sixty different journals published by qualified organizations which contain articles relating to psychology.

3. Dr. Max M. Kostick has written a short play, "Schools of Psychology," published by Applied Psychology Associates, 146 Lancaster Terrace, Brookline, Mass. 02146. It is suitable for class production and is designed to clarify what seem to be conflicting materials from three schools of psychology. (A *school of psychology* refers to a group of psychologists who adhere to a particular set of teachings.) You may want to organize a group of students to present the play.

4. One of the authors of this book, Dr. Louis Snellgrove, has also published a textbook entitled *Psychological Experiments and Demonstrations.* This book contains sections on "Meaningful statistics" and "Experimental design and procedures." The third section contains twenty-five demonstrations and experiments with complete descriptions of needed equipment and procedures. Most of the equipment involved is relatively inexpensive and some can be constructed by students and teachers. (It is published by McGraw-Hill Book Company, 330 West 42nd St., New York, N.Y. 10036.)

5. Ask several friends who have not studied psychology to define *mind*. Record their responses, bring them to class, and compare their definitions with the discussion of "mind" in the text.

6. The American Association for the Advancement of Science publishes *Science Books: A Quarterly Review.* Books on psychology are included in the reviews. The reviewers indicate whether they

17

recommend the books for use at the high school level.

7. *The Psychological Record* is an inexpensive journal published at Denison University, Granville, Ohio 43023. This journal costs $3.00 per year to students and high school libraries, by special arrangement. Your library or class might want to order this journal.

Suggestions for Further Reading

In addition to your study of this textbook, class discussions, lectures by your teacher, activities of various kinds, and experiments, you will wish to broaden your knowledge of psychology still further through supplemental reading. At the close of each chapter there will be "Suggestions for Further Reading."

Some of the books suggested are introductory college textbooks. Such books present much the same material as that presented in your textbook but treat it in more detail. Some stress the experimental method in psychology, and some stress problems of personal and social adjustment. For those of you who plan to go to college, these books will give a taste of the work at the next step up on the educational ladder.

Some of the suggested readings are taken from a list of readings recommended for high school students by a committee of the Division on the Teaching of Psychology, American Psychological Association. Other suggestions are taken from *An Inexpensive Science Library,* a publication of the American Association for the Advancement of Science and the National Science Foundation.

Do not consider these "Suggestions for Further Reading" as complete reference lists. Only limited space is available at the close of each chapter. New books and booklets are being published all the time. Your teacher or librarian might assist you in finding recent material. There is always new and interesting material to read in the field of psychology.

Butterfield, Herbert, *The Origins of Modern Science: 1300–1800,* rev. ed., Macmillan. A review indicating how such scientists as Galileo, Bacon, Copernicus, Newton, and others have changed the course of modern thought.

Daniel, Robert S., ed., *Contemporary Readings in General Psychology,* 2nd ed., Houghton Mifflin. This book offers seventy-five carefully selected readings, each written by or reporting the work of a recognized scientist. Although intended for college and university students, many of the articles can be read with interest and profit by high school students. For each unit in the textbook, a few articles are recommended because of their known special interest to students. However, from each part students and teachers will find many other articles which they will wish to read. Part I consists of six articles which fall under the heading, "Psychology Is a Scientific Enterprise"; and Part II consists of seven articles titled "Psychology Is the Science of the Behavior of Organisms." Recommended selections are: Rudolf Flesch, "The More or Less Scientific Method," pages 23–26; T. G. Andrews, "An Introduction to Psychological Methodology," pages 53–63.

Hilgard, Ernest R., and Richard C. Atkinson, *Introduction to Psychology,* 4th ed., Harcourt, Brace & World. This is an excellent introductory textbook for college classes in psychology and will serve to expand the material presented in high school courses. Especially recommended for reading at this time is Chapter 1, "Psychology as a Behavioral Science."

Kalish, Richard A., *The Psychology of Human Behavior,* Wadsworth. A new textbook written for introductory courses in psychology for students not planning to major in psychology. Read Chapter 1, "Psychology and Psychologists."

Leuba, Clarence, *Man: A General Psychology,* Holt, Rinehart & Winston. "The chief theme of this textbook is that man is an integrated bio-psycho-social organism." It contains more material from biology, anthropology, and sociology than do most introductory psychology textbooks. Note especially the following chapters: Chapter 2, "The Sciences of Man"; Chapter 3, "The Scientific Method in the Study of Man"; Chapter 24, "Toward a Science of Man."

Munn, Norman L., *Psychology,* 5th ed., Houghton Mifflin. This widely used college textbook stresses physiological aspects of psychology. At this point read Chapter 1, "The Science of Psychology." There is an abridged edition, *Introduction to Psychology,* which places less stress on physiological psychology.

Ogg, Elizabeth, *Psychologists in Action,* New York (Public Affairs Pamphlet No. 229).

Poincaré, Henri, *Science and Hypothesis,* Dover. A discussion of how science attacks its problems.

Ruch, Floyd L., *Psychology and Life,* 7th ed., Scott, Foresman. The title suggests the general orientation of this textbook, and students will find it very interesting. Chapter 1 is entitled "What Psychology Is and Does."

Sanford, Fillmore H., *Psychology: A Scientific Study of Man,* 2nd ed., Wadsworth. The author of this textbook has attempted to write first for reading and second for studying. For the present, read Chapter 1, "Knowing the Human Being," and Chapter 2, "Theories of People." Also, read Chapter 6, "Experimental Design and Psychological Statistics."

Sargent, Stephen S., and Kenneth R. Stafford, *Basic Teachings of the Great Psychologists,* Barnes & Noble. This book was written by a psychologist for the individual beginning his study of psychology.

The following books are suggested for general reference as you study psychology.

Candland, D. K., and J. F. Campbell, *Exploring Behavior,* Basic Books. This book will serve as a very valuable reference any time you contemplate a project involving research methods. It was written for use by high school students.

Crow, Lester D., and Alice Crow, *General Psychology,* Littlefield, Adams. This book will serve throughout your course as a guide to the basic principles of psychology. It includes self-scoring tests.

English, Horace B., and Ava C. English, *A Comprehensive Dictionary of Psychological and Psychoanalytical Terms,* McKay. A dictionary for the professional psychologist but useful for the beginning student. Definitions are very thorough and often point out differences in usage.

Harriman, Philip L., *Handbook of Psychological Terms,* Littlefield, Adams. A useful specialized dictionary.

————— *Modern Psychology,* Littlefield, Adams. An outline of the subject matter of psychology. You may wish to check yourself by taking the self-testing exercises.

Wilkening, Howard, *A Student's Psychology Handbook,* Chandler. Over seven hundred technical terms simply but carefully defined, plus some basic formulas used in the presentation and analysis of psychological statistics. A very good book for the beginning student.

Your attention is called to a series of paperbacks under the general title of *Vistas of Science.* These books are being written for the purpose of introducing high school students to exciting discoveries and important new applications in key science areas. Some of the books deal with aspects of psychology and related sciences. You should keep in touch with the new books as they are published by Scholastic Book Services, 904 Sylvan Ave., Englewood Cliffs, N.J. 07632.

CHAPTER 2

Misunderstood problems of psychology

We have been using the term "psychologist" so far to refer to a scientist with professional standards and proper training in a recognized college or university. Unfortunately, like the members of every profession, psychologists have the problem of combating charlatans, or persons who call themselves psychologists but who are not qualified to use that title.

There are some quacks who work around the fringes of psychology, preying on people who want advice about personal problems. Phrenologists, astrologers, numerologists, and others of their kind promise quick diagnosis, advice, and therapy. Having examined the bumps on your head, the phrenologist will claim that he is able to tell you all about yourself. The astrologer, who studies the positions of the stars, and the numerologist, who looks at the letters in your name, also make the same claims. Their "treatment" may consist of nothing more than telling you to think, "I am a success" or "I live gloriously." As any student of science knows, behavior is too complex to be understood in such simple terms. The mere fact that these quacks tell a troubled person exactly what to do is in itself an indication that they are not professionally trained. A trained psychologist helps troubled persons to develop insight into their own problems and to work out their own solutions.

Many of these quacks pass themselves off under titles that, to the uninformed, may sound impressive. Although such titles as "Doctor of Chiro-Deo-Therapy," or a "Certified Grapho-Analytical Psychologist," or "Doctor of Metaphysics" may sound like academic degrees, they were probably bought from one of the more than two hundred so-called schools or even colleges that are nothing but diploma- or degree-mills. In one of these schools, it is possible to get four "doctor's" degrees in twenty months at a mail-order cost of $250. An accredited Ph.D. normally requires a minimum of seven years of study beyond high school.

Anyone seeking to consult a psychologist should not hesitate to ask about the psychologist's qualifications. The well-trained and ethical psychologist will be glad to give this information. The quack will try to bluff and avoid giving direct answers, or he may claim to have training—but the education he reports is probably worthless.

The phrenologists, astrologers, and quacks who use mail-order degrees are sometimes called *pseudo-scientists*. They use some of the terms and even a few of the procedures of science, but their work is not scientific. Genuine scientists and pseudo-scientists occasionally are involved with common or overlapping fields. Hypnosis and telepathy ("mind reading") are two examples. These phenomena are studied seriously by reputable psychologists; at the same time they are often used as if they belonged in a carnival sideshow. In this chapter we shall consider these two topics and two others, psychoanalysis and instinct, which are equally misunderstood in popular talking and writing. Showing how psychologists work in these "mysterious" areas will help clarify the nature of scientific psychology.

PSYCHOANALYSIS

What is psychoanalysis? Many people confuse the science of psychology with *psychoanalysis* (sī'kō·ə·nal'ə·sis) —a method of treatment for mental disorders and a body of psychological theory. Psychoanalysis was developed under the leadership of Sigmund Freud (1856–1939), a Viennese physician. His work has been carried on and expanded by many students and followers.

Although, as we saw in Chapter 1, there is no need to bring the word "mind" into a definition of psychology, mind is a term which the psychoanalyst does use. According to early writings of the psychoanalysts, the "mind" may be divided into three levels or parts: (1) the conscious, (2) the preconscious —sometimes called foreconscious— and (3) the unconscious. The *conscious* includes everything that you are aware of at any given moment. An individual's conscious changes from one instant to the next. The *preconscious,* or foreconscious, includes everything that you can become aware of if and when you want to. For example, try to remember now what you had for breakfast this morning. With little trouble you can recall this information from the preconscious to the conscious. The *unconscious* contains all the information, desires, wishes, and concepts which you cannot recall to consciousness under ordinary circumstances— without inducement from psychoanalysis, psychotherapy, certain drugs, or some strong emotional shock.

Psychoanalysts also use the terms id, ego, and superego to explain the basis of an individual's personality. These terms, originated by Freud, have appeared extensively in recent writings. The *id* is located entirely in the unconscious and is governed by the "pleasure principle," which makes us want to seek out pleasure and avoid everything that might bring us any kind of pain. Since the id is concerned only with seeking pleasure, it has no direct contact with reality. Therefore, it has no way of knowing or caring about the consequences of acts. However, the id has indirect contact with reality through the ego and superego.

MISUNDERSTOOD PROBLEMS OF PSYCHOLOGY

Sigmund Freud's concept of personality, based on his theory of the unconscious, has deeply influenced contemporary thought. Many of his views resulted from analytic work with patients, conducted in this room.

Popularly, the term ego is used as a synonym for vanity; you have probably heard someone describe a conceited person by saying, "He has a terrific ego." Psychoanalysts, however, define the *ego* as the individual's conception of himself. It includes everything a person believes himself to be: a good person, honest, tall, short, intelligent, and so forth. Generally speaking, the self-concepts are consistent with one another. In other words, a person rarely believes himself to be both uninformed and informed in the same area (although he may believe himself to be better informed in one area than in another). The ego acts as a regulator, balancing the needs of the id with the demands of the conscience and of society and turning back or repressing impulses that would come into conflict with society or the person's conscience.

The third term, *superego,* corresponds roughly to what we commonly call "conscience" — the moral attitudes and values of the individual. Along with the ego, the superego also acts as a regulator on the id impulses. Individuals have a tendency to behave as their ego and superego dictate. It makes a difference that our behavior is usually regulated by these two concepts rather than by the id, since both the ego and superego are in contact with reality and can see the future consequences of acts. You will not need to use these terms in your course in psychology to any large extent, but you should be familiar with them. They are often used (and even more often misused) by pop-

22

ular writers, motion pictures, and television dramas. You should understand that they are all heuristic concepts and are not treated as scientific terms.

A simple example of these terms, as psychoanalysts use them, may help to clarify this complicated explanation of an individual's personality. You are taking an exam and wish to make a good grade by cheating. That wish is an unconscious id impulse. Suppose, also, you believe that it is wrong to cheat. Your belief represents your superego. At the same time, your ego tells you, "I am an honest person and honest people do not cheat." The result is that your ego and superego have regulated (inhibited, in this case) the id impulse to cheat. Or you may resort to another method of making a good grade—studying. If you study and make a better grade, you will have satisfied the id impulse without violating your self concept or moral attitude. Of course, as a rule you are not aware of any division of conscious and unconscious aspects of behavior in the millions of actions and decisions that occur from day to day. In Chapter 7 you will find a further discussion of how these terms relate to the development of behavior.

The terms "id," "ego," and "superego" are also useful in understanding somewhat more complex human behavior, such as conflict. For instance, suppose you are hungry and believe it is wrong to steal—but you have no money with which to buy food. Or suppose you are attracted to someone in your class—but that person is already going steady with your best friend. These are examples of conflicts between your id and your superego. Psychoanalysts explain mental illness as the inability of the ego to cope successfully with such conflicts.

Although psychoanalysis is not looked upon favorably by all psychologists, psychoanalysts must be given credit for helping us to appreciate the importance of an individual's childhood experiences upon his later life and for striving to understand and help their fellow men. Also, psychoanalysis has been very helpful in calling attention to the fact that emotional disturbances are often a result of the conflict between bodily needs and desires and the demands of social customs and rules.

Psychoanalysts place a great deal of importance on their interpretations of dreams. They believe that dreams often satisfy desires or wishes which have not been satisfied in the waking state, that the id is expressed more openly in dreams, when it is less restrained by the ego. For example, in a dream the individual may perform aggressive acts which he would not permit himself to do if he were awake. Even in dreams, however, such desires are often expressed indirectly in symbols. Only the trained psychoanalyst can interpret these symbols; certainly, dream analysis is not a matter for a beginner in the study of psychology.

HYPNOSIS

What is hypnosis? Popularly the word "hypnotism" is used synonymously with "hypnosis," although, strictly speaking, hypnotism refers to the study or practice of hypnosis rather than to

MISUNDERSTOOD PROBLEMS OF PSYCHOLOGY

the state of hypnosis itself. Sometimes hypnotism is called *mesmerism,* after Franz Anton Mesmer, an eighteenth-century Austrian physician who used hypnotic techniques (though he did not fully understand them).

Sometimes placed in the realm of mystery or magic, *hypnosis* is an artificially induced state, at times resembling sleep, although the biological processes in a hypnotized person are not exactly the same as those of a person in normal sleep. Furthermore, the person who has been hypnotized is usually very much open to suggestion, while the person in normal sleep is usually open to very little, if any, suggestion. Although the hypnotized person may appear to be asleep, he understands what is said to him and is able to carry out simple directions. The hypnotized person may be so much open to suggestion that he seems to have lost his ability to make judgments. He may believe almost anything that is told him and do almost anything requested of him. There are limits, however, to what he can be made to do.

How is hypnosis produced? There is no certain formula or mysterious technique to be followed in producing a state of hypnosis. Some psychologists induce a state of hypnosis in one way, some in another.

One instrument used in inducing hypnosis is an automatic variable strobe light. It consists of a light that flashes at a specific rate per second, while the subject stares fixedly at it. The flashing light is thought to block the *alpha wave,* one of the electrical waves sent out by the brain (see Chap-

ter 10, page 259). The alpha wave seems to be associated with sleep, because when the individual goes to sleep under ordinary circumstances, the alpha wave disappears. The blocking of the wave when the subject is awake tends to make him more relaxed and sleepy and therefore more susceptible to being hypnotized. The presence of the flashing lights also gives the subject something upon which he can concentrate. Other methods for producing hypnosis include the use of droning sounds and of specific objects, such as a pencil, upon which the subject directs his attention. Still other methods involve no mechanical aid of any kind. They merely use the spoken word, attempting to get the subject to concentrate upon a specific thought. Whatever the particular technique used, the fundamental procedure involves narrowing the subject's attention so that he is aware only of what the psychologist is saying to him. As the subject's attention is narrowed, he becomes less and less critical toward accepting the suggestions made to him.

Almost any person can hypnotize others if he knows how to do so and has the patience. There is no mysterious force involved. The suggestions can be placed on a phonograph record or tape recording, so that the "hypnotist" is not even present during the process of producing a hypnotic state. Of course, only a person with a thorough knowledge of psychology or medicine should attempt to practice hypnotism.

Who may be hypnotized? Some believe that only a person with a "weak

THE SCIENCE OF PSYCHOLOGY

will" can be hypnotized. As a matter of fact, most normal persons can be hypnotized if they are willing to be hypnotized, will allow sufficient time, and will cooperate in the process. The subject must be able to concentrate on what is said and done by the person who is about to hypnotize him. Very young children usually cannot concentrate for a period long enough to enable them to be hypnotized, and they are not sufficiently familiar with the language to understand all the suggestions made to them. The same may be said of mentally retarded persons and persons suffering from some forms of mental illness.

Another mistaken view of hypnosis is that you can be hypnotized without your knowledge. Perhaps you have read stories in which a "hypnotist" slipped behind his intended "victim" and hypnotized him before he ever knew what was happening. But by now you are aware that the person being hypnotized must concentrate on what the hypnotist is saying and doing. Obviously, if the "victim" does not know that the "hypnotist" is around, he cannot give the necessary cooperation and concentration. You need not fear, therefore, that anyone will hypnotize you without your knowledge and consent. Some evidence indicates that highly suggestible individuals may become hypnotized while trying not to be hypnotized and that individuals who have been hypnotized repeatedly by the same person may become hypnotized again at the sight of that person.

Still another notion is that a victim may be hypnotized and then left, never to awaken to normal life. Actually,

the person who has hypnotized another merely has to suggest to the other that he awaken, and he will do so. In case the victim is not told to awaken, he will eventually do so anyway, just as he would awaken from normal sleep.

As to the relationship between personality traits and hypnosis, there have been no significant consistent findings that any one pattern of personality traits is more susceptible to hypnosis than any other. How easily a specific individual can be hypnotized depends upon his desire, or fear, whether conscious or unconscious, to be put into a state of hypnosis and his ability to concentrate upon what the psychologist or hypnotist is saying and doing.

How do hypnotized persons behave? Perhaps you have never seen a demonstration of hypnosis. The following is some characteristic behavior often demonstrated in psychological laboratories.

After the person is put into a state of hypnosis, he can accept the suggestion that he will feel no pain when a pin is jabbed into his hand. A pin that is then stuck in his hand will not cause him to flinch or show any sign of pain. The pin does not "hurt" because the psychologist has told him that it will not hurt. Or the psychologist can tell the person that he is going to be stuck with a pin and that it will hurt. If the psychologist then touches the person with his finger, the person will jump and show all the signs of having experienced pain. The subject is unable to tell the difference between this suggested pain and real pain. At the present time, we do not understand nor can

MISUNDERSTOOD PROBLEMS OF PSYCHOLOGY

we adequately explain why this phenomenon takes place. Some experimental data reveal that nerve impulses do travel from the point of stimulation, such as the finger, to the brain and that the brain somehow denies the presence of the pain impulse to it. But we do not know how the person feels pain when there is no specific or known stimulation.

A hypnotized subject can, in some cases, give the license number of an automobile he owned or drove five or six years earlier, although in a normal waking state he may not even know the license number of his present car. He may be able to recall the name of the person who sat in front of him in the first grade in school, although in a normal state he may not be able to recall the name of the student who sat in front of him in class yesterday.

Remember, however, that although a person who is hypnotized can often recall facts from far back in his experience, he does not have any mysterious possession of facts he has never known or facts he has known only superficially. A psychologist demonstrating hypnotism once asked a woman whom he had hypnotized, "What was the license number on your car five years ago?" She seemed disturbed and did not answer for a minute. Finally she said, "I didn't have a car five years ago."

It is possible to suggest to a hypnotized person that he is to perform a particular act after he has been awakened. This procedure is called *post-hypnotic suggestion*. The following classroom demonstration was an example of this procedure. A psychologist hypnotized a student and suggested to him that he would perform a certain action after being awakened. It was suggested to the student that when the psychologist looked at his watch, the student was to jump up and yell very loudly, "Let's go!" When the subject was awakened, he remembered nothing of what had happened during his hypnotic state. Classwork was resumed. After some time the psychologist casually glanced at his watch. Instantly the student jumped to his feet and shouted, "Let's go!" Then he sat down in great confusion and embarrassment. He could not imagine why he had done such a silly thing.

In this instance, the suggested act was performed a short time after the subject was awakened from the hypnotic state. Other cases have been reported in which post-hypnotic suggestions were carried out months after the original suggestions were given.

Hypnosis can be divided into different degrees or states, such as "light," and "deep." Contrary to popular belief, the person being hypnotized into a "light" state of hypnosis is aware of what is going on around him. Those who have been hypnotized in this way report that it was very much like going to sleep. Perhaps you can remember that period of time, often called the "twilight zone" of sleep, in which you are on the verge of going to sleep or waking up and, although you are aware of what is going on around you, you find it very difficult to be fully awake.

Can a hypnotized person be made to commit a crime? On the basis of some experimental evidence, it seems that

THE SCIENCE OF PSYCHOLOGY

a hypnotized person will not perform a criminal act if he would not perform it under suitable circumstances in a normal waking state. For example, a hypnotized person with a dagger in his hand was told to stab his friend. He did so. In this case, however, the dagger was made of rubber. When given a real dagger, he refused to touch his friend. Although he was not told that one dagger was rubber and the other steel, the hypnotized person realized the difference and refused to do injury to another person.

During World War II, however, some work done with military personnel seemed to indicate that, at least under certain circumstances, crimes would be committed as a result of hypnotic suggestion. In one case an army private with an excellent military record was hypnotized. He was then told that when he opened his eyes, he would see an enemy soldier with a bayonet. Furthermore, he was told that the enemy soldier would kill him unless he could kill the enemy first. A lieutenant colonel was placed directly in front of the private, about ten feet away from him. The private opened his eyes and began to creep cautiously toward the "enemy." Suddenly he dived at the man, knocked him against the wall, and began strangling him with both his hands. It took three men to break the private's grip and pull him off the officer. Even then, the person who had hypnotized him had to quiet him down. The officer testified that the man's grip was strong and dangerous and that he might have been killed or injured if he had not been helped.

In the army it is a serious offense for an enlisted man to attack a commissioned officer. Certainly, without the hypnotic suggestion the private would not have done so. In this case the army private did not act contrary to his moral code, for he believed that he was attacking an enemy. Nevertheless, had it not been for the intervention of the three men, he probably would have committed the crime of murder as well as violated a military regulation.

Many factors make it difficult to discover if a hypnotized person can be made to commit a crime. For instance, there is the unconscious motivation of the individual. If the enlisted man had

Hypnosis was used as an anesthetic in this minor arm operation. The patient, a nurse, was able to return to work soon afterward.

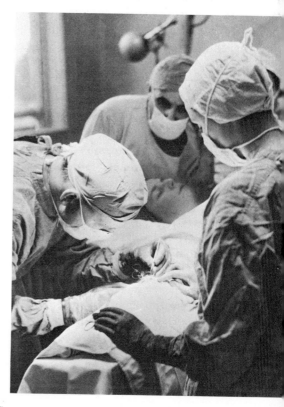

MISUNDERSTOOD PROBLEMS OF PSYCHOLOGY

a strong unconscious desire to attack or hurt an officer, would it be proper to state that hypnosis "made" him attack the officer? How would you determine if the enlisted man had such an unconscious motive? Finally, if the enlisted man conceived of himself as being in a dangerous situation and saw the officer as his enemy, and therefore attacked him, was he committing a "crime"? Self-defense is usually justifiable. Yet how could we know what the enlisted man saw and felt? Since it is very difficult, if not scientifically impossible, to answer these questions, you can understand the problem of ascertaining whether or not hypnosis can make a person commit a criminal offense.

Can animals be hypnotized? "Trance" states can be induced in some animals, but many psychologists question whether such behavior is equivalent to hypnotic states in humans. Stroking, scratching, or applying pressure to parts of an animal's body may have the effect of making him immobile. Suddenly turning an animal upside down or restraining his movements may also result in his remaining motionless for a period of time. But it is difficult to tell if the animal is actually hypnotized. Such behavior may result because it has survival value for wild animals. If a creature does not move, he may not be seen by his enemies. Some beasts of prey usually do not attack another animal that appears to be dead already.

What are some practical uses of hypnosis? The medical profession has evidence that hypnotic methods may be as effective as morphine and other opiates in minimizing pain with some patients. With other patients, though, hypnosis reduces suffering and discomfort but does not eliminate pain entirely. Hypnosis has been used to eliminate or reduce the pain of terminal cancer, severe burns, and childbirth. In some surgical cases, hypnosis has been used instead of a chemical anesthetic. Appendectomies have been performed with no anesthetic other than hypnosis. Instead of giving an anesthetic, dentists have suggested to hypnotized patients that they would feel no pain when their teeth were extracted; and the patients reported no pain.

Hypnosis may be used in the treatment of mental illness. Many persons have unreasonable fears which interfere with their lives. Such a fear may well have had its beginning in a single incident of early childhood. A person may be unable to recall the incident which originally produced this particular fear. Nevertheless, the incident continues to influence his behavior and to make his life unhappy. Under hypnosis he may recall the incident. Once the incident is identified, it can be dealt with. A course of explanation and suggestion will help the person overcome his fear. Psychologists have used hypnosis to get cooperation from otherwise resistant persons, such as an individual who refuses to cooperate in taking a test that will help in the study of his basic personality.

Lost articles have been found through the use of hypnosis. In a normal waking state a person may be unable to recall where he left an article, but under hypnosis he may easily recall where he put it. Obviously, if the article

THE SCIENCE OF PSYCHOLOGY

has been misplaced by someone else, the hypnotized person will not be able to relate where it is, since he has never known.

Because of the many uses of hypnosis and because it helps to give insight into behavior, psychologists have shown increasing interest in research in this area. The American Psychological Association recognizes the work of those psychologists who have diplomas granted by the American Board of Examiners in Psychological Hypnosis.

Why should hypnosis be used only by professional persons? A demonstration of hypnosis is always of interest. Perhaps for this reason hypnosis has all too often been used purely as a stunt for purposes of entertainment. Sometimes one sees advertisements for devices which are reported to enable the user to hypnotize any of his friends to the amazement of all. Other advertisements suggest that, for a fee, anyone will be taught to use hypnosis for such varied purposes as curing insomnia and allergies, preventing nervousness and speech disorders, and improving school marks and sales records. When hypnosis is used in these ways, it tends to give the incorrect impression that all psychology is concerned with entertainment or quackery rather than with the scientific study of behavior.

In one case a stage hypnotist put several high school students under hypnosis as part of his entertainment act at a high school show. After some of the students were put through the usual activities while in a state of hypnosis, one young girl began laughing and crying uncontrollably. The hypnotist tried to bring the girl out of her hypnotic state, but was unsuccessful. The young lady spent several weeks in a hospital in a coma, unable to communicate with anyone in any way. Although she slowly revived from the coma, she remained in a greatly disturbed emotional state for many weeks thereafter and underwent psychotherapy with a qualified psychologist. Her parents brought a lawsuit against the hypnotist, who was charged with assault. This hypnotist was not a qualified psychologist, for such a psychologist must abide by the APA Code of Ethics, which specifically states that a member may not use hypnosis for show or entertainment purposes.

The beginning student of psychology must recognize that a little knowledge may indeed be a dangerous thing. He is not prepared to carry out scientific experiments involving hypnosis. The use of hypnosis should be left to professional persons. In fact, some states even have legal restrictions concerning the use of hypnosis.

PARAPSYCHOLOGY

Parapsychology is the study of the two major subfields of extrasensory perception (ESP) and psychokinesis (sī′kō·ki·nē′sis) (PK). *Extrasensory perception* investigates experiences where it is said that knowledge is acquired independently of the known senses. Extrasensory literally means "outside the senses" or "apart from the senses." ESP is further subdivided into three areas: (1) *telepathy* (tĕ·lĕp′

à·thĭ), or the transfer of thought from one person to another without the use of the senses, (2) *clairvoyance,* or the extrasensory perception of objects rather than the thoughts of another person, and (3) *precognition,* or the perception of future events by ESP. The other major subdivision of parapsychology, *psychokinesis,* or PK, is the study of experiences in which the thought of an individual is said to influence the performance of some physical object or event.

The areas of parapsychology should not be confused with occultism, spiritualism, or mediums, which are, respectively, studies of the supernatural (ghosts, for example), the supposed control of the supernatural, and those who supposedly communicate with the dead.

We shall restrict ourselves to a discussion of only one of the above terms, telepathy.

What is telepathy? What is spoken of popularly as "mind reading" is referred to as "telepathy" in scientific writing. Alleged "mind reading" is a popular stunt for stage magicians, but telepathy is a subject for serious scientific study. *Telepathy* has been defined as the "communication of thought from 'mind' to 'mind' by other than the usual means of sensory stimulation." Sensory stimulation means the stimulation of a sense organ, such as the eye. Usually we communicate our thoughts either by means of vocal sounds (auditory stimuli) or by written words (visual stimuli). Theoretically, our thoughts may be communicated to others by means of any of the senses. In telepathy it is as-

sumed that thoughts are conveyed without the use of any of the senses.

How is telepathy explained? There is no need to assume that there are supernatural or mysterious explanations for telepathy, or "mind reading," for telepathy can be studied in the psychological laboratory. To date, there is no conclusive scientific evidence either for or against telepathy. But experiments have shown that what is often supposed to be extrasensory communication of thought is really sensory communication. That is, a person who appears to be "reading a mind" may actually be picking up cues from the other person's expression or motions.

In many instances, no doubt, you can tell whether your parents approve or disapprove of what you are doing, even if they say nothing or do not give any conscious sign. Perhaps you have learned that certain slight muscle movements around the mouth or on the forehead mean approval. Other slight muscle movements mean disapproval. Probably your parents are not aware that they make these slight muscular movements, and probably you were not aware of the fact when you learned to recognize them. Nevertheless, you have learned to "read their minds."

Why is coincidence often mistaken for telepathy? There are stories about friends, living hundreds of miles apart, who have not seen or written to each other for years writing to each other on the same date. Is this long-distance "mind reading"? There is no reason to assume that thought waves have

THE SCIENCE OF PSYCHOLOGY

The young man at the left tries to communicate the number and suit of a playing card to his partner in this experiment on telepathy.

been sent out and received. The fact that both wrote on the same date could be wholly accidental. But possibly both had just watched a show on television or read an item in the newspaper that reminded each of the other. Perhaps they were aware of being reminded in this way. Or possibly, years before, on a date that they had both made note of then, the two friends had had an interesting experience together. Although they may not be aware of it, the date in itself serves as the stimulus for each to think about the absent friend and thus to write him a letter.

The simultaneous writing of the two letters is so unusual that it is news. Each friend tells his acquaintances about the incident. People remember this case. But what about the thousands and thousands of friends who are separated, think of each other often, yet never write? On the other hand, out of the tens of thousands who actually write letters, it is likely that two people will write letters to each other at the same time by chance alone. When this event does occur, many people will tend to emphasize such an uncommon occurrence and completely ignore the other thousands of letters which were written on different dates. People tend to remember what seems to them to be unusual, while they tend to ignore the great mass of experiences that are not unusual.

What are the results of scientific experiments with telepathy? Various experimental studies of telepathy have been made. In one experiment ten books were placed in a row. The experimenter chose one of these books by secretly casting lots. Then he stood somewhat behind the subject and acted as a "mental" guide. He concentrated his thinking upon the book he had chosen by casting lots. This procedure was repeated a great many times. By pure mathematical chance the subject could have selected the correct book in 10 percent of the total number of tries. Yet in this experiment, he selected the correct book in 25 percent of the total number of tries. Was the subject reading the experimenter's mind, or was he getting slight sensory cues? Blinders were put on the subject so that he could not see the experimenter out of the corners of his eyes. Also, the subject's ears were plugged so that he could not hear any slight sounds made unintentionally by the experimenter. Under these conditions, which prevented sensory cues, his score for correct selection dropped to the pure mathematical chance of one out of ten.

You may wish to make an experimental study of telepathy. Directions for such an experiment are given in your *Record of Activities and Experiments*.

What is the judgment of scientists regarding telepathy? Telepathy is an unsolved problem of science. At one time a sampling of members of the American Psychological Association were asked to indicate whether or not they believed extrasensory perception to be an established fact. Only about 5 percent of these psychologists expressed the belief that extrasensory perception was an established fact; 25 to 35 percent regarded extrasensory perception as a likely possibility; the majority, however, merely regarded the investigation of such problems as a "legitimate scientific undertaking." That is, most psychologists were open-minded to the possibility that telepathy might prove to be a fact, but very few of them believed that sufficient accurate data were available to come to a conclusion now.

Although much scattered work is being done, only thirty or forty trained psychologists are investigating extrasensory perception. From the scientist's point of view, the problem is not one of converting doubters to believers in extrasensory perception; rather, the problem is the need for well-trained men to carry on research using the best of modern methods. Only after much research can the problem of telepathy and other areas of extrasensory perception be understood in scientific terms.

INSTINCT, OR SPECIES-SPECIFIC BEHAVIOR

The topic of instinct offers another illustration of the wide gap that often exists between popular beliefs and scientific theories. Many people attribute such things as mother love, competition, self-preservation, and war to "instincts." They assume that these kinds of behavior are inborn in all human beings and do not have to be learned.

This popular usage of the term "instinct" may have had its origin in a psychological theory that modern science has since abandoned. Some years ago psychologists believed they had discerned a number of human instincts, among them the mating, maternal, acquisitive (acquiring possessions), gregarious (being with other people), manipulative (using the hands to make things), and play instincts. Modern psychologists believe that more accurate explanations can be found for behavior, especially human behavior. So much of what man does depends on learning that it seems best not to call any of his behavior instinctive.

What do psychologists now mean by instinct? If they use the term at all, psychologists apply "instinct" to certain behavior of lower animals, not of human beings. Psychologists define *instinct* as a complex, organized, unlearned behavior pattern that applies to all members of the species. To be an instinct, the behavior of a given "species" must be found in all members of that species studied under experimental conditions. The nest-building of certain species of birds is an example. The behavior may not appear at birth, but as the organism matures, the pattern appears in practically complete form with no learning and little, if any, stimulation.

A brief explanation of the terms in the definition will clarify what is meant by an instinct. The term "complex" means that the behavior pattern has no simple explanation. As an example, one type of behavior that is often called "instinctive" is the reflex. A *reflex* is an automatic unlearned response, such as removing your finger from a hot stove. This type of behavior does not meet all our criteria for instinctive behavior. The reflexive type of behavior has a comparatively simple explana-

tion. For example, when you put your finger on a hot stove, by the time you feel the pain and begin to "think" about removing your finger, your muscles have already started the process of removing your finger from the stove because the "message" from the burned finger is sent to the brain and appropriate muscles at the same time. "Organized" means that each part of the behavior of the organism is related to the other parts; that is, it is not haphazard, or random, behavior. "Unlearned" means that the behavioral response is innate or inborn. The words "behavior" and "pattern" mean that the response must be observable and measurable and that it does recur in much the same way.

What are some examples of instinctive, or species-specific, behavior? Many psychologists prefer to use the term *species-specific behavior* as a modern substitute for the often misused "instinct." Hence this term will be used in our discussion as an equivalent for instinct.

Mud-dauber wasps construct curious little clay nests, or brooders, provisioned with live but paralyzed spiders for their young. The builders do not learn from older wasps how to fashion and stock their nests, for each generation dies before the succeeding generation comes out of the nest. By some means of heredity, this complex pattern of behavior is passed on from one generation to another. The same thing is true of burrowing wasps and their pattern of storing food.

Orioles build distinctive hanging nests, even though they have been

MISUNDERSTOOD PROBLEMS OF PSYCHOLOGY

raised in isolation from other orioles. It is true that the nests may vary slightly depending upon what nest-building material is available, but the general pattern of the nest is very characteristic of the species.

One psychologist points out that many fish construct nests in which to lay their eggs, but no two species make exactly the same kind of nest. For example, the African mouthbreeder digs a very simple pitlike nest in which the female deposits the eggs. The male then fertilizes the eggs and picks them up in his mouth, where he carries them until they hatch. The nest is not used again. On the other hand, the ten-spined stickleback builds a rather elaborate nest from small pieces of plants cemented together with a body fluid. The female swims inside the nest, deposits the eggs, and leaves. The male fertilizes the eggs and guards the nest.

Another example of instinctive, or species-specific, behavior is shown in an experiment in which ducks were reared in isolation to prevent their learning any behavior from other ducks. When the ducks were still young, one was taken to a field and put into a small cage. Prior to this time, a cardboard cutout had been prepared that looked like a chicken hawk in flight. This piece of cardboard was placed on the end of a long piece of string; the other end of the string was tied to a pole in the field with the caged duck. The pole was arranged so that when it revolved, the shadow of the cardboard (the independent variable) would pass over the duck's cage. To be sure that a shadow alone would not frighten the duck, the experimenter passed the shadow of another duck over the cage first. This did not disturb the duck. When, however, the shadow of the chicken hawk passed over the cage, the little duck became very much frightened (the dependent variable). He calmed down when the shadow of a duck passed over. But every time the shadow of the chicken hawk appeared, the duck became frightened. All other variables, such as noise, were controlled.

How was the duck able to tell the difference between the two shadows, unless he was born knowing the difference? Psychologists know no other explanation of the duck's behavior at the present time. Therefore, it may be stated that the duck instinctively knew the difference between the shadow of a chicken hawk, which represented a potential danger to the duck, and the shadow of another duck.

Is mating and maternal behavior instinctive or learned? Such lower mammals as the rat can mate, bear their young, and care for them without learning this behavior from an older rat. It is true that since young rats ordinarily associate with adult rats, the young would have the opportunity to learn how to mate and how to care for their offspring from observing the older generation. The only way to investigate the question is by carefully controlled scientific experimentation.

In one experiment, rats were reared in complete isolation from any other rats until they reached maturity. Then a male was placed in a cage with a female. The mating pattern was approxi-

THE SCIENCE OF PSYCHOLOGY

What Is Instinctive Behavior?

All the activities illustrated here were once — incorrectly — termed "instinctive." Now psychologists refer to eye-blinking (below) as a reflex. They question whether the behavior of migratory birds, which possibly use the sun and moon to navigate, is truly instinctive. Only the nesting habits of birds (above) still qualify as instinctive, or species-specific, behavior.

mately the same as that exhibited by rats who had had previous mating experience or had witnessed mating in others. Later, the female gave birth to the young, licked them, and bit off the umbilical cord. Then she built a nest, placed the young in the nest, and nursed them. The female rats exhibited this behavior whether or not they had ever observed such behavior in adult rats.

Although the female rat may never have had an opportunity to learn the specific acts of maternal care, we cannot be sure that there had been no opportunity for learning. It has been found that females reared under conditions in which the experimenter has made it impossible for them to groom their own bodies often do not clean and care for their newborn offspring. Evidently the experience of the rat in caring for her own body prepares her for caring for her young. Perhaps the isolated female rat had learned something of how to take care of her young from the experience of her own early life.

Can instinctive, or species-specific, behavior be altered? An experiment with moths has answered this question. There is a moth which lays its eggs on hackberry leaves. Each generation of females select hackberry leaves on which to deposit their eggs, even though leaves of other kinds are just as available. An experimenter found, however, that if he transferred the eggs from hackberry to apple leaves, the larvae still developed normally. Then when the adult females that spent their larval stage on apple leaves were given a choice of leaves on which to deposit their eggs, a high proportion of them selected apple leaves in preference to hackberry leaves. Thus, the experimenter was able to alter species-specific behavior in one generation.

Are there other explanations for some behavior popularly called instinctive? Experiments have shown that some behavior labeled "instinctive" can be explained in other terms. For example, many people would say that cats instinctively kill mice. If this were true, cats would kill mice, without training or experience in doing so, in 100 percent of their opportunities. A psychologist put this hypothesis to a test. Fifty-nine kittens were divided into three approximately equal groups. The kittens in one group lived alone and were kept from any possible contact with rats or mice. Later, when released in a cage with mice, 45 percent of the kittens killed mice. The kittens of the second group were raised in a cage with their mother and every fourth day saw their mother kill a rat or a mouse. When these kittens were released in a cage with mice, 85.7 percent of them killed the rodents. The kittens of the third group were raised in a cage with a rodent but never saw one killed by an adult cat. When the kittens of this third group were later placed in a cage with mice, only 16.7 percent of them killed mice.

It is clear that in no group did 100 percent of the kittens kill mice. In fact, in some cases the mice may have died as a consequence of too rough play on the part of the kittens rather than as a consequence of intentional killing. The evidence seems to indicate that kittens do not have an instinctive tendency to kill mice. But because of their speed, their claws, and their size, they may rather easily learn to do so. For instance, the kittens that saw their mothers kill mice were efficient in their mouse killing.

Studies with other animals suggest that some behavior commonly said to be instinctive might be explained better in terms of the body structure of the animal and in terms of learning. For example, you may have noticed that when horses are caught out in a field during a storm, they "instinctively" turn tail to the storm. People familiar with the habits of buffaloes report that these animals "instinctively" face a storm when caught out in the open. Is there some better explanation of such behavior than to say that it is instinctive? Colts, because of their structure, probably learn very early in life that it is more comfortable to turn tail to a storm than to have the storm beating in their faces. On the other hand, baby buffaloes, with their heavy coats of matted hair on head and shoulders, probably learn very early in life that it is more comfortable to face a storm than to turn tail to it. However, not all animal behavior has been explained in such simple terms of structure and learning.

For many years scientists have been fascinated by the navigating ability of migratory birds. At one time they were satisfied just to label this behavior instinctive. Today we have some evidence that birds use the sun in navigation, although we are still not sure exactly how they use it. It is known that

Kittens who have never seen a mouse may not try to kill one on first contact. Thus cats do not kill mice "instinctively."

birds flying over unfamiliar territory are less accurate in their flight on cloudy days than on sunny days. Other evidence indicates that birds use the stars in navigation. One scientist found that on clear nights caged migratory birds pointed themselves in the direction in which their species would normally migrate. On cloudy nights they did not point themselves so distinctly. In another phase of the experiment, the scientist took birds to a planetarium in which images of stars could be projected on the inside of a large dome. After some short exploratory flights,

MISUNDERSTOOD PROBLEMS OF PSYCHOLOGY

the birds took off in the direction normally followed by their species.

To sum up, scientists have shown that much behavior once called instinctive can be explained in terms of learning. But many questions, such as how birds navigate, remain to be answered. There is still much that we need to know about species-specific behavior in the lower animals, and the more complex behavior of humans is correspondingly more difficult to analyze. If you become sufficiently interested to go on to professional training in psychology, you may some day help to solve such puzzles. In the present state of knowledge, you will have to be cautious in using words like instinct. You have a right to question the scientific background of anyone who tries to explain human behavior in terms of "human instincts."

A major purpose of the two chapters in this unit has been to show the attitude of scientific psychologists toward their work. If you expect pat answers to complex problems, the science of psychology will disappoint you. If you want to find out what is now known and how it is known, if you want to know what steps are being taken to expand our knowledge of behavior, then psychology will be an absorbing and rewarding study.

Terms to Add to Your Vocabulary

alpha wave
clairvoyance
ego
extrasensory perception
hypnosis
id
instinct
mesmerism

parapsychology
post-hypnotic
 suggestion
precognition
preconscious
pseudo-scientist
psychoanalysis
psychokinesis

reflex
species-specific
 behavior
superego
telepathy
unconscious

Suggestions for Activities

1. Look for "Psychologists" in the classified section of your telephone directory or in the directory of the nearest large city. If there are psychologists or psychological services listed, what can you learn about the qualifications of the individuals named or involved? Also, if available in your school or public library, read the following articles: Henry P. David, "Phones, Phonies, and Psychologists," *American Psychologist*, vol. 9 (June 1954), pp. 237–40; Dell Lebo, "Degrees for Charlatans," *American Psychologist*, vol. 8 (June 1953), pp. 231–34; Henry P. David and Franklyn B. Springfield, "Phones, Phonies, and Psychologists: II. Four Years Later," *American Psychologist*, vol. 13 (February 1958), pp. 61–64; Alfred L. Brophy and Richard A. Durfee, "Mail-Order Training in Psychotherapy," *American Psychologist*, vol. 15 (June 1960), pp. 356–60. Skim three short articles on the use of the title "Doctor," *American Psychologist*, vol. 12 (January 1957), pp. 38–41.

THE SCIENCE OF PSYCHOLOGY

2. Try to find out whether or not your state has any regulations restricting the use of the title "Psychologist." If there are regulations, what qualifications do they require for psychologists? If there are no restrictions, you may be able to learn what psychologists in your state are doing to bring about a licensing law. Check recent issues of the *American Psychologist* for legislative activity and lists of states with legal restrictions.

3. Read some of the references given on hypnosis and make a list of all the reasons you can find why you should not allow anyone except a qualified psychologist to hypnotize you. Perhaps you can arrange with your teacher to give a report of your findings to the class.

4. If you have ever seen a demonstration of hypnosis, report on the demonstration. Was it done for entertainment purposes? Was anything done which might have been physically harmful? Was the hypnotized person asked to say or do anything which might have been embarrassing? What training in psychology did the person have who did the hypnotizing?

5. Many amateur entertainers mystify their audiences by giving demonstrations of "mind reading." Perhaps you can arrange such a demonstration in class. Will the entertainer admit that he is using one kind of trick or another, even though he may not be willing to tell his secret method of operation? Perhaps you can catch on to his trick anyway.

6. Ask your parents or friends who have not studied psychology to name both "human instincts" and instincts which only animals have. Make lists of these "instincts" and, in class, compare them with the lists obtained by others and with the textbook material on species-specific behavior.

7. Observe and report on what seems to be instinctive behavior in your pet dog or cat or in wild creatures. If possible, include very young animals in your observations. Can much of this behavior be explained in terms of learning?

Suggestions for Further Reading

Birney, Robert C., and Richard C. Teevan, *Instinct,* Van Nostrand.

Estabrooks, George H., *Hypnotism,* Dutton Everyman paperback.

Eysenck, Hans J., *Uses and Abuses of Psychology,* Penguin Books.

Hilgard, Ernest R., and Richard C. Atkinson, *Introduction to Psychology,* 4th ed., Harcourt, Brace & World. Pages 258–63 present material on hypnosis; pages 241–44 on extrasensory perception; pages 126–27 on instinctive behavior.

Marcuse, F. L., *Hypnosis: Fact and Fiction,* Penguin Books. This book will help to clear up your thinking on the subject of hypnosis but should not be used as a do-it-yourself handbook.

Munn, Norman L., *Psychology,* 5th ed., Houghton Mifflin. Page 171, mating (as related to instincts); pages 231–32, hypnosis as related to unconscious conflict; pages 17–19, hypnosis as related to studies of neurotic symptoms by Mesmer, Charcot, Janet, and Freud.

Rhine, J. B., and J. G. Pratt, *Parapsychology,* rev. ed., Charles C Thomas. See Chapter 1, "A Field of Science," and Chapter 2, "Objective Research Methods."

Ruch, Floyd L., *Psychology and Life,* 7th ed., Scott, Foresman. Chapter 3, "The Development of Behavior"; pages 71–74, "The Question of Instinct"; Chapter 14, "Mental Health and Therapy"; pages 521–23, "Hypnosis."

Singer, Charles, *From Magic to Science,* Dover. A general historical view of science and many little-known facts.

UNIT **2**

LEARNING

3

Principles of learning

As Chapter 1 explained, psychology deals with a vast topic—human behavior. One basic aspect of psychology and human behavior is the topic of learning. Learning plays a very important role in most behavior, from tying your shoes to writing a play to manning a space capsule. To illustrate the importance of learning, imagine what would happen if every twenty years everyone suddenly forgot everything that they had learned. How much progress would be made in a period of a thousand years? Obviously, not more than twenty years of progress could be made in any period of time, because everyone would have to start over after each twenty-year period. Another reason for taking up the topic of learning is that a study of some principles of learning should make your work in this course and other courses more efficient. Do not expect "six easy steps to mastering human knowledge"; psychology has not found any such short-cuts to success. But studying the scientific facts and principles given in this unit will give you a basis for improving your own study habits.

WHAT IS LEARNING?

You have been learning all your life, and you will continue to learn for the rest of your life. Learning is not restricted to what you do in school. It is true that some of your most contructive learning takes place in school —through books, laboratory work, shop work, and other activities. You also learn, however, in a less formal way from friends, movies, television, newspapers, and jobs. Before you started school, you were learning in your home and at play with other children.

Learning refers to relatively permanent changes in behavior that occur as a result of practice or other past experience. Characteristically, learning involves acquiring the ability to do something that you have not done before or at least the ability to use previously acquired reactions in new and different combinations. Some learning involves acquiring and using facts; some, acquiring and using skills.

Not all behavior has to be learned. Some behavior—like blinking your eyes when a puff of air strikes them—

occurs automatically. Such behavior does not require previous experience or practice. As we discussed in Chapter 2, this automatic bit of behavior is called a *reflex*. Still other unlearned behavior is mainly the result of physical growth and development. For example, as a baby grows and develops, he is able to crawl. We say, "The baby has learned to crawl," but what we really mean is that the child's nerves and muscles have developed to a point that makes crawling possible. In early adolescence a boy's voice changes, a result of the growth of his vocal cords. Such changes are due to physical growth and development rather than to learning. We shall discuss growth and development in Chapters 7, 9, and 10. In this chapter we shall restrict the term learning to refer to changes in behavior that are not reflexive and are not primarily the result of physical growth.

"TRIAL–AND–ERROR" LEARNING

Early in the twentieth century a great deal of experimental work placed animals and human beings in situations where they tried, over and over, to learn some desired bit of behavior. To a considerable extent, the subject of the experiment seemed to blunder onto the solution to his problem by trial and error. To provide an incentive for the subject's efforts, the experimenter gave food or some other reward for a correct response. For an incorrect response he often provided punishment, such as a low-voltage electric shock.

How were puzzle boxes used? Some of the early work on learning used puzzle boxes for experimental purposes. The boxes were so constructed that an animal placed in the box could turn a knob or push a latch that would allow him to escape. He was then rewarded with food. Typically, the animal made many trials and errors the first time he was put into the box, but eventually he happened to turn the knob. On subsequent trials the animal made fewer and fewer useless movements, or errors, until finally he could turn the knob immediately upon being placed in the box.

How were mazes used? Mazes were other devices used in much of the early experimental work on learning. A maze is simply a device having a series of pathways, some of which

Trial-and-error behavior consists of trying alternative responses and eliminating the errors until the problem is solved.

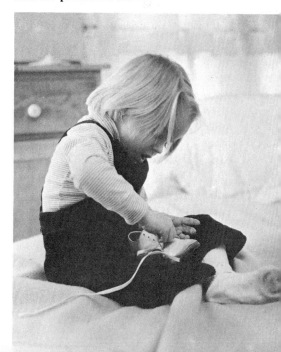

are blind alleys but one of which is the correct path to the goal. The animal or person is presented with the task of taking a path through the maze without entering any blind alleys. Many responses can be tried, but only one is correct.

In one of the early experiments (the research data were published in 1901), the psychologist placed a turtle in a maze that had been constructed in a box 3 feet long, 2 feet wide, and 10 inches deep. In one corner of the box there was a nest of damp grass, in which any turtle would like to hide himself. The arrangement of partitions in the box is shown in the diagram to the right. The turtle was placed in the box at the position shown in the illustration. Records were kept of his wanderings and of the time he took to reach the nest. As the table on the right indicates, it took the turtle 2,100 seconds to get from the starting point to the nest the first time he was placed in the box, 900 seconds the second time, and so on. On the fifth trial, however, the turtle took longer than he had on the third and fourth trials. Such irregularities are often found in studies of learning. At the beginning of the experiment, the turtle meandered about, making many trials and errors; he entered blind alleys; he backtracked. By the fiftieth trial he entered no blind alleys, did not backtrack, and went from his original position to the nest as directly as possible and as rapidly as his short legs would carry him. There was no doubt that the turtle had learned the solution to his problem.

Human beings have also been the subjects of laboratory experiments

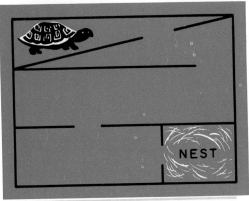

Data for the Turtle in the Maze

TRIAL	TIME TAKEN IN SECONDS
1st	2,100
2nd	900
3rd	300
4th	210
5th	420
10th	185
20th	45
30th	40
50th	35

with mazes. Some mazes are large enough to permit people to walk about in them, but other smaller mazes are not much bigger than a book. The subjects are blindfolded and asked to find their way with finger or stylus through a small maze consisting of grooved paths or raised ridges. When mazes of the same design are used with humans and with laboratory animals, the results do not differ greatly. People seem to make about the same number of trials and errors as the animals make. In fact, there have been some experiments reported in which rats had scores somewhat superior to those made by human beings.

Although research using mazes is not so common today as it was earlier in the century, students can still discover much about the learning process by performing simple experiments with mazes. Modern mazes are usually of the T or Y type; that is, the learner starts along a straight path but comes to a point where he must turn either left or right. Turning left, for example, may lead to no reward or even to punishment of some kind (often an electric shock); turning right may lead to a reward of some kind (often food, in the case of animal subjects). Even earthworms can learn such a simple maze.

Multiple-T mazes are usually used with higher animals and human beings. In performing experiments with such mazes, every turn in the wrong direction at each junction point is counted as an error. Today we usually use elimination of errors as a measure of learning rather than the counting of time spent, because otherwise the learner can speed up his movements without actually improving his learning.

Sometimes a double-alternation temporal maze is used. In such a maze the animal or person does not simply learn always to turn to the left or right at a given junction point. He must learn to turn to the left some of the time and to the right some of the time, in some definite pattern determined by the experimenter. Monkeys are able to learn such intricate sequences as *rrllrrllrrllrrll* (two turns to the right, two to the left, and so on). Human beings over four years of age can learn the solution to a dou-

Because this maze at Hampton Court, England, has such high hedges, people inside it cannot see the whole problem and must use trial-and-error learning to get out.

ble-alternation maze. Rats ordinarily cannot solve such a problem.

Today psychologists have other methods for studying learning. They speak in terms of conditioning rather than of the older trial-and-error learning. Many people use the term "conditioning" as if it were a synonym for learning. To the psychologist, however, conditioning has a specific technical meaning as one aspect of learning.

CLASSICAL CONDITIONING

Classical conditioning may be defined as a learning situation in which a response is evoked by a certain stimulus (which did not previously evoke it) as a result of combining this stimulus for a number of trials with a stimulus which normally did elicit that response. Although this definition may seem a bit difficult to understand, a few examples of classical conditioning will make it clear.

What was Pavlov's famous experiment? Have you ever felt your mouth water at the sight or smell or even the thought of a tasty bit of food? Ivan Pavlov (1849–1936), a Russian scientist, observed this "mouth watering" when he fed the dogs in his laboratory. He decided to follow up his observation by studying the phenomenon of salivation under controlled experimental conditions. Pavlov designed an apparatus which held the dog in a desired position. A tube attached to the dog's cheek near one of the salivary glands drained off the saliva and permitted accurate measurement of the flow. The apparatus was in a sound-proof room. There was a one-way-vision screen between the experimenter and the dog, which permitted the experimenter to see the dog, although the dog could not see the experimenter.

Powdered meat was placed in the mouth of the hungry dog and, as usual, saliva flowed. The flow of saliva became known as the *unconditioned response* (UCR)—the response that occurs normally, with no learning necessary. The meat Pavlov called the *unconditioned stimulus* (UCS) because it was the normal, unlearned agent for causing salivation. Next, the experimenter sounded a bell just before meat was delivered to the dog. Several more times he sounded the bell and presented the meat immediately after. Then, when he sounded the bell without presenting the meat, he found that the dog's saliva flowed. The dog had been conditioned to salivate at the sound of the bell. The sound of the bell had become a *conditioned*

Apparatus used by Pavlov for experiments in classical conditioning. The dog was observed through the panel; salivation was recorded automatically.

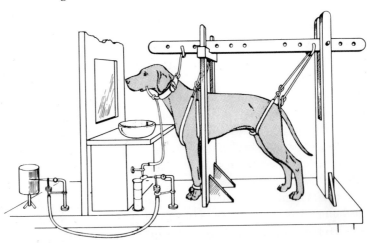

LEARNING

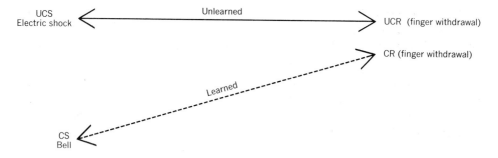

UCS
Electric shock

UCR (finger withdrawal)

Unlearned

CR (finger withdrawal)

Learned

CS
Bell

A diagram of classical conditioning

stimulus (CS) and the salivation at the sound had become a *conditioned response* (CR). A new association had been formed.

Are there other conditioning experiments? It is easy to demonstrate classical conditioning. A subject is seated with one arm resting on a table. Electrodes are attached so that he can receive a safe but noticeable shock through his hand and finger. When he gets a shock, he normally jerks his finger without having to learn to do so.

At the beginning of the experiment, the subject hears a bell rung. He does not jerk his finger, because he has no reason to give such a response. Next, the bell is rung and a shock is given almost at the same time. This bell-followed-by-shock routine is repeated a number of times, to which the subject always responds by a finger jerk. Then, although the subject does not know what is going to happen, he hears the bell rung but does not receive the accompanying shock. Again, he jerks his finger. Conditioning has taken place.

In summary, remember that the UCS

(unconditioned stimulus) is a stimulus which normally evokes a UCR (unconditioned response); that is, the UCR is an unlearned response to the UCS. The CS (conditioned stimulus) is a stimulus which is associated with the UCS and eventually evokes a CR (conditioned response), which is similar to but not identical with the UCR. The CR is usually weaker in strength than the UCR. The diagram shown above will help you to understand the procedures. The dotted line indicates that the connection between the CS and the CR is learned.

Are there practical applications of classical conditioning? Classical conditioning has been used for practical purposes outside the laboratory. In one case a baby girl showed none of the usual reactions to sound. The parents, afraid that she was deaf, asked a psychologist to determine whether or not the baby could hear. When a bell was rung, the baby made no observable responses. The sole of her foot was then scratched with a pin. She drew up her leg and cried. Then the bell was rung and the baby's

PRINCIPLES OF LEARNING

foot was scratched at practically the same time. After a considerable number of such pairings, the psychologist rang the bell without scratching the sole of the baby's foot. She drew up her leg and cried. A conditioned response had been formed. The anxious parents knew that their baby could hear, although for some unknown reason she had not been giving the usual responses to sound stimulation.

An interesting, common, and highly practical application of the principle of classical conditioning is the electrically charged wire fence for enclosing livestock. A fence with a few strands of charged wire, insulated at all points of contact with the fence posts, will serve as well as the much more expensive "hog-tight, bull-strong, and horse-high" fence. Animals that touch the charged wire receive a harmless but disagreeable shock. In some cases, even one experience of shock will condition an animal against trying to pass under, through, or over the fence. The expense of the conditioning will be slight, for current is used only during those instants when animals touch the fence. Soon all the animals in an enclosure become so well conditioned that they cannot be induced to go near the wire.

Another practical application is the use of a procedure known as counter-conditioning to eliminate undesirable behavior, such as alcoholism. *Counter-conditioning* consists of conditioning the stimulus to a different response, usually for the purpose of getting rid of certain learned, unacceptable behavior. The individual may be given a drug (emetine for alcoholics) which produces nausea when the individual tastes alcohol. Later, when he desires alcohol, he associates the feeling of nausea with alcohol and avoids drinking. Counter-conditioning is also used to reduce fear and anxiety. The procedures involved in counter-conditioning, however, when used alone, are criticized because they treat the symptoms of the undesirable behavior rather than the underlying causes. When used in conjunction with appropriate treatment of underlying causes, this method has more success, especially when the substituted desirable behavior is rewarded.

TECHNICAL TERMS RELATING TO CLASSICAL CONDITIONING

Psychologists use a number of technical terms in discussing classical conditioning. Five terms will be defined here: extinction, spontaneous recovery, reinforcement, generalization, and discrimination.

What is extinction and spontaneous recovery? When a conditioned stimulus (CS) is presented without the unconditioned stimulus (UCS), the conditioned response (CR) will gradually diminish and eventually cease. This process is called *extinction*. To illustrate extinction, we can refer to the bell-and-shock experiment previously described. If the bell (CS) is sounded a number of times without the shock (UCS) being given, the subject will cease to give the finger jerk (CR) when the bell is sounded. The conditioned response will have been extinguished. Referring to the practical case of the electrified fence, what may happen if the farmer turns off the current? The conditioned response (avoiding the fence) may last for a while, but if animals touch the fence accidently and are not shocked, the conditioned response will be weakened or will no longer be given. The fence will have lost its value because extinction has taken place.

After extinction has apparently occurred, however, if there is a rest period and then the conditioned stimulus is given, the conditioned response will reappear. The reappearance of the conditioned response without reinforcement is known as *spontaneous recovery*.

Both extinction and spontaneous recovery can be illustrated in graphic form (see below). At point *A* in the conditioning, the conditioned stimulus (CS) is presented without the unconditioned stimulus (UCS). The strength of the conditioned response (CR) may actually continue to increase for a few trials, but as the CS is continually pre-sented without the UCS, the strength of the CR will begin to decrease. This would be the beginning of the extinction period. Then, at point *B*, after a period of time and without any intervening reinforcement, the CS is presented to the subject. When this occurs, the CR will again appear in the subject's behavior as spontaneous recovery. For example, a rat conditioned to press a lever for food will, after a rest period, begin pushing the lever again, even though he receives no food. One way of measuring remembering is to compare the number of trials necessary for the organism to regain the original strength of the CR after extinction has taken place.

What is reinforcement? In classical conditioning the procedure of presenting the unconditioned stimulus immediately following the conditioned stimulus is called *reinforcement*. As the examples cited in the preceding pages have shown, the unconditioned stimulus (shock, for example) strength-

A diagram of extinction and spontaneous recovery

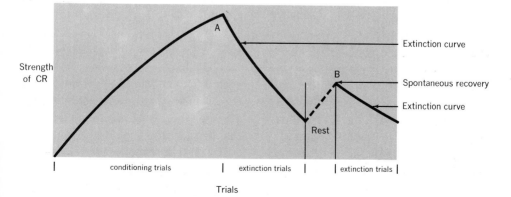

ens the tendency for the response (in this case, the finger jerk) to be made and thereby increases its probability of occurrence.

Reinforcement may be partial or intermittent. Once a conditioned response has been established, it will continue to be elicited when there is only occasional reinforcement with the unconditioned stimulus. The student who no longer jerks his finger because the bell has been sounded a number of times without the accompanying shock will begin jerking his finger again as soon as the bell and shock are paired one or more times.

In one well-known experiment, two groups of subjects were conditioned to blink their eyes when a light went on. One group had a puff of air (UCS) directed toward their eyes every time a light (CS) was turned on. Another group of subjects had the puff of air directed toward their eyes only half of the times the light was turned on. The group receiving reinforcement only half the time became conditioned almost as well as the group receiving reinforcement every time. Next the responses of both groups were extinguished by presenting the light without the puff of air. You would expect that the responses of subjects who had reinforcement every time would be extinguished more slowly than the responses of subjects who had reinforcement only half the time, but the opposite was true. Other experiments have borne out the fact that partial or intermittent reinforcement may result in greater persistence in behavior than does 100 percent reinforcement.

What is generalization? It might seem that learning in everyday life situations would require a tremendous number of different conditioning experiences. In a way this is true, but allowance must be made for generalization. When a conditioned response has been established to a certain stimulus, other similar stimuli will also bring about that response; that is, there will be *generalization*.

We know from experience that we perspire, "break out in a cold sweat," under severe emotional strain. This perspiration can be measured. In one experiment, individuals were given an electric shock severe enough to be unpleasant and even fear-producing. When they perspired, their skin response was measured. The electric shock (UCS) was then paired with a tone of a certain pitch (CS). Conditioning took place, and the subjects perspired to that particular tone even when the shock was not given. Next the particular tone was replaced by tones slightly higher and slightly lower, yet the conditioned response of perspiration continued. There had been generalization.

Then tones farther from the original tone were introduced. Although the skin response of perspiration was evoked by these tones, the reactions were less marked than those for the original tone. This experiment suggested the general rule that the greater the similarity between stimuli, the greater the generalization between them.

In another experiment, dogs were conditioned to salivate for the tone middle C. It was discovered that they

In this example of generalization, the child is responding wholeheartedly to an animal he has never seen before because it resembles an animal with which he has had pleasant experiences in the past.

salivated also for C sharp, D sharp, and even F.

Some of the fears of children may be understood in terms of stimulus generalization, as the following experiment suggests. A boy eleven months of age was shown a white rat. This seemed to be a pleasant experience, for he tried to play with the rat. It is known that small children are frightened by sudden loud noises. On one occasion just as the boy was shown the white rat, the experimenter produced a sudden loud noise. The boy shrank back. The white rat and noise were presented together a number of times. Conditioning took place, and the boy showed fear when the rat was presented even though the noise was not produced. Furthermore, he showed fear reactions to a white rabbit and other white or furry objects. He even feared a man with a white beard. Generalization had taken place. It is possible that some "foolish" fears of older children and adults can be explained in terms of generalization.

What is discrimination? In the previous section we noted that there is a tendency to respond to all stimuli of a similar kind in the same way. Related to, but also in contrast to, generalization we have discrimination. *Discrimination* refers to a tendency to respond to a particular stimulus in one way and to respond to similar stimuli in another way. Discrimination is established by reinforcing the desired response but withholding reinforcement for the generalized responses and thereby extinguishing them.

As we have seen, a dog can be conditioned to salivate at the sound of a bell. A tone of a certain pitch can be used instead of the bell to produce the conditioned response of salivating. Now if we present a tone somewhat different from the original tone, the dog will salivate to it. This is an example of generalization. If, however, we present food (reinforcement) whenever the first tone is sounded but do not present food when the second tone is sounded, the dog will soon salivate to the first tone only. There will be discrimination.

A child learns to respond by saying "Daddy" at the sight of his father, but for a while there is likely to be amusing generalization as he applies the term to any man he sees. However, the response "Daddy" is reinforced by some expression of pleasure on the part of the parents only when the child applies it to his father; it is not reinforced for other men. Soon there is discrimination, and the term "Daddy" is applied only to the father.

Perhaps you have already observed the fact that extinction, spontaneous recovery, generalization, discrimination, and the original acquisition of a response are all accomplished by furnishing or by withholding reinforcement for the response. The point at which reinforcement occurs in the conditioning process is one of the major differences between classical and operant conditioning.

OPERANT CONDITIONING

$S \rightarrow R$ reinf

Of more relevance to formal learning than classical conditioning is operant conditioning. The word "operant" is used because the subject "operates" on the environment to bring about a result. In everyday learning we are more likely to encounter cases of operant conditioning than of classical conditioning. *Operant conditioning* may be defined as the strengthening of a stimulus-response association by following the response with a reinforcing stimulus. The stimulus is reinforcing if it strengthens the response that precedes it, thus increasing the probability of the response occurring. (In some books you may find the term "instrumental conditioning" or "instrumental learning" used instead of operant conditioning or operant learning.)

What are some differences between classical and operant conditioning? An illustration will help to make clear the distinction between classical and operant conditioning. In an experimental setup, a dog has two electrodes attached to one of his feet. Whenever the current is turned on, the dog receives a shock (UCS) and so lifts his foot (UCR). If a bell is sounded (CS) each time the dog is shocked, he will soon be conditioned to lift his foot (CR) when the bell is sounded, even though he is not shocked. This is a case of classical conditioning.

Instead of attaching both electrodes to the dog's foot, we can attach one electrode to his foot and have him stand with his paw on the other electrode. Again we can condition the dog to lift his foot to the sound of a bell by ringing the bell and giving the shock just a moment later. If, however, the dog happens to lift his foot just as the bell sounds, he does not receive a shock. The dog soon learns to operate on his environment by lifting his paw for the bell and thus avoiding the shock. The dog's action prevents him from having an unpleasant experience. This is operant conditioning. A variation on the above experiment would be to sound the bell and give the shock at fixed intervals, say every thirty seconds. Soon the dog will learn to lift his paw just before it is time for the shock.

Many of the same principles that apply to classical conditioning also apply to operant conditioning, but there are important differences. The experiment just described illustrates one significant difference. The dog in this experiment is an "operator," not just a salivator or foot-raiser. In operant conditioning, the dog takes a larger role in the procedure. Another difference is that in classical conditioning the unconditioned stimulus, such as an electric shock, is specifically known, but in operant conditioning the unconditioned stimulus must be inferred. For example, in operant conditioning when a rat presses a lever (conditioned response) to obtain food (reinforcement), the unconditioned stimulus may be inferred to be hunger. Further examples of the operant principle follow. They will illustrate other important differences between operant conditioning and classical conditioning.

What are some operant conditioning experiments with animals? A contempo-

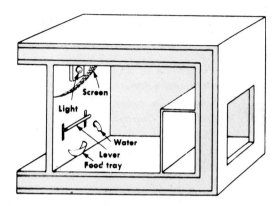

This "Skinner box" is used for animal experiments in operant conditioning.

rary psychologist, Professor B. F. Skinner, has done a great deal of work on operant conditioning. For animal experiments he developed a box (above), one side of which contained a protruding bar with a food cup below. When a hungry rat was placed in the box, the rat began to explore it. In the course of his wandering, he usually pushed the bar by accident. The apparatus was designed so that whenever the bar was pressed, a pellet of food fell into the cup. After a few such experiences of pressing the bar and receiving food, the hungry rat was conditioned to press the bar in order to get the food. He operated on the environment in order to bring about a desired result.

In another experiment a pigeon was taught to make complete turns in a clockwise direction. Making complete clockwise turns is not part of a pigeon's unlearned behavior. When first placed in the conditioning box, the pigeon merely wandered about, but in a relatively short time he learned that he could obtain food in the box. Then the psychologist began training him. Of course, the pigeon had no way of knowing that he was supposed to turn clockwise, but in the course of his random movements he chanced to turn a few degrees in a clockwise direction. Immediately the psychologist reinforced this behavior with some grain.

The pigeon continued to make random movements, but each time he turned a bit more in a clockwise direction, the movement was reinforced. The pigeon received grain for a quarter turn, for between a quarter and a half turn, and so on to a complete clockwise turn. Obviously, movements in a counterclockwise direction were never reinforced. Soon the pigeon was regularly making clockwise turns in order to get food—and sometimes even double clockwise turns. This experiment illustrates an important distinction between operant and classical conditioning. During classical conditioning the order of events is stimulus-reinforcement-response (with the UCS as the reinforcement). To insure that the response occurs, reinforcement is given before each response. During operant conditioning, however, the order is stimulus-response-reinforcement. Reinforcement follows the response, and it follows only a correct response.

Can operant conditioning be used for animal training? Using their knowledge of operant conditioning, modern psychologists have been able to train animals more efficiently than old-time professional animal trainers, although animal trainers have often used principles of operant conditioning without knowing it. The psychologists simply reinforce those responses that meet their requirements and extinguish all others by withholding reinforcement. For example, two psychologists trained a hen to play a five-note tune on a small piano. They provided reinforcement in the form of grain for desired responses as they occurred in correct order. Of course, no grain was presented for undesired behavior.

These same psychologists trained "Priscilla the Fastidious Pig" to turn on the radio, eat breakfast at a table, pick up dirty clothes and put them in a hamper, run the vacuum cleaner, pick out her favorite brand of feed from several different brands, and answer "Yes" or "No" (by lighting appropriate signs) to questions from the audience. Priscilla brought in the crowds at fairs, feed stores, and conventions, and she also appeared on television. Was Priscilla an unusual or "genius" pig? As a matter of fact, it was found necessary to train a new "Priscilla" every three to five months, not because each Priscilla failed in her act, but simply because she became too large for shipping purposes. With all due respect to the pigs, credit must be given to the psychologists and their knowledge of operant conditioning.

There is no reason to limit such operant conditioning of animals to stunts for entertainment purposes. Training dogs and horses for work on the farm can be done more efficiently by operant conditioning than by old-time methods. Dogs can be trained in this way for both hunting and guarding.

During World War II, Professor Skinner placed pigeons in missiles and conditioned them to guide the missiles onto targets. Although such trained pigeons were not used in actual combat, this experimental work suggested the possibilities of using carefully conditioned animals to replace heavy electronic equipment. In more recent years monkeys, chimpanzees, and other animals have been conditioned to carry out tasks and make reports during exploratory space flights.

In a recent experiment pigeons were taught to select visually "rejects" among drug-capsules, for example, a capsule that had a double cap or a rough edge. Capsules were viewed through a glass by the pigeons, who rejected capsules by pecking on the glass (they did not in any way touch the capsules). The pigeons were able to differentiate between acceptable and unacceptable capsules on a 99-percent correct basis within one week of daily training. They were reinforced only when they correctly selected a "reject," which had been mixed in a random order with acceptable capsules and placed on an endless conveyor belt during the training period. Later on, when the pigeons would be viewing the inspection line, to prevent a pigeon from selecting every capsule as a reject and thereby receiving reinforcement, two pigeons could be used to inspect each capsule. Each would be rewarded only when they both agreed to reject a capsule (there would be no way to know which capsules actually were rejects on an inspection line in a factory). Because of some of the problems involved, such as the huge number of pigeons needed to inspect the more than 20 million capsules manufactured

in one day, pigeons were never put to work on an actual inspection line. Although at first it may seem foolish to try to teach animals to perform such tasks, remember that man has domesticated and trained many animals to perform tasks previously performed by man.

Is operant conditioning used with human beings? Operant conditioning is no more limited to animals than is classical conditioning. In one experiment, the subjects were asked to make up sentences using words printed on cards. Each card contained a verb and six pronouns — *he, I, she, they, we,* and *you.* Each sentence had to contain one of the pronouns and the verb. The experimenter provided reinforcement by saying "Good" whenever a sentence containing the pronouns *I* or *we* was given. The production of sentences containing the other pronouns was not reinforced. In the course of eighty trials, there was a steady increase in the number of sentences containing *I* and *we,* whereas with a control group of subjects, to whom no reinforcement was given, there was no increase. Reinforcing desired responses is a standard procedure in teaching.

In another experiment, a psychologist and his subject carried on an informal conversation. Whenever the subject used a sentence beginning with "I think," "I believe," or a similar expression, the psychologist reinforced it by saying "You're right" or by otherwise expressing agreement. No reinforcement was given for other sentences. The record showed a steady increase in the number of sentences beginning with "I think" and similar expressions. Chairmen of committees and leaders of discussion groups may use this technique to encourage discussion.

Some of the terms which are used in classical conditioning are also used in operant conditioning; for example, extinction, spontaneous recovery, reinforcement, generalization, and discrimination. In this section we shall see how these words are used in operant conditioning.

Extinction and spontaneous recovery. In classical conditioning, extinction takes place if the conditioned stimulus is repeated without repeating the unconditioned stimulus. Likewise, a learned response in operant conditioning can be extinguished by withholding reinforcement. A pigeon that has been conditioned to make clockwise turns ceases to do so if he no longer gets food whenever he makes such a turn. The extinguished response of clockwise turns will reappear spontaneously after a period of time when the pigeon is again placed in the cage or experimental situation, however.

We have already considered the experiment in which subjects were conditioned to express their opinions by reinforcing all statements which began with "I think," "I believe," and so on. In a later part of the experiment, no reinforcement was given following such statements; that is, the experimenter simply said nothing when such

sentences were used. There was a marked drop in the number of sentences beginning with "I think" and the like. The chairman of a committee or the leader of a discussion group might use this technique to squelch some members of the group who were taking too much of the group's time for their personal opinions. Spontaneous recovery can be seen in these cases, too, when the group meets once more, and some of the same individuals again begin talking too much.

Reinforcement. In classical conditioning, reinforcement often comes in the form of an unpleasant sensation—for example, shock. You may already have recognized, however, that in operant conditioning a response is typically reinforced with a reward—for example, food. The reinforcement is *positive* if presenting it strengthens a response, as in the case of giving the pigeon food. The reinforcement is *negative* if removing it strengthens a response, as in the turning off of a somewhat unpleasant electrical stimulation. In either case the reinforcement amounts to a reward.

In everyday life outside the laboratory or experimental setup, animals and men continue to perform many acts even though there is only partial or intermittent reinforcement. The gambler continues to put his money in the slot-machine or to play the roulette wheel even though such behavior is reinforced by winning only a small part of the time.

It is possible that intermittent reinforcement may account for superstitions. What might be called superstitious behavior has even been observed in animals. A pigeon was placed in a cage where, at regular intervals determined entirely by a clock mechanism, food was made available for a short time regardless of what the pigeon was doing at the time. Since one pigeon happened to be making a certain kind of head movement just prior to when the food was presented, his head movement was reinforced. He repeated this behavior and again the behavior happened to be reinforced. Even though such reinforcement happened only at occasional intervals and the head movements were often followed by no reinforcement, the pigeon continued the head movements. He acted as though making head movements caused food to be presented.

The gambler rolling his dice may show superstitious behavior similar to that of the pigeon. On one play he snaps his fingers just after he has rolled the dice, and the number he wants happens to appear. Although undesired numbers appear following subsequent finger snappings, once in a while his snapping behavior happens to be reinforced. Hence, he goes through the ritual each time he throws the dice. He acts as though snapping his fingers after the dice have left his hand in some way causes the dice to stop in a desired position.

A pigeon can be conditioned to peck at an illuminated disk in order to get food. After this behavior has been conditioned, it is not necessary to give the pigeon food every time he pecks at the disk in order to have him continue pecking at it. In one experiment, a pigeon was rewarded with food only 12 times an hour (about every five minutes), although he pecked at the disk about 6,000 times an hour. Some pigeons have been kept pecking at an illuminated disk several thousand times with only one reinforcement of food. There is experimental evidence that other animals, and man, too, will perform faster and over longer periods of no reinforcement when the initial response has been established under partial reinforcement!

Knowledge of intermittent reinforcement can assist a person in understanding and controlling his habits. Habits are tendencies toward a particular kind of behavior that have become relatively fixed by repeated performance. An individual's habits may be undesirable or desirable from his own viewpoint and from the point of view of society. He may wish to break some habits and develop others.

As a consequence of published research on the possible harmful effects of smoking, a smoker may desire to break this habit. This particular bit of behavior has been reinforced so many times that extinction may be difficult. Suppose that a person wishes to stop smoking but decides to start out by limiting his smoking to once a day or even to once a week. Knowledge of the effects of intermittent reinforcement suggests that even occasional smoking will keep the undesired habit in force. On the other hand, intermittent reinforcement can be used to keep desired behavior in force.

Secondary reinforcement. Instead of being a direct reward (food reinforces a pigeon's turning), reinforcement can have a secondary stage. A *secondary reinforcement* has been associated with something which does satisfy needs to the extent that the secondary reinforcement is able to act as a reward by itself. This is best explained by an illustrative experiment. As a result of operant conditioning, chimpanzees learned that if poker chips were inserted in a vending machine, raisins would come out. They formed an association between poker chips and raisins (which they liked to eat). Next the experimenters required the chimpanzees to do certain work, such as moving a lever, in order to get poker chips. In one test, three of the four chimpanzees worked as

This chimpanzee has learned to work for poker chips, which he can insert in the "Chimp-o-mat" to obtain food.

hard for poker chips as they did for raisins. They had formed an association between work and poker chips. Poker chips had already been linked with raisins. The poker chips then had a secondary reinforcement value, though in themselves they had no direct value to the chimpanzees. The poker chips had acquired a value similar to the value that money has for humans.

Money is a good example of a secondary reinforcer. To maintain his family, a man must provide food, clothing, and shelter for them. However, when he works, he does not earn these items directly. Instead he earns money which he can then use to buy these necessities.

There was a thought-provoking aspect to the experiment with chimpanzees. After these animals had learned to work for "money," the experimenters gave the chimpanzees poker chips before beginning the sessions during which the animals could secure more chips by working at the machines. The amount of work done was reduced from that which was done ordinarily when there was no "handout." One animal ordinarily worked for about twenty chips at a single work session. When, however, the experimenter gave him thirty chips before he began the work session, he would work for only about three chips. Perhaps these effects of a handout involve a principle which also applies to human behavior.

Generalization and discrimination. In our discussion of classical conditioning, we spoke of generalization and discrimination (pages 50–52). Both generalization and discrimination are demonstrated in operant conditioning by the way the chimpanzees could learn to use poker chips for money. After the chimpanzees learned that a poker chip of one color was good for a raisin, they would work for poker chips of another color. This was generalization. If, however, a chip of a certain color was regularly reinforced with food and a chip of another color was not reinforced with food, discrimination developed. They learned not to work for chips that could not be used to obtain food.

OPERANT CONDITIONING AND PUNISHMENT

As you have been studying about operant conditioning, you may have noted that reward for desired behavior has been used rather than punishment for unwanted behavior. Even in the case of the dog conditioned to lift his paw in order to avoid a shock, the animal is rewarded by not being punished. In classical conditioning, on the other hand, he is shocked whenever the bell sounds.

Is reward more effective than punishment? Punishment for doing that which is considered undesirable is our traditional method for training children and adults as well as animals. We may punish the dog that does not obey a command. Parents punish a small child because he refuses to take his medicine. Society punishes adults with fines if they drive too fast. Operant conditioning suggests the possibility that it might be better to reinforce desired behavior

rather than to punish undesired behavior. We might pat or feed our dog for obeying the command, give a child a little treat whenever he takes his medicine without a fuss, or give citations for careful driving.

As we have seen, hungry rats can be conditioned to press bars if that behavior is reinforced with food. We can test the strength of this learning by seeing how long it takes to extinguish the behavior when no food is given. If, during extinction, we slap the rat for pressing the bar, will it cease pressing the bar more quickly than a rat that is not slapped? There is evidence that the bar-pressing response of the slapped rat is not extinguished with any fewer responses than is the bar pressing of the rat that is not punished. By analogy, we might question the effectiveness of some systems of punishment used with many criminals.

Punishment effectively stops undesirable behavior, but the behavior may reappear if punishment ceases. Also, punishment results in behavior which is less predictable than behavior which comes from rewarding desirable responses, because although punishment tells the individual what not to do, it often does not indicate what he should do. Nevertheless, threat of punishment is an important factor in our lives. The person who feels his skin begin to scorch from the sun seeks the shade to avoid becoming sunburned, and the driver of a speeding car slows down when he sees a policeman because of the threat of punishment. Furthermore, mild punishment is useful to a child if it helps him learn essential caution, say, about fire, hot water, and traffic. The experimental evidence does suggest, however, that punishment extinguishes behavior only sometimes, while reward usually reinforces behavior. Therefore, in many cases we might well use reward for desired behavior rather than punishment for undesired behavior.

PROGRAMED LEARNING

Now that we have finished a quick survey of operant conditioning and terms related to it, let us look at an interesting and important use to which operant conditioning has been put—programed learning.

What is programed learning?   As students of psychology, you should know something of how modern knowledge of the learning process is applied to teaching methods. In the discussion of operant conditioning, you saw how man and animals can be taught particular behavior by being presented with stimuli, making responses to those stimuli, and having their correct responses reinforced. Thus they learn the desired behavior. Programed learning has its basis in this technique.

In programed learning, subject matter is presented to the learner in a series of small steps, technically called *frames*. Each of the frames presents the learner with material which requires him to make an active response, either by answering a question or completing a statement. Programed materials are so written that the learner knows immediately whether or not he has given a correct response; if he is right, his behavior is immediately reinforced by the knowledge that he is right. This immediate knowledge of results is in contrast to the usual method of preparing a lesson and not discovering until the next day whether or not the material is correct. In fact, in the traditional method of study the student may not know whether he is correct or incorrect until several weeks later when he takes an examination and receives his grade.

The steps, or frames, of programed materials are so arranged that the student is not likely to make many errors, but if he does make an error, he discovers it immediately and so does not go on in the wrong direction. He spends his time learning what he should learn rather than unlearning what he stumbled onto by error.

The student using programed materials is in much the same kind of learning situation as the student who has a private tutor sitting beside him. Both the tutor and programed subject matter present material when, and only when, the learner is ready for it. They both help the learner to respond correctly by giving him hints, promptings, and suggestions. Both provide immediate knowledge of results—that is, they tell the learner whether his responses are right or wrong.

There are two basic ways to arrange programed material: according to the linear program or according to the branching program. In the *linear* program, the individual moves step by step in a line through the material regardless of whether his answers are right or wrong. In the *branching* type of program, the student is given an alternative sequence depending upon his answer. If he responds correctly, he is presented with the next question, and if he does exceptionally well, he may be given an opportunity to skip some material. On the other hand, if he makes an error, he will be branched off into some supplementary material on the subject that he answered incorrectly. For example, if a child learning to read has trouble with the word "church" in a sentence, he may be shown a picture of a church. If he still cannot read the word, he will receive another branch of instructional material. Whereas students occasionally become bored with linear programing, they generally find branched programing more stimulating. Since branching programs are more intricate, they usually require an automated device. Which kind of programing is used depends to a large extent upon the subject matter to be taught.

What are teaching machines? *Teaching machines* are mechanical devices designed to present programed material to the learner. A teaching machine can be elaborate, with electric power and complex recording devices, or it can be simple, with hand operation taking the place of electrical gadgets. The planning of the programed material the machine presents is far more important than the complexity of the machine.

In some teaching machines a question is asked or an incomplete sentence is presented in a window at the left of the machine, and the student writes his answer beside it. By means of a lever, he can then move his answer to a position under a transparent cover. At the same time the correct answer is moved into view. If his answer agrees with the correct answer, he can go on to new material. In some cases, the teaching machine is a computer, which sends out instructions on a screen or through earphones at an individual student station. The student responds on a special typewriter or writes on the screen with a special pen. His response is evaluated by the computer and determines which item in the lesson sequence he will receive next. Whatever the form of the teaching machine, it is based on what has been learned through research on the learning process.

Some people are wary of the idea of teaching machines. They look on teaching machines as a recent fad, although psychologists have been working to develop such machines since 1926. The skeptics insist that a personal teacher-student relationship is necessary for any and all kinds of learning to take place. Some seem to fear that teaching machines will take over completely, and that schoolhouses will become nothing more than factories with rows and rows of machines at which students work. Perhaps there will be no teachers around—just a mechanic in case a machine goes out of order.

The same kind of fear was expressed in industry when complex machines began doing much of the routine work that had previously required many man-hours of individual labor. Of course, today we know that men operate the machines and are able to work far more efficiently than they ever could without such machines. There is no reason to believe that teaching machines will replace good teachers. Teachers will be freed from time-con-

Programed Instruction

Teaching machines, programed books, and computer-assisted instruction all rely on operant conditioning. After completing each sentence on manual teaching machines (above), in programed books (below) — covering the left column, or at computerized outlet stations (right), the student uncovers, or is given, the correct answer and his correct response is reinforced. Most programs move step-by-step and elicit correct responses. In addition, computer-assisted instruction provides a "branch" of supplementary material to help students who answer incorrectly (top right).

change	**1.** *Learning* is a *relatively permanent change* in *behavior* that occurs as the result of *practice*. Thus learning is not a behavior — it is a_____in behavior.
permanent	**2.** Learning is a relatively_____change in behavior. This excludes temporary states such as fatigue or adaptation.
practice	**3.** Learning occurs as a result of_____. The idea here is to exclude from the definition of learning anything that has to do with maturation.
relatively **change, behavior** **practice**	**4.** Therefore we say that learning is a_____permanent _____in_____that occurs as the result of _____.

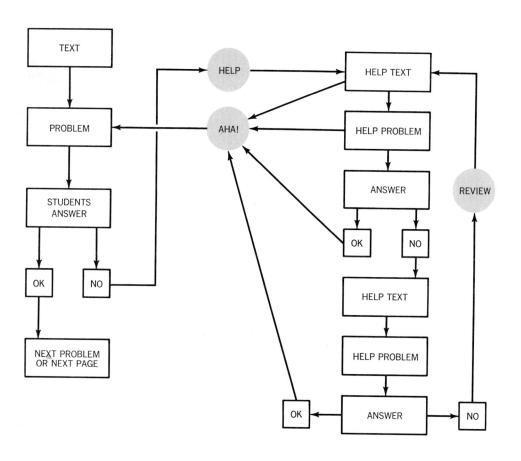

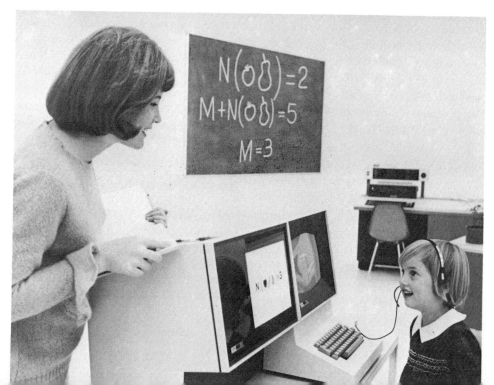

suming work on routine drilling in arithmetic combinations, spelling, formulas, and foreign language vocabulary. They will have more time for personal teacher-student relationships, which are important in the development of well-rounded, truly educated students.

There is a great deal of evidence that teaching machines can do a good job in education from kindergarten to college and beyond. To take just one example, a group of adults, using a teaching machine, were able to learn as much German vocabulary in 48 hours of instruction as college students ordinarily learn in an entire semester.

What are programed books? In programed books, there are a number of frames on each page. The correct response to each frame may appear next to or below the frame on the same page, or it may appear on the next page. In using a programed book, the student indicates what he believes to be the correct response to a frame, looks next to or below the frame (where the answer has been under some cover, such as a strip of cardboard), or turns to the next page, and immediately learns if his response is correct. Perhaps you are asking, "What prevents the student from looking at the answer before he writes his response, and merely copying the correct response in the blank?" The answer is that there is nothing to prevent the student from uncovering the answers and cheating himself in this way. A programed book is designed to encourage the student in his learning by breaking the process into simple steps and reinforcing the correct re-

sponse at each step. The book, however, cannot force the student to learn. If he looks ahead for answers, he is failing to make use of an aid to efficient learning.

Although they cannot replace classroom teachers, under some circumstances programed books and teaching machines may be able to teach more efficiently. Both programed books and teaching machines permit the learner to progress at his own speed, neither holding back the rapid learner nor forcing the slow learner to advance more rapidly than is reasonable for him. In working with individuals who are physically handicapped so that they move awkwardly and respond very slowly, the teacher, in spite of himself, may become impatient or otherwise discourage the slow-moving individual. Programed books and teaching machines cannot become impatient, no matter how slowly the learner responds. In industry each new employee has to learn many facts, and it would be expensive to provide a teacher for each new employee. The military services also have a great deal of technical material that must be taught to new men in a time-saving and efficient manner. Programed books and teaching machines are part of the answer to efficient learning of much new material.

LEARNING BY INSIGHT

Early in this chapter we saw how a learner may find the solution to his problem by blundering on it through trial and error. Then we went on to classical conditioning, in which an individual learns a specific response by having it paired several times with a specific stimulus. In operant conditioning the individual learns to respond in a particular way because that response is reinforced after he makes it. Now we turn to yet another way that an individual learns a particular response —through insight.

What is meant by insight? Often the word "insight" is used to refer to an almost mysterious understanding of the inner nature of things, an understanding that comes without previous experience or thinking. Psychologists cannot accept such a meaning for the word. To the psychologist, *insight* is the relatively sudden perception of relationships which results in the prompt solution of a problem. It is not a blind, chance hitting upon a solution to a problem. Although insight is often a relatively sudden perception which follows a period of little or no apparent progress, it is based on previous experience. Actually, the perception may appear somewhat gradually in the sense that an individual may see a number of minor relationships before he has the final insight into the problem.

Are there animal experiments that illustrate insight? One psychologist placed fruit beyond a chimpanzee's reach outside his cage. Within the cage there were two bamboo sticks, neither of which was long enough to reach the fruit. The chimpanzee nevertheless tried first one stick and then the other. He even pushed one stick with the other toward the fruit, but of course this did not permit the animal to rake in the fruit. The chimpanzee seemed to give up in his attempt to solve the problem.

Later, while playing with the sticks, the chimpanzee happened to hold one in such a way that it came into a straight line with the other. The chimpanzee pushed the thinner stick into a hole in the end of the thicker stick. Now there was a new relationship or pattern. Instead of two short sticks which could not be used to get the fruit, there was one long stick. The chimpanzee jumped up, ran to the side of the cage, and used this long stick to rake in the fruit. This successful bit of behavior was reinforced by the reward of eating the fruit. Thus, we could say that the chimpanzee would be conditioned to repeat his efforts. The basic learning in this case, however, depended upon the animal's solving his own problem, after a considerable time, by insight. You will note that the sudden solution was preceded by various attempts to use the sticks. Trying solutions that did not work may have helped the animal find the workable answer.

What are some examples of human insight? Soon after the publication of the above research, another psychologist carried out similar experiments with children of preschool age. In one case a toy was placed outside a child's playpen, where the child could not reach it with his hands. Some children spent a great deal of time trying vainly to reach the toy with their hands even though there was a stick in plain sight in the pen. Other children seemed to spend a while "sizing up the situation." Then they would pick up the stick and rake in the toy.

In this experiment of learning by insight, the chimpanzee is faced with the problem of obtaining fruit that is out of reach. Then he has insight.

Have you ever had insight into some problem, say a problem in a mathematics course? Perhaps you worked and worked on the problem, using methods you had learned previously. There were many trials that were not reinforced by the satisfaction of solution. Then, perhaps rather suddenly, you saw a relationship that you had not seen before and the whole problem became clear. Maybe you said, "Aha, I see it! How simple! How could I have been so dumb as not to see the solution in the first place?" You were not being "dumb"; you simply had not reached the point of insight into the problem. Insight has been referred to as the "Aha" experience.

What causes the learner to have insight? Even in what seem to be sud-

den perceptions, the subject has had some previous experience with the tools involved in the problem. The chimpanzee and the children had had previous experiences with sticks. The student has had much previous experience with mathematical processes and principles. Also, the subjects have had the experience of making several incorrect attempts and have therefore already ruled out some possibilities.

What appears to be a sudden solution to a problem may not be as sudden as it appears. We speak of behavior that is not easily observable by another person as *implicit behavior*. As an example of such behavior, the individual may sit and think about his problem. He may say to himself, "If I try method A, I'll run into difficulty W; if I try method B, I'll run into diffi-

He begins to pile up crates beneath the fruit. Finally, he climbs onto the
top crate and grabs the bananas, which are now within his reach.

culty X. Will I run into difficulty if I use method C? Aha! That is the method that will solve the problem." To an observer, it might seem that there was sudden insight without any previous experience, but there had been previous experience – thinking. Here is an important difference between insightful learning and many cases of conditioning. All learning involves some thinking, but when a situation is worked out through insight, the learner is often aware of steps in his thinking. In conditioning, on the other hand, the learner is hardly likely to recall that he said to himself, "I see a light. The light is associated with a shock. I will jerk my finger." Further discussion of thinking will be found in Chapter 5.

Human subjects can be asked about their thinking experiences, but with animals we have to depend upon observable behavior. The behavior may not be easily observable, but by using special instruments and techniques, we may be able to record and observe behavior that would not be noticed otherwise. In one experiment rats were required to learn to choose from a row of four doors the one door that would give access to food. One door was white, one medium gray, one light gray, and one black. The food was always behind the white door. The experimenter was able to count the number of times that each rat looked back and forth from one door to another. He spoke of such looking back and forth as "vicarious trial and error." A casual observer might have said that the rat learned suddenly to go to the white door without any trial-and-error expe-

PRINCIPLES OF LEARNING

rience. The experiment suggests, however, that looking at the gray and black doors was a substitute for trying them.

Insight, then, is not to be thought of as something that comes "out of the blue." To make a practical application, a student cannot expect to start an examination unprepared, thinking he can solve problems by insight. To have insight, he needs preparatory experience with the material covered in the course.

Terms to Add to Your Vocabulary

branching program
classical conditioning
conditioned response (CR)
conditioned stimulus (CS)
counter-conditioning
discrimination
extinction
frame

generalization
implicit behavior
insight
learning
linear program
negative reinforcement
operant conditioning
positive reinforcement

programed book
programed learning
reinforcement
secondary reinforcement
spontaneous recovery
teaching machine
unconditioned response (UCR)
unconditioned stimulus (UCS)

Suggestions for Activities

1. Cut out of cardboard or paper two crosses similar to the ones shown below. The crosses are to be of equal size. Cut each along the dotted line. Fit the four pieces together to form a square. Note how you go about the solution. Do you learn how to solve the puzzle by trial and error, by insight, or by a combination of both? Do you talk to yourself as you work? Give the puzzle to a friend. Does he suddenly see the relationship and say, "Oh, I see"?

   (In case you are unable to solve the problem, the solution is given on page 70. Do not look at it until you have done your best.)

2. Make a multiple-T maze (perhaps like the one on page 69) by tacking or gluing strips of wood on a 12-inch square sheet of plywood. The strips can be $\frac{1}{4}$ inch wide by $\frac{1}{4}$ inch high. Blindfold a subject, place his finger at the starting point, and tell him to find his way to the goal end of the maze. Count the number of times he turns in the incorrect direction whenever he must choose between left and right at the cross of a T. Repeat the runs through the maze as many times as possible in the time available or until the subject makes no errors for several runs.

   The experiment can be varied by making a maze in which the subject must turn to the left at the first choice, to the right at the second, to the left at the third, and so on. You could have some other pattern such as *llrrllrrll*. Does the subject "catch on" to the pattern? With some subjects you might reinforce desired behavior by saying "good" as soon as they start in the correct direction. Does this immediate reinforcement result in more efficient learning?

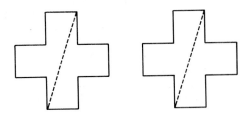

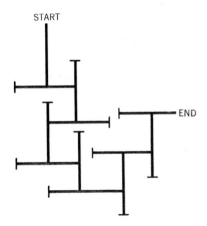

START

END

3. Another type of finger maze can be constructed by gluing straight pieces of a wire coathanger onto a piece of wood. They can be glued in a Y- or a T-maze pattern. Round each end of the wire off before joining them together, so that the person will not scratch his finger or have a clue to the correct turn in the maze. When you construct such a maze, do not give away the sequence of turns to anyone. Have several blindfolded individuals begin at the "start" point and proceed to the "end" as quickly as possible. Keep count of the number of correct and incorrect responses per trial and the number of seconds it takes the person to go from the beginning of the maze to the end. To have learned the maze, each person must go through at least two consecutive trials without error. Have as many persons learn the maze as time permits, making certain that each remaining subject does not see the maze before his turn.

Make a graph and include the mean number of errors per trial and the mean number of correct responses. Also include the mean time per trial for all subjects. In graphing the data, place trials on the horizontal or bottom axis (abscissa) and the frequency of errors, correct responses, and time on the vertical axis (ordinate). What shape does the curve have? Where did the fastest and slowest learning take place?

4. Try this simple conditioning experiment with one or more children. Place one of your hands flat on a table and have the child do the same. Instruct him to raise his hand every time you raise your hand. After a few such trials, begin using your other hand to tap on the table with a pencil about a second before you lift your hand. After a number of such trials, does the child begin to raise his hand following the pencil tap but before you lift your hand? Tap the pencil without raising your hand. Does the child lift his hand? Continue to tap the pencil without raising your hand. Does the child cease raising his hand? Can you provide an explanation of this experiment in technical terms?

5. If you have a pet that has some behavior you dislike, try to eliminate the behavior by using the principles of operant conditioning. Remember not to cause the animal any physical pain. Perhaps you might scold your pet when he has the undesirable behavior, and reward him when he behaves the way you would like. Keep an accurate record of your activities and the responses of your pet, and write a report on procedures and outcomes. Also, read "How to Teach Animals" in Daniel's *Contemporary Readings in General Psychology* for helpful information.

6. Teaching machines of one kind or another have become rather popular. Sometimes they are put on the market as educational toys. Possibly you have such devices at home. Bring them to class and study them in the light of what you now know about the learning process. To what extent is the learner likely to make errors? How is reinforcement given? Is there provision for omitting material once it has been learned? On the basis of your experience with the machines, do you consider them efficient? Does their effectiveness decrease as you continue to use them? If so, how do you account for the decrease?

7. Does your school make use of any programed books? If you are able to locate any, bring such books to class for study and discussion based on what you know about operant conditioning. In your opinion, do such books promote more efficient learning than traditional textbooks? Would you care to use them exclusively, that is, without the more traditional kind of textbook and without a classroom teacher?

8. If available, secure nail or other mechanical puzzles from your local variety store. Work in pairs, one student serving as experimenter and the other as subject. Measure the times required for successive solutions of a given puzzle. Possibly you may be able to count the number of trials made. The subject should be encouraged to talk aloud as he works. Evidences of insight may be noted.

Suggestions for Further Reading

Birney, Robert C., and Richard C. Teevan, eds., *Reinforcement,* Van Nostrand.

Daniel, Robert S., ed., *Contemporary Readings in General Psychology,* 2nd ed., Houghton Mifflin. Pages 95–98, "How to Teach Animals" (an article by B. F. Skinner telling how to apply principles of conditioning to the training of pets).

Hilgard, Ernest R., and Richard C. Atkinson, *Introduction to Psychology,* 4th ed., Harcourt, Brace & World. Chapter 11, "The Nature of Learning"; and Chapter 13, "The Management of Learning."

Kalish, Richard A., *The Psychology of Human Behavior,* Wadsworth. Chapter 4, "Principles of Learning and Their Application."

Keller, Fred S., *Learning: Reinforcement Theory,* Random House paperback.

Leuba, Clarence, *Man: A General Psychology,* Holt, Rinehart & Winston. Chapter 12, "Learning: Connecting Responses to Situations"; Chapter 13, "Learning: Selective Strengthening of Responses."

Lindgren, Henry C., Donn Byrne, and Lewis Petrinovich, *Psychology: An Introduction to a Behavioral Science,* 2nd ed., John Wiley. Chapter 4, "Learning."

Lumsdaine, A. A., and Robert Glaser, eds., *Teaching Machines and Programmed Learning: A Source Book,* Department of Audiovisual Instruction, National Education Association. Although a technical book, parts of it will be of interest to students as well as to teachers.

McKeachie, Wilbert J., and Charlotte L. Doyle, *Psychology,* Addison-Wesley. Chapter 5, "An Introduction to Learning"; and Chapter 8, pages 260–85, "Action: Learning and Performance."

Munn, Norman L., *Psychology,* 5th ed., Houghton Mifflin. Chapter 10, "The Learning Process"; and Chapter 11, "Foundations of Learning."

Ruch, Floyd L., *Psychology and Life,* 7th ed., Scott, Foresman. Chapter 6, "Defining and Measuring Learning and Retention."

Sanford, Fillmore H., *Psychology: A Scientific Study of Man,* 2nd ed., Wadsworth. Chapter 12, "Basic Processes of Learning."

Skinner, B. F., "Teaching Machines," *Scientific American,* 1961, 205: 91–102.

Whittaker, James O., et al., *Introduction to Psychology,* W. B. Saunders. Chapter 10, "Principles of Learning"; and Chapter 11, "Human Learning and Retention."

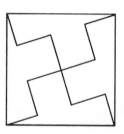

Answer to puzzle on page 68

How to learn efficiently

This chapter continues to examine the topic of learning, putting special emphasis on applying the principles of learning to the business of being a student. Most of the topics in this chapter can be applied directly to school work and to the role of the learner. In conditioning experiments, learning sometimes seems to be a matter of what is done to a subject. But in operant conditioning, and still more in insight, learning involves active work on the part of the learner. It is particularly true in school that learning is something you do, not something that is done to you and for you.

As you read this chapter, watch for answers to this question: How can I make my learning most efficient? The most conscientious students can give only a part of the hours in a day to study. The time available should be used with all possible efficiency.

We will begin this chapter with a topic of wide importance in education —transfer of training.

TRANSFER

Will a person's study of Latin help him with English, with other languages,

with science? Will learning to reason in geometry help an individual to develop the kind of reasoning required to argue a law case? That is, will learning in one field transfer to other fields? In an earlier day many teachers believed that transfer of training was a key to education. They spoke of a "mind" consisting of a number of faculties, such as reasoning and memory. They believed that hard drill in certain subjects would develop and discipline these faculties. Thus, they believed that if a student mastered Latin, he would increase his general ability in languages. Present-day psychologists do not believe that there are faculties that can be developed by exercise as muscles might be. Experiments have shown that studying Latin does not seem to cause any general improvement in using languages. Latin does help, however, with words in other languages that are derived from Latin. That is, transfer of training is not the key to all learning problems, but it is an important factor in learning. Transfer takes place from one specific experience to another—from learning Latin vocabulary to learning Spanish vocabulary, for example.

Transfer may be defined, then, as the effect of previous learning on later learning or later performance. Improvement in a given bit of learning as a result of earlier learning is called *positive transfer*. It is also possible, however, that earlier learning may interfere with the learning of new material. This occurrence is known as *negative transfer*.

Why do we often depend upon positive transfer? The importance of positive transfer can be seen from a review of the topic of generalization (Chapter 3, pages 50–51, 58–59). As noted, chimpanzees that have learned to work for a poker chip of one color will work for chips of other colors. To use an obvious example from human learning, a child who has learned to write with a pencil on paper can also write with chalk on a blackboard. Generalization of this kind saves much time in learning.

Schools do not maintain that the way to learn Spanish is to study Latin and hope for positive transfer. The way to learn Spanish is to study that language. For practical reasons, however, schools try to foster transfer whenever it can be useful. For example, since the technical school can seldom afford the expensive equipment found in industry, it makes use of less expensive equipment to teach basic principles and trusts that there will be positive transfer. Since the medical student cannot begin practicing surgery with living persons, he works with animals and cadavers, later transferring this experience to living human patients. The soldier cannot be given direct combat experience as part of his training because of the danger involved, but he is trained under conditions which approximate actual war conditions as closely as possible on the basis that there will be transfer in an actual war. The person learning to drive an automobile cannot be permitted to go out on the highway in heavy traffic for his first experience. In some driver-training courses, he is seated in a carlike apparatus, from which he watches a moving picture taken from a car in actual highway operation. In the safety of his simulated car, he learns something of how to drive under conditions in which he can evaluate his own correct and incorrect performances. Later this training transfers to actual automobile operation. In this same way, your study of the psychology of learning will transfer to all of your courses and make you a more efficient student.

What does the experimental evidence show about transfer? Over the years many experimental studies have produced a great deal of evidence that learning in one situation will transfer to other situations, although the amount of transfer is often not as extensive as was once assumed. Two of these studies will be mentioned here.

Every experienced typist knows that there is some, although possibly slight, difficulty in changing from one kind of typewriter to another—for example, in changing from an electric to a manual typewriter. That is, there is some negative transfer. On the other hand, there is a great deal of positive transfer, for a person does not have to learn the entire skill of typing each time he changes typewriters.

The army relies on positive transfer between the training soldiers receive under conditions simulating combat and their behavior in an actual war.

Radiomen in the navy are required to have, among other skills, some proficiency in typing. One experiment involved two groups of men matched for age, years of educational background, general ability, and radio code aptitude. Members of the control group began training on manual typewriters while members of the experimental group began training on electric typewriters. After three weeks of basic typing instruction, the experimental group was changed to manual typewriters. Both groups were tested at frequent intervals. The experimental group showed a marked drop in performance on the first test after changing to manual typewriters. On the whole, though, there was considerable positive transfer because the experimental group had learned key placement on the electric typewriter and therefore knew the key placement on the manual typewriter. There was some negative transfer, however, since the "feel" of the two kinds of typewriters is different. For example, the person who has learned to type on an electric machine strikes the keys with less force and reaches a shorter distance from key to key than he would in typing on a manual machine.

Evidence suggests that knowledge of facts and principles can transfer to practical problems. One psychologist was interested in measuring the extent to which training in facts and principles of human behavior would transfer to

HOW TO LEARN EFFICIENTLY

the practical problems of diagnosing difficulties and assisting the individuals having such difficulties. College students taking courses concerned with adolescent behavior, educational psychology, and mental hygiene were tested not only with the usual subject-matter tests but also with case-study tests in which they could apply what they knew. The data indicated that although knowledge of facts and principles about adolescent behavior was positively related to ability to diagnose specific cases and apply appropriate remedial procedures, the relationship was not great. Perhaps the courses should have been taught with more emphasis on transfer.

How are stimulus-response relationships involved in transfer? Many instances of transfer can be understood in terms of associations between stimuli and responses. The highest positive transfer results when the stimuli and responses of two tasks are identical. Thus, to learn to type on an electric typewriter, an individual does better to practice on an electric typewriter than to practice on a manual one. Although not so highly positive, transfer is also positive when the individual is learning to make old responses to new stimuli. For example, a psychologist asked a group of subjects to learn paired lists of nonsense syllables. If you care to try a similar experiment, make a list such as gak-bic, zuf-lar, and so on. Later, ask your subjects to learn lists such as sen-bic, zyz-lar, and so forth. You will note that the stimulus syllable gak is first followed by the response syllable bic. Later a new stimulus syllable sen

is followed by the old response bic. In other words, you will be asking your subjects to learn old responses to new stimuli. The psychologist found that if his subjects had had a considerable amount of practice on the original list, there was positive transfer; that is, they learned the second list more easily for having learned the first list.

If you have already studied a foreign language (for example, Spanish) and plan to study another foreign language (for example, French), you can expect some positive transfer. While studying Spanish, you learned to attach masculine and feminine articles to nouns. While studying French, you will learn to attach masculine and feminine articles (similar old responses) to new nouns.

As a rule, learning to make new responses to old stimuli results in negative transfer. Continuing your experiment, you could have a group of subjects learn paired lists of nonsense syllables (gak-bic, zuf-lar, and so on) thoroughly. Then ask your subjects to learn such lists as gak-zam, zuf-reg. You will note that the stimulus syllable gak is first followed by the response syllable bic. Later the same stimulus syllable gak is followed by a new response syllable, zam. In other words, you will be asking your subjects to learn new responses to old stimuli. The psychologist who carried out a carefully controlled similar experiment found that there was negative transfer. That is, his subjects learned the second list with more difficulty because they had learned the first list.

If you have already studied Spanish and plan to study French, you may experience some negative transfer. When asked to give the French equivalent (response) for a certain English word (stimulus), you may find yourself giving the Spanish word rather than the French word. For "dog" you may say "perro" instead of "chien." You will have been asked to learn a new response to an old stimulus, with a resulting negative transfer.

The experienced driver who buys a new car does not have to learn to drive all over again. The stimuli presented by the various levers, pedals, and knobs are similar on all cars, and so are the responses necessary to control cars. There is a great deal of positive transfer but some negative transfer—a driver may find himself turning on the windshield wipers instead of the headlights.

Another way to express the relationship of stimuli and responses to positive and negative transfer is by using symbols. If we allow S_1 to represent the original stimulus, R_1 the original response, S_2 a different stimulus, and R_2 a different response, we can diagram the relationship. Then, $S_1 - R_1$ becomes the original stimulus-response situation; $S_1 - R_2$ is a situation involving the original stimulus but a different response to the same stimulus; and $S_2 - R_1$ is a stimulus different from the original but where the same response is given.

For example, a red light (S_1) previously evoked a braking action (R_1), but in an experimental situation the subject must now put the brakes on (R_1) to a green light (S_2). In such a situation as $S_2 - R_1$ there will be some positive transfer, for when new stim-

uli are used, positive transfer will result in most cases if the response remains the same, as the diagram below indicates. If, however, the individual had to make a new response (pressing the accelerator — R_2) to the old stimulus (red light — S_1), there would probably be negative transfer. Generally, when stimuli are the same, as responses to the stimuli become more different, negative transfer will increase. The situation could be diagramed in the following way:

$$S_1 - R_1$$
positive transfer
$$S_2 - R_1$$

$$S_1 - R_1$$
negative transfer
$$S_1 - R_2$$

How can the amount of transfer be increased? Many experiments, as well as everyday observations, show that transfer can and does occur, but those who teach and those who learn must not assume that there is automatic spread of training and experience from one field to another. They must strive to secure such transfer.

Modern educators recognize the need for coordinated training in both theory and practice. Laboratory courses and projects of various kinds are designed to promote transfer from theories to everyday life situations. Summertime work can be used not only to earn money but also to give a student experience in transferring what he has learned in class to practical business situations.

At the university level, medical students are required to have, in addition to their classwork, actual practical experience with persons who are ill. Dental students are required to apply their knowledge to persons in need of dental care. Individuals who plan to become teachers not only study psychology and other subjects to learn how to teach but also have actual experience in teaching, under supervision.

A broad background of learning is conducive to transfer. The more we know, the easier it is to learn related material. A good background in mathematics makes learning a science easier because there are so many elements in common. College students often find that after the first few courses in a subject field, later courses in that field are somewhat easier because of transfer.

A student's attitude toward transfer is very important. Although some transfer will take place without an active effort on your part, it is much more likely to occur if you strive for it. The influence of attitudes toward transfer has been demonstrated with college students. Three groups of students were each divided into two equivalent sections. One section in each of the three groups was told that their previous training would help them in a new task about to be assigned; that is, it was suggested that their previous training would transfer. The other sections were given no such suggestion. On the new task, the three sections with favorable attitudes toward transfer made superior records compared with those of the three sections in which no one had suggested that there would be transfer. One way to use

learning time efficiently is to look for similarities in various courses and for applications outside of school—to apply principles learned in one situation to other situations.

In the future, positive transfer will probably become more important in the educational process. With the constant increase in knowledge of the contents of various courses such as biology, chemistry, physics, and psychology, it will become more and more difficult for any one teacher to try to teach all information in any one course. Therefore, what an individual learns in one course will have to transfer and relate to other courses to a greater extent than happens today. For example, emphasis upon the scientific method as one way of discovering information and facts would transfer to many different courses.

OTHER FACTORS IN LEARNING EFFICIENCY

Striving for transfer is only one of many ways to make efficient use of the time available for learning. Several of the many other topics psychologists have studied will be discussed here, along with notes on the experimental evidence and on practical applications.

1. Motivation

How important is motivation? The section on transfer stressed that striving for transfer is important. This idea suggests the importance of wanting to learn, of being motivated. In psychology, *motivation* refers to behavior that is regulated in such a way as to satisfy the needs of an individual. It is concerned with the goals toward which one is working. This concept is basic in psychology; nevertheless, we shall limit our discussion to satisfying needs and working toward goals through efficiency of study. Incidentally, there is some evidence that girls are more highly motivated toward academic achievement than are boys. You may wish to discuss this point in class.

Although a certain amount of incidental learning may take place without our intending to learn, the intent to learn is essential to efficient studying. The student who is motivated takes an active interest in his work and therefore is much more likely to succeed than the student with a passive attitude. Sometimes students become indifferent to certain courses because they have studied some of the same subject matter in other courses or have learned it outside the school; the work is too easy for them. Sometimes they become indifferent because they become lost early in the course. They say, "The teacher goes way over my head." Sometimes subject matter does not seem interesting and students become bored. Whenever a student finds his work too easy, too difficult, or boring, he is likely to become passive rather than active in his studying. In such a case, the student must remember that he can become more active. Textbooks usually offer suggestions for further reading. Teachers are glad to suggest additional reading or other activities that will be more difficult or easier or clearer, depending upon what the student needs.

Many times students feel virtuous when they put a book aside and say, "There, I have read my lesson for tomorrow!" Such reading may have been passive, a mere "soaking up" process. Have you ever read a page and then realized that you had only a vague idea of what it said? Experimental evidence has shown the value of reviewing and reciting to yourself as you read. In reading or any other kind of study, take an active role in what you are learning.

The most immediate kind of motivation in day-to-day schoolwork comes from being given immediate knowledge of results when you make reponses in class. For example, if you answer a teacher's question correctly, knowing immediately that you are correct not only reinforces that correct response but also helps to maintain your satisfaction with and interest in the learning. Immediate knowledge of results is very important for motivation as well as for reinforcement. (We shall discuss knowledge of results in more detail later in this chapter.)

Effective motivation for learning comes from the fact that a student sees his studying as a means to achieve his goal — a professional career, for example. Short-range motivating devices are often useful, however. As well as providing a means for checking on progress, tests and examinations play a role in motivating learning. Many teachers give weekly or biweekly tests. They believe that such frequent testing provides continuous motivation and, at the same time, serves to diagnose difficulties and to suggest remedial steps. There is much to be said for frequent testing, although there can

HOW TO LEARN EFFICIENTLY

be drawbacks. The student must guard against a tendency to feel, "Well, that's over!" after each test. He may fail to fit each part on which he has been tested into the total structure of the course.

Examination results are turned into grades, and striving for passing grades or honor grades motivates many students. Report cards or other notices to parents may also act to spur the learner on. A certificate or diploma may become a goal in itself. Of course, such a document is essential for many fields, including professional careers. To some people, however, just getting a "sheepskin" to hang on the wall provides a real—though superficial—kind of motivation.

Does competition motivate learning? In our culture, competition generally can be relied upon to provide motivation. Athletic events, sales contests in business, team rivalry in fund drives for charity, and student rivalry for high grades and honors are all examples of competition which provides motivation. Psychologists have studied competition in learning situations. In one experiment, 814 children served as subjects. They were striving to develop proficiency in adding. For the control part of the experiment, the children were first told that they were to work simply for practice. The mean (popularly called the average; see the Appendix) number of examples they worked per minute was 41.4. In another part of the experiment, cooperative effort was encouraged. The children were told that their individual scores would count toward their class average and that there would be a prize for the best class. The mean score was 43.9. In still another part of the experiment, the children were told that they were being tested in order to see who could add fastest in the school, second fastest, and so on. There were individual prizes for those with the best scores. The mean score was 46.6. Certainly this experiment suggests the motivational value of competition for children in our culture. It should be added that a follow-up study found that cooperation could be effective under some conditions, for example, when boys were competing against girls.

Competition is not an unmixed blessing. We tend to overlook the effects of competition on those who do not win. Students have spent many bitter hours in disappointment because they did not quite make the grades they strove for or were not elected to some honor group. The student who barely makes the coveted honor may have been no better a student than the one who did not quite make it; every teacher must use a cut-off point in deciding between A's and B's, between B's and C's, and between which grades earn honors and which do not.

Remember that an individual can always compete with his own previous record—and win. In the long run, such competition may well be worth more to the individual than competition against a fellow student and may result in happier interpersonal relationships. The student who can set realistic goals for himself and can succeed in achieving them is likely to remain highly motivated.

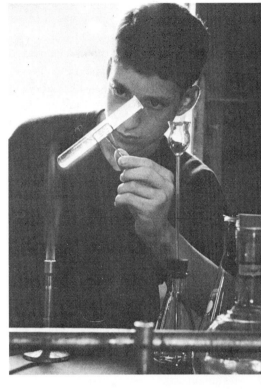

Motivation

What motivates an individual to learn? One factor that motivates a person in our society is competition. A boy strives to excel as a football player because he wants to be on the winning team. Interest is another motivation to learn. The boy who is actively interested in a subject or activity, such as a lab project, will learn more about that subject than someone who is indifferent to it. A third kind of motivation consists of gaining immediate knowledge of results. A student who is immediately informed by the teacher that he has given the correct answer becomes highly motivated to learn other correct responses.

2. Meaningfulness

How important is meaningfulness in learning? Experimental evidence as well as everyday experience leads us to believe that meaningful material is much easier to learn than nonsense material. The psychologist may ask his subjects to learn nonsense syllables for experimental purposes, but in school studies and everyday experiences we are more likely to work with material that is meaningful and therefore relatively easy to learn. Even though the value of meaningfulness in learning is rather obvious, it is worthwhile to sum up a few suggestions concerning the importance of meaningfulness in your studies.

The greater the variety of experiences a student may have, the easier future learning will be. That is, the more basic information a student has, the more meaning he will find in each new chapter or book or course. The student who tries to "get by" with just as little subject-matter learning as possible is likely to find increasing difficulty as he goes on to more advanced courses or practical applications.

Insofar as basic principles and rules in a subject field are understood, new material in that field will be relatively easy to learn. The student who neglects the early lessons in a mathematics course is almost sure to run into great difficulty later on. Mathematical formulas can be little more than nonsense material if basic principles are not understood. The student who neglects fundamental rules of grammar is not likely to finish his study of a foreign language with flying colors.

Material for which the "why" is understood is relatively easy to learn. In this book, many experiments and other illustrations are quoted or mentioned so that you will understand why psychologists are able to state conclusions and make recommendations.

Material for which there is an immediate application, or for which some application seems likely in the future, is easier to understand and learn than material which is "purely theoretical." Sometimes students despair of certain courses because they do not see any use for the material they are asked to learn. Often teachers can help them to see applications for what seems to be general or theoretical material.

3. Knowledge of Results

Why does it help to have knowledge of results? Although sometimes persons and animals seem to learn in spite of unfavorable learning conditions, they learn more efficiently under favorable conditions. One condition that can be relied upon to increase learning efficiency is to have knowledge of the results of the learning effort. Sometimes knowledge of results is spoken of as *psychological feedback.* We have already seen that teaching machines and programed books are designed to provide immediate knowledge of the results of learning experiences (pages 60–64). Now we shall examine further experimental evidence.

During World War II the Army Air Force was concerned with teaching men to operate machine guns in bombers. For most of the training period, it was not practical to have the men ac-

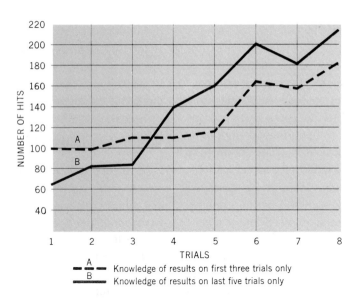

Effect of immediate knowledge of results on gunnery performance

tually fire at targets. Therefore, a training device was developed that would simulate combat conditions. Moving pictures were used to show attacks by enemy fighters. The soldier was equipped with a special "gun" so constructed that not only the number of shots fired was recorded but also the number of shots that would have hit the attacking plane had the gun been a real one. The apparatus was made with a "beep" tone that could be sounded whenever a hit was made. The instructor controlled the beep signal, which he could turn on and off at will. When it was turned on, the gunner could tell immediately that he was firing correctly; that is, he had knowledge of results. When the beep tone was turned off, he had no way of knowing immediately whether or not he had made a hit.

In this training experiment, 64 men were used as subjects and each was given eight training sessions on the apparatus. The men were divided into two groups. Group A heard the beep tone for hits on their first three trials, but the sound was turned off on their last five trials. The men of Group B were not given the beep tones for hits on the first three trials but were given the tones on the last five trials. The data from this experiment are shown graphically in the figure above. As long as Group A had knowledge of results, it was superior to Group B, but when Group B had knowledge of results and Group A did not, Group B became superior.

How does knowledge of results affect school learning? The teaching of gunners, as just described, was a practical application of psychology during the war. Our basic concern however, is with applications as they affect you as a student. You should make use of the principle that knowledge of results aids learning when you take an examination. Unfortunately, many students do not bother to check over examinations in order to see which questions they fail to answer correctly. Their interest seems to be in their grade rather than in improved learning. For best results, knowledge of correct and incorrect answers should be obtained as soon as possible after the completion of an examination. Some teachers make it a practice to have a key available for students to study as soon as examination papers are handed in. Pages in the textbook or other sources of information are indicated on the key so that the students can check their answers.

One experiment, using freshman students in a college chemistry course, was conducted over an entire semester. Some students checked the answers to short tests as soon as they handed in their papers. Other students did not have knowledge of results until the next meeting of the class. The students who had immediate knowledge of their results on short tests made significantly higher grades on the final examination than did students who had to wait until the next meeting of the class to learn the results of their tests.

Objective tests do not give the student an opportunity to express himself in well-organized fashion, but they can be used very effectively to provide immediate knowledge of results. One testing device requires the student to punch holes in a special answer sheet. A red dot appears whenever the correct answer is punched, thus providing immediate knowledge of results. One psychologist developed an answer sheet in which, when the student marked his choice of answers, the mark turned blue if the answer was correct but red if the answer was incorrect.

4. Massed vs. Distributed Practice

Massed practice refers to the running together of practice sessions during which material is being learned. *Distributed practice* refers to a type of practice in which the sessions are spaced with rest periods.

Which type of practice is more efficient? There was a time when the answer to this question was simply that distributed practice results in more efficient learning than does massed practice. Modern research has indicated, however, that there is no such simple answer. The question is complicated by such factors as the following: in massed practice, fatigue may reduce efficiency; in distributed practice, forgetting is likely to occur between sessions; in massed practice, the student may become bored; but, on the other hand, he may become bored if a learning task stretches over too long a period of time because practice is spaced. Probably the best answer is that the relative efficiency of massed and distributed practice depends upon the type of learning task involved.

Much experimental work has been done on practice in learning motor skills. These experiments have often been performed using mazes, tracking (the subject must keep a stylus in contact with a moving target), or mirror tracing, as in the experiment on page 44 of the *Record of Activities and Experiments*. In general, the research literature suggests that in learning a motor skill, performance is superior under conditions of distributed practice, particularly during the early stages of learning.

In a classic experiment carried out early in this century, a psychologist assigned his subjects the task of transcribing words into numbers according to a code. There were four groups, each of which practiced a total of 120 minutes. Group I practiced 10 minutes twice a day for six days, Group II practiced 20 minutes a day for six days, Group III practiced 40 minutes every other day, and Group IV practiced 2 hours at one sitting. The resulting data, shown on the graph below, certainly suggest that distributed practice is more effective for this simple task than is massed practice.

For more complex learning, however, results are different, as the following experiment shows. Subjects were required to learn to make a nonsense-syllable response to certain symbols. The subjects were divided into six groups. Three groups learned under conditions of massed practice, massed to the extent that there were only eight seconds between trials. The other three groups learned under conditions of distributed practice—two minutes between trials. Three tasks differing in complexity were assigned to each group. One task consisted of a simple association. A symbol was presented alone, but after two seconds a nonsense syllable was presented with it. Later the subject was required to in-

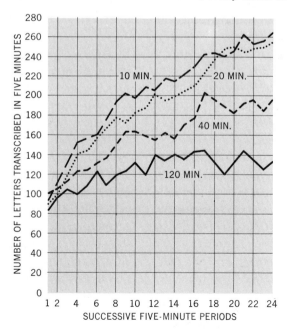

Relative effectiveness of variously distributed practice periods

SUCCESSIVE FIVE-MINUTE PERIODS

NUMBER OF LETTERS TRANSCRIBED IN FIVE MINUTES

HOW TO LEARN EFFICIENTLY

dicate the correct nonsense syllable when only the stimulus symbol was presented. The second task was similar except that each stimulus symbol was combined with two response terms, only one of which was correct. The third task was similar, but there were three choices.

The table to the right indicates the mean number of trials required for the subjects to be able to give one recitation without errors. For both the massed and distributed practice groups, the number of trials required increased as the complexity of the problem increased. Also, the difference between massed and distributed practice groups decreased as the task became more complex. There is further evidence that in complex learning, where the seeing of relationships is important, massed learning may be superior to distributed learning.

What are some practical suggestions about massed and distributed practice? In general, research literature indicates that in learning which is largely a matter of skill, as is typing, some form of distributed practice is best. This is especially true during the early periods of practice, although at later stages more massed practice may be desirable. In the learning of serial material, that is, material which requires that certain responses be made in a prescribed order, as in a poem, the evidence seems to suggest the superiority of distributed practice. In nonserial learning, where responses are independent of each other, as in a vocabulary list, the superiority of distributed practice is less pronounced than in serial learning. As

Mean Number of Trials Required to Learn Certain Nonsense Material Under Conditions of Massed and Distributed Practice

	NUMBER OF CHOICES		
	ONE	TWO	THREE
Massed practice	26.85	37.45	40.70
Distributed practice	21.05	34.00	39.40

learning becomes more and more complex, and as the individual seeks to learn ideas and principles, the advantage of distributed over massed practice becomes less. In fact, experimental evidence seems to indicate that the best procedure is massed practice at first, followed by distributed practice.

Perhaps you hoped to find a simple formula that would enable you to set up an efficient study schedule. Learning is too complex for any simple, invariable rules. Nevertheless, the suggestions just given can be helpful to you. And future research may give us more definite suggestions.

5. Whole Learning vs. Part Learning

Requiring students to memorize a great deal of material verbatim is less common than it was many years ago, but some such requirements still exist. The music student must memorize long passages of music to play in a concert. The student of dramatics must memorize his speeches and possibly the speeches of his fellow actors. The student in literature courses may be required to memorize selected passages. Many times foreign language vocabulary must be memorized.

For the student striving to be efficient in his work, the question is raised, "Should I try to learn this material as a whole or should I break it up into parts and learn it part by part?" There was a time when psychologists felt that experimental evidence indicated very clearly that it was more efficient to learn an entire selection as a whole rather than to break it down into parts and finally combine the parts into a whole. More recent evidence has indicated that there are too many variables involved to permit any sweeping general rule in favor of the whole method. Whether or not the whole method is superior to the part method seems to be related to the general intellectual ability of the learner. For example, we have evidence that the whole method is more efficient for children of superior intellectual ability than for children of normal ability. Also, the more a learner uses the whole method, the more effective it becomes for him. In cases in which the learner is using distributed practice, the whole method seems to be superior to the part method.

What are some practical suggestions about whole and part learning? Some students work more efficiently when using the whole method than when using the part method, but there are some students who work more efficiently if they use the part method. You will need to determine for yourself which method is better for you, and you cannot depend upon your general impression. You will have to test out both methods with a variety of subjects. Keep track of the time spent, and try to check your learning by seeing how much you remember and what grades you get.

Most students find that they can learn meaningful passages more efficiently by the whole method than by the part method. On the other hand, disconnected material, such as a foreign language vocabulary, probably can be learned as efficiently, and perhaps more efficiently, by the part method.

For the student who needs frequent encouragement, there is often an advantage in the part method because his learning is reinforced at frequent intervals. He can feel that he is "getting someplace." Therefore, he is less likely to become discouraged. The part method, however, imposes the additional task of eventually putting the parts together to make a whole.

Using the whole method does not necessarily imply studying a whole assignment as a unit. A given assignment may consist of two or more logical units. When the student learns one of these logical parts, he is learning a psychological whole even though it is not the complete assignment.

For greatest learning efficiency, the whole and part methods may be combined. In many learning situations it is probably best to begin with the whole method, while feeling free to concentrate at any time upon a particularly difficult or important part. By using the part method with the difficult sections, the learner need not spend time going over material he already knows well. At the end of his study session, however, he should round out his learning with a brief return to the whole method to review and to check on his learning.

6. Mnemonic Devices

How reliable are mnemonic devices? In an attempt to be efficient in his learning, a student may sometimes turn to *mnemonic* (nē·mon′ik) *devices* such as catchwords, jingles, and formulas to help him recall particular facts. No doubt you know the little jingle beginning, "Thirty days hath September, April, June, and November." The jingle helps you remember the facts. The rhyming of *two* and *blue* may help one to remember that Columbus discovered America in 1492:

> In fourteen hundred ninety-two
> Columbus sailed the ocean blue.

However, there is the story of the schoolboy who put down 1493 on his examination paper because

> In fourteen hundred ninety-three
> Columbus sailed the deep blue sea.

The possibility of making such mistakes is always present when we depend on mnemonic devices.

Mnemonic devices may save time for the moment, but they often waste time in the long run. There is always the danger that a person will apply more effort to learning the mnemonic device than to the facts he should learn. If he were to spend the time learning logical relationships between facts or ideas that he spends on learning nonlogical mnemonic devices. he would often produce far more effective results.

Although mnemonic devices may be used with some value in the learning of simple facts, they cannot be used successfully in more complicated learn-

Concert pianists, such as Van Cliburn, must learn many long passages of music. When memorizing a new piece of music, pianists often combine the whole and part method of learning.

ing processes. Anyone who attempts to depend upon mnemonic devices in such subjects as geometry, history, and literature will soon become bogged down in the devices. He will miss the point of the matter to be learned. Correct methods of study are far surer and are easier in the end than trick "memory aids." The efficient student resorts to mnemonic devices sparingly.

7. Overlearning

What is the value of overlearning? Suppose you have to memorize a poem or a speech or a vocabulary list. You study until you can close your book and recite the material without a mistake. Why study more? There is experimental evidence that materials learned to the level of a single perfect recitation are forgotten more rapidly than materials that are studied more thoroughly, or *overlearned*. The student who studies only to the point of being able to recite the material perfectly one time will probably find that he can no longer repeat it perfectly when the day comes for an examination.

In a classic experiment on overlearning, adults were asked to learn lists consisting of 12 nouns of one syllable each. Some of the lists were repeated over and over until the subject had learned them well enough to repeat them once without error. As soon as he met this criterion, he studied these particular lists no further. For other lists, the subject went on with his repetitions to the extent of 50 percent overlearning. For example, if four repetitions had been required in order to meet the criterion of one errorless

repetition, the subject went on to a total of six repetitions. For still other lists, the subject went on to the extent of 100 percent overlearning; if four repetitions had been required in order to meet the criterion, the subject went on to a total of eight repetitions. Learning was measured at intervals for twenty-eight days by testing how much of the lists the subjects could remember. The resulting data are shown in the figure on page 88.

From this graph you will note that overlearning results in a material increase in what is remembered, especially over longer periods of time. Note also, however, that a law of diminishing returns seems to be operating. There is less difference in the amount remembered between 50 percent overlearning and 100 percent overlearning than there is between no overlearning and 50 percent overlearning. The results of overlearning carried to 200 percent bear out the generalization about diminishing returns. The student with practically unlimited time available might improve his grades somewhat by going over his lessons time after time after time. For the student who must budget his time, some overlearning is clearly indicated, but he must recognize the fact of diminishing returns. Poring over the same material hour after hour may make the student feel virtuous, but he is paying a high price for an increasingly smaller return.

The above experiment is not to be taken as evidence of how much overlearning you should attempt to do in your schoolwork. If you thoroughly understand the material you are studying, and if it is material which involves

HOW TO LEARN EFFICIENTLY

understanding relationships rather than material which requires rote learning, you may need very little time for over-learning.

8. Latent Learning

What is latent learning? There is some evidence that learning takes place in the absence of reinforcement but is utilized only when reinforcement is given. Such learning is spoken of as *latent learning*. There is experimental evidence that animals learn even though they are not rewarded. Three groups of rats were tested in maze running. One of the groups was permitted to wander through a maze but was never rewarded with food. (Some psychologists feel that the handling the rats received from the experimenters served as reward, even though they may have received no food.) Another group was always fed upon completing the run of the maze. A third group was permitted to wander about in the maze for ten days but was not rewarded until the eleventh day. Upon being presented with food reinforcement, this third group quickly took the short path through the maze, equaling or even excelling the maze-running ability of the group which had been reinforced from the first.

In our everyday activities we have many experiences in which we do not seem to learn but later find that some learning has taken place. We may feel that we have learned practically nothing on certain days or in certain classes. Yet there may have been latent learning. It is encouraging to realize that this learning may be there at some later time when it is needed.

THE PROGRESS OF LEARNING

Thus far we have discussed a number of the problems and techniques involved in learning. Now we shall consider the whole process of learning a set of facts or a skill. How fast should

Retention following no overlearning and two degrees of overlearning

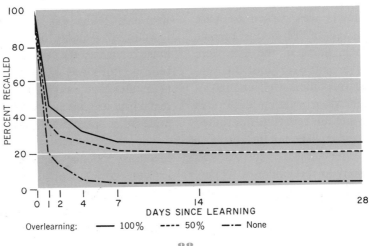

LEARNING

that process be? Should we expect to improve at a steady rate until we achieve mastery?

Graphs of learning can show us how learning progresses. We encountered graphs which show the progress of learning when we studied knowledge of results in gunnery training and in massed and distributed practice. To keep track of the progress of learning, experimenters plot their data on graphs.

As you perhaps noticed on the learning graphs mentioned above, the amount of learning is usually shown on the vertical axis, and the amount and kind of practice is shown on the horizontal axis; the dependent variable is indicated on the vertical axis and the independent variable on the horizontal axis. Take a look at the learning graph on page 81 showing the effects of knowledge of results in gunnery training. The dependent variable, the amount of learning (indicated by the number of hits) is plotted on the vertical axis. The independent variable (the number of trials, controlled by the experimenter) is plotted on the horizontal axis.

There is some reason to believe that if we are able to measure the process of learning a skill or set of facts from the very beginning to at least a fair degree of mastery, the graph of our data would show an S-shaped (sigmoid) curve, as indicated in the figure above. Learning progress is generally very slow at first, then speeds up, and finally slows down. Suppose that we were to measure the complete process of how an individual learns his native language. The newborn infant exercises his vocal cords. Soon

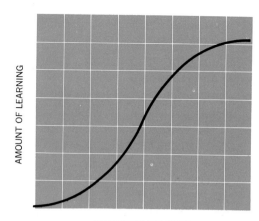

AMOUNT OF PRACTICE

he hears sounds. He is learning, although very slowly, to speak the language he hears. There are great individual differences, but generally the first word is uttered somewhere between eight and twenty months of age. The child continues to make meaningful sounds. By the age of four he may have a vocabulary of more than 1,500 words. During his school years, his vocabulary continues to grow at a fairly steady rate. Then there is a slowing down in the acquisition of vocabulary, although he adds new words to his vocabulary and drops some old words throughout his life.

Graphs of learning data for an individual are characteristically irregular. One day he may not have as good a record as on a previous day. Perhaps the learning process is itself irregular, or perhaps the irregularity is a result of inability to measure all that is really taking place as a person learns.

What are positive, uniform, and negative acceleration? Some experiments on learning result in curves that show increasing returns. Such learning curves are said to show *positive acceleration*.

HOW TO LEARN EFFICIENTLY

They resemble the first part of the S-shaped curve. Some experiments on learning result in curves which show *uniform acceleration,* that is, the same amount of improvement for equal units of practice. They resemble the middle of the S-shaped curve. Still other experiments result in curves that show decreasing returns. They are said to show *negative acceleration.* They resemble the last part of the S-shaped curve. Most learning curves are of the last-mentioned shape, probably because measurement does not begin until after much of the total learning has been completed. Also, the learner may be reaching his limit; for example, a typist may be reaching the point beyond which his fingers will not move more rapidly. (Most of us, however, cease to improve long before we reach this limit.)

Sometimes students become discouraged because they slow up in a given learning process. The discouragement may not be warranted. They may be nearing the end of the total learning process, or at least they may have reached a fair degree of mastery. On the other hand, the slowing up may be just a temporary phenomenon.

What is a plateau?   Occasionally, but not frequently, one or more plateaus may be found in a learning graph. A *plateau* is a period of little or no apparent progress in learning. It is preceded by measurable learning and is followed by measurable learning. A plateau is more likely to be found in data that is based on learning a complex skill than in data that is based on learning a simple skill.

At one time the progress made by workers learning a particular industrial job was studied. Part of the data obtained from this study are shown in the graph on page 91. Note that the rapid initial learning was followed by a plateau (marked off by the two broken vertical lines). Note, too, that there was further rise in skill following the plateau.

If you ever learned to type, do you think data on your progress might have shown a plateau? Individuals who learn to ski often feel that they go through a period that would appear on a graph as a plateau. Did you have a plateau while learning to play a musical instrument? If you are a radio "ham," you may have had a plateau in your learning of the code.

Why may there be a plateau?   A number of possible explanations have been offered for the plateau that is found in some learning graphs. It has been said that a plateau is likely to occur when the learner becomes bored. The beginning student of typing is quite enthusiastic; he is on his way to a good job, and his motivation is high. In time, however, the novelty wears off, he becomes discouraged, he loses interest, and his progress levels off. It may be, of course, that the plateau is a cause of boredom rather than a consequence of it. At any rate, a short period of no practice may be helpful. During this rest period, detrimental habits may be extinguished. The learner may return to the original practice material with renewed enthusiasm. A graph of his learning will show that he then leaves the plateau.

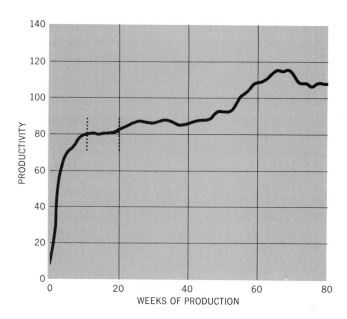

Progress in learning a particular industrial job

A plateau may occur when the learner has to discover a more efficient work method. For example, some individuals learn to type by the hunt-and-peck system. They may achieve considerable speed with this system, but they do not become truly good typists. If they decide to become good typists, they must change to the touch system. A plateau may occur as the change is made, but as they acquire skill in the touch system, they leave the plateau. Lessons from a skilled teacher may help an individual to leave a plateau. If, for example, your progress in learning to play a musical instrument has leveled off, a music teacher might help by instructing you to change the position of your hands or of the mouthpiece on your lips.

A plateau may appear because the learner has not understood earlier material. Sometimes a course has to move so rapidly from one topic to another that the learner does not master each step as it is presented. He will leave the plateau when he assimilates this earlier material.

A plateau may occur because the learner becomes tense. He feels that he is "dumb" because he isn't making progress. Knowing that a plateau is only a temporary thing and that further progress will come will relieve tension and help the learner rise above the plateau.

It is encouraging to realize that the plateau may not represent an actual lack of improvement. It is true that the learning curve levels off temporarily, but it may be that if we could measure the learning process more accurately and in more detail, we would find that progress is steady. The ap-

HOW TO LEARN EFFICIENTLY

parent plateau might be eliminated.

Throughout your study of psychology you will find many different kinds of curves and graphs. The Appendix has additional information on how to draw and interpret curves.

REMEMBERING

Inherent in the discussion of learning has been the idea of remembering. We learn with the thought that at some time later we shall be able to recall what we have learned. In this section we shall consider some of the experimental work that has been done on retention — on what is retained or remembered. To be studied scientifically, retention must be measured. Psychologists have performed experiments using many methods of measuring memory over the years; we shall consider three basic methods here.

What is the method of relearning? The method of relearning, sometimes called the "method of savings," can be illustrated by reference to a classic experiment by the German psychologist Hermann Ebbinghaus. In order to avoid the effects of previous learning, he introduced the use of nonsense syllables in his experiments on learning. Serving as his own subject, he memorized lists of nonsense syllables, carefully recording the amount of time required to learn each list to the point of making two errorless recitations. This point can be designated as the *point of immediate recall*. Following various intervals, he relearned the lists, again keeping a record of the time required. The difference between the time required for the

original learning and the time required for relearning was a measure of retention. The table below summarizes his data in terms of percent of material retained when measured by this method.

Retention of Lists of Nonsense Syllables, as Measured by Ebbinghaus

INTERVAL BETWEEN LEARNING AND RELEARNING	PERCENT RETAINED
None (immediate recall)	100
20 minutes	58
1 hour	44
9 hours	36
24 hours	34
2 days	28
6 days	25
31 days	21

Are these data disturbing? Are you asking yourself, "Why bother to learn? I'll forget most of what I learn in a month anyway." Note that this experiment employed nonsense syllables; there is greater retention for meaningful material.

Another well-known experiment indicates that material that has once been learned can be relearned with less effort than material not learned previously, even though the original learning occurred early in life and a long interval elapsed between learning and relearning. A psychologist read selected passages of Greek to his child when the child was between fifteen and thirty-six months of age. Each day for three months, passages were read to the child. At the end of each three months, new passages were selected and read. When the child was eight and one-half years of age and again when he was fourteen years of age, he was required to memorize these same passages. In addition, at these ages he was required to memorize new Greek passages of equal length and apparently of equal difficulty. At eight and one-half years, 317 repetitions were required to memorize the passages that had been heard in early childhood, but 435 repetitions were required to memorize the new passages. In other words, 27 percent fewer repetitions were required for the passages heard in infancy. It is true that by the age of fourteen years the saving was reduced to 8 percent, but the remarkable fact is that there was retention for what was obviously nonsense material to the young child.

Sometimes students become pleasantly aware of the fact that they have actually retained learned material which they believed had been "completely" forgotten. Perhaps you have studied a foreign language in high school. Later in college or while traveling you may need to read, write, or speak this language. At first it may seem that you have completely forgotten your high school language training. Yet it takes much less time to relearn vocabulary than to learn a comparable amount of vocabulary in a language that you have never studied.

What is the method of recall? In this method of studying retention, the individual is simply asked to reproduce something he has learned in the past. For a laboratory experiment a subject is asked to learn a list of nonsense syllables or words. Later his retention is measured by giving him the first syllable or word and asking him to respond with the remainder of the list. By dividing the number of items he can reproduce by the number of items originally learned, you obtain a retention score expressed as a percentage.

A more refined method of measuring recall involves anticipation. Again a list of nonsense syllables or words is learned. Later the syllables or words are exposed one at a time through the aperture of a memory drum, a device consisting of a drum on which is placed the material to be learned. As the drum revolves, each item is exposed briefly through a small opening. In an anticipation experiment, syllables or words are exposed at intervals of a few seconds, in the same order as in the list the subject has learned. During this interval the subject tries to anticipate what the next syllable or word will be.

As students, you have a great deal of experience with the recall method of measuring retention of learned material. In a French class, for example, you may be asked to conjugate the verb *faire*. Following this minimal stimulus, you try to recall the various forms of the verb. In history class you may be expected to trace the course of the Industrial Revolution — to recall many names, dates, and events. Essay examination questions are typically used to measure retention by the method of recall. Perhaps you have often felt that you really know much more than you were able to recall during an examination.

What is the method of recognition? Following an examination, you have probably talked over the questions and

HOW TO LEARN EFFICIENTLY

answers with some of your classmates. Perhaps there was one question for which you could recall practically no material. The friend mentions the answer he gave, and you recognize immediately that his answer represents what you had learned but could not recall. We can usually recognize far more than we can recall.

Objective examination questions are typically used to measure retention by the method of recognition. For example, an objective test may contain such a question as this:

The strengthening of a stimulus-response association by following the response with a reinforcing stimulus which strengthens the response that precedes it is a definition of what kind of conditioning? (A) Classical. (B) Pavlovian. (C) Operant. (D) Respondent.

Is it not easier to recognize the correct response to this question than it would be to recall the response to the question, "How can we define operant conditioning?"

Objective examinations can cover many more points than essay examinations. The student has a better chance to indicate just how much of the material he has retained. If he has forgotten two or three points out of a hundred on an objective examination, he still earns a very good score. If he has forgotten two or three points on an essay examination, and if these two or three points happen to be stressed, his score is not an accurate measure of his total retention for the material in the course. Yet it is also true that objective examinations do not give the student an opportunity to organize and express his thinking in the form in which he will do most of his reporting throughout life. A good examination program combines essay and objective questions; that is, it uses both the method of recall and the method of recognition.

Is an extensive vocabulary an aid to retention? Language assists us in remembering specific material. This was demonstrated in an experiment involving the naming of colors. The psychologists performing the experiment pointed out that humans are able to distinguish about 7,500,000 different "colors." However, the English language has less than 4,000 names for colors and only about 8 names occur very commonly (red, orange, yellow, green, blue, purple, pink, brown). The subjects for the experiment were college students, all of whom spoke English as their native language and none of whom was color-blind. Selected groups of 4 colors were shown to each subject. Then the subject was shown a card containing 120 colors and was asked to identify the 4 he had just seen. Data indicated that those colors that were easiest to recognize were those most easily named.

The same experiment was carried out with Zuñi Indians. In the language of the Zuñi Indians, there is but a single name for the colors we denote as orange and yellow. Although English-speaking subjects never confused orange and yellow in the recognition test, Zuñi subjects frequently did so. That is, both the laboratory study and the field study indicated an agreement between vocabulary and ability to remember (recognize) a color. The practical suggestion that can be based on this experiment is that students should learn the vocabulary of each field they study. This book lists vocabulary at the end of each chapter.

Are general ideas or exact words easier to remember? Sometimes, in a sincere effort to do good work, students attempt to memorize verbatim the material in their textbooks. Often upon examination they are greatly disturbed to find that they cannot recall material studied in this way. Psychologists have found that longtime retention is greater for general essential ideas that have been mastered than for statements that have merely been learned verbatim.

In one scientific study, students were required to recognize the correctness or incorrectness of statements based on a passage they had read previously. That is, retention was measured. Some of the statements they were asked to recognize were worded exactly as they had been stated in the passage; others were worded differently, although ex-

pressing the same general idea as that of the original passage. Retention was measured at various intervals over a period of seventy days. The results are shown graphically in the figure below.

In this experiment there was actually a rise in retention of essential ideas and facts for a number of days following the reading of the passage. This rise occurred even though retention of essential ideas was at first somewhat lower than verbatim retention. Some loss followed the initial rise in retention of essential ideas, but this loss was slight compared with the loss for verbatim retention. In your studying, do you merely try to memorize "what the book says," or do you try to understand the fundamental meaning of what you read?

Can we remember what is heard during sleep? It has been estimated that in a normal lifetime a person spends approximately twenty-two years sleeping. If some of this time can be salvaged for learning purposes, total learning—and

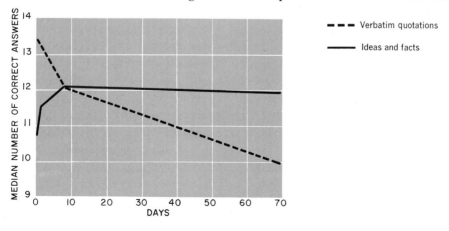

Retention of general ideas compared with retention of exact words

- - - Verbatim quotations

——— Ideas and facts

free time for recreation—can be increased. Some research reports seem to show that people can remember what they hear while asleep. For example, two psychologists attempted to teach the words of three songs, each one eight to twenty-seven lines in length, to a lightly sleeping woman by playing each song to her five times a night for three successive nights. She did not know the songs before the experiment began, but following the sleep training she was able to write the lyrics for two of the songs without error and for the other song with only minor errors.

Such reports seem impressive and may be cited in advertising for commercial devices which, the manufacturers claim, will teach a person while he is asleep. After reviewing the literature on learning during sleep, however, psychologists have concluded that it is highly speculative whether or not the studies reported to date have presented any acceptable evidence that learning during sleep is possible. Experiments in recent years have suggested that sleep can be divided into four stages, of which the lightest sleep is the first stage and the deepest sleep is the fourth stage. It has been shown that subjects can discriminate auditory signals during a light stage of sleep and that spoken personal names are incorporated into dreams when presented during a period when the subject is dreaming. But there are still insufficient data regarding learning during sleep. The individual who spends his time learning while awake will still learn more than the one who spends an equal amount of time trying to learn when

asleep. At any rate, the student certainly should not depend upon having someone read his textbooks to him during the night.

FORGETTING

Why do we forget? There are several theories to answer this question, none of which seem to adequately answer all of the problems involved. Nevertheless, we shall examine six of these basic theories: (1) elapse of time, (2) inattention, (3) retroactive inhibition, (4) proactive inhibition, (5) motivated forgetting and (6) distortion of the memory trace.

1. *Elapse of time*. One of the oldest theories of forgetting is based on the belief that when we learn, a *memory trace* is laid down in the nervous system and especially in the brain. Learning causes a physical change in the brain and nervous system that disappears with the passage of time. The elapse of time brings about a fading of the memory trace, which is sometimes called "organic decay." To date there is little evidence to support this belief. One argument against this theory is that some apparently "lost" event is later remembered. Particularly in old age, individuals can often remember events that happened when they were much younger. For example, there is a record of one man who, at the age of ninety, suddenly recalled a poem of eight lines which he had learned at the age of fifteen. He could not remember having reheard the poem during the interval of seventy-five years.

2. *Inattention*. Another reason for some forgetting is thought to be based

on a lack of attentiveness when we are supposed to be learning. For example, when we are introduced to someone, unless we are paying close attention, it is sometimes very difficult, if not impossible, to recall the person's name after a few seconds.

3. *Retroactive inhibition.* The theory that new learning may interfere with old learning is called *retroactive inhibition.* For example, in one experiment subjects were required to learn a list of nonsense syllables (List A) and then learn a different list of nonsense syllables (List B), after which they were required to recall List A. A control group, who learned only the nonsense syllables on List A, was able to recall more of List A than the experimental group. The control group did not have any new learning to interfere with their memory of List A.

Another example of retroactive inhibition is one experimental study in which subjects were asked to memorize lists of adjectives. Following this learning, other learning activities were introduced which consisted of the following lists: (1) adjectives that were synonyms of the original list, (2) adjectives that were antonyms of the original list, (3) adjectives that were unrelated in meaning to the original adjectives, (4) nonsense syllables, and (5) three-place numbers. Following the original learning, the subjects were divided into groups. Each of five groups learned a different one of these five lists, while one group of subjects rested after the original learning and made no attempt to learn another list of any kind. The percentages of recall following the rest and following various learn-

Why do students sometimes forget previously learned material on an exam?

ing activities are indicated in the table on the next page. The interval of time between original learning and recall was ten minutes. Certainly the data in this table suggest that retroactive inhibition is greatest when the original learning is followed by the learning of very similar material. Also, note the effect on recall of rest following the original learning.

HOW TO LEARN EFFICIENTLY

Retention of Original Learning Following Rest or Other Learning

INTERVAL ACTIVITY	PERCENT RETAINED
Rest (no further learning)	45
Learning:	
Digits	37
Nonsense syllables	26
Unrelated adjectives	22
Antonyms	18
Synonyms	12

4. *Proactive inhibition.* Proactive inhibition is similar to retroactive inhibition, except that the sequence of the interference of learning material is reversed. That is, *proactive inhibition* is the interference of earlier learning with later learning. In one experiment subjects first learned List A, next List B, and then were asked to recall List B. A control group showed that the prior learning of List A did interfere with the recall of List B. Actually evidence has shown that experience with learning lists does improve the learning of new lists, but it also shows that past experience in learning of such lists interferes with the recall of lists or information of a similar nature. Such interference is considerably less, however, when the material learned is meaningful. Also, through overlearning the individual becomes much less susceptible to interference.

5. *Motivated forgetting.* An important aspect of forgetting not previously stated is the individual's motives. One instance in which an individual is motivated to forget is *repression,* an unconscious process by which we make memories inaccessible to recall, presumably because we become uncomfortable when we do recall them. Such memories are not lost because of an organic decay or time lapse, since under hypnosis these memories can be recalled. In one experiment subjects were hypnotized and told that upon waking they would not be able to remember certain critical words suggested to them while under hypnosis. When the subjects awoke, hints were given to them, but they could not remember the critical words. The cues for the critical words were not consciously recognized by the subjects in their wakened state. In order to prove, however, that these words were not permanently forgotten, the subjects had also been given a post-hypnotic suggestion that when they were given permission to remember the words, they would be able to do so. When the subjects received verbal permission to remember, they did recall all of the repressed words.

6. *Distortion of the memory trace.* In more recent years there has been considerable progress in experiments analyzing memory on a biochemical basis. Although this theory is much too complex to present in detail, a general explanation will be given. In an experiment with flatworms which had learned the conditioned response of contraction to a light, a substance containing ribonucleic acid (RNA) was taken from their bodies and injected into untrained organisms. The untrained but injected organisms were subjected to the same classical conditioning procedures as the original flatworms and learned the response much faster than a control group which had RNA injected from

untrained organisms. A similar experiment was performed on rats with the same results. It is thought that the RNA molecules contain a biochemical substance related to the specific learning task of the animals. Although some later experiments have failed to support the original data, the role of RNA in memory involves some intriguing possibilities. For example, if it were proven that data are stored in an RNA molecule for specific learning tasks, it would be theoretically possible to inject knowledge about psychology from the RNA of a psychologist! The memory trace could be changed through the injection of certain RNA molecules. For the present, however, students will still have to resort to the more difficult task of studying to gain their knowledge.

It is known that electroconvulsive shock (ECS) is related to retention. ECS involves the administering of an electric current which produces immediate temporary unconsciousness in the organism. Different rats that had learned a task were given ECS at various intervals after learning the task. It was found that there was a relationship between retention of the learning and when ECS was given after the learning. The shorter the time interval between the learning and the ECS, the less the rats retained, as measured by relearning. Perhaps the ECS destroyed the memory trace before it became part of the long-term memory, a phrase explained below. In terms of RNA, perhaps there was a biochemical disruption of the RNA molecule that contained the data involved in the learning of the task.

What are long-term memory and short-term memory? One theory hypothesizes that there are actually two kinds of memory, one for short-term memory (STM) and another for long-term memory (LTM). Every bit of information we receive, according to this theory, is stored for a very short period of time in STM, where it may or may not be coded and eventually stored in LTM. (*Coding* refers to the process of transforming one type of energy into another.) While the information is in STM, it can be recalled perfectly. Because of its limited capacity and the flow of new information arriving constantly from the senses, STM can store information only briefly. If information is successfully coded, it can be stored in LTM, which is analogous to a large storage room. The question then is, "Why is it difficult to recall some information from LTM?" One possible answer is that some information never reaches LTM. Another conceivable explanation is that there is no sufficient stimulus present for the individual to locate the information properly once it is stored in LTM. It is one thing to store information away and still another to find it at a later time, especially when it can be filed under many different headings.

No single belief or theory can answer all questions related to forgetting, just as no single learning theory can presently account for all the processes involved in learning. At present we must use a number of different approaches to explain forgetting, although all the approaches agree that forgetting is an active process, not a passive one.

How does sleep affect retention? In a previously mentioned experiment on retention of learning following rest (see page 97), we saw experimental evidence that learning followed by rest is retained better than learning followed by activity. We usually seem to rest most completely when we sleep. Therefore, is retention of learning followed by sleep markedly greater than retention of learning followed by waking activity? To answer this question, six subjects were tested twenty-four, forty-eight, seventy-two, and ninety-six hours after the original learning. There was consistently greater retention of learning in sessions followed by sleep. Other experiments indicate that details of organized material are remembered better if the learning is followed by sleep rather than by waking activity but that essential items are retained about as well after remaining awake as after sleeping.

Would it be best to have periods of relaxation after each class period? In practical school situations, such a plan is not possible. Experimental evidence and the experience of teachers suggest, however, that after a student learns one set of materials he should then, if possible, learn a very different kind of material. You may wish to make use of this practical suggestion for planning your study schedule. In fact, by applying the different principles of learning and forgetting you have just studied, you can improve your learning and retention considerably.

Terms to Add to Your Vocabulary

coding
distributed practice
electroconvulsive shock (ECS)
latent learning
long-term memory (LTM)
massed practice
memory trace
mnemonic device
motivation
negative acceleration

negative transfer
nonsense syllable
overlearning
part learning
plateau
positive acceleration
positive transfer
proactive inhibition
psychological feedback
repression

retention
retroactive inhibition
ribonucleic acid (RNA)
selective forgetting
short-term memory (STM)
transfer
uniform acceleration
whole learning

Suggestions for Activities

1. Have a Latin teacher talk to your class about the value of his subject for high school students. Does he point out the possibilities of transfer of training? What do students who have taken Latin think of the transfer value of the subject?

2. The following experiment will demonstrate the effects of active versus passive attitudes in learning. The teacher or some member of the class should select two passages of poetry by the same author that seem to be of equal difficulty. One

passage should be marked A and the other B. The passages should be eight lines in length. In some random way, divide the class into two groups. Members of Group I should read and reread the A passage as often as possible in a fixed period of time, say three minutes. The members of this group should be instructed to make no effort to recall the material as they read. Group II should read and reread the A passage as often as possible in a fixed period of time equal to half the time allowed Group I, say one and a half minutes. The members of Group II should then spend the other half of the time in actively reciting the passage to themselves. In this recitation time, they should read two lines at a time, close their eyes and try to recite these lines, then go on to the next two lines, and so on. Immediately following the period of reading or reading-study, have members of both groups write as much of the poem as they can remember. The score for each individual is the number of words which he can recall correctly.

In a second part of the experiment, use the B passage and reverse the procedure. Group II should spend the entire time reading and rereading the material without making any attempts at recall. Group I should divide reading and reciting as Group II did in the first part of the experiment. Data can be secured in the same way as for the first part. Do the combined data suggest any tentative conclusions?

Can you improve the experiment by using four groups of subjects?

3. Ask your parents, other relatives, and friends what mnemonic devices they use now or have used in the past. Make a collection of these devices. Then put together a class scrapbook on the basis of the material brought in by various students. How many of the mnemonic devices represent efficient learning procedure? How many are more trouble than they are worth?

4. Make a weekly work-study-play schedule for yourself and follow the schedule for several weeks. Does such a schedule result in more efficient study? Does it result in more time for recreation?

5. Write a sentence that contains ten words on an index card. Take ten different words and write them in a random order on another card. Then select someone who is not taking and has not had this course and for ten seconds show him the card with the ten randomly written words. Afterward, ask him to write down as many words as he can remember. Next present the card with words in sentence form for ten seconds and ask him to write down these words. On which list did he remember more words? Ask him to explain why.

6. Take fifty small index cards and number them from 1 to 50. Divide a table top in half by placing a small board or a piece of string down the middle so that there is a right side and a left side. Next shuffle the cards thoroughly. Hand the cards to someone and instruct him to place all even-numbered cards on the right side of the table and all odd-numbered cards on the left side, as fast as he can without making any mistakes. If he places a card on the wrong side, he must replace it on the correct side. Time him to see how fast he can correctly place all cards on the table. Repeat this same procedure for at least ten trials, timing each trial, or until there is no further decrease in time for three consecutive trials. Then have the person reverse the order of placing the cards on the table; even-numbered cards on the left side and odd-numbered cards on the right. What happens to the time it took to place the cards? For Trial 3, have him put the even-numbered cards on the left side and the odd-numbered cards on the right, using the same number of trials as were used for the reverse procedures at the beginning. Did he learn fastest in the Trial 3 procedures? How do you explain your results?

HOW TO LEARN EFFICIENTLY

7. Try to recite some rather long bit of poetry that you learned in elementary school or earlier. Probably you have forgotten much of it. Undertake to relearn the poetry, noting to what extent you are able to say, "It came back to me." Then try to memorize an equally long piece of poetry that is new to you. After one week, try to recite both passages. Which passage took the most time to memorize, the one that you were relearning, or the one that you were learning for the first time? Which passage did you retain best after one week?

8. At the end of each chapter in this book is a list of words to be added to your vocabulary. Secure a card index or possibly an indexed blank book. Record words from preceding lists which you believe you might have difficulty using in your own writing about or discussion of psychology. Record the meaning for each word. Add to this list as you continue with your study of psychology. Frequent study of this index list and review of it near the close of the semester will be excellent preparation for a final exam as well as for long-time retention.

Suggestions for Further Reading

Daniel, Robert S., ed., *Contemporary Readings in General Psychology,* 2nd ed., Houghton Mifflin. Pages 106–09. "Memory Systems in the Brain"; pages 110–14, "Information and Memory"; pages 115–18, "Where Were You on the Night of April 23, 1935?" (How reliable is court testimony?)

Hilgard, Ernest R., and Richard C. Atkinson, *Introduction to Psychology,* 4th ed., Harcourt, Brace & World. Chapter 12, "Remembering and Forgetting"; Chapter 13, "The Management of Learning."

Kalish, Richard A., *The Psychology of Human Behavior,* Wadsworth. Chapter 4, "Principles of Learning and Their Application"; Appendix II, "Study Methods."

Kendler, Howard H., *Basic Psychology,* Appleton-Century-Crofts. Chapter 10, "Learning and Forgetting."

Leuba, Clarence, *Man: A General Psychology,* Holt, Rinehart & Winston. Chapter 14, "Remembering and Forgetting."

Lindgren, Henry C., Donn Byrne, and Lewis Petrinovich, *Psychology: An Introduction to a Behavioral Science,* 2nd ed., John Wiley. Chapter 4, "Learning."

McKeachie, Wilbert J., and Charlotte L. Doyle, *Psychology,* Addison-Wesley. Chapter 9, "Cognition: Memory, Language, and Meaning," pages 302–24.

Mahoney, Harold J., and T. L. Engle, *Points for Decision,* rev. ed., Harcourt Brace & World. Chapter 11, "In-School Problems." This guidance book discusses some of the same problems you discuss in your course in psychology but less technically.

Meenes, Max, *Studying and Learning,* Random House paperback. Written for high school seniors.

Munn, Norman L., *Psychology,* 5th ed., Houghton Mifflin. Chapter 10, "The Learning Process"; Chapter 11, "Foundations of Learning"; Chapter 12, "Remembering and Forgetting."

Ruch, Floyd L., *Psychology and Life,* 7th ed., Scott, Foresman. Chapter 7, "The Management of Learning and Retention."

Sanford, Fillmore H., *Psychology: A Scientific Study of Man,* 2nd ed., Wadsworth. Chapter 13, "The Management of Learning."

Staton, Thomas, *How to Learn Faster and Better,* Educations Aids, Montgomery, Alabama.

Whittaker, James O., et al., *Introduction to Psychology,* W. B. Saunders. Chapter 10, "Principles of Learning"; Chapter 11, "Human Learning and Retention."

5

The process of thinking

Many topics in Chapters 3 and 4 imply thinking. At the level of conditioning, learning may appear to be an almost automatic business of pairing bells and food or lights and shock. Most learning, however, involves remembering and using past experience. The ability to recall a tune or a name or a formula or to recognize and define a foreign word implies that certain processes are going on within the learner. Through some activity within the human organism, principles learned in mathematics can be transferred to computing batting averages or analyzing the school budget. You can use words and numbers to work on problems "in your head," and you can talk about them or write them down. This kind of activity involves thinking.

Just what is thinking? For many centuries philosophers and scientists have been concerned with understanding thought. In modern times psychologists have been trying to understand, explain, and define thinking. But do not hope that psychology can tell you all about thinking. The human organism is so complex that even the most complicated electronic computer is simple by comparison.

Much remains to be learned about thinking behavior. Research in thinking has, however, produced many useful and interesting studies, some of which are included in this chapter. Chapter 5 also offers suggestions for efficient student performance, since school learning involves much reasoning, concept developing, and other thinking.

BASIC ELEMENTS OF THINKING

How is thinking defined? In psychological dictionaries and textbooks, definitions of thinking differ, but they usually share certain basic elements. To begin with, thinking is a form of behavior and as such is subject to psychological study. It is true that many other forms of behavior, such as heavy muscular activity, are much easier to observe and study. Sometimes thinking is referred to as *implicit behavior*—behavior that is not directly observable but that can be inferred from observable facts. If we watch a child solve a puzzle, we can observe his movements, and from them we infer that he is thinking.

Thinking implies more than mere perception—more than simply becoming aware of objects, qualities, or relations by means of the sense organs. It also implies more than the mere manipulation of objects. Indeed, in actuality, thinking implies the manipulation of symbols.

We may define *thinking,* then, as implicit activity by means of which an organism becomes aware of and manipulates past experience through the use of symbols.

What is a symbol?   Suppose that while attending a basketball game you see some red-and-white ribbon being worn by another student. You think, "He attends West Side High School." The

The shapes of international traffic signs, as well as the drawings, are symbols. What do these shapes and drawings represent? (Answers on page 133.)

red-and-white ribbon makes you think he attends West Side High School because red and white are the colors of that school. The red-and-white ribbon is a symbol representing that high school—its teams, student body, teachers, and building. A *symbol,* then, is anything that becomes a representative substitute for something else. Flags, pins, colors, and badges frequently serve as symbols for organizations of people. Gestures, diagrams, pictures, and numbers may serve as symbols in our thinking.

Letters and the words they form are symbols. On a white page you see the black marks MAN, and these marks convey a meaning to you. These marks, arranged as they are, have become a symbol for a specific class of organism. On another white page you see a black mark, 人. Probably this mark has no meaning for you because you are not familiar with Chinese symbols, or ideographs. To the person familiar with Chinese ideographs, 人 suggests or represents man; it is a representative substitute for man. The ideograph 山 is a representative substitute for a mountain to those who read Chinese. To us, the printed word or symbol "mountain" has more meaning.

We recognize the symbols "man" and "mountain" rather than 人 and 山 because our past experience has taught us printed words rather than ideographs. Therefore, using past experience is another element in thinking. If we see that a bolt needs tightening, we think of the word or symbol "wrench." Our past experience tells us that we need to make use of the object for which the word "wrench" is the symbol. In other words, thinking about what we are to do involves manipulating our past experience to work out a solution to a current problem.

How important to thinking is language?
The development of language and the development of thinking are closely related. Vocabulary has been described as the stock in trade of the thinker. This statement is obvious to anyone who has had the pleasure of observing the development of children. Sometimes we are amused by what seems to be the child's incorrect usage of words, but we are always amazed at the rapidity with which a normal child's vocabulary develops. As a rule, the vocabulary development of retarded children is much slower than that of normal children. Every teacher of retarded children is acutely aware of the limitations in language, and so in thinking, of such children. On the other hand, the vocabulary development of very superior children is much more rapid than that of normal children, and teachers are often amazed at the superior child's ability to think more clearly than most children of their age.

A child's use of words, as well as the number of words in his vocabulary, changes as he grows older and develops thinking ability. Early in his development, the child uses a single word instead of a sentence. "Drink" may mean "I want a drink." The single-word sentence is characteristic of the child of eighteen months, but by the age of three years, the average sentence contains three or four words. By the age of five years, the child is probably using sentences of four or five words, and by the time he is in the third grade his sentences have increased in average length to about ten words. When he is completing high school, his sentences are almost twice as long as when he was in the third grade.

CONCEPTS

Concepts are important in thinking. A *concept* is the meaning which an individual attaches to the qualities or characteristics that are common to otherwise diverse objects, situations, or events. In forming a concept, an individual thinks of similarities and groupings, and associates them with a word or other symbol which he can use thereafter to describe other similar objects, situations, or events.

In what way are an apple and a banana alike? If asked this question, either small children or adults of very limited intellectual ability are likely to insist that an apple and a banana are not alike, that one is round and the other is long. Of course, an apple and a banana are both part of the concept of fruit. Furthermore, the concept of fruit can be applied to other objects: oranges, pears, pineapples, grapes, apricots, avocados, lemons, figs. As one advances in his thinking and areas of knowledge, his concepts become more specific. To the botanist, all seed-bearing plants produce fruits. Although a tomato is commonly called a vegetable, the botanist's concept of fruit would cause him to classify the tomato as a fruit.

Adults often develop concepts by looking up a definition in a dictionary.

THE PROCESS OF THINKING

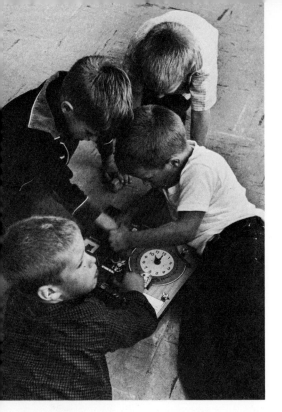

Here children play a game with a clock designed to help them in their formation of a concept of time.

for example, that potatoes and carrots are both vegetables. By the time the child is four and one-half years of age, he is able to grasp second-hierarchy concepts, such as potatoes are vegetables, apples are fruit, and both vegetables and fruit are food.

To understand the concept of time requires a long period of development. Probably the child has a concept of morning and afternoon by the time he is four years of age, but the concept of the days of the week is usually not achieved until a year later. More difficult concepts involving the use of the clock and calendar come afterward for normal children and still later for retarded individuals. For example, it has been found that mentally retarded adults with an average age of twenty-six have developed concepts of time using clocks and calendars that are equal to concepts developed by normal children between eight and nine years of age.

The text of this book, the glossary, and your teacher provide you with definitions to guide you in your formation of concepts.

How do children form concepts? The concepts of the small child are usually self-centered, since they grow out of the experiences that satisfy his needs. As he gets older, his concepts become more impersonal and, at the same time, more accurate. Ability to develop concepts progresses from simple to complex levels. What are called first-hierarchy concepts are commonly developed at about twenty-six months of age. The child of this age recognizes,

Can concept formation be studied in the laboratory? There is evidence that animals can develop concepts. In one experiment, rats were required to develop a concept of triangularity. They were shown cards bearing triangles, rectangles, circles, and other geometric figures. Whenever a rat jumped to a card bearing a triangle, it was rewarded. Whenever it jumped to a card bearing any other geometric figures, it was punished. Eventually, the rats learned to jump only to cards containing the original triangle or to cards showing other kinds of triangles. In some way these rats had developed a concept of triangularity.

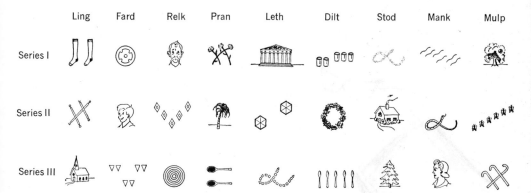

	Ling	Fard	Relk	Pran	Leth	Dilt	Stod	Mank	Mulp
Series I									
Series II									
Series III									

These drawings were used to study concept formation in adults. Each non-sense syllable represents a concept illustrated by the figure in Series I which appears below it. Look at each figure in Series I and find the matching concept in Series II and in Series III. What concept does each syllable represent? (Answers on page 108.)

One psychologist, working with human subjects, presented them with material which was similar to the figure below. He asked them to identify the characteristics that distinguished DAX from non-DAX, and then to define the nonsense syllable *DAX*. What does *DAX* mean? Did you note that all the figures at the left are similar in certain respects? Did you note that all the figures at the right are similar in some respects to those at the left but at the same time are different in at least one important respect? The psychologist who reported this experiment found that many subjects could correctly identify figures that are *DAX* even though they could not express the principle in words. Did you verbalize your concept? Did you spend most of

What do you think DAX are? (Answer in text on page 108.)

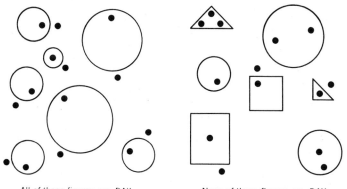

All of these figures are DAX .   None of these figures are DAX .

THE PROCESS OF THINKING

your time looking at the figures on the left or looking at the figures on the right? It was found that the subjects in the reported experiment learned much more from studying the positive examples at the left than from studying the negative examples at the right.

Practical advice about concepts. The experiments mentioned above may have given the impression that the development of concepts is a simple and short-time experience. On the contrary, we develop and even change many of our concepts over days, months, and years. In the formation of concepts, it is very important for the individual to have wide and varied experiences. Sometimes high school and college students become too narrow in their training, taking only subjects that seem to have immediate practical value and avoiding subjects that will give them experiences in a wide variety of situations. In the course of a lifetime, we must learn thousands of concepts, which should include broad as well as specialized concepts. (DAX are circles that have one dot on the inside and one dot on the outside.)

UNCRITICAL THINKING

Man is very proud of his ability to think and justifiably so when he compares himself with lower animals. Yet when he compares some of his thought

---

The syllables represent concepts of concrete objects, spatial forms, and numerical quantities: Ling—2; Fard—circularity; Relk—face; Pran—one line crossing two lines; Leth—building; Dilt—5; Stod—a looped form; Mank—6; Mulp—tree.

processes with mature thinking, man is far less proud. The concepts developed in childhood are selfish, for the child tends to think of himself as the center of the world. As we grow more mature, we learn to respect the importance of other individuals and of social institutions. Unfortunately, our thinking often continues to be limited, such as when we feel sure that we go to the best school, that the political party to which we belong is the only one that can govern wisely, or that our family is better than other families in the neighborhood. Sometimes we swing the other way and say, probably without meaning it, that our school is the worst in the world, that our political party is totally corrupt, and so on.

We are capable of thinking about schools, political parties, and families critically. Although we are indeed capable of comparing them and finding both good and bad features, all too often we do not bother to think critically. It is frequently easier to accept incomplete information than to search for more complete information. Our friends may be prejudiced, too. As long as we associate only with people who have prejudices similar to our own, we are likely to retain our uncritical thinking. We shall give further consideration to prejudices in Chapter 18; here we shall note the risks of childish thinking in adults.

What is wrong with "all-or-nothing" thinking? Popular fiction, movies, television, and other mass media may frequently encourage us to go all out one way or the other in our thinking. The child watching the thrilling television program is apt to think that there are just two kinds of persons in the world, the "good guys" and the "bad guys." He may not realize that goodness-badness is a continuum — that bad guys have some good characteristics and that good guys have some bad characteristics.

As the individual matures, he becomes interested in romantic stories, movies, and television programs. He comes to believe that he must be either completely in love or not in love at all. This pose seems to be easier than thinking about friendships in general and evaluating romance in the framework of general social relationships. (We shall discuss friendships, love, and marriage in Chapters 13 and 16, giving further attention to problems created by thinking in narrow categories.)

Individuals tend to think that they have either good jobs or bad jobs. This "all-or-nothing" thinking is easier than evaluating their jobs in the light of what various jobs offer and what sort of job they can reasonably hope to get. (We shall consider job evaluation in more detail in Chapter 19.)

How is coincidence confused with cause? Sometimes events seem to "go together," as when there is a spell of cold, wet weather and a large number of people have head colds. We often jump to the conclusion that the cold weather caused the colds, but this is not a scientific conclusion unless we have screened out all other causes. We would also need to know how many people actually had colds before and after the bad weather. To assume that

One example of uncritical thinking is this adulation by masses of people for a man who will lead their country to destruction.

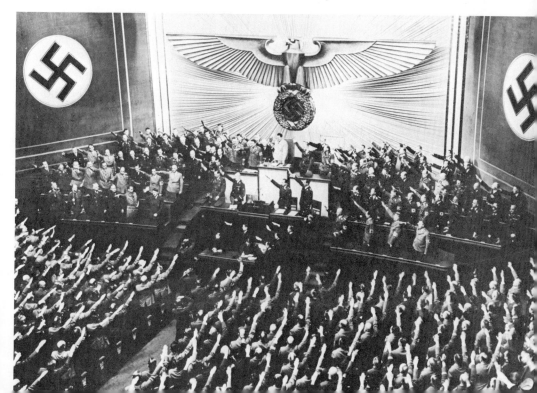

because B is found with A, A caused B is uncritical thinking. Both A and B might be related to or caused by C. For example, statistics indicate that church weddings are less likely to be followed by divorce than are weddings not performed in churches. Uncritical thinking might suggest that our divorce problem would be lessened by urging, or even requiring, all couples to be married in churches. The basic factor, of course, is that persons who have fairly stable home backgrounds and religious beliefs tend to marry in a church. Stable home backgrounds and religious beliefs are factors which often contribute to stable marriages.

What are delusions? Perhaps the most extreme examples of uncritical thinking are to be found in the delusions of mentally ill persons. A *delusion* is a false belief which persists in spite of evidence to the contrary. The ill person may insist that he is a great general who is being held prisoner in a concentration camp. It can be pointed out to him that he has no military record and that the hospital in which he finds himself has practically none of the characteristics of a concentration camp, but he continues to think of himself as a great general being persecuted by the enemy. He is incapable of critical thinking.

To cite a much less extreme case, students sometimes insist that they are brilliant but that all the teachers "have it in for them." It can be pointed out to them that they have done poorly on objective, standardized tests in which no teacher judgments were involved. It can be pointed out that teachers have

asked them to come in for personal help. Nevertheless, they continue with their uncritical thinking.

CREATIVE THINKING

Sometimes schools are criticized for not producing students who can do truly creative thinking. Our schools are said to turn out technicians but not creative thinkers. It has been estimated that of all the individuals who have lived in historical times, only about two in a million have become truly distinguished for their creative thinking. But even if really great artistic and scientific creativity were possible for only two in a million, most of us are capable of some creative thinking. Schoolwork often calls for creativity.

In creative thinking, the individual strives to discover new solutions to problems, to see new relationships, or to find new modes of artistic expression. He tries to discover new and better ways of achieving goals. His thinking brings into existence something which is new for society, or at least for himself. For contrast, consider "do-it-yourself" kits. We buy the parts, we follow the directions, and behold — we have made a radio, we have constructed a useful piece of furniture, or we have cooked an edible meal. Perhaps we buy a numbered canvas and a set of correspondingly numbered bottles of paint, and we paint a picture. Such activities may be fun, they may serve as recreation, and they may produce useful results, but they do not give us the opportunity to do creative thinking. Similarly, in laboratory or shop courses it is possible to follow directions and get by—or to try to do more and thus to learn more.

What is artistic creativity? The true artist does more than copy nature; he creates. Like the scientist, he recombines or reorganizes ideas according to some specific pattern in an attempt to achieve some goal or to solve some problem. Can such a process be measured? One psychologist developed a test in which the subject was required to recombine familiar ideas according to certain patterns. In one part of the test, the subject was told to recombine given lists of words into as many meaningful, grammatical sentences as possible. For example, how many sentences can you make using the following ten words: *men, sky, is, fight, that, the, slow, bright, of, far?* In another part of the test, the subject was asked to make as many pieces of furniture or house furnishings as possible out of ten blocks. The complete test was administered to professional artists, college art majors, and college students not majoring in art. The mean scores of both the professional artists and art majors were significantly higher than the mean scores of the college students not majoring in art. They displayed more creativity as measured by the test.

What are the steps in creative thinking? In various courses you may be asked to write term papers. In laboratory or shop courses, you may be asked to design new apparatus or tools. After school days, your job may require that you devote some of your time to creative thinking. For example, you may be asked to prepare constructive reports and to preside at meetings in which plans and policies are discussed. Many individuals have found that the following four steps are helpful to all creative thinking.

1. *Preparation.* Preparation in creative thinking may be a very long process, possibly requiring weeks, months, or years. Although Einstein wrote his famous creative treatise on relativity in a few weeks, he had spent seven years in preparation for the writing. Such extended study is not possible in all creative work, but preparation does mean enough time for a "soaking up" process. The individual reads widely, he may attend lectures, he talks with others interested in the problem, he strives to have personal experience in the field about which he is thinking. He often finds it useful to keep a card index of notes and lists of references. No doubt, he will follow some blind leads, since he will have such a mass of material that he will be likely to be confused. Such confusion should not be discouraging, however, for it seems to be a normal part of the process of creative thinking.

2. *Incubation.* After collecting many facts and opinions during the stage of preparation, creative thinkers usually find it helpful to put their work aside for a while and do something else, such as engaging in some recreational activity. They have their equipment at hand, and they have at least a rough map of the road they are to follow, but before setting out on their journey, they consciously take time to permit their thinking to incubate. Perhaps this period of incubation is an application of

THE PROCESS OF THINKING

the principle of distributed learning discussed in Chapter 4.

The period of incubation is not a matter of resting because the individual is tired, discouraged, or bored. It is a definite step in the process of creative thinking. During this period of incubation, the individual does not try to think about his problem, even though he may find himself thinking about it in a rather enjoyable way at odd times.

An application to schoolwork should be noted here. All too often students leave the writing of term papers and other creative work until it is nearly time to hand the assignment in. They procrastinate; they do not complete the preparation stage early enough to allow for a period of incubation. The absence of this important step often causes their reports to be little more than jumbles of facts and opinions, representing only the preparation stage of the creative process.

3. *Inspiration.* There is nothing magical about inspiration as the term is used here. It is simply a rather sudden solution of a problem already studied. The thinker may not be able to trace the steps by which he has reached his solution, but his inspiration has followed preparation and incubation. There is a dropping out of irrelevant material, a seeing of new relationships. Often the new ideas come very rapidly and, although still difficult, thinking becomes enjoyable as the goal is neared.

The student who puts off all preparation of a report until the last minute may hope to have a sudden inspiration and be able to write a brilliant report, but he is doomed to disappointment. He is neglecting the first two essential steps in creative thinking. Unfortunately, some school assignments are of such a nature that the student merely collects facts in a routine manner without ever being required to see new relationships, without ever having the pleasant experience of inspiration.

4. *Verification and revision.* All too often the student is satisfied to stop with the step of inspiration—if he gets that far in his attempt at creative thinking. More work is needed, however. In scientific thinking, the inspiration may have been incorrect or only partly correct. Objective data will have to confirm the correctness of the inspiration. The scientist will have to go to his laboratory and verify his hypothesis or theory by experimentation. He will have to add to his observations. He may need to read further about the thinking of others along similar lines, and then revise his thinking a number of times. The creative artist will need to check and recheck his work in order to be sure that he has achieved the artistic effect he wanted. Probably he will make at least minor changes as a result of this verification process.

The four distinct steps that seem to be necessary for creative thinking are difficult steps. The thinker who follows them can, however, look for the reward of knowing that he is out of the rut, that he has achieved something truly worthwhile.

Does "brainstorming" help creative thinking? *Brainstorming* is a popular term for a method of thinking in which an individual attempts to solve problems by listing all the possible solutions that occur to him, without attempting to evaluate his solutions until some later time. In one experiment two groups of college students, matched on the basis of grades, age, and sex, acted as subjects. The following brainstorming instructions were given to the first group:

"You are to list all the ideas that come to your mind, without judging them in any way. Forget about the quality of the ideas entirely. We will count only quantity on this task. Express any idea which comes to your mind. As you go along, you may combine or modify any of the ideas which you have already listed, in order to produce additional ideas. Remember that quantity and freedom of expression without evaluation are the key points."

To the second group the instructions were: "You are to list all the good ideas you can think up. Your score will be the total number of good ideas. Don't put down any idea unless you feel it is a good one."

The results indicated that significantly more ideas of good quality were produced under brainstorming instructions than under nonbrainstorming instructions. Why? The men performing the experiment suggested that in the customary course of our thinking, we tend to inhibit ideas because we are afraid of criticism by others or even by ourselves. Brainstorming seems to reduce this fear and thereby encourages more ideas, including better ideas. Creative thinkers may make many false starts on the way, but they successfully get out of the rut of everyday thinking.

What are some characteristics of a creative person? From past experimental data psychologists know that some individuals are more creative than others. Because creative persons contribute a great deal to society, it is important to determine if creative individuals have any behavior characteristics in common.

One way of determining characteristics of creative persons is to select a group of such persons and study them at length and in detail. Several different studies have shown that creative individuals are more flexible, have a good sense of humor, are more willing to analyze their own impulses, are independent in both thought and action, and prefer the complex rather than the ordinary. Such individuals also tend to devote less than the average amount of time to social behavior, perhaps because of the amount of time and energy that goes into their work. The important question, however, is whether they became creative and then developed the tendency to devote energy to work or whether they became creative as a result of strong devotion to and concentration on their work. Although we do not know the answer today, longitudinal studies are presently under way which may eventually answer such questions. By studying creativity in young children and continuing the studies as these children grow into adults, we may discover what conditions promote creativity.

Perhaps you are wondering why intelligence has not been listed as a major aspect of creativity. Although there is a positive relationship between the two, the correlation is not very high over the

Creative Thinkers

Each of these individuals has developed his own distinctive style of creative expression. Sculptor Henry Moore (above) is constructing a statue that will reflect his artistic style. The Beatles (below) have changed the sound of popular music with their style of musical expression. In architecture, Frank Lloyd Wright (right) has contributed new solutions to the problems of designing buildings. By her dancing, teaching, and choreography, Martha Graham (upper right) has brought originality to the field of modern dance. And Albert Einstein (lower right) has revolutionized theoretical physics with his scientific creativity.

entire range of intelligence; and for individuals with high IQ's, the relationship between creativity and intelligence is very small. It seems that motivation and personality are more important variables in the creativity of individuals with high IQ's. Nevertheless, a basic level of superior intelligence seems to be necessary for creativity. There is little, if any, creativity in a school for retarded individuals.

Even though creative individuals do tend to have the characteristics described, you should be extremely hesitant about categorizing individuals one way or another. Simply because a person possesses the aspects described does not automatically make him creative, nor does a lack of such characteristics guarantee that he is not creative. Although studies of creativity are providing new concepts and information in this area, there is still much to be learned about creativity and how to adequately measure and promote it.

IMAGINING

Formerly, psychologists spent a great deal of time discussing whether thinking involved having images of one kind or another. It seems evident that most, if not all, individuals do have some imagery. A popular phrase used to describe imagery is "seeing with the mind's eye." Can you picture how the breakfast table looked this morning? Can you recall the sound of the voice of a good friend? Such images occur in normal thinking.

What are eidetic images?   Particularly vivid images are called eidetic (ī·det′ik) images. An *eidetic image* is an image which is so vivid that it almost seems to the individual that he is having a sensory experience, though he recognizes that he is not. The person with eidetic imagery is popularly said to have a "photographic mind." Some examples will clarify the term "eidetic imagery."

Studies of eidetic imagery are often conducted by showing a picture to subjects for a short length of time, say thirty seconds or less. Then the picture is taken away and the subject is asked to report on the details in the picture. The picture may contain an unusual word or a word in a foreign language. The subject with clear eidetic imagery will be able to spell the word both forward and backward. Why? He can "see it."

One psychologist tells of a law student suspected of cheating on an examination. One of the questions on the examination asked for a detailed account of a law case given in the textbook. The student's answer to this question was a word-for-word reproduction of the case in the textbook. Of course, the professor assumed that the student had had his textbook open during the examination, but the student denied the charge. He said that just before the examination he had looked over the case and then on the examination had been able to call up such a clear image of the page that he could "copy" it on the examination paper. Since the members of the faculty committee investigating the case were skeptical, they decided to test the student. He was given a page of unfamiliar material and permitted to study it for five minutes. At the end of that time the material was taken away and he was asked to reproduce it. He did so—reproducing some four hundred words without a single error. Even punctuation was exactly the same.

Eidetic imagery is most common in the visual field but may occur in other fields. For example, a music teacher who was also a composer made it a rule not to use any printed music material in his teaching. He simply wrote off on ruled paper the music he thought the student needed for practice. Once, while writing out music for a student, the teacher hesitated a minute or so and then went ahead with his writing. The student asked, "Why did you have to stop, and how were you able to go ahead with your writing?" The reply was, "I had forgotten just how that part went, but as soon as I heard the orchestra play it, I could write it for you."

How valuable is eidetic imagery? Eidetic imagery might be useful for examinations, but having such imagery is not necessarily a mark of superior intellectual ability. In fact, there is some evidence that persons who regularly engage in the highest and most abstract kind of thinking are not likely to use visual imagery. As you have grown older and have turned to more and more abstract thinking, you probably have less vivid imagery than you had as a child. Eidetic imagery is more common in children than in adults.

Psychologists believe that most individuals have at least some experiences involving images and that such images may be helpful in some kinds of thinking. However, psychologists today tend to consider that images play a minor rather than a major role in thinking.

What does the psychologist mean by imagination? The word "imagination" implies having images, but today psychologists do not stress this meaning of the word. To persons untrained in psychology, the word "imagination" often carries an almost supernatural connotation. A person is supposed to be able to imagine anything. But to the psychologist, *imagination* is the reproduction and reorganization of past experiences into a present ideational experience.

We may imagine what we are going to do next week, next month, or a year from now, but the imagined future experiences are based on our past experiences. Television programs suggest what it will be like when man lands on some other planet. In these programs the conditions found on the other planet and the organisms living there are somewhat different from those on earth, but the influence of earthly experiences is clearly discernible. An eyewitness account of another planet may well indicate conditions beyond our present wildest imagination.

In some cases imagination is spoken of as *autistic thinking*. In such thinking, the individual remakes his world into a place which is more like the world in which he wishes to live than is his real world. In some cases the word *fantasy* is used to describe imaginative and usually pleasant thinking in which the individual finds relief from his frustrations by living in a visionary world of his own. All such

THE PROCESS OF THINKING

Daydreaming is desirable if it leads to constructive action, but excessive daydreaming is often an escape from action.

thinking can be discussed under the heading of daydreams.

Are daydreams undesirable? The young person may daydream of marrying a beautiful actress or handsome actor of movie or television fame, ignoring the fact that in the theatrical arts there are just not enough such persons available for the youthful population. The high school student may daydream of having a job with a tremendously high salary, ignoring the fact that such jobs are limited to a very small percentage of the population and only to persons with years of business experience.

Sometimes individuals become concerned over their daydreams. They may even fear that daydreams indicate that they are becoming mentally ill. Such fears are unwarranted. In fact, daydreaming is normal. It takes considerable intellectual ability to produce elaborate daydreams.

Whether a daydream is psychologically desirable or undesirable can be determined only by a study of the daydream and the conditions under which it occurs. If the daydream becomes an end in itself, so that the individual ceases to try to succeed in the world of reality, the desirability of his thinking should be questioned. On the other hand, the daydream may be little more than an inexpensive form of entertainment and no more undesirable than temporarily losing oneself in a movie or television program. And daydreaming that leads to action can be highly desirable. The daydream may be less restrained than careful planning, but in many ways it is a form of planning. The high school student may daydream about his later college, vocational, marital, and social successes. As long as he works toward the fulfillment of these successes, his daydreams are constructive. If, however, the student finds his successes in daydreams so pleasant that he does not bother to prepare for his future college career or vocation or take part in present social activities, his thinking becomes very undesirable. Further consideration of thinking that does not stay close to reality can be found in Chapter 14 (pages 383–86).

REASONING

Obviously, one form of thinking is reasoning. In *reasoning,* a present problem is solved on the basis of general principles derived from at least two previous experiences. The new solution is not a mere reproduction of earlier solutions. It represents the adapting of earlier solutions to fit the present problem.

Although man is considered to have more ability to reason than have lower animals, some psychologists have secured experimental evidence which, they contend, demonstrates that animals can solve problems involving very simple reasoning. Other psychologists, however, are not sure that such thinking should be called reasoning. Therefore, we shall concentrate on experimental evidence based on human subjects.

How well do children reason? A psychologist carried out an experiment de-

signed to find out to what extent a child could reason out how to get to a desired toy. The figure below shows a simple version of the apparatus used. A child could walk through the various pathways. Entrance to any pathway was from a booth partitioned off by curtains. For a first experience the child was permitted to explore the apparatus. Then he was removed through the exit to pathway Y. Next he was taken around the outside of the apparatus to the booth permitting entrance to pathway W. There he encountered a toy windmill that would play a tune, much to the delight of the child. This was his second experience.

The child was then taken to the booth permitting entrance to pathway X and told to find the windmill. Note that he could not go directly to the windmill without combining his first and second experiences — knowledge of the apparatus and knowledge of where the windmill was. It was found that in-

Apparatus used to test reasoning ability in children

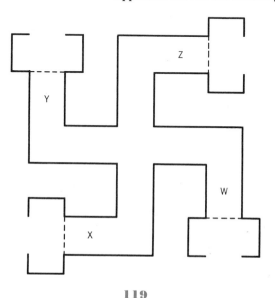

THE PROCESS OF THINKING

Computers now cannot perform all the thinking processes of which human beings are capable, but there are certain parallels between the operation of high-speed computers and human thinking. Computers can store information, "recall" material, and make calculations.

creasing age was accompanied by increasing ability to do this simple kind of reasoning. In some of his experiments, the psychologist found that the percentage of children who could combine such isolated experiences increased from about 20 percent at four years of age to 71 percent at six years of age. By eight years, 100 percent of the children could do this kind of reasoning.

How well do college students reason?
In another experiment conducted by the psychologist just mentioned, 384 students in introductory psychology classes were used as subjects. The psychologist was interested in learning whether or not instruction on how to reason would improve the solution of

problems involving reasoning—that is, would there be transfer?

The students were given three kinds of problems to solve, of which only one will be described here. A string was fastened to the ceiling and was of such length that the end came to the top of a stationary table in the room. Another string, six feet in length, was fastened to the wall six feet above the floor. The problem was to tie the two strings together. Conditions were so arranged that when the subject held one of the strings, he could not reach the other. Several solutions were demonstrated, one of them being to tie one of the strings to a chair and then place the chair halfway between the two positions. However, the students were not permitted to use this answer or any version of it in their solutions. Available in the room were such materials as washers, pliers, bolts, and chalk. How would you have solved the problem? The desired solution was to convert one of the strings into a pendulum by means of a weight available in the room.

The students were divided into two groups. The control group went to work on the problem without any suggestions on how to reason. The experimental group was given a lecture on reasoning. On the string problem there was very little difference in percentage of correct solutions by the two groups. For the experiment as a whole, however, the mean percent of correct solutions by the control group was 39.7, for the experimental group 49.2. The instruction in how to reason seemed to have made a difference. In the above experiment it was assumed that the two groups were equal in general ability, an assumption that might or might not have been correct. In a refinement of the experiment, 169 students attacked problems in different orders. Thus, the same students served in both control and experimental groups. In this case, data revealed that the lecture on reasoning about doubled the successes.

You might like to try one of the problems used in this part of the experiment. Above are three rows of three dots each. Your problem is to pass through each of the dots with four straight lines without lifting the pencil from the paper and without retracing any line. (Copy the dots on a separate piece of paper, so that you need not write in your book. You will find the solution on page 130.)

write in your book. You will find the solution on page 130.)

What are inductive and deductive reasoning? Reasoning is often described in terms of two types—inductive reasoning and deductive reasoning. To understand these two types of reasoning, let us use the hypothetical experiment on the relation between insufficient sleep and low exam grades described on pages 9–11 in Chapter 1. In *induction,* the thinking moves from specific cases to general principles. The thinker discovers common characteristics in otherwise separate and unique events. For example, suppose that, before formulating his hypothesis, the psychologist noticed that students who were tired when they came into an exam seemed to score low grades on it, even though they were prepared. By induction, then, he might reason from the specific cases of low-scoring students being tired to the general principle that insufficient sleep caused the students to make low scores.

On the other hand, the psychologist may have arrived at his hypothesis by deductive reasoning. In *deduction,* the thinking moves from general principles to specific cases or consequences. The psychologist may have begun his thinking with the general principle that people who are tired are less efficient than are those who are not tired. He then may have deduced that in the specific cases where students are tired, they will not perform well on exams, even when prepared for them.

In our daily problem solving, we seldom reason a problem through by using only the inductive or only the deductive method. We change from one form to the other and back again many times as we think through our problems. In Chapter 12 we shall examine how individuals reason when faced with conflicts and frustrations.

Does group reasoning have advantages over individual reasoning? Attention has been focused on how reasoning is done by individuals thinking as individuals. What is the result if individuals combine their thinking and try to solve a problem as a group?

Probably you have had some experience working on committees, or have served as chairman of a committee. Have you ever become disgusted with the way in which committees work? Have you ever felt that you could have solved a problem all by yourself in less time and to better advantage than did a committee? Did someone on the committee express what to him seemed an excellent idea, only to have someone else disagree quite violently? Members of the committee took one side of the argument and refused to back down in their "reasoning." No doubt some members felt inadequate and were defending themselves rather than trying to think through the problem before the group.

Committee work can be very exasperating.

Although group efforts to solve problems are sometimes exasperating, there is evidence that under some circumstances individuals working as a group can do a better job in solving problems than can the same individuals working as individuals. In one experiment the subjects were divided into two groups. During the first half of the experiment, groups composed of four individuals attempted to solve some difficult problems, while other individuals worked by themselves on the problems. In the second half of the experiment, the persons who had worked in groups now worked as individuals, and those who had worked as individuals now worked in groups. Of course, a different set of problems was used for the second half of the experiment. The percentage of correct solutions for the group efforts was 53 as compared with 7.9 percent for the individual efforts. Furthermore, notes kept on the solutions attempted indicated that individuals working alone tended to make more errors in the earlier steps of the solutions than in the group situations. When an individual made an incorrect suggestion in the group situation, others would point out the fallacy and no further time would be spent on that lead. The individual working alone had no one to check his thinking and prevent the attempted solution from going far in the wrong direction before the error was detected. Whether a group solution to a problem will be more efficient than an individual solution depends upon the abilities and training of the individuals in the group.

APPLYING PRINCIPLES OF LEARNING TO STUDYING AND TAKING EXAMINATIONS

The three chapters in this unit are devoted to learning and thinking—basic topics for psychology and basic techniques for the student. To round out Unit Two, here are some specific suggestions on applying the principles of learning to reading—a major part of study—and to taking examinations.

What are some suggestions for efficient reading? The following are suggestions that can apply to any and all reading.

1. *Do not read all pages of all books.* Since your study time is usually limited, do not read a whole book if only part of the book is pertinent to your needs. How can a student know where the material he needs appears in the book? A few minutes spent scanning the table of contents may save hours of ineffective reading. If he is seeking material on a specific topic, the student will be able to tell by glancing at the index of the book whether or not that topic is treated.

Often, reading the first and the last sentences of a paragraph in a book or a magazine will give you an idea of the contents of the entire paragraph. If, as a result of this quick survey, you think that the entire paragraph should be read, you can then read it with care. Otherwise, go on without taking time to read the entire paragraph. A heading or a caption may show whether it is necessary to read that section in a book or a magazine article. The first and the last pages will often indicate whether you should take time to read the entire chapter or article.

2. *Do not read all books the same way.* Vary your method of reading according to the kind of material being read. Francis Bacon expressed this idea very aptly with the words, "Some books are to be tasted, others to be swallowed, and some few to be chewed and digested."

Today, teachers tend to place less emphasis on the mastery of a text and more emphasis on reading from a wide variety of sources. History teachers still ask students to study a text, but the text serves as a foundation for wider reading and not as the only essential reading. When possible, students are asked to read original documents of history. They are often asked to read historical novels, too, for a more personal view of history. Certainly anyone would use different techniques in reading a history text than he would in reading a historical novel.

3. *Mark important points.* Underline important points in books and magazines you own. Make notes in the margins. You may not and should not write in library books or magazines or in books rented from school. You can, however, make your own books and magazines more valuable by underlining and by making notes in the margins.

You will notice that in this text there are many headings and subheadings to make it easy to find important topics.

4. *Develop your vocabulary.* Reading is always slow for a person who is not familiar with the words used. This is especially noticeable in reading a foreign language, but it is also true in reading English. Use the dictionary!

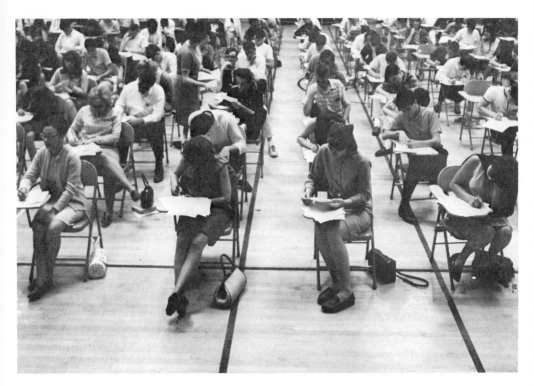

Students are likely to do well on an exam if they are well rested, emotionally calm, and have studied and reviewed the material.

Whenever you have to look up a word in the dictionary, write that word and its meaning in an alphabetically arranged notebook or on a card. Review the words that you list until you have mastered them. In time you will find that you have to look up fewer and fewer words. As a result, you will become a more efficient student. Be sure that you know the meanings of the psychological terms listed in the vocabulary at the end of each chapter in this book. Definitions for many of them are given in the glossary at the back of the book.

5. *Try to understand what you read.* Read with the intention of understanding the ideas expressed, not with the intention of virtually memorizing the words used. Before beginning to read an article or a chapter, ask yourself questions on what you expect to find. For instance, the following: "What were the factors leading to America's entrance into World War I?" "What persons or groups favored entering that war?" "What persons or groups were opposed?" "What reasons were advanced by each side?" Material that you understand is retained better than material merely learned by rote. Moreover, to study a book without understanding it is like practicing an incorrect response.

Study tables and graphs with care, to assure understanding of what you read. Sometimes students skip tables and graphs under the false impression that they are saving time in reading. Tables and graphs are put in books and magazine articles because they give added clarity to facts dealt with in the text.

Do not count on a "photographic mind" or on mnemonic devices. Learning the basic principles is more efficient than using devices in terms of time and retention.

6. *Recite to yourself as you read.* As soon as you finish reading a section or other logical unit of a book or a magazine article, close the book or the magazine. Then recite to yourself the important points in the material you have just read. In order not to lose your place, slip a piece of paper or your finger between the pages. If you find that some points are not clear, open your book and check up on them.

At first thought it might seem that stopping to recite to yourself is a waste of time when you have much reading to do, but, as already noted on page 87, there is evidence that reviewing and self-checking increases efficiency of learning.

7. *React to what you read.* You must be motivated to be an active learner. Definitely react to what you have read. Not only should you recite what the author has said, but you should also try to imagine new situations or conditions. Compare what an author says on a given subject with your own ideas as they were before you did your reading and as they are after. Ask yourself such questions as these: Do I agree with what the author has said? What sort of reasoning does he use? Are there any signs of all-or-nothing thinking or other confused thinking? Has the author presented valid evidence to support his statements? Does he present all the facts, or does he omit those that conflict with his point of view? Has he left out topics on which I want information? If all or part of the book is well documented and useful, how can I transfer the information to other courses or apply it in my own life now?

8. *Take the right kind of notes.* Before the invention of printing, it was necessary for monks to spend many hours, days, and months in copying manuscripts. Judging from the notes that some students take, a teacher is tempted to believe that they are living in the Middle Ages. As suggested, important points may be marked in books and journals that you own. When reading library books and journals, you may not mark them. But you can, and often should, take some notes on what you read. These notes should usually be in outline form, with possibly a few quotations of important key sentences. Do not try to copy the book. The outline should be made after you have read, or at least have skimmed through, the entire material or a large unit of it. You should survey a whole unit before you try to learn the details of any one part. If you attempt to take notes as you go along in the first survey of the material, you will probably include many unimportant and even confusing details.

In the event that you want to preserve an entire page of material verbatim, there are frequently copying

THE PROCESS OF THINKING

machines available in libraries where you can have a copy made.

What are some suggestions on preparing for examinations? The basic preparation for any examination is efficient daily study, using the principles already discussed. As already noted, you cannot have inspiration without preparation and incubation. However, a few suggestions on techniques for immediate preparation for and actual taking of examinations may be helpful.

1. *Watch your physical condition.* In the days preceding an examination or examination period, take time for sufficient exercise. Eat meals regularly. Secure sufficient sleep for several nights before — and especially the night before — the examination period. The inefficient student may feel that he is being virtuous by staying up until the "wee small hours" the night before an examination. Actually he is only adding to his inefficiency.

2. *Be emotionally well prepared.* It is easy to say, "Do not worry about the examinations." But how can you prevent worrying? Worry is a form of fear. If anyone worries about an examination, it is because he is afraid that he will not pass it or at least will not do well. Careful study long in advance and efficient review just before the examination are the best ways to prevent worry. Remember that a good examination will give you an opportunity to demonstrate how much you know. The examination is not designed as a trap to catch the good student who has failed to grasp one minor point. Most students pass most examinations. It is those who have not tried or who have been grossly inefficient in their study who are likely to have the lowest scores. Students who have done their best may not be "perfect," but they are not likely to earn very low scores.

3. *Do not attempt to cram* in the last minute or two, or even hour or two, before the examination. You have often seen students with their books open, trying to "stuff in" facts up until the very second the examination begins. Very seldom does such a student pick up any new information in this way; he is more likely to become confused and emotionally upset.

Students sometimes are too excited to sleep well before an examination. In that case they should relax and rest as much as possible. They should not worry about the fact of not sleeping. Although sleep is considered best, there is evidence that thorough relaxation is almost as effective.

4. *Go to the examination prepared to work.* Be sure to know ahead of time what equipment you will need. Check it. Pen? Ink? Several sharpened pencils? Eraser? Paper? Compass, ruler, graph paper? Teachers understandably become unhappy with students who frequently come to examinations without the proper implements.

What are some hints on taking examinations? If you go to an exam well prepared, the next problem is to make use of your abilities and time.

1. *Do not try to bluff.* Experienced teachers have been known to say, "The less a student knows, the more he writes"; that is, some unprepared students try to bluff by writing and writing

and writing, even though what they write is scarcely related to the question. The teacher can soon tell if a student has written a lot because he knew a great deal about the answer or because he knew nothing about the answer. You will be respected more as a student if you do not answer at all than if you try to hide ignorance under meaningless writing.

Do not pretend that a question is not clear just because you do not know the answer. Sometimes questions are not clear. If so, the teacher will be glad to explain any really uncertain statements. However, the teacher often learns what a student does not know by the questions he asks about the questions. The time to ask questions is in the regular class periods before the examination.

2. *Follow these rules in answering essay questions.* Some examination questions ask the student to explain, summarize, compare, critically evaluate, discuss, describe, outline, illustrate, trace, define, or prove some point. Be sure to do what is asked. If told to define, do not merely illustrate. If told to compare, do not merely explain one part.

   a. *Read all questions* on the examination before beginning to answer any. Otherwise you may waste time bringing out a point in one answer that should be brought out in answering another question. As you read over the questions, jot down any points that you wish to be sure to include in any given answer. Pause to jot down for the proper question any thoughts that occur to you as you write other answers. Otherwise, under the pressure of the examination you may not think of the point again until after you have handed in your paper.

   b. *Outline,* at least in your thinking, an answer before beginning to write it. Otherwise you are likely to ramble, thus breaking one of the rules of good English composition.

   c. *Use technical terms* — provided you know their meanings. They express ideas more clearly than nontechnical terms.

   d. *Leave some space at the end of each answer.* You should re-read your examination paper before handing it in. When you do so, a point may occur to you that you will wish to add to an answer. Put it in the space left for such an emergency rather than in the margin or between lines.

   e. *Apply the rules of grammar, spelling, and punctuation* to any subject field in which you are writing.

3. *Remember these hints for answering objective examinations.* Sometimes students say that they prefer essay questions to objective questions. This may mean that they think they can bluff better on an essay than on an objective examination. On the other hand, it is true that there is much value in being able to recall and write down in organized fashion what you have learned. We have noted that objective

THE PROCESS OF THINKING

examinations, since they require recognition rather than pure recall, may be easier than essay examinations. Studies have shown, however, that there is usually a great similarity between marks on essay and objective examinations.

a. *Mark answers clearly.* Follow directions. A statement marked "True" that you meant to be "False" can only be considered incorrect. On examinations scored by stencils or by machine, answers not clearly indicated according to the directions are counted as omitted. If you wish to change an answer, be sure that you erase the old answer thoroughly.

b. *Lightly check any answers of which you are uncertain.* Later you can go back and either verify or change your answers. Questions answered in the meantime may have helped to clear up these previously doubtful answers. The previous section advised reading all questions on an essay examination before answering any. As a rule, this advice does not apply to objective questions. Probably you would not have time to read all questions twice.

c. *Be careful in answering true-false or yes-no questions.* True-false and yes-no questions are usually not so desirable as other objective questions; but since they do have some value, they are used. There are various ways of scoring answers to such questions. Sometimes the student is simply scored on the number of correct answers. Sometimes his score is the number of correct minus the number of incorrect responses. The latter method of scoring is designed to discourage guessing. The former enables the student to answer on the basis of "hunches"—that is, in terms of partial knowledge. Probably in the long run well-prepared students will "guess" correctly at certain answers more often than poorly prepared students. Try to find out how true-false and yes-no answers are to be scored. Govern your answering of doubtful questions accordingly.

d. *Watch for sweeping generalizations.* In true-false questions, especially in the social sciences, statements containing such terms as *always, never, invariably, without question, everyone,* and *no one* are likely to be false. Sweeping statements are usually false because there are so many points about which we are still uncertain. On the other hand, questions containing such terms as *there is some evidence that, some authorities say that, generally, frequently,* and *sometimes* are likely to be true. Watching for such terms may help the student in answering doubtful questions. However, a guide such as this is no substitute for accurate and thorough knowledge.

e. *Watch for partial truths.* Most

true-false questions are to be answered as either true or false. Sometimes the directions indicate "usually true" or "usually false." If the directions indicate either purely true or purely false, it is well to remember that if a statement is almost but not quite true, it is false. Sometimes questions are designated as *true-otherwise* rather than as true-false. A statement may not be true and yet not exactly false — it is otherwise. Be sure to note whether the directions are for true-false or for true-otherwise.

f. *Watch the directions when answering multiple-choice questions.* In multiple-choice questions, you may be instructed to choose just one of the several answers given. Or you may be directed to select the two or possibly more best answers. In either case, be sure to note the directions. To give more answers than the instructions indicate will mean that the answers will be counted as incorrect, even though they may include the correct answers.

g. *Analyze multiple-choice questions.* A multiple-choice question may seem hopeless at first glance. If, however, you will begin by checking off any answers that are clearly incorrect, you will limit the choices. You will run a much better chance of giving the correct answer than if you try to choose from all the answers given.

h. *Be systematic when answering matching questions.* In answering matching questions, you should work down one column looking for matches in the other column. Random looking around in the hopes of finding matches is an inefficient use of time and is confusing. It is better to mark those matches of which you are certain and to fill in lightly those of which you are less sure. This method reduces the possibilities of choice for those items about which you are quite uncertain. Eventually, by being systematic, you may be able to make all matches correctly, even though at first the question seemed somewhat overwhelming.

i. *Change answers if you are sure you made a mistake.* Frequently the question is asked, "Should a person change his answers, or is the first impression more likely to be correct?" If the first answer has been just a "guess," the first impression will probably have a slight advantage. You should not, however, hesitate to change answers if you believe you have made an error. One psychologist studied 28,000 answers on true-false and multiple-choice questions. He found that the majority of students raised their scores by changing answers which they believed to be incorrect. Only one fourth of them lowered their scores by making such changes. Do not change answers just to

THE PROCESS OF THINKING

be changing them, hoping that luck will be on your side. But do not hesitate to make changes if you have reason to do so.

4. *Budget your time on an examination.* Before beginning to answer questions on an examination, essay or objective, look over the entire exam. Note about how long you will have to answer each question. The teacher cannot learn what you know about a topic unless you answer the question concerning it. To spend most of your time on the first question or two and then rush through as many remaining questions as possible will not give a true picture of your knowledge.

In answering objective questions, remember that all answers will probably have the same value in the total score. There is some virtue in working out the answer to a difficult question. In an examination, however, it is foolish to spend so much time on one question that you do not have time to answer twenty-five or thirty others that you could have answered readily and correctly.

Whether the examination is an essay or an objective test, budget your time. Save a little time to go back over your paper and clear up doubtful points or complete uncertain answers.

5. *Profit from your mistakes.* We have already stressed the importance of psychological feedback — knowledge of results. Examinations are part of the learning process. Check over your errors, and learn why certain answers were incorrect or inferior. Otherwise you may never clear up incorrect impressions.

Terms to Add to Your Vocabulary

all-or-nothing thinking	deduction	incubation
autistic thinking	delusion	induction
"brainstorming"	eidetic imagery	inspiration
concept	fantasy	reasoning
concept formation	imagination	symbol
creative thinking	implicit behavior	thinking

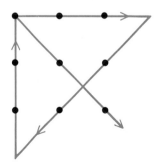

Answer to problem on page 121. If you were unable to solve this problem, was it because you thought only in terms of keeping all your lines within the area bordered by the dots? The instructions did not make this a requirement.

Suggestions for Activities

1. Some members of the class may present a short play in pantomime. Is such symbolization as efficient as word symbols in conveying ideas?

2. Arrange to listen in on some children's conversations for short periods of time, say five minutes. Record everything that is said. If available, a tape recorder will make the job easier. How many different words did each child use? Did older children use more words than younger children? Were there any examples of questionable or incorrect usages of words? Report your findings to the class.

3. You may wish to arrange to take the *Watson-Glaser Critical Thinking Appraisal,* published by Harcourt, Brace & World. It measures five aspects of the ability to think critically: to draw sound inferences from a statement of facts; to recognize assumptions implied by a statement; to reason logically by deduction; to reason logically by interpretation; to discriminate between strong and weak arguments. The test can be completed in a fifty-minute class period.

4. Read a newspaper editorial and analyze it. An editorial concerned with some political problem may be of special interest. On the whole, is the editorial sound? Are there any evidences of uncritical thinking?

5. Bring to class examples of newspaper or magazine advertising for coffee, tea, cola drinks, tobacco, and alcoholic beverages. Note such advertising on radio and television. Are the statements in the advertising justified on the basis of scientifically determined facts? Do advertisers sometimes use language to induce uncritical thinking on the part of the public?

6. If you know someone who has a baby of about five or six months of age, with the permission of parents and in familiar surroundings to the baby, preferably in his own home, perform the following. You will need two pieces of cloth and an interesting small toy or object. Seat the baby about halfway between the two pieces of cloth, which are placed on either side of the baby. While the baby is looking, hide the toy under one cloth, perhaps the one on his right side. Allow the baby time to reach under the cloth and retrieve the toy. Also, let him play with the toy for several minutes. Then take the toy away from him and slowly hide it under the cloth on his left side while he is watching. Where does the baby look for the toy? After you have finished, give the toy to the baby and let him play with it. If time permits, select various individuals who are older and repeat the same procedures. Do you notice any differences in reasoning ability as evidenced by where babies look for the toy as age increases?

7. Have one student demonstrate inductive reasoning in geometry. Have another student demonstrate deductive reasoning in geometry. Can you give examples of such reasoning in literature? What sort of reasoning is demonstrated in Poe's tale *The Gold-Bug?*

8. Present the following to someone who is not taking this course:

> All A is B.
> All C is B.
> Therefore, some C is A.

Ask the person if, according to the statements, the conclusion is true. To show that it is not true on the basis of the premises alone, show the person the following diagram.

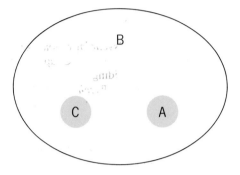

From the diagram it can be seen that B is only something that A and C share in common with each other. The conclusion stated above is, therefore, incorrect.

9. What do high school students daydream about? Have a locked ballot box where it is easily accessible. Ask students to deposit frank statements about their daydreams. It might be well to require that the papers be typed in order to assure anonymity. Students who are just trying to be funny may submit some statements, but these can be thrown out. How many of the daydreams seem to be ends in themselves? How many seem to be related to planning for the future? Do some seem to be just a form of entertainment?

10. If you have not already done so, take a standardized reading test. At what grade level do you read? Is there any difference between your reading speed level and your comprehension level? What specific steps can you take to improve your speed of reading level and your comprehension level? What specific steps can you take to improve your reading ability?

Near the close of the semester, retake the test in order to measure your improvement. Note any possible need for still further improvement.

11. Take one of the standardized study-habits inventories which your teacher will be able to recommend. Such inventories will enable you to make some analysis of your strong and weak study habits. Also, they may offer specific directions on how to increase your study efficiency.

Toward the end of the course, retake the inventory. Note your improvement, and note any inefficient habits you may still have at that time.

12. Secure copies of any objective examinations that may be available. Try to secure tests, or parts of tests, illustrating as many as possible of the following kinds of objective questions: true-false, multiple-choice, single-word completion, multiple-word completion, matching, analogy, listing, and rearrangement.

Make a class scrapbook of such questions. Study the various forms of questions and the various ways in which some of the forms can be answered.

Add to the scrapbook any samples of separate standard answer sheets that may be available, including some that can be scored electrically.

13. Have someone time you as you read several pages silently. Then select an equal number of pages elsewhere in the same book and be timed as you read them aloud. These pages should be of as nearly as possible the same difficulty as those read silently. Was there much difference in the two times? If not, how do you account for the fact? What can you do to improve your speed of silent reading?

Suggestions for Further Reading

Coleman, James, *Personality Dynamics and Effective Behavior,* Scott, Foresman. Part III, "Resources for Effective Living," considers intellectual competence under such topics as learning, problem solving, decision making, and creative thinking.

Daniel, Robert S., ed., *Contemporary Readings in General Psychology,* 2nd ed., Houghton Mifflin. Pages 153–57, "What Makes a Person Creative?"; pages 174–77, "How Children Form Mathematical Concepts."

Gerken, C. d'A., *Study Your Way Through School,* Science Research Associates.

Hardy, Lois, *How to Study in High School,* Pacific Books.

Heston, Joseph C., *How to Take a Test,* Science Research Associates.

Hilgard, Ernest R., and Richard C. Atkinson, *Introduction to Psychology,* 4th ed., Harcourt, Brace & World. Chapter 14, "Thinking, Language, and Problem Solving."

Hook, Julius N., *How to Write Better Examinations,* Barnes & Noble.

Kendler, Howard H., *Basic Psychology,* Appleton-Century-Crofts. Chapter 11, "Verbal Behavior and Problem Solving."

Leuba, Clarence, *Man: A General Psychology,* Holt, Rinehart & Winston. Pages 387–404, "Symbols in Perception and Thinking"; Chapter 16, "Thought Sequences and Their Determinants."

Lindgren, Henry C., Donn Byrne, and Lewis Petrinovich, *Psychology: An Introduction to a Behavioral Science,* 2nd ed., John Wiley. Chapter 14, "Communication."

McKeachie, Wilbert J., and Charlotte L. Doyle, *Psychology,* Addison-Wesley. Pages 364–69, "The Development of Thinking."

Morgan, Clifford T., and J. Deese, *How to Study,* McGraw-Hill.

Morgan, Clifford T., and Richard A. King, *Introduction to Psychology,* 3rd ed., McGraw-Hill. Chapter 5, "Thinking and Language."

Munn, Norman L., *Psychology,* 5th ed., Houghton Mifflin. Chapter 13, "Thinking"; Chapter 14, "Communication and Language."

Ruch, Floyd L., *Psychology and Life,* 7th ed., Scott, Foresman. Chapter 10, "Thinking and Deciding."

Sanford, Fillmore H., *Psychology: A Scientific Study of Man,* 2nd ed., Wadsworth. Chapter 14, "Higher Mental Processes."

Seidman, Jerome, ed., *The Adolescent: A Book of Readings,* rev. ed., Holt, Rinehart & Winston. Although written for teachers, this book contains some helpful suggestions for students; pages 408–20, "Relieving Anxiety in Classroom Examinations"; pages 421–25, "A Further Investigation of the Relationship Between Anxiety and Classroom Examination Performance."

Shanner, William, *A Guide to Logical Thinking,* Science Research Associates.

Thompson, Robert, *The Psychology of Thinking,* Penguin Books.

Whittaker, James O., et al., *Introduction to Psychology,* W. B. Saunders. Chapter 12, "Thinking."

Witty, Paul, *How to Become a Better Reader,* Science Research Associates. This book is written for high school juniors and seniors as well as for college students. It contains practical reading lessons, general reading exercises, a reading progress folder, and a list of suggested books to read.

Answer to symbols on page 104. Shapes: triangular traffic signs are for danger; circular signs for driving instruction; rectangular for information. Drawings: ⪚ sign indicates curves; line through horn means horn blowing is prohibited; P signifies authorized parking; walking figure means pedestrians crossing.

UNDERSTANDING HUMAN BEHAVIOR

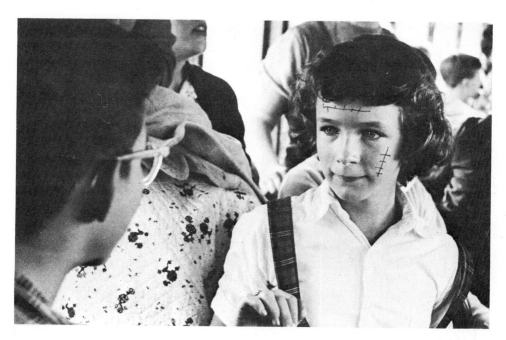

6

Understanding personality

There are many words in our language that are used vaguely, and even incorrectly, in everyday speech. Yet to psychologists these terms have definite, scientific meanings. Several such words—for instance, "instinct"—have already been discussed. Another misunderstood word is "personality." What is the popular use of this term? And how does it differ from the scientific meaning?

THE POPULAR VS. THE SCIENTIFIC VIEW OF PERSONALITY

In the popular view, personality is a wonderful quality we all want to have. The ambition of many Americans is to possess a "winning" or "charming" or "dynamic" personality. Unfortunately, not everyone—so goes the mistaken popular view—has this almost magical advantage.

What is the popular concept of personality? Advertising has helped to formulate the concept of personality that many people hold. Magazines, television, and Sunday newspapers run some advertisements in the form of romantic picture-stories. Scene 1—A pretty girl is sitting at home, crying. She has no boyfriends, no social life, no date for the big dance. Scene 2—A friend drops a hint, or the girl overhears two friends talking in the next room. Scene 3—The girl is brushing her teeth with "Dento" toothpaste, washing her hair with "Sudso" shampoo, eating "Atomic" vitamin pills, or covering her face with "Madame X's Skin Revitalizer." Scene 4—The girl, greatly cheered up and wearing a new dress, is surrounded by handsome young men. They are often in evening dress, they always look like movie stars, and they want nothing so much as to dance with the girl. Now she is popular because her skin is clear, her hair is shiny, she has a sparkling smile and boundless energy; in short, she has "personality." Advertising asks us to believe that we can buy personality—in a large economy-size bottle from the corner drugstore.

What is the psychological definition of personality? Actually, "personality" is difficult to define, and psychologists differ somewhat in their definitions. It may be said, however, that *personality* is the sum total of an individual's reactions to his environment as determined by his perceptions and by his reactions to his perceptions. Personality is, therefore, the unique or individual pattern of a person's life. It is the fundamental organization of an individual's characteristic adjustment to his environment. Total adjustment includes the individual's characteristic attitudes toward others, his habits of thought and ways of expression, his interests and ambitions, his plan of life, and his attitude toward life in general. It is an error to think of personality as one quality that some persons have and others lack. Everyone has a pattern of life and reacts to his environment, and therefore everyone has a personality.

Perhaps you have noted that the word "character," often used in connection with personality, has not been mentioned. This is a very popular word referring to the general moral and ethical outlook and the social conduct of an individual. Certainly psychologists are concerned about such aspects of life, but they include them under the general term "personality" rather than under the somewhat confusing popular word "character."

THE DEVELOPMENT OF PERSONALITY

How does personality develop? How do our patterns of behavior build up? From the definition of personality, it is obvious that there can be no simple answer to these questions. Personality is very complex, and many factors, such as intellectual ability (see Chap-

ter 8), biological foundations of heredity (Chapter 9), and certain anatomical and physiological factors (Chapter 10), influence its development. Here we will briefly mention additional factors in the development of personality.

The early years of life are very important to the development of personality. Even during the first few weeks of life, infants differ in their behavior (although such differences are primarily biologically determined). For example, some will cry, others will not cry; some infants are active, others are more passive. Distinctive patterns of adjusting to the environment are seen by the fourth month of life or slightly later. During the first half of the first year of life, behavior starts to become individualized as the infant reacts to food, clothing, light, dark, and so on. The child begins to show that complex pattern called "personality." As we shall see in Chapter 7, there is evidence that personality patterns established in the early years of a child's life usually persist into adult years, although the way in which these personality patterns are expressed may change, and experiences in later life, such as contacts in business, churches, and clubs, can greatly modify them.

How does the home affect personality? In America the home plays a major role in the development of personality because basic foundations of personality are laid down early in life, and most of the child's early life is spent in the home. Different home environments produce different personalities. Some parents constantly tell their children what they must not do, rather than showing them what they should do. Such repressive treatment by parents may have undesirable effects, causing the child to be defiant or to withdraw from contacts with other people or to live in a world of daydreams. Some parents make nearly all the decisions for their children, while others give children an opportunity to make decisions for themselves. What suit or dress the child wears each day or whether he eats oatmeal or cornflakes for breakfast is not important, but it is very important for the child to develop habits of making decisions because such habits are basic to the development of a personality marked by independence.

Affection in the home has a strong bearing on the personality development of children. By affection in the home we mean the degree to which children feel free to confide their problems to their parents, the degree to which parents are interested in and recognize the work and play of the children, and the degree to which there is mutual sharing of work and play in the family. In one psychological study, a group of ten-year-old children were asked to rate the degree of affection in their family relations. It was found that children who had indicated that there was a great deal of genuine affection in their family relations tended to be responsible and honest in their social relationships, whereas children from homes with little family affection were more likely to be irresponsible and dishonest.

How does his society influence an individual's personality? At first, a child learns something of his society through his home life. Then, as he grows older, he has more and more social contacts outside the home. His personality development is shaped by his contacts in the schoolroom, on the playground, in a church, and in play activities with children in the neighborhood. Through his home and social contacts he gradually learns what is expected of him as a member of the society in which he lives. The social group in which the child is reared will help him learn ways of behaving that are accepted by his society. To understand an individual's behavior we must also understand the society in which the child is reared.

Perhaps we can get a good idea of how much a society influences personality by looking at some ways in which societies, or large groups of people who share common traits, customs, or ways of behaving, may differ from one another.

In some societies of the world we do not find the striving for financial "success" that is so characteristic of the United States; for example, in the case of the Balinese, orthodox Hindu, and Hopi Indians. In other societies an individual's life work is determined by the occupational group into which he is born—if he is born a farmer's son, he will be a farmer. Societies may differ from one another in a multitude of ways, such as the amount of emphasis they place on individual achievement, worth and rights of the individual, education, marriage, standards of individual achievement, and money or material wealth. The types of achievement emphasized and the amount of emphasis placed on these areas by the

UNDERSTANDING HUMAN BEHAVIOR

Influences
on Personality

Three of the most important influences on the development of an individual's personality are his family, the school, and society. During the child's early years, when basic personality patterns are usually formed, his parents and siblings exert the greatest influence. Then, as the child goes to school, his teachers and schoolmates become instrumental in his development. Most of his life, an individual is influenced by his social group. Social patterns in Algeria (right), for example, produce a personality development different from ours.

society will help determine the personality of its members.

There are also differences between social groups within a society. Too often we tend to judge members of another group on the basis of the standards of the group to which we personally belong. The group's standards influence personality to the extent that the personality development of members of different social groups often reflect the differences in standards set by their groups.

In summary, remember that personality is determined by the home in which the person is reared, as well as the social group with which he associates, and the society in which he is raised. If you had been reared in a different society and a different geographical setting, you might have a quite different personality.

THE NORMAL DISTRIBUTION

To follow psychological work in the field of personality, some knowledge of a normal distribution, or normal frequency distribution, is helpful.

What is a normal frequency distribution? You have probably observed in your classes that on the average, when grades are given on a test, a few of the students are given A's and a few are given F's (or whatever the failing mark is), but most of the grades fall somewhere between these two extremes. It would be rather unusual if everyone received an A on a test or if almost everyone failed it.

One of the authors of this book has made a study of the grades given in all classes in a certain high school. Below is a table showing the 6,087 final grades which the 800 students in that school received at the end of the semester.

A Frequency Distribution of Final Grades

GRADE	A	B	C	D	F
Number	572	1,229	1,896	1,821	569
Percent	9.4	20.2	31.1	29.9	9.3

In the table, beside "Number," you can see the number of times each grade occurred; that is, you can see the frequency with which it occurred. We therefore say that this table shows a *frequency distribution*. We can plot this frequency distribution on a graph (Figure A, on the opposite page), placing a dot in the appropriate place to show how often each score occurred.

As you can see from this graph, most of the grades were in the middle of the range—B, C, and D. Comparatively few grades were in the highest and lowest categories—A and F. This distribution partially resembles what is called a *normal distribution,* or a *normal frequency distribution.* A normal distribution of data usually, although not always, results when a large number of psychological data are plotted. By connecting the dots on a graph (Figure B) of such a distribution, we almost get a *normal distribution curve,* sometimes known as a *normal curve,* which is bell-shaped.

A normal curve has some definite characteristics. (1) It has one high point in the center of the curve, with the lines sloping downward smoothly on both sides. (2) It is bilaterally symmetrical, one side being the mirrored image of the other. Each dot on one side of the high point is matched by another dot at the same height on the other side. (3) It is bell-shaped. The sides of the graph are steep near the high point but level off as they approach the bottom. (4) The ends of the curve never touch the base lines. (5) The mean, median, and mode, all measures of central tendency, are numerically the same (see the Appendix). Actually, a true normal curve exists only in theory, but generally the larger the number of scores, grades, or other data which are plotted, the closer the distribution comes to being a normal curve. The scores of more than one million military personnel have been plotted to produce a curve that is close to a normal curve but that did not form a perfect normal curve.

Psychological measurements are not the only data that show normal distribution and a normal curve. Whenever a large number of measures of biological events are collected, they too are found to have a normal distribution and to

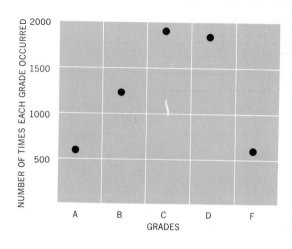

Figure A

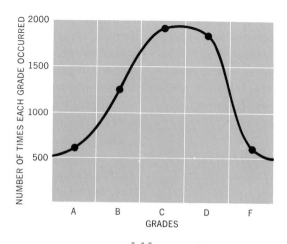

Figure B

UNDERSTANDING PERSONALITY

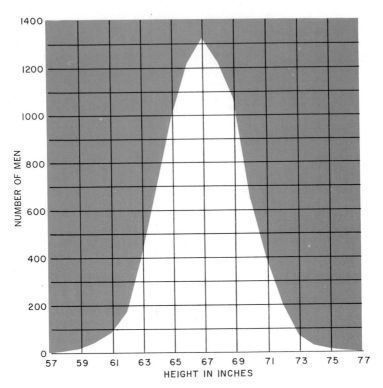

Normal distribution curve for data on height

resemble, when graphed, a normal distribution curve. In 1883, scientists measured the height of 8,585 adult men. The data they collected are shown graphically above.

In the following pages, which discuss "introversion-extroversion" and other terms used in personality study, you will note examples of normal distribution and normal curves. For further information on these important concepts, see the Appendix.

SOME THEORIES OF PERSONALITY

Through the years, as psychologists have sought to learn about personality,

they have introduced several theories to explain its nature. We shall now consider a few of these theories.

What is a trait theory of personality? A *trait* is a more or less permanent pattern of behavior. Traits are categories of an individual's personality which can be observed, described, and measured. Therefore, we can use traits to indicate similarities and differences between people.

One study has shown that the English language includes approximately 18,000 terms, mostly adjectives, which describe what might be called traits of personality. There is much overlapping in meaning among these terms.

UNDERSTANDING HUMAN BEHAVIOR

One trait theory, based on statistical analysis, speaks of *primary traits*—traits which are characteristic of most individuals in a society. There are about a dozen primary personality traits, traits which appear in various independent research studies of personality. Traits are usually expressed as pairs of words of opposite meaning, presuming that individuals vary, anywhere from one extreme to the other, in the degree to which they have a particular trait. Therefore, traits are generally described in the same way as those listed below.

What is the introvert-extrovert theory?
An early theory of personality which persists today, at least in popular thinking and generally without the sanction of psychologists, is one originated by the Swiss psychiatrist Carl Jung (yo͞ong). He classified persons as introverts or extroverts (sometimes spelled "extraverts"). By introverts, he meant those people who were very self-centered and shy. By extroverts, he meant those who were very socially centered and active. Another way of explaining these terms is to state that someone who responds primarily to internal stimuli, such as his own ideas, is an introvert and someone who responds primarily to external stimuli, such as ideas from others and social situations, is an extrovert.

Primary Personality Traits

1. Easygoing, genial, friendly	*as opposed to*	1. Inflexible, hostile, suspicious
2. Intelligent, independent, thoughtful		2. Foolish, frivolous, slipshod
3. Emotionally stable, realistic, patient		3. Evasive, emotionally changeable, unrealistic
4. Emotionally hypersensitive, high-strung, excitable		4. Phlegmatic, tolerant, self-controlled
5. Dominant, self-assertive, headstrong		5. Submissive, self-effacing, sensitive
6. Cheerful, sociable, optimistic		6. Unhappy, seclusive, pessimistic
7. Conscientious, reliable, painstaking		7. Impulsive, irresponsible, fickle
8. Friendly, trustful, curious		8. Suspicious, cynical, inhibited
9. Tenderhearted, sympathetic, idealistic		9. Hard-boiled, poised, unemotional
10. Vigorous, energetic, alert		10. Languid, slow, absent-minded
11. Trained and cultured, esthetic, conscientious		11. Uncultured, impulsive, narrow
12. Adventurous, carefree, cooperative		12. Frustrated, reserved, withdrawn

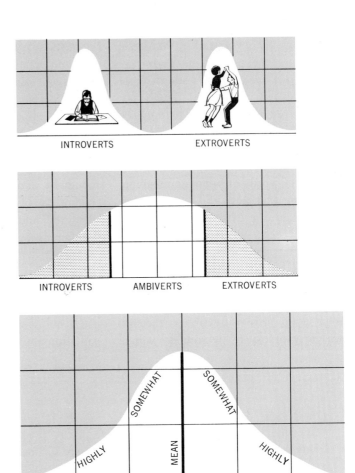

Figure A

INTROVERTS   EXTROVERTS

Figure B

INTROVERTS   AMBIVERTS   EXTROVERTS

Figure C

SOMEWHAT   SOMEWHAT

HIGHLY   MEAN   HIGHLY

INTROVERTED   EXTROVERTED

There is one serious criticism of a scheme of classification such as that proposed by Jung. It tends to make us believe that persons can be separated into definite types or classes, that a person is in one class or another, and there is no overlapping. Figure A, shown above, represents such a classification. Introverts and extroverts appear in distinct distributions, with a definite separation between the two types or classes.

The tendency to put persons into categories or types is very common.

Thus we sometimes hear the expression "Oh, you are just the type that would do that!" Persons are far too complicated to be classified into types in any such simple manner. The work of the psychologist would be much easier if he could readily classify persons. But individuals are very complex. No matter how the psychologist measures individuals, he will not find any completely and clearly separable types.

It has been suggested that Jung's classification can be improved by introducing a large middle group. These persons may be called *ambiverts.* In that case we might have such a classification as that shown in Figure B (page 144). Note that according to this figure all classes are presumed to fall into a normal frequency distribution. The distinctions between classes are indicated merely by dividing lines.

Today it is not considered scientific to think of individuals as belonging in classes of introverts, extroverts, and ambiverts, as in Figures A and B. We can just as easily and more scientifically think of them as being distributed by small degrees along a normal frequency curve like the one shown in Figure C where there are no definite categories or boundaries. Figure C illustrates the advantage of speaking of persons as being introverted or extroverted instead of calling them introverts or extroverts. If we say that an individual is *introverted,* we do not mean that he is being put in a type. We mean that of all his habits of action and thought, most center around himself. If we say that an individual is *extroverted,* we mean that most of his habits of action and thought are centered around other people.

How introverted or extroverted we are can be judged from our relative position on the curve. Do we have more self-centered habits and fewer socially centered habits than most persons? If so, we would be to the left of the center (the "mean," or average) in Figure C. If we have more socially centered habits and fewer self-centered habits than most persons, we would be

Many efforts have been made to relate an individual's personality to the structure of his body. One well-known theory is W. H. Sheldon's classification of body types. Sheldon rated individuals on the basis of three basic body types, shown below. He then found a correlation between each body type and certain personality traits. The endomorph, who has a round, soft body, is sociable, conventional, loves to eat, and seeks bodily comforts. The mesomorph, who is very muscular, likes strenuous exercise and is adventurous, energetic, and direct. The ectomorph, who has a thin, linear physique, is sensitive, shy, given to worry, and fearful of groups.

ENDOMORPH

MESOMORPH

ECTOMORPH

UNDERSTANDING PERSONALITY

to the right of the average. How far to the left or the right of the average we are is determined by what proportion of our habits are self-centered or socially centered. These distinctive tendencies of habits are spoken of as traits.

What are some characteristics of introversion-extroversion? Psychologists have made up lists of activities, interests, and attitudes which reflect introversion and extroversion. Among the traits the psychologists have considered characteristic of *introversion* are having "feelings" hurt easily, daydreaming frequently, blushing often, keeping in the background on social occasions, suffering from stage fright, showing reluctance about making friends (especially with the opposite sex), worrying over possible misfortunes, being unable to make decisions, being critical of others, showing excessive concern over gossip, taking meticulous care of personal property, responding excessively to praise.

Traits considered characteristic of *extroversion* are not having "feelings" hurt easily, seldom daydreaming, making friends easily, being the "life of the party," being free from excessive worrying, laughing frequently and easily, preferring oral reports rather than written reports, accepting orders from others as a matter of course, preferring work involving social contacts rather than confining details, avoiding indulgence in self-pity, being a good loser.

Some psychologists have tried to break down introversion-extroversion into several independent traits such as social introversion-extroversion, emotional introversion-extroversion, and

intellectual introversion-extroversion. Some psychologists question whether we should even think of extroversion and introversion as extremes of the same dimension of personality. There is some evidence that extroversion and introversion may be differently manifested in men and women and that extroversion and introversion may be differently manifested in well-adjusted and maladjusted individuals.

Certainly, the words "introversion" and "extroversion" must be used with care. We must not speak of individuals as belonging to the introvert type or the extrovert type. Remember the definition of "personality" as the fundamental organization of an individual's characteristic adjustments to his environment. Personality can never be reduced to a few simple terms.

CORRELATION

Before taking up the methods by which psychologists measure personality, you should understand a statistical method known as correlation, which helps psychologists interpret their findings.

What is correlation? *Statistics*, used in all sciences, is the mathematical procedures for gathering, organizing, analyzing, and interpreting data. In studying scientific measures of personality — and in much other work with psychology — you will find references to a statistical device known as *correlation* (kôr′ə·lā′shən). Psychologists often use correlation to tell how much relationship there is between two scores. It must be noted that correlation merely

UNDERSTANDING HUMAN BEHAVIOR

indicates that there is a relationship between two things or events, but it does not necessarily mean that there is a cause-and-effect relationship. The primary purpose of correlation is to obtain a prediction of one variable in relation to another.

In case you wish to correlate data obtained in your classes, you will find a simple mathematical technique for computing degree of correlation explained in the Appendix.

But without going into the mathematical details, a word will be said now about the meaning of correlation, so that you will understand certain statistics quoted in this book and in other scientific sources.

Suppose that a high school class takes two tests, one in physics and one in advanced algebra. Would those who earned high scores in physics tend to make high scores in algebra, would they tend to make low scores in algebra, or would there be no relationship between scores on the two tests? A single number, called a *coefficient of correlation,* can be used to express whatever relationship may exist. Suppose that the student who scored highest on the physics test scored highest on the algebra test, that the student who scored next to highest on the physics test scored next to highest on the algebra test, and so on down to the student who scored lowest on the physics test and also lowest on the algebra test. Such a result would produce a coefficient of correlation of +1.00 (note that this is not one hundred), indicating a perfect positive relationship. Suppose, instead, that the student who scored highest on the physics test

scored lowest on the algebra test, that the student who scored next to highest on the physics test scored next to lowest on the algebra test, and so on to the student who scored lowest on the physics test and highest on the algebra test. Such a result would produce a coefficient of correlation of −1.00, indicating a perfect negative relationship. A negative coefficient, which shows a relationship in reverse, is just as indicative of a relationship as the corresponding positive coefficient. Whether a correlation coefficient is positive or negative indicates the direction of the relationship between two such variables as the scores on a physics and algebra test. The size of the coefficient indicates the degree of relationship. In statistics the coefficient of correlation is usually designated by the letter r. Thus we would say that r may theoretically exist from +1.00 to −1.00, but in actual practice such perfect relationships are not found.

There is no simple rule for interpreting a given coefficient of correlation. For our purposes, however, there are these general rules: Coefficients, either positive or negative, of .90 and above indicate a very close relationship. Coefficients between .70 and .90 indicate a very strong trend of agreement—although of less importance than those of .90 and above. Coefficients between .50 and .70 are quite common in practice and indicate a relationship of some importance. Going down the scale from .50, there is decreasing importance until .00 is reached, which indicates that there is no relationship.

Either small positive or small negative coefficients may be a result of pure

UNDERSTANDING PERSONALITY

chance, not indicating any true relationship. In practice, the coefficient of correlation between any two tests is nearly always positive.

There are three points that you must remember when interpreting any given coefficient of correlation: (1) A coefficient of correlation is not a percentage and cannot be interpreted as such. (2) The extent of correlation does not follow closely its numerical size. For example, a coefficient of +.80 or −.80 is considerably more than twice as important as a coefficient of +.40 or −.40. (3) A causal relationship must not be inferred between variables on the basis of correlation.

The following pages will take up five techniques psychologists use to measure personality: ratings, inventories, interviewing, behavior sampling, and projective techniques. Notice how correlation is employed in these studies.

SCIENTIFIC TECHNIQUES FOR MEASURING PERSONALITY

Some psychologists prefer to speak of evaluation rather than measurement of personality, especially when the individual is being considered in a broad social setting. Sometimes the term "assessment" is used for any procedure designed to describe an individual's characteristic behavior. But whatever terms they use to describe the process, psychologists employ similar techniques in their efforts to measure personality.

1. Ratings

What is rating? *Rating* refers to assigning a rank or a score to an individual. This method of measuring personality is often used in business and in schools.

An executive may be asked to rate the salesmen under his supervision on such personality traits as friendliness, courtesy, and honesty. Foremen in industry may rate the men working under their supervision. By this means, the men with the most promising personalities can be selected for and promoted to those positions in which a pleasing personality is especially desirable. For example, in one industry the coefficient of correlation between the high ratings on seven traits of personality and recommendations for promotions to more responsible positions was +.81.

In many schools the development of desirable student personalities is recognized as being as important as, or more important than, developing skill in solving quadratic equations, declining Latin nouns, or knowing outstanding dates in history. It is much easier to measure ability in algebra, Latin, and history than it is to measure personality patterns. Yet schools often do the best they can to measure personality by having each teacher rate his students on selected personality traits.

What is the order-of-merit method of rating? There are a number of techniques for rating. One is known as the *order-of-merit method*. In using this technique, the raters assign numbers, beginning with *1*, to the persons they are rating. Suppose that you are trying to find the most courteous person in the class. Each one who is judging the group will assign a number to each member of the group. Suppose that

UNDERSTANDING HUMAN BEHAVIOR

Judge A decides from his knowledge of the behavior of Henry Smith that Henry is the most courteous boy in the class—then he will assign Henry the number *1*. If he thinks Mary Jones is the next most courteous person in the class, he will assign her the number *2*, and so forth.

This technique is easy to use if you write the name of each person on a separate slip. Then you can sort and re-sort the slips until you have them in the correct order from highest to lowest, according to the best of your ability to judge. Then put a number *1* on the highest slip, number *2* on the second, and so on. Several judges rank the group. The rating of each individual on each trait is the average of all his scores on that trait. Such a technique can be used only where the group to be rated is relatively small.

What is a graphic rating scale? Another rating technique makes use of a *graphic rating scale*. For each trait considered, a line is drawn. The rater indicates on the line where he thinks the given individual stands. For example, suppose that you are going to rate a person on leadership. The total line represents the range from never being a leader to always being a leader. It helps to put short descriptive phrases under parts of the line, as in the following illustration:

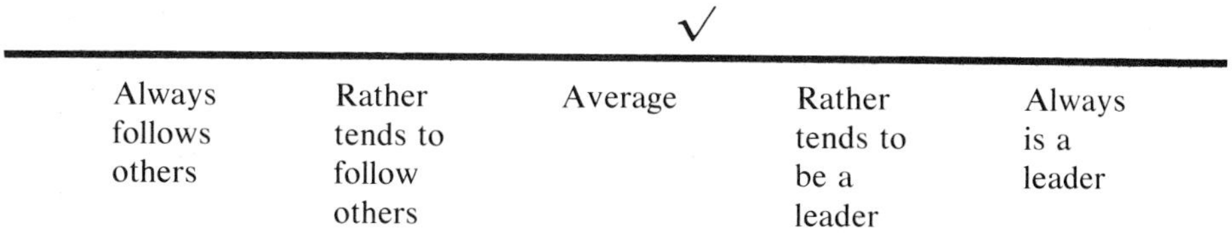

| Always follows others | Rather tends to follow others | Average | Rather tends to be a leader | Always is a leader |

The check mark in the illustration would indicate that the rater believed the person he was rating was slightly above the average in leadership.

Sometimes the line is divided into a number of compartments. The rater does not indicate a point on a line but merely checks the compartment which best fits. Usually there are five or seven compartments. An odd number makes it a bit easier to remember the normal frequency distribution while rating.

There are not very many persons who can judge accurately more than seven differences.

The foregoing two schemes for rating are not the only ones in use, but they illustrate the general method and will be suitable for your use in class experiments.

What dangers must be guarded against in rating? Several precautions must be taken whenever an individual is called

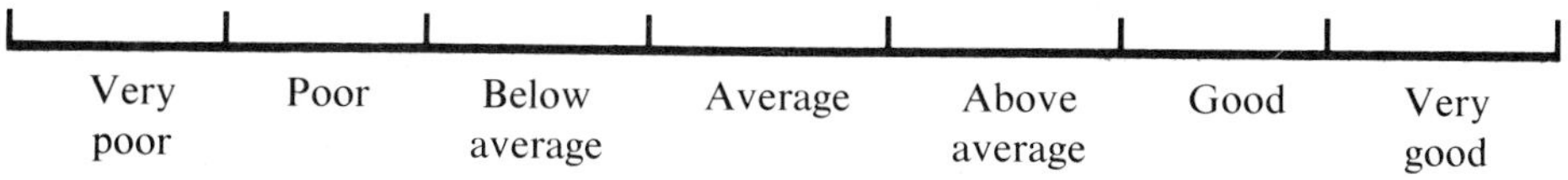

| Very poor | Poor | Below average | Average | Above average | Good | Very good |

UNDERSTANDING PERSONALITY

upon to rate others on traits of personality, regardless of which method is used.

First, be careful not to overrate. Psychologists have found that unless a person is very careful to take into account the normal frequency distribution, he will overrate most persons on most traits. One of the authors of this text once made a study of the rating of 345 high school students. Their teachers rated these students each semester on ten personality traits. For example, one trait was appearance. The judgment of best in appearance was weighted 5, the next 4, and so on to 1 for the poorest in appearance. According to the normal frequency distribution, the average score should have been 3, but the author found the average score to be 3.84. That is, the teachers were overrating the students in appearance. The same was true for all other traits. Possibly, in the traits rated, the students were above the average of the community as a whole, but the teachers had been told to rate on the basis of the high school population only. Psychologists speak of this tendency to overrate as the *generosity error*.

Second, be careful of the halo effect. The word "halo" is used here in a technical sense, but it is related to the common use of the word meaning the circle of light around a saint's head in a picture. Psychologists use the term *halo effect* to describe the tendency to rate a person high on all traits because he makes a favorable general impression. The term also describes the tendency to rate someone low on all traits because he makes an unfavorable general impression. In short, the halo effect is the tendency of general impressions to spread to specific traits or even the tendency of the impression made by one trait to spread to other traits.

For example, businessmen find it difficult to rate salesmen on specific personality traits without being influenced by their sales records. A man who has been bringing in large orders is very apt to be rated high in all personality traits. A man who has a poor sales record is very apt to be rated low in all personality traits. Although such high and low ratings may be justified, if the sales records were to get mixed up, the ratings might be quite different. That is, there is apt to be a halo effect from the sales record.

Such a halo effect can be overcome, in part, by rating all individuals on one trait before going on to the next trait. For example, the business executive should rate all salesmen on initiative, then rate all of them on dependability, and so forth. He should not rate one man on all traits, then another on all traits. By concentrating on one trait at a time, the executive can make more accurate judgments.

Although we assume that there is some halo effect, the correlation between traits may actually be in the people being rated, rather than in the rating process. For example, it may well be that the salesmen with the best sales records actually are the ones with the most pleasing personalities. Teachers find it difficult to rate pupils on traits of personality without being influenced by their classwork. But perhaps there is considerable correlation between personality and classroom achievement.

The halo effect is especially likely to be present if the name of the trait to be rated is not clearly defined in the thinking of the rater. For example, "character" is often a vaguely used word. If a rater is asked to rate individuals on this trait, his rating is likely to be a carry-over from his general impression of the individual.

Be careful also of a third error, the *stereotype*. We tend to apply to an individual the judgments we have previously formed of his racial, national, or social group. For example, we may have formed a stereotype judgment of the Chinese. If we meet a Chinese person, we are apt to assume that he "runs true to type." If we attempt to rate him, there is danger that we shall do so in terms of our prejudices and biases toward all Chinese rather than on the basis of his personal characteristics. If we have time to learn to know him well before we attempt to rate him, we are likely to find that he does not conform to our previous stereotyped idea of Chinese people. Knowing of the error of the stereotype, a rater can be on his guard against it.

There is a fourth error to be guarded against in rating — the error of the *type,* or *pigeonhole*. If we recognize that personality traits are probably distributed according to normal frequency, we shall not rate individuals as the blond type or the brunette type, as the good type or the bad type, as an introvert or an extrovert. To do so would immediately introduce an error in our judgment.

Finally, there is the danger that when we rate another person, we may attribute to him our own characteristics, or

The halo effect can influence how applicants are rated during an audition for a high school play.

their opposites. If we are very thrifty, we rate him as being very thrifty or else very wasteful. If we are very neat in dress, we are likely to regard him as similar to ourselves or very slovenly.

Rating is not a perfect measure of personality. If, however, the raters are trained in rating and if the technique is carefully developed, it is a useful psychological tool.

Regardless of the scheme of rating used, the one essential requirement is that those who do the rating must have had an opportunity to observe and know the individuals they are rating. Sometimes it is impossible to find enough judges who know the individuals to be rated and who are willing to take the time and effort necessary to rate them. How can psychologists get a measure of personality in such cases?

The following method was devised for this situation.

2. Inventories

The word "inventory" is derived from the Latin word *inventarium* and means literally "to find out." Psychologists use the word to refer to a measuring device enabling one to find out about an individual's personality, especially his ability to adjust to his environment.

The use of inventories to measure personality stems from studies made during World War I. The hundreds of thousands of men who entered the United States Army in 1917–18 differed greatly in their total personality patterns. Some fitted themselves into army life easily. Others adjusted with some but not too much difficulty. Still others found it almost impossible to adjust to the army and the war. It was clearly necessary "to find out" which men would make good front-line fighters and which ones would not.

A committee went to work to devise a method for measuring personality on a large scale. From studies of those men who had difficulty in adjusting to army life, the committee made up a list of 116 questions. For example: "Can you stand pain quietly? Can you stand the sight of blood? Can you stand disgusting smells?" All questions were to be answered "Yes" or "No."

After the war, the list was adapted for civilian use, and schools and businesses took up the inventory method. The military services made some further use of personality inventories during World War II, although they put a good deal of emphasis on psychiatric interviews.

How are inventories made up and scored? Lists of inventory questions are known by various names: personality inventories, personality schedules, personality questionnaires. They are designed to measure various aspects of personality or the general adjustment of an individual to his environment. They are all based on the statistical theory of *sampling*. That is, from all the habits of overt action and thought that a person may have, one hundred to two hundred habits are selected to obtain a good cross section of what all his habits are like.

So that inventories are easy to score, the answers are often given by drawing a circle around a "Yes," a "No," or a "?" Then, by means of a scoring key, the answers are measured and a score is obtained.

Inventories were first developed as group measures of personality. In more recent years some inventories have been developed for individual administration; that is, the psychologist gives the inventory to one individual at a time. In one of these individual inventories, the psychologist gives to the person whose personality is being measured a box containing 550 cards. Each card bears a statement somewhat similar to those found on group inventories. He then files these cards under three headings: "True," "False," "Cannot say." By means of a scoring technique, the psychologist is able to tell a good deal about the individual's personality from the cards he filed under each heading. Psychologists find such indi-

UNDERSTANDING HUMAN BEHAVIOR

vidually administered inventories more valuable than group-administered inventories for the study of personality, although there is a group form for this particular inventory.

One of the objections to the inventory method is that the individual can quite often, when he deems it desirable, bias the results of an inventory. For example, an individual might be asked to answer either "True" or "False" to the following question: "Do you dislike your brother or sister?" Perhaps the individual actually dislikes his sister, but, believing that the answer "True" is socially unacceptable, he answers "False."

A device which has attempted to overcome this objection to inventories is the Edwards Personal Preference Schedule. In this inventory the individual has to choose between two statements, both of which are favorable, or both of which are unfavorable. For example, he may be asked to choose between the following:

A. I sometimes feel that I want to hurt others
B. I feel inferior to others

Another device used by some inventories is to include "lie" questions. One personality inventory contains fifteen questions to which the answers, if inconsistent with the large majority of other answers, indicate that the person taking the test is lying and cause the examiner to be suspicious of the scores on other parts of the inventory.

How important are inventory scores? You should be cautioned about personality inventory scores. Do not take them too seriously. Always remember, when considering scores on inventories, that they are not like the scores on school tests. They do not represent right or wrong; they merely indicate the trend of the habits of action and thought of the individual. There is no such thing as a passing or failing grade. Inventories are of value in helping us to understand one personality as compared with the personalities of others, but they are not examinations on which anyone can be "flunked."

Even comparing the score of an individual with the scores made by others must be done with caution. What might appear to be an undesirable response for a person belonging to one social group might not be an undesirable response for a person belonging to a different social group. At one time several personality inventories were given to a group of Chinese students. A first glance at the data seemed to suggest that these Chinese individuals had undesirable traits of personality. One of the questions asked was, "Do you allow others to push ahead of you in line?" In terms of American standards, since the person who permits others to crowd in ahead of him is considered to be too timid and submissive, the desirable answer is "No." In terms of Chinese standards, the desirable answer is "Yes." In the traditional Chinese culture, people gather around together and do not form lines as we do. The Chinese believe that if an individual crowds ahead, there must be a very special reason and deference should be given him.

Furthermore, inventories are measures of habits, and habits can be

UNDERSTANDING PERSONALITY

Because of cultural differences between Chinese and American families, caution should be used in giving the same personality inventory to both groups.

to think about his answers very long, he may indicate the kind of personality he would like to have rather than the kind of personality he does have at the time. In answering the questions on an inventory, it is best to work rather rapidly. On such a "test," a person's first impression is probably a better indication of his personality than a response which he has taken time to "think out."

Remember that personality inventories are crude measures at best, although they are of value if properly administered and interpreted by a psychologist.

3. Interviewing

Sometimes interviewing is used as a technique for measuring personality. Many employers and employment managers believe that they can "size up" the personality and other qualifications of an applicant for a job in just a few minutes by means of a personal interview. Something about an individual's personality can be learned from an interview. However, a general "sizing up" of a person in this way may give a far from valid impression of his personality.

Why is interviewing not always a valid measure? We noted certain precautions to be taken in rating individuals (pages 149–51) and we need to take these same precautions when interviewing. The following experiment demonstrates that interviewing is not always a valid way of evaluating personality. Twelve sales managers in an automobile organization were asked to

changed. Some of the unscientific attempts to measure personality suggest that we are born with fixed personality patterns and are doomed to go through life with them. Psychology has no such pessimistic point of view. Recent research has indicated that significant changes in habits and attitudes may continue to occur in the adult years of life. Such changes may even mean the difference between a personality that is pleasing and happy and one that is not.

Scores on an inventory are of value only insofar as the individual has answered the questions frankly and honestly. Even then, especially if he stops interview 57 applicants for sales positions. These sales managers were accustomed to "sizing up" men and selecting those whose personalities indicated that they were suited for positions as salesmen. Each sales manager interviewed each one of the 57 applicants. Then, without consulting anyone, he ranked the applicants in order of desirability for sales positions. That is, if a sales manager believed an applicant to be the best prospect of all, he gave the applicant a rank of 1. The applicant he judged to be the next best he gave a rank of 2, and so on down to a rank of 57 for the applicant he judged to be least desirable of all the applicants.

When psychologists compared the rankings of the sales managers, they found many differences. For example, one applicant had been given the following rankings: 1, 2, 6, 9, 10, 16, 20, 21, 26, 28, 53, 57. One of the sales managers had thought him the best prospect, and another had thought him the worst—on the basis of the interview. Another applicant had been ranked 2, 4, 9, 13, 16, 16, 19, 28, 32, 33, 46, 55. Thus, one applicant might be judged very desirable by some sales managers, very undesirable by other sales managers, and intermediate in desirability by still others. Certainly "sizing up" of men, even by these experienced interviewers, did not give consistent results.

How has interviewing been improved?
Since World War II, interviewing techniques have improved considerably. The principal difficulty with interviewing had been that so much depended upon the judgment of the interviewer. Psychologists found that judgments made following interviews become more valid if they are guided by the two previously discussed techniques for measuring personality—inventories and rating scales.

The interviewer may use a list of questions, some of which are similar to those asked on inventories. In a skillfully conducted interview these questions, which are given orally, may be answered more frankly and honestly than if they were merely printed questions to be answered by pencil marks. The interviewer can explain questions not fully understood and get more complete answers from the person being interviewed.

The interviewer may use a rating scale to record his estimate of the degree to which the individual being interviewed has certain traits of personality. The rating scale is used during the interview or immediately following it. Judgments recorded while they are fresh are probably superior to those based on memory of past impressions.

In one wartime situation candidates for commissions were interviewed and rating scales were used. The interviewers worked independently but used the same rating scales. Correlation between ratings of these interviewers was $+.83$ in one case and $+.85$ in another.

Psychologists have found that they can obtain more valid measures if several interviewers of an individual pool their findings. Interviewers should have access to and use any information about an individual that may be available. Also, it is helpful to recheck

UNDERSTANDING PERSONALITY

interviews. Rechecking has become possible in recent years with the improvement of tape-recording equipment. Tape recordings can be made of interviews an hour or more in length. When interviewers play back these recordings, they can correct any wrong first impressions. They can note any points they missed during the original interview. Other trained interviewers can listen to the interview and add their judgments to those of the original interviewer. Usually the recording microphone is concealed, so that the person being interviewed is not bothered by the thought that every word is being recorded.

As commonly used (by employment managers, for example), interviewing can scarcely be considered "a scientific attempt to measure personality." However, interviewing by scientific methods is another matter. Interviews handled by well-trained interviewers who use modern techniques may be able to measure personality as well as, or even better than, ratings or inventories can.

We should add that interviews have another use besides measuring personality. They are sometimes valuable in the treatment of patients with emotional or "nervous" troubles. Psychoanalysts and clinical psychologists often use interviews for purposes of therapy.

4. Behavior Sampling

Another technique which psychologists use to measure aspects of personality is quite different from the three techniques described previously. In this fourth method no one's opinion is asked about another person, nor does the person answer questions about himself. Instead, a sampling of actual behavior is measured or recorded.

To secure a measure of a person's honesty, a psychologist can set up a sample situation in which the person

In this example of behavior sampling, a boy is given toys with which he can act out his problems, as a psychologist (left) observes his behavior.

may be dishonest if he wishes. Then the extent of his honesty can be measured. For example, he may be given a chance to steal a small amount of money. The circumstances are arranged to lead him to believe that no one will be able to detect that he has stolen. To measure the trait of leadership, the psychologist can create a sample situation in which an individual can demonstrate his ability to lead. The extent to which a person lies may be measured by counting the lies he tells in a given number of answers to questions.

How can cheating in schoolwork be measured? Cheating in schoolwork is measured by setting up an experimental situation in which pupils can cheat if they wish to do so. One favorite method is to give a test in some subject, collect the papers, and carefully make a record of right and wrong answers. The papers must be scored without indicating in any way on the papers that they have been scored. The next day the teacher returns the papers to the class. The pupils then score their own papers, assuming that the teacher will collect them and record the marks in the grade book. Perhaps the teacher leaves the room for a few minutes, to give the pupils an opportunity to cheat. The pupil-scored papers are then collected. Whatever differences there are between the scores the pupils set down when marking the papers and the previous scores are a measure of cheating — unless there were actual errors in marking.

The work of two psychologists who studied cheating by school children provides an interesting illustration of the use of behavior sampling. The psychologists gave the children an opportunity to cheat on school tests. They were interested in comparing children who varied in their general intelligence. We shall discuss general intelligence in Chapter 8, but for the present we shall simply understand that A represents the highest intelligence, B the next highest, and so on down to E. The data obtained are indicated in part in the table below, which should be read as follows: 21 percent of the children of highest (A) intelligence cheated on school tests, 31 percent of the next to the highest (B) group cheated, and so on.

Intelligence and Cheating in School Tests

INTELLIGENCE	PERCENT CHEATING
A	21
B	31
C+	30
C	46
C−	49
D	70
E	82

In terms of correlation, the psychologists found that the coefficient of correlation between cheating and intelligence was −.493. The minus sign indicates that the lower the children were in intelligence, the more they tended to cheat in schoolwork. Probably the children of low intelligence were unable to compete successfully in schoolwork. Hence, they resorted to cheating in order to get better marks.

How can cheating in games be measured? The same two psychologists conducted research on the relation between intelligence and cheating in party games. They measured cheating in party games, for example, by asking blindfolded children to pin an arrow as near as possible to the bull's-eye of a target. The blindfold was so arranged that the child could see under it if he tried to do so — and some children did. The coefficient of correlation between this kind of cheating and intelligence was +.05. That is, there was no relationship between intelligence and cheating in this situation. The explanation is probably that the children of low intelligence were able to compete successfully in party games without cheating. Hence, they did not cheat. Also, unfortunately, some children feel that cheating in schoolwork is the accepted thing — but that cheating in games is dishonorable.

How have psychologists measured public honesty? An experiment performed with "lost" letters is of interest in connection with our study of behavior sampling. Stamped, addressed, sealed letters were dropped at various locations on busy city sidewalks. Each envelope contained only a trivial message and had no return address. Eighty-five percent of these letters were put in a mailbox by the persons who found them. Other letters were "lost" in the same way, but these letters contained a lead slug the size of a half-dollar. A note in the sealed envelope indicated that the lead slug was of value only to the person to whom the letter was addressed. Only 54 percent of these "lost" letters were mailed. Of those mailed, 13 percent had been opened before being mailed.

The persons who found letters were not asked whether or not they were honest about mailing found letters. They were not rated by others. Instead, a situation was designed in which they had an opportunity to demonstrate their honesty. If several such tests could have been given to these same individuals, some interesting individual differences in honesty might have been discovered.

What caution is needed in interpreting behavior samplings? Behavior samplings are valuable in the scientific measurement of personality, but they must not be interpreted too broadly. Although psychologists strive for samplings that are *representative* of a person's behavior, that is, whether the person would behave similarly in a similar situation, you cannot assume that because a trait is shown in one situation, it will necessarily be shown in all situations. Children who cheat in schoolwork may not cheat in party games or in athletic contests. People who are dishonest about letters found in the street may not be dishonest in other matters. Such traits are, however, probably representative enough so that behavior samplings can be of considerable value to the psychologist in his study of personality.

What is the critical incident technique? Closely related to such behavior sampling as has just been described is the *critical incident technique*. In this technique individuals are asked to report direct observations of samples of human behavior. The incidents reported are "critical" in the sense that they must have occurred in a situation where the purpose and intent of the acts seemed clear to the observer.

One study sought to learn what kinds of men tended to be good foremen in a given industry. Foremen and staff personnel were asked to report incidents of both desirable and undesirable behavior on the part of foremen as they had observed such behavior. Their directions for reporting incidents included such statements as: "Think of a time when a foreman has done something that you felt should be encouraged because it seemed in your opinion to be an example of good foremanship"; "Think of a time when a foreman did something that you thought was not up to par." Typical incidents thus collected were selected and classified for a *Performance Record for Foremen and Supervisors,* a booklet which served as a kind of textbook for foremen.

5. Projective Techniques

What is projection? *Projection* is the process whereby an individual attributes elements in his own personality to other persons or to objects in his environment. It is mainly the undesirable elements of one's personality that he tends to project. For example, the student who is careless in his work may say that the teacher is so careless that she cannot teach him anything. He projects a trait of his own personality into the personality of the teacher. The individual who is dishonest tends to project this trait into the personality of others. He is likely to say, "Everybody is dishonest."

It should be noted that an individual is not aware of the fact that he is projecting his own characteristics to others. The careless student does not realize that he is attributing carelessness to his teacher because he himself is careless. The person who says that everyone is dishonest is not aware of the fact that he is seeing his own dishonesty reflected.

At one time a psychologist asked some college students to adjust a spot of light so that it appeared to be equal to the size of a penny, nickel, dime, or quarter. There were no coins present, so that the students had to adjust the light according to their remembered impressions of the sizes of these coins. Their adjustments of the light spots were quite accurate; that is, they made a spot of light about the right size for a penny, for a nickel, for a dime, and for a quarter. Then the students were hypnotized and told that they were very poor, that it was very difficult for them to secure money, and so on. While hypnotized, they were again asked to adjust the size of the spot of light so that it appeared to be equal to the sizes of the various coins. In their "poor" state the students' adjustments of the light spots were consistently larger than in the normal waking state. Again they were hypnotized, but this time they were told that they were rich, that there was more than enough money for their every need, and so on. And again they were asked to adjust the spot of light until it appeared to be equal to the sizes of the coins. In the

UNDERSTANDING PERSONALITY

"rich" state, their light adjustments were consistently smaller than in the normal waking state. How these students perceived the spots of light depended upon their wants, needs, interests, attitudes, and values at the time they adjusted the light.

How do psychologists use inkblot tests? Projection can be demonstrated by a simple experiment. Place several drops of ink on a sheet of paper and fold the paper in half. The ink will blot and give an irregular but symmetrical design.

Show your inkblot to a friend and ask him to tell you what he "sees" in this "picture." Show the blot to several others and ask them what they "see." You will probably find that different persons interpret the inkblot in quite different ways. An individual who has had much experience with animals may see some kind of animal in a given blot. An individual who has studied designing may see a basic pattern for wallpaper in the same inkblot. What anyone sees in the inkblot depends to some extent upon his own capacities and experiences; that is, what he sees is, in reality, a projection of his own thoughts.

A Swiss psychiatrist, Hermann Rorschach (rôr′shäk), developed an inkblot test that some psychologists find very useful in studying personality. The individual whose personality pattern is being studied is shown a series of ten standardized blots, one at a time. He is asked to respond by telling and describing the things and ideas that each inkblot suggests to him.

Although the administering and scoring of this test are standardized, a dif-

ficulty arises in the interpretation of the responses. The lack of objective ways of interpreting responses has led to disagreement among some psychologists as to the validity of such responses to indicate personality.

One attempt made to utilize some of the hypotheses underlying the Rorschach test, and at the same time provide an objective comparison of scores, uses forty-five inkblots. Whereas an unlimited number of responses are allowed on the Rorschach test, on this test the subject is allowed only one response per card. The score of the individual can be compared directly with the responses of one or more norm groups (comparison groups). For example, the scores of a college student can be compared with that of other college students or to a known group of schizophrenics.

Some attempts have been made to modify the individual Rorschach test so that it could be used as a group test, but such group forms have not proved very successful.

What are some other projective techniques? Some psychologists use pictures of clouds and ask individuals to relate what they see in the clouds. Other psychologists use series of rather vague pictures involving persons, animals, and objects. They instruct their subjects to tell stories suggested by the pictures. Sometimes the psychologist merely begins telling a story without a picture and then asks the subject to complete the story. The themes of these stories and the characters involved tell the psychologist a great deal about the personalities of the persons telling the stories. For example, suppose that a boy tells a story in which the hero, who is so small that he has difficulty in defending himself, suddenly learns how to fight and goes about knocking down boys twice his size. The psychologist would have reason to believe that the teller of this story felt himself to be inferior. In his story he was projecting this feeling of inferiority onto the hero. Also, he was expressing his own desire to be superior.

In one set of pictures used as a test the "hero" and all other characters are dogs, but the individual looking at the pictures interprets the behavior of the dogs in terms of his own feelings, habits of thinking, and attitudes.

Sometimes children are given toys to play with as they wish. During the play a psychologist observes many elements involved in the personality of the child. For example, suppose the child builds a house with a fence around it and says, "This is my house and I am building a high fence around it so that other kids can't come in and bother me." The psychologist will have reason to believe the child is introverted.

Still other projective techniques are used by psychologists. For instance, individuals may be asked to draw pictures and tell the stories behind the pictures. In other cases the individual is given a background picture, such as a living room, a forest, an attic, a schoolroom, or a street scene. These pictures contain no people, but the individual is given cutout figures of men, women, and children of various races, animals, and so on. He is then asked to place these figures on the background pic-

As the subject tells a story about this picture, he will reveal personality traits useful to the psychologist.

tures and tell the stories of the pictures. Finger painting has also been used as a projective technique. Or the first part of sentences may be given and the individual asked to complete the sentences. Dreams have been studied as projections. Whatever the specific technique, all projective techniques give the individual a great deal of freedom in expressing himself.

How do projective techniques measure personality? Can projective techniques measure personality? That is, can they tell how much of a certain trait there is in an individual's personality? At present, projective techniques are more useful for finding the kind of personality traits someone has than for measuring their intensity.

For the clinical psychologist treating personality maladjustments, it may

UNDERSTANDING PERSONALITY

be enough to know the quality of a person's traits. It is better, however, to know the quality and to be able to measure quantity. Psychologists are developing various schemes to measure the replies to projective tests. Inkblots, pictures, and toy arrangements have been used with thousands of persons. Psychologists have found that a large number of people tend to give the same response. This response can be taken as a rough sort of "normal," or average, answer (although it should not be inferred that there are right or wrong answers to projective tests). We can then compare any individual's test with these "normal" answers. Thus, we can roughly measure how an individual compares with other persons.

There is another way of measuring replies to projective tests. A psychologist can count the number of times that one thought shows up in stories. Suppose that in nine out of ten stories John Doe expresses a feeling of inferiority. But Richard Roe expresses inferiority in only one out of ten stories. How often a certain feeling or attitude is expressed is a measure of the extent of each person's feeling, say, of inferiority.

In scoring responses to inkblots, the psychologist may obtain measures of quantity by several means. He may calculate the percentage of responses concerned with the blots as a whole. Then he may calculate the percentage of responses concerned with details to be seen within the blots. He may count the responses indicating movement of the figures in the blots and the responses based on the seeing of the colored parts of the blots. Then he may compute the ratio of one total to the other. He may note whether responses are original or popular, for example, whether they are such as occur only once in every one hundred records, or once in every six records. The interpretation of the scores is much more difficult than the scoring itself.

Psychologists have still other techniques for the measurement of personality. However, the five methods discussed in this section—ratings, inventories, interviewing, behavior sampling, and projective techniques—are the most widely used.

Terms to Add to Your Vocabulary

ambiversion	interviewing	primary trait
assessment	introversion	projection
behavior sampling	inventory	projective techniques
coefficient of correlation	mean	rating
correlation	negative correlation	Rorschach inkblot
critical incident technique	normal curve	sampling
extroversion (extraversion)	normal frequency distribution	statistics
generosity error	order-of-merit method	stereotype
graphic rating scale	personality	trait
halo effect	positive correlation	

UNDERSTANDING HUMAN BEHAVIOR

Suggestions for Activities

1. Write a brief autobiography, stressing the events in your life which you believe have especially influenced the development of your personality.

2. Measure the heights or weights of a large number of male or female students. Make a graph of the data. Since average measurements for the sexes differ somewhat, it will be best not to include both sexes in one group. If you find that your data do not give a bell-shaped graph, you should seek the explanation. There is always some special reason for a biological distribution that does not form a normal curve.

3. Consult the Appendix for information on the rank-order method of correlation, then perform a correlation procedure on the heights and weights of individuals in the above activity. Is there a positive or negative relationship between height and weight? Is there a difference between the correlation coefficient for males and females?

4. Select a child you know very well. With permission of his or her parents but without the child's knowledge, observe the child's behavior, take notes, and then try to describe his or her personality from your first observation. Observe the behavior of the child several additional times. At the end of all the observations, describe what you believe to be the personality of the child. Did any of your original beliefs about the child change? Did you notice any personality "traits" you were not aware of at first?

5. Have friends write a paragraph on the personality traits they associate with a very muscular individual. Do they agree on traits? Could all muscular persons have similar personalities?

6. Your teacher may be able to obtain from records on objective tests the scores made by a large number of pupils. If so, graph the data. Is the distribution normal? If not, how do you account for the fact that it is not normal?

7. If possible, take and score one of the commercially available personality inventories, for example, the *Gordon Personal Profile and Personal Inventory,* published by Harcourt, Brace & World. To what extent do you think it gives a true picture of your personality?

8. Assume that you are a school counselor and that a student has been referred to you. You wish to assess the personality of this student. List and describe which method or methods you would use. What would help you decide which method or methods to use?

9. Have someone in your class "lose" a number of notes or letters around the school. The notes or letters should be sealed in some way and should bear the names and locker numbers of members of your class. How many of the total "lost" are turned over to the addresses? Have they been opened?

10. Sometimes it is said that an author "writes himself into his work." Write down your impression of the personality of some author, such as Ernest Hemingway, whose writings you have studied in an English course. Then check biographical and autobiographical material in order to learn to what extent the author seems to have projected himself into his writings.

11. Fold a sheet of white paper, open it, place two or three drops of black ink near the crease, and fold it over again. Have several persons describe the ink-blot which you have made. What do

they see in it? Are there individual differences? (Of course, you are not prepared to attempt a personality analysis. Furthermore, you must remember that your inkblot is not a standardized one.)

12. Using an overhead projector, display a homemade inkblot on a screen for one minute and have others write down what they see. Their papers should not include their names but should indicate whether the individual is male or female. Collect all the papers and divide them into two stacks, one for male responses and the other for females. Are there any differences between male and female responses? Can you see what others saw in the inkblot?

13. Find a picture showing several children, preferably children of both sexes. Show the picture to a number of children. Ask them to tell you about the picture—what has happened in the past, what the children are thinking about, what is going to happen in the future. Are there marked individual differences in the reactions of the children to whom you show your picture? Is there any evidence that a given child is identifying himself with a child in the picture? (You cannot make an analysis of personality on the basis of just one nonstandardized picture. You will, however, gain some idea of how individual differences may be tested by such techniques.)

Suggestions for Further Reading

Clark, Thaddeus B., *What Is Honesty?* Science Research Associates.

Daniel, Robert S., ed., *Contemporary Readings in General Psychology,* 2nd ed., Houghton Mifflin. Pages 224–27, "What People Dream About."

Henry, William E., *Exploring Your Personality,* Science Research Associates.

Hilgard, Ernest R., and Richard C. Atkinson, *Introduction to Psychology,* 4th ed., Harcourt, Brace & World. Pages 403–04, "The Normal Distribution"; pages 409–14, "The Coefficient of Correlation and Its Interpretation"; Chapter 18, "Theories of Personality"; Chapter 19, "Personality Appraisal."

Kendler, Howard H., *Basic Psychology,* Appleton-Century-Crofts. Chapter 13, "Personality."

Leuba, Clarence, *Man: A General Psychology,* Holt, Rinehart & Winston. Chapter 18, "Personality and Its Assessment"; pages 545–49, "Change and Stability in Personality."

Lindgren, Henry C., Donn Byrne, and Lewis Petrinovich, *Psychology: An Introduction to a Behavioral Science,* 2nd ed., John Wiley. Chapter 11, "Person-

ality: The Organization of Behavior."

McKeachie, Wilbert J., and Charlotte L. Doyle, *Psychology,* Addison-Wesley. Chapter 2, "The Cultural Background of Behavior"; Chapter 12, "The Person: Personality Characteristics and Their Assessment."

Munn, Norman L., *Psychology,* 5th ed., Houghton Mifflin. Pages 74–75, correlation; Chapter 9, "Personality."

Ruch, Floyd L., *Psychology and Life,* 7th ed., Scott, Foresman. Pages 145–53, a description of various techniques for measuring personality; pages 139–45, the normal distribution.

Sanford, Fillmore H., *Psychology: A Scientific Study of Man,* 2nd ed., Wadsworth. Pages 145–47, tests of personality; Chapter 15, "Personality."

Seidman, Jerome, ed., *The Adolescent: A Book of Readings,* rev. ed., Holt, Rinehart & Winston. Pages 605–17, "Children's Attitudes Toward Peers and Parents as Revealed by Sentence Completions."

Whittaker, James O., et al., *Introduction to Psychology,* W. B. Saunders. Chapter 17, "Personality."

CHAPTER 7

How behavior develops

Having investigated some basic material on personality and its measurement in Chapter 6, we are now ready to consider how human behavior develops. Behavior follows certain patterns of development, which can be observed, studied, and defined. In this chapter we shall discuss general principles of development under the six categories of physical, motor, emotional, social, personality, and mental development. We shall mention some characteristic changes that take place in each individual as he develops. Since this chapter gives a general picture of development, it contains some material which is discussed in greater detail elsewhere in the book.

DEVELOPMENT

Why study development? There are several very important reasons for studying the various areas of development. In the first place, we can learn what patterns of behavior usually develop and thus establish standards for comparing behavior. Once we have standards of behavior for various age groups, we have a general idea of what

to expect of the individual. And when we know what behavior to expect, we can help prepare the individual for the next step in his development.

For example, if we know in advance that the usual pattern of behavior is for the average child to walk alone and without support at about fourteen months of age, we are able to provide him with ample opportunity to begin to learn this motor task a little before fourteen months. In this way the child can be given a chance to develop at his own rate with adequate preparation. Or, in the area of intellectual development, by knowing when a mental trait, such as learning to tell time, begins to develop, we can assign the child tasks related to this trait and thus help him in the process of achieving his potential ability. If, however, we expect too little of a child, or too much, we could easily upset his developmental schedule. We should always remember that each person is an individual with his own developmental schedule and pattern. Also, only experts in this field, such as psychologists and psychiatrists, are qualified to make interpretative judgments about whether the individual is developing faster or slower than the average person in his age group.

How is maturation related to development? To understand human development, it is important to see its relationship to maturation. *Maturation* is the potential development of the individual as set by heredity. It is a fact that no individual can develop a specific trait until he is physiologically ready to develop that trait. For example, regardless of how hard you try to teach him, no baby can learn to walk before he has developed the muscles and neurons that control his walking. The readiness of various parts of the body to perform more complex movements is determined by the degree of maturation of these parts.

Maturation is necessary not only for physical and motor development but also for the development of mental traits. For instance, it is a waste of time to try to teach a child to read if he is not mature enough for it. Remember, though, that some individuals develop faster and some more slowly than others. Not all children are at the same level of maturation at the same age. Since new evidence from psychologists on the individual's readiness to learn is constantly being discovered, the future should bring an increased understanding of the relationship of maturation to development.

What are some general principles of development? Perhaps the most important single statement that can be made about development is that development follows a predictable pattern. One illustration of such a predictable pattern is seen in the early physical development of infants. In babies development spreads downward from the head, which develops first, to the feet. If you observe a newborn infant you will notice that he develops control of his eyes first, then learns to turn his head and then his trunk, and finally gains control over his legs and can walk. In babies development also proceeds outward from the central axis of the body to the hands and feet. For example, the newborn baby first moves his arms in a very general way and then begins to control his elbows and hands and finally his specific finger movements. These are two patterns of physical development in infants that are predictable.

Another principle of development is that the individual first develops general responses and then proceeds to specific responses. This principle becomes evident if you watch a very young baby trying to reach for a toy. His efforts seem to involve using his entire body. When you observe the same baby a few months afterward, you will see him use more specific parts of his body to reach the toy. Later on, he will be even more specific in his responses and will use only those parts of his body actually needed to obtain the toy.

A third characteristic of development is that it is a continuous process. The expression "stages of development" incorrectly implies that developmental tasks have a definite starting and stopping point. There is no one specific point at which a task suddenly appears or disappears. Some behavior may seem to appear all at once, but, in

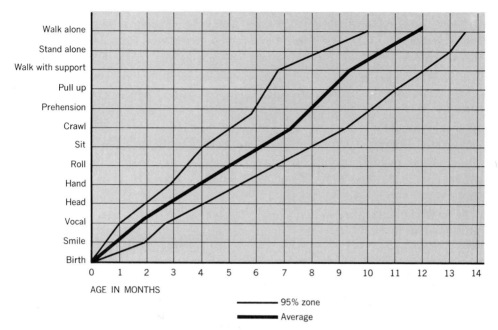

A developmental graph for the first year of life. The thick line shows the average age for these achievements; the thin lines indicate the age span within which the developmental graphs for 95 percent of the babies fell.

fact, this behavior has been developing slowly for some time. This is true of all developmental tasks. Nevertheless, it is convenient to group the occurrence of various developmental changes into stages as long as you remember that there are no specific dividing lines between these stages.

A fourth principle of development is that some individuals have a different rate of development. The pattern of development is similar for most people, but the amount of time required in developing may vary in different individuals. If there is some prenatal or natal damage of the central nervous system or glands, it can cause a faster or slower rate of development, depending upon the specific type of damage

and when it takes place. For example, improper functioning of the pituitary gland can cause a noticeable change in the rate of development. When the gland secretes too little, the individual may develop as a miniature but normally proportioned adult. When the pituitary secretes too much, the individual may develop as an unusually tall adult.

There is a relationship between mental ability and the rate of physical development. The child with a high potential mental ability has a tendency to grow physically faster than the average for his age group. It should be noted in passing that not only can the rate of physical development differ among individuals but also that differ-

HOW BEHAVIOR DEVELOPS

ent parts of the body will develop at different rates.

Another characteristic of development is that each stage has unique features. Each stage is expressed differently, depending upon the society and upon the period of development involved. One of the best examples is the so-called rebellion period of adolescence, which seems to be a unique feature of our own society and culture.

A final characteristic is that early development is more important than later development. For example, consider the theoretical isolation of an individual at various periods of his development. Compare the effects on intelligence of isolating a child for a year between his first and second birthdays and isolating the same person for a year at the age of twenty. Although the latter isolation would certainly influence the person's development, the earlier isolation period would have a much greater and more lasting effect on the development of his behavior.

How do psychologists study development of the individual? One of the oldest methods of studying behavior and development of the individual is that of observation. In the beginning this method was used mainly by unskilled persons, without the benefit of controlled experimental conditions, and therefore it yielded inconsistent results. Modern methods of observing behavior, however, make use of more standardized procedures and produce more objective, unbiased results.

One of the best-known American psychologists to study behavior through observation was Arnold Gesell. He developed not only specific techniques but also a special room for observing the behavior of infants and small children. (See picture on page 169.) This room was dome-shaped with transparent walls. It was located inside a larger room from which skilled observers could watch what the children were doing. Children within the smaller room could not see the observers through the transparent walls, because the outer room was darkened and the smaller room well lit. Tape recorders, still cameras, and movie cameras were installed in the smaller room to provide a permanent record of the observed behavior. By observing a large number of individuals at different age levels, Gesell was able to establish norms of behavior.

Another means of studying the behavior and development of the individual is through the *longitudinal method,* which involves selecting a group of individuals and studying the development of their behavior over a considerable period of time. In some longitudinal studies individuals have been observed from birth to adulthood. The method has the following limitations, however: (1) it is time-consuming; (2) it can be very expensive; (3) it must face the difficulty of keeping the same group together over a period of time, since some individuals may move to another location during the study; and (4) the individuals chosen for study may not be a representative sample of their age group. Nevertheless, the longitudinal method has the important advantage of providing psychologists with information on specific changes in behavior and development.

UNDERSTANDING HUMAN BEHAVIOR

The *cross-sectional method* selects different individuals of different ages in order to study groups at various age levels simultaneously. For example, different groups of three-, four-, five-, and six-year-old children can be selected and studied at the same time. This method has the major advantage of reducing the amount of time necessary for the study. However, it shares one of the limitations of the longitudinal method—the difficulty and necessity of selecting groups which are representative of their age levels. If the groups are not representative, norms of behavior cannot be established, and the conclusions of the study cannot be considered valid for the age levels involved.

In addition to the different methods to be used, the choice of subjects is an essential part of the study of development. The study of animals has the advantage that animals can be subjected to certain controlled conditions of deprivation, such as isolation, to find out what the effects would be upon behavior and development. Animals can be experimentally deprived of any combination of their senses to see what effect this would have on development. Also, animals can be restrained in certain motor areas, such as preventing them from having any exercise and practice, to see what happens to behavior or development. In one experiment, chimpanzees were reared in isolation and later allowed to mix socially with other chimpanzees. It was found that their motor activities were normal but that they were socially inept at getting along with the other chimpanzees.

Gesell's one-way-vision observation dome permits observers to study and record behavior under controlled conditions.

For both ethical and moral reasons, it is obvious that human beings cannot be treated as animals. Most parents and most societies would not permit their children to be completely isolated for the first five years of life. Nevertheless, it is also clear that psychologists are ethically able to study human beings while using enough experimental controls to be consistent. The study of identical twins is useful because with identical twins the hereditary factors are held constant. Therefore, any differences in development must be due to environmental factors. Certain environmental factors can then be regulated and studied to see their influence on the individual's development.

PHYSICAL DEVELOPMENT

How does body development affect the individual? *Physical development* is the growth of an individual's body. A child who develops physically faster than the norm for his age will be able to do things better and more quickly than others of his age group. His superior physical capabilities will influence his popularity, which could be increased by his achievements or decreased if he became a bully. The individual has the choice of using his greater strength to help others, to be sought after by his fellow playmates to be on "their side" because he can run faster and hit harder, or to force others to obey him. How he is accepted by others will have an effect on what he thinks of himself. If the individual is handicapped by inadequate physical development, others may make fun of him, which also influences his concept of himself.

From these few examples it is clear that physical development does play an important role in how the person sees himself and how others see him, both of which affect his adjustment to the world around him. The individual can be psychologically affected by even a rather slight abnormality in his physical growth pattern.

Remember, however, that there is a considerable amount of variation within any age group. The figures given in this chapter represent the average for each age-level state. The simple fact that certain individuals are taller or shorter than the average for their age group should never be taken as a sign that they are not accepted by the group or will not be liked for their good qualities.

What changes occur in the physical development of height and weight? The two most frequently cited examples of an individual's physical growth are height and weight. Both height and weight have a developmental pattern of increasing in spurts, with the greatest percentage of growth in the earliest stages. In the case of height, the average newborn baby is slightly less than 20 inches tall. Tremendous growth in height occurs during the first year, when the average increase is 50 percent. At the end of the third year, the average person is half as tall as he will be as an adult. By the fifth year, he is twice as tall as he was at birth.

During the elementary school years the height of the individual will increase very slowly compared with the preschool years. But during the puberty stage (from about age eleven to fifteen for girls and twelve to sixteen for boys), there is a spurt in height growth for both males and females. Increases in height then become smaller.

The average male grows in height at a slightly slower rate than the female until the puberty stage, when he catches up with and passes the female. By the time the male reaches adulthood, he will be approximately 4 to 5 inches taller than the female. He will average between 70 and 71 inches in height, whereas the adult female will be about 66 inches. (The averages of heights have increased over the years.)

Several general principles emerge from the preceding data: (1) the greatest rate of growth for both sexes occurs during the preschool years; (2) increases in height slow down during the first six years of school, after which there is an upsurge in growth, followed by a leveling off in the late teens; (3) girls grow faster in height than boys until the puberty stage, when boys not only catch up but surpass girls in height; and (4) the average adult male is about 4 to 5 inches taller than the average female.

In the case of weight, the average newborn baby will weigh about 7 pounds (although newborn infants may weigh anywhere from about 3 to 16 pounds). The general principles regarding rate of development of height also apply to weight. The largest percentage increase in weight will occur during the first five years of life, so that by age five the average person will weigh about five times what he weighed at birth. During the next seven years his weight will more than double.

The average newborn male baby is slightly heavier than the female. The female will equal and then surpass the male in weight at about ten years of age, but the male will catch up at about age fourteen and remain heavier than the female throughout life.

During adulthood the individual will gain weight. As the person approaches the middle-age period, an excessive amount of fat may accumulate. Later, however, as the individual reaches old age, he will lose weight, largely because of loss of body fluids and the various chemical changes associated with advanced age. Of course, at every age, exercise, a proper diet,

and good psychological adjustment all play important roles in keeping the individual trim and fit.

When individuals are overweight, the relationship between their weight and psychological adjustment should not be overlooked. People with anxiety, guilt, and other disturbing feelings sometimes have a tendency to overeat. Have you ever noticed how you frequently become hungry before and during exams or when watching your favorite team play ball? Observe the large amount of food consumed at ball games. It is not true, however, that every overweight person is distressed, because other factors can and do cause them to be overweight. Some people have glandular trouble that results in an overweight condition; others develop habits of overeating from their parents.

How does development of teeth affect the individual? As you probably know, almost everyone develops two sets of teeth during his life — so-called baby teeth and permanent teeth. The baby teeth begin to form even before birth, but they do not actually break through the gums until about the seventh month after birth. The permanent teeth begin to appear and push the temporary teeth out shortly before the average child enters first grade. Although most people have only one set of permanent teeth, a few individuals have been known to cut a second set of permanent teeth. The last of the permanent teeth to appear are the wisdom teeth, which begin to come through in the late teens. There are exceptions, however—some individ-

HOW BEHAVIOR DEVELOPS

uals never grow wisdom teeth at all; for others, they do not appear until late in life. As the individual lives through middle age, he may lose some permanent teeth. He may even eventually lose all of them. Yet with improved dental techniques and excellent dental care, some people may keep their permanent teeth all their life.

The development of adequate teeth affects the behavior of the individual. The way his teeth grow can influence whether a person smiles or how he talks. For example, teeth with wide spaces between them (diastema) can cause a person to hiss when talking. This development can affect both the individual's speech and his pattern of behavior. Using braces on the teeth often corrects many dental faults. If braces are used properly before the teens, the individual's whole personality may benefit.

How do physical defects affect the individual? Physical defects are caused by such things as hereditary factors, an accident which may occur before, during, or after birth, and psychological factors. The most common cause of defects is physical in origin. Some physical defects, however, such as stuttering, have a psychological basis. Usually those individuals who stutter do so only when they are anxious, frightened, worried, or similarly upset. When they are singing, talking about their hobbies, or doing anything else in which they are genuinely interested, they do not stutter. Stuttering seems to be characteristic of civilized societies, since it does not usually exist in the more primitive so-

cieties. Surprisingly, slightly more than 85 percent of all American children stutter before they are three years old. As the child grows up and adapts increasingly to his home environment, his stuttering will usually disappear. It is rare in adults.

The effect of physical defects upon the individual will depend upon the type of defect, when it occurs, how others regard it, and how the individual himself sees it. If the defect is a serious one, such as amputation of an arm or leg, the effect upon the individual will be greater than with a less serious defect. If the physical defect occurs early in life, thereby giving the person a longer period of time to adjust, it will not affect him as much as if it occurs during the teens. If others regard the defect as relatively unimportant and react toward the person in this way, they will affect the person's own viewpoint of his defect. Probably, though, the most important single factor is the individual's own attitude toward his defect. A relatively minor defect that the person regards as a major catastrophe can seriously affect his psychological adjustment.

Remember that an individual's attitude toward himself is largely determined by how others react to him. The attitude and behavior of his parents, siblings, playmates, and teachers will significantly influence the person's own attitude toward the defect. For example, if his parents regard a physical defect, such as deformed legs, as a social disgrace and try to hide their child from social contacts, they are very likely to influence the child to regard the defect as they do. Some-

UNDERSTANDING HUMAN BEHAVIOR

times, unfortunately, parents of a handicapped child will become frustrated by their child's defect and take their frustration out on him.

You should remember that your behavior toward a handicapped individual will play a part in how he regards himself. It is a sign of your personal adjustment when you react toward a handicapped individual with friendliness instead of pity. Some people make fun of handicapped individuals as a way of boosting themselves. If you criticize and find fault with others, ask yourself why you do it. Or if you hear others criticizing, think, "Why are they doing this?"

MOTOR DEVELOPMENT

Motor development is development of control over the muscles of the body. Motor development is a very important area in the total development of an individual. It is related to good physical and mental health, socialization, and the development of the person's concept of himself. The same general principles of development stated at the beginning of this chapter apply to this area as well. As you remember, these principles are that development follows a predictable pattern, proceeds from general to specific responses, is a continuous process, involves different rates of development, has unique features for each stage, and is more important early in life than it is later on.

How is motor development related to the individual's general development? If the motor development of an indi-

vidual is slower than his age group, he may not be invited to participate in games and activities as much as the more fully developed person. As a result he may decide that he does not want to join in. By not trying to participate, he will miss the exercise and practice necessary for better physical development and motor coordination. If he lacks sufficient muscular coordination for his age group, he will feel left out of activities, which will affect his view of himself. Motor development, like physical development, influences the person's concept of himself.

Motor development becomes increasingly important during the school years. In high school muscular coordination is especially necessary for participation in activities which require more precise motor skills, such as football, baseball, and track and field, and for social activities, such as dancing. Many other activities during this period of life, such as learning to drive a car, also require motor coordination and good reaction time.

At various stages of life, motor development contributes to the individual's growing awareness of himself as an independent person. The young child gains a feeling of independence when he learns to do things for himself. A simple act such as learning to tie a knot in his shoelaces is a rewarding experience for him because it means that he no longer has to depend upon someone else. Early in life, individuals have a strong tendency and desire to be independent, which becomes frustrating when they realize that they cannot be truly independent.

Motor Development

The development of an individual's motor ability is clearly visible in these pictures. A very young child does not have the coordination to use a spoon. By the age of five, however, the child has enough muscular control of his fingers to learn to write. The motor skills of a six-year-old are not developed enough to permit him to play games such as badminton with a great deal of accuracy. But by adolescence most individuals have sufficient motor ability to execute the precise, graceful, intricate movements performed by ballet dancers.

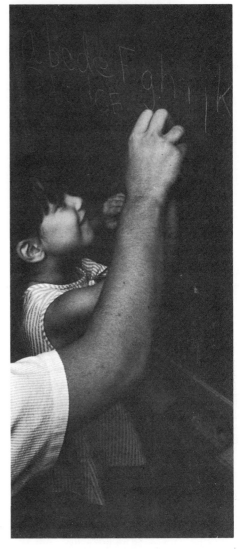

In the adolescent stage the desire for independence and the accompanying frustration becomes even more intense.

Another area in which motor development is important is socialization. The newborn infant is totally dependent on others. He cannot move to others; they must move toward him. As he develops control over motor activities, he can crawl, walk, and eventually run to others.

The development of the motor skills required in locomotion allows an individual to increase the number of people, events, and situations with which he comes in contact.

As was previously mentioned, motor development is also very influential in the individual's self-concept. If

he has slow motor development, the individual may begin to think that he is below average and decide that he should not join in games or activities. Or he may decide to overcompensate for his slow development by participating in as many motor-related activities as possible. Remember, however, that by far the biggest factor here is how the individual regards himself, not how others see him. He reacts to how he thinks others see him, although the way that others actually behave toward him does affect the individual as he forms his own concept of himself. If discrepancies or differences exist between how he believes others see him and the way that they actually do see him, the individual will be frustrated. An awkward person who believes that he has very good coordination will encounter frustration. Similarly, an individual who thinks that he is a very careful person but constantly falls down because of a lack of coordination is faced with a discrepancy between his actual behavior and his self-concept, which is unpleasant for the person. The more discrepancies that exist between what is actually true about ourselves and what we think is true, the more frustrated we will be.

What is the sequence of motor development in a baby? Motor development in the head region takes place at a very rapid rate after birth. The newborn baby can hold his head up for a short period of time, although it is not until about the sixth month that he can hold it up while lying down. Control over eye movements occurs within the first few months. By the third month the baby is capable of performing fairly complex eye movements, such as remaining focused on a moving object as it goes across his field of vision (horizontal eye pursuit develops first, then vertical, then circular). Babies can perform a type of smile (a reflex) within the first two weeks after birth, although smiling as a specific response to stimulation by another person does not occur until about the third month.

In accordance with the sequence of physical development that proceeds from the head downward, the trunk area develops next. Before he can learn to turn over completely, the baby must first learn to control his head movements, which requires using his neck muscles. Learning to turn over is a gradual response, in which the baby first turns over from his side to his back, then turns from back to side, and eventually succeeds in making a complete turn. He cannot sit without support until he has full control over his trunk, which does not occur in the average baby until about the tenth month.

With regard to the sequence of physical development that proceeds from the body's central axis to the arms and hands, the average baby will make some general responses to an object placed in front of him by the third month. The baby is able to see the object before he has the coordination to reach it. The two-month-old baby looks as if he is using his entire body when he reaches for an object, but he will not be able to grasp objects until about the fourth month. In picking up objects the thumb must work in coordination with and opposition to fingers, which occurs about the ninth month.

Most individuals are physically ready to walk between nine and fifteen months of age, but they usually progress through a crawling, creeping, and standing-alone stage before actually walking. In the crawling stage the body is pulled along the floor or bed, while in the creeping stage the trunk is lifted free of the floor. The average baby first begins to walk with support when he is about a year old. Most babies walk within one month after they reach the standing-alone stage; within two months almost all are doing so.

What are characteristics of motor development in childhood, adolescence, and old age? Motor development in early and late childhood increases more slowly than in the period immediately after birth, but it does continue to increase. There is a popular misconception that during adolescence individuals are awkward and clumsy. On the contrary, many studies have shown that during this time motor coordination shows significant increases. Instead, the concept of awkwardness in adolescence seems to be due to the individual's lack of assurance toward himself and his abilities. It arises from his self-concept rather than from any lack of motor control. In this sense, adolescence may be regarded as a period of testing in which the individual tries out various patterns of behavior and sometimes seems to give the appearance of a lack of coordination.

The development of an individual's motor abilities generally increases until approximately the early to middle twenties. There is a slight decline until the age of fifty and more of a decline to age sixty-five, after which the decline of motor abilities often becomes considerably more rapid. Employers and industries have long used this decline in later years to support the idea of retirement. Yet by setting an age for retirement, they are overlooking individual differences, which are very large within any age group. Although variations in some older people are not so large as those in younger groups, some older individuals maintain a high level of performance even at the age of seventy.

Are there differences in the motor abilities of males and females? In general, there are no significant differences between the development of motor skills in males and females in the early years.

As individuals mature, however, some types of motor skills become more socially acceptable for one sex than for the other. For example, running, jumping, and climbing are associated with boys; and knitting, crocheting, and sewing are considered more appropriate for girls.

Differences in motor skills begin to appear at about five years of age. From that time on, boys start to become more efficient in those tasks which require strength, endurance, and speed. The differences become more noticeable during and after puberty, when muscular growth increases considerably more for boys than for girls. On the other hand, girls from about the age of five onward show a superior ability in tasks which require very precise muscle movements, such as finger dexterity. For instance, as a hobby some girls make tiny, intricate designs in needlepoint with great ease. These differences between boys and girls increase as they grow older.

EMOTIONAL DEVELOPMENT

Emotional development involves the individual's awareness and expression of an affective experience, which might be pleasurable or not pleasurable, mild or intense. Emotions are something we all have. The kinds of emotions we feel play a large part in how we get along with others and how well we get along with ourselves. An individual whose life is dominated by unpleasant emotions will be an unhappy person. Those people for whom the majority of emotions are pleasant will lead a relatively happy life.

HOW BEHAVIOR DEVELOPS

Just as important as the kinds of emotions an individual feels is the way in which he handles his emotions. Two individuals can have the same physiological emotional condition, but one may handle it in an acceptable fashion and the other may not. For example, one student may become angry with his teacher and express his anger in words, whereas another student may became angry and smash a window, throw books on the floor, or perform some other unsuitable act to get rid of the anger.

Emotions involve physiological changes in the body, such as the secretion of adrenalin into the bloodstream, which can be partially counteracted by exercise. The next time you become angry, try running or some other form of strenuous exercise and see how long the anger lasts. Do not try to drive an automobile, however, for the emotional state of anger and the need to be careful while driving a car are not very compatible. You might well have an unconscious tendency to use the automobile as an instrument of revenge or aggression.

What emotions are present at birth? No specific emotions can be determined in the newborn infant. The only discernible emotion observed is a general state of excitement, which diffuses into distress and delight shortly after birth. Although distress appears a little before delight, both are present by the end of the third month. The former is characterized by muscular tension and crying; the latter by muscular relaxation and smiling. By the sixth month fear, disgust, and anger

appear, and by the end of the first year elation and affection are present.

When young children become angry, they are likely to show overt aggressive or hostile behavior. As they grow older they soon learn that this type of behavior is not socially acceptable and begin to hide it. The overt behavior eventually will become hidden and be manifested in pouting, which may continue even when the individual has reached adulthood.

In middle age the male becomes less aggressive and hostile than he was earlier, which is usually attributed to a decline in physical strength. This change is more noticeable in the later years of life, when a man becomes considerably less able to defend himself physically. The emotions which were evoked by distress early in life, such as grief, self-pity, and boredom, seem to take on a more personal character in later years. That is, his emotions are more related to himself as an individual and less involved with the social world around him.

Are emotions learned? It was once thought that some emotions were innate, or present at birth. These emotions were believed to be fear, rage, and love. Fear could be elicited by a sudden loud noise or loss of support, rage by restriction of body movement, and love by stroking and petting the infant. More recently, however, several studies have shown that a specific emotion cannot be identified in the newborn infant.

One of the best-known experiments on innate emotions was conducted by the psychologist John B. Watson. He selected a baby who was referred to as Albert. Since Albert was reared primarily in a hospital nursery (his mother worked in the same hospital), his life had remained more sheltered and restricted than the early lives of most children. Therefore, he had less opportunity than most babies of having learned emotions.

As part of the experiment, Watson presented Albert with several objects, among which was a white rat. Little Albert showed no initial fear response to any of the objects, including the white rat. Watson then presented the white rat to Albert accompanied by a loud sudden noise that frightened Albert. This procedure was repeated several times. Eventually, whenever he saw the white rat, Albert showed fear. Albert had learned to associate the sudden loud noise with the white rat. This is a clear example of how an emotion can be learned. In this case the learning was achieved through classical conditioning.

Approximate ages when emotions emerge during the first two years of life

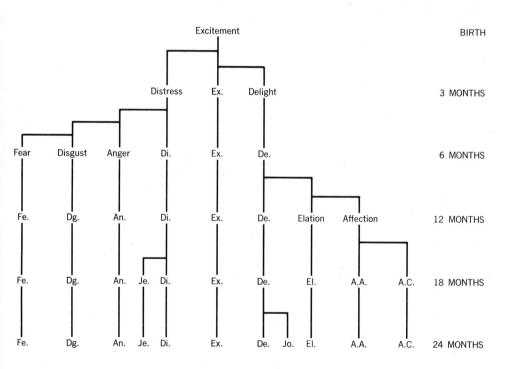

A.A.	affection for adults	Dg.	disgust	Fe.	fear
A.C.	affection for children	Di.	distress	Je.	jealousy
An.	anger	El.	elation	Jo.	joy
De.	delight	Ex.	excitement		

HOW BEHAVIOR DEVELOPS

There was another interesting outcome of the experiment. Albert had learned to fear not only the white rat but also anything that resembled it, such as a Santa Claus mask with a white beard, even though these things had not been associated with the noise or with the rat during the experiment. In other words, Albert had generalized fear from the rat to other things. This is known technically as *stimulus generalization*. However, Watson was able to recondition Albert so that the baby no longer feared the rat, by keeping him in the presence of the rat while Albert performed a pleasant task, such as eating.

Many times we dislike something or someone but do not know why. An individual who dislikes or is uneasy in the presence of someone with a mustache, for example, may have had some earlier unhappy experience with a man who wore a mustache. Later, he may generalize from that one person to all similar individuals. This may be one way in which individuals develop prejudices against an entire ethnic group.

Although all emotions are probably learned, they are not learned exclusively from personal experiences. Much emotional learning occurs by imitation of the behavior and acceptance of the attitudes of others as thoroughly as if the emotion had been experienced by the individual himself. Some young children hate spinach and other types of food, but upon examination it sometimes turns out that they have never tried the food. They have learned from others that it does not taste good. Would you eat fried snake meat or chocolate-covered ants? Probably not, even though you may never have tried them, and even though some people in other countries consider them great delicacies. We learn emotions from the people around us—our parents, siblings, friends, and teachers. Children also have attitudes similar to their parents because they both share some of the same emotional stimuli.

What are some common emotions? Everyone shows fear, love, anxiety, worry, anger, or jealousy, although different people show varying amounts of each emotion at different times. The young infant probably fears nothing until his mental development increases to the point where he recognizes the potential danger of an object, event, or situation, such as patting a horse that could bite him. Most children fear specific things, such as snakes, spiders, or worms. During the preadolescent period, the child comes to have more generalized fear, such as worry and anxiety.

Although an individual can probably learn to fear anything, he usually follows a pattern of fears that changes with the different stages of life. Young children fear such things as strange people, unfamiliar animals and objects, and the dark. Ironically, the young child shows more fear than he did as a baby or will show later in life. This is probably because a baby has no understanding of danger, and an older child is able to separate real and imagined dangers more fully. The older child's increase in reasoning can differentiate the real from the unreal and dissolve

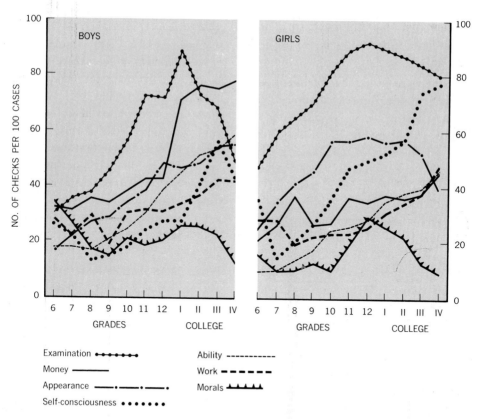

NO. OF CHECKS PER 100 CASES

BOYS

GIRLS

GRADES · COLLEGE

GRADES · COLLEGE

Examination ●●●●●●
Money ————
Appearance ——·——·——·
Self-consciousness ●●●●●●

Ability -----------
Work ■ ■ ■ ■ ■ ■
Morals ▲▲▲▲▲

Age trends in worries during adolescence and early adulthood

some fears that were due to ignorance.

The number of fears diminishes after the child enters school. Perhaps the increase in the socialization process as a result of going to school helps the child to overcome fears, especially when he learns from his schoolmates that some of his fears have no basis. Also, there is a change in the type of fear. The child shifts his emphasis from fears of tangible things to imaginary fears.

As the individual grows older, he begins to develop fears involving social situations and things he cannot understand at the time, such as thunder and lightning and death. The high school student develops a fear of failing courses, or being "different." As an adult, the person begins to fear loss of security and, especially in the case of males, sexual inadequacy. In old age there is an increase in the fear of death, losing a job, and financial problems.

Although they are negligible early in life, sex differences in fears develop during later years. Girls have a tendency to be more afraid of insects and spiders than boys, who are more afraid of wild animals. Perhaps some girls are afraid of insects or spiders because they believe it is expected of them,

HOW BEHAVIOR DEVELOPS

while boys might be "sissies" if they were afraid of the same things as girls.

Worry is a subacute form of fear involving something that might or could happen in the future. It differs from anxiety in that worry is usually associated with a specific thing, like a test, lack of money, or adequate grades, whereas anxiety has no specific attachment. Anxiety involves a feeling of dread, that something bad is going to happen but you have no idea what it is or when it will take place.

Worry is not found in babies, because it does not have a special stimulus to cause it. Everyone else, even the most well-adjusted individual, worries about something. Early in life most worries center around the home and school. School becomes the source for an increasing number of the child's worries as he progresses through different grades.

Worry is a common emotion shared by all, but it is one emotion that most people could do without. Worrying itself accomplishes nothing. The only time that it is justified is when it can do some good. In most cases, however, when you are worrying about something, it is too late to improve the situation. For example, worrying about a test while you are taking it does no good—it is too late; unless your worrying makes you study harder for the next test, it has not done any good. Worrying helps only when it leads to constructive behavior. It is the same as a test score, which has no value in itself. It is only what is done with the score that is important. The score, like worrying, is a means to an end, never an end in itself.

SOCIAL DEVELOPMENT

Social development involves learning to act and live in a culture or society as a member of that society. Sometimes it necessitates learning to inhibit your impulses; at other times it requires doing things that you may not like. An individual becomes a sociable person through associations with other people, from whom he learns cultural habits, mores, and what is right and wrong in that society.

When does social behavior appear? Social behavior first appears early in life, when the average baby is about two months old. The baby will cry when an adult leaves him and smile when the person returns. Children under one year of age will pay attention to the presence of another child, but they will not interact with two children at the same time until about thirty months of age.

Two of the most obvious social traits that appear in preschool children are dominance and submissiveness. To determine which children are primarily dominant and which are submissive, observe their behavior in a group. As the members of the group change and new members are added, however, some previously dominant children may become submissive, and some submissive children may become dominant.

During the preschool years the child will undergo three stages of interaction with adults: (1) dependence, (2) resistance, and (3) cooperation. Early in life the child passively accepts his dependence upon adults.

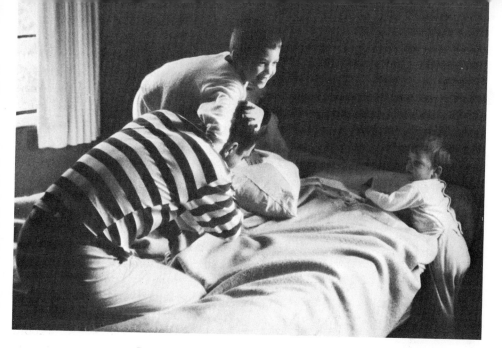

During the preschool years children learn most of their social behavior from contact with the other members of their family.

At two years of age he reaches a stage of resistance and rebels against adult standards. This is sometimes called the "I, me, mine" or "Let me do it!" stage. This stage occurs when the child begins to realize that he is a separate individual with certain rights and privileges. It can be a very confusing time of life, for the child must learn that although he does have rights, he also must have limits placed on his behavior. In the third stage the child becomes more cooperative and friendly as he begins to accept the limits imposed on him.

What social changes occur during the early school years? During the early school years, during grades 1 to 6, several social situations arise that were present to a small degree before but now begin to change the child. As the child enters school, he is confronted with conflicting ideas and attitudes to a larger degree than in the past. Meeting new people, being exposed to the educational process, and having to leave home for a large amount of time each day bring about confusing situations for the child. It is at about this point that children begin to develop a disregard for adult standards and adopt those of the peer group. These attitudes increase and reach a peak in the adolescent period, which occurs at the junior and senior high school level.

During the preschool years and up to about the second grade, the child disregards the sex of playmates. Then, at about the age of eight, males start to choose males and females to choose females. Between this age level and the puberty stage, the two sexes develop disrespect, even hostility, for

183

Between the ages of about eight to twelve, girls usually prefer associations with other girls, and sometimes form cliques.

but such social behavior is primarily for fun-and-games type of activities. These associations do not have the organization or leaders that gangs have during the adolescent period.

What are some characteristics of the social behavior of adolescents? The adolescent period is the time when the individual grows out of childhood into adulthood—usually referred to as the teen years. It is characterized by the individual's striving to be independent from the home but recognizing that complete independence is impossible at this time. The individual rebels. Sometimes he chooses to rebel over minor things, such as how late he can stay out at night. Parents often fail to recognize their children's growing need for independence. Adolescents often fail to recognize that their parents are trying to protect them. When neither parent nor offspring recognize the other's point of view, both are destined to experience frustration.

During adolescence individuals are prone to join groups which are more organized and have stronger leadership and loyalties than the groups they joined during the early school years and which sometimes come into conflict with adults. The most extreme adolescent group is the street gang. However, most adolescents do not join gangs. Instead, many form *cliques,* which are small groups of individuals up to about a dozen in number, bound together by common interests and shared activities. Cliques spring up in schools, neighborhoods, and places of recreational activities.

each other, preferring to associate with members of their own sex. Since girls reach the pubertal stage of development about one to two years earlier than males, during their early teens girls will begin to develop an interest in boys which will not be returned until the boys are some two or three years older. The earlier attraction of girls toward boys is probably one major reason that some girls in their early teens date boys who are two or three years older. At this stage, boys their own age are simply not interested in girls.

The desire of individuals to associate with members of their own sex during the early school years leads to the formation of gangs and cliques,

In adolescence, joining groups gives the individual a chance to identify with other people and to learn new ideas and attitudes. Groups aid adolescents in forming standards—good and bad alike—which will help serve as guides for behavior in later life. Therefore, adolescents should think carefully in selecting which organizations and groups they will join.

One of the most characteristic social developments during this period is the development of heterosexual interests. Generally, the individual passes through a hero-worship stage, then the so-called puppy-love stage, and finally the more intense romantic-love stage.

The first stage, which occurs in the early teens, is characterized by a strong attraction toward someone of the same or opposite sex and is based primarily on great admiration of the person. This person, who is usually older, may be a movie or television star, athletic hero, singer, or a successful person in some other area. Individuals move out of this stage into the puppy-love stage during junior high school and early senior high school years. The affection then turns from an older person to a member of the opposite sex close to the individual's own age. In female behavior this new interest is shown when girls begin to use make-up, which is one way of making themselves more attractive to the opposite sex, as well as a way to conform to the standards of their age group. In a male this new interest can be seen by an increased desire to show that he is a man, which may cause him to start shaving before his beard has

really grown. The last stage, romantic love, starts in late adolescence and is a more intense, stable, and mature affection. The individuals begin to "go steady." They center more of their behavior around activities in which both partners can participate. Interest in other members of the opposite sex decreases as attention is focused primarily on one individual.

What are the characteristics of social development in adulthood and old age? The years beyond the teens to the late sixties are chiefly concerned with finding and keeping a job, getting married, and raising a family. This can be a very confusing, frustrating, yet rewarding time of life.

Choosing a vocation can be a difficult decision. Unfortunately, many individuals fail to adequately explore occupational choices during high

Many adolescents develop an interest in members of the opposite sex. Some center their attention on just one person.

school, although such exploration is increasing as counselors and guidance personnel help students with the problem. Many students in college also have difficulty in deciding on a vocation. Sometimes individuals select a job not because they like it but because it pays a high salary. As a result, the individual may become dissatisfied with his job, and this dissatisfaction and frustration may carry over into other areas of his life.

Marriage represents the culmination of the development of heterosexual interests. With marriage comes the responsibility of a spouse and a family. Marriage often means the end of an individual's membership in some of his former social groups, but it also usually leads to participation with new groups, such as other married couples of about the same age. The level of happiness changes during the course of married life, depending to some degree upon the circumstances and expectations of the people involved.

As the individual approaches old age, he experiences changes in his physiological, emotional, and mental development. He feels more and more alone. The individual begins to fear losing his job and having to retire. Often individuals look forward to retirement—until that time of life approaches. When a person has worked long and hard at a job and suddenly finds himself with his time completely free, he may enjoy it very much—at least at first. Doing nothing can be very boring, however, especially if you have been forced to retire. If you find this hard to believe, try to sit down and do nothing for one hour. Do not move or talk, just breathe. You will then have some idea of what many people feel when they are forced to retire. Thus, it is very important that individuals prepare themselves for retirement by learning new things and developing some interesting hobby. Otherwise, with their children married and away from home, this can become a very lonely time of life.

A wife usually outlives her husband by several years, which makes old age an even more trying time for the woman. The life expectancy for women in the United States is more than seventy-four years. (Compare this life expectancy and the accompanying problems with the situation in countries where the life expectancy is in the middle thirties. You can see how the differences in development between individuals in their seventies and in their thirties affect the problems of these two life expectancy groups.)

HOW PERSONALITY DEVELOPS

Each individual has a personality. His *personality* is the unique organization of an individual's characteristics of adjustment that sets him apart from other individuals. Although individuals' personalities may differ greatly, they have some similar developmental patterns.

The word "personality" closely resembles the Latin word *persona*, which means a mask. In earlier times a persona was a mask that actors wore on the stage so that the audience could tell what part the actors were playing or what emotion they were displaying.

UNDERSTANDING HUMAN BEHAVIOR

If the actor wanted to show joy or happiness, he wore a mask with a smile. If he were playing the part of a monster, he wore a mask resembling a monster. Thus, personality is something that each individual shows to other people so they can tell what kind of person he is. There are, however, deeper underlying aspects of an individual's personality that others do not see. In fact, there are parts of his personality that the individual may not be aware of himself. Because of the complex nature of these underlying aspects of personality, only the more obvious parts of personality will be discussed in this section.

Where does our personality come from? It was once thought that each individual's personality was biologically inherited from his parents. Today, however, psychologists believe that most of personality is learned.

The most important influence on the early development of personality is the parents. If the parents are happy and well-adjusted, then the personalities of their children will tend to be happy and well-adjusted, too. As the child grows older, his playmates and schoolmates will also help to form his personality, as will most people with whom the individual comes into contact. It is the early preschool years that are by far the most important in the formation of personality. Therefore, our discussion here will deal mainly with that period.

How does self-concept affect personality? The self-concept is the core or center of personality. In order fully to understand the relationship of the self-concept to personality, however, it is useful to study several other concepts that help to explain how the personality is constructed.

Freud emphasized that early childhood was very important in the forming of personality, a statement that psychologists today accept as fact. Freud believed that an individual's personality was made up of his id, ego, and superego. The *id* is interested in only one thing—whatever brings the individual pleasure. Since the id is innate, or present at birth, the newborn infant is a good example of pure id. As the child grows older, part of his id splits off and becomes the ego, or self-concept.

The *ego* includes everything that the individual believes about himself. Do you think that you are honest or a cheat, tall or short, smart or dumb? Your ego provides you with the answer. The ego also includes what you assume other people think of you. The development of the ego occurs during the first few years of life, when the child reaches the "I, me, mine" stage. Part of the ego then becomes the *superego,* commonly known as "conscience," which tells us right from wrong.

The individual's self-concept governs to a large extent how he behaves. There is a strong tendency to do things that agree with, support, or reinforce the ego. If you see yourself as an honest person, the chances are you will not cheat on an exam when given the opportunity, since you are honest and you believe that honest people do not cheat. Also, your superego would probably tell you that it is morally wrong to cheat.

Formation of the ego involves learning, whether from the attitudes of others or from personal experiences. Parents are the first and most important factor in the development of the child's ego. If parents consistently tell their son, "You are a failure," they are very likely to convince him that this is true. They do not even need to express it verbally. A parent can suggest to the child that he is a failure, unable to do anything well, by not letting the child attempt to do something, for example, like trying to build a model car. Because they think that the activity is too hard for the child and he may fail, they take the model car parts away from him without an explanation. If they do this every time the child starts something, the child may develop the attitude that he cannot do anything well. This attitude could become part of his self-concept.

Our self-concept is learned not only from parents but also from everyone with whom we come in contact—teachers, peer groups, siblings, and other relatives. Anything or anyone that disagrees with our self-concept will cause us to defend our ego. If you believe that you are very smart and someone tells you that you are stupid, your self-concept will be disturbed, and you will probably want to contradict the person. If you believe that you are honest, but you cheat on an exam, you may feel guilty or try to excuse this behavior. The self-concept does not necessarily agree with cultural values. For example, a person who sees himself as the best hubcap stealer in the world will be angry or hurt if you say he is not a good hubcap stealer. The point is that the self-concept is defended because of contradictory statements between what the person believes and what others tell him or what his own behavior tells him is true.

The individual who has the wrong self-concept is more unhappy, tense, and worried than someone whose self-concept is accurate. The self-concept is "wrong" when it does not present a true picture of the person. When you constantly have to defend your self-concept against others or against your own contradictory behavior you have little time to do anything else. On the other hand, a well-adjusted individual has the ability to change his self-concept throughout life. He can do this even in a case where his self-concept was once true but is true no longer, now that he is older. For example, as the fast, well-coordinated young person eventually reaches middle age, his abilities based on speed and coordination begin to decrease and he cannot keep up the pace of his earlier days. To be accurate, his self-concept would change, too.

How much does personality change? Surprisingly, the basic personality structure of the individual is laid down before he enters school. After he enters school, his personality changes very little, although specific ways of behaving or responding may change as he grows older. Unless he undergoes strong emotional shock or psychotherapy, however, his pattern of responding will change very little during the rest of his life. In general, as the

UNDERSTANDING HUMAN BEHAVIOR

individual grows older, his personality becomes more stable, and significant changes are harder to make; but this does not mean that the individual's personality is fixed at any single period of life. It merely means that it remains much the same after the first few years of life.

One study of individuals from birth to age fifteen indicated that general ways of behaving in a situation changed very little during those fifteen years. The baby who showed fear and screamed when he was a year old showed fear and ran away at the age of two. Although there was a modification in the specific response because the child had learned to run, the general pattern of behavior was the same.

MENTAL DEVELOPMENT

Another fundamental aspect of human development is the development of an individual's mental abilities. It is important because it has such a decisive effect upon the individual's total development. *Mental development* refers to the increase and decline of the traits and abilities that comprise an individual's intelligence.

What are some problems in studying the development of mental abilities? It is very difficult to determine specific mental traits in infants. At present, measuring the intelligence of babies relies heavily upon the measurement of motor abilities, which have a small but positive correlation with intelligence scores later in life. Measuring mental abilities is further complicated by the problem of comparing the results of

different intelligence tests, since not all intelligence tests measure precisely the same things. Therefore, some changes may show up in the specific traits used to describe the development of intelligence simply because different tests were used at the various age levels. Another factor complicating the description of intelligence over a long period of time is that a longitudinal study over a period of sixty-five years takes exactly that long to make. To avoid waiting for so long a time for conclusions, psychologists have turned to cross-sectional studies for a large part of the data on this subject. This section will emphasize the aspects of mental growth that psychologists agree upon most.

How do mental traits develop and decline? One of the first mental abilities that appears in babies is memory. The baby learns that certain faces, such as those of his parents, are associated with pleasant things. Learning plays a major role in the baby's mental development, as it does in other areas of development.

Some other mental traits may exist within the individual but do not show up in his behavior because he lacks the physical growth to express them. For example, the mental ability to solve the problem of getting from one place to another and then returning to the same place by another route might be present, but the behavior cannot occur until the individual has been able to learn to crawl.

Regardless of when mental traits appear, once they have appeared, they continue to grow rapidly until the av-

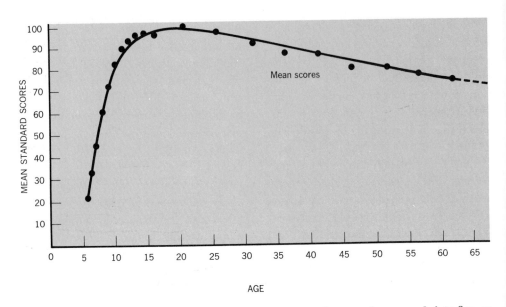

Changes in intelligence scores between the ages of seven and sixty-five, as measured by the Wechsler-Bellevue test

erage individual reaches his early twenties. As he passes through the twenties, some mental traits will "hold up" well, while others will begin a fast decline. However, each mental trait will eventually decline in the individual. The following summary list can be used as a general guide:

1. Verbal ability increases until the early thirties, although it increases less rapidly in the middle and late twenties.
2. Perception of spatial relations significantly slows down in the early twenties, levels off in the late twenties, and begins to decline sharply in the early thirties.
3. Reasoning ability begins to decline in the late teens or early twenties.
4. Numerical ability increases to the middle forties and then declines.
5. Word fluency rises until the early

thirties, declines for a few years, rises, and then begins a continuous decline in the early forties.

Generally, the earliest and fastest decline of abilities after early adulthood occurs in the areas of intelligence involving speed in solving problems and abstract reasoning. Those abilities which rely primarily on verbal skills, previous experience, and judgment decline more slowly and later in life.

The increase and decline of mental traits differ according to the composite intelligence score of the individual. Those who are above average will have a sharper rise in the development of mental traits, and their abilities will increase or hold up longer than for the average person. For those below average intellectual ability, the development of traits will reach a peak sooner and more slowly, and will decline faster.

This does not mean that older persons know less than they did earlier or that they do not continue to learn. What decreases is the individual's readiness to learn and the speed with which he can perform tasks.

In summary, remember that specific mental traits differ according to how fast they develop, when their peak performance level is reached, and the rate at which they decline. Overall intellectual development increases for the average person until about the early twenties. It begins to decline slowly up to the early thirties and then more quickly until the sixties, when the decline is most rapid. Also, do not forget that there are important differences among individuals: the higher the intellectual ability, the more rapid the development of individual traits, the higher the peak performance reached, and the slower the decline. For those below average intellectual ability, the reverse is true. Although there are individual differences in the extent of mental abilities, the pattern of mental development generally is the same. This is true of all the areas of development discussed in this chapter.

Changes in primary mental traits during the adult years

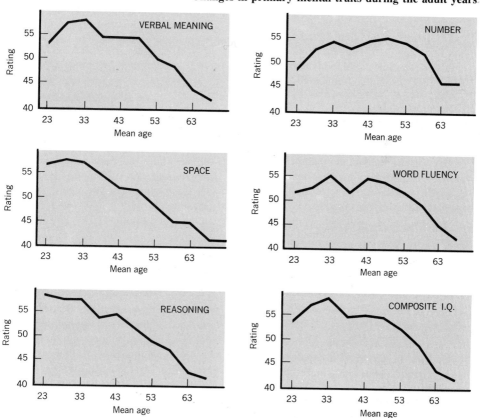

Terms to Add to Your Vocabulary

As is true of some of the information in this chapter, some of these vocabulary terms appear elsewhere in this book.

anxiety
clique
cross-sectional approach
development
ego
id

longitudinal approach
maturation
mental traits
observation
persona
self-concept

socialization
stimulus generalization
superego
worry

Suggestions for Activities

1. Try to remember how you developed in height in elementary school and even further back if possible. Perhaps your parents kept a "baby book" which would have a record of your height at different ages. Describe in a report this area of development and if you felt, at different ages, that you were above or below average in developing. What effect might your feelings at that time have had upon your present self-concept? Has your study of psychology helped you in evaluating your present self-concept?

2. If you know of someone who has a physical handicap and is not known to others in your school or class, write a report on the individual's handicap and how you think he views his own handicap. Be very careful in selecting the person and drawing any conclusions. If such a person is not available, imagine that you personally have developed a physical handicap and write a report on how you would react and adjust to it. Be as honest as you can in describing the handicap and how you would feel about it.

3. Ask your local hospital if they will give you the weight and height of male and female babies born in the hospital during the past year, or earlier if the data are available. Determine the mean height and weight for males and females separately. Do your data agree or disagree with the data in this chapter? How much variation in height and weight did you find? What principles can you give as illustrated in this chapter?

4. If you have a tape recorder or one is available, record the voices and speech of children of different age groups. For example, record children whose ages range from one to five years. What changes can you detect in the number of words used at each age level? the structure of sentences? level of difficulty of the words used? What other changes do you find?

5. Obtain some old movies of friends or members of your own family. By watching the movies, can you detect any differences in motor activities, such as running and jumping? Did you find any examples to illustrate any of the principles of development in this chapter?

6. If you have identical twins in your school whom you know personally, describe your observations of the twins, such as similarity of clothing, interests, courses taken in school, and attendance at social events. Be sure that you have the consent of the twins and that no embarrassment to them will result. Do the twins agree or disagree in these areas? Stress any differences you might find.

7. If you have an opportunity to do so, with the parents' consent, pick up a small child to whom you are a stranger. Does the child cry or try to escape? Do reactions to strangers vary with age? If you do not have an opportunity to carry out this activity yourself, you may observe others picking up children to whom they are strangers. For example, as part of the baptismal service in some churches, the clergyman takes a child in his arms. Do children of various ages react differently in this strange situation?

8. Select any two beliefs, interests, or attitudes that you have and try to determine how they specifically came about. When did they originate and how did they develop?

9. Select five things that you worry about quite often. Describe your feelings about each one. To what extent, if any, has the worrying changed your behavior? Has your study of psychology helped you to understand some of your worries? Compare with worries of other students. Is there any agreement?

Suggestions for Further Reading

Hilgard, Ernest R., and Richard C. Atkinson, *Introduction to Psychology,* 4th ed., Harcourt, Brace & World. Chapter 3, "Infancy and Childhood"; Chapter 4, "Adolescence and Adulthood"; Chapter 7, "Emotion"; Chapter 16, "Ability Testing and Intelligence," pages 429–30, "Changes in Adult Intelligence."

Hurlock, E. B., *Child Development,* 4th ed., McGraw-Hill. Chapters 1–11: A detailed account of the developmental aspects of the individual from birth to adolescence.

Kalish, Richard A., *The Psychology of Human Behavior,* Wadsworth. Chapter 6, "The Earliest Years"; Chapter 7, "The Developing Child and His Relationships"; Chapter 11, "The Mature Years," pages 246–53."

Lindgren, Henry C., Donn Byrne, and Lewis Petrinovich, *Psychology: An Introduction to a Behavioral Science,* 2nd ed., John Wiley. Chapter 2, "Infancy and Childhood"; Chapter 3, "Adolescence and Adulthood."

Meyer, W. J., *Developmental Psychology,* Center for Applied Research in Education, 1964. Short book dealing with general principles of behavior development.

Morgan, Clifford T., and Richard A. King, *Introduction to Psychology,* 3rd ed., McGraw-Hill. Chapter 2, "Maturation and Development," pages 57–68, "Development in Sensory, Motor, Language, and Intelligence"; Chapter 7, "Emotion," pages 238–52, "Emotional Development"; Chapter 13, "Personality," pages 490–93, "Personality Development."

Munn, Norman L., *Psychology,* 5th ed., Houghton Mifflin. Chapter 4, "How Individual Differences Originate," pages 104–11, "Motor Development"; Chapter 5, "Intelligence," pages 136–42, "Intellectual Development"; Chapter 7, "Feeling and Emotion," pages 209–14, "Emotional Development"; Chapter 9, "Personality," pages 255–62, "Personality Development."

Ruch, Floyd L., *Psychology and Life,* 7th ed., Scott, Foresman. Chapter 3, "The Development of Behavior."

Sanford, Fillmore H., *Psychology: A Scientific Study of Man,* 2nd ed., Wadsworth. Chapter 3, "The Developing Organism."

Whittaker, James O., et al., *Introduction to Psychology,* W. B. Saunders. Chapter 3, "The Development of Behavior"; Chapter 5, "Feelings and Emotions"; Chapter 16, "Individual and Group Differences," page 459, "Intellectual Development."

CHAPTER 8

Measuring intellectual ability

THE MEANING OF INTELLIGENCE

How is intelligence defined? It is very difficult to give a satisfactory definition of intelligence. One definition is that *intelligence* is the ability of an organism to adapt itself adequately to both the old and especially the new situations in its environment. An individual is intelligent to the extent that he can quickly and successfully adjust to situations on the basis of his past learning and his present grasp of the problems he encounters. One psychologist has defined intelligence as "the ability to see what ought to be done and how to do it." Adjusting to the environment is the primary characteristic. Later in this chapter, however, we shall describe more specifically some of the essential factors involved in intelligence.

Note that there is no mention of school attendance in either of these definitions. It is true that schools help us adapt ourselves to the world we live in. To take but one example, schools and colleges help us get better-paying jobs —and thereby to afford better homes,

food, and clothing. Yet intelligence can be found where there are no schools. An Eskimo who could kill game and build huts was adjusted to his surroundings. He was showing intelligent behavior even though he might never have had any formal schooling.

To make a successful adjustment to American society — to live in what we call comfort — it is usually necessary to be able to earn money, but the signs of intelligence and a successful adjustment in one society do not necessarily apply to some other society. For example, to a Pygmy, hunting skill might be more valuable than a million dollars. A Pygmy may have intelligently fitted himself for living in his environment without even knowing what money is.

The highly intelligent person is able to assimilate and retain many facts. Remembering useful facts is very necessary in our crowded, mechanized world. In order to move about successfully, we have to remember bus and train schedules, school hours, traffic rules, dates, meetings, telephone numbers. Yet it is possible to be a "walking encyclopedia" and still not be very successful in adjusting to new situations.

The highly intelligent person not only retains many facts; he also manipulates them and his ideas about them so as to come up with new solutions to his problems. He sees new meaningful relationships. On the other hand, persons of low intellectual ability forget many facts which they have learned and often do not use facts which they remember. They do what they are told to do but are often quite content to sit and do nothing. If they make mistakes, they may be quite unaware of their errors. There is much more to intelligent behavior than appears in one glance at our definition of "intelligence."

We all recognize that some persons are better able to adapt themselves to their environment than others. Popularly, some persons are called "smart," others "dumb," and some "average." To be scientific, we must describe intelligence in much more specific terms, and must measure it objectively. In this chapter we shall learn how psychologists study intelligence.

How many factors make up intelligence?

When items from various tests of intelligence are treated statistically, intelligence can be broken down into a number of factors. To date, psychologists have found that there are about 80 such factors; that is, there are at least 80 ways of being intelligent. Further research may result in breaking intelligence down into 120 or more abilities. The same essential factors have been found on the basis of tests given to children five and six years of age, to high school students, and to adults.

One psychologist, Dr. L. L. Thurstone, has identified these seven primary factors: the space factor, the number factor, the verbal comprehension factor, the verbal fluency factor, the memory factor, the reasoning factor, and the perceptual factor.

If you have studied plane and solid geometry, you have had much experience in visualizing flat figures and solid objects. Some students like mechanical drawing more than do other students because they are better able to visualize what they are drawing. Individuals differ in their ability to visualize flat figures or solid objects. Hence psychologists speak of the *space factor* in intelligence.

Some individuals have more facility than others in doing simple numerical tasks. Psychologists have found that there is a *number factor* in intelligence. A good cashier or bookkeeper would probably have facility in this factor. On the other hand, it might be that a person who is not high in the number factor could do very well in advanced theoretical mathematics courses.

It has been found that some individuals do very well in tests of vocabulary, verbal reasoning, interpretation of proverbs, comprehension of difficult prose passages, and so on. They have facility in understanding verbal material. Psychologists speak of a *verbal comprehension factor* in intelligence. A related factor is that of *verbal fluency*. Some individuals are much more able than others to express themselves orally and in writing. Individuals who are of superior ability in these two factors usually do well in schoolwork. The reason is that so much of our tradi-

Facets of Intelligence

Some individuals show greater facility than others in various areas of intelligence. The intelligence factor in which they excel often determines their occupation. An individual who is superior in verbal fluency may well become a writer, such as Ernest Hemingway (above). The student who is good at mechanical drawing and design, indicating that he scores high in the space factor of intelligence, is apt to succeed at engineering or architecture. Some persons with a facility in the memory factor become well-known actors, such as Sidney Poitier (top right). Others, having an ability with numbers, might become proficient in accounting.

tional schoolwork involves reading, understanding what is read, and answering oral or written questions.

There is evidence that persons differ in their ability to remember. Perhaps you know people who seem to remember names, dates, and facts of all kinds with ease. Facility in this respect is often an advantage. A person with an unusual memory may be envied by others, but he does not necessarily have *general* intellectual superiority. He is probably superior in the *memory factor* of intelligence.

Some individuals have more ability than others in *inductive reasoning*.

That is, they can take a problem or a set of facts and discover the rule or principle involved. Some have ability in applying general principles to particular cases or problems—that is, in *deductive reasoning* (see pages 121–22). There is some evidence that inductive and deductive reasoning are related to two separate factors in intelligence. We shall, however, consider them together as the *reasoning factor*.

The seventh factor is called the *perceptual factor*. Some individuals have more facility than others in grasping visual details and in noting similarities and differences between pictures. For

example, when being tested for this factor, the subject may be asked to mark pictures that are exactly alike, although in actuality they are part of a series of very similar but slightly different pictures. It should be noted that tests for the perceptual factor are not always included among the batteries of tests designed to measure primary mental abilities.

Originally some psychologists thought that these seven primary factors that make up intelligence were independent of one another; that is, they were "pure" factors. More recent evidence has become available, however,

that indicates that these factors are related to each other, for when the factors are correlated, the result is a positive correlation. Nevertheless, it is still possible that the factors are primary ones, but that the tests presently available to measure the factors are not pure enough adequately to isolate the factors.

How can we apply knowledge of factors in intelligence? All too often it has been assumed that a child who is "bright" in some ways must of necessity be bright in all ways. Conversely, it is assumed that a child dull in some ways must be dull in all ways. These are wrong assumptions. In actual fact, a child may be bright in one factor of intelligence, yet dull in another. It is well known, for example, that some children can do well in arts and crafts but have great difficulty in other subjects because they cannot read efficiently. Eventually teachers may be able to fit their methods of teaching to each child's ability in certain factors of intelligence. We cannot, however, completely overlook the fact that there may be a general factor, that is, a general intellectual ability.

Knowledge of factors of intelligence may be of value to young people in selecting a lifework. For example, students of superior ability in the verbal factors would probably do well to consider writing or journalism. Students superior in the visualizing (space) and reasoning factors might well consider engineering or work in the physical sciences. However, in our present state of knowledge there are no tests that can tell a young person exactly what vocation he should choose. Many of the factors involved cannot be measured by present tests.

Another great advantage in recognizing the various factors in intelligence has to do with mental health. It may be that many children fail in schoolwork, become discouraged, and develop feelings of inferiority because they are forced to try to succeed in the wrong field. They should be given an opportunity to excel in the field of their greatest ability. Individuals may go through life unhappy and discouraged because they have drifted into a vocation for which they are not suited.

However, as one psychologist has said, "The best position for educators to take is that possibly every intellectual factor can be developed in individuals at least to some extent by learning." *

INDIVIDUAL TESTS OF INTELLIGENCE

Measurement is a very important part of scientific study. Psychologists have devoted years of work to devising tests to measure intelligence.

How did intelligence tests originate? A number of attempts were made to secure measures of general intelligence before a really workable test was devised. Intelligence tests in the form generally used today have developed from the work of Alfred Binet (bē·ne′), a French physician and psychologist. Binet was assisted by another French physician and psychologist, Théodore Simon (sē·môn′).

After much careful study and research, these men published their first test of intelligence in 1905. This test consisted of thirty tasks to be performed by children. These were not the kinds of tasks that the children were required to learn in school. On the contrary, they were simple tasks that the children would be likely to know from their everyday experiences without formal teaching.

Binet and Simon made two important revisions of their test. The final one was published in 1911, the year of

* J. P. Guilford, "Three Faces of Intellect." *American Psychologist*, Vol. 14 (1959), p. 478.

UNDERSTANDING HUMAN BEHAVIOR

Binet's death. In both revisions the tasks were arranged in groups from age three to adulthood.

In selecting the tasks to be assigned to each age group, Binet and Simon did not depend upon their own judgment of what children of a given age should be able to do. Such a procedure would not have been scientific. Instead, they tested a large number of children on all the tasks in their list. If at least half of presumably normal children at a given age passed a task, the task was considered to be correctly placed for that age. For example, they found that about one-half of all children five years of age could count four coins, that most children four years of age could not do so, and that the task was too easy for most children six years of age. Thus, they found that the task was suitable for testing five-year-olds.

What is a child's mental age (MA)? Today we often speak of the mental age (MA) of a child as well as of his chronological age (CA). An individual's *chronological age* is the number of years, months, and days since his birth. An individual's *mental age* is determined by his ability to perform such tasks as are given in intelligence tests.

If a child's performance on a mental ability test is median for children who are exactly four years old, the child is said to have a mental age of four years. By *median* is meant that there are just as many scores above an individual's score as there are below his score. (For a fuller explanation, see the Appendix.) If his performance is equal to the median performance of children exactly five years old, he is said to have a mental age of five years, and so on.

A child's performance may equal the median performance of six-year-olds. He may, therefore, have a mental age of six years, regardless of the fact that chronologically he is only four or five years old. Or he may have a mental age of six even though he is chronologically seven or eight.

Suppose that there are three children whose chronological ages are exactly four, five, and six years, respectively. Furthermore, suppose that each child is given an intelligence test such as Binet and Simon devised. The tests may show that each child can do the tasks that most children five years of age can do and that not one of the three children can do better. All three children are said to have mental ages of five years, regardless of the fact that they differ in chronological ages.

In summary, the mental age can be said to represent an individual's present level of mental functioning, as determined by his scores on a standardized test of intelligence.

What are some individual intelligence tests for Americans? American psychologists soon became very interested in the work of Binet, and they began using the Binet-Simon tests with American children. These tests were translated from French into English and adjusted to fit the conditions of American life.

One of a number of American psychologists who became involved in the problem of the measurement of intelligence was Lewis M. Terman of Stanford University. In 1916 he published the *Stanford Revision of the Binet-*

Individual intelligence tests are useful for determining how well a child can perform in school.

Simon Test. This test consisted of ninety items arranged by years, covering a range from three years of age to superior-adult ability. The *Stanford Revision* has been used extensively in schools and psychological clinics in America. In 1937 Terman published another revision of the test, with a range of from two years of age to superior-adult ability. In 1960, following the death of Dr. Terman, a third revision was published. Both these later revisions are known as the *Revised Stanford-Binet*.

Two other widely used individual tests of intelligence are the *Wechsler Intelligence Scale for Children* (WISC) and the *Wechsler Adult Intelligence Scale* (WAIS). Both tests are composed of two parts: one section on verbal ability and the other on performance. A measure of intellectual ability is obtained for each part individually. The total is then based on a composite score of the two parts combined. The two parts are made up of six verbal and five performance subtests. These subtests measure verbal ability, auditory memory, numerical ability, reasoning, comprehension, general information, perceptual-motor ability, and other factors. The WISC is designed to measure intelligence of individuals from ages two through fifteen years of age; the WAIS measures individuals who are sixteen years of age and older. One difference between these tests and the *Revised Stanford-Binet* is that on the latter test, items measuring different factors (such as verbal and numerical ability) are mixed together within any single age grouping, whereas on the Wechsler tests all similar items are given under one heading, in an order starting with easy questions and proceeding to very difficult ones.

What are performance tests of intelligence? Sometimes psychologists wish to determine the intelligence of someone who has a different cultural background, is handicapped by a lack of understanding of the English language, or is too young to know the language, such as an infant or baby. Performance tests, occasionally known as "nonverbal" tests, are designed to be administered to these persons. Such tests are usually of the form-board or picture-comple-

UNDERSTANDING HUMAN BEHAVIOR

tion type. The form board consists of a board with recesses into which the individual must insert variously shaped forms. The picture-completion test is one in which the person must select certain parts that will complete a picture. The results of performance tests alone do not correlate as highly as do verbal test results with the combined verbal and performance test results. Most psychologists prefer to use tests which measure both verbal and performance aspects of intelligence.

One factor on the *Wechsler* and *Revised Stanford-Binet* tests is auditory memory. Testing auditory memory is also useful for measuring individuals who do not speak the English language. The test requires little or no verbal instructions by the examiner (person giving the test). For example, the examiner can tap on a desk three times with a pencil point, as the subject listens and watches. Then the examiner hands the pencil to the subject and indicates that he is to repeat the same tapping. After the subject repeats the same number of taps, the examiner repeats the taps but lengthens the number of digits presented. For example, tap three times, pause, then tap two more times. The examiner, of course, has tapped out the digits 3–2. The number of digits presented can be lengthened to make any combination of numbers, although in this kind of test for auditory memory, the digit 5 is usually the highest digit tapped out. Each digit can be reused within a single series, however, so that the length of the series can be quite long (1–4–3–2–2–5). Notice that it makes no difference what language the subject

uses for the digits, as long as he repeats the same number of taps as the examiner in the same groupings.

GROUP TESTS OF INTELLIGENCE

All the measuring devices mentioned so far have been individual tests; that is, the examiner gives the test to one individual at a time. Obviously, any extensive program of individual testing requires many trained clinical psychologists and a great deal of time and money.

How has the army used group intelligence tests? During World War I the army was faced with the problem of testing the intelligence of many thousands of men. There was work in the army that could be done by men of very low general intelligence, other work for men of very high general intelligence, and all kinds of jobs between these extremes that required men of all degrees of intelligence. In the rush of the war, there was not enough time, nor were there enough trained psychologists, to give individual tests to all the men. A group of psychologists was called together to construct group tests of intelligence for use by the American army.

In all, 1,726,966 enlisted men and officers were tested during World War I. When the Armistice was signed, the large-scale intelligence testing in the army came to a close for a time. However, the foundation had been laid, and work in group intelligence testing continued in other fields, especially in the schools.

MEASURING INTELLECTUAL ABILITY

In World War II our army used a somewhat different testing program. For four and a half years, men entering the army were given the *Army General Classification Test.* This was a test of "general learning ability" or, more specifically, of "ability to learn quickly the duties of a soldier." More than ten million soldiers took this particular test. The test was of the four-choice multiple-choice variety, with a time limit of forty minutes. Designed to measure primarily three factors of intelligence, it consisted of the following kinds of items: (1) vocabulary, (2) arithmetical computation and problem solving, and (3) spatial items.

The major use made of test scores was in the selection of men for the large number of specialist training courses required by technical modern warfare. It was found that men who made high scores on this test were likely to make good commissioned and noncommissioned officers or highly skilled specialists. (Ability in leadership as well as tested intelligence was found to be important for officers. See Chapter 13.) Men who had somewhat lower scores made very good basic soldiers. They were often able to profit by training in the less highly technical fields. Men who had still lower scores made good basic soldiers or were placed on necessary but unskilled jobs. For men who neither spoke nor wrote English or who were illiterate, there was a *Visual Classification Test.* Since the war, a civilian edition of the *Army General Classification Test* has become available for aid in solving the many peacetime problems of guidance, selection, and placement.

How do schools use group intelligence tests? Schools have used group intelligence tests quite extensively since the 1920's. You have probably taken at least one of these tests some time during your school career. School officials use these test scores to get a rough measure of each student's intellectual ability. They can then group students into fast, average, and slow learning sections and adjust instructional methods accordingly. Although much can be said for this educational practice, teaching and learning involve so many variables that sectioning on the basis of group intelligence-test scores alone may lead to situations which do not serve the best interest of individual children. For all children presenting unusual problems, group intelligence tests should be followed by individual tests, administered and interpreted by trained psychologists.

Group intelligence tests for school use have both advantages and disadvantages as compared with individual intelligence tests. There are not enough trained psychologists to enable schools to give each child an individual test, and even were enough psychologists available, the cost per student would be prohibitive for most schools. Group intelligence tests can be administered and scored by school administrators and classroom teachers who are not trained psychologists and who are already salaried employees of the school system. A large number of children can be tested at one time, and their papers can be scored easily, often by a machine.

Offsetting these advantages is the fact that a group test may not give a

UNDERSTANDING HUMAN BEHAVIOR

very valid measure of a given child's intellectual ability. He may be emotionally upset or not feeling well at the time the test is administered, he may fail to understand directions, or he may not be motivated to do his best. In some cases children have achieved high scores because they managed to copy from the papers of other children! The trained psychologist administering an individual test can avoid such conditions as these.

As you can see, from the practical point of view of the school, group intelligence tests have many advantages; from the point of view of the individual child needing guidance and assistance, they may have some disadvantages.

No psychologist claims that his test, whether an individual or group test, is a perfect measure of general intelligence or of any factor in intelligence. Yet tests are accurate enough to give a mathematical measure. That is, a psychologist does not estimate intelligence by saying that John Doe is "very bright" or "very dumb." Instead, through the use of tests, the psychologist can express John Doe's intelligence by a number.

One word of caution about intelligence tests and the measurements they give. Such tests are very valuable in the hands of a trained psychologist, but they should never be used or interpreted by untrained individuals.

THE INTELLIGENCE QUOTIENT (IQ)

A term often used to give a mathematical measure of intelligence is the "intelligence quotient," or IQ. Perhaps you have the impression that an IQ is some kind of mysterious mental X-ray picture. As a matter of fact, an *intelligence quotient* is merely the ratio between a person's mental age and his chronological age. It is expressed by the following formula:

Intelligence quotient

$$= \frac{\text{mental age}}{\text{chronological age}} \times 100$$

$$IQ = \frac{MA}{CA} \times 100$$

In a preceding section you learned the meaning of the two terms "mental age" and "chronological age." Here is a convenient way to express the ratio between them.

How is an IQ calculated? Suppose an intelligence test shows that a child can do what the average, or median, child eight years of age can do. That is, he has a mental age of eight years. Furthermore, suppose that his chronological age is also eight years. That is, it is just eight years since he was born. To find his intelligence quotient, divide his mental age by his chronological age and multiply by 100; thus —

$$IQ = \frac{MA}{CA} \times 100 = \frac{8}{8} \times 100 = 100$$

The 100 in the formula is simply for the purpose of enabling psychologists to express an IQ without using a decimal point — merely a matter of convenience.

Let us take another example. Suppose that a child has a mental age of twelve and that his chronological age is also twelve. Again his IQ would be 100. In other words, if a child can do on an intelligence test what the median child of his chronological age can do—that is, if his mental age and chronological age are exactly equal—his IQ is 100.

Now suppose an intelligence test given to a child indicates that he can do what the median child six years of age can do. That is, his MA is six years. However, his birth record shows that he is chronologically eight years of age. His intelligence quotient would be computed as follows:

$$IQ = \frac{MA}{CA} \times 100 = \frac{6}{8} \times 100 = 75$$

Suppose another child takes an intelligence test which indicates that his MA is six years. His chronological age, however, is four years. What is his IQ?

$$IQ = \frac{MA}{CA} \times 100 = \frac{6}{4} \times 100 = 150$$

To sum up, if a person can do less on an intelligence test than the average, or median, person of his chronological age, he has an IQ below 100. If he can do more than the average, or median, person of his chronological age, he has an IQ above 100.

Although the concept of the IQ is often useful in measuring the intellectual ability of children, the IQ as a measure of adult ability is subject to various errors and is approximate only. For example, an individual's chronological age continues to change, although, as we shall see later in this chapter, his mental age becomes relatively stable after a certain point. Therefore, the method of computing IQ which we just studied is no longer useful, because it presumes that both chronological age and mental age as measured by tests are continuing to grow. Then, too, adults are usually tested for ability in specific fields rather than for the general ability which tests designed for children measure. For these reasons, psychologists have refined their methods of computing the IQ. In fact, in the latest (1960) revision of the Stanford-Binet, special statistical adjustments (rather than the ratio of MA to CA) are employed to determine a person's IQ.

The concept of mental age was never used in deriving an individual's IQ on the Wechsler tests. The test results are based on standard scores. If a person scores at the mean for his chronological age group, he has an IQ of 100; if he scores one standard deviation above the mean raw score for his age group, his IQ is 115, and an IQ of 85 is represented by the person scoring one standard deviation below the mean raw score of his age group. Nevertheless, in the Wechsler tests as well as in the others, intelligence still involves estimating one's intellectual ability in relation to that of other persons of the same chronological age.

Does the IQ remain constant through life? The IQ of an individual tends to remain approximately constant—that is, approximately the same—throughout his life. Suppose a child whose chronological age is three takes an intelligence test and shows a mental age of three; that is, his IQ is 100. When he is five, tests show that his mental age is five; his IQ is again 100. When tested at age ten, he also shows an IQ of 100. In such a case it would be said that the IQ is constant—that it has remained the same. Actually, such a close correspondence in IQ from year to year is seldom, if ever, found. But in the majority of cases the IQ does not vary more than about five points above or below its median value from year to year.

There is considerable evidence that tests of babies and preschool children do not predict later intelligence test scores very well. During an individual's early years, test results indicate that the IQ may vary considerably rather than remain constant, although the variation may be due, at least to some extent, to the inadequacy of the tests used to measure intelligence during the very early years of life.

Today, psychologists are less certain about the constancy of the IQ than they were a number of years ago. We have spoken of the group tests of intellectual ability that were developed and administered during World War I (page 201). Thirty years after they had taken one of the Army tests when entering college in 1919, a group of 127 men took the same test again. Although the correlation for the test-retest was +.77, as a whole, the group increased their scores over the period of thirty years. These were college-trained men who, as a consequence of their training, had tended to live in challenging environments. Probably persons of higher intellectual ability do tend to remain intellectually alert longer than persons of lesser ability, but there is some evidence that even retarded individuals improve in intelligence-test scores as they grow older, providing they live in an environment which is challenging to them.

There is even evidence that a change in motivation of a person taking an intelligence test can result in some change in IQ. One scientist says that students are not likely to exert their full powers in a test conducted merely in the interests of some psychologist's research. He has found that when a student's admittance to some school or university depends on his intelligence-test score, the score may rise to ten IQ points higher than when the student takes the test merely for the sake of a research study.

The problem of the constancy of the IQ is very closely related to a bigger problem—the relative influences of heredity and environment in the development of an individual—as we shall see in the next chapter.

At what age do we reach mental maturity? As a person grows up, he continues to learn more and more about how to adjust himself to his surroundings. Thus, he is able to do (let us say) eight-year-old work at age eight, ten-year-old work at age ten, and twelve-year-old work at age twelve. His IQ remains constant because each year he is able to answer more questions on an intelligence test. That is, his mental age keeps up with his chronological age.

Psychologists have said there comes a time, however, when he is no longer able to improve appreciably in his ability to answer questions on an intelligence test. When a person ceases to improve his score as he grows older, we say he has reached *mental maturity* or *intellectual maturity*. Some psychologists have placed this age as early as sixteen or even thirteen, some as late as the mid-twenties. Of course, the idea of intellectual maturity does not imply that an individual cannot learn after reaching such maturity. He may show great improvement in his ability to answer questions in specific fields such as science, language, history, commerce, and other branches of study or business.

We have evidence that some factors of intellectual ability tend to remain relatively high as an individual grows older, whereas ability in other factors tends to decline. Number ability and vocabulary tend to remain high even though ability for new learning and reasoning decline.

The question as to the age at which individuals achieve mental maturity is not one for which a simple answer can be given. The age seems to differ greatly from individual to individual but, as we have seen, it is probably later in life for persons of superior ability than for persons of quite limited ability.

Do IQ's follow the normal distribution curve? As intelligence tests are constructed, when a large number of individuals are measured in various ways and the results are plotted on graphs, the curves tend to be normal frequency curves. In one study of 2,904 children, the distribution of IQ's produced the curve shown in the graph on the top of page 207.

Sometimes it is convenient to apply descriptive terms to IQ ranges. One classification is given in the table on this page. Psychologists are not agreed on all the descriptive terms used here.

"Feeble-mindedness," for example, is a legal term, still used in some states, to describe the condition of those individuals who are of such subnormal intellectual ability that they are judged to be in need of special care and training in order to adjust to their environments. Psychologists prefer to use the term "mental retardation."

Descriptive Classification of Intelligence Quotients

IQ	DESCRIPTION
180 and above	Genius
140–179	Very superior, or gifted
120–139	Superior
110–119	High average
90–109	Average, or normal
80–89	Low normal, or dull
70–79	Borderline
Below 70	Feeble-minded, or mentally retarded

You will note that in this classification IQ's from 90 to 109 are described as average, or normal. Nearly half of all individuals tested (actually $46\frac{1}{2}$ percent) have IQ's in this range. Although it is not indicated in the table, we know that about one third of all persons have IQ's between 100 and 116 and that about one third have IQ's between 84 and 100.

It is necessary to be very cautious in using a descriptive classification of IQ's. You have seen that there are no sharp divisions, or types, in the normal frequency distribution. Furthermore, the IQ is, at best, a rough measure of intelligence. It certainly would be unscientific to say that an individual with an IQ of 110 is of high

UNDERSTANDING HUMAN BEHAVIOR

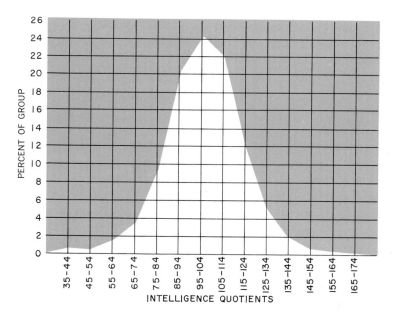

Graph of IQ distribution for 2,904 children

average intelligence, while an individual with an IQ of 109 is of only average intelligence. Such a strict classification of intellectual abilities would fail to take account of social elements such as home, school, and community. These elements are not adequately measured by present intelligence tests. Furthermore, it would not take account of the fact that an individual may vary somewhat in his test score from one testing to another.

Measures of intelligence are valuable, but much harm can be done by persons who try to classify individuals strictly on the basis of such measures alone. No one should be either alarmed or discouraged if he finds that his IQ is not as high as he might have hoped. Remember that many elements besides IQ contribute to success and happiness.

PRACTICAL APPLICATIONS OF INTELLIGENCE TESTS

The development of intelligence tests led overoptimistic persons to believe that a simple method had been found for fitting everyone into a suitable place in life. Actually, human beings are far too complicated for any simple procedure in arranging their lives. Nevertheless, on the basis of intelligence tests, many sound suggestions can be made for guidance of school and adult living.

How do schools use intelligence tests? Some schoolwork requires greater ability (either in general intelligence or in specific factors) than does other schoolwork. To give a child of high intellectual ability work requiring very little such ability is as great a mistake as to give a child of low intellectual ability

MEASURING INTELLECTUAL ABILITY

work requiring high ability. In neither case are the children happy in their work. Children need to be classified so that they may be given suitable schoolwork. With the development of group intelligence tests, it became possible to test and consequently to classify many children at one time and at relatively little cost to the schools.

Some modern group tests are so constructed that they measure not only general intelligence but also factors in intelligence. For example, verbal and nonverbal factors may be measured. In a discussion of intelligence tests, it should be noted that, strictly speaking, the term "IQ" should be used only with reference to individual tests of the Binet type. Some group tests, however, do attempt to indicate a score somewhat comparable to an IQ. Today many elementary schools, high schools, and colleges give some kind of individual or group intelligence test as part of the regular work of the school.

A psychologist is often called upon to advise parents and teachers about the school possibilities of particular children. Children with IQ's below 50 will probably never be able to do even first-grade work satisfactorily. Those with IQ's in the 50's may be able to do schoolwork through the second grade but can go no further. Children with IQ's from 60 to 65 are also very limited in their scholastic ability. No matter how long they stay in school, they cannot do satisfactory work beyond the third grade. Children with IQ's in the 70's cannot satisfactorily do higher than fourth- or fifth-grade work; those with IQ's in the 80's can probably complete the seventh and perhaps the eighth grade. Pupils with IQ's from 90 to 110 or above can do high school work, although those near the 90 mark will probably have some difficulty. Individuals with IQ's of 115 and above can do college work satisfactorily. There is even some evidence that students with IQ's in the neighborhood of 100 can do acceptable college work, especially for the first year or two, depending on the standards of the college and the willingness of the student to work hard.

Do IQ's correlate with school grades? Many studies have been made of this problem: What is the relationship between intelligence, as measured by intelligence tests, and ability to be educated, as measured by subject-matter tests and school marks? In the elementary school, psychologists have found that achievement in classwork and intelligence-test scores correlate about $+.75$. This means that, by giving an intelligence test early in the school life of a child or early in a school year, the teacher will be able to predict with considerable accuracy the quality of work the child will be able to do. Of course, the teacher will not expect so much of the child of low intelligence as she will of the child of high intelligence. Since the correlation is not perfect, however, she will have to recognize that factors other than intelligence are involved in schoolwork. Furthermore, predictions of school success should never be made on the basis of a single intelligence-test score, especially a score from a group test.

Prediction of school achievement from intelligence-test scores is less certain at the high school level than at the elementary school level. Correlations from +.60 to +.65 are usually found between high school achievement and intelligence-test scores.

There are two reasons for the correlation's being lower at the high school than at the elementary school level. One is that students of low intelligence usually drop out of school at the first opportunity. Consequently high school students form a more homogeneous group than do elementary school students; that is, there is less range in intellectual ability within the group. The majority of students at the high school level are of average or higher intellectual ability. Thus, it is harder to distinguish between them and harder to predict that one will do better than another.

A second reason for the lower correlation at the high school level is that more factors are involved in high school achievement than in elementary achievement. In elementary schools all students must learn basic facts and skills. The subjects studied are much the same for everyone. High school students have some opportunity to choose the subjects they wish to study. Consequently, interest plays a greater part in determining achievement than it does at the elementary level. The high school student has more opportunities for social life than the elementary school student. If the high school student indulges in too much social life, his school success will not be very closely related to his intellectual ability. High school students often have jobs outside school hours. If these jobs take time that should be devoted to study, the relationship between school

success and intelligence will be lessened. Students in elementary schools usually have only minor jobs, if any, aside from their schoolwork. Private lessons in music, dancing, and the like, may reduce the correlation between school achievement and intellectual ability, if these activities take a great deal of time.

At the college level, correlations between achievement in classwork and intelligence-test scores are usually found to be about +.50. The college group is even more homogeneous in intellectual ability than is the high school group. Persons not in the upper levels of intelligence usually do not attempt to go to college. Also, college students have much more freedom than high school students. If a college student does not wish to study, he does not have to do so, for the professors do not stand over him to make sure that he studies. In many cases the college student lives away from home. If he has not learned to take care of himself, he may indulge in excessive social activities or just plain loafing, because his parents are not present to make him study. Furthermore, students differ in the way they respond to the stress of college examinations. There is evidence that students who have records of good marks in college tend to improve under stress, whereas students who get poor marks show a decrease in quality of work under such pressure. Perhaps, at least to some extent, some students obtain poor marks because of the stressful nature of college examinations rather than because of lack of intellectual ability. All such factors tend to reduce the correlation between intellectual ability and school achievement.

Intelligence tests have proved to be of great value in helping teachers and administrators in their tremendously important task of guiding students. In some cases too much confidence has been placed in the score on a single test. Sometimes teachers and administrators have failed to recognize the importance for school success of the various factors in intelligence and of elements other than intellectual ability. Nevertheless, when properly used, intelligence tests are one of the major contributions of psychologists to the work of the schools.

Can intelligence tests be used in industry? Business executives sometimes ask psychologists to help them by devising and giving intelligence tests to their employees and to applicants for positions. In most cases of industrial intelligence testing, group tests are used. Although applicants may be tested one at a time as they appear, for convenience they are given group tests rather than individual tests.

One psychologist gave intelligence tests to a group of clerical workers. He compared their scores with the percentage of turnover for a period of thirty months. (*Turnover* means the rate at which employees leave jobs and are replaced by others.) The clerical work was graded into five degrees of difficulty. Grade A was the lowest grade, the work consisting simply of opening mail. Grade B work required more ability than Grade A work, Grade C required more than Grade B, and so on up to Grade E. The individuals in

Grade E work were private secretaries with very responsible positions. The percent of turnover for each grade of work was computed for individuals who had test scores of 80 points or less and for those who had scores of 110 points or more. (Note that these scores are not IQ's.) The table on page 211 indicates the results.

As you can see, persons of low intellectual ability tended to remain in the lower-grade jobs, but persons of high intellectual ability quit these jobs. On the other hand, persons of low intellectual ability tended not to remain in the higher-grade jobs, whereas those of high intellectual ability tended to keep the better jobs.

It must be admitted, however, that quite a number of studies have shown very little, if any, correlation between general intelligence and degree of proficiency or success in particular jobs. There seems to be much waste of intellectual ability in industry. The student of superior ability should resolve that he will not permit himself to be kept in a job that does not challenge his intellectual ability.

What is the relation of intelligence to vocations? Many studies have shown that, on the average, men engaged in the professions tend to have higher intelligence-test scores than men in clerical and business positions. In turn, clerical workers and businessmen tend to have higher scores than skilled laborers. Skilled laborers tend to have higher scores than semiskilled laborers. The lowest average scores are made by unskilled laborers. This relationship of intelligence to vocation was first noted

UNDERSTANDING HUMAN BEHAVIOR

**Turnover for Various Grades of Clerical Workers
of High and Low Intelligence-Test Scores**

GRADE OF WORK	PERCENT TURNOVER FOR INTELLIGENCE-TEST SCORES OF 80 POINTS OR LESS	PERCENT TURNOVER FOR INTELLIGENCE-TEST SCORES OF 110 POINTS OR MORE
A	37	100
B	62	100
C	50	72
D	58	53
E	66	41

during World War I, when soldiers were classified according to their vocations in civilian life, and intelligence-test scores for each vocation were assembled. This relationship was found to hold true in many studies made during the interval between wars. Data obtained in World War II show the same sort of pattern.

For the soldiers of World War II, the *Army General Classification Test* (AGCT) scores were analyzed according to vocational groups. From a long list of vocations, sixteen have been selected and are presented in the table on page 212. In reading this table, keep in mind that the scores are not IQ's (although the average score for all men taking the test was 100).

There was much overlapping of high and low scores among vocations. For example, one-fourth of the men preparing to be doctors had scores of 120 or lower, and one-fourth of them had scores of 135 or higher. One-fourth of the tabulating-machine operators had scores of 111 or lower. On the other hand, one-fourth of them had scores of 127 and higher — that is, equal to or higher than the average for the young medical men. One-fourth of the airplane-engine mechanics had scores of 94 or lower, yet one-fourth of them had scores of 120 or higher. That is, one-fourth of these mechanics had scores equal to or higher than the average for tabulating-machine operators and equal to or higher than the lowest fourth of the medical students.

The median scores on page 212 are *average scores*. That is, about one-half of the men in each group had scores lower than each score noted in the table, and about one-half had higher scores. Within any vocation there are various levels of proficiency. An accountant may be little more than a routine bookkeeper — or he may be a man working with the most complicated business problems. A carpenter may be a man who does little more than saw boards and drive nails — or he may be a businessman of high caliber.

There is a relationship between the kind of work a person can do successfully and his ability as measured by intelligence tests. Always remember, however, that many elements other than general intelligence are involved in success in any vocation. An individual may be appreciably below the test score average for a given vocation,

MEASURING INTELLECTUAL ABILITY

VOCATIONAL GROUP	25TH PERCENTILE	MEDIAN SCORE	75TH PERCENTILE
Accountant	123	129	137
Medical student	120	127	135
Teacher	117	124	132
Lawyer	118	124	132
Stenographer	115	122	130
Tabulating-machine operator	111	120	127
Cashier	107	117	127
Store manager	104	115	124
Toolmaker	101	112	123
Salesclerk	95	109	119
Airplane-engine mechanic	94	108	120
General carpenter	86	101	113
Light-truck driver	80	95	109
Laborer	76	93	108
Miner	75	87	103
Lumberjack	70	85	100

but if he is sufficiently enthusiastic and willing to work hard, he can be reasonably successful. As we shall explain in the last chapter, there are elements other than intellectual ability to consider when selecting your life work.

MENTAL RETARDATION

The table on page 206 indicates that individuals with IQ's below 70 are often spoken of as being mentally retarded. Measurement of the IQ alone, however, is insufficient to determine whether or not a person is mentally retarded. In fact, psychologists often try to get away from this tendency to think of mental retardation in terms of IQ. Social factors are very important in determining whether or not a given person should be classified as retarded. Nevertheless, IQ's are helpful in making a diagnosis and will be examined, along with social factors, in our study of mental retardation.

Mental retardation is a great social problem. It has been estimated that about 3 percent of the population of the United States are mentally retarded. Where are they to be found? Government reports indicate that there are only about 220,000 mentally retarded individuals being cared for and trained in institutions. Of this number, about 10,000 are in special private schools for the retarded. Unfortunately, about 48,000 of these individuals are in psychiatric hospitals rather than in special institutions for the retarded. Still other mentally retarded persons may be found in prisons, reform schools, infirmaries, and social welfare institutions.

The great majority of mentally retarded individuals are not institutionalized. There are three commonly described levels: mild, moderate, and severe retardation. People have social contacts with some higher-level retarded persons nearly every day without recognizing them as retarded.

What are the characteristics of severely retarded persons? In your everyday experiences you probably seldom see a severely retarded individual. These persons are nearly always cared for in special institutions. It is estimated that they constitute only a tiny fraction of all mentally retarded individuals. Some are so low in intellectual ability that they cannot understand the most simple statements or utter simple words. Often they cannot wash and dress themselves; some cannot learn to eat and drink or take care of their other bodily needs without assistance. If permitted to be out of institutions, they would not know enough to avoid the ordinary dangers of life. If able to walk, they would be likely to walk directly in front of speeding cars. They are custodial cases; that is, they must be cared for by others, and no amount of training will make independent, self-supporting citizens of them. Sometimes the term *profoundly retarded* is applied to those very severely retarded individuals with an IQ below 20, who show practically no response to stimulation from their environment.

Severely retarded persons are usually considered to be persons with IQ's between 20 and 34. As to their ability to answer questions on an intelligence test, the highest of them can do no better than a normal three-year-old child. That is, even though the individual may be an adult twenty or twenty-five years of age, he can do no better on an intelligence test than a normal child who is just learning to talk well.

What abilities are shown by moderately retarded persons? Moderately retarded persons have more ability to adjust to life than do severely retarded individuals. They are unable to respond in any satisfactory way to the teaching of ordinary school subjects. However, in special schools for the training of the retarded they can be taught to take care of themselves to a certain extent — to avoid the common dangers of life, to feed, dress, and wash themselves — and to help in the work of the institution — to polish floors, make beds, set tables, help in a laundry, and perform other simple routine tasks. But they must have someone watch over them all the time and tell them just how and when to do things.

After a period of training, some are able to return to their homes, provided that the parents are willing to assume the responsibility of supervising their activities. They may help with tasks in the home or do other useful work under supervision. They seldom, however, can be entirely self-supporting.

In terms of IQ, moderately retarded individuals range from about 35 to 49. As adults, their mental ages range from about four years to about seven years. More individuals are moderately retarded than are severely retarded, but the moderately retarded still constitute only a small percentage of all mentally retarded persons.

What are mildly retarded persons like? Persons who have IQ's ranging from about 50 to about 70 are usually considered mildly retarded. The great majority of all mentally retarded persons are in this group. Many of them are not in institutions but are abroad in the community. The mental ages of adult mildly retarded persons are usually between eight and twelve years.

Mildly retarded children are unable to progress normally in ordinary schools. In special ungraded classes and after much time and effort, they may learn to read, to write or print, and to do simple arithmetic problems. Ordinarily, they are not able to progress beyond the level of the fourth grade, no matter how long they remain in school.

Can a mildly retarded person live as a self-supporting citizen? In schools designed to help them, mildly retarded persons can be trained so that they are able to return to their home communities and take their places in society as self-supporting citizens. Of course, they can never become professional

The drawings below provide some idea of the different levels of mental retardation. They were done by three mentally retarded individuals, each of whom was asked to draw a person. The figure at the left was drawn by a severely retarded twenty-three-year-old man. The center picture is the work of a moderately retarded twenty-six-year-old woman. The picture at the right, which is the most lifelike of the three, was drawn by a mildly retarded eighteen-year-old man.

people or business leaders. They can, however, earn their living as domestic servants, farm hands (not farmers), day laborers, routine factory hands, and so on.

Unfortunately, citizens of the community do not always give the mentally retarded individual a fair chance to earn a living. A case in point is that of a young man who had been trained to do farm work in a school for the retarded. Then the school found a farmer who needed someone to help with the chores and do other jobs around the farm. The young man was placed on "convalescent leave" and went to live with and work for the farmer.

All went well for a while. His work was satisfactory, and he was happy. Sometimes on Saturday afternoons he went to a small town nearby for a little recreation. In time, people in the town learned that he had been in a school for the mentally retarded, and some of the town loafers (probably not too far from being retarded themselves) began to tease him and call him such names as "dummy" and "fool." The young man resented this treatment, and he cannot be blamed for wanting to retaliate a bit. However, the resulting minor disturbance was blamed entirely on him. Not long afterward, he was sent back to the school for the retarded. The farmer lost a good hand, the young man lost his pleasant noninstitutional life, and the citizens of the state lost money, for they had to pay taxes to keep the young man in the institution.

You should question the motives of those who tease retarded or dull individuals. Probably those who do the

teasing feel inferior in their own accomplishments. It gives them a certain amount of satisfaction to find someone who is even "dumber" than they are. They enjoy a temporary feeling of superiority when they mock and torment a retarded person.

Do mildly retarded persons make good social adjustments? Some adults with IQ's in the 60's are able to make their way in their home communities, though they are probably thought of as dull or "odd." Other persons with IQ's in the 70's have to be removed from the community and placed in institutions. Why must one individual be institutionalized when he has a higher IQ than does an individual who is not institutionalized? Much depends upon emotional stability. Some mildly retarded persons are well-behaved, fairly industrious, and inoffensive, while others are easily upset and are constantly getting into social trouble. The well-behaved have adjusted sufficiently to remain in the community, but for the good of society, the less well-controlled individuals must be placed in institutions.

How well a mildly retarded individual adjusts socially depends in large part upon the home. Many dull or mildly retarded children and young persons are committed to institutions because parents are unable or unwilling to help them. Others just as dull may be loved and cared for in their homes. Hence, they never have to be institutionalized, at least as long as the parents or brothers and sisters live. There is no substitute for a good home. Nevertheless, friends and so-

Mildly retarded children can help do household chores. A mentally retarded boy (left) dries the dishes with his younger, normal, brother.

cial agencies can do much to help mildly retarded and dull individuals adjust to their environments.

Sometimes mildly retarded individuals run afoul of the law. Because they may not be capable of understanding moral and legal obligations or of foreseeing the consequences of their actions, they may commit a crime. Also, they are often anxious to please others or to feel important, and they may be persuaded by an unscrupulous person to break the law. It is entirely wrong, however, to conclude that all retarded persons are criminals. In fact, many such individuals strive in their simple way to be honest, law-abiding citizens.

In an earlier day the terms "idiot," "imbecile," and "moron" were used to refer roughly to what we have called severe, moderate, and mild retardation, respectively. These earlier classification terms were often based primarily on IQ rather than including important social adjustment. Furthermore, these earlier terms have come to have unfortunate connotations. As a result, psychologists tend not to use them today.

What can mentally retarded persons learn? In recent years educators have become more aware of the possibilities of providing special classes for the mentally retarded.

Classes for mildly retarded individuals deal primarily with programs emphasizing social skills, the use of money, and the development of simple occupational skills. Such classes are designed for the mentally retarded who are "educable." These persons are capable of learning some of the simple processes involved in such subjects as reading and arithmetic.

Classes for the moderately retarded have more limited objectives, although as adults these persons can be taught to take care of themselves and to work in unskilled or semiskilled occupations with supervision.

The severely retarded can be taught, as adults, to maintain some self-care under constant supervision; that is, they are "trainable." Some experimental data from recent studies indicate that operant conditioning procedures may be used to some extent to train the severely retarded.

The profoundly retarded may develop some motor and speech abilities, but they are incapable of self-help and need complete care and supervision even in adult life.

Since more emphasis today is being placed on the social aspects of the retarded person, there are more programs for educating and training such persons for self-help and, if possible, for the utilization of abilities in unskilled or semiskilled occupations. The goal is to equip the individual to lead a more constructive life in the community. Such procedures represent a considerable advance from the days when mentally retarded persons were put into an institution where very little attempt was made to train or educate them.

With further strides in the methods of training and educating retarded persons, perhaps more such individuals will be able to live in society as constructive citizens.

Are the causes of mental retardation known? For what reasons are millions of Americans mentally retarded? At the present time there are more than one hundred known or suspected causes of mental retardation, yet it is very difficult and sometimes impossible to determine the precise causes in a specific case. Although mental retardation does run in families, and many medical men and psychologists believe that heredity is the basic factor in causing mental retardation, there are other known causes. Some of these other known causes are related to environmental factors. We shall learn more about heredity and environment in the following chapter.

Injury before, during, or shortly after birth is responsible for some cases of retardation. Toxic agents, such as carbon monoxide and lead, may lead to brain damage in an unborn child. Biochemical factors, genetic-chromosomal factors, and premature birth cause some of the other cases of mental retardation. If, early in her pregnancy, the mother develops a syphilitic or other infection, such as measles, she may have a retarded child. Also, certain glandular deficiencies are present in some mentally retarded persons. Yet, despite all these possible causes, in many cases the specific cause of mental retardation is unknown.

Mental retardation, especially at the severe and moderate levels, may appear in any family even though there are no known cases of it in the family history. The presence of such a child in an otherwise normal or superior family is tragic, but the child should never be considered a disgrace. If some member of the family is blind, deaf, or crippled, he is not considered a disgrace — he is helped and treated with sympathy. The same help and sympathy must be given to an individual who is mentally retarded.

Can mental retardation be cured? Although much can be done through training retarded persons, there is at present no known way of "curing" those who have serious brain damage. Drugs, individual psychotherapy, and special education programs are useful in helping the mentally retarded to make a better adjustment in their social life, but these procedures are not designed to cure the disorder. Administration of thyroxin (the active hormone of the thyroid gland) has produced, in some cases, significant improvement of a specific type of mental retardation (cretinism). Also, surgical techniques have been devised for treating hydrocephalus, a condition in which an abnormal amount of fluid in the brain results in an extremely large head. Special diets have brought about an improvement of some cases of phenylketonuria (fen'əl·kē·tōn·yŏŏr'ē·ə) (PKU), which is caused by the lack of a certain chemical substance in the body. Early diagnosis is extremely important if treatment is to be of maximum value in those cases where a treatment exists that can help. Within recent years there has been progress with mental retardation. Hopefully, future psychological and medical research will enable us to improve the condition of retarded persons much beyond what is possible at present.

SUPERIOR INTELLIGENCE

Individuals of very superior intelligence are correctly termed abnormal, as are mentally retarded persons. The "gifted" are above the average, while the mentally retarded are below the average. Psychologists make even less attempt to classify persons of very superior intelligence than they make to classify mentally retarded persons. The term *gifted* is often applied, however, to the six persons in a thousand who have IQ's of 140 or more. At the far reaches of this group is the one person in a million with an IQ of 180 or more who is spoken of as a *genius*.

In what way do some individuals show their intellectual superiority as children? Just as mental retardation is often apparent very early in life, so is intellectual superiority. Studies that have been made of the early lives of men who have become prominent indicate that in many cases these persons showed remarkable intellectual ability as children. For example, Charles Dickens was reading such books as *Robinson Crusoe, Don Quixote,* and *The Vicar of Wakefield* before he was seven years old.

A well-known Swiss psychologist, Jean Piaget (pē·ə·jā'), at the age of ten wrote a short article that was published in a natural history journal. In his early teens he began a series of authoritative

UNDERSTANDING HUMAN BEHAVIOR

articles on local mollusks, and at nineteen he wrote a philosophical novel that was later published.

Sir Francis Galton, a nineteenth-century English scientist of great brilliance, could pick out and name the capital letters when he was twelve months old. He could identify both capitals and small letters at the age of eighteen months. By the age of thirty months he read a book, and at three years he could sign his name. The day before his fifth birthday, he wrote the following letter to his sister:

My dear Adele:
I am 4 years old and I can read any English book. I can say all the Latin Substantives and Adjectives and active verbs besides 52 lines of Latin poetry. I can cast up any sum in addition and can multiply by 2, 3, 4, 5, 6, 7, 8, 9, 10, 11.
I can also say the pence table. I read French a little and I know the clock.

Francis Galton
Febuary 15, 1827

Perhaps this letter shows a bit of childish bragging. Francis himself realized that he might have overstated his ability a bit, for in the original letter he crossed out the 9 and 11 in the list of numbers he could multiply. Nevertheless, we must recognize that Galton was a genius. Compare this letter with one "written" by an average child at about the time of his fifth birthday. It is true that Galton misspelled "February," but high school students have often made the identical error. If Galton could have been tested by modern means, his IQ would probably have been about 200.

One of the authors once tested a six-year-old boy with an IQ of 175. Despite his age, this young man was collecting butterflies, mounting them in a professional collection box, and labeling them with their Latin names. He accomplished this entirely on his own, using a university library to find the correct names of the butterflies. Some of the answers he gave to questions on the *Revised Stanford-Binet* were correctly given in Spanish. It turned out that he was in his first year of studying Spanish and doing excellent work. Upon further questioning, it was found that he was learning Spanish from his older sister; she was seven years old and in her second year of Spanish, which she was studying on her own with the aid of Spanish phonograph records. The sister, who was tested by a different examiner at the same time as her brother, had an IQ of 176.

Is the gifted child superior in all ways? Children of very superior intelligence are popularly supposed to be frail, sickly, maladjusted in schoolwork, and hard to get along with. Lewis M. Terman, with other psychologists' cooperation, made an extensive study of one thousand children of very superior intelligence. Terman found that, as a rule, mentally superior children are also physically superior. For example, he found that on the average they are taller and heavier and have greater lung capacity, greater width of shoulders, and greater muscular strength than other children of their ages. Sometimes it is said that children of very superior intelligence do not do well in schoolwork, or possibly do well in only one subject. Terman found that 85 percent of his superior group were further along in school than most children of their ages. None of the superior group were held back in school. Their schoolwork tended to be of superior quality in all lines of study rather than in just one line. The superior children read on a wide range of topics, especially on science, history, travel, biography, informational fiction, poetry, and drama. As a rule, their social interests were normal, and they were not regarded as peculiar by their fellow students and friends.

Sometimes it is said that children of very superior intelligence do not live up to the promise of their childhood and become inferior in ability and even mentally ill as they mature. Terman kept in touch with individuals of this superior group and found that they continued to be superior as they grew older. Many of them entered the professions. They went far in formal education, 48 percent of the men and 27 percent of the women obtaining advanced academic degrees (higher than the bachelor's degree obtained after four years of college work). They wrote books and magazine articles. They married and evidently lived happily, for their divorce rate was lower than for the general public. The percentage who became mentally ill was lower than for the population as a whole. They made good, or at least comfortable, salaries.

Unfortunately, society often does not pay as much attention to its very superior children and adults as it does to mentally retarded persons. In many schools superior children are forced to waste a good deal of time while the remainder of the class catches up with them. They are often much more neglected (in terms of their potentialities) than are dull children. In adult life superior individuals often have to spend a large part of their time in relatively trivial tasks in order to make a living rather than spending this time doing work more in keeping with their abilities and more profitable for society.

Do students of superior ability live up to their potentials? In one research study, high school students of superior intellectual ability (all with IQ's over 110) were studied in order to learn whether or not their school achievements were as high as could be reasonably expected of them. They were divided into two groups on the basis of their high school records. One group was designated as "underachievers" because each member had a grade-point average below the mean of his class. The other group was designated as "achievers" because each member had a grade-point average above the mean of his class. There were more boys than girls classified as underachievers.

Following the selection of students in these two groups, their academic records were traced from the time each had entered the first grade. For the boys, data indicated that the underachievers, as compared with the achievers, had been obtaining grades below their ability since the first grade. For girls, the data indicated that the underachievers, as compared with the achievers, had been obtaining grades significantly below their ability level since the ninth grade and had tended to do so since the sixth grade.

UNDERSTANDING HUMAN BEHAVIOR

In another research study, female college students who earned higher grades than might be expected of them in terms of their intellectual abilities were compared with students who earned grades lower than might be expected of them. The overachievers, as compared to the underachievers, were found to have stronger motivation for studying. They tended to be more self-confident and to have greater capacity for working under pressure. The underachievers showed a marked tendency to procrastinate, to rely upon external pressures to make them complete their assignments, and to be critical of educational methods.

The results of one other study on intellectual achievement indicated that underachievers were less desirous of continuing their education, had more withdrawal tendencies, were more antisocial than the average student, and came from families with a lower educational level and fewer books. Overachievers, on the other hand, tended to like mathematics and to come from homes where family members attended church more frequently.

According to most studies of underachievement and overachievement, approximately 10 to 15 percent of a school population is underachieving, although the specific percentage depends largely upon which method is used to select individuals as underachievers. From the data just given on underachievers, however, do not assume that underachievement causes the various tendencies mentioned; the tendencies may either result from or be caused by underachievement. What does seem apparent is that individuals

Children who are given an opportunity to have varied experiences often develop new interests and are stimulated to learn.

who come from homes which stimulate them to achieve, to be motivated, and to continue their education have distinct advantages over those individuals who come from homes where this stimulation is lacking.

MEASURING INTELLECTUAL ABILITY

Terms to Add to Your Vocabulary

average score
chronological age
educable
genius
gifted
intelligence
intelligence quotient

median
mental age
mental (intellectual) ability
mental retardation
mildly retarded
moderately retarded
performance test

profoundly retarded
Revised Stanford-Binet
severely retarded
trainable
Wechsler Adult Intelligence Scale
Wechsler Intelligence Scale
    for Children

Suggestions for Activities

1. Review the seven primary factors of intelligence given in this chapter. Consult references listed for further information on these factors. Make up a short test consisting of two or three items for each factor, which you believe might measure the factors. Remember, however, that your "test" is not really an intelligence test and may not measure the factors. Nevertheless, try out your questions on several persons just to note individual differences in responses.

2. Consult several references given at the end of this chapter and find more specific and detailed information on the construction of the Stanford-Binet tests. Make a report on your findings.

3. If convenient, have a psychologist administer at least part of a Stanford-Binet or other individual intelligence test to some child. For professional reasons, the psychologist would not be able to give you the child's IQ. But you would learn something of how such tests are given and of the skill required to use them.

4. Your teacher may be able to arrange for you to score a few group tests that have been administered to children in elementary school. If so, the children's papers should be identified by numbers rather than by names. Make up distribution graphs of the resulting scores. Attempt to interpret the scores, always keeping in mind the limitations of your training. Do not take tests out of the classroom or show them to anyone not in your psychology class!

5. If your school has a counselor, psychologist, or guidance teacher, make an appointment and ask what tests are given in your school and how the results are used in the school. Ask particularly about intelligence tests.

6. Find out if your city or town has special education programs for the mentally retarded. If possible, determine what criteria are used in selecting individuals to participate in the programs. Also, you might wish to find out what training or care for the mentally retarded your state provides.

7. If it can be arranged, visit a school for the mentally retarded in order to see how these people are cared for and trained.

8. Someone in the class might write to the Superintendent of Documents, U.S. Government Printing Office, Washington, D.C. 20402, for the most recent book entitled *Patients in Mental Institutions,* U.S. Department of Commerce, Bureau of the Census. This

UNDERSTANDING HUMAN BEHAVIOR

book offers a wealth of statistics on the mentally retarded. National and separate state statistics are given. Members of the class can make many interesting graphs from data in this book. The book can be used again when you study Chapter 15, "Mental Illness."

9. Write a theme on the life of some great scientist or other person who can be classed as a genius. Note especially evidences of superior intellectual ability in childhood.

10. Write a frank evaluation of yourself as a student. Do you believe that you are an underachiever or an overachiever? Are you "in a rut"? Do you like to study (most of the time)? Do your teachers have to use pressure in order to get you to study? Are you self-confident? Do you tend to procrastinate? Are you frequently critical of the school in general and of certain teachers? Do you "blow up" on examinations so that you don't do as well as you are capable of doing? You may have taken one or more group intelligence tests, or even an individual test, although probably you were not told your score. Do you think such tests really measured your potentialities?

Suggestions for Further Reading

Byrne, Katharine M., and John Byrne, *You and Your Mental Abilities*, Science Research Associates.

Daniel, Robert S., ed., *Contemporary Readings in General Psychology*, 2nd ed., Houghton Mifflin. Part IV, "Behavior Is Variable," consists of eight articles, of which the following are recommended; pages 127–32, National Education Association, "Your Child's Intelligence"; pages 140–42, Leonard Carmichael, "Are the Sexes Really Equal?"; pages 146–51, Sidney L. Pressey, "Concerning the Nature and Nurture of Genius."

Hilgard, Ernest R., and Richard C. Atkinson, *Introduction to Psychology*, 4th ed., Harcourt, Brace & World. Chapter 16, "Ability Testing and Intelligence."

Leuba, Clarence, *Man: A General Psychology*, Holt, Rinehart & Winston. Pages 492–500, "Intelligence Tests"; pages 514–16, "Changes with Age in Intellectual and Learning Abilities"; pages 561–63, "The Mentally Deficient."

Lindgren, Henry C., Donn Byrne, and Lewis F. Petrinovich, *Psychology: An Introduction to a Behavioral Science*, John Wiley. Chapter 10, "Intelligence and Creativity."

McKeachie, Wilbert J., and Charlotte L. Doyle, *Psychology*, Addison-Wesley. Pages 353–63, "Individual Differences in Problem Solving."

Munn, Norman L., *Psychology*, 5th ed., Houghton Mifflin. Chapter 5, "Intelligence."

Ruch, Floyd L., *Psychology and Life*, 7th ed., Scott, Foresman. Pages 153–70, "Traditional Means of Testing Intelligence," "Primary Mental Abilities," and "The Determinants of Intelligence."

Sanford, Fillmore H., *Psychology: A Scientific Study of Man*, 2nd ed., Wadsworth. Chapter 7, "Intelligence."

Seidman, Jerome, ed., *The Adolescent: A Book of Readings*, rev. ed., Holt, Rinehart & Winston. Pages 184–98, "A New Look at the Curve of Intelligence"; pages 198–217, "Three Faces of Intellect"; pages 823–33, "The Gifted Group at Mid-Life: Fulfillment of Promise."

Spencer, Lyle M., and Ruth Dunbar, *Making the Most of Your Intelligence*, Science Research Associates.

Whittaker, James O., et al., *Introduction to Psychology*, W. B. Saunders. Pages 458–75, "Intelligence."

Witty, Paul, *Helping the Gifted Child*, Science Research Associates.

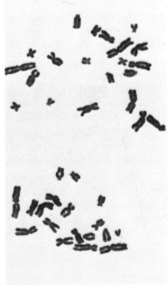

PATTERNS OF BEHAVIOR

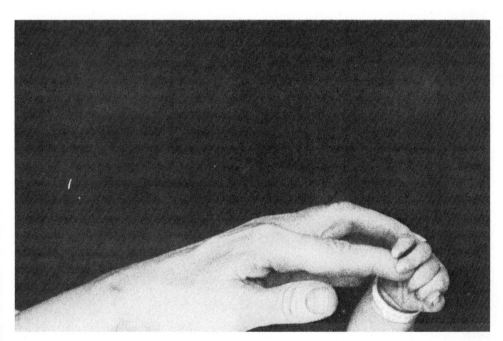

9

Heredity and environment

Billy has been warned repeatedly concerning his misconduct in school. The teacher has now decided to ask Billy's mother to come in and talk over the situation with her in an effort to arrive at an understanding of—and with—Billy. The mother admits that Billy's behavior is not what she would like it to be. Then she confides to the teacher, "Poor boy, he comes by it naturally; everyone on his father's side of the family is like that." If it is Billy's father who comes to school, the observation will probably be, "Poor boy, he comes by it naturally; everyone on his mother's side of the family is like that." Both parents are accounting for Billy's present behavior by his heredity—although there is disagreement concerning which side of his ancestry is responsible for his good traits and which for his bad traits.

Or the parents may say, "Oh, yes! We know Billy is bad. But all the other children in the neighborhood are bad, and Billy learns his naughtiness from them." That is, they account for Billy's present behavior in terms of his environment rather than in terms of his heredity.

HEREDITY OR ENVIRONMENT?

The question is often asked, "Which is the more important factor in the development of the individual, his heredity or his environment?" Is he to be understood more in terms of what he has received biologically from his ancestors, or more in terms of the external forces, conditions, and influences that surround him and affect his activities? Although you may hear the problem expressed in terms of nature and nurture instead of heredity and environment, the meaning is the same. Psychologists have been very much interested in this question and have done a great deal of work in trying to answer it. Let us look at some of the evidence.

What are Mendel's laws of heredity? Often it is said of a child, "He is the very picture of his father (or mother)." This remark implies that in some way he has inherited outstanding physical features from one side of his family or the other. How does this inheritance take place?

Gregor Mendel, an abbot in Moravia

(later included in Czechoslovakia), was very much interested in this problem and carried out a series of experiments in his monastery garden. During a period of eight years, he observed more than 10,000 specimens of garden peas and recorded his observations. When his results were published in 1866, little attention was paid to these important findings. Since then, however, scientists have found a great deal to say about the famous Mendelian laws of heredity.

Mendel spoke of the separate features of parents as *unit characters*. He said that unit characters are passed on to children independently and as wholes, sometimes becoming apparent in the first generation, sometimes not appearing until later generations. Characteristics that appear in all individuals of the first generation of descendants are said to be *dominant* characteristics. Those which are latent and do not appear in the first generation of descendants, although they may appear in subsequent generations, are said to be *recessive* characteristics. A few dominant and recessive characteristics in man are as follows:

DOMINANT	RECESSIVE
Brown eyes	Blue eyes
Curly hair	Straight hair
Dark hair	Light hair
Dark skin	Light skin

Mendel's law may be seen operating in domestic animals. For example, if a rose-comb black bantam is crossed with a rose-comb white bantam, all the offspring of the first generation will be black. (For this kind of chicken, black is dominant and white is recessive.)

Now if these black offspring are crossed, part of their offspring will be black and part will be white, the ratio of black to white being approximately three to one. That is, the hereditary units ultimately reappear without change, even though there is an apparent absence of these characteristics in the generation of the first cross. It should be added that sometimes a characteristic is neither dominant nor recessive. For example, there is a species of poultry in which the mating of a black with a splashed-white fowl produces blue offspring. In human beings we find blue-eyed children born to parents both of whom have brown eyes. We know, therefore, that somewhere in the ancestry of the blue-eyed child there were blue eyes and that this characteristic has been passed down from one generation to another as a recessive characteristic. Remember that as far as physical appearance is concerned, it is impossible to distinguish between persons who have "pure" brown eyes and persons who have brown eyes but carry recessive determiners for blue eyes. The laws of heredity are complicated; for further information on them, turn to a text in biology.

How are characteristics passed on from one generation to another? In reproduction the female contributes an egg cell (ovum), and the male contributes a sperm cell, or spermatozoon (spûr′mə·tə·zō′on). Although the egg cell is very, very small (smaller than a period on this page), it is still many times larger than the sperm cell. When a sperm cell enters an egg cell, fertilization occurs.

HEREDITY AND ENVIRONMENT

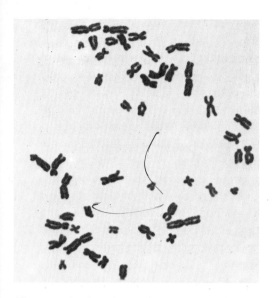

These are human chromosomes, magnified 2,000 times. Ordinarily each human cell contains 46 chromosomes. A new individual inherits 23 from each parent.

What are chromosomes and genes? Most cells of the body contain rod-shaped "colored bodies" called *chromosomes* (krō′mə·sōms). There is evidence that 46 chromosomes exist in each cell. These chromosomes are in pairs. Prior to fertilization, the number of chromosomes in the egg and sperm cells segregate so that one of each pair finds itself in different daughter cells; the net effect of this is that each sperm and egg contains 23 chromosomes. When the sperm fertilizes the egg, the fertilized egg cell contains 46 chromosomes, or 23 pairs. By a process of cell division, more and more cells are formed. Each new cell in the human species normally contains 46 chromosomes. In other species, the number of chromosomes in each cell is different from the number in the human species;

for example, the crayfish has 100 pairs; the moth, 31 pairs; the salamander, 14 pairs; the mosquito, 6 pairs. Recent investigations have revealed that approximately 95 percent of all mongoloids have 47 chromosomes instead of the usual 46. Thus, a study of chromosomes as they relate to mongolism suggests that possession of an extra chromosome may even be responsible for this type of mental retardation. Chromosomes often provide an explanation of some physical irregularity present at birth.

It was thought for a while that heredity could be understood in terms of combinations of the chromosomes. It is now known that heredity is far too complicated to be explained in such simple terms. Scientists now speak of tiny parts within each chromosome called *genes* (jēns). The term "genetics," which stands for the branch of biology dealing with the scientific investigation of the mechanisms of heredity, comes from the word "genes." In the human species there are probably at least a thousand genes in each of the 46 chromosomes. An individual's genetic make-up for any characteristic is called a genotype (jen′ə·tīp). A *genotype* refers either to the sum of all the biological characteristics that an individual is capable of transmitting to his or her offspring, or to a single such characteristic. Thus, if one parent contributes a gene for blue eyes and the other parent contributes a gene for brown eyes, the fertilized egg contains brown-blue as a genotype for eye color. The actual, observable characteristic which an individual manifests is called a *phenotype* (fē′nə·tīp). Thus, although an individual's genotype for eye color is brown-blue, his actual eye color or phenotype will be brown. If the pair of genes an individual receives from his parents differ, the one which always wins out (and therefore becomes the phenotype) is said to be dominant, the one which does not exhibit itself is said to be recessive.

How do genes determine your biological development?

In recent years new evidence has been discovered on genes and the specific procedures of how a single cell ultimately develops into an extremely complex adult being. The primary chemical which seems to be the basis for all genetic action is called *deoxyribonucleic* (dē·ok′sē·rī′bō·nōō·klē′ik) *acid* (DNA). This substance is found in the nucleus of every cell in all living organisms. DNA is responsible for forming another similar chemical known as *ribonucleic* (rī′bō·nōō·klē′ik) *acid* (RNA). In some as yet unknown way DNA gives special "hereditary instructions" for the cellular development of the organism, and these instructions are partially carried out by RNA. What results is the development of all the cells of the body, some of which make up the hands, others the brain, still others the nerves, and so on.

Although the processes of DNA and RNA are not yet fully understood and in any case cannot be discussed at length in this text, perhaps a rough analogy will help you to understand the extreme complexity of heredity. Compare a single cell of one person to a large business that would employ every living person in the world today. The business is run by one person (compa-rable to DNA), who gives orders. The orders are followed in a precise way and at the exact time they are supposed to be carried out. The boss gives instructions to subordinates, without whom the work could not be done, and they in turn carry instructions elsewhere. Although some of the instructions are to be carried out immediately and others may have to be delayed for months, all must be carried out exactly how and when they should be; otherwise the result may be ruinous to part of the company, or to the entire business. In biological development, if the instructions are not obeyed, the result may be a deformed arm, green rather than blue eyes, mental deficiency, or death. Since the average adult is made up of billions of cells, having different functions, all of which receive instructions for development from DNA, you can see that the process is very complicated indeed.

The potential importance of the discovery of both DNA and RNA is that once we know how these substances give instructions and how the instructions are carried out, we may be able to correct faulty growth in mankind. For instance, we may eventually be able to correct inherited abnormalities.

Actually each human father has genes which can combine in several million different ways, as does each mother. The genes of both can be theoretically combined in over one hundred thousand billion different ways. Unless you are an identical twin, probably no other person in the world has or ever had your genetic make-up. No one exactly like you will ever read the words on this or any other page with

HEREDITY AND ENVIRONMENT

precisely the same background that you have. In other words, you are literally a unique individual. The biological and environmental factors which have combined to make you a unique person are so complex as to be almost unbelievable.

Do we inherit characteristics from our parents or from remote ancestors? It is customary to say that parents reproduce themselves in their children, but in terms of biological heredity, it is not correct. When a man and a wife have children, they do not reproduce themselves. They merely pass on to their children some of those characteristics which they received from their parents, and so on back through all the generations of life. Therefore, it is not strictly correct to speak of a child as inheriting tallness, musical ability, or any other specific trait from his parents. The genes within the chromosomes within the reproductive cells are not believed to be changed by the individual carrying them. Instead, parents transmit to their children, unchanged, genes which they have inherited from their own parents.

A characteristic acquired by parents themselves and not possessed by preceding generations is not transmitted by heredity. A man and his wife may have spent years in the serious study of music, yet their child will not know one note from another—unless he is taught, just as other children are taught whose parents were not musicians. One biologist cut off the tails of mice for twenty generations, yet each new litter of mice appeared with full-length tails. For generations Chinese women bound

their feet; but each baby—girl or boy—was born with normal feet.

Whenever we say that a child inherits such-and-such characteristics from his father, we mean from the ancestors on his father's side. If a father and child, or a mother and child, look alike, it is because they have a common ancestry rather than because the parent in some way reproduces his appearance in the child. We can say that a child inherits characteristics from his parents only if we mean that the parents were the immediate carriers of the characteristics of their ancestors.

Does the mother influence the unborn child? There is a very common superstition that the thoughts of a pregnant woman affect the unborn baby she is carrying in her body. It is said that if the mother reads good literature, the child will of necessity have literary ability; that if the mother reads crime stories and sees crime movies, the child is likely to become a criminal. It is said that if the mother looks intently at strawberries, the child will be born with a red spot, which—by a stretch of the imagination—may appear to be a picture of a strawberry. All these ideas are groundless. Scientists know that there is absolutely no connection between the nervous system of the mother and the nervous system of the fetus developing in her body.

This statement does not mean that the mother has no influence on the developing baby. Although the blood of the mother does not flow through the veins of the child, some things do pass from the mother to the child. Some disease germs, such as those of diphthe-

PATTERNS OF BEHAVIOR

ria, typhoid, and syphilis, may succeed in passing from the body of the mother to the body of the child. It is believed by some biologists that if the mother worries a great deal or has a severe emotional shock, the chemicals formed in her body as a result of this worry or shock may be carried to and affect her unborn child. Of course, the health of the mother affects the health of the developing child; if the mother damages her health, by excessive use of alcohol, for example, the child is affected. Poisons in the mother's system or narcotics like opium or morphine in excessive doses may also cause damage to the child.

Such influences as these are of environment and not of heredity. They may affect the child long before his birth, but his heredity was complete at conception. After conception, for nine months the child lives in the limited environment of the mother's body.

Birth itself is only an incident in life; it is not the beginning of life. Conditions at the time of birth may, however, have a great influence on the infant's later life. The infant may be damaged in the birth process. Research at a medical school gives some indication that very rapid births or births in which the infant is deprived of oxygen for a time (anoxia) may result in damage which causes the child's IQ to be lower than that of a child born under more normal conditions. Since, however, the medical school also found that some children of well above normal intellectual ability were born under these adverse conditions, it concluded that parents need not be overanxious in cases of unusual birth conditions.

If you are especially interested in biology, you will wish to study more about reproduction and the laws of heredity. For our purposes it is not necessary to go into a further discussion of the biology of heredity. Instead, we shall turn to some of the studies of heredity that are particularly important for the science of psychology.

STUDIES EMPHASIZING THE IMPORTANCE OF HEREDITY

One way to study the effects of heredity is to trace a family tree. It is sometimes assumed that whatever similarity there is among members of a family is largely due to common heredity. Many studies of family histories have been made. We shall investigate to what degree the results of these studies are scientific.

What do animal experiments show? First, let us look at an experiment with subhuman animals. One psychologist took 142 rats at random and set them the task of learning to run through a maze in order to secure food. He found that the rats differed greatly in ability, just as human beings differ in ability. Some rats entered as few as seven or eight blind alleys. Others, with no greater opportunity to make errors, made as many as 214 entrances into blind alleys. Thus, it seemed that some rats were more intelligent than others.

The psychologist segregated the bright rats and let them mate and then permitted the mediocre and dull rats to mate. This selective breeding went on for eight generations. Descendants of the original bright rats always bred with other descendants of the original bright rats; dull and mediocre rats always bred with other descendants of the original dull and mediocre rats. By the end of the eight generations, there was practically no overlapping of the two lines of descendants so far as ability to learn a maze was concerned. That is, the descendants of the original bright rats were very bright; the descendants of the dull and mediocre rats were very dull. The dullest of the bright group was about as bright as the brightest of the dull group.

Selective breeding was continued through the eighteenth generation but resulted in no greater differences than those found in the eighth generation. Then the bright and the dull rats were mated. The offspring, when tested in the maze, showed a distribution much like that with which the experiment began. That is, there were some dull rats and some bright rats, but most of the rats were in between the extremes.

This experiment is very impressive, but the data must be interpreted with caution. Further experimentation with the two strains of rats revealed that the bright rats were much more active than the dull rats, thus achieving higher scores. Possibly it was this capacity for activity which was transmitted from one generation to the next rather than a general intellectual ability. When the two strains of rats were tested on a variety of other learning tasks not so dependent upon mere activity, the bright rats were not necessarily bright nor were the dull rats necessarily dull. In a more recent experiment, however, a maze was used in which scores were not so directly related to activity, and

breeding was more carefully controlled. Nevertheless, in a few generations there was a distinct separation of the scores made by the bright strain as compared with the scores made by the dull strain. From these and other animal experiments, it seems clear that learning capacities are inherited to some extent.

Although such experiments cannot be carried out with human beings, it is possible to work backward and study interesting family trees.

What do studies of human families show? There was a time when psychologists and sociologists placed a great deal of confidence in studies which have been made of family trees. These studies were often quoted as "proof" of the great importance of heredity. In them, the descendants of selected families were traced through a number of generations. It was found that when one or both parents were considered mentally retarded, they tended to produce a larger percentage of mentally retarded children than would be expected in the general population. Conversely, tracings of the family trees of unusually intelligent couples have resulted in descendants who became top public officials, college professors, lawyers, physicians, and clergymen.

Are studies of family trees scientific proof of the importance of heredity? At first glance, tracings of family trees seem to indicate that heredity plays almost an all-important part in the development of any individual. Certainly, heredity is important, but there are at

PATTERNS OF BEHAVIOR

least three reasons why such studies are no longer considered of great scientific value.

1. The men making these studies were not always as scientific as they should have been in collecting their data. In many cases they depended upon hearsay rather than upon carefully collected facts.

2. There was a tendency to omit cases that did not prove the point. For example, all undesirable members of a family with some history of mental retardation were noted with care, but not so much attention was paid to the normal or superior members of the family.

3. Probably the most serious criticism of these studies is that no account was taken of environment. That is, the children of unusually bright or unusually dull parents grew up in that particular environment. Would the results have been the same if, in some way, exceptionally intelligent children could have been raised in the homes of mentally retarded families?

Because of the many uncontrolled variables in the tracing of family trees, these studies are not regarded as scientific evidence today.

Are there practical applications for controlling heredity? In a province in northern Italy, there existed for many years an excessive number of mentally retarded persons of a certain kind. Then, beginning in 1890, these mentally retarded persons were prevented from marrying. Within twenty years this form of mental retardation had almost disappeared from the province. Although this study was not made with the scientific care used in the study of

Assume that the figure below represents a hypothetical family's genetic make-up for hair color. Assume, too, that black represents the dominant gene, dark hair, and that gray represents the recessive gene, light hair. What, then, is the genotype for hair color for each member of the family? What is the phenotype for each? (Answers appear on page 234.)

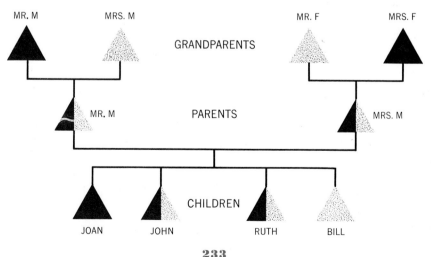

rats which we noted on pages 231–32, it does show the great importance of heredity.

Eugenics (yōō·jen'iks) is the science dealing with methods for improving the hereditary qualities of a species, especially of the human species. One method some eugenicists advocate is the method described above – that of preventing defective people from reproducing. Some states in the United States now have laws providing for the sterilization of certain defective people, so that they cannot reproduce. Others interested in eugenics try to educate the public to the value of choosing marriage partners with good hereditary background.

Eugenics is a controversial subject – one in which legal, social, and religious as well as scientific attitudes enter. You should be reminded, however, of our discussion of mental retardation in Chapter 8, in which you learned that some married couples of normal or superior intelligence may produce a mentally retarded child, since many defective characteristics are recessive. Eugenics could not control these cases.

Also, as mentioned in our discussion of family trees, we cannot be sure to what extent defective characteristics are hereditary unless we are able to control environmental factors.

Much research in the area of human heredity still needs to be done. Per-haps some of you will be geneticists and will contribute to this research.

STUDIES EMPHASIZING THE IMPORTANCE OF ENVIRONMENT

It is impossible to go around taking children out of their homes and putting them in other homes in order to see what effect another environment will have on them. But sometimes children are raised in homes other than those of their biological parents. Psychologists have made careful studies of some of these cases. As was pointed out in Chapter 8, the IQ tends to remain constant, but changes in environment can have some influence on IQ.

Can a change in home conditions cause a change in IQ? In one case a study was made of twenty-six children in an orphanage. This particular orphanage was conducted with little thought for the welfare of the children. There was overcrowding, those in charge were not trained for the work, play and study equipment was lacking or very poor, the children received very little individual attention. Upon entering the orphanage, the children all had IQ's of 80 or above, the average IQ being 90. After these children had lived in the undesirable environment for less than two years, their average IQ dropped 16 points, that is, to 74. An IQ of 74 is not so far above what is generally considered mental retardation. Yet none of the children gave indications of mental retardation before living in the poor environment of the orphanage.

Answers to problem on page 233 (genotypes precede phenotypes): Grandparents – Mr. M and Mrs. F, dark-dark, dark; Mrs. M and Mr. F, light-light, light. Parents – Mr. M and Mrs. M, dark-light, dark. Children – Joan, dark-dark, dark; John and Ruth, dark-light, dark; Bill, light-light, light.

How do various community environments affect children? Children living in five "hollows" in a mountainous section of Virginia were studied because their home and community environments differed radically.

One hollow consisted of a few scattered families living in an area so isolated that it did not even have a road to the outside world. There was neither a school nor a church, and none of the citizens could read or write.

A second hollow was connected with the outside world by a rocky mountain trail. Occasionally, the townspeople held meetings in a combined church and schoolhouse, and a few of the men could read and write.

A third hollow could be reached by automobile, although the road was a very poor one. There were a combined church and school and a general store which contained the post office. The people of this community did most of their buying from mail-order catalogues, and they sold some agricultural products.

A fourth hollow could be reached by a fair road connecting with a state highway. There was daily mail service. About 75 percent of the people could read, and they kept in touch with events by means of newspapers. There was an organized school in session seven months out of the year.

The fifth community was on a hard-surfaced road. There was a modern school, and church services were held regularly. The people kept in touch with events by means of newspapers, magazines, radios, and automobile travel. This community was a rather typical small American town.

When the children in these five communities were given intelligence tests, it was found that there was a direct relationship between scores and the conditions under which the children lived. The more isolated the hollow, the lower the intelligence-test scores.

There was no reason to believe that the poor performance of the children in the isolated hollows could be blamed on "poor heredity." The children in the remote hollows were all from the same general ancestral background as the children living in the fifth community. Limitations of the environment—lack of schools, books, social life, and so forth—seemed the most plausible explanation.

How do different socioeconomic levels affect test scores? In one testing survey which involved several hundred students, all students in a school system were tested at the twelfth, ninth, sixth, and third grades. The students at each grade level were composed of individuals representing two different backgrounds and socioeconomic levels. Group A represented those from a higher socioeconomic level than Group B. When the scores of twelfth-grade students were compared, Group A achieved at the twelfth-grade level and Group B scored at the sixth-grade level, a difference of six years. The difference between scores of the two groups at the ninth-grade level was three years; at the sixth-grade level, only one and a half years; and at the third-grade level only nine months. In other words, at every three-grade decrease, the difference between the groups was divided in half. If this

What influence do these neighborhoods have on the children who play in them? Psychology seeks to determine how and to what extent environment affects behavior.

progression had continued to the first-grade level, where tests were not given to the students, theoretically there would have been no appreciable difference between the groups.

The question is, "If the two groups showed no appreciable difference at the first grade but did at the twelfth grade, what caused the difference?" Did the difference in background cause the difference in scores, or was it that Group B had a lower potential as determined by heredity? These questions, like many others, cannot be adequately answered at the present time. Perhaps in the future, as we gather more data, we shall be better able to provide more scientific conclusions.

What further study of environment is needed? Most studies showing the importance of environment have been concerned primarily with measurement of intelligence. At present, psycholo-gists feel that they know how to measure intelligence much better than they know how to measure personality, social habits, and attitudes. For that reason, most of the studies of the influence of environment have been limited to intelligence. Although it is valuable to know about changes in IQ as measured by tests, one must always remember that saying an IQ increases is not necessarily the same as saying that there has been an improvement in the way the individual adjusts to his environment. Furthermore, there are many other aspects of personality that should be studied. Some experiments with small children have indicated that shyness and lack of self-confidence can be overcome by means of environment. In the experiments, the children were given opportunities to do things and to do them well. More studies will be made in the future on many phases of the effects of environment.

STUDIES OF TWINS

You have seen that some studies show the tremendous importance of heredity, while others show the tremendous importance of environment. It would be ideal for purposes of research if we could permit a group of babies to grow up under one environment, then, by some magic, change them back to babies again and let them grow up under a very different environment. In this way we could determine the effects of different environments when the hereditary basis was the same. Quite obviously, such an experiment is impossible. Fortunately, however, studies of twins go a long way toward giving us the answers desired.

In the United States twins occur about once in every ninety births. Some twins dress alike and act very much alike. They may be so similar in appearance that their friends cannot tell them apart. Other twins look no more alike than any two brothers, two sisters, or brother and sister.

What is the difference between fraternal and identical twins? There are two kinds of twins, fraternal and identical. *Fraternal twins* are children of the same parents who simply happen to be conceived and born at approximately the same time. In terms of heredity they are no more alike than other children of the same parents. Two ova (eggs) were fertilized by two sperms, and two individuals developed from the start. There may be two boys or two girls, or there may be a boy and a girl. Sometimes fraternal twins decide that they wish to appear very

much alike. A typical case is that of two high school girls, who are fraternal twins. There is some resemblance between them, as there often is between two sisters, but their faces and figures differ. However, they do not like to admit this. They dress absolutely alike (one has to have her dresses slightly tight, and the other slightly loose), they go to the same places, they study the same subjects in school.

If a psychologist makes a study of fraternal twins, he cannot tell with any certainty how much of their individual development is due to heredity and how much is due to environment. Their environments are often similar, and in some cases every effort is made to have their environments as nearly alike as possible. There is not a good opportunity for a scientific measure of the relative influences of environment and heredity.

From a scientific point of view, psychologists are much more interested in identical twins than in fraternal twins. *Identical twins* result from a single ovum, which is fertilized by a single sperm. Seemingly, one new life is started. Then, for some reason not yet known, this cell divides and two individuals develop instead of one. Since both of the individuals come from a single fertilized cell, it is believed that they have the same heredity. They are always of the same sex. There is great similarity in such characteristics as eye color, skin color, hair form, length and shape of fingers, height, weight, body shape, and facial details. These are the twins that look so very much alike. Since identical twins have the same heredity, whatever differences may

HEREDITY AND ENVIRONMENT

appear in them must be due to the influence of environment.

How much alike are twins reared together? A number of scientific studies have been made of twins and of siblings other than twins. (*Siblings* [sib′ lingz] are children of the same parents, whether twins or not, and regardless of sex.) In general it has been found that identical twins are much more alike than fraternal twins and that in many cases fraternal twins are more alike than siblings who are not twins.

In IQ, pairs of identical twins tend to differ, on the average, about 5 points. Pairs of fraternal twins differ about 9 points, while other siblings differ about 11 points. Unrelated pairs of individuals selected at random tend to differ about 15 points. The difference in IQ's for identical twins (5 points) is no greater than is often found for two tests given to one individual. Furthermore, one study of 150 pairs of identical and fraternal twins showed that identical twins were much more alike in each of the primary mental abilities (see page 195 in Chapter 8) than were fraternal twins. Thus, it seems that identical twins, having the same heredity, are much more alike than the other pairs of children who have different heredities.

Secondly, fraternal twins are more alike than siblings who are not twins. This difference cannot be accounted for in terms of heredity, for there is no reason to believe that fraternal twins have common heredity to a greater extent than any two children of the same parents. However, fraternal twins probably have a more common environment than other siblings. Identical twins are likely to have a still more common environment.

Most pairs of twins, both identical and fraternal, are reared in the same homes, go to the same schools, attend the same social events, and so on. They

Although these quintuplets look alike and are the same age, the boy's heredity is no more similar to his sisters' than that of ordinary siblings.

are of the same age and so have a more common environment than siblings who are not twins.

At first thought it might seem that siblings other than twins reared in the same home would have just as similar an environment as twins reared in the same home, but this is not the case. Suppose there are two boys in a family, one twelve years of age, the other nine. The one twelve years of age has had three years of the home environment which his younger brother has not had. Furthermore, the twelve-year-old boy has a younger brother in his environment. The nine-year-old has an older brother in his environment. If the two children are of different sexes, one has a younger brother or sister and the other has an older brother or sister. These circumstances all make differences in what seem otherwise to be very similar environments.

How much alike are twins reared in different environments? In most cases identical twins live in very similar environments. Once in a while, however, it does happen that identical twins are separated early in life and grow up in quite different environments.

Scientists succeeded in finding nineteen pairs of identical twins who had been separated early in life and who were at least twelve years of age when studied. Thus, there had been a considerable length of time in which environment had had a chance to play its part in their development. Now there was an opportunity to study the effects of different environments with individuals having the same heredity. In several cases the twins grew up in total ignorance of each other's existence. The average difference between the IQ's of these nineteen pairs of twins was 8.2, as against about 5 for identical twins living together.

This difference of 8.2 points in IQ can perhaps be accounted for in terms of a few of the nineteen pairs. In these few cases there had been marked differences in educational opportunity. Except for the few cases of very unequal educational opportunities, the rest of the pairs of identical twins differed only 5.5 points on the average. This is almost the same difference that has been noted for identical twins reared in the same homes. Furthermore, the difference of 8.2 points for all pairs of identical twins reared apart is less than that usually found between siblings living in the same home environments (11 points). Certainly it is less than the 15 points found on the average for unrelated individuals living in different home environments. This study seems to suggest that heredity is a very important factor in the development of the individual, regardless of the influences of the environment.

Some of the data presented in this section are summarized in the first table on page 240. Obviously no figure can be put in the middle space of the top row, because identical twins cannot live in the same family otherwise than as twins. In the top horizontal row of the table, note that the factor of heredity seems to be strong, regardless of differences in environment. The bottom horizontal row indicates that greater similarity in environment tends to make fraternal twins more alike than siblings other than twins raised in the same

Point Differences in IQ for Various Combinations
of Hereditary and Environmental Influences
(a Summary of Scientific Studies)

	LIVING TOGETHER AS TWINS	LIVING MERELY IN THE SAME FAMILY	LIVING IN DIFFERENT FAMILIES
Identical heredity	5 (Identical twins)	(Could be no such condition)	8.2 (5.5 for most cases)
Nonidentical heredity	9 (Fraternal twins)	11 (Siblings) Nontwin	15 (Unrelated)

home. Nontwin siblings, remember, differ no more in heredity than do fraternal twins. The greatest difference is found where both heredity and environment are different — that is, among unrelated individuals living in different families.

How much correlation is there in height and weight for twins? Further light is thrown on the influence of heredity and environment by studying various physical measurements of twins reared together and twins reared apart. The coefficient of correlation for height of identical twins reared together has been found to be +.981; for identical twins reared apart, +.969. Fraternal twins reared together show a correla-

tion for height of +.934. Height is determined primarily by heredity. Note that identical twins, even when living apart, are more alike in height than fraternal twins living together.

Weight is determined in part by heredity and in part by the kind and amount of food eaten. The coefficient of correlation for weight of identical twins reared together has been found to be +.973; for identical twins reared apart, +.886. For fraternal twins reared together, the correlation was found to be +.900.

How much correlation is there in intelligence and school achievement for twins? A British scientist made very extensive studies concerned with the

Correlation Between Measures of Intelligence and School
Achievement for Twins and Nontwins

	IDENTICAL TWINS TOGETHER	IDENTICAL TWINS APART	FRATERNAL TWINS TOGETHER	NONTWIN SIBLINGS TOGETHER	NONTWIN SIBLINGS APART	UNRELATED CHILDREN TOGETHER
Intelligence	+.925	+.876	+.551	+.538	+.517	+.269
School achievement	+.898	+.681	+.831	+.814	+.526	+.535

PATTERNS OF BEHAVIOR

inheritance of mental ability. He succeeded in finding over thirty cases of identical twins brought up in different environments. Part of his data is summarized in a table (page 240, bottom) so that you can compare identical twins reared together and apart. The table also gives coefficients of correlation for nontwin siblings reared together and apart. Finally, data are given for unrelated children who have been reared together. You will note that for intelligence as measured by intelligence tests, the correlation for identical twins, even when reared apart, is very high. It is almost as high as for successive testings of the same individuals. For school achievement, the correlation is much lower for identical twins reared separately than for those reared together. In fact, this correlation is lower than for fraternal twins and nontwin siblings reared together.

What can be learned from case studies of twins raised in separate homes? The study of twins is interesting, not only in terms of average figures and general conclusions but also in terms of specific cases. One example is the case studies of identical twin boys who were born in a mountain village in Tennessee and whose mother died at the time they were born. The paternal grandparents adopted one, known in psychological writings as R. The maternal grandparents adopted the other, known as J. The grandparents who took J were industrious and gave him many advantages. He was graduated from high school and became an engineer. He was fond of reading good literature.

The grandparents who took R were

rather shiftless. The grandfather tried blacksmithing, working on the railroad, and coal mining, but he did not stick to any kind of work. R attended school for eight grades but was not interested in schoolwork. Something of his environment can be seen from the fact that in the community in which he lived school was in session for only five months of the year. After leaving school, R did some work of various kinds, but he seemed to avoid all work as much as possible. At the age of twenty-seven, J's IQ was found to be 96 and R's 77 (Stanford-Binet).

What conclusions have been reached from studies of twins? As a result of their studies of twins, some psychologists have reached certain tentative conclusions: that physical characteristics are least likely to be affected by environment; that intelligence, as measured by the IQ, is more likely to be affected; that education and achievement are still more likely to be affected; that personality is most likely to be affected.

MOTIVATION

Psychologists who study motivation can tell us a great deal about the influences of heredity and of environment on an individual. As you saw in Chapter 4, motivation refers to the regulation of behavior that satisfies needs and leads toward goals. By studying motivation, psychologists can understand something of the conditions which predispose individuals to one kind of behavior rather than toward another. How an individual behaves is determined in part by biological drives and in part by social considerations.

All men, as well as lower animals, have certain biological drives which are to be understood in terms of inherited structures. Biological drives which serve to motivate man are the drives for nourishment, water, oxygen, elimination, and reproduction. Man is also motivated to keep his body at a comfortable temperature and to provide sleep and other rest for his body. The biological drives help man and lower animals to maintain their bodies in a state of equilibrium.

How an individual satisfies these drives depends on his learning from his social environment. For example, let us consider an individual who is motivated by hunger. He may work for the money with which to buy food, or he may steal to eat; he may eat his food according to accepted rules of table etiquette, or he may stuff it into his mouth; he may insist that his meat be well cooked, or he may prefer to eat it raw.

Man is also motivated by psychological and social drives. For example, he has the need for the security found in group living (gregariousness). Man forms social groups varying from the family to international organizations. The infant's group living is limited to the mother and other individuals in the family circle. These individuals satisfy the infant's early biological needs, but soon he learns to value companionship even when it is not necessary for the satisfaction of his biological needs. It is not necessary to think of our desire for group living as inborn or inherited, but rather we should think of it as learned behavior, and as growing out of a period of dependence through which we all pass.

Throughout your present study of psychology, you will find many references to motivation. If you do supplementary reading in more advanced textbooks, you may find a different organization of material. Perhaps there will be several chapters devoted to a unit on motivation instead of a discussion of the topic throughout the book. In your supplementary reading you may find certain differences in the definitions given for such terms as motivation and drives. Psychologists have not yet fully agreed on the definitions for these terms. Nevertheless, you will find much interesting evidence from experiments and from many field studies concerning the general problem of motivation.

MATURATION

A study of heredity must include a study of a process which is determined by heredity — maturation. You may recall that in Chapter 7 we spoke of changes in a human being which result from physical growth and development. This process of physical growth and development of an organism over a period of time is called *maturation*.

Maturation is not the same as learning, since changes due to maturation are determined by heredity. For example, a newborn baby cannot learn to walk, no matter how much instruction he is given. Only when his body structure has developed sufficiently as a result of maturation can he be taught to walk.

PATTERNS OF BEHAVIOR

Different species of animals have different rates of maturation as a result of heredity. An eight-week-old puppy can run about, eat from a dish, and do most of the things he will do as a grown dog. An eight-week-old baby, on the other hand, is still quite helpless and could not survive if he were not cared for. Dogs mature more rapidly than do human beings—but, of course, their capacity for development is far more limited.

An experiment with a simple organism. How do organisms such as salamanders "learn" to swim? In one experiment, a large group of salamander eggs was divided into two groups. One group served as a control for the experiment. The eggs of this group were placed in ordinary water and permitted to develop as they normally do in nature. The other group of eggs served as the experimental group. These eggs were placed in a drug solution which did not interfere with the normal processes of growth but which did paralyze the animals so that they could not move. The control group developed the usual swimming ability. After these salamanders had been swimming for five days, the ones that had been in the drug solution were removed and placed in ordinary water. Within thirty minutes they were able to swim about with as much ease as the members of the control group that had had five days' practice. Apparently the development of a salamander's ability to swim depends upon maturation rather than upon practice or learning.

Why did it take these experimental salamanders about thirty minutes to

The difference in maturation rates between horses and human beings is evident: a foal is able to gallop shortly after birth, whereas many children cannot walk unsupported for a year.

develop swimming? Why didn't they swim as soon as they were placed in ordinary water? What effect did the drug have? To answer these questions, the experimenters placed in the drug solution other animals which had been raised in ordinary water and had developed normal swimming. Of course, they now became motionless. After twenty-four hours in the drug solution, they were put back in ordinary water. It took them up to thirty minutes to regain swimming ability.

What is imprinting? Have you ever seen baby chicks following their mother around the barnyard? Perhaps you assumed that such following was "natural," without realizing that there was involved a very interesting relationship between maturation and learning. Psychologists use the word *imprinting* to refer to a special kind of very rapid learning that takes place in some animals—notably birds—at an early stage of their development. A specific reward or reinforcement is not involved. Imprinting does involve presenting to the animal a large moving object. Also, imprinting may take place only at the time maturation makes it possible. Such learning is relatively •insusceptible to forgetting or extinction.

As early as 1873, it was noted that incubator-hatched chicks tended to follow the first moving object to which they were exposed. Much more recently, another scientist reported that goslings followed the first large moving object they saw—in this case, the scientist, and would have nothing to do with their mother when she appeared later on. In one experiment, the scientist imprinted a group of goslings upon himself and imprinted another group of goslings upon their mother. All of the goslings were placed together under a box while the mother goose and the scientist stood nearby. When the mother started to walk away, so did the scientist but in a different direction. The box was lifted. The goslings imprinted upon their mother followed her, and the goslings imprinted upon the scientist followed him.

Imprinting varies with the age of the animal and the conditions of the imprinting. For example, with ducklings the tendency to follow is strongest when imprinting occurs thirteen to sixteen hours after hatching. Merely allowing the bird to see a large moving object does not necessarily produce imprinting. The young bird must spend effort to stay near its object. In one experiment, ducklings were imprinted on a large wooden decoy duck which was moved mechanically around a circular track. Those required to walk only a few feet showed less strength of imprinting than those required to walk one hundred feet.

Wouldn't it make an interesting experiment for a fair or other exhibit

"They think I'm their mother."

to imprint baby chicks on a mother duck and to imprint ducklings on a hen? Such a demonstration might be quite disturbing to people who had thought it was "natural" for baby chicks to follow a hen and for ducklings to follow a duck.

What does maturation have to do with human learning? In order to answer this question, we must turn to some experimental studies. In one experiment identical twin babies were used. At the age of forty-six weeks, one of the twin girls was given an opportunity to climb a set of stairs. She did not climb any of them. She was then given training in climbing stairs, and after four weeks of such training she was able to climb the stairs without assistance. The other twin was not given any experience with stairs until she was fifty-three weeks of age. In her first test at this age she climbed the stairs unaided in 45 seconds. After two weeks of training, this twin, who had had no training until she was fifty-three weeks of age, was actually climbing stairs better than her twin, who had had five weeks of training. Remember that these were identical twins and therefore had the same heredity.

Another study of twins has a bearing on our question. Twin boys, Johnny and Jimmy, were placed under very different environmental conditions at the age of twenty days and were used as experimental subjects until they were about two years of age. It was thought that these boys were identical twins, but later it was found that they were fraternal twins. Neverthe-

less, the study does contribute to our understanding of the importance of maturation and of environment. Johnny was given training in such acts as diving, swimming, roller skating, and use of language. By the age of eight months he swam 7 feet; at eighteen months he swam 50 feet. At fifteen months he would dive headfirst from a springboard 5 feet above the water. Before most children can walk, Johnny was learning to roller skate, and before he was two years of age, he was quite a proficient skater. Johnny was trained largely on the sink-or-swim basis. That is, he was made to face hardships in the hope that he would be bold and self-reliant.

Jimmy had no such special training and could not perform the acts Johnny could perform. Furthermore, Jimmy would not even attempt these acts. That Jimmy was more timid than Johnny may well be explained by the difference in their training.

It is significant to note that the training given Johnny did not make him permanently superior to Jimmy in such behavior as crawling and creeping, sitting up, reaching and grasping objects. Maturation in itself seemed to produce these activities. Training did make Johnny superior to Jimmy in the less essential skills such as swimming, diving, and skating. We must not, however, overlook the fact that later, when he was given an opportunity to learn these activities, Jimmy usually acquired them more easily than had Johnny at an earlier age, owing to the fact that he was more mature when he undertook the learning.

We shall consider just one more

illustration of the effects of maturation. Traditionally, Hopi Indian babies are attached to cradle boards for most of their first nine months of life and so have very little opportunity to exercise the muscles to be used in later walking. Some Hopi Indians, however, allow their babies to move about freely, unconfined by cradle boards. In one study it was found that both Hopi babies raised in the traditional way and Hopi babies who moved about "learned" to walk at almost exactly the same age (about fifteen months).

Can maturation be depended upon to guarantee learning? The importance of maturation is receiving more and more attention in modern education. For example, at what age should a child be taught to read? There is no simple answer. The answer depends in part upon the degree of maturation of the child. Some children are ready to read at an earlier age than other children because of their more rapid biological growth rate. Children do not, however, suddenly mature into being able to read without training. How soon a child learns to read depends in part upon how much he is read to before he is able to read himself. The child growing up in a home where there is a good deal of reading and other broadening experiences will wish to learn to read at an earlier age than a child growing up in a home where reading is neglected and where life is very monotonous. Learning to read is influenced partly by the processes of maturation and partly by environmental influences.

The child may be forced to learn to read at an early age, but he can learn more efficiently if he has achieved a sufficient degree of maturation before instruction in reading is given.

In general, we can say that human learning is too complex to be accounted for solely in terms of maturation, but learning does take place most efficiently when the environmental stimulation is keyed to the degree of maturation of the individual.

The discussion of maturation has led us a little nearer to an understanding of the effects of heredity and environment on individuals. Before attempting to reach any general conclusions about the comparative importance of heredity and environment, we might consider some studies of extremely unusual cases.

UNUSUAL STUDIES

You have seen that children raised in foster homes serve well as subjects for studies in the effects of environment. There have been documented cases of some individuals who were reared as foster children of animals and of others who, in some way, managed to survive alone in the forest. After these individuals were discovered, attempts were made to teach them to speak, read, and perform the usual social customs of civilized life. Few of the attempts were successful, however. These persons continued to function and perform as animals in many ways; they were human only in shape. The essential question involved is whether the lack of early training, guidance, and association with other humans resulted in behavior resembling that of a mentally retarded individual or whether the individuals were retarded before being reared by animals or before roaming the forests alone. Wild animals cannot be thoroughly trained unless they are captured soon after birth. The early years are very important in child training. These "wild" children may have been so impressed with their early training that later attempts to train them in the ways of human society were not very successful.

Owing to the lack of adequate data, no one knows whether to account for the behavior of these "wild" children in terms of heredity or environment. It is obviously out of the question to abandon children of known heredity in forests in order to learn what will happen to them—or to place one child of a pair of identical twins in a human home and abandon the other to the home of a wolf or other animal.

What about the other side of the story? What about placing a nonhuman animal in a human environment?

What would happen to an ape raised with a child? Many persons keep animal pets in close contact with human environment. Even so, the animals are treated as animals rather than as human beings. They are taught tricks and seem to learn a great deal about human customs, but fundamentally they are treated like nonhuman animals. What would be the result if a nonhuman animal were placed in a human home and treated just as a human child is treated? Such an experiment has been performed.

A professor of psychology and his wife undertook to rear a baby female chimpanzee with their own baby boy. When the experiment began, the baby chimpanzee, named Gua, was seven and one-half months of age; the baby boy, Donald, was ten months old. The two lived together as playmates and as the "children" of the psychologist and his wife for nine months.

Gua learned to walk like a human being instead of like a chimpanzee. She learned bladder control and to use the toilet—well but not perfectly. She kissed and hugged. Gua understood 95 words by the end of the nine-month experiment (Donald could understand 107). She did not learn to speak (although in a similar experiment made more recently a chimpanzee named Viki was taught to say four words). On the other hand, she was able to eat with a spoon and drink from a glass at an earlier age than Donald. Since chimpanzees mature more rapidly than do human beings, Gua could learn certain bits of behavior before Donald, although in time Donald caught up and surpassed her.

Gua never behaved altogether like a human being. In those acts in which anatomical structure was important for performance, her behavior remained apelike. Yet some of her behavior was very much like a human being's. That is, both heredity and environment were involved in her development.

In all studies of human children living with nonhuman animals and of nonhuman animals living with human beings, both heredity and environment play a part.

PRACTICAL CONCLUSIONS

Is it possible to tell whether heredity is more important than environment, or vice versa? Now look back at the question at the beginning of this chapter: "Which is the more important factor in the development of the individual, his heredity or his environment?" To help answer this question, compare an individual with a rectangle. Which is the more important factor in a rectangle, its base or its altitude? Obviously we cannot have a rectangle without both base and altitude. Neither can we have an individual without both heredity and environment. Did you ever see an individual without any environment? Did you ever see an individual who did not have ancestors? We might represent an individual by a four-sided figure, with heredity as the base and environment as the altitude, as in the figure below.

Although we cannot have a rectangle without both a base and an altitude, the base and the altitude can vary in length. A rectangle may have a narrow base and a high altitude, or a wide base and a low altitude, as shown in the figure on page 249.

An individual may have an inferior heredity and a superior environment, or an individual may have a superior heredity and an inferior environment. Suppose there are two individuals with approximately equally good heredity. One is placed in a rich cultural environment, the other in a poor cultural environment. The resulting total individuals will be quite different. Or suppose two individuals with considerably different heredities are placed in approximately the same environments. The individuals will be quite different, owing to the factor of heredity.

Psychologists do not know enough about either heredity or environment to speak in terms of specific measurable units. Hence, it is not possible to say that one individual's environment is three times as good as another's or that one individual's heredity is twice as good as another's. Neither can it be said that as a result of both heredity and environment, one total individual is, for example, three times as capable as another. Individuals cannot be appraised by a geometrical formula. The analogy to rectangles suggests, however, the related contributions of heredity and environment to the development of the individual.

How important are eugenics and euthenics? The farmer who tries to improve his crops must take account

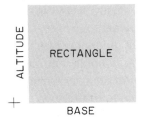

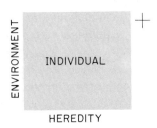

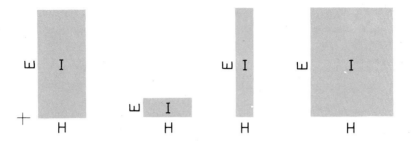

of both heredity and environment. If, for example, he is trying to raise premium corn, he will first carefully select the best seeds available and then plant them in rich soil. He may have to improve the soil environment by fertilizing it, and he will have to plow the soil. By combining good seed (heredity) and good soil (environment), he can expect to secure premium corn. In raising premium cattle, the farmer must mate good stock and then give the resulting cattle every advantage in food and shelter.

Human beings are often not as careful in their own mating as the farmer is in cattle mating or in the selection of seeds for planting. Eugenics (page 234) aims at the improvement of the human race by calling attention to the importance of heredity.

In trying to improve the human race, we should give careful consideration to the factor of environment. Individuals reared under poor social conditions, as in slums, cannot be expected to develop into individuals as desirable as those reared under good social conditions. Unfortunately, again, society is often not as careful of human environment as the farmer is of the environment that he provides for his premium stock. Yet by means of edu-

cation, religion and ethics, social work, and medicine, the human species can be improved. The branch of applied science that aims at the improvement of man by regulating his environment is called *euthenics* (yōo·then'iks).

As society is now constituted, persons of inferior abilities tend to intermarry. They frequently have many children who are usually reared in inferior environments. Since both heredity and environment are inferior, socially undesirable individuals are often the result.

Persons of superior abilities tend to intermarry and have relatively few children. These children are usually reared in superior environments. Since both heredity and environment are superior, socially desirable individuals are the usual result.

Go back to the case of Billy, who misbehaved in school (page 226). Was that misbehavior owing to heredity or environment? Perhaps Billy inherited a small body; he is shorter and weighs less than the other boys his age. Perhaps where Billy lives, the larger boys make fun of him and make him feel inferior. Billy does not wish to be the subject of jokes about his size, does not wish to feel inferior. He believes that by misbehaving in school, he will cause the other children to think that he is tough. If Billy's heredity had been different, he might not have had the small body and would not have been the subject of jokes about his size. If Billy's heredity had been the same but he had lived in a community where other children did not make fun of him, his misbehavior would not have developed. In effect, his present behavior is to be understood in terms of both his heredity and his environment. Heredity and environment always interact.

Terms to Add to Your Vocabulary

chromosomes
deoxyribonucleic acid (DNA)
dominant characteristics
environment
eugenics
euthenics
fraternal twins

genes
genetics
genotype
heredity
identical twins
imprinting
maturation

phenotype
recessive characteristics
ribonucleic acid (RNA)
siblings
unit characters

Suggestions for Activities

1. Write a history of your family. You may wish to include charts similar to the ones shown in Chapter 9 of your *Record of Activities and Experiments*. The history should include such physical characteristics as heights, weights, eye colors, hair colors, and possibly body builds. Also, include records of the vocational activities, social achievements (for example, public offices held), religious affiliations and activities, travel experiences, homes lived in, military services, schools attended, and so on. There may be stories of personal happenings which you will wish to include. In writing your history, you will need to confer with your parents, grandparents, aunts and uncles, and other relatives. There may be family records to which you can refer. You may wish to consult official public documents. Pictures of living members of the family should be included and, also, if available, pictures of members of the family no longer living. Your history will be of value to you now as you study the influences of heredity and environment. In time, it may become a valuable document in the family archives.

2. If you live in a large city, or when you visit one, travel through one or more areas of homes belonging to people in the higher socio-economic levels. Then travel through the poorer areas of the city. Contrast the homes, the schools, the churches, the stores, the recreational facilities. Is there a difference in the personal appearances of the children and adults to be seen on the streets? To what extent do you think the adult lives of the children will be influenced by their environments? You may wish to take some pictures to illustrate your report, but take care not to offend anyone, especially in the poorer districts.

3. Write a report on your pet dog, cat, or other animal. To what extent do you treat him like a human being? In what ways does he show the effects of your humanlike treatment? To what extent

does the animal continue to act like most animals of his species?

4. If you live in a rural area, study the inheritance of various physical features as they may be noted in livestock. You may wish to make charts for animals similar to those on page 97 of your *Record of Activities and Experiments*.

5. Find and bring to class any family albums that may be available. Can you trace any physical characteristics from these pictures?

6. If you know identical or fraternal twins who are willing to cooperate and who will not be embarrassed, compare a few physical measurements and personality inventory scores for them. Although your measurements will not be statistically significant, they may prove to be of considerable interest.

7. Visit a farm or zoo in order to observe the behavior of young animals, especially of the bird family. Do you note any indications of imprinting? Are there any of the young of one species being cared for by mothers of another species? If you live on a farm, try to imprint ducklings or chicks on some animal other than their mother or on some large moving object.

Suggestions for Further Reading

Coleman, James, *Personality Dynamics and Effective Behavior*, Scott, Foresman. Part I, "The Human System," discusses the mechanics of heredity and the role of heredity in development, as well as the roles of physical and sociocultural environments in development.

Hilgard, Ernest R., and Richard C. Atkinson, *Introduction to Psychology*, 4th ed., Harcourt, Brace & World. Chapter 6, "Human Motivation"; Chapter 17, "Behavior Genetics."

Itard, Jean-Marc-Gaspard (English translation by George and Muriel Humphrey), *The Wild Boy of Aveyron*, Appleton-Century-Crofts. A paperback edition of this famous account of an inarticulate, and probably mentally retarded, child found roaming in a French forest in 1799.

Kalish, Richard A., *The Psychology of Human Behavior*, Wadsworth. Chapter 5, "An Introduction to Human Personality and Development," especially pages 96–104.

McKeachie, Wilbert J., and Charlotte L. Doyle, *Psychology*, Addison-Wesley. Chapter 4, "Heredity and Maturation."

Mead, Margaret, *New Lives for Old*, New American Library (Mentor Books). The effects of environmental influences on a primitive people.

Montagu, Ashley, *Human Heredity*, rev. ed., New American Library.

Morgan, Clifford T., and Richard A. King, *Introduction to Psychology*, 3rd ed., McGraw-Hill. Chapter 2, "Maturation and Development."

Munn, Norman L., *Psychology*, 5th ed., Houghton Mifflin. Chapter 4, "How Individual Differences Originate."

Ruch, Floyd L., *Psychology and Life*, 7th ed., Scott, Foresman. Chapter 3, "The Development of Behavior," pages 74–82, "The Mechanism of Heredity," and "Inherited Structures."

Sanford, Fillmore H., *Psychology: A Scientific Study of Man*, 2nd ed., Wadsworth. Chapter 3, "The Developing Organism."

Singh, J. A. L., and Robert M. Zingg, *Wolf-Children and Feral Man*, Shoe String Press. This book includes material by Reverend Singh, the missionary who cared for the "wolf-children" of India, as well as accounts of other individuals who have lived wild or isolated lives.

Whittaker, James O., et al., *Introduction to Psychology*, W. B. Saunders. Chapter 3, "The Development of Behavior."

CHAPTER 10

Biological influences on behavior

In Chapters 7 and 9 you have seen something of the biological facts of heredity and of how the body matures and otherwise responds to its environment. Genetics is not the only branch of biology which is of particular interest to psychologists. In this chapter, and in the one following it, we shall give further attention to the relationship between an organism and its environment. We shall be concerned with how the body functions, that is, with the branch of biology called *physiology*.

Our bodies are very complex, and the operations of all parts are related. Anything that affects one part of your body affects all parts. Suppose that you run a mile. You run with your legs, but are your legs the only parts of you that tire? After running, can you lift heavy weights just as easily as you could lift them before you ran the mile? Does your heart beat at the same rate it did before you ran? Is your breathing the same as before? Of course, your entire body has been affected. How?

Much of the unification of our bodily activity is to be accounted for in terms of the circulation of the blood. When you run, fatigue chemicals are formed in the muscles of your legs. They are carried to all parts of your body by means of the bloodstream. Your whole body becomes tired.

Other factors in the unification of bodily activity are the nervous system and the glands. You may have learned something about the nervous system and glands in elementary school. If you have studied biology in high school, you have given more detailed attention to these parts of the body and their functioning in man and other organisms. For further information on anatomy and physiology, you can turn to college textbooks devoted to those subjects. A study of psychology will also give you some fundamental knowledge on how the human body functions.

THE NERVOUS SYSTEM

A major regulator of the body's activities, and therefore of behavior, is the nervous system. We shall now examine the divisions and functioning of the nervous system.

What are the central and peripheral nervous systems? In terms of its structure in the body, the nervous system has two main divisions—the central nervous system and the peripheral nervous system.

The illustration to the right will help you to recall important parts of the central and peripheral nervous systems. Perhaps you were taught to think of the central and peripheral nervous systems as being something like a telephone system. Suppose you become ill. You can go to a telephone and turn a dial, or push a series of buttons, or ask for a number. The message is carried through the exchange office and out to a physician's office. Soon the physician is on his way. Or suppose you hear good news. You call up a friend, and he shares your joy. The telephone system helps to tie all parts of the community together.

In the body, the *central nervous system* functions to connect the parts of the body. The central nervous system is made up of the brain and the spinal cord. The brain and the spinal cord are both parts of one unit, as is shown in the figure to the right. The *peripheral nervous system* consists of nerve fibers running to and from the central nervous system.

The central and peripheral nervous systems act as connecting and coordinating systems between the sense organs and the muscles and glands. A

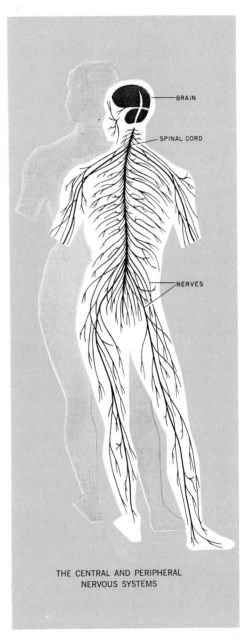

THE CENTRAL AND PERIPHERAL
NERVOUS SYSTEMS

When a sense organ is stimulated, a nerve impulse passes along the peripheral nerves to various parts of the central nervous system. The brain and spinal cord then send nerve impulses back out to the organ. When, for example, you touch a hot object, a "message" is sent to the central nervous system, which then sends out a motor response to the muscles of your arm and hand by way of the peripheral nervous system—and you jerk your hand away from the hot object.

rose thorn pricks your hand. A "message" is carried to the brain and out to a muscle. Instantly you jerk your hand away from the rosebush. Or someone makes an insulting remark about you. A "message" is carried from your organs of hearing to your brain and out to a gland. You say that you are emotionally upset.

The comparison to a telephone system is useful, but it must not be carried too far. For one thing, the central nervous system of the body is infinitely more delicate, and for another thing, it is far more complicated than any telephone system in the world. One student of the nervous system has suggested that we imagine a man from Mars suddenly taken from his planet and placed in the heart of the New York City telephone system. Our Martian knows absolutely nothing about telephone systems or even about electricity. Nevertheless, he undertakes to figure out just how the telephone system works in all its details. He must learn how electricity operates. He must trace out all of the millions of telephone wires, must learn how all the instruments work. Our man from Mars has a tremendously difficult task ahead of him. Nevertheless, his job is very simple compared with the task scientists face in trying to trace out and understand the workings of the nervous system in a human body. Today much is known about the structure and operation of the nervous system, but there is an almost infinite amount yet to be learned.

There is another reason for not carrying the analogy of a telephone system too far. A telephone system is, in a way, passive. It is all set to connect you with your friends if you wish to be connected, but when you are not using it, it is inactive. The nervous system is part of a living organism, and as such it is always active. Physiologists have definite evidence that, although the kind of activity may vary, the nervous system is always active, even when a person is asleep or under an anesthetic — or knocked unconscious.

What is the autonomic nervous system? In terms of function, part of the central and peripheral nervous systems regulates the activities of the vital organs. We call the part of the nervous system which performs this regulating function the *autonomic* (ô′tə·nom′ik) *nervous system*. It acts somewhat, but not entirely, independently of the central nervous system. Ordinarily we are not aware of its activity. It regulates the activity of those organs necessary for life and reproduction, namely, the lungs, the stomach, the intestines, the heart, the liver, the eliminative organs, and the reproductive organs.

Under most circumstances we cannot voluntarily control the activities regulated by the autonomic nervous system, but in an activity like breathing, which can be voluntarily regulated for a short period of time, we do have control temporarily. A few persons are able voluntarily to slow down or speed up the rate of their heartbeat, but most of us do not have this kind of control over our autonomic nervous system.

The autonomic nervous system is divided into two divisions: the sympathetic and the parasympathetic. The *sympathetic system* acts as a unit, and in emotional excitement it speeds up the heart, dilates the arteries of the muscles and heart, causes adrenalin to be secreted, makes the person perspire, and produces many other physiological reactions associated with emotion. In one way this system has "sympathy" for the individual during an emotion and tries to help him perform better. It serves to mobilize the individual during emotion. The *parasympathetic system* acts, most of the time, in opposition to the sympathetic; that is, it slows down the heart and, in general, maintains the ordinary body functions, such as producing saliva and aiding digestion. Although, as stated, the two systems function primarily in opposition to each other, they also can work together or follow a sequential pattern. The total workings of these two systems are not yet completely understood.

THE BRAIN

In our discussion of the central nervous system, we saw that the brain is an important part of it. Now let us examine the role that the brain plays in behavior.

Is there any relation between brain size and intelligence? Can a person's intelligence be judged from the size of his brain? To find out, students of anatomy have examined the brains of deceased individuals.

It has been found that on the average the brains of adult men weigh about 48 ounces, while the brains of adult women weigh about 44 ounces. From this particular scientific fact some men have jumped to the conclusion that men must be more intelligent than women. However, many studies of intelligence, as measured by tests, school marks, and success in life show that on the average women are just as intelligent as men. It is the quality of brain structure that is important, rather than the quantity. Why should anyone expect the brains of women to weigh as much as the brains of men? The average total weight of women is less than the average total weight of men. The weights of women's brains are as great in proportion to total body weight as are the weights of men's brains.

Are the brains of very intelligent persons heavier than the brains of mentally retarded persons? The heaviest brain ever found was that of a moderately retarded individual, a London newsboy, whose brain weighed 80 ounces (almost twice as much as the average). The lightest brain ever found was also that of a moderately retarded person. In schools for the mentally retarded may be found individuals with both abnormally large heads and abnormally small heads. One scientist measured the brains of 125 persons, including individuals who were severely and moderately retarded, criminals, and persons of ordinary intelligence. In each case the brains were heavier than those attributed to such distinguished men as Thackeray, Webster, and Napoleon. Individuals differ in the sizes of their brains. Yet there is no reason to believe that one individual is less intelligent than another because his brain is smaller.

Nevertheless, on the average, the brains of civilized races are somewhat heavier than those of primitive races. It has been found that the average brain weight of individuals who are intelligent enough to live normal social and economic lives is slightly heavier than the average brain weight of those individuals who are so lacking in intellectual ability that they must be cared for in institutions.

In some studies brain size has been judged from head measurements of living persons (a rough measure at best), and the intelligence of these same individuals has been measured by intelligence tests. Positive correlations of from .10 to .15 have been found. Such correlations show only a very slight relationship—certainly nothing significant. The findings of psychologists on this point have been well summed up in the statement, "You can't judge a man's mind by the size of his hat."

Are intelligence and thinking related to specific parts of the brain? In the illustration below is a diagram of the human brain, with the various parts labeled. In what part of the brain does man do this or that kind of thinking? Man does not think with his brain alone; the brain is simply one part of the entire organism. However, the brain is such an important unifying center for the entire organism that it must be given special consideration as a mechanism for thinking.

Surgeons have found that if parts of the cortex (the outer layer of the cerebrum) are stimulated with a very mild electric current, specific muscular contractions will occur. If one particular spot is stimulated, the toes will be moved. Stimulation of another spot produces movement of the forearm, stimulation of still another spot produces movement of the neck, and so on. Also, sensations are known to be rather definitely localized in the brain. For example, an area at the back of the cerebrum functions in vision; an area on each side is especially related to hearing (see diagram on page 257).

The more complicated processes of thinking are not so clearly localized.

The human brain

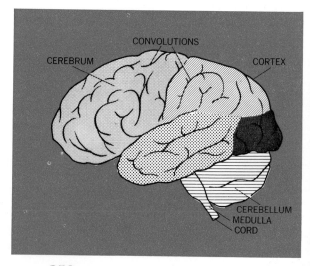

LOBES OF THE BRAIN

Frontal Temporal
Parietal Occipital

Experiments with nonhuman animals have suggested that the complicated processes of thinking are to a considerable extent spread over the entire cerebrum. Much of the activity of the human brain seems to be best understood in terms of either total or at least widespread patterns of activity. In some cases destruction of parts of the cortex does not seem to result in loss of general intellectual ability. In one case a man was struck across the forehead with a crowbar, and a large part of the frontal lobes was destroyed. (The brain is divided down the center from front to rear into two symmetrical hemispheres. The frontal lobes are found in both hemispheres at the front of the brain.) Physicians succeeded in preventing infection, and the man recovered. He was able to go about his daily work as usual. It should be noted that he was a laborer and his work did not involve abstract thinking.

A number of experiments performed in recent years on rats, porpoises, and other animals indicate that there are "pleasure" and "pain" areas in the brain. When electrical stimulation of the "pleasure" area was used as the only reward for behavioral responses, stimulation resulted in the learning of the responses. In stimulating a certain area (the septal region) of the brain of mental patients, some remarkable changes in behavior have occurred. (The septal region is located deep within the brain, between the two hemispheres, approximately where the frontal, parietal, and temporal lobes join, if the brain is viewed from the side.) Some patients became more alert and less frightened than before

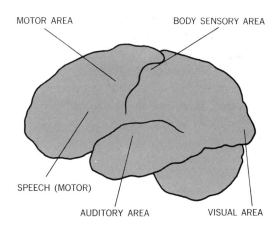

Localized functions in the human cortex

electrical stimulation, recognizing people they had previously ignored. Although in most cases results have been favorable, some patients have reported unfavorable sensations. But work in this area has only begun, and much data are yet to be gained and analyzed before more meaningful conclusions can be drawn about electrical stimulation of the brain.

Studies have been made in which general intelligence tests, such as the Stanford-Binet, have been given both before and after brain surgery. Destruction of parts of the cortex did not usually result in loss of intellectual ability as it is measured by tests of general intelligence.

There is still a good deal to learn about the relationship between various kinds of thinking and specific parts of the brain.

Can the lower animals think? Can your pet dog or cat — or any other lower animal — think? It is true that man's brain, especially the cerebrum, is more highly developed than the brain of any other species. But the fact is that animals other than man do have brains, including cerebrums. Indeed, some animals have more brain than man. An elephant's brain weighs about 10 pounds, and a whale's brain weighs about 14 pounds. Are elephants and whales therefore more intelligent than men? Are they better able to think than men? Certainly we have no evidence of such superiority—in fact, quite the contrary. We should remember, however, that the brains of elephants and whales weigh far less than do the brains of men in proportion to total bodily weight.

Experiments with animals have shown that they can and do think to an extent. We have direct evidence that there is a relationship between brain activity and learning in animals. One psychologist has demonstrated that if electrodes are placed in a certain region of the brain and an electrical stimulation is given, a thoroughly satiated rat will begin eating again. Furthermore, if the rat has been trained to open a hinged door in order to secure food, electrical stimulation results in the rat's opening the door, that is, in carrying out a learned activity.

Man, in his thinking, has one great advantage over other animals. He has developed a very complicated spoken and written language, and much of his thinking is done in terms of language. Some lower animals can communicate with their own species more than was once believed, but they are not known to have a language that compares in complexity and sophistication to the speech of man.

How is personality related to the brain? It has been found that if the cortex in one frontal lobe becomes diseased or is removed, no marked change in personality occurs. If both frontal lobes are destroyed, however, very considerable alteration in personality may result. The behavior of the individual often becomes rather childish; he becomes boastful about his imagined greatness. He may become immoral and antisocial in general. In many ways his behavior resembles that found in cases of paresis, a form of mental illness described in Chapter 15. In a preceding paragraph we mentioned the case of a man whose frontal lobes were partially destroyed by a crowbar. After the accident, his emotional behavior was less well controlled. His temper became more violent. Similar changes, although milder, occur in disease or removal of the temporal lobes. (The temporal lobes are located on the lower sides of both hemispheres of the brain.) Disorders or destruction of other lobes of the brain do not result in such personality changes.

What is the EEG? Television programs and the better popular magazines are doing much to acquaint the layman with modern scientific and technical terms. You may have heard of the EEG. These initials refer to an instrument called an "electroencephalograph," or to the record made by the instrument, an *electroencephalogram*. An *electroencephalograph* is used to record a person's brain-wave patterns on a chart. When electrodes from the EEG are placed on a person's scalp over various parts of the cortex, the instrument makes a recording of the electrochemical changes which constitute his brain activity. The recordings change as the activity of the individual changes: the record made by the EEG for a sleeping person will be different from the record made for the same person when he is awake. It will change when he performs arithmetical calculations or when he tries to remember something. Research with the EEG has not progressed far enough to permit any general conclusions concerning the relationship between activity of the cortex and personality. There is some evidence, however, that many—but not all—children showing socially undesirable behavior have abnormal patterns of activity in the cortex. Adult criminals and some persons with severe mental disorders often show abnormal patterns, also.

The physician uses the EEG to assist him in finding the location of brain tumors. Also, he uses it in his study of cases of convulsive disorders, popularly called epilepsy. Sometimes the EEG is the first indication the physician has that his patient has some disturbance of a convulsive nature. The EEG of a person having an epileptic seizure is quite different from the EEG of that person at other times. Even when an epileptic person is not having an epileptic seizure, his EEG often differs from the EEG's of persons not subject to this illness. About 10 percent of the population show brain wave patterns which indicate that they are more susceptible to seizures than those with normal EEG patterns.

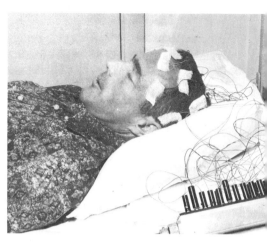

The electroencephalograph is being used to record an astronaut's brain waves during a preflight physical examination.

We shall refer to epilepsy again in Chapter 15.

The EEG has found a number of uses in psychological work. While awake an individual shows an *alpha wave*, which has a frequency of approximately ten pulsations per second. When a person is relaxed, the alpha wave is less noticeable, and when he is asleep, it disappears entirely. Thus, in experiments the disappearance of the alpha wave may be used to indicate that a person is asleep. Also, EEG records have helped psychologists find differences between hypnosis and sleep, since EEG patterns of individuals under hypnosis are not like those of the same person when he is actually asleep. Finally, the EEG has shown that brain wave patterns are not so well developed when human subjects are tense, worried, or apprehensive as when they are relaxed. Theoretically, EEG records can be used as part of lie detection, which will be discussed later; but the EEG patterns are not understood well enough at the present time to incorporate them into the more established ways of measuring emotional responses.

REACTION TIME

Men and women engaged in psychological research and others engaged in biological and medical research have done a vast amount of experimentation in their studies of the nervous systems of men and other organisms. Psychologists, in particular, have done much experimental work in the measurement of reaction time. *Reaction time* refers to the interval of time between the onset of a stimulus and the beginning of the observer's overt response. It is a measure of the time required for a nerve impulse to travel from a sense organ to the brain and out to a muscle.

How is reaction time measured by laboratory experiments? One simple laboratory experiment consists in having a person press a key as soon as he sees a light flash on. When he presses the key, an electrical contact is made. A very delicate instrument measures the length of time between the flashing of the light and the pressing of the key by the subject. The time required for this simple reaction is usually from 150 to 225 thousandths of a second. In other experiments the subject is told to press the key as soon as he hears a specified sound (usually a buzzing sound produced in headphones fitted over his ears).

The reaction time in this case is usually from 120 to 180 thousandths of a second. Reactions to smells, tastes, pain, cold, and warmth are considerably slower; that is, these other sensory reactions take a longer reaction time.

The experiment can be varied. For example, the subject can be told to press a key as soon as he sees a red light but not to press it if he sees a green light. Reactions of this kind take more time than reactions where no discrimination is involved. Sometimes the subject is told to press a key with one hand as soon as he sees a red light and to press a key with the other hand as soon as he sees a green light. In this last-named test, since the choice is more complex, it requires a still longer time for reaction to take place.

To a limited extent, practice in making a reaction tends to shorten reaction time. The stronger the stimulus, the faster is the reaction time, although the intensity of the stimulus of light does not make much difference. There is evidence that high altitude and sudden changes in direction lengthen reaction time. The reaction time of a young adult is faster than the reaction times of both small children and older persons.

How fast are reactions in automobile driving? Suppose that a traffic signal turns red, a child steps into the street, or a car suddenly turns out from a side street. How long will it take a driver to release his foot from the accelerator pedal and apply the brake pedal? Individuals differ in this as in other reaction times. One automobile-driving test is simply a reaction-time experiment. The person being tested sits in a seat similar to the seat of a car. In front of him are a steering wheel and brake and accelerator pedals, just as they are found in an automobile. Through the windshield he can see a traffic light. He is told to take hold of the steering wheel, put his foot on the accelerator pedal, and "drive along" until the traffic signal turns red. Then he is to put on the brake as quickly as possible. A recording instrument indicates the time required.

The average reaction time for getting the foot pressed against the brake pedal is about .45 second. How far would a car traveling 40 miles an hour go during this very short time? Forty miles an hour is 211,200 feet an hour, or 3,520 feet a minute, or 58.67 feet a second. In .45 second a car would travel 26.40 feet. A car traveling 70 miles an hour would go 46.20 feet in this same length of time. Of course, the activity in this .45 second is only the beginning of the process of stopping the car. The brake pedal must be pushed down and held down until the car is brought to a stop. Also, reaction time under actual driving conditions is probably longer than in a driving-test apparatus.

There is scientific evidence that the reaction time in applying the brake is much longer if the driver is not concentrating on his driving. If a person is concentrating his attention on the steering wheel rather than on the foot pedals, his reaction time is lengthened by between .10 and .15 second. The time is lengthened far more if he is paying attention to friends in the car rather than to his driving. When a driver is fatigued, his reaction time is longer than when he is fresh. If he has consumed alcoholic beverages, his reaction time is greatly lengthened. In fact, anyone who drives a car after indulging in alcoholic drinks may be said to be a potential murderer. The smoking of marijuana cigarettes is another factor that greatly lengthens reaction time.

Reaction time is one element in driving efficiency. No thorough studies have been made, however, of the correlation between reaction time and accident proneness. There are also other factors that are very important in influencing ability to drive efficiently — for instance, vision and hearing efficiency, which will be discussed in Chapter 11. Some persons can drive quite well as long as everything is in good order. In an emergency they become so emotionally upset that they lose control of the car. Tests have been devised in which "accidents" occur. There may be a crashing noise, the windshield may swing backward, the seat may be tipped. Can the driver continue to drive under such circumstances, or does he lose control? Such questions are of vital importance because automobile driving is a very important aspect of transportation, in which most of us take part or will take part.

If such persons as aviators, railroad engineers, and automobile drivers have slow reaction times, they are probably more likely to have accidents than persons with fast reaction times. We do not, however, have definite evidence that an individual's reaction time is, by itself, a valid test of his overall ability

BIOLOGICAL INFLUENCES ON BEHAVIOR

to do such work. There are many other important factors involved.

What factors affect reaction time? There are wide variations in reaction time for each individual. The reaction time may even be different for the same individual, depending upon the combination of factors and upon the type of situation. The factors that combine to affect reaction time can be separated and examined. One such factor is the specific sense, such as vision or hearing involved. Reaction time for sound, for example, is faster than that for light and, surprisingly, slowest for pain. Another factor is the complexity of the stimulus situation. For example, in everyday life, where there is reaction to a variety of stimuli, reaction time is slower than it is in typical laboratory experiments, where most stimuli are controlled. Similarity of stimuli affect reaction time, in that the closer stimuli resemble each other, the longer the reaction time.

Other factors act to lessen the reaction time. For instance, as the strength and duration of the stimulus increases, the reaction time becomes shorter. The reaction time also tends to decrease with increased practice and strong motivation. Reaction time shortens, too, if the individual is prepared to react, for example, a runner starting at the sound of a gun. Have you ever noticed that a starter at a track meet usually varies the time between "On your mark . . . set . . ." and the firing of the gun? If the warning time were always the same, the runners might respond to the time interval and not to the sound of the gun. In reaction-time experi-ments, varying the warning period is very important unless constancy is desired as part of the experiment.

There are many other factors which affect reaction time, such as fatigue, length of time vigilance has occurred, drugs, and alcohol, all of which have a tendency to make reaction time longer. Finally, one more factor, which has the effect of lengthening reaction time, is acceleration. It has gained increased importance in more recent years. Acceleration has become more important not only for aircraft pilots, as the speed of aircrafts grows ever faster, but also for astronauts. When a vehicle suddenly changes direction at high speed, or changes from a stationary to a moving state, as when pilots take off from carriers or land on them, reaction time slows down.

GLANDS

Early in this chapter we spoke of the glands as being a factor in the unification of bodily activity. There are two kinds of glands in the body—duct glands and ductless glands.

What are duct glands? *Duct glands* are those which empty their contents through small openings, or ducts, onto the surface of the body or into body cavities. Since duct glands do not secrete their products directly into the bloodstream, they are often spoken of as glands of external secretion. On a warm day you become aware of your sweat glands, which are important in eliminating fatigue products from the body. Whenever you get a tiny object in your eye, you become aware of your tear glands. When you put food in your mouth, or sometimes when you just think about food, the salivary glands pour saliva into the mouth cavity. After food is swallowed, the contents of other duct glands are poured into the stomach and small intestine so that the food may be digested.

What are ductless glands? Although the duct glands are very important, psychologists are even more interested in the ductless glands. *Ductless glands* have no openings or ducts through which they can pour their contents. Because they secrete their products directly into the bloodstream, they are sometimes referred to as glands of internal secretion, or *endocrine* (en' dō·krin) glands. The chemical substances they produce are known as *hormones* (hôr'mōnz). The hormones are absorbed directly into the bloodstream without having to be emptied through openings or ducts. The word "hormone" is derived from a Greek word which means "to excite" or "to stir up." You will note, as you read about various endocrine glands, that it is a descriptively accurate name for their products.

The illustration to the right shows that there are several ductless glands. (It should be mentioned that the pancreas is only in part a ductless gland; another part of the pancreas functions as a duct gland, pouring its product into the small intestine to aid digestion.) Of the ductless glands shown in the illustration, we shall be concerned with the effects of five — the thyroid, the parathyroid, the pituitary, the adrenals, and the gonads.

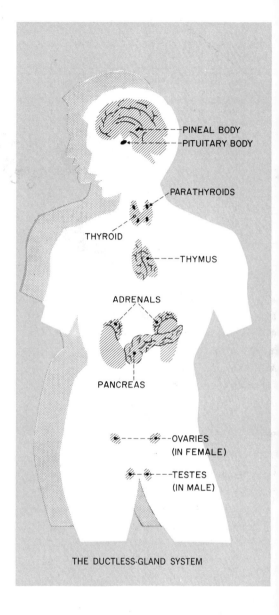

THE DUCTLESS-GLAND SYSTEM

The ductless glands are important regulators of the body, and their activity has a considerable influence on behavior. Because each individual personality consists of an interplay between such biological factors and outside social factors, psychologists study the relationship in order to understand the total personality of an individual.

How do the thyroid and parathyroid glands affect behavior? The *thyroid* (thī′roid) *gland* is located in the neck in front of the windpipe. Normally it weighs less than an ounce. One important element in the hormone produced by this gland is iodine.

If the thyroid gland becomes underactive (in hypothyroidism), the individual tends to become lazy and dull. If the underactivity of the gland dates from infancy, a condition known as *cretinism* (krē′tən·iz′əm) results. If you visit a school for the mentally retarded, you are almost certain to see a number of cretins. The cretin is dwarfed, with a thickset body. The legs are short and bowed, the feet and hands are stubby, the hair is coarse, and the skin is a sickly yellow.

Sometimes there is overactivity of the thyroid gland (hyperthyroidism), as in some cases of goiter (goi′tər), when the gland may become greatly enlarged and very prominent. Individuals suffering from hyperthyroidism are very restless and excitable, have difficulty in sleeping, tend to be irritable, and seem to work with untiring energy.

Close to the thyroid glands are two pairs of small glands called *parathyroid glands*. Their hormone regulates the utilization of calcium in the body. When there is a lack of this hormone, a condition known as *tetany* appears. It is characterized by intermittent, involuntary muscle twitching and spasms.

How does the pituitary gland influence growth? The *pituitary* (pi·tōō′ə·ter′ē) *gland* is attached to the underside of the brain. Part of this gland has great influence on bodily growth. If there is overactivity of the gland in childhood, giantism results. There is a record of one young man who at the age of nineteen years was 8 feet, 6 inches tall and was still growing at the rate of 2 inches a year. He weighed 435 pounds and wore size 36 shoes. Although very large, he was not unusually strong. For a time he played basketball. "But it's too easy," he said. "I'd stand down near the net, someone would throw me the ball, and I'd drop it in. I don't think the other teams liked it much." This giant's parents and brothers and sisters were all of a normal size. At birth he himself was of normal size ($8\frac{1}{2}$ pounds); it was a hyperpituitary condition that produced his great height.

Giants have difficulty in obtaining work other than that of exhibiting themselves in sideshows at carnivals. A skillful surgeon can remove some of the excess glandular substance and so prevent giantism, if the hyperpituitary condition is discovered early and is promptly brought to his attention.

In a case of underactivity of part of the pituitary gland in childhood, the individual becomes a dwarf or midget. Many dwarfs or midgets, unlike cretins, have well-proportioned or reasonably well-proportioned bodies. Administration of pituitary extract to an afflicted child will do much to promote normal growth. In one case an infantile, emaciated eighteen-year-old boy was treated with pituitary extract. He had not grown for eight years. Yet, within four and a half months after treatment began, he had matured sexually and had grown two inches taller.

If the part of the pituitary gland that influences growth functions normally until after an individual has matured, and if the gland then becomes overactive, gigantic height does not result. Instead, such effects appear as greatly enlarged hands and feet, arms capable of reaching to the knees, a massive jaw, a bulging chest, and bowed back. An individual so afflicted may sometimes be seen in sideshows labeled "Gorilla Man."

Such persons often show unusual personality patterns as well as strange anatomical patterns. Because of their physical development, the giant, the dwarf, and the "gorilla man" cannot always have normal social contacts. But if anyone happens to know such individuals, he can help to make their lives happier by treating them like normal persons as far as possible. He should never make fun of their peculiarities, although he does recognize them.

How does the adrenal gland function in cases of fear and excitement? Located near each kidney is a small gland called the *adrenal* (ə·drē′nəl) *gland*. It is composed of two parts and really should be thought of as two separate glands, although it is usually referred to as one.

One psychologist tells the story of a young woman who was a musician. She was very fond of a piano that was in her home. It was a heavy piano, which she could not move. Whenever she wanted to dust behind the piano she had to have someone move it for her. One day the house caught fire. No one else was at home, and it seemed that her piano was going to be burned. In her excitement she moved the piano across the room and out the door to safety. Had she been pretending when she required someone to move the piano for her on cleaning days? No, under the excitement and fear of the fire she was able to do something that she actually could not do under normal conditions. Activity of the adrenal glands was in part responsible for the change.

Under the excitement of anger or fear, one part of the adrenal gland becomes quite active. As it releases its hormone (adrenalin) into the bloodstream, a number of changes take place in the body: the heartbeat increases in speed and strength, the stomach temporarily ceases activity, the pupils of the eyes become dilated, the blood coagulates easily, the individual may perspire freely, feelings of fatigue vanish, breathing is speeded up. All these bodily changes would help an individual to survive in case of emergency. He would be better able to fight, to run from danger, to keep from bleeding to death. The individual is prepared by the adrenal gland for short-time emergency activity.

Injections of the adrenal hormone have been used with some success in "bringing persons back to life" after appearances seemed to indicate that they had died.

The hormone (cortisone) produced by the other part of the adrenal gland helps the individual to resist infection. Also it seems to play an important

BIOLOGICAL INFLUENCES ON BEHAVIOR

The adrenal gland often releases a hormone, adrenalin, in moments of danger. Adrenalin makes available extra energy for escape.

part in preparing the individual for long-continued muscular activity. If the amount of the hormone produced is very small, blood circulation is impaired, sex activities decrease, the individual becomes weak. Death follows, unless the hormone is administered artificially.

If an excess of this hormone is produced, the individual shows increased sexual development, regardless of how young he is. An excess may also pro-duce masculine characteristics in a woman: her figure will tend to lose its curved lines, her voice will become deeper, and a beard will grow. Again a gland is responsible for a sideshow exhibit, "The Bearded Lady."

What are the functions of the gonads? The *gonads* (gō′nadz) — sometimes called the sex, or puberty, glands — supply the sperm and egg cells for repro-duction. In addition, they produce hor-mones that have an important effect on the personality development of the individual. Although the sex hormones are present in childhood, production of the hormone is increased during adolescence, causing the de-velopment of the biologically mature man and woman.

The behavior of a male horse that has had the gonads removed is quite different from that of a stallion. If the gonads are removed from female animals, male characteristics often develop. For example, if the ovaries are removed from ducks and pheas-ants, the birds soon develop the char-acteristic male plumage. If the sex glands from male rats are transplanted into female rats from which the ovaries have been removed, the female rats will begin to show behavior charac-teristic of male rats.

Of necessity, this discussion of the ductless glands has been brief and non-technical. Some important glands have not even been mentioned. You have seen that particular glands produce particular effects on individuals. But always bear in mind that the glands interact on one another. Furthermore, the glands are only part of the total individual. In organisms as complex as human beings, social factors as well as physiological factors are important in development.

Has man's changing environment affected glandular activity? It is impossible to place large groups of human subjects in experimental and control environments over a long period of time in order to learn what effects the experimental environment has on individuals. Such studies can be made, however, with lower animals, such as the rat. There are two kinds of Norway rats: wild and domesticated. Scientists from many fields of biological, medical, and psychological research have, for a long time, used Norway rats in their laboratories. Thus some Norway rats have been domesticated for a hundred years. They have lived in the very "soft" environment of a laboratory, where they have been fed and cared for, as compared with the environment of wild rats.

One advantage in studying the Norway rat is that there is some control over hereditary factors. This rat does not mate with rats who are not of the Norway strain.

One psychologist compared domesticated Norway rats from his laboratory colony, which had been in existence for over thirty-six years, with wild Norway rats trapped in alleys and yards. After making a careful, comparative study of his domesticated and wild rats, he reached these tentative conclusions: (1) The adrenal glands in domesticated rats are smaller and less effective than in wild rats. (2) The thyroid glands are less active in domesticated than in wild rats. (3) The gonads develop earlier, function with greater regularity, and bring about a much greater fertility in domesticated than in wild rats.

It might be added that he found the brains of domesticated rats smaller in weight than the brains of wild rats. He believed that the brains of domesticated rats function less effectively because these rats are more subject to convulsions than are wild rats.

The psychologist reporting the above comparison raises the question, "To what extent has civilization brought about changes in man parallel to those produced in the rat by domestication?" He points out that today great physical energy is not needed. In many ways man lives in a very "soft" environment. The psychologist concluded his report with the questions "Where are we going? What is our destiny?"

HOW DO EXTERNAL FACTORS, SUCH AS TEMPERATURE, AFFECT BEHAVIOR?

In a discussion of the functioning of the body in the environment, it is important to examine the effect of outside factors, such as temperature and humidity. Another question is how drugs affect efficiency. A third point to consider is how the body reacts to loss of sleep.

What effects do air circulation, temperature, and humidity have on efficiency of work? There is considerable experimental evidence to support the common observation that work effi-

When mountain climbers go above 22,000 feet, fatigue, cold, and lack of oxygen often cause them to experience delusions.

ciency is influenced by such factors as circulation of air, temperature, and humidity. Men training to be airplane pilots are often given tests in which they work under conditions of lower-than-normal oxygen supply. These tests show that as oxygen supply diminishes, tremors appear and movements become jerky and overvigorous. Also, subjects become less and less alert as the amount of oxygen in the air is decreased, although they may not realize that their efficiency is decreasing. Men on climbing expeditions high in the mountains, where the oxygen supply is decreased, tend to think slowly.

Men in military service may be called upon to work under conditions of severe cold. Is their efficiency affected by low temperature? In one military research study, 620 soldiers were subjected to a variety of temperatures and wind speeds. Temperatures down to 35° Fahrenheit and probably to 50° below zero did not affect reaction speed, providing there was low wind speed (not greater than 5 miles per hour); but at wind speeds of 10 miles per hour or greater in low temperatures, there was a significant decrease in reaction speed. Part of the loss in reaction speed could be overcome by introducing mild exercise.

In another military study, data indicated that manual dexterity is not significantly affected by temperatures ranging from 25° to 100° F. or by variations in time of exposure from 40 to 120 minutes. There is evidence, however, of significant impairment of dexterity with the bare hands following exposure for at least a half hour to temperatures between 14° and 20° F.

Most individuals living in hot and humid climates do not display the initiative found in individuals living in cooler and drier climates. Industrial studies have shown that the introduction of ventilating and temperature control systems is often followed by increased work efficiency, fewer accidents, and less time off because of employee illness. We cannot be sure, however, that the increased efficiency was purely a result of physiological conditions.

In one study subjects were tested in a poorly ventilated room where the temperature was 86° F. and the humidity was 80 percent. They were asked to do such work as solving multiplication problems "in their heads" and finding words opposite in meaning to given words. The experiment was conducted for four hours a day on five consecutive days. Also, the subjects were tested in a well-ventilated room where the temperature was 68° F. and the humidity was 50 percent. Certainly the second condition was more comfortable for working than the first, yet there was no essential difference in work efficiency under the two conditions. We can think efficiently on hot, humid days in poorly ventilated rooms if we have sufficient desire to do so. Office workers and students may become uncomfortable and stop working under such circumstances, but the statement "I just can't work in this atmosphere" is probably not scientifically correct.

What is the effect of alcohol on efficiency? It is difficult to obtain truly scientific data on the effects of alcohol. Those who are opposed to alcohol shower us with printed matter pointing out the ill effects resulting from its use. On the other hand, the advertisements of distillers, wine producers, and brewers sometimes suggest that desirable effects result from the use of their products.

Since the beginning of recorded history, some men have reacted to their difficulties by trying to reduce or distort their awareness of them. Many have used alcohol to escape their problems instead of trying to overcome them.

There is no doubt that large dosages of alcohol result in socially undesirable behavior. The intoxicated man lying on the floor in a stupor is certainly incapable of doing work either efficiently or inefficiently. Studies have been made of the effects of varying amounts of alcohol on vocational efficiency. In one experiment young men stenographers were given carefully controlled dosages of diluted pure alcohol. Following heavy dosages their speed in copying material fell off only a few percent, but errors increased as much as 72 percent.

The workman who has used alcohol will probably insist that he has been stimulated by it and that as a result his work is more efficient. Scientific evidence is to the contrary. Alcohol produces a false sense of well-being and efficiency, but actually it is a depressant rather than a stimulant. Many physicians classify alcohol as an anesthetic drug. The user becomes less alert, responds more slowly, and is less dependable. Alcohol dulls judgment, and the drinker is likely to take foolish risks.

What are the effects of caffeine? Caffeine is a stimulant drug found in many popular beverages—coffee and tea especially, but also chocolate, cocoa, and the "cola" drinks. Advertisers for drinks not containing caffeine take care to suggest that their drinks do not keep people awake or make them "nervous."

In one scientific study, subjects were asked to swallow capsules for a period of forty days. On some days these contained caffeine varying in amount from two to six grains. On other days they contained, rather than caffeine, a milk sugar similar in appearance to the caffeine. The subjects did not know when they took caffeine and when they took the milk sugar. Each day they were given various kinds of tests. It was found that small doses (not exceeding three grains) of caffeine increased the speed of typing, but larger doses decreased the speed. The number of errors decreased for all sizes of doses of caffeine. Speed of movement, as measured by tapping, was increased by all sizes of doses. Steadiness of movement was decreased following the taking of caffeine. In fact, slight tremors were found following doses of from one to four grains, and more pronounced tremors followed larger doses. Ability in addition of figures was increased by all sizes of doses. In general, it was found that caffeine tends to produce heightened efficiency, at least for a few hours immediately following the dose. In small doses, caffeine is usually thought to be a mild stimulant, but we do not know what effect longtime use of caffeine has on an individual. Some evidence suggests that the continued use of caffeine drinks is detrimental. Carefully controlled experimentation in this field is needed.

It is known that for some persons caffeine reduces sleep efficiency. Of course, a person who is tired from loss of sleep cannot work efficiently. You may hear people say, "This idea that coffee keeps people awake is all imagination. I drink it three or four times a day and it never affects my sleep." The statement that coffee never affects a person's sleep would probably be found to be false under conditions of careful scientific investigation. A habitual user of caffeine may notice no effect on sleep, but a person not used to the drug may be kept awake by it. The person who does not use caffeine drinks regularly can rely on them for a temporary lift in emergency situations.

How much is known about the effects of tobacco? There is a great deal of discussion about the effects of tobacco, and both those favoring smoking and those not favoring smoking present evidence selected to reinforce their points of view. In the past few years, research has been conducted on a possible relationship between smoking and lung cancer. More investigation is needed in this area, and further research is in progress.

There is no present evidence for a "smoker's personality"; that is, research studies do not indicate a cause-and-effect relationship between psychological characteristics and smoking behavior. Evidence is lacking that smokers differ from nonsmokers in intellectual ability. For young normal subjects, smokers show more anxieties than nonsmokers, but this does not necessarily indicate a cause-and-effect relationship. Smoking may cause nervous tension, nervous tension may result in smoking, or they may be mutually causative.

There is some evidence that nonsmokers among adolescent boys make, on the average, higher marks in school, fail less often, and make better scores on psychological tests than do occasional smokers and habitual smokers. However, smoking and poor scholarship do not always go together. In fact, in some cases studies of scholastic averages have favored smokers.

Considering how widely smoking is

practiced, all too little is known about its effect on behavior.

How important is sleep? In many cases production in a factory tends to be low on Monday. By Tuesday or Wednesday workmen seem to be "warmed up," with production at a maximum for the week. Possibly the low production on Monday is to be accounted for by the hypothesis that Saturday and Sunday nights may be spent in prolonged and tiring entertainment. The resulting loss of sleep shows up in inefficient production on Monday.

Various tests indicate that loss of sleep is followed by inefficient performance, although highly motivated individuals can do remarkably well following periods of continued wakefulness, even in work involving concentration. There is evidence, however, that efficiency of work is maintained only through the expenditure of a great amount of energy.

A person may lose sleep in two ways. He may go without any sleep for a long period, or he may sleep much less than usual for a period of several nights. In one experiment subjects were kept awake continuously for 72 hours. They were under constant medical supervision during this dangerous experiment, but even with this precaution some fainted upon the conclusion of the experiment. Again, subjects reduced the amount of their sleep from about 8 hours to about 5 hours a night for a period of five nights. In both cases the subjects were given various tests before and after the periods of no sleep or reduced sleep.

Intelligence-test scores dropped 24.5 percent following a period of 72 hours without sleep but dropped only 14.9 percent following five nights with only 5 hours' sleep each night. The corresponding percentages for decrease in ability to solve addition problems were 13.8 and 3.1 percent, respectively. How much the individual swayed forward and backward when trying to stand still was measured. After 72 hours without sleep, there was a 51.8 percent loss in control of bodily swaying. After five nights of 5 hours' sleep each there was a loss of only 6.1 percent.

The individual who loses much sleep is likely to be less efficient in thinking and in work involving more apparent physical activity than is the individual who sleeps regularly and for a sufficient length of time.

A number of scientific studies have shown that sleep is most sound at the end of the first hour of sleep and for a short time thereafter. By the end of the third hour sleep is usually lighter. Emergencies will arise wherein it is absolutely impossible to get normal amounts of sleep. In such cases, as experiments indicate, it is better to take a number of short naps than to try to use all available sleeping time in one period.

Are dreams really necessary? In recent years several interesting experiments have been performed on the relationship between sleep and dreams. In early experiments one of the major problems was to determine if and when an individual was asleep. At one time EEG records alone were used to determine whether or not the subject was asleep and how deeply he was sleeping. Today noises of graded intensities are also used to determine the depth of sleep, on the assumption that the louder the noise required to awaken a sleeper, the deeper asleep the subject. The intensity of the stimulus needed to awaken the individual is rigidly controlled.

From this and other evidence, psychologists speak of four stages of sleep. Stages 1 and 2 indicate a light sleep, and Stages 3 and 4 represent deeper sleep.

The general pattern of sleep, which varies not only for the same individual from one night to the next but also from one individual to another, is that sleep occurs in cycles. The individual goes from an awake state into Stage 1, then into Stages 2 and 3, and finally into Stage 4, the deepest stage of sleep. As individuals fall asleep, they progress rapidly through the different stages, reaching Stage 4 in about forty-five minutes. After spending about fifteen to twenty minutes in Stage 4, they go, either directly or indirectly, back to Stage 1 or 2. A few minutes later they begin the second cycle of sleep. Most individuals have four or five cycles each night. With each succeeding cycle, the individual spends less and less time in deep sleep and more and more time in lighter sleep.

In Stage 1 sleep, which is the lightest sleep according to EEG records, subjects have rapid eye movements (REM's), which are found primarily in this stage and are associated with dreaming. It is during Stage 1 sleep that *paradoxical sleep* occurs; that is, although the person is supposed to be in the lightest sleep at this stage, when he is having REM's he is harder to arouse, indicating deeper sleep. Even those individuals who deny that they dream quite frequently report dreaming if they are awakened when they are having rapid eye movements. On the other hand, individuals who are awakened while not having rapid eye movements rarely report dreaming. From this and other data it has been shown that dreams may last from a few minutes to more than an hour. This finding is contrary to beliefs held by some psychologists only a few years ago, when dreams were thought to last only a few seconds. It is a good example of how new evidence changes ideas and concepts and therefore why scientists must be willing to remain flexible in their thinking.

In one experiment subjects were deprived of their dreams by awakening them during REM's; it was found that when they were allowed to sleep later they dreamed longer — sometimes twice as long as their normal dreaming. It has also been found that those deprived of dreams have temporary changes in behavior during their waking hours, such as greater irritability, difficulty in concentrating, and some memory lapses. These changes disappear, however, when the subjects are allowed to sleep undisturbed, during which time they dream more frequently. It is as if they were trying to "catch up" on their dreaming. Perhaps you may wonder whether the disturbance of sleep and not the disturbance of dreams might have produced these data. Experimenters eliminated this possibility by awakening subjects during periods of no REM's, which resulted in no increase in dreams and no changes in behavior during the day when the subjects were awake.

The evidence available today indicates that dreams seem necessary for sleep, that probably everyone does dream—some remember them and some do not—and that while dreaming, the individual is harder to awaken. It is also interesting to note that cats have REM's when they are asleep, during which time movement of their whiskers and tails occurs. Could the cat be dreaming of chasing a mouse?

EMOTIONAL BEHAVIOR

Suppose that some morning an impressive legal-size envelope arrives in the mail. You open it—and learn that an uncle you never knew has left you $10,000 in his will. Would you be happily excited? Would your heart beat faster? Would you rush about, telling your friends?

If you were driving a car and some careless driver almost struck your car, would you gasp? do some rapid and forceful turning of the wheel and jamming down of the brake pedal? be angry? Unprepared-for experiences are likely to produce emotional disturbances.

Usually emotional disturbances have survival value. They enable the individual to run away from danger or to fight against that which threatens him. If the emotional disturbance is too intense, he may "freeze" in his tracks, he may be too frightened to run or fight. In some animals, such "paralysis" may have survival value because by remaining motionless the animal may escape the notice of his enemies. As you saw in Chapter 2, the term "trance state" has sometimes been applied to this behavior. Such "paralysis" in man might have value in certain war situations or in jungle travel, but ordinarily he is more likely to survive if he runs from or fights back against some physical danger.

Sometimes we hear it said that a given individual is "cold," that he has no emotions. Again, we may hear someone referred to as being very emotional. Such expressions are popular but not scientific. Everyone experiences emotion. Some persons express their emotional states more noticeably than others.

What does an emotional state involve? Think about some emotional experience which you have had recently. In terms of your body's reactions, the kind of emotion—fear, anger, despair, being in love—is not very important. Did your heart "pound" so loudly that you were afraid others could hear it? Did you gasp? Did you turn pale or red? Did you become nauseated? Did you break out in a "cold sweat"? No doubt you were aware of some of these symptoms.

If you go on to study psychology in college, you will learn about various theories that have been proposed to explain emotional states. For our purposes, it is enough to say that emotional states involve the entire body. We know that the autonomic nervous system (pages 254–55), the glands (pages 262–67), and the viscera (stomach, lungs, heart, and other internal organs) are involved in emotional behavior. A part of the brain called the *hypothalamus* is involved in emotional states. The cerebral cortex is also involved. We think about our emotional experiences and so prolong them. On the other hand, there is evidence that the cortex decreases the intensity of emotional expressions, for in an animal whose cerebral cortex has been removed, emotional states are more intense than before such surgery.

Later, in Chapter 14, we shall consider some specific emotional problems which many persons have. For the present, we can simply say that an *emotional state* involves widespread physiological changes which are either pleasant or unpleasant to the individual experiencing such a state.

How can emotional states be produced in the laboratory? How can emotional states be studied scientifically? It is difficult to produce genuine emotional states in the laboratory. An experimenter may say to his subject, "Be afraid now." In order to cooperate in the experiment, the subject may try to be afraid, but he is not actually afraid. On the other hand, the psychologist cannot be present with his measuring instruments when someone is having a narrow escape from an accident on the highway. A young man cannot be connected with scientific instruments while he sincerely proposes marriage to a girl. Such records would be interesting, but they cannot be obtained. It is possible, however, to set up some laboratory situations in which an individual may actually experience an emotional state.

In order to obtain a genuine emotional response, it is essential that the subject being experimented upon be unprepared for what happens to him. Sometimes a gun is fired behind his back, or he is given an unexpected electrical shock, or he is stuck with a pin, or he is told funny stories – while he incorrectly believes that the experiment has not actually begun.

One psychologist produced an emotional state in his subjects by means of the following experimental technique. The subject was required to sit alone in a dark room for a considerable amount of time. Then suddenly and unexpectedly his chair fell backward through an arc of about 60 degrees. The complete falling of the chair was prevented by a powerful door check. The subject was not hurt, but he was frightened. He screamed, struggled to escape, and called for help; he had a genuine emotional experience.

How can emotional states be measured? From experience, you know that under emotional excitement of any kind your breathing rhythm is different from its usual rhythm. The next time you see an exciting motion picture, notice how those about you gasp and hold their breath at the critical moments. In the laboratory, breathing is measured by means of specially designed instruments, which make a record of breathing rate on a revolving drum.

Using these recording instruments, one psychologist found that at the blast of an auto horn, sounded suddenly while his subjects were seated quietly before the instruments, breathing was momentarily checked. Then breathing

A boy's emotional states differ with regard to the physiological changes, amount of activity, and degree of pleasantness or unpleasantness involved.

was resumed at a rate greater than normal, and was also deepened.

Have you ever had a narrow escape and, after the danger had passed, noticed how rapidly your heart was beating? In the laboratory the rate of the pulse is measured by an instrument which is usually fitted over the radial artery—the artery seen so easily in the wrist. Records of the rate of beat are made on a revolving drum.

One psychologist gave his subjects an electric shock as an emotion-producing stimulus. Also he produced a state of "excited expectancy" by telling each subject that he was about to receive a severe electric shock. One minute after telling the subject that he would receive a shock, he actually gave the shock. There was a decided increase in pulse rate during the interval of expectancy and a still further increase when the shock was given. There is also an increase in blood pressure during an exciting emotional experience such as anger or fear.

Under one emotion-producing situation or another, a person may break out in a "cold sweat," have "goose-flesh," turn pale, experience a feeling of either warmth or coldness, have a tingling sensation in the skin. Psychologists measure skin changes under emotion-producing conditions by means of a technique known as the *galvanic skin response,* or GSR. In this technique two electrodes are pressed against the skin. One electrode may be placed on the left hand and the other on the right. Then a very weak electric current (2 to $3\frac{1}{2}$ volts) is passed through the body. Under some conditions more resistance is offered to the passage of this current than under other conditions. When a person is asleep, resistance is great, whereas just following vigorous exercise resistance is much reduced. Under emotional excitement the amount of resistance offered to the passage of an electric current is reduced, due partly to increased sweat secretion. The amount of electricity passing through a given circuit is measured by means of an instrument called a *galvanometer*. Using this instrument, one psychologist secured the record shown below. In this case a decrease in resistance, indicated by a rise in the line, resulted from the emotion-producing stimulus of an unexpected scream. Following this decreased resistance, which began soon after the scream, there was a gradual return toward normal. There are other techniques for measuring psychological changes occurring in emotional states, but we need not go into them here.

How do anger and fear affect digestion?
Perhaps after some intense emotional experience you have noticed that your stomach is upset. Psychologists have found that under emotion-producing

Record of a galvanic skin response following an emotion-producing scream

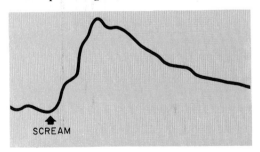

SCREAM

situations, normal digestive processes are interrupted. For example, a cat may be placed under a fluoroscope so that the stomach movements can be seen and studied. Before being placed on the machine, the cat is given food containing a substance that shows up on the fluoroscope. Under normal conditions, churning movements of the stomach are to be noted. A dog is brought into the room and permitted to bark at the cat. Presumably, the cat is having an emotional experience. His fur stands on end, he arches his back, he spits. The fluoroscope shows that the churning movements of his stomach stop. Even though the dog is taken from the room, the churning movements are not likely to begin again for about fifteen minutes. Also, it is known from other experiments that under such conditions of anger, the movements of the intestine stop and that the gastric juice ceases to flow into the stomach.

If we wish to avoid digestive disturbances, we should take care not to become angry for some time after eating. It has been found that digestive processes cease in dogs for as long as three hours after the dogs have been placed in strange surroundings. Perhaps this experience with dogs is analogous to the loss of appetite and nausea noted in the emotional experience of homesickness.

Uncertainty and fear may result in ulcers, not only for human beings but for laboratory animals. For example, in one experiment two groups of rats were used. For one group, every time a light was turned on, the rats were given an electric shock, but when a buzzer was sounded, they were never shocked. For the other group, half the number of times the light was turned on the animals were shocked, and half the time when the buzzer sounded they were shocked. Both groups received the same total amount of stimulation from light, buzzer, and shock. For rats of the first group, the shock was predictable; that is, they learned when it was going to occur. For the rats in the second group, the shock was unpredictable, they could not learn when it was going to occur. This second group developed significantly more ulcers than the first group.

Can emotions be judged from facial expressions? Some things can be learned about emotional states without using instruments. This is especially easy with children, for children have not learned to hide their emotional states. If you are playing a card game with a child and he happens to receive a very good hand, you may note that he smiles slightly. He straightens up, he is eager to play. If he receives a poor hand, he scowls, he pouts, he slumps down in his chair. Playing cards with an adult, you probably cannot learn the nature of his hand by observing his behavior. He has learned to keep a "poker face." At a basketball game the spectators dance up and down, they shout, they laugh. Under some conditions the same individuals may sob, wring their hands, and cry.

We can observe manifestations of emotion, but we must be very cautious in interpreting our observations. An adult goes to a party and has a very dull evening. Nevertheless, as he leaves he brings his face into a smile and tells the hostess that he has had a very pleasant time. Could we, unless we knew him very well, tell about his emotional experience by observing his expressions?

How do individuals differ in their responses to stressful situations? Although in many ways it is difficult to differentiate between various emotional states in terms of physiological changes, scientists are making some progress along this line. In one very carefully conducted research study, college medical students were subjected to two kinds of emotional stress-producing situations, and certain physiological changes were measured. In one situation, the students were asked to do computation problems which became progressively more and more difficult. As the students began to miss the answers, they were subjected to insults and sarcastic remarks. In the other situation, the students were asked to give some material aloud as rapidly and accurately as possible. They spoke into a "sonic-confuser," which fed their vocalizations back to their ears with a slight delay. This delayed feedback caused stammering and other speech irregularities and was very annoying. Under such a condition, the students tended to slow down in their speech, but whenever they did so they were given a mild electric shock.

Following such treatment, the students were asked to report how they felt about the situations. There were three principle kinds of reactions.

1. *Anger-out.* These students reported that they were angry and that their anger was directed against the

situation or against the experimenter.

2. *Anger-in.* These students reported that they were angry but that their anger was directed against themselves.

3. *Anxiety.* These students reported that the situation made them anxious, frightened, and even panicky.

The experimenters made various physiological measurements before, during, and following the stress-provoking situations. One measurement was of the amount of blood being forced out of the heart. The students who expressed "anger-out" showed the least change from their pre-situation to post-situation measurements. Another physiological measurement was of blood chemistry. The students expressing "anger-out" showed excessive amounts of noradrenalin in the blood. (Noradrenalin produces very little disturbance.) "Anger-in" and especially the "anxiety" students showed greater changes in heart activity. Also, both the "anger-in" and "anxiety" students showed an increase in the amount of adrenalin in the blood. You will remember that adrenalin is secreted in emergency situations (page 265). In general, this research suggests that individuals who become angry at external situations do not react in an emergency manner but that individuals who become angry at themselves or those who become anxious react as they would in an emergency.

Physiological changes do not entirely explain emotional states. In fact, the research just mentioned included a study of the family backgrounds of the students. There was evidence that "anger-out" students tended to have stern, authoritative fathers, "anger-in" students tended to have parents who were affectionate and who shared their authority, and "anxiety" students tended to come from families in which the mother exercised most of the authority. Evidently, how an individual responds to stress situations depends in part upon his childhood background.

It is of interest to note that "anger-out" is a more primitive, less civilized, more childish way of responding to stress situations than is "anger-in" or "anxiety." As the individual adjusts to social life, he must learn to curb his hostile, "anger-out" impulses. As a consequence, he is likely to direct his anger against himself or to become anxious, conditions not conducive to the best mental health. (We shall discuss mental health in Unit 5.)

How does the lie detector work? The best-known application of measurement of emotional states is that provided by the lie detector. Many times newspaper accounts of crimes state that a lie detector was used on a suspected person. A lie detector is often employed in cases of crime. It is used as a matter of routine in many police systems, not only to detect the guilty but also to eliminate from suspicion those who are innocent.

The lie detector is not a mysterious mind-reading, or conscience-measuring, machine. In fact, it does not measure lying at all. As you have seen, emotions are to be explained largely in terms of physiological changes. Telling a lie is usually an emotional experience. The lie detector merely measures some of the physiological changes that take place in an individual under the emotional stress of lying.

Adults are often capable of masking their emotional states with regard to facial and other bodily expression. Some people can "lie without batting an eye." Even under close scrutiny no one can tell from outward manifestations that they are lying. Furthermore, a lie may be so carefully planned that the story itself contains no logical errors. How can a machine detect lying that cannot be detected by a careful observer experienced in questioning criminal suspects?

Some lie detectors measure three physiological factors: blood pressure, pulse, and breathing. Blood pressure seems to be an especially sensitive indicator of the emotional state produced by lying. It has been found that blood pressure usually will rise 8 millimeters or more under the emotional stress of lying. Not only is the rate of breathing usually affected, but the pattern of breathing is also often changed when a person tells a lie. Under normal conditions the ratio of inspiration to expiration is about one to two; that is, inspiration takes about half as long as expiration. When a person tells a lie, the inspiration-expiration ratio tends to decrease; that is, the person takes relatively less time for inspiration and more for expiration.

Some lie detectors measure changes in the skin resistance offered to the passage of a weak electric current—the galvanic skin response. Police may use a modern instrument combining the features of the two kinds of lie detectors just mentioned.

When changes occur in the "suspect's" body, the lines drawn by the lie detector deviate from their usual pattern.

How is the lie detector used? In the psychological laboratory the lie detector is often demonstrated with students as subjects. The lie detector is so sensitive that very reliable results can be secured even with mild emotional states. One common laboratory experiment involves selecting a student who is to represent an accused person. The teacher or another student represents the policeman. The accused is given a dozen or so playing cards. He is asked to pick one of the cards and show it to the class but not to the policeman. The card is then put back in the pack, and the pack is thoroughly shuffled. The accused is connected to the lie detector and told, "You are going to be shown each card in the pack. For each one you will be asked, 'Was it this one?' You are to answer 'No' for each card, including the one you actually did select and show to the class."

BIOLOGICAL INFLUENCES ON BEHAVIOR

Next, the policeman shows the accused each card in turn, as it comes up in the deck. Meanwhile, he watches the lines recorded on the lie detector. For one card he will probably note a rise in blood pressure, a change in rate of heartbeat, and a difference in breathing. There will probably be a decrease in the resistance offered to the passage of a weak electric current. He goes on with the pack of cards and the blood pressure, heartbeat, breathing, and resistance return to normal. The policeman has good reason to believe that the accused was lying when he said "No" to the card at which the physiological changes occurred. In fact, the chances of detecting a lie by this means are about nine out of ten. If simply lying about a card can produce measurable physiological changes, is it not reasonable to believe that a lie told by a man accused of some serious crime would produce these changes?

In actual police work a suspected person is asked a number of questions. Usually the questions are asked in such a way that they can be answered by a simple "Yes" or "No." Some of these questions have nothing to do with the crime that is being investigated. They are routine questions about age, place of residence, place of employment, and so forth. Inserted among these routine questions are some questions directly or indirectly related to the crime under inquiry. Physiological changes denote lying.

Sometimes the suspect is read a list of details related to the crime. He is told that hidden among other items is one which is "critical," that is, one which can be known only to an individual implicated in the crime. Furthermore, he is told that he will be questioned about this critical item. If the person is guilty, changes will be noted at the critical point in the record. For example, the suspect's blood pressure will rise to a point just following the significant detail and will then decrease and remain level.

Questions or the giving of detailed items may not be necessary. In one famous case it was believed that a murder had been committed, but the body had not been found. A man suspected of the crime was connected to a lie detector. A map of the city in which the crime was believed to have been committed was spread out before him. The examiner pointed with his pencil to various parts of the map. It was noticed that whenever the pencil was pointed toward a particular suburb of the city, the suspected man's blood pressure rose. The examiner went over this section of the map in detail and noted changes in blood pressure. One spot showed the greatest physiological disturbance. Later the body of the murdered person was found at this place. The suspect did not even have to tell a lie in order to give himself away to the police.

Can the lie detector be wrong? Can a person fool the lie detector? In the great majority of cases the answer is "No." Can a criminal practice so that his blood pressure, rate of heartbeat, and breathing will not change when he tells a lie? No, because such physiological changes take place regardless of any desire to prevent them. It is true that to some extent a person can control his breathing, but the mere fact that a suspect held his breath or breathed abnormally would lead the police officer to suspect that he was trying to hide a lie.

Even practice with the lie detector does not seem to enable anyone to fool the instrument. There is a record of a student who had had much experience with a lie detector in connection with some of his college courses. He knew about the theory and practice of the instrument. Later he was suspected of having stolen some property. He was subjected to a test with a lie detector. Although he lied as carefully as possible and tried to control his physiological processes, the machine gave him away. He had actually stolen.

What are the chances of an innocent person being emotionally upset when attached to a lie detector? Is he not likely to show physiological changes that might suggest guilt? There is some possibility of this. The lie detector does not give 100 percent proof. However, the innocent suspected person tends to be tense throughout the whole examination. Wouldn't you feel tense and excited if you were suspected of a crime and the police were questioning you, even though you were entirely innocent? This tenseness and excitement is reflected on the record of the lie detector, but it tends to remain constant throughout the examination. A person actually guilty will become especially tense when questions concerning the crime are asked. He will tend to relax when routine questions are asked. This change from tenseness to relaxation is indicated by fluctuations in the lie-detector record. The innocent sus-

pected person has practically nothing to fear from the lie detector, which will help to remove suspicion from him. A guilty person has just cause to fear and hate the lie detector.

The lie detector is a very valuable instrument in the hands of the police. Law enforcement authorities cannot be 100 percent sure of results with it. When used by a qualified person, however, lie detectors are accurate about 75 percent of the time; that is, they will accurately detect lying in about three out of four individuals. This type of data has been obtained primarily from experimental situations, where the liars were known for certain. In actual practice, of course, as in criminal investigations, there is no way of knowing for certain which one of the four individuals the lie detector will not work on. But neither is it certain that 100 percent correctness can be secured by any other method. So far, lie-detector findings are only rarely admitted as evidence in a court trial — although other findings, probably much less reliable, are used.

What is pupillometrics? *Pupillometrics* (pyōō′pə·lō·met′riks) is a new method used in measuring physiological changes during emotion, based on the principle that the pupil of the eye enlarges when a person receives a pleasant stimulus and contracts when he receives an unpleasant stimulus. An instrument has been developed which photographs and enlarges the pupil of a subject as stimuli are presented. Eventually, pupillometrics may make it possible to present a potential patient for psychotherapy with a series of pictures showing unpleasant situations and, by observing his pupil, to determine which picture evokes an unpleasant emotion in the subject. The method has a distinct advantage over galvanic skin response and most other physiological measures of emotion because the pupil contracts and dilates to specific emotions, unpleasant and pleasant, respectively, whereas other physiological measures indicate only that an emotion has occurred.

Later, when we discuss problems of mental health, we shall have much more to say about emotional behavior.

Terms to Add to Your Vocabulary

adrenal gland	emotional state	parathyroid glands
alpha wave	endocrine glands	peripheral nervous system
autonomic nervous system	frontal lobes	pituitary gland
central nervous system	galvanic skin response (GSR)	pupillometrics
cerebrum	galvanometer	rapid eye movements (REM)
cortex (cerebral)	gonads	reaction time
cretinism	hormones	sympathetic nervous system
duct glands	hypothalamus	temporal lobes
ductless glands	paradoxical sleep	tetany
electroencephalogram (EEG)	parasympathetic nervous	thyroid gland
electroencephalograph (EEG)	system	

Suggestions for Activities

1. Secure data from your local police officials on reaction time for drivers and stopping distances for motor vehicles. A motor club may be able to furnish this material, too. Make graphs showing these data.

2. Take the pulse of a friend under normal conditions. When he is very excited, take it again and note the difference. You may find it necessary to produce the excitement—for example, by making a sudden loud noise.

3. If you are a candid-camera fan, take some unposed pictures of persons in various emotional states. For example, at athletic contests when the home team is winning and when it is losing. Cover all such pictures except for the face. Have friends say what emotion they think was being expressed. When the environmental situation is not known, many errors are made in judging emotional states from facial expressions.

4. If possible, have local or state police demonstrate a lie detector.

5. With a stopwatch, record the sprinting times for several athletes or other students. Each person should start sprints under two different conditions. For several sprints he should concentrate on listening for the starting signal. For the same number of other sprints, he should concentrate on the motor act of starting. Average both sets of data. Does the difference in starting set make any difference in the time required for the sprint?

6. Select several pictures which are emotionally neutral, others which show pleasant emotions, and still others displaying unpleasant emotions. A photograph of an automobile accident from a newspaper might represent the unpleasant picture. A pleasant picture might be of a person with whom your potential subject is "going steady," or dating rather frequently. Shuffle the pictures without letting anyone see them and then ask your subject to look at them one at a time — for about fifteen seconds each. Without seeing which picture the subject is looking at, watch the pupil of one eye. Do you notice any difference in pupil size when the subject looks at the automobile accident? at the picture of the person with whom the subject is going steady? Remember that this may not work, as the difference in pupil size may be very small. Looking at the pupil through a magnifying glass may help. Also, remember that you are performing procedures to demonstrate principles used in psychology and that you should do nothing which might embarrass anyone, especially your subject.

Suggestions for Further Reading

Daniel, Robert S., ed., *Contemporary Readings in General Psychology,* 2nd ed., Houghton Mifflin. Pages 191–95, "The Evolution of Mind"; pages 267–75, "A Biologist Looks at Human Nature"; pages 279–80, "The Physical Basis of Mind: A Philosopher's Symposium."

Hilgard, Ernest R., and Richard C. Atkinson, *Introduction to Psychology,* 4th ed., Harcourt, Brace & World. Chapter 2, "The Behaving Organism"; Chapter 7, "Emotion"; Chapter 10, "States of Awareness."

Kendler, Howard H., *Basic Psychology,* Appleton-Century-Crofts. Chapter 5, "The Biological Foundations of Behavior."

Leuba, Clarence, *Man: A General Psychology,* Holt, Rinehart & Winston. Chapter 4, "Body Needs and Behavior"; Chapter 7, "Reactions to Stress: Body Defenses and Primitive Emotion"; pages 233–50, "Sensory, Nervous, and Muscular Mechanisms"; Chapter 11, "The Brain and Behavior: Further Aspects."

Lindgren, Henry C., Donn Byrne, and Lewis Petrinovich, *Psychology: An Introduction to a Behavioral Science,* 2nd ed., John Wiley. Chapter 5, "Neural Aspects of Behavior"; Chapter 8, "Emotion and Emotional Behavior."

McKeachie, Wilbert J., and Charlotte L. Doyle, *Psychology,* Addison-Wesley.

Chapter 3, "The Biological Background of Behavior."

Mason, A. Stuart, *Health and Hormones,* Penguin Books.

Morgan, Clifford T., and Richard A. King, *Introduction to Psychology,* 3rd ed., Mc-Graw-Hill. Chapter 19, "Nervous System and Internal Environment"; Chapter 20, "Physiological Basis of Behavior."

Munn, Norman L., *Psychology,* 5th ed., Houghton Mifflin. Chapter 2, "The Human Organism"; Chapter 7, "Feeling and Emotion."

Ruch, Floyd L., *Psychology and Life,* 7th ed., Scott, Foresman. Chapter 2, "The Biological Basis of Behavior"; Chapter 9, "Observation and Action," especially pages 328–31, "Perception Under Unusual Conditions"; Chapter 12, "Emotion."

Sanford, Fillmore H., *Psychology: A Scientific Study of Man,* 2nd ed., Wadsworth. Chapter 4, "Biological Base for Integrated Behavior"; Chapter 9, "Emotions."

Whittaker, James O., et al., *Introduction to Psychology,* W. B. Saunders. Chapter 2, "Biological Foundations of Behavior"; Chapter 5, "Feelings and Emotions."

Young, John Z., *Doubt and Certainty in Science: A Biologist's Reflections on the Brain,* Oxford University Press.

11

Getting to know your environment

By what means do we become aware of our environment? Very likely you have been told that there are five senses: those of seeing (vision), hearing, feeling (touch), smelling, and tasting. But we probably have at least eleven senses, and maybe even twenty or more.

In other courses, such as biology, you have probably studied about the sense organs of man and other organisms. If you have studied physics, you know something of how sense organs are stimulated, especially by light and sound. We shall not go into the details of vision, hearing, smelling, tasting, touching, and so on, in this textbook. Instead, we shall limit our discussion to some interesting applications of what is known about sensation and perception.

If you are using the *Record of Activities and Experiments* which accompanies this textbook, you will have some interesting experiences and will learn more about how we come to know our environment. For those of you who are especially interested, college textbooks in psychology often discuss sensation and perception in considerable detail.

SENSATION AND PERCEPTION

Look at the figure below. What does this simple drawing represent? Decide for yourself. Now check with others in the class and see whether you all agree. Unless some have seen the figure before, each student will probably explain the drawing in a different way. One may say that it represents lightning striking a tree, another may think that it represents part of a hayrake, another may guess that it is a Chinese ideograph, and still another may think that it is a figure for a proposition in geometry.

Why does one student interpret the drawing as lightning striking a tree? And why does another see in it the teeth of an implement mounted on a rod? The only explanation can be in

What is it?

terms of the previous experiences of the individuals. Perhaps the first person has recently seen a tree struck by lightning, while the second has witnessed the harvesting of a hay crop. The third person may have been examining a Chinese laundry ticket; the fourth may have been leafing through a plane geometry textbook.

The drawing is intended to suggest an old-time soldier starting off to war. The vertical line represents a doorpost. The soldier himself has passed through the door, but his gun barrel with bayonet attached is still in sight. Farther down is a small part of the soldier's faithful dog. You might think up pictures of your own and try them out on your friends.

When you looked at the drawing on page 284, your eyes were stimulated by light. Thus, you had a visual sensation. When sound waves reach your ears, you have an auditory sensation. The word *sensation* is used by psychologists to refer to the physiological arousal of a sense organ by a stimulus.

Each sense has its own sense organ, its own nerve pathways, and its own centers in the brain, all of which together constitute a *sensory mechanism*. The sense organ is just one part of the sensory mechanism. This *visual mechanism* consists of the eye (the sense organ), the optic nerve, and the part of the brain that organizes visual impulses. The *auditory mechanism* consists of the ear (the sense organ), the auditory nerve, and the part of the brain that organizes auditory impulses.

Psychologists use the word *perception* to refer to sensation plus meaning. When you looked at the figure on page 284, you interpreted it — you put meaning into it — according to your previous experiences. For our purposes it is not necessary to distinguish sharply between sensation and perception. Both are factors in the process of getting in touch with our environment.

An additional concept which psychologists use in studying the senses is *absolute threshold,* which is the minimum amount of stimulus that a subject can detect. In some studies it is important to know how much a stimulus must be changed before the subject is aware that the stimulus has been changed. The amount of change necessary for a subject to notice the change in stimulation is known as a *difference threshold.* (You may come across the word "limen" in your supplementary reading, since it is sometimes used as a substitute for "threshold.")

Another phenomenon associated with the senses is *sensory adaptation,* that is, the adjustment of a particular sense to stimulation. Using controlled conditions it is possible to determine specific aspects of sensory adaptation, such as the length of time it takes for adaptation to occur under different amounts of stimulation. Some examples of sensory adaptation are the adjustment of your eyes to a dimly lit room, or the fact that an obnoxious odor becomes less noticeable after a short period of time.

VISION

Although psychologists have studied many aspects of vision, we shall discuss only eye movements in reading,

GETTING TO KNOW YOUR ENVIRONMENT

color and color blindness, perceiving depth with a stereoscope, and optical illusions.

How do the eyes move during reading? Try this simple experiment. Ask a friend to read a bit of easy fiction while you watch the movements of his eyes. The best way to do this is to stand back of your friend and hold a mirror at an angle on the desk on which his book rests. By adjusting the mirror, you can easily observe his eye movements.

Perhaps you will be surprised to learn that his eyes move by jerks rather than steadily. He will look at one word or phrase, then move his eyes and look at another word or phrase, and so on across the line. Then he will make a return sweep to the beginning of the next line and move across it by jerks. Read-

A good reader made this pattern of eye movements. The fewer fixations, or stops, there are per line, the more efficiently the person is reading.

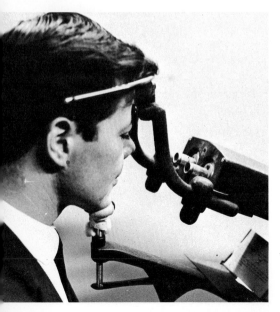

This instrument is an ophthalmograph, used to photograph the eye movements of a person as he reads.

ing is actually done while the eyes are stationary, for images which are moving on the retina are indistinguishable. In reading we spend from 90 to 95 percent of our time with eyes practically stationary. The remaining small part of the time is used for eye movements.

Try to count the number of movements made in each line by your friend. Then have him read in a technical book such as a chemistry or a mathematics text. Did he make more stops (fixations) per line? Most persons do when reading difficult material.

Watch the eye movements of a young child who has only recently learned to read. Does he make more fixations per line than an older person? Most children do. Part of the secret of becoming an efficient reader is to make fewer and fewer fixations per line.

A record of eye movements can be made on a motion-picture film by means of an instrument designed to produce such records. The illustration to the left shows the record of the movements of the two eyes of a superior high school student as he read seven lines. The fixations and movements of the eyes were recorded as a series of "stairsteps." Note the return sweep to the beginning of each new line. In reading a newspaper a good reader's eyes will make from three to six fixations per line. Since so much schoolwork is based on reading, efficiency as a student is determined in large measure by efficiency in reading. Do not be concerned, however, about your eye movements in reading. There was a time when much attention was given to training poor readers to move their eyes efficiently. Now it has been found that inefficient eye movements are a symptom of poor reading rather than a cause of it.

Teachers who specialize in helping students correct poor reading habits use various techniques in their work. Anyone can improve his reading speed by simply trying to read easy material more rapidly than usual. (Of course, technical material should not be read at a rapid rate.) In one study, poor readers were told, "Read anything—read enjoyable things—read and talk about it—just read." In less than three months, 75 percent of them had brought their reading-test scores up to normal. Developing an extensive vocabulary improves reading skill because more words are understood without having to stop to analyze them.

What is the physical nature of color?
Three basic terms are used in describing colors: "hue," "brightness," and "saturation." You will find the following discussion of these terms more understandable if you refer to the illustrations of the color circle, the visible spectrum of hues, and the color solid, which shows the three dimensions of color, on pages 294–95. (A color solid is shaped like a double cone.)

Hue refers to the quality of redness, blueness, yellowness, or greenness that differentiates one color from another; it is what most people commonly call "color." Sunlight can be broken up into different hues, as, for example, in a rainbow. The complete arrangement of hues visible to the human eye is called the *visible spectrum*. Arranged according to wavelengths, the spectrum has red on one end and on the other end, violet. In the spectrum, red shades off into orange, which shades into yellow, and then green, blue, and violet. There are no sharp dividing lines between the colors in the visible spectrum; as many as 150 distinct hues can be observed. These hues can be thought of as arranged around a circle. Purple is indicated on the circle, but purple is not a color of the spectrum. However, because it can be formed by mixing red and blue lights, which are on the spectrum, it is included in the color circle.

In determining the ability of an individual to distinguish between different hues, or colors, psychologists use the concept of just-noticeable-difference. A single stimulus is presented to a subject and then is changed by a very small amount. The minimum amount of change in the stimulus necessary for the subject to be able to de-

GETTING TO KNOW YOUR ENVIRONMENT

tect a change is called *just-noticeable-difference.* (The difference threshold [page 285] is the amount of change necessary for the subject to detect a just-noticeable-difference 50 percent of the time.)

Brightness refers to the sensation of lightness or darkness of any color or gray. Note on the diagram of the color solid that the vertical axis runs from white at the top to black at the bottom. Between the black and white poles of a color solid are shades of gray. As hues approach white at the top of the color solid, they become progressively lighter. Note on the color solid that the blue toward the top of the solid is lighter than the blue farther down. The lighter the color, the brighter it is. Note also that hues become progressively darker as they approach the black at the bottom of the color solid.

Saturation refers to the purity of a hue. Look again at the diagram of the color solid and note how saturation is represented on it. As a hue runs from the outermost point on the color solid toward the center, it progressively loses its purity and becomes grayer. We say that it has become less saturated.

The partial vertical cross section of the color solid illustrates both saturation and brightness. Notice how red diminishes in its amount of redness, or saturation, as it approaches the vertical axis. You can also see how red increases in brightness (becomes lighter) as it moves up toward white at the top of the axis and decreases in brightness (becomes darker) as it moves down toward black at the bottom of the axis.

An example will help to explain saturation still further. A seamstress makes a dress and puts away scraps of the material for use as patches. Later, the scraps of cloth are brought out for use as patching material. But the scraps no longer match the dress! The dress has been exposed to sunlight and washing. It has faded, while the scrap that was packed away in the dark is as fresh as when new. In technical terms, the faded dress is less saturated than the scrap.

Colors opposite each other on the color circle are said to be *complementary;* that is, when mixed together, they give gray. Does this seem strange? Would you mix blue and yellow paint to form gray? Of course that would give green paint, but mixing paint is somewhat different from mixing light. To mix light, disks of colored paper are placed on a wheel, and the wheel is rotated rapidly; or else different-colored lights are projected on a screen. In this discussion of color we are mixing lights, not pigments.

When two colors on the color circle are mixed together but are not opposite each other, the resulting hue will be between the two hues. The saturation of the color will be closest to that color which has the greater proportion in the mixture. These statements represent what is called the *Law of Intermediates.* As an example, if you were to mix blue and red, the result would be purple. Mixing yellow and red would result in orange. If yellow made up 60 percent of the mixture and red 40 percent, the saturation would be more yellow than red.

What are some favorite colors and color combinations? Do you like colored objects better than black-gray-white objects? What is your favorite color? In one experiment, colored papers and gray papers were held before babies. The babies showed greater interest in the colored papers than in the gray ones. Red seems to be the favorite color of small children; as they grow older, they prefer blue. For American adults, blue is the favorite color of most persons; yellow is the least preferred color. South of the Mexican border, red is the preferred color. Apparently our color preferences are culturally determined, at least after infancy.

However, it must be noted that a color which would be pleasing in one situation may not be pleasing in another. A boy may like one color for the dress of a girl friend and yet not want to be seen in a suit of the same color. A house made of grass-green bricks might be considered to show lack of taste on the part of the builder, yet most people like green grass.

In many cases it is necessary to use two colors together, as in advertisements, in school colors, and in clothes. As a rule, a combination of two colors is pleasing if the colors are opposite each other on the color wheel. Blue and an orange-yellow would make pleasing school colors; so would red and blue-green or purple and yellow-green. If it is desired to use three colors together, a simple rule can be followed. Select colors equidistant on the color wheel. If you have studied geometry, you have learned how to inscribe an equilateral triangle in a circle. The vertices of any such inscribed triangle would fall at points which would give a pleasing combination of three colors. Notice how these rules of color combination are used in advertising signs. To a considerable extent they are applied in the color schemes of women's clothing, although fashion may dictate that almost any combinations are pleasing. Thus we may see tints of blue and purple, red and purple, or almost any other combination in women's dresses.

Saturation must be considered when choosing pleasing color combinations. As a rule, red and yellow are said to be too close together on the color wheel to give a pleasing combination. If, however, both the red and the yellow are of very weak saturation (pastel tints), they may give a pleasing effect when used together.

What are some practical applications of color? A number of years ago a large mail-order house included in its catalogue two different pages on which skirts were advertised. The skirts on the two pages were identical in style and were practically the same in price and quality. One page presented the skirts in black, white, and intermediate grays; the other page showed the skirts in colors. It costs far more to print a page in color than to print it in black-gray-white. Do sales justify the additional expense? The orders from the page in colors were ten times as great as the orders from the page in black, white, and gray. There is a record of one company which increased its sales of a given product 1,000 percent merely by changing the color of the wrapper.

It may be said that a great deal of modern advertising has two functions: (1) to interest nonusers of the product in buying it and (2) to preserve and enhance the pride of ownership for those who have already purchased the product. In both cases, it is essential to associate the name of the brand with the product. In one experiment, 992 persons were asked to look through a book bound with twenty full-page advertisements from recent issues of a magazine having a very high circulation. The advertisements were for a wide variety of products: soft drinks, cigarettes, cosmetics, medicine, and so on. The individuals lived in ten cities scattered throughout the United States. They were divided into two groups matched for sex, age, economic status, and amount of formal schooling. One group saw ads which were in color, the other saw ads which were in black and white. In this experiment the independent variable was the color (which refers to both red, green, yellow, etc., and to black, gray, and white) of the ads, and the dependent variable was the effect of such color in arousing interest or pride for the product advertised. The investigators concluded that in the promotion of a new brand, where the primary purpose was to interest nonusers, colored advertising was not necessarily greatly superior to black-gray-white advertising. On the other hand, where the primary purpose was to keep alive and enhance the reputation for quality so that owners would be proud of their purchases, colored advertising seemed to have an advantage over black-gray-white advertising.

There are many other practical applications of color. For instance, color may determine how often a public room is used. One manufacturer decorated the women's cafeteria in his factory in light blue, a favorite color of Americans. Nevertheless, the women complained that the room was cold. Many insisted that it was necessary for them to wear their coats while eating. The thermometer showed that the room was at a comfortable temperature. The manufacturer had the room trimmed in orange and had orange slipcovers placed on the chairs. The women no longer complained of the coldness of the room and no longer found it necessary to wear coats while eating. The thermometer indicated that the temperature was the same as before. In another industry, the walls of the recreation room were painted oyster white. The room was seldom used by the employees until it was repainted in a soft rose.

What is color blindness, or color weakness? We have been assuming that any person who is not completely blind can see colors as well as any other person. Unfortunately, this is not true. There are some persons who cannot distinguish all the colors most of us can distinguish. Popularly, such persons are said to be color-blind, although more strictly they should be said to be "color weak."

There are two kinds of color blindness: total color blindness and red-green color blindness. Those persons who are only red-green blind can still distinguish blue and yellow. To the totally color-blind person, the world appears like a black-and-white snapshot or an uncolored motion picture. To the red-green color-blind person, a scene wholly in blue and yellow would appear just the same as to a person who is not color-blind. Red and green, however, would appear to him as a dull yellow-gray. Very few persons are totally color-blind. Interestingly enough, there are a few individuals who are color-blind in one eye but have normal color vision in the other eye.

Color blindness is inherited and is definitely related to sex. It is generally estimated that from 6 to 8 percent of men are color-blind, at least to some extent. Practically no women are color-blind, yet color blindness is inherited through the female side of the family. Thus, a color-blind man will have a daughter who has normal vision, but his grandson (not granddaughter) may be color-blind.

One of the tests usually given to applicants for driving licenses, as well as to railroad employees and airplane pilots, is a test for color blindness. Such tests often consist of numbers, letters, or curved pathways differing in color or shade from the background on which they are printed. For example, there may be a number made up of faint red dots on a background of light green dots (page 293). The person with normal vision can see and report a numeral without difficulty, but the color-blind individual is unable to distinguish the red numeral from the green background.

Is color blindness a serious handicap?
Although a color-blind person is somewhat handicapped, the handicap is serious in only a few occupations. Railroad men must not be color-blind, for ability to distinguish between red and green is extremely important in that work. For the same reason navigators and pilots must not be color-blind. Telephone circuits are often traced by means of colored, plastic-coated insulation over the wires; therefore, a telephone repairman who was color-blind might have difficulty. A color-blind house painter would have to rely on another person in matching colors. A color-blind florist might make strange color combinations in floral pieces.

Under some circumstances, color blindness may be an asset rather than a liability. It has been suggested that every well-organized clothing store should have one or two color-blind employees to use throughout the store in matching brightness. They would not confuse brightness and color, as so many persons of normal vision do. In military situations it has been found that color-blind men can sometimes detect camouflage when men of normal color vision cannot do so.

The most common handicap for the color-blind person is in the serious business of driving an automobile. He may not be able to tell which is the red light and which is the green. It must be understood that he would have no difficulty in distinguishing between the light that was lighted and the one that was not. This would be a matter of brightness, not of hue; and the color-blind person can distinguish brightness without difficulty. Sometimes double red lights are used for stop and single green lights are used for go, so that the

GETTING TO KNOW YOUR ENVIRONMENT

color-blind person can differentiate by the number of signals. In addition, blue is occasionally added to the green filter in traffic lights, and orange to the red, which enables the red-green color-blind person, who sees the blue and orange as colors, to distinguish between the two signals.

How does a stereoscope assist in the perceiving of three dimensions? Although we are able to perceive depth as well as length and width when we use only one eye (monocular vision), our perception of depth is improved by looking at any object with both eyes (binocular vision).

Before the days of the popular movies and television, many a parlor had a stereoscope and a set of stereoscopic cards. Members of the family and friends entertained themselves by looking at pictures through this instrument. Today we have compact stereoscopes with the pictures, in color, mounted on a disk so that they can easily be brought into view one after the other by pressing a lever.

The stereoscope is so arranged that the right eye can see only the right-hand picture on the stereoscopic card, and the left eye can see only the left-hand picture. A stereoscope and the kind of card that is used with this instrument are shown below.

Amateur photographers sometimes prepare stereoscopic cards from pictures that they take with a special cam-

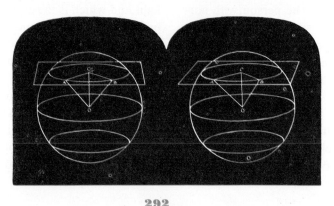

PATTERNS OF BEHAVIOR

era or with ordinary cameras. A special camera for taking stereoscopic pictures is really two cameras in one. There are two lenses, two shutters, and two films. The two instruments are mounted in a single frame. Their lenses are about the same distance apart as the human eyes.

Any ordinary camera can be used to make stereoscopic pictures. Merely take a picture; then move the camera to one side about 3 inches and take another picture. There must be no up or down movement. When the pictures are printed, they will at first glance appear to be alike; but careful scrutiny will show that they are slightly different, for they were taken from slightly different angles. Now mount these pictures side by side on a cardboard of the proper size to fit in a stereoscope. A little experimentation will enable you to mount them so that when viewed through the stereoscope, they will appear as one picture rather than as two. Be sure to mount the picture taken when the camera was at the left so that it will be in front of the left eye. The picture taken when the camera was at the right must be in front of the right eye.

When you look at a stereoscopic card through the stereoscope, the picture stands out clearly in three dimensions. You might say, "It seems as if I were actually looking at the scene." This merely means that the stereoscope permits you to see the picture as you should see the scene with your two eyes.

How can stereoscopic pictures be used by physicians, teachers, and others?

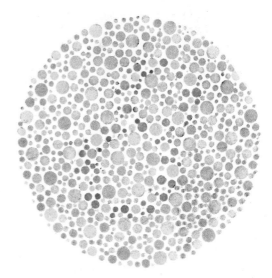

This is a plate from the Ishihara Test for color blindness. When a person with normal color vision looks at the plate, he sees a figure 8. The person with red-green blindness sees a figure 3. A person who is totally color-blind sees no figure at all.

Physicians sometimes make use of the principle of stereoscopic vision. Suppose that a physician has reason to believe that a man has tuberculosis. He can have simple X-ray pictures taken, which may tell him something about the location of the infected part or parts. However, he may be able to make a better diagnosis if he has a stereoscopic X-ray picture taken. Such a picture is merely two X-ray pictures taken with cameras a few inches apart. The developed plates are then placed in a specially constructed stereoscope, with the result that the physician is able to see the patient's lungs in three dimensions.

Also, physicians often use stereoscopic picture cards to give patients special exercises for the eye muscles.

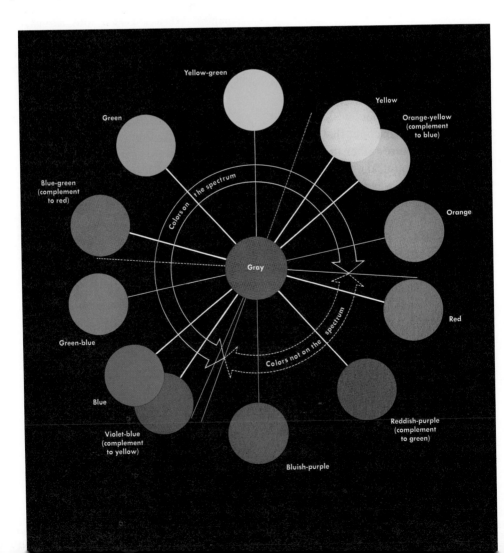

Violet   Blue   Green   Yellow   Orange   Red

Colors produced by light waves may be arranged according to the length of the light waves, as in the solar spectrum above, or may be arranged around the circumference of a circle to form a color wheel, as shown below. The solar spectrum results when sunlight is sent through a prism. The colors of the spectrum are in the same order as can be seen in a rainbow. When color light waves are arranged in a circle, those colors opposite each other, known as complementary colors, will mix into a neutral gray. Some colors—certain purples and reds—do not exist on the spectrum, but are included in the color circle because they can be produced by mixing spectral lights.

Yellow-green

Green

Yellow

Orange-yellow
(complement
to blue)

Blue-green
(complement
to red)

Colors on the spectrum

Orange

Gray

Red

Green-blue

Colors not on the spectrum

Blue

Reddish-purple
(complement
to green)

Violet-blue
(complement
to yellow)

Bluish-purple

The lights of two non-complementary colors can be mixed to produce a third color, as shown on the right: red and green lights fuse into yellow; green and bluish-purple yield blue. The mixture of any two of these colors combines to give the complement of the third color, as seen in the triangular sections.

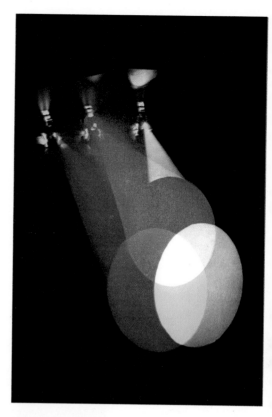

The color solid (or color cone) below illustrates the three dimensions of color. The circumference of the cone shows hue; the radius shows saturation; and the vertical axis shows brightness. The vertical slice (foreground) for the hue red gives the brightness range vertically, from light (top) to dark (bottom), and presents the saturation range horizontally, running from "pure" red (on the right) toward gray (on the left).

GETTING TO KNOW YOUR ENVIRONMENT

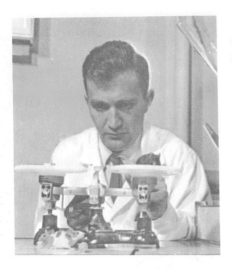

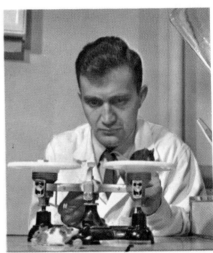

The many colors that show in the final version of the photograph above result from the use of only three different color inks. Before the ink is applied, however, the original image is photographed through three filters to produce three different color negatives. These negatives are obtained by putting filters over the lens of a camera so that only one color can come through at a time. Often a fourth negative, for black, is also made. When these negatives are printed with the three color inks—red, yellow, and blue—and with black ink, one on top of the other, the photograph is reproduced on the page in full color. If a part of the original photograph is green, that part will appear on both the yellow negative and the blue negative, and the two inks will combine to form green on the finished reproduction. Other colors are reproduced by the same process of first separating by filter, and then recombining by ink.

PATTERNS OF BEHAVIOR

A patient can be given exercise in looking from distant mountains to nearby objects without leaving the doctor's office by merely looking at stereoscopic cards showing such distant and near objects.

Many times students have difficulty in their study of solid geometry because they cannot see the figure on the flat page of the book as representing a figure in three dimensions. Stereoscopic pictures of the common figures in solid geometry can be purchased. When the student looks at these figures through a stereoscope, he can get a much better understanding of the three dimensions of such figures.

Stereoscopic pictures taken in many parts of the world are available and are used by teachers in giving children correct concepts of three-dimensional space. There are stereoscopic books for children printed in two colors and accompanied by a two-color viewer.

In peacetime exploration and in military reconnaissance work, it is often impractical to survey an area by means of the usual transit-and-measuring-chain technique. Stereoscopic pictures can be made of the desired area from an airplane. When viewed through a stereoscope, the resulting pictures not only give the flat layout of the ground but also provide some measure of the heights of mountains, buildings, and other objects.

What are optical illusions? Sometimes we make mistakes in our perceptions.

False perceptions of stimuli of any kind are referred to as *illusions*. If the false perception is in the field of vision, it is called an *optical illusion*.

Above are two horizontal lines, exactly equal in length. The images of these two horizontal lines are equal, but we perceive one as longer than the other. Why? We do not restrict our attention to the horizontal lines themselves. Instead, we look at the entire figures. One entire figure is longer than the other, and we interpret this to mean that one horizontal line is longer than the other. Some other optical illusions are given on page 299. Their effect is achieved by creating total figures that produce a distorted perception of part of the figures.

What is the difference between an illusion and a hallucination? As we have just seen, an illusion is a false perception of an external stimulus. On the other hand, a faulty senselike perception for which there is no external stimulus is called a *hallucination*. Some mentally ill persons "hear" voices speaking to them, although there are no voices or other sounds which might be interpreted as voices. They may have "visions" of persons long since dead. The subjects in the study of sensory deprivation (page 313) also had hallucinations. It is possible to produce hallucinations by means of such drugs as LSD–25, but such drugs should be taken only under rigid and well-qualified supervision. Hallucinations are usually along auditory or visual lines but may be related to any sensory field. A mentally ill person may "feel" someone place a hand on his shoulder, although there is no one near him.

Suppose a person is walking along the street and "sees" a snake on the sidewalk. Such an experience may be either an illusion or a hallucination. If a branch has fallen off a tree and the person mistakes it for a snake, he is having an illusion. If there is no branch, or no other object which might be mistaken for a snake, the person is having a hallucination.

A word sometimes confused with "illusion," and even with "hallucination," is "delusion," which, as we saw in Chapter 5, on page 110, is a false belief.

Why are illusions useful in designing clothes and in camouflage? Every day we see examples of the practical applications of illusions. Much of our clothing is selected with the intention of giving impressions that are not exactly in harmony with actuality. A girl who is tall and very thin may wish to give the impression that she is of average height and weight. She should, then, wear clothing in which lines tend to run horizontally rather than vertically. People will see her as a number of short units rather than as one long figure. On the other hand, a girl who is short and somewhat heavy may wish to give the impression that she is of average height and weight—or even tall and slender. She should wear clothing in which the lines tend to run vertically rather than horizontally. She should wear a one-piece dress rather than a skirt and blouse. People will then see her as one figure rather than as several short units.

Young men and women who are somewhat smaller than their classmates will appear sturdier and larger in light-colored than in dark clothing. Persons who are larger than their fellows can give the impression of being smaller than they actually are by wearing dark clothing. Baseball players usually wear light-colored uniforms. Officials, in order not to be confused with players, usually wear dark jackets and trousers. Have you noticed, during games, that the players often appear to be larger than the officials? After a game, when both players and officials are dressed in the usual street clothing, there may be no apparent difference in their sizes.

Camouflage is simply a matter of illusion. In time of war, a tank which can be perceived as a tank by enemy observers is sure to become the object of artillery fire. Painting the tank with splotches of various colors causes the outline of the tank to become less distinct, and therefore a more difficult target. In recent wars camouflage has been applied very extensively. For example, ponchos for jungle fighters were of a mottled green-brown color. Naval vessels were given various different arrangements of paint. Important buildings and factories were painted and altered to blend with the surrounding landscape.

How do magicians use illusion? Sometimes a professional magician makes use of illusions in his performance. For example, he may show the audience a

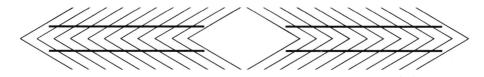

Are these horizontal lines parallel? Measure their width at both ends.

Which of these lines is longer? Measure them.

nail. He then proceeds to pass the nail through his finger—or rather, that is what the audience perceives. Actually he has two nails. The one shown to the audience is a regular nail. The magician skillfully exchanges this nail for one composed of two ends of a nail with a curved piece of metal joining them. The audience sees the head of the nail on one side of his finger and the point on the other side of his finger. The curved piece joining the two ends cannot be seen, so the nail is falsely perceived as passing through the magician's finger. This trick depends upon an optical illusion.

All of the magician's success is not to be accounted for in terms of such simple illusions. Much of it is based on his ability to guide the attention of his audience.

What is the illusion of apparent motion?
The ordinary "movie" is not literally a moving picture; the impression of continuous motion is merely an optical illusion. The motion-picture projector throws a picture on the screen, then it shuts off the light and leaves the screen dark; next it throws a slightly different picture on the screen, then it shuts off

the light and the screen is dark again; and so on, throughout the show. You say that you have seen a moving picture. Actually, you have seen a series of still pictures. The pictures were thrown on the screen at the rate of twenty-four per second. This rate was so rapid that you did not perceive the separate pictures but experienced the illusion of motion.

Advertisers often use the illusion of motion in electrically operated signs, whether with incandescent bulbs or neon tubes. For example, one bus company often has a neon sign showing a lighted figure of a greyhound running. The dog is shown with his legs in one position. The light in these legs is turned off and the light in another pair of legs is turned on. Then the light in the first pair is turned on again and that in the second pair turned off, and so on. We "see" the dog running; that is, we have an optical illusion. Other electrically operated signs show wheels turning and liquids pouring.

Psychologists have given the name *phi phenomenon* to the mistaking of apparent motion for real motion. (*Phi* [fī or fē] is merely a Greek letter used for convenience.)

GETTING TO KNOW YOUR ENVIRONMENT

HEARING

There is a great deal of interesting and technical material on the subject of hearing, but here we shall limit ourselves to a brief discussion of what we hear, known as sound, and to three interesting aspects of hearing: absolute pitch, noise, and the problem of deafness.

What are pitch, loudness, and timbre? Sound may be discussed in terms of pitch, loudness, and timbre. Some sounds are of high pitch, others of low pitch. We can distinguish between the pitch of a cornet and the pitch of a bass horn. A sound with a clearly marked pitch is called a *tone*. The *pitch* of a tone is determined by the rate or frequency of vibration of the sound wave. The greater the frequency of vibration, the higher the pitch of the tone. Conversely, the lesser the frequency of vibration, the lower the tone.

Although sound can carry through such substances as water and metal, most sound waves that we hear travel through the air. Man cannot hear all the vibrations that reach his ear but is limited to those from about 20 to about 20,000 vibrations per second. Some individuals cannot hear sounds above 15,000 to 16,000 vibrations per second. As a person grows older, the pitch of the tones he hears is not so high as the pitch he could hear in his youth. On the other hand, there is some evidence that older people lose their hearing partially because of the culture in which Americans and Europeans live. Tests for the hearing of individuals in a primitive culture have shown that

these individuals do not lose their hearing for higher frequencies. Our loss of hearing such frequencies in later years may be due in part to the rather noisy environment in which we live.

In the case of animals, dogs can hear sounds above 25,000 vibrations per second; bats are able to hear sounds of 40,000 to 50,000 vibrations per second. Yet turtles' ears are highly sensitive only to waves ranging from about 100 to 700 vibrations per second. They cannot normally hear above 3,000 vibrations.

The range of hearing (for frequency) is determined by presenting a tone of a specified frequency to an animal, rewarding him for responding to the sound, then presenting a tone of a slightly higher frequency and rewarding him for his response to it. This procedure is continued until the animal no longer responds to the frequency. The same steps are used to determine the lowest level of hearing except that the tone is presented in decreasing stages until the animal no longer responds.

The *loudness* of a tone is determined primarily by the height, or amplitude, of the vibrations of the sound wave. The greater the amplitude of the waves, the louder is the sound.

Suppose that you are blindfolded. You hear middle C produced by a violin, a cornet, and a human voice. Suppose further that this is a carefully controlled experiment. The three sounds are of exactly the same loudness as well as of the same pitch. Could you distinguish the sources of the three sounds? The distinctive quality of tones is known as *timbre*

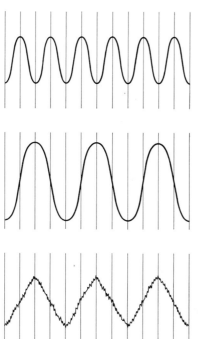

PITCH
determined by the
frequency of vibration

LOUDNESS
determined by the
amplitude of the
vibrations

TIMBRE
determined by the
overtone pattern
of the vibrations

In this graphic comparison of the properties of sound waves, pitch is represented by the frequency of the waves, loudness by the height of the waves, and timbre by the complexity of the wave pattern.

and depends primarily upon the overtone pattern of the sound waves.

The human voice, most musical instruments, and other sources of sound give off overtones as well as their fundamental tone. For example, when a tone is played on a violin, you hear not only the fundamental tone but also a number of overtones. The human voice is very rich in overtones. Were it not for the differing overtones in the voices of our friends, we could not tell one voice from another. In fact, each individual has a characteristic voice sound pattern which identifies him even if he attempts to conceal or change his voice sound.

What is absolute pitch? You may have heard discussion of whether or not some individuals have *absolute pitch.* "Absolute pitch" means (1) the ability of an individual to name correctly a particular tone that is sung or played without comparing it with any other heard tone or (2) the ability to reproduce a designated tone after a considerable period of time. It should be noted, however, that although a person with absolute pitch can tell what note on a scale is being played, he cannot tell how many vibrations per second it is.

Some psychologists believe that absolute pitch is inherited. This ability

GETTING TO KNOW YOUR ENVIRONMENT

Why do most people prefer the sound of music being performed to the sound of unrelated vibrations of noise?

seems to run in families (even without training). Also, it seems to be present in connection with the first musical experience of some individuals. On the other hand, there is some experimental evidence that ability in pitch discrimination is widely distributed. It appears that pitch-naming ability can be improved, to a certain extent, by training. In one study, sixteen persons were trained in discrimination of absolute pitch. When they were tested a year later, their retention of the ability was still high. In another study, however, individual improvement in discrimination of absolute pitch was largely lost after several years during which there was no practice. More research is needed concerning absolute pitch.

It is of interest to note that white notes on the piano are more often correctly judged than black notes. Also, notes in the middle range are judged more accurately than those in the extreme range. One psychologist found that a bass player was better in judging tones in the lower range than in the rest of the scale. A violinist was better in judging tones in the upper range. Certainly, such reports suggest that judgment is best with respect to notes with which the individual is associated most frequently. That is, ability in absolute pitch appears to be a product, at least in part, of learning.

Why is music pleasant and noise a problem? Both music and noise are produced by vibrations in the air. In many cases it is difficult to distinguish between the two. The sounds made by a modern dance orchestra may be music to the dancers and a horrible noise to the musician trained in classical music. The sounds from a typical apartment house full of radios playing at top volume would be classed as noise, although each of the radios in itself might be playing music. In general, noises produce unpleasant experiences, whereas music produces pleasant experiences. The sensation of noise is stimulated by sound waves of irregular and unrelated frequencies. In other words, noise differs from tone in that noise has no clearly defined pitch.

No careful study has been made of the relationship between personality pattern and the emotional effect of noise. It is known, however, that individuals differ greatly in the extent to

PATTERNS OF BEHAVIOR

which they are annoyed by noise. Individuals are often able to adapt themselves to noise if necessary. For example, in one bit of research, Air Force ROTC students were given certain material to learn and recall. They were subjected to a high-intensity noise similar to that created by a jet aircraft engine. The noise had no significant effect on their ability to recall the learned material. They reported some early disturbance due to the noise but said that they adapted quickly and ceased to perceive the noise as an annoying sensation. There is even some research suggesting that, for certain tasks, noise apparently improves performance.

Nevertheless, noise is a serious social problem, especially in thickly settled communities. In progressive cities, definite campaigns to reduce noise are under way. In some cities it is against the law to sound an automobile horn except in an emergency. In most cities it is against the law to drive a car without a muffler on it. Police action may be brought against persons who insist on playing their radios or televisions at full blast during all hours of the day and night. There is even some evidence that damage to hearing may result from repeated attendance at places where extremely loud music is played.

How much does noise affect business efficiency? Noise is a serious business problem. Owners of city real estate find their property decreasing in value because people are moving to the suburbs partly to escape city noise. Some persons who would otherwise prefer to live in apartment houses move into private houses because there is less noise.

One psychologist had typists work under ordinary conditions of office noise. A "noise machine" reproduced the sounds occurring in the usual busy office. The psychologist kept a record of the amount of typing accomplished. By means of an ingenious device, he measured the amount of oxygen consumed during typing. On other days the same typists worked in the same room and with the same noise machine going. However, the walls were covered with panels of a sound-absorbing

Sound waves of street noises (top and middle) and of a pure tone

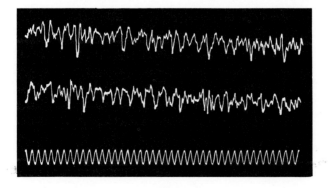

GETTING TO KNOW YOUR ENVIRONMENT

material that was estimated to reduce by about 50 percent the sound heard in the room. Again, records were made of the amount of typing done and the amount of oxygen consumed.

The average time for typing a letter under the noisy conditions was 162 seconds. Under reduced-noise conditions the average time was 155 seconds —a gain of 4.3 percent. Furthermore, it was found that 19 percent more energy, as measured by oxygen consumption, was used under the noisy conditions than under the more quiet conditions. Also, there was some evidence suggesting this conclusion: The speedier the worker is, the more adversely his output is affected by the distractions of noises.

It has been found that noise is especially annoying when it is unexpected, when it spreads and reverberates, when it is judged to be unnecessary, and when it indicates malfunctioning of mechanical equipment. Irregular, variable sounds are more annoying than steady ones. High-pitched sounds tend to be more annoying than low-pitched sounds.

Intense noise, even when it has no apparent effect on efficiency of performance, tends to produce discomfort, irritability, and distraction. It is known that loud or intermittent sounds tend to produce changes in blood pressure, gastric secretion, pulse rate, perspiration of the palms, respiration, muscle tension, and electroencephalographic recordings. Reduction of noise is not only a matter of an individual's personal comfort and health; it is also a matter of dollars-and-cents efficiency in terms of output.

Is deafness a serious problem? There are varying degrees and kinds of deafness. Some persons are tone deaf; that is, although they can hear sounds, they have very poor pitch discrimination. If you sound two notes on the piano, they will be unable to tell which is the higher of the two. They can appreciate the rhythm in music even though they cannot appreciate the melody. Obviously, such persons could not become great musicians. Also, they would find it practically impossible to acquire correct intonation in a foreign language.

The word "deafness" is used most commonly to refer to the condition of persons who are "hard of hearing"— that is, those who cannot detect faint sounds that can be heard easily by persons of normal hearing ability. This deafness may be for the whole range of pitch, or it may be limited to particular parts of the total range of sounds. Old persons are often unable to hear either high-pitched or low-pitched sounds. At one time the hearing of over a million persons was tested. It was found that 1 out of 25 persons had difficulty in hearing in auditoriums; 1 in 125 had trouble in hearing face-to-face conversation; 1 in 400 had difficulty in hearing over the telephone.

We all sympathize with the person who is blind, but we are not always so considerate of the person who is deaf. Blindness can be recognized quite easily. Yet the fact of another's deafness may not impress itself on a person who has normal hearing ability. The associates of a deaf person may think that he is ignoring them when he does not enter into their conversation. Or they may think that he is not very intelligent, because he does not respond to their questions. If he does respond, his answer may be confused because he did not hear all of the question clearly. Many times deaf children have been thought to be dull and have failed to be promoted in school. The teachers thought that they were of low intelligence or that they did not pay attention to what was said in class. Oftentimes tests reveal that children thought to be stupid really have normal ability to learn but are unable to hear what is said in school and at home.

It is necessary to raise the voice in talking to individuals who are hard of hearing. This attracts the attention of everyone in the room, both to the speaker and to the deaf person. They both feel conspicuous. The person of normal hearing ability will perhaps stop trying to talk to the deaf person. The deaf person will probably withdraw into his own little world rather than suffer further embarrassment. On occasion he may see people talking. Being unable to hear what they say, he may suspect that they are making fun of him. Deafness may be a serious handicap in the development of a desirable personality.

How can a deaf person overcome his handicap? The person who has defective hearing can fill a very important place in the world. You have seen that work is done more efficiently under quiet conditions than under noisy conditions. Thomas Edison was very hard of hearing, but he found this circumstance to be an advantage to him insofar as his work was concerned. He

Although handicapped by deafness, this girl can learn to speak by making use of her other senses.

was not distracted from work on his inventions by the noise and conversation around him. Persons who are hard of hearing often make excellent bookkeepers, typists, printers, and machinists. They live and concentrate in a quiet world of their own. They may not be expected to do so well in work requiring social contacts.

In many cases the personal, social, and vocational handicaps of deficient hearing may to a great extent be overcome. The social field is broad for the deaf person who learns lip reading. He can understand what is being said from the movements of the lips of a speaker. He cannot understand what is said in the dark, for he "hears" with his eyes.

Once "ear trumpets" were used by the deaf. Modern electrical devices are much more efficient and are small and

GETTING TO KNOW YOUR ENVIRONMENT

inconspicuous. Unfortunately, some persons, especially young people, hesitate to wear hearing aids because they are afraid that wearing an aid will interfere with their popularity. Probably the truth is that their personality, and their popularity, are much more adversely affected by deafness than by wearing a small and nearly unnoticeable hearing aid. In fact, with the new microelectronic circuits available today, some hearing aids are almost undetectable.

OTHER SENSE FIELDS

We shall not attempt to go into detail concerning other sense fields; nevertheless, a few comments about these other fields may stimulate you to read more about them.

Smell. Of course, man has a sense of smell, although it is not as keen as in some other animals. A good bloodhound, for example, can trace a person for miles by the faint odor remaining on the trail.

Our sense of smell comes from receptors in the upper part of the nose which are easily stimulated by gases. There have been various attempts to classify the odors which we sense. One classification suggests that there are six fundamental odors: spicy, burnt, resinous, flowery, fruity, putrid. Most persons consider some of these odors to be pleasing and others displeasing. Another classification system suggests only four primary odors: acid (vinegar), burnt (roast coffee), fragrant (musk), caprylic (goaty).

Some psychologists and physiologists attempt to explain smelling in terms of chemical reactions taking place at the receptors, while others suggest that smelling is to be understood in terms of heat radiation. If you are studying chemistry, you may wish to do further reading on the identification of gases in terms of different absorptions of infrared radiation.

Tobacco companies frequently use the word "aroma" in their advertising. It might be added here that most of the "odor" appeal is in the advertising rather than in the tobacco itself. In spite of advertising claims, most blindfolded subjects cannot differentiate among brands of tobacco. In one experiment blindfolded subjects used a pipe. Sometimes the pipe contained tobacco, and they actually smoked. At other times the pipe contained a hot electric coil, and the subjects merely "smoked" warm air. They could not tell the difference between the warm air and tobacco smoke. One subject insisted on blowing smoke rings when in reality there was nothing but warm air in the pipe. However, there was a slight odor of smoke in the room from a pipe smoked by another person.

Taste. For most people, taste is primarily a means of getting enjoyment from the environment. Taste is related to the sense of smell, and much of the "taste" of food is really the smell of that food. You have probably noticed that when you have a "cold in the nose," your appreciation of taste is greatly diminished.

A substance must be in liquid form in order to be tasted. The liquid is supplied either by the substance itself or by the saliva. Wipe the surface of your tongue dry with a clean cloth, and then place a lump of sugar or salt on the tip of the tongue. You will not be able to taste it until enough saliva forms to produce ·a solution of sugar or salt which seeps down to the *taste buds* below the surface of the tongue. Insoluble substances cannot be tasted.

There are about 245 taste buds located for the most part on the top and sides of the tongue. These taste buds can be divided into four specific classes: sweet, sour, bitter, salty; that is, there are four primary taste sensations. Taste buds at the tip of the tongue are especially sensitive to sweet solutions, those along the sides are especially sensitive to sour solutions, and those at the back of the tongue are especially sensitive to bitter solutions. Taste buds especially sensitive to salt solutions are located on the tip and sides of the tongue.

Taste buds are made up of taste cells, which vary in their responsiveness to the four basic taste qualities. For example, some taste cells respond to sugar and salt, while other cells may respond only to salt. Since the cells of a taste bud vary in sensitivity, some doubt exists over whether there are specific taste buds for any particular taste quality. Obviously, there is no simple explanation of taste; it, like all our senses, is a very complex and important aspect of behavior.

Taste sensitivity varies with changing circumstances. Very old persons sometimes completely lose their sense of taste. An aged person may observe that a food is tasteless, while a young person will say that the same food is highly seasoned. When adults feel sorry for children who are given well-cooked but unseasoned food, their sympathy is wasted, for the child probably gets as many pleasant sensations from the unseasoned food as an adult gets from rather highly seasoned food. Following smoking there is a temporary reduction in the sensitivity of all taste buds. For this reason, some gourmet clubs will not permit their members to smoke during a gourmet banquet.

Some persons make a serious business of their sense of taste and work as professional tasters. Manufacturers of tea, coffee, soft drinks, and alcoholic beverages hire professional tasters to judge their products. Most of us do not attempt to make the fine discriminations in taste which these professionals make.

The skin senses. You will note that this section is entitled "skin senses" rather than "skin sense" or "sense of touch." There are four kinds of skin receptors—those sensitive to cold, to warmth, to pain, and to pressure. The various types of skin receptors can be demonstrated by touching the skin with such instruments as cooled or warmed nails, needles, and hairs. You can easily demonstrate these skin senses for yourself. For example a number of points on the skin can be touched with a nail (not very sharp) which has been placed in cold water for a while. As some spots are touched, a sensation of cold will be produced, while other spots will merely yield a pressure sensation. Certain spots respond to low and high temperatures but not to intermediate temperatures (an *intermedi-*

GETTING TO KNOW YOUR ENVIRONMENT

ate temperature is the approximate temperature of the skin under normal conditions). Although there are only four primary skin sensations, our daily experiences of touch are always complex. Experiences such as tickle, smoothness, roughness, and wetness involve combinations of the primary skin sensations.

The sense of pressure is especially valuable to a blind person who seeks to overcome his visual handicap. The blind person is able to read by means of his sense of pressure as he moves his fingers across a page of Braille, a system of raised dots. There is a record of a blind and deaf woman who had so learned to use her sense of pressure that she could recognize, a year later, the hand of a person with whom she had shaken hands once.

Kinesthetic sense. The *kinesthetic sense,* or the muscle, tendon, and joint sense, is important in determining body movement and position. A person can move parts of his body without the use of his eyes. This can be easily demonstrated by having someone place your arm in a specific position while you are blindfolded or have your eyes closed. You will have no trouble in recognizing the position in which your arm has been placed.

Equilibrium. The sense of *equilibrium,* which tells an individual where his body is in space, is governed by the inner ear (part of the auditory system), and is used to aid the person in maintaining body position. It is this sense that, when disturbed, produces "motion sickness."

THE PERCEPTION OF TIME AND SPACE

Can an individual "perceive" time? You are aware of the passing of time and may be able to estimate the passing of time fairly accurately without resorting to watches, clocks, or calendars. How? We have no special sense organ for the perception of time but depend upon cues from various sense organs and upon the complexity of our thought processes.

Certain individuals, in some unknown way, perceive the passage of time while asleep. For example, these individuals can go to sleep at night with the intention of awakening without the aid of an alarm clock or any other device at some predetermined time the following morning. It is surprising how close to that set time they awaken. They can wake up at a preestablished time even in a strange place, which eliminates the possibility that they use the cues of specific ordinary noises of their regular sleeping room to awaken them.

Time, at least for the individual, is relative. Depending upon the circumstances, a few minutes may seem like an hour, and sometimes an hour may seem like a few minutes. During an interesting lecture, time seems to pass quickly—much more than during a dull one. In one experiment, subjects of different ages were asked to indicate how long ago a day, a week, the last Christmas, and eight years ago seemed to them, by marking on a line these comparative time spans. The older the subject, the shorter the distance marked on the line to represent the passage of one week. That is, a week ago for the oldest subject seemed only a short distance away, compared with the length of time it seemed for the youngest person.

What is space perception? We perceive space by using cues in our environment to achieve an awareness of distance and depth. What are some of the cues which individuals use to perceive distance and depth? One of the ways in which we perceive distance and depth is the movements of our eye muscles. When our eyes follow a moving object, certain muscles cause the lens of the eyes to become flatter as the object moves into the distance or to bulge outward when the object comes close. The movement of eye muscles can be easily demonstrated by holding a finger at arm's length and moving it slowly toward the nose. Our pupils will converge, or come closer together. This cue to distance is called *convergence.*

If one object blocks the view of another, it is assumed that the object blocking the view is closer than the one behind it. This cue is known as *interposition.*

Another cue is that of movement. If we move, those objects near us seem to move past us, while those at a distance seem to remain still or to move by us much more slowly. For example, when you are riding in a car, the edge of the road seems to go by very fast, whereas objects in the distance seem to stand still or to move very slowly.

Other cues are linear and atmospheric perspective. In *linear perspective,* objects appear to be closer together the farther away they are. For example, railroad tracks seem to meet in the distance, and telephone poles seem to get closer together. In *atmospheric perspective,* objects that are blurred or hazy from smoke or dust in the air appear to be farther away than objects which can be seen clearly.

The perception of light, texture, and size also helps us determine distance and depth. For instance, the effect of light and shadow upon objects is a cue for judging depth. Or, if the texture of an object can be seen clearly, the ob-

Our perception that these railroad tracks become smaller and eventually meet gives us an awareness of distance.

ject appears to be closer than when its texture cannot be as distinctly defined. Size constancy, too, helps us determine the size of objects because when we learn that a specific object or person has a certain size, we tend to see it or him as having the same size, even if viewed from a distance. For example, if you saw an unfamiliar adult at a distance of 200 yards, would you guess his height as 5 or 6 inches? The chances are that you would probably guess in terms of feet, not inches.

Another cue can be illustrated by this example—that of using standards or familiar objects to judge distance. If a close friend of yours were standing beside the stranger, and you knew the height of your friend, your guess of the stranger's height would probably be much closer to his actual height, since you have a standard by which to compare heights. If you are unfamiliar with an object and have no standard of comparison close to it, it is very difficult to judge its size or distance accurately. For example, you would find it very difficult to guess the distance or size of a wire with the sky as a background unless you could determine its texture or use other cues.

Using both eyes when looking at an object gives you a cue to the distance of the object, because you have two retinal images. Each eye has a slightly different view of the scene, which is called *retinal disparity* (sometimes called *binocular disparity*).

In briefly discussing the cues for space perception, we have seen that the following cues are used: convergence, interposition, movement, linear perspective, atmospheric perspective, light, texture, size constancy, standards or familiarity of objects, and retinal disparity. It is possible to identify several of these cues in one situation. Artists quite often use most of these cues to give depth to their paintings. The next time you look at a painting, try to determine the cues used by the artist to give you the perception of depth and distance.

Are these spatial cues learned or innate? At the present time we cannot adequately answer this question. However, interesting experiments have been performed in recent years which suggest that there may be some innate patterning of the brain for depth perception.

Several studies have been performed with varying species of young organisms, using a "visual cliff." This apparatus consists of a large piece of heavy glass several feet off the floor. A textured piece of linoleum is glued directly underneath one end of the glass. At the other end of the glass, the linoleum drops away to give the appearance of a cliff, although the glass is still present over that end. Viewed from above, one area appears to be a cliff, while another is seen as a shallow area.

When infants of six to fourteen months of age were placed on the glass, almost all of them refused to cross the "cliff," even when called by their mother on the other side. The infants would cross the "shallow" end very readily. Some infants would pat the sheet of glass over the cliff but still would not cross, refusing to believe their sense of touch. They preferred to

PATTERNS OF BEHAVIOR

Because he perceives that one end of the "visual cliff" drops off several feet, the infant refuses to move onto that end, although he can feel that it is covered by a glass surface.

rely more on their sense of vision than on touch. Studies such as this have been performed with chickens, goats, lambs, and kittens, with approximately the same results. Rats, which depend a good deal upon touch with their whiskers, will cross the cliff side if they can first feel the glass with their whiskers. If, however, the glass over the cliff is dropped several inches so that the rat, who stays on a platform or shelf above, cannot touch the glass with his whiskers, he will cross only the shallow side. Although the studies seem to indicate that the perception of certain depth scenes, such as a "visual cliff," may be present early in life, at this time we do not know which cues the sub-

jects under study used in order to perceive depth.

SENSORY DEPRIVATION AND SUBLIMINAL PERCEPTION

Now that you have learned something of the senses and their importance, what is the result of depriving an organism of its senses? To answer this question, it is helpful to realize how sensitive individuals are to stimuli. A person's senses are capable of responding to very little stimulation. For example, the average person is so sensitive to light that he can see the glare of a match at a distance of about thirty miles on a clear dark night. The sense

tion? We cannot, of course, deprive human beings of a sense early in life and then restore this sense to find out what effect sensory deprivation has upon individuals. There is, however, one study of adults who were born blind because of cataracts of the lens. After their cataracts were removed by surgery, these persons were able to see for the first time. They were found to have great difficulty in distinguishing differences between forms, such as a circle and square. They also had difficulty in remembering people's faces.

One way to brainwash an individual is to enforce an absence of almost all sensory stimuli for long periods of time.

of touch is such that a person can detect the wing of a fly falling on his cheek. He can smell a single drop of perfume when it is diffused into a six-room apartment. Taste is so well defined that a person can detect a teaspoon of sugar stirred into two gallons of water. In a quiet room, you can hear a ticking watch at a distance of twenty feet. Thus, our senses are able to detect a very small amount of stimulation. Remember, however, that sensitivity can vary with different people and with such factors as age, and stimulation of the involved sense immediately before experimentation.

Several studies of sensory deprivation have been made with animals as subjects. The results of such studies with dogs indicate that when they are deprived of normal stimulation early in life, the dogs have great difficulty in learning to avoid painful stimuli or objects which are associated with the painful stimulus. Studies with monkeys show that their social behavior is affected by sensory deprivation. Normal social behavior of monkeys depends upon more than a mother-infant relationship; it seems to require other sensory stimuli as well. One group of monkeys was divided into mother-infant pairs, and each pair was put into an isolated cage. These pairs of monkeys were reared in a very limited environment, while another group was reared in a richer, more varied environment, which included toys, climbing facilities, and the sights and sounds of other monkeys and people. Those reared in isolation developed a stronger than normal attachment to their mothers. The mothers encouraged this attachment by using more punishment on their infants and by not allowing their infants to explore the limited environment, which helps to bring about independence from the mother.

The evidence presently available seems to indicate that early, and especially prolonged, sensory deprivation does influence the normal development of the individual. However, much additional information and evidence are yet to be gathered before we can adequately begin to understand the full effects and meaning of sensory deprivation.

Is sensory deprivation pleasant or unpleasant? What would it be like to be deprived of many of our sensory experiences? This may become a very practical problem in the years ahead as man travels far into space. His trip is going to take a long time, and after he is on his way, his sensory experiences are going to be very limited. At first thought, it might seem that the trip would be a very restful and pleasant experience with no annoying sights, noises, or odors. However, we do have experimental evidence suggesting that the experience may be far from pleasant unless research can alter these conditions.

Students were hired to take part in an experiment in which each one was confined for several days and nights in a small, soundproof room. Each one wore frosted glass goggles so that he could not distinguish patterns even though there was some light in the room. His hands and arms were covered so that he had very little perception through touch. He lay on his bed and did as little as possible. Such sensory deprivation proved to be very disturbing to the students. They complained of being unable to concentrate, their ability to solve simple problems declined, they became bored, and they imagined that they saw and heard things. Some became so confused that they had difficulty in finding their way home when they left the laboratory.

Sensory deprivation is one technique of brainwashing. Prisoners are isolated in dark rooms with a minimum of stimulation. In time, many of them will agree to almost any suggestion and will even confess to crimes they did not commit in order to be relieved from the horror of sensory and social deprivation.

There is experimental evidence that sensory deprivation results in retardation of learning. Five groups of rats were trained in a multiple-T maze. One group of rats learned the maze very quickly. These rats had full use of all their senses. Another group was deprived of the use of vision. They made more errors in learning the maze than did the first group. A third group was deprived of both vision and hearing, and they made still more errors. A fourth group was deprived of vision and the sense of smell. They made more errors than the rats deprived of vision and hearing. Finally, one group of rats was deprived of vision, hearing, and the sense of smell. They made the most errors of any group; in fact, their learning was very limited.

We know that persons deprived of vision or hearing are handicapped in their learning. If a person is deprived of both these senses, as in the case of Helen Keller, learning becomes a difficult process because most of it must come through the sense of touch.

What is subliminal perception? We have said that perception refers to sensation plus the way in which we interpret the sensation. Stimuli may be so weak that we are not aware of the sensations that they are arousing. Yet our perception of them may influence our thoughts or overt behavior. This perception of sensation aroused by stimuli too weak to be specifically reported by an individual is called *subliminal perception*.

Although psychologists have studied subliminal perception for many years, the public became keenly interested in it a few years ago when a report claimed that such phrases as "Eat Popcorn" and "Drink Brand X" (a soft drink) had been flashed on the screen during the showing of a motion picture in a theater. As a result, the report said, popcorn sales increased 50 percent and sales of the soft drink increased 18 percent. It was said, on the basis of some very questionable and incomplete data, that the phrases were flashed on the screen for only 1/3,000 second so that the audience was not aware of seeing them. Nevertheless, because of the rise in sales, the members of the audience were thought to have perceived them.

Some advertising men anticipated that this report might be the basis of a whole new field for their efforts. Some individuals were quite alarmed by the report. They saw in it possibilities for dangerous social controls. It was said that elections might be controlled by one political party flashing "Vote Republican" or "Vote Democratic" on the television screens of the nation during campaign years. It was said that an enemy agent might succeed in influencing our attitudes by flashing his propaganda in movies and television programs.

There are many variables which must be taken into account for successful subliminal stimulation, such as the strength of the stimulus itself, the speed at which the stimulus is given, the nature of the stimulation immediately following the subliminal stimulation, and the general train of thought in which the viewer has been engaged. In general, psychologists seriously question the effectiveness of subliminal stimulation under most conditions to influence behavior. Certainly, it seems that stimulation of which we are aware is more effective in influencing behavior than is subliminal stimulation. At any rate, much more research is needed before we can speak with certainty on possibilities of and conditions for subliminal stimulation.

Terms to Add to Your Vocabulary

absolute pitch	brightness	difference threshold
absolute threshold	color blindness (weakness)	equilibrium sense
atmospheric perspective	complementary colors	hallucination
binocular vision	convergence	hue

illusion
interposition
just-noticeable-difference
kinesthetic sense
Law of Intermediates
linear perspective
loudness
monocular vision
noise

perception
phi phenomenon
pitch
retinal disparity
saturation
sensation
sensory adaptation
sensory deprivation
size constancy

skin senses
stereoscope
subliminal perception
taste buds
timbre
tone
visible spectrum

Suggestions for Activities

1. Using sheets of colored paper, cut out one 6-inch square each of red, yellow, blue, and green. Mount these on a piece of white paper so that they are about 2 inches apart. Late some afternoon, place the large sheet of paper containing the colored squares in the sunlight. At about ten-minute intervals while the sun is going down, look at the squares one at a time. Do you notice any change in the saturation of the colors? Does one color seem to remain clearer than the others as the sun goes down? As illumination decreases, the cones do not receive enough light to be stimulated. Sensitivity to red is lost first, then yellow, blue, and finally green. (For a further explanation of this occurrence, look up the Purkinje phenomenon in a college textbook, such as Norman Munn's *Psychology.*)

2. Borrow the color-mixing wheel from your school science department. Mix complementary colors, red and blue, black and white, black and various colors, white and various colors.

3. Secure two focusing floodlights or slide projectors. Over the lens of one place a yellow filter (yellow cellophane will do) so that you can project a yellow circle of light on a white screen, such as a movie screen. Over the other floodlight, place a blue filter so that you can project a blue circle of light on the same screen. Now move the projectors

so that the two circles of light overlap. You have added light waves. What is the result? Next, use only one floodlight or projector. Place both the yellow and blue filters over the lens and project on the screen. You have subtracted light waves. What is the result? Is there any relation to the mixing of paints?

4. Cut a hole about an inch in diameter in the center of a piece of white cardboard. Under this hole you can place pieces of paper of various colors, especially red, green, blue, and yellow. Gaze at one such color fixedly for about forty seconds, trying not to blink or change your focus. Have someone tell you when the time is up and then shift your gaze to any place on the white cardboard. Is the color of the afterimage the same as the one at which you had been gazing? If not, can you find it on the color circle on page 294? What term is used to apply to such colors? Rest your eyes for several minutes and then try gazing at another color.

5. Perhaps an amateur magician can give a short performance before the class. He may be induced to explain one or two of the illusions he uses.

6. Try this simple demonstration of the phi phenomenon. Hold your forefinger at arm's length and focus on it. Al-

ternately close your right and left eyes without moving your finger. Do you have a perception of motion, although there is no actual movement of the stimulus object?

7. If possible, borrow or buy a set of records entitled "The Science of Sound," available through Folkways Records, and play them for the class. If time does not permit the class to hear the entire set, listen to the records yourself several times and either give a report to the class, or select sections to play in class.

8. Secure a sample of Braille printing. If it can be arranged, have a person who can read Braille give a demonstration and tell of his experiences with this kind of reading.

9. Have you ever had difficulty in seeing objects when you first enter a darkened movie theater but found that later you could see them without difficulty? Your eyes had become adapted to the dim illumination. You can easily demonstrate visual adaption to different amounts of light by closing one eye for about ten or fifteen minutes before entering a dimly lit room. When you enter the room, keep your eye closed for a minute longer. The room will appear dark when you use the eye which you kept open. Then open your closed eye, and close the one which you kept open. Can you see more clearly?

10. To demonstrate body adaptation to temperature, place three bowls in a row. Pour very warm but not scalding water in one bowl, pour very cold water in another bowl, and water at about body temperature in the third bowl. Place and keep one hand in the bowl of very warm water and the other in the bowl of cold water for several minutes. Then put both hands in the water which is at body temperature.

Does this water feel warm to one hand and cold to the other? For several minutes keep both hands in this body-temperature water. What happens?

11. Secure two or three paintings, including one landscape, from the art department, or have students bring some prints or paintings from home. What cues have the artists used to create the perception of depth?

12. To demonstrate perception with both eyes as opposed to perception with only one eye, try the following. Select a room which has a number of obstacles in it, close one eye, and walk around the room between the obstacles. Most people find it more difficult to thread their way through the room with one eye than when they use both eyes. Your two eyes give you stereoscopic vision, or a three-dimensional perception of space. Of course, in using both eyes, you also have a wider field of vision.

13. Select a variety of short articles which would take about fifteen minutes to read. Without letting your subjects know what you are looking for, ask them to pick any one article which they think would be most interesting to them. Before they start reading, ask them to tell you, as they read, when they believe thirty seconds, two minutes, five minutes, and finally ten minutes have passed. Then have each subject read the article out loud, mentioning when he thinks these particular periods of time have passed. The subjects may or may not complete the article.

   Next, select some dull articles and ask the same subjects to let you know when they believe the various time periods have passed. Remember that what you think is dull may be interesting to someone else. You might have boys read an article on female hair styles and girls read an article on fishing. Or you might have the subjects select articles they think would be the most boring to read.

Does the time seem to pass more quickly for the subjects when they are interested in what they are reading?

Suggestions for Further Reading

Buddenbrock, Wolfgang von, *The Senses,* University of Michigan Press. This book deals with the functioning of eight senses in man and other organisms.

Daniel, Robert S., ed., *Contemporary Readings in General Psychology,* 2nd ed., Houghton Mifflin. Part VII contains nine articles on "The Behaving Organism Is Biological." You will profit from the following four articles on sensation and perception: pages 293–95, "How Much Can We See?"; pages 295–98, "Vision and Behavior"; pages 299–302, "Fingertip Sight: Fact or Fiction?"; pages 303–06, "Why We Have Two Ears."

Griffin, Donald R., *Echoes of Bats and Men,* Doubleday. A discussion of how bats and other animals use echoes to navigate and how man uses radar and sonar.

Hilgard, Ernest R., and Richard C. Atkinson, *Introduction to Psychology,* 4th ed., Harcourt, Brace & World. Chapter 8, "The Sensory Basis of Perceiving"; Chapter 9, "The Perception of Objects and Events."

Kalish, Richard A., *The Psychology of Human Behavior,* Wadsworth. Chapter 3, "Perceiving and the Environment."

Kendler, Howard H., *Basic Psychology,* Appleton-Century-Crofts. Chapter 6, "Sensation"; Chapter 8, "Perception."

Leuba, Clarence, *Man: A General Psychology,* Holt, Rinehart & Winston. Pages 226–33, "Sense Organs, Muscles, and Their Nerves"; pages 369–87, "The Influence of Imagery on Perception" and "Motor Sets and Attitudes as Symbols Influencing Behavior"; pages 426–29, "A Note on Early Man's Artistic Creativity."

Lindgren, Henry C., Donn Byrne, and Lewis F. Petrinovich, *Psychology: An Introduction to a Behavioral Science,* 2nd ed., John Wiley. Pages 125–32, "Physiological Aspects of Sensation"; Chapter 6, "Perception."

McKeachie, Wilbert J., and Charlotte L. Doyle, *Psychology,* Addison-Wesley. Chapter 6, "Perception."

Minnaert, M., *The Nature of Light and Colour in the Open Air,* Dover. A physicist explains many everyday phenomena.

Morgan, Clifford T., and Richard A. King, *Introduction to Psychology,* 3rd ed., McGraw-Hill. Chapter 8, "Sensory Processes and Vision"; Chapter 9, "Hearing and the Other Senses"; Chapter 10, "Perception."

Munn, Norman L., *Psychology,* 5th ed., Houghton Mifflin. Chapter 15, "Knowing Our World"; Chapter 16, "Attending and Perceiving."

Ruch, Floyd L., *Psychology and Life,* 7th ed., Scott, Foresman. Chapter 8, "Stimulation and Sensation"; Chapter 9, "Observation and Action."

Ruechardt, Edward, *Light, Visible and Invisible,* University of Michigan Press. Facts about light and its uses, for the student interested in both physics and psychology.

Sanford, Fillmore H., *Psychology: A Scientific Study of Man,* 2nd ed., Wadsworth. Chapter 10, "Sensations"; Chapter 11, "Perception."

Teevan, Richard C., and Robert C. Birney, eds., *Color Vision,* Van Nostrand.

Van Bergeijk, Willem A., John R. Pierce, and Edward E. David, Jr., *Waves and the Ear,* Doubleday. For the student wishing to relate physics to psychology.

Whittaker, James O., et al., *Introduction to Psychology,* W. B. Saunders, Chapter 13, "The Sensory Basis of Perceiving"; Chapter 14, "Perception."

MENTAL HEALTH

12

Adjusting to your social environment

In this unit on mental health, no sharp line will be drawn between physical health and mental health. Most factors that contribute to physical health contribute also to mental health. You have probably studied some of these factors in hygiene or physical education courses. Chapters 12, 13, 14, and 15 will deal with the factors involved in preserving what is often called "mental health."

What does it mean to be in good mental health? A person in good mental health is well-adjusted to his social environment, both from his own point of view and from the points of view of others. He is able to live with his fellow men without undue stresses, strains, and conflicts. He finds life satisfying and pleasant most of the time. He lives in such a way as to make life satisfying and pleasant for others. Certainly mental health is a goal worth striving for.

High school students, like everyone else, face many problems which make it difficult for them to achieve the goal of mental health. In fact, because you are changing so rapidly and are approaching adult status, you seem to encounter difficult situations rather frequently. You run head-on into many frustrating circumstances and situations involving conflict. As a result, you may become emotionally upset. You must learn when to control your emotional reactions.

FRUSTRATION AND CONFLICT

A person is said to be frustrated whenever any of his goal-directed activities are slowed up, rendered difficult, or are made impossible. Our society is so complex and our goals are so elaborate that most persons experience many frustrating situations. An individual must learn that he cannot always have what he wants when he wants it. Each of us develops characteristic patterns of responding to frustrating situations, and sometimes these patterns are not conducive to mental health.

Are there experimental studies of frustration? One classical study was concerned with the effects of frustration on the behavior of preschool children. The children were invited to enter a room where there were toys which had some parts missing. The children did play with these defective toys, however, and seemed to enjoy their play activities. During this time, skilled observers rated each child according to the constructiveness of his play activities. The children were then allowed to enter the other side of the room, which had been blocked from view by a screen. In this side of the room the children found much more attractive and interesting toys. They were allowed to play with these toys for a short period of time, after which they were returned to the other side of the room and separated from these new toys by a wire screen. They could now see the new toys but could not reach them because of the physical barrier. Of course, this caused the children to be frustrated. Observers again rated the children according to the constructiveness of their play. The level of constructiveness was now much lower for the children as a group. Some of the children attacked the wire screen, others asked for help from adults, some tried to leave the room, some showed regressive behavior, such as whining like younger children, and others went back to playing with toys from which parts were missing. On the other hand, a few of the children showed an increase in constructive play. These are some of the ways in which individuals may react to a frustrating situation.

What are some frustrating situations in everyday life? There are many kinds of frustrating situations. Our physical environment often places obstacles in our paths as we work toward goals. Perhaps, since you are going to have a very full and energy-consuming day

tomorrow, you decide to go to bed early and get plenty of sleep. But the neighbors have a big party which lasts far into the night, and the noise makes sleep impossible. Or for a week you have planned a picnic, but on the big day it rains. Perhaps you are in a hurry to get to a football game, but heavy traffic allows you only to inch along. Undoubtedly you can think of many other examples.

Frustration also may come from social regulations and conditions. You would like to take an active part in city, state, or national politics, yet the law says you are not old enough to vote. Possibly you would like to marry at once and establish a home of your own, but social pressures and economic factors may prevent your taking such steps. You may wish to get a full-time job and make enough money to buy a new car, more clothes, a television set of your own, but social pressure dictates that you remain in school. You would like to travel extensively and have many new experiences, but parents, schools, and financial problems keep you at home doing the usual things. Perhaps you would like to plan ahead for college work or marriage soon after you complete your high school course, but there is the consideration of your military service.

Frustration may be a consequence of personal limitations, too. A boy who wishes to play football is too small to meet the coach's requirements. A girl who wants to be a fashion model just does not meet the usual qualifications. A student who wants to attend a certain college with very high entrance requirements and limited en-

ADJUSTING TO YOUR SOCIAL ENVIRONMENT

rollment does not have the grades to compete successfully with other applicants.

Adolescents have to face many frustrating situations, and many pages of this psychology textbook deal with problems related to frustration: difficulty in learning which prevents you from achieving certain goals in school, circumstances which may keep you from achieving popularity and leadership, physical handicaps which limit your activities, environmental factors which hinder you.

What is frustration tolerance? Psychologists use the term *frustration tolerance* to indicate the ability of an individual to withstand frustration without becoming maladjusted or unduly upset emotionally. When a turtle meets a situation with which it cannot cope, it withdraws into its shell. When a person encounters a frustrating situation, he may "withdraw into his shell"; that is, he may not be able to tolerate the frustration. On the other hand, the person who is in good mental health accepts frustration as one of the realities of life. He may have to readjust his goals and his plans for achieving these goals, but he does not feel that everything is hopeless. He may begin by tolerating little frustrations without becoming upset—a shoestring breaks when he is in a hurry. Frustrating situations seem less frustrating when one realizes that they are normal, that everyone experiences them.

What are some conflicting situations? Sometimes frustration results not so much from being prevented from doing something; it may result when you have to choose between alternatives. Conflict is often very frustrating. In such a simple matter as buying an article at a store, you often have to decide between the expensive and the inexpensive, between the good-looking article of poor quality and the less attractive article of good quality. The frustration occurs because if you have to choose between one of two articles, the purchase of one becomes a barrier to purchasing the other.

Many young persons are faced with making the decision between early marriage and continued schooling. There is a conflict, and the decision may be very difficult. Popularly such conflict is expressed by the saying "You can't have your cake and eat it too."

Young persons of late high school and early college age are faced with many other conflicts. They must decide whether to go on with formal schooling or not go on, whether to leave home in order to get a good job elsewhere or to remain at home and accept an inferior job, whether to go along with the crowd using alcoholic beverages or not to go along, whether to act like a child or to act like an adult, and so on. There are many points for decision. In Chapter 14 we shall consider some conflicts that arise between adolescents and their parents, and between adolescents and their brothers and sisters.

Psychologists often speak of three kinds of conflicting situations: the approach-approach, avoidance-avoidance, and approach-avoidance.

What is approach-approach conflict? When you are faced with two attractive choices which are mutually exclusive, you are torn between them. Both are positively attractive. You would like to do both, but you can't. This is called an *approach-approach conflict*.

There is the story of the donkey standing halfway between two very attractive bales of hay, but in this approach-approach conflict he starved to death because he couldn't decide which way to go. A boy knows two very attractive girls. He would like to take both of them to a formal prom, but two girls with one boy is just not accepted behavior for such an event. Since he can't decide which one to approach, he stays home alone the night of the big dance. A girl wishes to buy a new formal for a prom and finds two that are equally attractive in design, quality, and price. Since she can't decide which one to buy, she does not buy either.

Actually, in everyday life, circumstances intervene which often cause us to make a decision. Probably the donkey would have moved around a bit, and as he moved nearer one bale of hay, that bale would have seemed more attractive. He would have approached it and feasted instead of starved. The boy might just have happened to meet one of the two girls in the hall, stopped to talk a minute, mentioned the prom, and his whole problem would have been solved. If she said, "Yes, thank you!" the conflict was over. If she said, "No, thank you!" the conflict was likewise over, because now he could approach the other girl for a date. The girl trying to buy a formal might have been influenced by the saleswoman who merely said, "You look very nice in that one." In many approach-ap-

proach conflicts, we vacillate for a short time and then make a decision.

In one experiment, rats were taught to receive food placed at one end of an alley. The rats were put into a harness, which was attached to a spring scale so that the pull on the harness could be measured in grams. The rats could be stopped at any point in the alley — either close to the place of reward or far from it. From this experiment it was shown that the closer the rats came to the place where they had been rewarded (approach behavior), the harder they pulled. Evidently, once an approach has been decided on, the strength of the approach increases in direct relation to the nearness of the goal.

What is avoidance-avoidance conflict? When you are faced with two alternatives that are equally unattractive, you are facing an *avoidance-avoidance*

The harness on this rat is attached to a scale, which measures the strength of his approach or avoidance behavior.

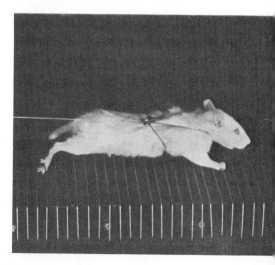

ADJUSTING TO YOUR SOCIAL ENVIRONMENT

In this approach-avoidance situation the boy wants to touch the goat, yet is apprehensive about moving closer to him.

conflict. To use the popular expression, you find yourself "between the devil and the deep blue sea." As a student, you may be faced with the unpleasant thought of having to study for an examination on an evening when there is a special program on television. An equally unpleasant thought is that if you don't study, you may fail the exam, fail the course, and fail to graduate. You would like to avoid both situations — studying and failing the exam. Maybe you go to your room and sit down to study but cannot keep from thinking about what you are missing, so you go to the living room and watch the television program. However, you cannot enjoy the program because you keep thinking about the possibility of failing. Back you go to your room and

open the book — then back to the living room. Such vacillation is very unpleasant. You would like to "leave the field" — to use a psychological expression. You decide to take a walk, you drift off into a daydream, you remember a chore that needs your attention. You try to avoid both the thought of study and the thought of failing.

In another experiment using rats in a harness (so that the strength of their pull could be measured), the rats were given a shock at one end of an alley. In this experiment the rats pulled away from the point of shock (avoidance behavior). The closer to the shock point, the harder they pulled away; the farther away from the shock point, the less hard they pulled away. It would seem that the strength of avoidance behavior increases as the subject gets nearer and nearer to the experience he seeks to avoid.

What is approach-avoidance conflict? Sometimes you are attracted by a certain situation, and, at the same time you are repelled by it. This is *approach-avoidance conflict*. You would like to approach a particular goal, but at the same time you would like to avoid it. It has both positive and negative value for you. Psychologists apply the term *ambivalence* (am·biv′ə·ləns) to this tendency to be pulled in opposite directions, to like and dislike at the same time. For example, you are at the beach, and a swim with your friends seems most attractive. You run up to the water's edge and a little wave goes over your feet. The water is terribly cold. A swim suddenly seems like something to avoid rather than something to approach. You run back on the beach. Your friends call. You approach the water again, but it hasn't warmed up any. You run back on the beach, and so on. You are faced with an approach-avoidance conflict.

Perhaps you are trying to decide whether or not to apply for admission to college. You have heard a great deal about the pleasures and advantages of college life, and you would like to approach it. However, you have heard of the long hours of study, of difficult examinations, and of the heavy expense involved. You would like to avoid these unpleasant features.

Life is full of conflicting situations, and many times a person is at least temporarily frustrated. How will he respond to such conflict? By highly emotional but ineffective behavior or by relatively calm and effective behavior? Conflicts are unpleasant, but the individual in good mental health can take them in his stride.

DESIRABLE WAYS OF RESPONDING TO FRUSTRATION AND CONFLICT

When a person is frustrated or runs into conflicts, he may become quite aggressive. He may respond either by trying to do something to his environment to change it so that he can achieve his goals or by adjusting his goals to the environment. Following are a number of suggestions which you may wish to consider as you meet frustrations and conflicts in your life.

Tackle the problem even though it appears almost hopeless. It takes de-termination to pitch into a problem that seems almost hopeless. At one time a psychologist developed a kind of test of "spunk," or will power. The individual being tested was asked to stand on a small platform with his heels off the floor. The apparatus was so made that when the individual's heels touched the floor, a bell rang and the test was stopped. Although it might seem that standing on the balls of the feet might require a great deal of physical strength, this is not the case. The test depends far more on the ability to endure discomfort in order to make a good score. It was found that a group of normal young persons could remain off their heels from 12 minutes to $2\frac{1}{2}$ hours, with an average of 36 minutes. They had determination. A group of delinquent boys from a reform school were tested with the same apparatus. Their time ranged from $2\frac{1}{2}$ minutes to 53 minutes, with an average of 15 minutes. They lacked the "will power" to endure discomfort to achieve a goal.

Ask other people for help. Asking for help is a satisfactory way of responding to a difficulty, providing you ask only for help rather than ask someone else to solve your problem for you (page 340).

Your family is an ever-ready source of help. You may feel that your parents do not understand you and are at the bottom of most of your frustrations. Nevertheless, in the great majority of cases, they are not only ready but anxious to help you. In one study in which high school students were asked where they turned for help in overcoming obstacles, 37 percent said that they turned to their families for help in cases where the problem involved conflict with family standards.

Lack of sufficient money can be very frustrating. In the study just mentioned, 51 percent of the students found that they could get help from their schools, and 18 percent found that individuals or groups within the community were ready to help them.

You may feel frustrated in your social life because you do not know how to act in accord with accepted social rules. Of the high school students mentioned above, 67 percent found their schools a source of help in learning social techniques.

If you feel blocked in reaching your goals because of health or physical development, you can turn to your family physician, school health department, or community health center for help.

Your friends and classmates are a potential source of help. They are near your own age and so may have a good deal of insight which an older person could not have. A give-and-take discussion may indicate that your frustrations and conflicts are shared by others. You may be able to help each other.

Work with others. Many jobs or decisions are just too big for one person. If he attempts them by himself, he soon feels frustrated and develops feelings of inferiority. Working with others on a common problem is not a way of running away from the problem. Oftentimes it is a way of attacking the problem in an efficient way. Good athletic teams consist of individuals who have learned to work together when faced with opposition.

The student who is having difficulty in some school subject may help solve his problem by working with another student — provided they work together rather than gossip together. Students with financial difficulties can work with others in a Junior Achievement group. A person who is shy may find working on a committee a pleasant way to overcome this difficulty.

Search for a better way to meet the problem. Suppose that you are seeking an office job. Such a job will probably require skill in typing, but suppose you have no training in typing. Perhaps you have access to a typewriter and have spent many hours practicing on it. You have become quite proficient as a two-finger typist, but such typing is not likely to meet job requirements. You will be frustrated in getting a job. You can exercise your "will power" and pound the typewriter hour after hour, but you will not become a good typist. To overcome your frustration, you will have to learn another method of typing if you want to become an efficient typist.

Suppose that you are having difficulty with your schoolwork. You can spend long hours studying (and it does take time to study), but that may not be the answer to your problem. Perhaps you had better talk with each of your teachers in order to learn how best to study for each course. You may be able to increase your study efficiency, and thereby overcome your frustration, by reviewing the study suggestions in Chapter 5.

Know when to be flexible. Giving up whenever one is frustrated in reaching a goal is indicative of poor mental health, but there is no virtue in carrying out a poor decision. Suppose that you have decided to get a job as soon as you graduate from high school rather than to go to college. That may have been a wise decision. On the other hand, you may have made this decision when you were emotionally upset as the result of a poor grade or a "bawling out" at home. One night on a date you may have felt you were in love and decided to get married as soon as you graduate from high school. That may have been a wise decision or a foolish one. Decisions made under emotional stress are seldom made with due consideration for both sides of a problem. If you make a decision when you are emotionally upset, you will be wise to reconsider it objectively after you have calmed down. You will then be able to think of all possibilities with a problem-solving attitude and so make a wiser decision. We shall discuss control of emotional states later in this chapter.

In the past you may have made a decision with great care and in the light of all known facts. Today, new evidence may be available, so that you will need to change or alter your decision. You may have decided not to go to college, but college aptitude-test scores and an offer of a scholarship may indicate that you should reverse your decision. On the other hand, you may have decided to go to college on the basis of limited information about social activities and athletic teams. After you have the facts from your school counselor concerning your interests, aptitudes, and abilities, you may wish to reverse your decision.

A student who is having difficulty in a course may overcome his frustration by seeking help from the teacher.

A wise man often changes his plans. A foolish man may never change his plans, or he may change them with every passing fancy. As you consider adjusting your goals, be sure that you have real reasons for doing so, not just rationalizations (pages 341–44).

Consider alternatives. Sometimes frustrations cannot be overcome directly. You may have to detour. Under proper control, making a detour may be the best possible solution to frustration. So important is this topic of compensation that we shall devote considerable space to it in a later section of this chapter.

For the present, we shall turn to some suggestions for controlling the emotional states that are likely to develop when you are faced with frustration and conflict.

CONTROLLING EMOTIONAL REACTIONS TO FRUSTRATION AND CONFLICT

Frustrating and conflicting situations can be very disturbing. Therefore, our emotions play a part in how we respond to these situations.

How do some individuals face emotional problems? One psychologist made a study of two groups of university students who were about nineteen years of age. The members of both groups filled out a preinterview questionnaire, indicating many facts about themselves and their attitudes toward certain personal and social problems. One group, whom we shall call the "unselected students," consisted of students who had the usual emotional problems of students but who were not unduly disturbed by them. The other group consisted of students who indicated that they had rather pronounced and persistent difficulties. These latter students will be referred to as "emotional students" – although, of course, the unselected students had emotional problems too.

The emotional students actually did not have more problems than the unselected students, but such problems as they did have were more persistent. Their attitudes toward these problems and their attacks upon them were not so satisfactory as were those of the unselected students. For example, only 6.3 percent of the emotional students reported that their emotional problems had arisen in connection with their life in college. Yet 15.4 percent of the unselected students reported such problems. That is, the unselected students were having to face new emotional problems in the university, whereas the problems of the emotional students had arisen earlier in life and under other circumstances.

Of the unselected students, 57.1 percent were making a positive attempt to overcome their problems, but only 34.3 percent of the emotional group were making such a positive attack. Of the unselected students, 20.5 percent said that it was difficult to overcome their emotional problems; 35.0 percent of the emotional students found it difficult.

It was not found that the students with emotional problems were from smaller towns or smaller high schools than the unselected students. Neither was there significant evidence that they differed from unselected students in financial background.

On the other hand, the unselected students were much better adjusted socially than the emotional students. For example, emotional students reported fewer friendships and acquaintances than did unselected students, as the table on page 329 shows. All figures are percentages; 3.8 percent of the emotional students reported that they had no friends, 30 percent said that they had few friends, and so on. (Some students did not answer all questions, so percents do not total 100.)

Of the unselected students, 73.0 percent of the men and 72.0 percent of the women considered ability to make friends as one of their greatest assets.

For the men and women with emotional problems, the corresponding figures were only 45.0 percent and 43.0 percent.

	UNSELECTED STUDENTS	EMOTIONAL STUDENTS
Friendships:		
None	0.0	3.8
Few	10.6	30.0
Average	61.0	45.7
Very many	25.9	15.7
Acquaintances:		
Very few	0.5	4.2
Several	5.3	7.1
Average	30.0	44.7
Very many	62.0	37.6

Many of the replies of these two groups of students are of considerable psychological interest. For example, 3 percent of the unselected students said that they were sensitive about unpopularity with members of their own sex, but 18 percent of the emotional students were sensitive about such unpopularity. The corresponding figures for sensitivity about unpopularity with the opposite sex were 8 percent and 16 percent, respectively. Five percent of the unselected students were bothered by feelings of inferiority, but 26 percent of the emotional students were bothered by such feelings. Of the unselected students, 26 percent said that they often procrastinated, but 40 percent of the emotional students admitted that they often put off doing those tasks which had to be done but could be postponed. In general, these students were faced with the same problems which you are considering in your course in psychology. The unselected students were enjoying better mental health than the emotional students. They were making a better adjustment to their frustrations and conflicts.

How may emotional reactions be helpful? Life would be very dull — and many worthwhile things would not be accomplished — if everyone repressed all of his emotional experiences. Romantic love would not be very romantic if the two persons merely sat down and made up a list of advantages and disadvantages of their marriage, computed the ratio of advantages to disadvantages, looked in a mathematical table to see if their ratio was sufficiently high to justify marriage, and then possibly went into marriage as a business enterprise.

In time of emergency, emotion often enables people to accomplish feats they could not accomplish otherwise. Members of a football team play a much harder game under the emotional excitement of close competition than when the opposing team is easy to defeat. The excitement of trying to break a record may give a trackman extra speed.

A student may say, "I'm too nervous even to take that test, let alone make a good grade." He means that he is emotionally too upset to take the test or to do well. He may even be somewhat nauseated, have a headache, or find that his hands are shaking. It is true that his anxiety may reduce his efficiency. There is psychological evidence that if a person is extremely anxious

ADJUSTING TO YOUR SOCIAL ENVIRONMENT

about doing well, his ability is impaired on even such a simple test as repeating lists of digits which he has just heard. On the other hand, there is reason to believe that mild reactions of the autonomic nervous system (pages 254–55) may result in increased efficiency.

In one study, two psychologists demonstrated that students with high grade averages in college tended to improve under stress. On the other hand, students with poor grade averages tended to show a decrease in ability under stress, even though they had as much intellectual ability, as measured by a college aptitude test, as did the good students. No doubt there are many situations in which individuals differ with respect to the effects of emotional reactions.

Emotionally toned thinking, however, is often not clear thinking and may lead to acts that will be regretted later. The individual striving to maintain good mental health must therefore learn when and how to control undesirable emotional reactions.

How can I control undesirable emotional reactions? "An ounce of prevention is worth a pound of cure." The physiological changes of emotional states cannot be readily "cured." Many times, however, they can be prevented from developing, or they can be minimized. Thus, emotional experiences are, to that extent, controlled.

The following suggestions will be of assistance to you as you attempt to control undesirable emotion.

1. *Recognize your emotional states as such.* It is easy to say, "Oh, I am not angry," or "I am not the least bit excited." But are you? Without the aid of measuring instruments, you can usually recognize that your heart is pounding, that your breathing pattern is not normal, that your face feels flushed, that you feel tense or perhaps feel that you have an unusual amount of energy. You may realize that the experience you are having is more pleasant or unpleasant than the situation warrants.

2. *Look ahead so that you can avoid situations likely to produce undesirable emotional states.* A student may "go to pieces" over an examination if he leaves preparation for it until the last minute. If he has looked ahead, planned for, and studied for the examination, he is not likely to become unduly disturbed by it. If a person knows that a group is likely to develop into a mob or do things of which he does not approve, he can control his emotion by not joining the group.

3. *Watch your physical condition.* When possible, undertake difficult tasks or attempt to solve problems that may be emotion-producing at the times when you are in your best physical condition. When a person is very tired or is just recovering from an illness, his body is not functioning at maximum efficiency. At such times he is easily upset emotionally. He should try to postpone difficult or troublesome tasks.

Furthermore, there is some evidence that even in normal health the body functions more efficiently at some times than at others. Periods of maximum and minimum bodily efficiency seem to pass in more or less regular cycles. Such fluctuations are related to emotional fluctuations. There is evidence that in even such a simple matter as strength of hand grip, an individual passes through cycles of greater and lesser strength.

The period from one peak of maximum bodily efficiency to another such peak is not the same for all individuals. The period seems to range from about three weeks to about nine weeks. An individual may be able to note his own cycle and arrange, as far as possible, to do his most difficult work and make his most troublesome decisions at times of maximum bodily efficiency. Of necessity, some matters cannot be postponed. Also, the length of the bodily cycle may be influenced by disturbing situations that arise. It certainly is a comfort to know, however, that, no matter how miserable you may feel at a given time, before too long you will feel better and will be able to meet emotion-producing problems with less strain.

A dark, lonely street becomes a less frightening experience when the outward display of fear is kept under control.

4. *Exercise some restraint in the overt expression of undesirable emotion.* The purpose of such restraint is to minimize physiological reactions. It has been found that the full expression of fear and anger in animals prolongs the internal physiological changes, resulting in maximum total emotional behavior. The angry person who grits his teeth and clenches his fists is more likely to lose control of himself than the person who refrains from these outward expressions of anger.

Anyone may be frightened as he walks down a dark street. It will help to minimize the emotion of fear if he refrains from walking more rapidly than normal. There is value for emotional control in "whistling in the dark" —that is, in putting on the outward ap-

pearance of an emotion quite different from the one that is actually being experienced. There is value in the old saying "Count ten before you strike."

Control of the outward expression of emotion is very helpful in social situations. If you show that you are angry, others are likely to become angry. Soon a vicious circle of anger develops. On the other hand, if you can suggest by outward behavior that you are calm (even though you are angry), others are not nearly so likely to become angry.

If one person shows by his actions that he is afraid, others are likely to become afraid. It should be added, however, that war experience has demonstrated that under some conditions there is value in admitting fear and talking over the matter with others who

Active participation in sports can be a good outlet for expending an excess amount of energy produced by an emotional situation.

are afraid. It helps a man to realize that he is not alone in his fear, that he is not abnormal.

5. *Remove yourself from situations that are producing undesirable emotional states.* If you find that you are losing your temper in an argument, tactfully change the subject, or excuse yourself on some pretext until you can cool off. If you find that the work you are doing is making you "nervous," take a little time off to eat lunch, talk with someone, or in some other way get away from the work for a short time.

6. *Expend in some socially approved manner the energy aroused in an undesirable emotional experience.* You may become very angry at someone.

Physiologically you are prepared to fight, but the energy can be expended on a punching bag, on a pile of wood to be sawed, or in taking a long walk. Books have been written, pictures painted, and music composed at intervals when individuals were working off thwarted or undesirable emotion. The person who is disappointed in romantic love may turn to social welfare or religious work in order to redirect the energy which would have gone into romance.

Psychologists use the word *sublimation* to refer to the redirecting of emotion from socially unacceptable forms of expression into approved channels. Sublimation is an adjustive process in which a desirable form of behavior is substituted for one that is undesirable. Psychoanalysts use the word to refer especially to the redirection of the sex drive into socially approved behavior.

7. *If possible, set a deadline for the solution of emotional problems.* In many cases, emotional experiences become more and more disturbing with the passing of time. Therefore, it is wise to allow sufficient time to study a problem but with a deadline for the solution. Otherwise you may drag on and on and become more and more upset.

One advantage of setting a deadline for solution of a problem is that it will help you to get started on your attack. Nothing leads to greater emotional upset than worrying about a problem but doing nothing about it. Sometimes tension can be reduced by writing down the advantages and disadvantages for each side of a conflict. It may help to tell a friend that you plan to reach a decision and will let him know the results by a certain time.

After meeting your deadline for a decision, turn your thoughts elsewhere. Relax! Don't keep reopening the case unless new and important evidence is presented. Even though the decision has been an important one, everything in your life does not depend upon it. If you do make a mistake, you may be able to modify your decision in the future. Even if you are unable to modify it, you will not be the first person in the world to have made an unfortunate decision.

Do all adults reach emotional maturity? As a person grows older, he normally tends to develop better and better emotional control, but some persons mature in terms of general bodily development without maturing emotionally. Even as adults they have temper tantrums, they pity themselves, they are easily frightened and express their fright in childish ways, they are constantly seeking sympathy.

Psychologists have found that children and emotionally immature adults are characterized by certain behavior: (1) intolerance of discomfort and demand for immediate relief; (2) demand for immediate satisfaction of their desires; (3) explosive behavior such as "flying off the handle," temper tantrums, sudden and copious crying; (4) demand for personal satisfactions regardless of the inconvenience and even discomfort which such demands may bring to others. You will note examples of these characteristics in small children. Note the same characteristics in adults who are emotionally immature.

Have you any characteristics of emotional immaturity?

What are the characteristics of an emotionally mature person? One psychologist has characterized the emotionally mature person in these terms: (1) he can endure pain and suffering (when necessary) with courage and fortitude; (2) he can wait for rewards and look at situations from a long-range view; (3) he is able to take an active interest in the life and welfare of others. This definition sounds very much like our definition of mental health. The adult who enjoys good mental health is emotionally mature.

Some individuals seem to find it more difficult than others to achieve emotional maturity. We cannot say how much of the difficulty is a consequence of inherited physiological factors and how much is a consequence of early childhood conditioning. At any rate, so long as a person is doing his best to achieve emotional maturity, he should not worry if he is easily moved to tears, if he is upset by the sight of suffering, or if he has to make considerable effort to control his temper. Many other people have as much difficulty as he.

Furthermore, there is some evidence that many individuals who tend to become emotionally upset rather easily nevertheless are able to meet real emergencies with surprising calmness. In times of crisis and tragedy, they do with dispatch and efficiency whatever must be done. They may go through emergency situations more calmly than persons who generally appear much more emotionally stable.

ADJUSTING TO YOUR SOCIAL ENVIRONMENT

OTHER WAYS OF RESPONDING TO FRUSTRATION AND CONFLICT

We have considered desirable ways of responding to frustrations and conflicts. We have noted desirable ways of controlling emotional reactions. Now, we shall turn to other ways of responding to frustrations and conflicts. Some of these ways may be either desirable or undesirable, depending upon how and to what degree they are used.

Doing something else. Psychologists use the word *compensation* to refer to an attempt to make up for a deficiency in one field by expending extra effort and energy over a prolonged period in order to excel in some other field. Compensation may be a very desirable way of meeting frustrations. It may lead toward good mental health. A person may consciously set out to compensate for some deficiency, or he may compensate without being aware of the fact that he is doing so. Compensation may also be used in unfortunate ways.

Compensatory (kəm·pen′sə·tôr′ē) behavior may lead to constructive activities that leave a person better off than before he experienced frustration in reaching his original goal. A member of a high school football team had polio. The result was that he could never play football or any other strenuous game again. He might have compensated by becoming a ping-pong player, but even in this relatively mild game his physical deficiency would have meant a very hard uphill fight and one probably not worth the price.

His interests were in athletics, and he did not wish to change his interests just because he could no longer play strenuous games. While still in high school, he became the sports reporter for the school paper. After graduation he worked his way up as a reporter on a city newspaper. He has now become well known as a sportscaster on a television program. He has many friends among sports fans. Once in a while, his most intimate friends hear him say, "Gee, I wish I could get out there and play myself," but he knows and admits that he cannot play. He has compensated for his physical handicap in a desirable way. In terms of lifelong happiness and financial income, he is probably better off than if he had been able to continue as an athlete.

He might have compensated in an undesirable way. He might have decided that since he couldn't play, he would make money out of sports by gambling. He could have gone in for "fixing" games so that the player or team on which he bet would be sure to win. He would have compensated for his deficiency but at the expense of becoming dishonest, of losing friends, and of degrading the thing in which he was most interested.

A person may recognize that he does not have the size or strength to be a varsity player. He may compensate by being a good player on some minor team. He may compensate by becoming a skilled chess player. He can enjoy himself and enrich his social life regardless of which game he plays. Yet he might have compensated in an undesirable way — by bullying and mistreating smaller and weaker boys in an attempt to feel superior.

A student may realize and admit that even though he tries very hard, he just can't be a superior student. He may compensate by becoming superior in some other field in which he does have ability. For example, a girl was just getting by in most subjects in high school in spite of her best efforts. For a while she did become very much interested in the chemistry course when the teacher talked about and demonstrated chemical processes involved in photography. In fact, the girl made a B in chemistry for that grading period, and B's were scarce on her record. She began developing and printing pictures at home. She borrowed and studied library books on photography. She joined a local camera club. Several of her pictures were published in the school annual, and one was in the rotogravure section of a Sunday newspaper. She had compensated for her lack of general scholastic ability. She had developed an interesting and, possibly, a profitable hobby.

Compensation for none-too-good schoolwork might have taken an undesirable turn. According to records in the guidance office, this girl possessed only average intellectual ability, and her school record seemed to bear out test scores. In spite of this, she might have set out to prove to herself that she was a genius. She might even have said that in chemistry the teacher and the textbook were all wrong. In that case she would never have learned all the things that she found so useful in photography. Belittling others is a common but unfortunate kind of compensation.

There are many ways in which a person can compensate: the person who is not very attractive physically can compensate by being very friendly and helpful; the student who does not do well in vocational subjects may compensate by doing well in the more academic subjects and vice versa; the person who, for some reason, is unable to have children of his or her own may compensate by being a Scout leader or playground supervisor caring for other people's children; the person who is unable to travel can compensate by reading books and magazines about travel. You can make a long list of ways in which an individual can compensate for feelings of frustration and inferiority. If the compensations are to further mental health, they must be socially approved. In Chapter 18, "Social Attitudes and Social Problems," we shall see that delinquent behavior may often be understood in terms of undesirable compensation.

Compensation can be overdone. The shy student may try so hard to compensate for his lack of social life that he studies excessively, even to the point of not getting sufficient healthful exercise and eliminating what little social life he did have. The poor student may try so hard to compensate for his lack of scholastic ability that he joins every available club or other social organization. He is out every night. His schoolwork drops still lower. Both the student who studies almost all the time and the student who engages in excessive social activity are overcompensating for their respective deficiencies.

Did you ever hear a boy say, "I'm the dumbest person in school," or a girl say, "All the other girls are so much prettier than I am"? Did they expect you to agree with them? Did they want you to say, "I'd hate to see them come any dumber," or "I can't imagine anyone uglier than you"? On the contrary, they hoped you would say, "Oh, you're one of the smartest boys in school," or "I think you're the prettiest girl in the whole world." Self-repudiation, that is, "running yourself down," often indicates over-compensation.

Joining and identifying with organizations. The word *identification* refers to the achieving of satisfaction from the successes of other individuals or groups. Small boys identify themselves with their fathers, and small girls identify themselves with their mothers. Later, they may identify themselves with their teachers or with the heroes or heroines of the movies, the theater, or television programs. By putting themselves, in imagination, in the place of an older and admired person, they can achieve some vicarious satisfaction.

As we become more mature, we tend to identify ourselves with organizations rather than with individuals. A person may join a club, lodge, church, or other social group because, by so doing, he can enjoy the social life and do his part in carrying out the worthwhile objectives of the organization. On the other hand, he may identify himself with an organization for the feeling of superiority such membership gives him, rather than for the good he can do for the organization. A student may join a school club only because it is the largest or most popular club in school. A high school graduate may choose a college because it has a very good football team and he can say, *"We* are the strongest team in the conference" (even though he may not play and takes physical education only because it is required).

We all do a certain amount of identifying, but the person who finds himself deriving too much glory from the accomplishments of another or who finds himself joining organizations solely for the prestige he will derive from membership should strive for more personal success.

Attributing your own emotions and intentions to someone else. When a person perceives in other people certain traits or motives in which he feels himself to be inferior, he is demonstrating *projection*. He may blame others for his shortcomings or difficulties, or he may attribute to others his own unacceptable desires. A student yields to the temptation of cheating on an examination. To relieve his feeling of guilt, he says, "Everybody else in the class cheats. I even saw Evelyn cheating and she is on the honor roll." He had arranged to have a neighbor drop a slip containing the most important answers so that he could pick it up. But to minimize his guilt, he says, "When Evelyn borrowed a pencil during the exam, I'm sure she looked at my paper." An irritable person may accuse others of being irritable. An impolite person may accuse other people of rudeness.

We may gain a bit of temporary relief from our feelings of frustration and inferiority when we project our traits and motives onto others, but the person striving for good mental health tries to correct his faults rather than to see them in others.

Refusing to change. When faced by frustrating or conflicting situations, some individuals respond by simply continuing in a blind way with their past behavior patterns, making no attempt to adjust to new conditions. A person has difficulty in being socially accepted, possibly because of the careless way in which he dresses. Instead of trying to learn why he is not readily accepted, he goes ahead doggedly trying to enter social groups without improving his appearance. A student has difficulty with a particular kind of algebra problem. Instead of trying to work out a new plan of attack, he plunges ahead with the same incorrect approach time after time.

Psychologists use the term *stereotyped behavior* to refer to inflexible behavior, that is, behavior which is not altered by circumstances.

"Forgetting" the incident. One way of getting around frustrations and conflicts is to "forget" them. As we saw in Chapter 4, we do forget many things, but when we "forget" because the original thoughts are painful to us, we are demonstrating *repression* rather than true forgetting. Psychologists often use the term "repression" in a very special and technical way. For our purposes, however, we can say that repression is selective forgetting. We "forget" that which is unpleasant for us to remember.

Perhaps you have had some very embarrassing experience in the classroom. For weeks you were kidded about the unfortunate incident. Life became rather unhappy. You might say to yourself, "I'll just forget the incident." If by "forget" you meant that you were going to try to think of other things and take the kidding good-naturedly, you were making a good adjustment. If, without saying "I'll forget," you began to avoid situations which reminded you of the unfortunate incident, you were repressing your thoughts of the incident.

Probably we all repress some undesirable thoughts, but if such "forgetting" becomes extreme, a person is mentally ill. After a painful incident some persons even "forget" their names, where they live, and experiences of their earlier life. For example, a young woman struck a man with her car and believed that she had killed him (although she had not). When picked up by the police for ignoring a stop sign, she could give them no information concerning her identity. She had "forgotten" her past, including the accident. It wasn't a matter of trying to fool the police. It wasn't until much later that they even thought of connecting her with the accident.

Running away from the situation. Sometimes an individual, when faced with personal problems, tries to evade unpleasant facts or responsibilities. He doesn't say, "I'll run away from the situation," but he does just that, nevertheless.

ADJUSTING TO YOUR SOCIAL ENVIRONMENT

The use of alcohol or drugs is often a way of running away from unpleasant situations. Certainly the person who is drunk or the person under the influence of a drug is not attacking his problems. The vagrant runs away from his frustrations and lives a life of irresponsibility. Sometimes sleep is used as an escape from problems, especially when it is brought on by the use of sleeping pills. The student who feels that he is frustrated and cannot succeed in his schoolwork may escape by quitting school, if he is old enough, or by being absent as much as possible, especially on the days when he should be taking tests. An individual whose love affair ends unpleasantly may run away from possible future unhappy situations by refusing to have dates.

Sometimes individuals regress, or return to earlier ways of behaving, to avoid their present problems. *Regression* is the escaping of present problems by returning to earlier-known ways of meeting frustrations. Older children sometimes become quite babyish in their behavior because they find the problems of an older child too difficult to face with comfort. Sometimes "tired businessmen" run away from their jobs and behave in a very childish manner at conventions or school reunions. Adolescents may resort to childish temper tantrums and fights rather than attacking their problems.

Occasional temporary regressions are not abnormal, although, as we shall see in Chapter 15, mental hospitals contain many persons who have run away from their frustrations. The person who drifts off into elaborate daydreams may be escaping from un-

pleasant situations. Another very common way of escaping problems is by *procrastination,* or delay.

Procrastinating to avoid doing something. By putting off a task, an individual gets temporary relief from a distressful situation. For the time being, he escapes an unpleasant task.

A person is especially likely to procrastinate if he has very high ambitions but feels inferior. He is not willing to test his strength because of fear of failure. For example, a high school senior said that he was very anxious to enter a certain college. Going to this college was a "must" on his list of ambitions. The college provided a very helpful scholarship, and several seniors were applying for it. This boy said, "I just have to win that scholarship," yet he also realized that someone else might win it. He put off filling out the necessary application blank. Finally, he filled out the blank and sent it in—two days after the deadline for applications. Of course, he didn't win the scholarship, but he could say, "I'd probably have received the scholarship if I had sent the blank in on time." Instead of facing a possible failure, he had run away from any possibility of success.

The student who puts off writing a theme or term paper escapes, for a time, what seems to be an unpleasant task. The longer the task is put off, the more unpleasant it becomes. In the meantime, he hurries from one task to another. He can say, "I just don't have time to write that paper." Finally, and at the last minute, he hurriedly gathers some material and writes the paper. Of course, the grade on the paper is poor.

Responses
to Frustration

Frustration is a blocking of activity that is directed toward some goal. One way in which a person may respond to frustration is by displaced aggression (top), as when the boy kicks his bicycle instead of the real source of his hostility. Another response is procrastination (middle), as when the student watches television to put off doing his homework. Compensation (below), in which an apprentice actor who would like to appear onstage compensates by working offstage, is yet another response.

He says, "I wouldn't have had the poorest grade in the class if I had had time to do enough work on the paper." He ignores the fact that he had done many other things while putting off the writing of the paper. He kids himself into believing he would have had a good paper if he had had more time, but in reality he had been running away from the task so that he would have an excuse for his failure. He was not in the best possible mental health.

Somewhat facetiously it has been said that "procrastination is the art of keeping up with yesterday." Probably everyone gets behind in some of his work at times. Sometimes it is not his fault, but the person who is generally behind in much of his work should ask himself, "Basically, why do I procrastinate? What is it that I am trying to run away from?" A frank answer to these questions may help him to improve his mental health.

Taking out your frustration on an innocent victim. Perhaps you have run into some difficulty at school. You were not prepared for class and had to remain after school to make up the work. You had planned to get home early, do the necessary studying, and then go to a show. Now your plans have been upset. As you come home, your faithful dog happily runs out to meet you. Instead of patting him, you kick the dog. You were angry at the teacher, but you could not give direct expression to your hostility by kicking the teacher, so instead you kicked your poor dog. A workman is bawled out by his boss. He would like to kick the boss, but that direct aggressive be-

havior would mean the loss of his job. He goes home and growls and snaps at his wife and children instead. A child is happily playing with his toys when he is told to put them away and go to bed. He is frustrated, but what can he do to his parents? He kicks the toys all over the floor and may even break some of them.

All of the situations described above show examples of what psychologists speak of as *displaced aggression*, meaning the transfer of hostility from the actual source of frustration to some innocent person or object. Popularly, displaced aggression is spoken of as "blowing off steam."

Letting someone else decide for you. Making a decision is often difficult and even painful. In order to avoid such difficulty, you can ask a friend for the answer to your problem: "What would you do if you were in my place?" How does he know what he would do if he were in your place? He is not and never has been in your place. Both his heredity and his environment are different from yours. His hopes and aspirations are different. Your friend can give you information and even make recommendations, but all too often when you ask for advice, you are really asking for a ready-made solution to your problem. You are not facing your own problem. You are escaping.

Letting chance decide for you. Instead of asking a friend to solve your problem, you may put the burden on mere chance. You can't decide whether to get a job after high school graduation or go to college. You flip a coin—

heads you go to college, tails you get a job. Of course you may question the decision of the coin, so you decide to make it two out of three. Maybe you had better flip it a hundred times, or a thousand or at least flip it until you remember that you are refusing to face your problem.

Rationalizing your behavior. Instead of actively attacking or plainly running away from his problems, a person may try to "explain" what he has done. He may rationalize. Psychologists use the word *rationalization* to refer to the kind of thinking people do when they explain their behavior in terms of socially approved and high-sounding reasons instead of real reasons. Unlike projection, in which the individual places blame for his shortcomings on another person or persons, rationalization does not necessarily involve another person. An individual often rationalizes his behavior by blaming an object or a set of circumstances.

Rationalizing is not the same as lying. The person who does the rationalizing deceives himself first and others (maybe) afterward. He is not willing to admit that he is wrong. Instead, he fools himself into accepting some explanation for his behavior which will save his "face," or pride.

The student who has neglected his work finds failing or poor marks on his report card. He feels that it will be necessary to explain these low marks to parents and friends. The real reason for his negligence is not a good one and will not be approved by his parents and friends. He "reasons out" more acceptable explanations for his low

marks. He says, "I did the work all right, but the questions on the test were very unfair," or "My classes are so dull that I can't possibly pay attention." By such defenses as these, he saves his pride in his own eyes, and he may even fool a few friends. But many persons will recognize immediately that he is rationalizing. They will note that his unwillingness to face the truth is a symptom of poor mental health.

Rationalization is not limited to persons of high school and college age. We see it developing in young children. A child asks for candy but is refused. Instead of facing the fact that although he would like to have some candy, he may not have it, he says, "Oh, I didn't want candy anyway. It always makes me sick." We see adults rationalizing, also. A man may stress the importance of honesty to his children. Then in his business he has a chance to make a profitable deal, providing he tells an outright lie or raises a false implication about the merchandise he is offering. He completes the dishonest transaction. Later a friend may accuse him of not living up to the principles he taught his children, or he may be troubled by questioning thoughts of his own. He is not willing to admit to himself or to others that he has been dishonest, for dishonesty is not approved by society. Possibly he rationalizes by saying, "Business is business. Anyone else would have done the same thing. The customer knew, or should have known, what he was buying. Anyway, I gave no written guarantee."

We must be careful not to condemn too freely in our thoughts the person

ADJUSTING TO YOUR SOCIAL ENVIRONMENT

we know to be rationalizing. Just as none of us is in perfect bodily health, none of us is in perfect mental health. We all rationalize.

We can get a better understanding of rationalization by noting two forms it often takes, "sour grapes" and "sweet lemons."

What is the "sour grapes" rationalization? The name *"sour grapes"* is given to the form of rationalization in which a person says that he does not want something which he cannot have. By finding fault with the unattainable object, a person makes it seem less appealing to himself. The term comes from the fable of the fox and the grapes —a fable attributed to Aesop, who lived twenty-five hundred years ago. The fox, unable to reach the grapes he desired, declared that they were sour. Maybe some of his fox friends believed that he didn't want the grapes. Probably most of them knew very well that he was rationalizing. (This fable is also a good example of anthropomorphism. See page 11.)

Have you ever known a case like the following? A student works hard hoping to receive grades that will put him on the Honor Roll. Yet he fails to make it by a narrow margin. He says, "I didn't care to get on the Honor Roll anyway. Only bookworms get on the Honor Roll." Of course, he would have been proud to see his name on the Honor Roll. Instead of admitting that he was sorry that he did not succeed and resolving to work even harder the next time, he tried to save his pride by offering to himself and to his friends a sour-grapes rationalization.

A boy asks a girl to go to a dance with him. For some reason she does not accept his invitation. Her refusal hurts his pride. Perhaps other fellows hear about it and tease him about having been turned down. Instead of admitting his situation and, perhaps, asking another girl, he says, "I didn't really want to go to that dance anyway. Besides, I wouldn't want to be seen on the dance floor with her. She is the poorest dancer in school. She is too short" (or tall, or fat, or skinny) — and so on.

What is the "sweet lemon" rationalization? Psychologists have given the name *"sweet lemon"* to the form of rationalization in which a person says that what he has, but doesn't really want, is just what he wants. The lemon is sour, but if we put sugar on it we may be able to take it with a fair degree of grace. If we add enough sugar, we may be able to make it appear to others and to ourselves that a lemon is exactly what we want.

Perhaps the student who doesn't quite make the Honor Roll says, "I am glad that I didn't get on the Honor Roll. I prefer to be one of the great mass of average students." In actuality he isn't glad at all; but by putting enough "sugar" on his disappointment he is able to stand the failure a bit more easily. Just possibly he is even able to fool some of his friends into believing him.

The boy who is refused when he asks a girl to attend a dance with him may say, "I am glad that she didn't accept. I thought I just had to ask her because no one else would. Now I can stay home and enjoy a nice long night of sleep."

The person who drives an out-of-date car says, "I wouldn't trade this old bus for any of the new models. I wouldn't accept a new model as a gift." In spite of this statement he enters an advertising contest in which the prize is a latest-model car. If he should win the contest, would he refuse to accept the new car?

Is it sometimes helpful to rationalize to cover disappointment? Under some circumstances one form of rationalization may afford a measure of relief from disappointment. Suppose that a student has striven hard to be elected to the position of editor of the school annual or some other school publication. Only one person can be given this honor. An unsuccessful candidate may be keenly disappointed. In his effort to console himself he may think, "Well, the job probably would involve too much time anyway; I'd have to sit up nights working at it." By looking at that side of the picture for a little while, he may succeed in overcoming his disappointment or at least in greatly lessening it. Finding relief from disappointment in that way may not be undesirable. It may even be helpful, provided a person (1) keeps such thoughts to himself, (2) recognizes that he is only consoling himself, and (3) resolves to try for success in some other field of endeavor.

Both sour-grapes and sweet-lemon rationalizations indicate that an individual is unwilling to face the unpleasant realities of life. Excessive rationalization is indicative of poor

mental health. From the point of view of mental hygiene, the sweet-lemon rationalization is probably more desirable than the sour-grapes rationalization. However, friends weary of sweet lemons as well as of sour grapes.

How do groups and nations rationalize? Social groups as well as individuals devise and accept rationalized explanations for their behavior.

Under the ancient law of Moses, a goat was selected, over whose head the high priest confessed the sins of his people. Then the "scapegoat" was driven into the wilderness, bearing with it, symbolically, all those sins. Today we refer to any individual or group blamed for the misdeeds or mistakes of others as a *scapegoat*. If civil authorities are unable to cope with the problems in a community, they do not like to admit their failure. They find it easy to place the blame on some weak minority group; this or that "element" becomes the scapegoat.

When a national leader is unable to cope with economic and social problems, he may not dare to admit his failure. He must rationalize and influence the public to rationalize with him.

We have many good illustrations of group rationalization in time of war. Most persons do not believe in killing other persons. Therefore, in order for a country to be led into war, the people must be taught to rationalize their war behavior. History is full of such instances.

The individual who is striving to achieve good mental health will take into account as many of his rationaliza-

ADJUSTING TO YOUR SOCIAL ENVIRONMENT

tions as possible. He will face reality, even though that reality is sometimes unpleasant, rather than excuse himself by offering plausible explanations for his conduct. When the majority of individuals act on these principles, it is more difficult for leaders to force a whole nation into an unjustified war.

Are defense mechanisms healthy or unhealthy? Such behavior as rationalization, projection, daydreaming or fantasy, regression, and repression is referred to as a defense mechanism. *Defense mechanisms* are ways of behavior that protect the individual's self-esteem, or ego. They are used by everyone to some degree and do not necessarily represent maladjusted behavior. It is the degree to which an individual employs these mechanisms that indicates the state of his mental health. For this reason, the specific mechanism or number of mechanisms used is not as important as the frequency and way in which the individual uses any one mechanism. An individual who uses five or six defense mechanisms may be in better mental health than someone who uses one mechanism over and over again and to an extreme degree.

Remember, also, that classifying defense mechanisms is arbitrary, since more than one mechanism is often involved in a given situation. Labeling behavior or classifying individuals into types is useful only for descriptive purposes; it often does not clearly explain the behavior of the individual. In order to explain behavior, we need to know much more about the person; we must consider his needs, his point of view, his motives, and many other factors. A mechanism may provide the individual with time to determine more adequate ways of behaving. Nevertheless, defense mechanisms should not be used as a permanent substitute for more direct ways of behaving and adjusting.

Terms to Add to Your Vocabulary

ambivalence	frustration	regression
approach-approach conflict	frustration tolerance	repression
approach-avoidance conflict	identification	scapegoat
avoidance-avoidance conflict	mental health	sour-grapes rationalization
compensation	procrastination	stereotyped behavior
defense mechanism	projection	sublimation
displaced aggression	rationalization	sweet-lemon rationalization

Suggestions for Activities

1. Perhaps you have studied a personality inventory or took one yourself in connection with Chapter 6. If so, you may wish to reconsider your score in the light of the present chapter. A number of such inventories include an

analysis of both personal and social adjustment.

If you have not taken such an inventory, you may wish to take the *Gordon Personal Profile,* published by Harcourt, Brace & World, Inc., which measures four aspects of personality: ascendancy, responsibility, emotional stability, and sociability.

2. Happiness depends not on the absence of conflicts but on how well you resolve conflicts. Often it is helpful to make a simple analysis of conflicts so that they can be faced more objectively. For a few days, jot down the nature of conflicting situations which you encounter and try to classify these conflicts as approach-approach, approach-avoidance, or avoidance-avoidance. Perhaps some of your conflicts are related to school situations and are common to a number of students. If they are not too personal, discuss them in class or in small groups. Does such a group approach help you with your individual conflicts? Does classifying them help?

3. Think of some very unpleasant emotional experience which you have had or which you have observed in someone else. Can you think of ways in which the emotion-arousing situation might have been avoided? What were the overt expressions of the emotional state? If the experience was your own, did you note any indications of visceral changes? What was done, or what should have been done, to control the expression of emotion? You may wish to make a class report describing the experience.

4. You may wish to write a report for an English or history class in which you portray the life of some person whose life seemed to be largely spent in compensating for a handicap, for example, Helen Keller, Thomas Edison, De-

mosthenes, Theodore Roosevelt.

Your report may be based on some character in literature; for example, in Shakespeare's *Richard III,* Gloucester compensates for a deformed and stunted body by shrewd striving for power.

5. Do you ever procrastinate? Do your friends ever procrastinate? Write a short report of a case of procrastination. Basically, why did you, or a friend, put off a job? Were results as good as they would have been if the job had been done more promptly?

6. For a period of one or two weeks, jot down frustrating situations which you experience, both those in which you are prevented from doing something you wish to do and those in which you are faced with a conflict. Such situations may involve schoolwork, dates, home activities, recreational activities, and so on. Draw up a four-column chart with the following headings: *Situation, Desirable Response, Questionable Response, Undesirable Response.* Down the side of the page, under the heading *Situation,* list the experiences which you have found frustrating or conflicting. Then for each situation, indicate how you responded to it, classifying your response under the heading which describes it. For those situations responded to in questionable or undesirable ways, indicate in red ink under *Desirable Response* how you might better have met the situation.

7. For one week, listen for and jot down apparent rationalizations that you hear. Some may be given by your friends or relatives, some may be overheard in the conversations of strangers, some may be detected in your own conversations. As far as you can judge, which ones are "sour grapes" and which ones are "sweet lemons"?

ADJUSTING TO YOUR SOCIAL ENVIRONMENT

8. For at least a period of a week, check newspapers for items suggesting group rationalizations. You might keep a file of such articles and compare the various rationalizations. Are there evidences of scapegoats? Examples of group rationalizations are especially easy to locate during the campaigns which precede a political election.

9. While watching sports events, such as boxing, wrestling, and auto racing, some individuals become very excited. If you have a chance to attend or watch such sports events (perhaps on television, or in movies), observe the people in the audience. What evidence can you find that they are identifying with the players?

Suggestions for Further Reading

Bergler, Edmund, *Tensions Can Be Reduced to Nuisances: A Technique for Not-Too-Neurotic People,* Collier.

Coleman, James, *Personality Dynamics and Effective Behavior,* Scott, Foresman. Part II, "The Dynamics of Individual and Group Behavior," a section including a discussion of frustration, conflict, stress, and breakdown under excessive stress.

Daniel, Robert S., ed., *Contemporary Readings in General Psychology,* 2nd ed., Houghton Mifflin. Pages 375–79, "Implications of Recent Advances in Prediction and Control of Behavior"; pages 408–10, "Four Great Lacks in Mental Health."

Hilgard, Ernest R., and Richard C. Atkinson, *Introduction to Psychology,* 4th ed., Harcourt, Brace & World. Chapter 20, "Conflict and Adjustment."

Kalish, Richard A., *The Psychology of Human Behavior,* Wadsworth. Chapter 12, "Emotions and Stress"; Chapter 13, "Reactions to Stress."

Leuba, Clarence, *Man: A General Psychology,* Holt, Rinehart & Winston. Chapter 8, "Understanding and Controlling Emotions"; Chapter 9, "Psychological Defenses Against Stress"; pages 549–50, "The Mature Personality"; pages 551–59, "Happy and Unhappy Personalities."

Lindgren, Henry C., Donn Byrne, and Lewis F. Petrinovich, *Psychology: An Introduction to a Behavioral Science,* 2nd ed., John Wiley. Chapter 12, "Personal Adjustment and Mental Hygiene."

McKeachie, Wilbert J., and Charlotte L. Doyle, *Psychology,* Addison-Wesley. Chapter 11, "Frustrations and the Mechanisms of Defense."

Menninger, William C., *Growing Up Emotionally,* Science Research Associates.

——— *Understanding Yourself,* Science Research Associates.

Morgan, Clifford T., and Richard A. King, *Introduction to Psychology,* 3rd ed., McGraw-Hill. Chapter 15, "Mental Health and Psychotherapy."

Munn, Norman L., *Psychology,* 5th ed., Houghton Mifflin, Chapter 8, "Conflict and Adjustment."

Ruch, Floyd L., *Psychology and Life,* 7th ed., Scott, Foresman. Chapter 13, "Reactions to Frustration."

Sanford, Fillmore H., *Psychology: A Scientific Study of Man,* 2nd ed., Wadsworth. Chapter 16, "The Adjusting Individual."

Seidman, Jerome, ed., *The Adolescent: A Book of Readings,* rev. ed., Holt, Rinehart & Winston. Pages 218–37, "The Course of Healthy Personality Development."

Thorman, George, *Toward Mental Health,* Public Affairs Pamphlet No. 120.

Tussing, Lyle, *Psychology for Better Living,* Wiley.

Whittaker, James O., et al., *Introduction to Psychology,* W. B. Saunders. Chapter 7, "Frustration and Conflict."

13

Friendship, popularity, and leadership

Adjusting to your social environment is a lifelong process. Everyone meets frustrating situations throughout his life, as we discussed in the last chapter. This chapter will focus on several specific areas—friendship, popularity, and leadership—in which adjustments to the social environment are necessary for the achievement of good mental health. We shall examine the development of friendly relationships and the characteristics of an individual's personality that cause other people to like him or be influenced by him.

HOW FRIENDSHIPS DEVELOP

Friendship may be defined as a pleasant relationship between two persons based on mutually reinforced behavior. It develops through learning experiences. The kind of behavior that takes place between two people is affected by reward or punishment, by positive or negative reinforcement. A friendship grows when the pleasant experiences between two individuals are mutually reinforced. Friendship also includes affection between two per-

sons, which means that there is some emotional involvement in the relationship. Friendship puts stress on emotion rather than on rational analysis and accumulation of knowledge about the other person (although knowing facts about a given person and deciding to be friendly with him or her often helps in forming friendships). Friendships established during high school years may last a lifetime or they may be of relatively short duration, but whatever the length of the friendship, at the time it is being experienced, the affection involved distinguishes friendship from casual relationships.

We shall make no attempt to distinguish sharply between friendship and love in this chapter, although we shall discuss romantic love in Chapter 16. Usually the mutual attraction is considered less intense in friendship than in love, but this is not necessarily so. Sometimes the term "love" is applied only to relationships between individuals of different sexes, and "friendship" is applied both to members of the same sex and members of the two sexes. Our main concern here, however, is that friendship and love are pleasant relationships between individuals.

Can we learn about friendship through experiments with animals?

Like any other kind of behavior, friendship can be studied experimentally. Although we usually think of friendship as a term that refers only to a human relationship, we can gain some understanding of friendship by studying animal behavior under experimentally controlled conditions.

In one experiment, puppies were reared in isolation. No puppy had an opportunity to play with or even fight with any other puppy. Furthermore, none had social contacts with human beings (although, of course, food and water were placed in each cage). Later, as mature dogs, because they had not had an opportunity to learn to be friendly, these animals were unable to learn to interact socially with other dogs or to respond affectionately to human beings. This experiment suggests that friendly behavior is behavior that is learned as animals — and human beings — mature.

Some very interesting work conducted with monkeys further indicates how important it is for young animals to receive attention and affection. In the following experiment, baby monkeys were reared with surrogate mothers. *Surrogate mothers* are artificial objects that take the place of the monkey's real mother. One surrogate mother was made from a block of wood, covered with sponge rubber and sheathed in a tan piece of terry cloth. Another surrogate mother was made of uncovered wire mesh. Both artificial mothers were warmed by a heat source, and both contained a bottle arranged so that an infant monkey could nurse from it.

Then baby monkeys, one by one, were placed in a cubicle with the two surrogate mothers. It was clear that they preferred the cloth-covered mother, because they spent far more time clinging to her than to the other artificial mother (see picture on page 349). When confronted with fear-producing stimuli, the infant monkeys showed a marked tendency to run to the cloth-covered mother rather than to the wire-mesh mother. As the psychologist conducting the experiment stated, "The wire mother is biologically adequate but psychologically inept."

In time these monkeys matured and were studied further. The adult monkeys that had been reared by surrogate mothers failed to develop healthy, friendly relationships with other monkeys. Mating behavior was not normal, although some of the females did have infants. These females were not very good mothers: they showed little affection for their babies. In fact, they avoided their offspring, pushed them away, and some even beat their infants or crushed them against the floor. They displayed what we would consider to be abnormal behavior in human beings. Instead of caring for their babies, the mothers would sit in their cages all day staring into space and would pay little, if any, attention to other living creatures. If approached by other monkeys or human beings, they would sometimes go into frenzies of rage so great that they would injure themselves. Their pattern of behavior suggests that in order to have friendly

MENTAL HEALTH

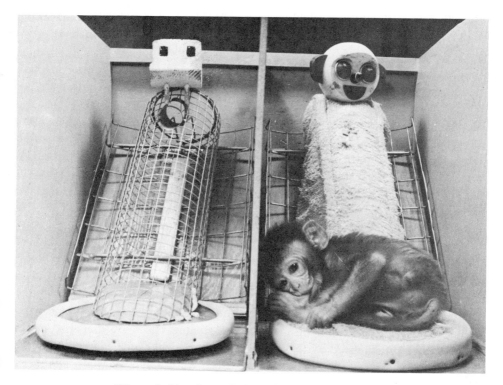

When afraid or in need of comfort, the infant monkey would choose to be close to the cloth-covered rather than the wire-mesh surrogate mother.

relationships, monkeys, and perhaps human beings, too, need affection in the early stages of development.

Can experiments with human infants be used to study friendship? Scientists cannot duplicate with human subjects the complete isolation they can impose on animals in an experiment, nor can they raise human infants with wood or wire-mesh surrogate mothers. But it is possible for scientists to study certain infants who have received very little maternal care. For example, during a war some infants are left without a family when their parents and other relatives are killed. These infants are usually sent to orphan homes, but with

so many of them and so few people to tend to them, these orphans may receive only the most essential care. In these orphan homes no one has time to cuddle the infants, fondle them, pet them, or sing to them. Babies growing up under such institutional care often develop slowly, both in bodily growth and intellectual functioning, and fail to show normal affectionate behavior.

Scientists are sometimes able to provide improved living conditions for a selected number of these infants being raised in an orphan home. In one experimental study a woman psychologist selected sixteen babies for special "mothering" care. These babies were not only bathed, diapered, and

FRIENDSHIP, POPULARITY, AND LEADERSHIP

fed, but they were soothed when they cried, they were held and played with, and they were responded to when they smiled or vocalized. This special care was provided $7\frac{1}{2}$ hours a day, five days a week, over a period of eight weeks. Although the other babies were not neglected in any way, they received only the essential care they had always been given. Since these other babies were not given special mothering care, they served as a control group.

Before, during, and after the period of experimentation, the babies were given various tests. To help attain valid results, the person who administered the tests was not the same person as the one who did the experimental mothering, so that the test scores were not influenced by the attitude of the experimenter.

One of the tests administered was for social responsiveness. In it the examiner performed a variety of acts, such as smiling and frowning at the baby and calling and talking to it. Before the eight-week experimental period began, experimental and control groups had been practically equal in scores on this test. When retested afterward, the experimental babies had scores indicating much more responsiveness than was the case for the control babies. In other words, after eight weeks the experimental group had become more friendly babies.

At the time these data were first published, many child psychologists believed that the children simply showed the need for and advantages of "mothering." A year later the children were retested. The experimental and control groups were now indistinguishable. Apparently the advantages of early stimulation were not maintained over the period of a year. The evidence also suggests that institutionalization did not have a lasting adverse effect on the behavior of the children, for the control group did not show the apathy or attention-seeking behavior often considered to be characteristic of institutionalized children. We do not yet have data, however, concerning the adult behavior of these individuals.

Another research project had somewhat similar results. Two groups of infants three months of age were used. One group consisted of infants who were being raised in an institution; the other group consisted of infants who were being raised by their parents in homes of high socioeconomic status. There were some marked differences in the environments of the two groups. For example, the own-home infants were played with by their parents seven times as often as the institutionalized infants. Yet tests revealed that the institutionalized infants actually smiled and vocalized more and, in general, were more responsive than the own-home infants.

Why these unexpected findings? We do not know for certain. Perhaps the institutionalized infants learned that they could get more attention by cooing and gurgling than was the case for own-home infants. Perhaps the fact that a number of persons cared for the institutionalized infants provided greater stimulation than in the case of the homes where just one person, the mother, provided most of the stimulation. At any rate, it seems that friendly babies need some sort of stimulating environment in which to grow up, and in our society this stimulation is usually accompanied by displays of affection.

How do friendships develop in childhood and adolescence? Friendships develop partly as a result of contact with an increasing number of other individuals of about the same age. As babies mature and become children, their social contacts expand. They change from playing alone to playing with one other child, to playing with two other children, and then to playing with three or more children. They establish contact with the children in the neighborhood. When they go to school, they have the opportunity to meet many more children. As they become adolescents and enter junior and senior high schools, their range of acquaintances expands even further. They often join various clubs and other social groups.

Along with contact another basic factor in the development of friendships is propinquity—the nearness in time and place that makes social contacts possible. But why do individuals develop friendships with certain individuals and not with others? A review of some of the research literature will help to answer this question.

One investigator measured friendships of children whose ages averaged three and a half years. Since these children were in a nursery school, it was easy to observe their social contacts with their peers. A count was kept of the number of times each child was with every other child, which was considered a measure of the degree of friendship. The most interesting finding was that at this early age children

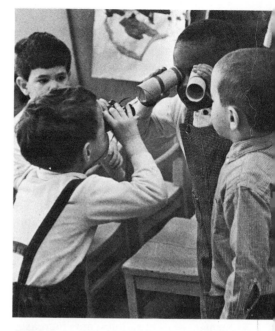

Children at the ages of four and five begin to enjoy the companionship of an increasing number of other children.

tended to form their strongest friendships with other children of their own sex.

As children grow older, the basis for forming friendships broadens. In one study, second-graders were asked to choose phrases which described their best friends. They tended to stress such phrases as "has lots of money to spend," "is good-looking," "has a nice home." When a group of sixth-graders was asked to describe their best friends, they tended to stress aspects of personality such as friendliness, cheerfulness, tidiness, and cleanliness.

In general, as children grow older they tend to quarrel less with their friends, although there is a difference between the two sexes: girls are less

FRIENDSHIP, POPULARITY, AND LEADERSHIP

quarrelsome than boys, and they have fewer outbursts of anger. At any given age during childhood, girls have more friends than boys.

As boys and girls approach adolescence, they tend to become more stable in their friendships. In one research study, children and adolescents were asked to indicate the names of their best friends. When they were asked to do so again two weeks later, 40 percent of the girls eleven years of age chose the same best friend, but more than 60 percent of the girls fifteen years of age chose the same best friend. For boys, the corresponding percentages were 50 and 60. Friendships were found to become more permanent as the adolescents increased in age. The oldest age studied in this particular research project was eighteen years.

To recapitulate, as children grow older, they tend to develop friendships in ever-widening social circles, they have more friends, they quarrel less with their friends, they shift the basis for forming friendships from superficial physical and social aspects to deeper aspects of personality, and their friendships become more stable. As children become adolescents, friendships include members of both sexes rather than remaining limited to mostly one sex.

How much of friendship is learned? Although affection may be partly a matter of maturation, the relationship of the individuals for whom we develop an affection and whom we call friends is determined mainly by conditioning. In infancy and babyhood our parents were instrumental in satisfying our physiological needs for food, drink, and bodily care, and as a result we developed affection for them. When we grew older, other adults and children satisfied our physical needs and our needs for companionship. In our experiences outside the home, we learned that interaction with some children and adults brought rewards and satisfactions of various kinds, and so we tended to seek reinforcement from them. If we had contacts with children, especially older children, who pushed or bossed us around or with adults who teased us, we soon learned to avoid them. We learned to form friendships with some children and adults and not with others.

Even though, as we have seen, friendships tend to become more stable as we grow older, we do continue to make new friends, and some who have been close friends may become mere acquaintances. Lack of contact with close friends or the sheer physical unavailability of friends we used to see frequently but who are no longer in the vicinity is a major factor in dissolution of friendships. High school and college class reunions are a lot of fun for a short period of time, but after an hour or two of pleasant exchange of memories individuals often find that there is little left to talk about. Perhaps their needs have changed, and the individuals no longer find the old friendships as mutually satisfying as they once were. If one or the other of a pair of friends gets little, if any, satisfaction from the friendship, or finds it frustrating because of quarrels or differences in social standards, their friendship is not likely to continue.

WHAT POPULARITY COSTS

Although popularity is closely related to friendship, the two are not synonymous. The personality traits that cause popularity are not necessarily the same as those that usually win friends. Some persons strive so hard to be popular that they lose most of their friends. Some persons become so obsessed with the idea of becoming popular that they are no longer well-adjusted. The adolescent who is very popular with his peers can be considered to be a social success, but this does not necessarily mean that he has achieved good personal adjustment. The person who makes tremendous effort to win popularity may lack confidence in himself. He may have so little assurance of personal worth that he strives constantly to prove by means of hard-won popularity that he is an adequate person.

Since a person's popularity depends upon his behavior in social situations, it is a suitable subject for psychological study and research. Unfortunately, psychologists have not been as much concerned with this aspect of behavior as with some other areas, so that the research literature is relatively limited. Nevertheless, we shall consider a few psychological reports and then turn to some of the personality characteristics that contribute to popularity. Finally, we shall discuss a number of techniques of developing a likable personality which can be used to increase one's popularity.

Individuals often strive to be popular and gain the admiration of others.

What is popularity? If a person has many admirers, or is esteemed by many individuals who feel that the person has a pleasing personality, he or she is said to be *popular*. Too often we compare ourselves with a few persons who are outstandingly popular and fail to consider that most persons we know probably have no more friends or admirers than we ourselves have. In reality, the evidence seems to suggest just the opposite: that popularity has a normal distribution (pages 140–42).

Psychological research suggests that individuals who are highly popular with the members of one group are likely to be popular with members of other groups. This finding indicates that common requirements for popularity exist among various groups, which

FRIENDSHIP, POPULARITY, AND LEADERSHIP

means that popularity does have traits that can be described and that pertain to popular members. Popular individuals have developed social skills and likable characteristics, so that they can recruit friends from a wide range of acquaintances. Yet even these persons do not appeal to all their acquaintances and may even be thoroughly disliked by a few.

Do I want to pay the price of popularity? Those who deviate very much from group norms are likely to be rejected by most members of the group, whereas individuals who conform to group norms tend to become popular. Most persons tend to go along with the group in order to achieve some degree of popularity. Yet if the norms of a group differ to a considerable extent from those to which he is accustomed, a person may deliberately choose not to attempt to be popular in that group. For example, he may not try to be popular in a group whose social behavior is contrary to the teaching of his religious faith. Or if a person is deeply interested in science or some other scholarly pursuit, he may not care to be popular in a group that professes to hate anyone who rises above mediocrity in such intellectual endeavors.

A number of general statements have been made about popularity, most of which have been based on research studies without including the supporting evidence. Now that we have established that it can be measured by its common traits, we shall consider in greater detail several of the studies that have been done on popularity.

To what extent is a girl's happiness related to her popularity with boys? One, but only one, measure of popularity is the frequency with which individuals have dates. One study in Chicago involved two groups of high school girls between the ages of thirteen and eighteen. Some of the girls in each group indicated that they had at least one date a week: that is, they were "popular" with boys. Other girls were "less popular" with boys, having dates less than once a week.

All the girls were asked to indicate what kind of song hits they liked. Of all the songs that become popular each year, about three-fourths deal with romantic love. In some of these songs, designated as "happy songs," the persons are very happy in their love lives. In other songs, designated as "blues songs," either the boy or the girl is unhappy in his or her romantic relationships.

To what extent was popularity with boys related to the kinds of songs preferred? The study's hypothesis was that girls having many dates would prefer "happy songs" and girls having infrequent dates would prefer "blues songs." Data for one neighborhood is given in the table on page 355.

The data do not bear out the original hypothesis. Popular girls preferred sad songs and less-popular girls preferred happy songs. It should be noted, however, that the number of subjects in each group was small.

It was then thought that the neighborhood in which the girls lived might be a factor relating to their song preferences. In another neighborhood of the same city, 50 popular and 27 less-popular girls were asked to indicate which kinds of songs they preferred. The girls in this neighborhood came from homes of a higher socioeconomic level than did the girls in the first group. Presumably, they came from a happier neighborhood than the girls in the other group. Their answers indicated that 76 percent of the popular girls and 67 percent of the less popular girls preferred "happy songs." In all, 73 percent of the girls from the happier neighborhood preferred "happy songs" as compared with 43 percent of the girls from the less happy neighborhood. Neighborhood norms evidently did bear some relation to song preferences. In the less happy neighborhood, the popular girls went along in their song preferences with the general tone of the neighborhood in which they lived. The ties to neighborhood norms were stronger than popularity in influencing which songs girls liked.

Although their popularity with boys may not ensure their happiness, adolescent and college-age girls are usually conscious of whether or not boys like them. High school girls seem to consider popularity with boys in a more purposeful and mature way than high school boys view being popular with girls. Possibly girls need this

popularity to maintain their own self-regard. College women, too, have a desire to be popular with men. In one study of female college freshmen 29.5 percent reported that their belief that they were unpopular with men was the basis for unhappiness in their lives. By the time these women were juniors, 66.4 percent reported holding this view. Unpopularity with men appears to be an important source of unhappiness among college women.

How is athletic ability related to popularity? Among adolescents, athletic ability seems to be a major factor in determining an individual's popularity. On the other hand, studiousness seems to have only a small positive relationship to popularity and in some schools may even tend to make a person unpopular. Of course, when there is such unpopularity, envy could well be the cause of it.

Some adults condemn students for this frivolous popularity of athletes. If, however, they glance through a newspaper, listen to a radio, or watch television, they will notice that adolescents reflect the attitudes of adults on this subject. Mass media give far more time and space to major-league baseball, golf, and football than to the

Preference of High School Girls for "Happy Songs" and "Blues Songs," as Related to Their Popularity with Boys

PREFERENCE	POPULAR GIRLS		LESS-POPULAR GIRLS		BOTH	
	NO.	PERCENT	NO.	PERCENT	NO.	PERCENT
Happy songs	7	23	14	74	21	43
Blues songs	23	77	5	26	28	57
Total	30	100	19	100	49	100

FRIENDSHIP, POPULARITY, AND LEADERSHIP

Average Ratings on Social Acceptability
for Eight Hypothetical Students

COMBINATION OF TRAITS	GIRLS	BOYS
Brilliant, nonstudious, athletic	31.36	25.28
Average, nonstudious, athletic	29.04	23.14
Average, studious, athletic	26.10	22.27
Brilliant, studious, athletic	23.66	23.83
Brilliant, nonstudious, nonathletic	14.27	9.24
Average, nonstudious, nonathletic	10.68	10.61
Average, studious, nonathletic	8.86	8.02
Brilliant, studious, nonathletic	1.58	2.83

scholarly, creative activities of scientists, artists, and literary persons.

Eleventh-grade students in a big-city high school were asked to express their attitudes toward eight hypothetical students with various combinations of athletic ability, brilliance (intellectual ability) and studiousness. The range of possible scores on the scale of acceptability (popularity) was from positive 46 to negative 46. There were 305 girls and 310 boys participating in the research. Their average ratings for various combinations of hypothetical students appear in the table above. The scores for girls are given in rank order, but you can see that the rank order for boys differs only slightly.

Both boys and girls consistently rated athletes higher than nonathletes in social acceptability (popularity). Students who themselves had good scholastic records placed about the same value on athletic popularity as did students with lower scholastic records. Athletes are popular regardless of whether they are considered to be of high or average intellectual ability and whether they are considered to be studious or nonstudious.

At this point you may wish to consider two questions for discussion. Do some students become athletes because they are popular, or do they become popular because they are athletes? Do some individuals become studious because they are not very popular, trying to obtain recognition through academic channels, or do they become less popular as a result of their studiousness?

WAYS TO BECOME POPULAR

Regardless of whether or not you like the data presented concerning girls' popularity with boys and the popularity of athletes, you would probably like to be somewhat more popular than you are at present. Therefore we shall turn to some suggestions on how to develop personal qualities that are likely to enhance your chances of being popular.

Some books suggest that in order to be popular a person must develop two quite distinct patterns of social behavior: one for use with members of his own sex and one for use with members of the other sex. It is true that social conventions and rules of etiquette require people to behave somewhat differently according to whether they are in male or female company, but the basic behavior that makes a person pleasing to members of one sex will make him pleasing to members of the other sex as well.

What are some basic elements of a pleasing personality? A pleasing personality is too fundamental to be developed by any simple bag of social tricks. The development of a truly pleasing personality is the work of a lifetime. It is worthwhile, however, to think over the following points:

1. *Sincerity.* We must strive for genuine friendliness rather than for the mere superficial aspects of friendliness. There is no place for insincerity in friendship. The making of acquaintances for business purposes or from any selfish standpoint lacks the sincerity involved in the process of really making friends.

2. *A basic guiding philosophy.* The person who has no basic guiding philosophy of life is not likely to attract friends. He is undependable. Whether or not we accept the details of a person's philosophy, we admire the person who has definite and essentially worthy ideals that he upholds.

The individual seeking to develop qualities that will attract friends must begin with a concern for the general good as the foundation of his personality, using honesty as the cornerstone. He must set for himself the standard of sticking with a task even though it may occasionally be unpleasant. He has a responsibility to himself and to any task he undertakes, and he does not merely try to get by.

But setting standards is not enough. A person must live up to his standards, which must become part of his life plan. Some persons find a basic guiding philosophy of life in their religion.

3. *Unselfishness.* In order to have friends, it is absolutely necessary to be of help to others. In fact, a person must sometimes go out of his way to help others. At times he must be willing to sacrifice his own comfort and wishes for the comfort and needs of others, without expecting favors in return.

4. *A tendency to look for good in people.* It is quite easy to find fault with people. In many ways others do not live up to our standards, as we ourselves often fail to do our best. It is not always easy to find admirable qualities in others, but they are almost always there. If a person is seeking friends, it is absolutely necessary for him to look for good in other people.

5. *Cheerfulness.* People judge a smiling face to be more friendly than a serious one. Life has its unpleasant as well as its pleasant sides, but the person who smiles has gone a long way in making friends.

If you can relate humorous incidents so that people will really enjoy hearing about them, do so, but do not force a story into a conversation. Let your narrative have a point and be in good taste. There is an "art of being humorous in an agreeable way." Develop a healthy sense of humor. Learn to laugh at jokes on yourself, but do not laugh at cruel or embarrassing jokes on others. Remember that being cheerful does not necessarily mean that you must tell jokes continually. The person who can comfort, gladden, encourage, and help others by actions and words is a cheerful person.

6. *Control of emotions and moods.* The person who "flies off the handle" and has his "feelings hurt" easily is not likely to attract friends.

Control, rather than repress, emotions. On a picnic the girl who screams at the sight of a worm may be considered amusing the first few times. If she keeps it up, however, she will be considered a nuisance. If she is afraid of worms, she will make more friends by quietly moving away from the offending situation than by giving free vent to her emotion. The person who goes into raptures of joy over the least bit of good news is likely to repel rather than attract friends. On the other hand, the person who shows neither pleasant nor unpleasant emotional reactions is likely to be considered dull and a poor prospect as a friend.

A *mood* is a mild emotional state that lingers on for some time after the emotion-producing situation has passed. In fact, a person may not even be aware of the emotional circumstance that is the basis of a given mood. Perhaps you failed in an examination yesterday, and ever since you have had the "blues." While you have the blues, you are invited to a party. You refuse, saying, "I just don't feel like going." By not controlling the mood you may weaken a friendship and lose an opportunity to make more friends.

Possibly the basketball team has just won a decisive victory over its traditional rival, with the result that for several days you are in a jolly mood. Gai-

ety usually attracts friends, but if others wish to be serious, your jollity may be unwelcome. Always remember that others may not be in the same mood you are in, and they may not wish to share your mood of the moment.

7. *Self-respect.* People do not like a cringing individual. You cannot expect others to respect you and be a friend unless you respect yourself. Others will not think your friendship worthwhile unless you consider yourself a worthwhile person. Make a list of your good points, of things that you can do well, of ways in which you excel, but keep this list where only you will see it. Friends will be attracted to you if you respect yourself but not if you brag about yourself.

What are some techniques for helping others to like us? A person may know quite well the basic principles of helping others to like him. And yet, unless he knows some of the techniques of developing a pleasing personality, he is not likely to be successful in winning friends. It is valuable to consider some of the techniques for helping others to like us. No doubt you will think of other points which should be added to the following list of suggestions.

1. *Help to build up the self-respect of the other person.* People tend to have a friendly feeling toward those who make them feel good about themselves. Pay deserved compliments. A girl wearing a new, becoming dress or the student who has just won a contest will appreciate a compliment from you. Furthermore, the person will tend to like you for having made it.

If you can by an action of yours give recognition to excellence in another, the action will speak louder than words. There is no subtler or more satisfactory way of paying a deserved compliment.

When you are engaged in conversation, pay attention to and take an interest in what the other person has to say. It is very disconcerting to talk to someone and find that he has not been listening to what you have been saying. Or, the other way around, perhaps someone has been telling you about an interesting school event. When he finishes, you ask a question that he has just answered. Such lack of attention to what the other person is saying is not conducive to building up his self-respect. It does not help him to like you.

Do not talk too much about yourself. You have probably heard about the conceited movie star who says, "We've been talking the whole time about me. Let's talk about you. How did you like my new picture?" If a person talks too much about himself, he may give the impression that he is bragging to bolster a self-esteem that in reality is weak. The persons "talked at" become bored, if not mildly resentful. It has been said that a bore is an individual who insists on discussing his headache when you are just dying to talk about yours.

Ask for a few favors. The asking of too many favors is sure to repel friends, but the exchange of legitimate favors is a great aid to friendship. There should be a spirit of give and take, although not a trading spirit. To ask a favor of another is to imply that he has some ability, or whatever it may be, that we do not possess; thus, we increase his

One technique for being well-liked is to listen carefully and respond sincerely when your advice is sought.

self-respect. However, you should never ask someone to do for you anything that he might consider unethical or that you would not want to do for him. He might, indeed, do the thing asked and yet lose respect for you because you asked it.

Ask for needed advice, information, and opinion. The boy who honestly says to a female fellow student, "This geometry proposition is hard for me. I would appreciate your help," is likely to get the help he needs. Chances are that the girl will find her pride bolstered and will be pleased that the favor was asked.

If you are facing a serious decision, the advice of a friend can help. He will feel proud that you want his views.

Try to remember names and faces. Although it is very easy to forget the name of someone you have met, the

FRIENDSHIP, POPULARITY, AND LEADERSHIP

individual may construe your forgetting as an indication that you did not think his name worth remembering. You may find it helpful to keep a little pocket notebook for entering names and brief descriptions of persons you meet.

2. *Be tactful.* "Tact" is an overworked word. Nevertheless, we shall use it to mean the ability to say or do what is best or most suitable under delicate or difficult circumstances.

A person who uses tact does not step on other people's toes. When one person does not agree with another, he may express his feeling in either a tactless or a tactful way. Small children who have not yet learned to be tactful—and careless adults as well—may say, "Aw, you don't know what you're talking about." Doesn't this insult the other person? A more tactful person would say, "I don't understand what you're talking about." When you say "I don't understand" rather than "you don't know," you encourage the other person to explain his views more clearly. Instead of angry disagreement, you may provoke a fruitful discussion.

The tactful person is careful not to criticize too much. He is careful not to speak out of turn. Tact often calls for leaving unsaid those words which are true but unkind and unhelpful.

3. *Develop some skill in several forms of social recreation.* The person who prefers a game of solitaire to a game of bridge is not going to have the opportunity for making friends that the person will have who plays bridge at least reasonably well. The person who plays on some amateur basketball or softball team will probably have more friends than the person who spends his time at an exercising machine in his own basement or attic. The person who plays in an orchestra or band will have more opportunities to make friends than the person who keeps his musical ability to himself.

Dancing is necessarily a social recreation. In most communities it is one of the surest ways of meeting people and giving them an opportunity to learn to like you.

Some persons use reading, plays, and music for recreation. If you wish to be more interesting to such persons, you must be somewhat familiar with recent books, plays, and music so that you can talk with them about their interests.

4. *Be familiar with and practice the common rules of etiquette.* Etiquette does not apply only to behavior at formal dinners and dances. Etiquette refers to the rules of conduct in any social situation. Its purpose is to make social contacts run smoothly and pleasantly.

A sincere concern for the convenience of others is the basic rule of etiquette. A person who feels this concern will probably have pleasing manners, even though he does not follow all the rules in books on etiquette. Nevertheless, conformity to such rules will help to make an individual more likable.

5. *Make the most of your personal appearance.* Develop your good points and minimize whatever features or qualities are less attractive. It is not necessary to be either pretty or handsome in order to appear attractive.

Cover or ignore defects. A girl who

happens to have beautiful hair but large ears can arrange her hair so that it will show to best advantage and at the same time cover her ears. If defects cannot be removed or hidden, ignore them, as your friends probably do.

Keep in good physical condition. For maximum attractiveness, maintain good health. Proper rest and diet will keep you feeling well and looking well.

Select clothing that is becoming to you. This does not mean that you must have expensive clothing or, if you are a girl, that you need to spend a lot of time in the beauty parlor. Every student, no matter what sort of income his family has, can and should keep up his appearance so that those with whom he associates will not feel apologetic on his behalf. It doesn't take money to keep fingernails clean and hair combed, to brush clothing, or to sew a rip.

Many a young man has said that a young woman he liked failed to like him because he did not have as much money for clothes as some others did. Perhaps the real trouble was that he had been careless about the little, inexpensive points of personal appearance, the simple personal chores, and had embarrassed the girl before her friends by this inconsiderate behavior.

6. *Avoid unpleasant mannerisms.* People often develop little habits of which they are unaware yet which are very noticeable and annoying to their acquaintances and friends. Some of the most common unpleasant mannerisms are meaningless grinning, twitching, pulling the ears, sniffling, fussing with a tooth, blowing the nose noisily, shrugging the shoulders meaninglessly, puffing out the cheeks, fidgeting, chewing gum without letup. Usually such habits can be eliminated if a person is aware of them and strives to break them.

7. *Develop pleasing habits of speech.* The person with a nasal, gruff, high-pitched, strident, or whispering voice may find it difficult to attract friends. Through practice an individual can do much to overcome poor voice habits, especially if he seeks the advice of someone trained in techniques of speech correction. For example, the so-called nasal voice can be improved by developing the habit of keeping the throat open and lips rounded while speaking. A speech correctionist can also help the person who stutters.

The use of profanity is likely to be embarrassing and objectionable to others, especially to those of the opposite sex. The person striving to develop a pleasing personality is careful to avoid this unpleasant habit.

The person seeking to develop pleasing habits of speech must not only watch the quality of his voice but must also be careful to use correct English. Other persons are often attracted or repelled on the basis of correctness of speech. Slurring words and dropping word endings are unappealing habits, and, of course, baby talk should be limited to babies.

The techniques we have considered are not mere tricks for winning friends. Apply them with the purpose of making yourself a more agreeable person. Soon you will be applying them as a matter of course; they will become part of your pleasing personality.

CHARACTERISTICS OF LEADERSHIP

In a group of friends, usually one person stands out as a leader. In school and college classes, in church organizations, in the community, in the nation, and even in international politics, there are a few individuals who lead the others. Yet a surprisingly small number of recognized leaders exist in any one field, whatever that field may be—art, music, science, literature, or any other area of knowledge and skill.

Occasionally, in small, unstructured groups, two leaders emerge. One leader may have a pleasing personality and be popular with the members of the group. He is able to settle arguments tactfully between members of the group or between cliques in the group. At times he may even be able to prevent the group from disbanding. The other leader may be less popular but more able to guide the group's thinking because of his superior ideas and carefully thought-out plans.

People become leaders for a variety of reasons. The individual who leads because he has the characteristics of leadership behavior is probably enjoying good mental health. But some individuals strive to achieve positions of leadership because, whether they realize it or not, they feel inferior and wish to be a "leader" in order to bolster their self-esteem. They want to acquire followers so that they will feel less inadequate. These individuals are probably not enjoying good mental health. They are not likely to have many friends or to be very popular.

What are the characteristics of a true leader? A true leader is an individual who exerts great influence upon his group. He initiates, organizes, and directs group activity. He guides the thinking of his group and plays a major role in formulating goals and in inspiring the members to work toward these goals.

In popular usage the word "leader" refers to anyone who may happen to hold high office in a club, in public life, in business, or in some other field. Sometimes, though, people who hold office do not lead. For example, some politicians do not really help to mold public opinion; they merely follow it. At the other end of the scale are many so-called leaders in education, industry, and so on, who dominate rather than lead others. Obviously, such people do not qualify as true leaders.

A true leader is responsible to those both within his group and those outside it. He must lead the members of his group toward goals which are consistent with their own welfare. But he must also see that these goals and the way in which the group works toward them do not run counter to the welfare of those outside the group. A good union leader directs the members of his union toward goals which will produce desirable benefits for them. Yet, at the same time, he thinks of the general welfare of all citizens and avoids advocating measures which would upset the economic health of the nation. Leaders in school athletics strive to produce winning teams which will bring recognition and honor to their respective schools but not at the expense of the broader objectives of education.

What functions do leaders perform?
As we have seen, the leader of a group may be designated as such by his assigned role as an officer of the group, or he may emerge as the leader in a group with no predetermined structure. Regardless of how leadership comes about, psychologists have suggested that leaders serve a great many different functions in the group. Some of these leadership functions are as follows:

1. Executive
2. Planner
3. Policymaker
4. Expert
5. External group representative
6. Controller of group relations
7. Purveyor of punishments and rewards
8. Arbitrator and mediator
9. Exemplar, or model
10. Substitute for individual responsibility
11. Ideologist
12. Father figure
13. Scapegoat

Of course, not all leaders carry out all these functions in a given group, and the relative importance of each function may vary from group to group. Such groups as large business organizations assign vice presidents and other officers to specific functions. You may wish to relate the functions just listed to the activities of certain leaders in school, business, or governmental organizations.

Is there a specific kind of personality for leadership? Research on the subject indicates that there are seven aspects of personality related to leadership, some being more strongly related than others. These personality aspects are (1) intellectual ability, (2) good personal adjustment, (3) extroversion, (4) dominance, (5) masculinity, (6) a tendency not to be conservative, and (7) sensitivity to interpersonal relationships.

However, leadership is always relative to the situation. The same individual may be a leader in one social group and a follower in another social group. Or, as group goals change, an individual may alternate between the role of leader and follower in the same group. Nevertheless, one research study reported an average correlation of .67 in leadership ratings for the same person when placed in groups that were confronted with different tasks. It would seem that those persons accustomed to being leaders in one group may show leadership tendencies in various groups.

Is leadership in high school related to leadership later in life? In one research study, the leadership qualities of 956 Air Force cadets were compared with their participation in high school extracurricular or cocurricular activities. Each cadet indicated the high school activities in which he had engaged: football, basketball, track, debating team, chorus or glee club, science club, hobby or interest club, student government, or class office. A measure of leadership was obtained by asking each man to rank-order every

A good leader encourages other members of his group to express their
ideas. He is receptive to both criticisms and suggestions.

other man in his group on the basis
of leadership potential. (Such judgments are called *peer judgments*. A
peer is a person considered to be
one's equal or a companion or associate
on the same general level of age or
ability.)

Positive, but low, correlations were
found between leadership potential and
most major sports and athletic honors;
that is, there was some tendency for
men with high school athletic records
to be considered leaders in the Air
Force school. Participation or honors
in nonathletic activities were less pre-
dictive.

The researchers then studied
whether the size of the high school
that the cadets had attended was related to their leadership ability.
Students in small high schools usually
have fewer activities available to them
than have students in large schools,
but possibly they have more opportunity to participate in the available
activities. The cadets were divided
into two groups—those with fewer
than one hundred members in their
high school graduating class and those
whose high school class had numbered
one hundred or more. In general,
participation in activities in large and
small high schools was about equally
related to cadet leadership, although
there were the following exceptions.
In small high schools, being a member
of the debating team was positively
related to cadet leadership to a greater
extent than it was in large high schools.
Being an officer or a member of the
student government was positively related to leadership for cadets from large
high schools but not for those from
small schools.

Some activities which one might assume would show a positive correlation with leadership among students from either small or large schools were found to show no relationship whatsoever. Some of these activities were president of an interest club, hobby club, language club, or science club, or being editor of the school newspaper or yearbook. Why are these activities not related to leadership? We do not know. Possibly students with relatively low leadership ability go into such activities. Then too, leadership is relative to the situation. For example, the leader in a high school science club may have achieved that position because of above-average knowledge in science, a factor which may not necessarily make him stand out as a leader in a group of men preparing for careers in aviation.

Remember also that we have been considering only one kind of adult leadership — military leadership. Adult leaders in other areas may have somewhat different characteristics, and may show a closer relationship to leadership ability in high school.

What are some personal characteristics of executives? In another study 258 businessmen were divided into two groups: (1) company officers and supervisors, (2) personnel who were not officers or supervisors. All the men were given a personality inventory. It was found that the company officers and supervisors tended to be less neurotic, less introverted, more dominant, more self-confident, and more self-sufficient than the men who did not hold such positions.

One psychologist studied the interests of 500 successful public administrators. These men held offices pertaining to such public functions as public health, welfare, taxation, city management, and hospital administration. Some of the men were in senior positions of great responsibility and high salary. Others held junior administrative positions of less responsibility and lower salary. The interests of the senior administrators tended to be similar to the interests of presidents of manufacturing concerns. They had interests of a scientific nature, and they were interested in influencing people. The junior administrators had more of the interests of social workers, production managers, general office workers, and skilled workmen. Both groups of men were carrying on necessary and important work.

Executives and other leaders are often of superior general intellectual ability — but not necessarily so. Leaders in public life have been found to range all the way from dull-normal intellectual ability to genius. Promotions are often made simply to reward men for years of service. In many cases, men are promoted to senior administrative positions even though their interests and qualifications do not necessarily fit them for any such advancement.

In general, leaders in business and public life need the ability to provide an atmosphere of approval for those working under their leadership. In order to provide this atmosphere of approval, they must give men definite directions, so that the men know what is expected of them. They must develop schemes of measurement, so that men know how well they are succeeding in their work. They must explain reasons for rules and regulations.

Workmen should be given an opportunity to participate in the solution of problems affecting them. The good leader delegates responsibility to subordinates as they become ready to assume such responsibility. In short, the good administrator leads rather than drives those working with him.

What is the difference between a democratic leader, an autocratic leader, and a laissez-faire leader? A democratic leader works with his group. Although at times he may have special guidance responsibilities, he generally participates as a member of the group. He may suggest certain policies, but he welcomes and appreciates contributions by the other members. The autocratic leader, on the other hand, directs the operation of his group with a firm hand. He formulates policies and gives detailed and frequent directions, but he is essentially outside the group and neither asks for nor welcomes suggestions from the members.

We might speak of a third kind of leader—the laissez-faire (les'ā·fâr') leader, although he is not really a moving force in his group. (*Laissez-faire* is a French term meaning "let do," in other words, "Let people do whatever they wish.") He is a leader who tends to stand by passively without exerting influence on his group, although he is willing to give information or help if asked for such assistance.

In one well-known investigation, the behavior of boys was studied in three kinds of social climates. The boys were formed into clubs, those in the various clubs being matched so that they were as nearly alike as possible. They worked under adult leaders who played the roles of democratic, autocratic, and laissez-faire leaders.

Under democratic leadership the boys showed initiative in making plans; they worked happily and vigorously, used their time to good advantage, were friendly toward one another and toward the leader, and worked well even when the leader left the room.

Under autocratic leadership there was much hostility, and certain boys became scapegoats (see page 343). The boys worked, but the work was done apathetically, that is, with little enthusiasm. Work stopped and aggression broke out whenever the leader left the room.

Under laissez-faire leadership, group interest lagged. Individuals tended to work for themselves rather than for the group.

When the boys were asked which kind of leader they liked best, they indicated that they much preferred the democratic kind of leader.

Can techniques of leadership be learned? Psychologists cannot accept the popular view that some persons are "born leaders," in the sense that they inherit qualities of leadership. Techniques of leadership are learned. This learning may begin very early in life and continue through the years without the individual giving any conscious thought to the matter. If, however, a person is not a leader but aspires to be one, he can deliberately undertake to develop qualities of leadership. He can do much to develop a strong and healthy body. He can set himself the task of developing skills that will win him the deserved respect of others.

Two psychologists asked themselves this question: "Can social leadership be improved by instruction in its technique?" To answer this question, they had students in a high school rate each other on leadership. Next they divided the students into two groups. The groups were so selected that they were equal to each other in leadership qualities as indicated by the ratings. In a series of eleven conferences held during the seven months that followed, the students in one group were given instructions in the qualities and techniques of leadership. Students in the other group were given no such training. At the end of the seven months, the students again rated one another on leadership. This time the mean rating of those students who had had training in qualities and techniques of leadership was appreciably higher than the mean rating of those who had not had this training.

One of the techniques which has proved effective in training for leadership is *role playing*. In this technique a situation is outlined, and individuals take on the roles of the people who would be involved in it. Without rehearsing or using a prepared script, the role players act as people in a real-life situation, assuming their feelings, attitudes, and characteristics. For example, one way of training supervisors for business is to have the trainees act out certain situations involving interpersonal relationships between supervisors and those under them. One

trainee assumes the part of a supervisor, and the others play the parts of workers under him. Not only does the individual playing the role of a supervisor learn how to handle the problems of those under his supervision, but those playing the roles of the non-supervisory personnel learn to understand something of the feelings and attitudes of the employees whom they will be supervising.

Teachers are in positions of leadership. Sometimes part of the training for teaching consists in having one prospective teacher act out the role of a teacher while others assume the roles of students. Such role playing is very likely to give prospective teachers a new insight into problems of student-teacher relationships and thus make them better leaders.

Does an individual's position in the group affect whether he becomes a leader? There is some evidence that an individual can become a leader by being placed in a position where he is given the opportunities to assume leadership. In one well-known experiment, groups of five students each were seated in one of the arrangements shown in the figure on page 368. Each of the arrangements was tested with five different groups. The students were seated in separate cubicles. They could communicate only with those whose cubicles connected with theirs and only by sending written notes through slots in the cubicle walls. For example, in the circle arrangement, A could communicate with both B and E. In the next arrangement to the right, a "chain," A could communi-

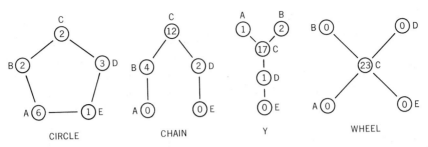

Four different seating arrangements by which groups can communicate

cate only with B, although B could communicate with both A and C. In the other two arrangements, the Y and the wheel, A could communicate only with C. What were the communication possibilities for C in each of these groupings?

The groups were assigned a task. Each student was given a card on which had been printed five out of a possible six symbols. Only one symbol appeared on all five cards. The students had to pass information to one another so that they could learn which symbol appeared on all of their cards. After fifteen trials each student was asked, "Did your group have a recognized leader? If so, who?" The students in the circle arrangement had a great deal of difficulty in answering this question and only about half of them identified any leader. Those they did name as leaders were distributed among each of the positions in the circle. On the other hand, almost all of the students in the wheel situation were able to identify a leader, and they unanimously selected the person at the center of the group. The numbers in the circles in the figure above indicate the number of times the students in that position were identified as the

leader by the members of their group.

We must be careful not to jump to conclusions on the basis of this experiment, although other experiments have tended to verify it. Yet it does seem that the individual whose position gives him the most opportunity to communicate with others is likely to be thought of as a leader regardless of his personal qualities.

Leaders are needed. There is evidence that persons can be trained for positions of leadership. Do not forget, however, that everyone is a follower in many situations. Psychologists need to study the characteristics of good followers as well as the characteristics of good leaders.

Do people think less of an individual if he is not a leader? Obviously, most individuals in most situations are followers rather than leaders. Furthermore, most individuals show at least one of the functions of leadership in one or more small groups or subgroups. Since practically everyone is a follower, and many followers qualify as partial leaders, statistically speaking, there is no justification for looking down on those who are regarded as followers rather than as leaders.

MENTAL HEALTH

The relatively few studies done on followership seem to bear out the fact that individuals are not thought any less of for being followers. At one time each Naval cadet graduating from Officer Candidate School was asked to nominate three of his classmates whom he considered to be the best-qualified men to lead a special military mission. Then each cadet was asked to think of himself as the leader of the mission and to choose the three cadets he would want to be part of his unit. Finally, each cadet was asked to name his three best friends. The relationships between the various combinations of those chosen as leaders, followers, and friends are indicated in terms of coefficients of correlation:

Leaders	0.92	Followers
Leaders	0.47	Friends
Friends	0.55	Followers

Very clearly, each cadet tended to choose the same individuals to be his leaders and his followers. There was no indication of looking down upon followers, even in this group of men specially trained to be leaders. Also, you will note that friendship was not the chief factor in choosing either leaders or followers. A man might consider another man as one of his best friends without thinking of him either as a leader or as a follower. It would also seem that the selection of leaders and followers was not a matter of mere popularity.

We can conclude from this chapter that to achieve good mental health, you should have friends, enjoy some popularity, and exercise some degree of leadership. However, these desires should take their rightful place in your program of mental health rather than become ends in themselves.

In a racing shell the crew members are followers, obeying the orders of their coxswain, but they are a decisive part of any victory.

FRIENDSHIP, POPULARITY, AND LEADERSHIP

Terms to Add to Your Vocabulary

autocratic leader
democratic leader
friendship
laissez-faire leader

mood
"mothering"
peer judgments
popularity

role playing
self-respect
surrogate
tact

Suggestions for Activities

1. Decide who are your present three best friends. Hand in an unsigned slip of paper on which you have written your own sex, the sex of each friend, and how far each lives from your home. Then find the range and the median distances of friends for the class as a whole. Are there any sex differences? Think back to your childhood at the time just before you started going to school or kindergarten. Did your three best friends at that time live closer to your home than do your current friends? You may wish to secure similar data for your last year in elementary school. At that time did your friends live farther from your home than they did before you started going to school? How do present distances compare with either of the previous periods in your life? Do you think the next five years will bring any great differences?

2. Indicate, on an unsigned piece of paper, how long you have known each of your three best friends and how long each has been one of your best friends. You may wish to secure similar data from your own experiences when you were in some specific grade in elementary school, or you may wish to secure such data from some group of children in elementary school at the present time. Statistical treatment of the data should provide interesting information on the stability of friendships. Do you think four or five years from now you will have the same friends that you have at the present?

3. In class discussion or a written report analyze a case of friendship as portrayed in some piece of literature, such as George Eliot's *Silas Marner*. What factors contribute to the friendship, and what causes friendship to dissolve?

4. Through class discussion, prepare a list of items of personal behavior that class members have found to be especially pleasing in their best friends. From this list jot down those items that apply to a very good friend of yours. Show the class-prepared list to this friend and ask him or her to check the items that he or she believes apply to you. Compare your list of items with the ones he or she has checked. Are there some items that are in both lists? Are there some items not in both lists? Both similarities and differences may enter into the formation of a friendship.

5. Discuss steps that are being taken to promote friendliness among nations and among citizens of different nations. You may be able to arrange correspondence with students in some other country.

6. From class discussion, make up a list of unpleasant mannerisms which mem-

bers of the class have noted in others, such as sniffling, frequent and ill-concealed yawning, fingernail-biting, and so on. Make a note of the items which you frankly think apply to yourself. Then ask two or three of your friends to check the unpleasant mannerisms which they have noted in you. First assure them that you are striving to develop a more pleasing personality and that you will not take offense. From your list and the lists provided by your friends, you can set about changing certain undesirable habits.

7. Make a list of characteristics of several young men who are leaders in your class social activities. Do the same for young women. Make similar lists for persons who hold an office by virtue of outstanding ability along some line. Are there outstanding differences between the characteristics of social leaders and of those who hold office because of their ability? Are there sex differences? For your own sex, which characteristics apply to you personally?

8. Have a business leader or military officer speak to the class about his experiences in leading other men.

9. Visit a playground where you can observe children engaged in free play. Do any of the children show evidences of leadership? If so, can you offer a possible explanation in terms of their home background?

10. Have a few selected students act out a spontaneous play in which one person assumes the role of leader and the others the roles of followers. Have another group of students do the same, but this second group should not have seen the play by the first group. Were there differences in qualities of leadership and followership? Were there evidences of democratic, autocratic, or laissez-faire leadership?

Suggestions for Further Reading

Bell, Wendell, Richard J. Hill, and Charles R. Wright, *Public Leadership,* Chandler. A review of information on both public leadership and citizen participation in public affairs.

Hertz, Barbara V., *Where Are Your Manners?* Science Research Associates.

Leuba, Clarence, *Man: A General Psychology,* Holt, Rinehart & Winston. Chapter 22, "Different Types of Groups and Their Functioning."

Mahoney, Harold J., and T. L. Engle, *Points for Decision,* rev. ed., Harcourt, Brace & World. Chapter 3, "Getting Along with the Crowd."

Menninger, William C., *Making and Keeping Friends,* Science Research Associates.

Munn, Norman L., *Psychology,* 5th ed., Houghton Mifflin. Pages 548–63 of Chapter 17, "Social Behavior."

Northway, Mary, *What Is Popularity?* Science Research Associates.

Ruch, Floyd L., *Psychology and Life,* 7th ed., Scott, Foresman. Pages 562–71, "Effective Leadership."

Sanford, Fillmore H. *Psychology: A Scientific Study of Man,* 2nd ed., Wadsworth. Pages 546–53, "Leadership."

Seidman, Jerome M., ed. *The Adolescent: A Book of Readings,* rev. ed., Holt, Rinehart & Winston. Pages 567–78, "The Expressed Standards of Behavior of High School Students, Teachers, and Parents."

Shacter, Helen, *Getting Along with Others,* Science Research Associates.

Stevens, Patricia, *Guide to Good Grooming,* Science Research Associates.

Wrenn, C. Gilbert, *How to Increase Your Self-Confidence,* Science Research Associates.

14

Some emotional problems of high school students

Because society often fails to recognize the physical and social maturation of adolescents and because adolescents often fail to recognize that they are not completely mature, young people may have some more intense emotional problems than do persons in earlier and later periods of life. Several problems which have been shown to be rather common during adolescence will be discussed in this chapter.

FEELINGS OF INFERIORITY

Persons of all ages believe that they are inferior to others in some ways, but such "feelings" are likely to be more common in young people than in children or older adults.

Are feelings of inferiority abnormal? A feeling that one is inferior to other individuals in certain areas is normal, and is desirable from the point of view of mental health. We should all feel inferior to some persons in some ways. If you were invited to go into the prize ring with a professional boxer, no doubt you would and should feel inferior. On the other hand, the boxer might well be and feel inferior to you in certain other areas. A person in good mental health is not disturbed by the fact that he is inferior to others in some ways.

Feelings of inferiority are characterized by a general feeling of worthlessness. Popularly feelings of inferiority are often referred to as an "inferiority complex." As the individual looks about at his associates, he feels that he compares very unfavorably with them. Actually the comparison may mean only that he or she is different from others. As you know from your study of psychology, individuals differ in many ways, but all too often adolescents fail to recognize this and feel that to be different is to be regarded unfavorably. As one becomes still more mature, he has less tendency to be bothered by the fact that he is different. In fact, he may recognize that he is making his most worthwhile contribution to society by being different from others in certain ways.

It is not uncommon for anyone to feel rather worthless at times, but for the person in good mental health, such a feeling is temporary. The adolescent is especially likely to feel temporarily worthless as he tries to make the transition between childhood and full adulthood. Basically, the young man or woman is asking, "Who am I?" or "What is my role in society?" In a relatively few years he or she will be established in adult life, will have a job, will probably be married and have a family, and will be participating in worthwhile community activities. He will feel worthwhile rather than worthless. If, however, the feelings of inferiority—of worthlessness—continue throughout life, the individual is indeed in poor mental health.

Should physical abnormalities cause feelings of inferiority? In many cases a physical defect may serve as a foundation for excessive feelings of inferiority. The individual who has crossed eyes, a harelip, a hunched back, or defective hearing or who is crippled does have a physical defect. That is a fact, but it is not a fact that an obvious physical defect leads to inferior attainments in all fields of endeavor. If possible, the defect should be corrected. If it cannot be corrected, the individual must face his situation squarely. He must recognize that he is not the only individual who has some physical defect. He must realize that others have succeeded in spite of physical handicaps. He must understand that although he happens to be inferior in one physical way, he may be outstanding in other ways.

Sometimes there is no defective physical structure but merely an unusual physical development. A boy may happen to be of very small physi-cal stature. Although he may not be able to make a varsity athletic team, he need not feel excessively inferior. One high school student, who described himself as a "runt," desired to play football, which was out of the question. Nevertheless, he went out for football practice. He listened to all the coach's instructions. He studied rule books and books on techniques of playing. He became a local authority on football. Members of the team came to him for advice on the interpretation of rules. He planned some of the plays the team used. Whenever the coach could not be present at practice, this "runt" took charge. At the end of the season, he was awarded an honorary athletic letter and was recognized as the one individual who had done most to ensure success for the team. Because he was physically small, he might have felt inferior to others, but he didn't. He chose a special field in which he could be superior.

Often high school students are unnecessarily concerned about what seems to them to be abnormal physical development. An individual who is smaller or larger than his classmates at one time may not always be so. During late elementary or high school years, most individuals take a rather sudden spurt in growth. A girl may gain her full height before some of the boys in her class catch up with or surpass her in size. A boy may be slow in growing. Neither boys nor girls should worry about differences in height.

Not every student can play on the varsity team, but every student can find some extracurricular activity in which he can excel. He may play in

SOME EMOTIONAL PROBLEMS OF HIGH SCHOOL STUDENTS

the band, he may be on the debating team, he may work on the school paper or yearbook.

How important is glamour? Sometimes girls feel that they are not attractive unless they resemble motion picture actresses or television stars. They forget that make-up artists and good photographers can work marvels and that these stars may not be so glamorous in private life.

The fact is, however, that some girls are too thin, too tall, too short, or too heavy to resemble the actresses they would like to resemble. Should this make them feel inferior in every way? No doubt they are superior to their movie-star heroines in many ways. Certainly in social adjustment and true happiness, they may become greatly superior to some highly publicized stars. The girl who does not have the particular qualities of a motion-picture star should do all that she can to make herself attractive in her own right and in conformity with her own general personality pattern. She should strive to excel in some field or fields in which stunning or exotic or borrowed looks are not a necessity.

Some people delight in referring to companions by such nicknames as "Skinny," "Longlegs," "Shorty," "Dumpy," and so on. They say, "Oh, he doesn't mind being called 'Shorty.'" Possibly the person who is of short stature does not resent being called "Shorty." On the other hand, he may dislike the nickname more than anyone realizes. Such a nickname may tend to develop feelings of inferiority. Those who apply uncomplimentary nicknames to others may be trying to make themselves feel superior by calling attention to inferiorities in others; they may be trying to cover their own feelings of inferiority. Persons who are thoughtful of others are very sparing in their use of derisive nicknames.

How does clothing affect feelings of inferiority? Clothing, as well as physical structure, has much to do with appearance. It is not strictly true that "clothes make the man." Nevertheless, clothing often does serve as a basis for excessive feelings of inferiority — or for feelings of self-confidence.

In choosing clothes, you may wish to follow these two fundamental principles: (1) Clothing should be somewhat similar to that worn by most members of the social group to which you belong; (2) there should be some element of individuality expressed in the clothing. Note that cost is not a necessary factor in either of these fundamental principles of dress. Sometimes young persons feel inferior because their clothing has not cost as much as the clothes worn by some of their companions. Such a feeling is unwarranted so long as the clothing has been chosen in accordance with the two basic principles listed above. Persons suffering from excessive feelings of inferiority tend to overdress. Those persons who do not feel inferior are glad to dress in conformity with the standards set by the social group to which they belong.

How can we prevent social prejudices from causing feelings of inferiority? Excessive feelings of inferiority may develop from social factors. In one study of college students, it was found that 32 percent of the inferiority disturbances were attributed to social causes. In Chapter 18 we shall see how prejudices develop against particular social groups. If a person happens to belong to a group against which prejudices have been developed, there is danger that he will develop excessive feelings of inferiority. Members of religious or racial groups that happen to be in the minority anywhere and members of some nationalities (especially in time of war) must be constantly on guard not to develop feelings of inferiority which may spread to all their activities. They must face the unfortunate fact that unjust prejudices exist. Also, they ought to keep in mind the fact that they can contribute and achieve much and even win great acclaim in spite of the handicaps that such prejudices impose.

Young persons may develop feelings of inferiority because they are not familiar with accepted forms of etiquette. Fortunately, the remedy in such cases is simple. High school and college libraries and public libraries contain books that tell how to act in various social situations. Time spent in studying such books, followed by practice of the principles they lay down, may be considered as time spent in developing good mental health.

Should poor school marks be taken as a proof of inferiority? Sometimes students develop a feeling that they are inferior in every way if they cannot make high marks in all school subjects. From your study of the normal frequency distribution, you know that relatively few individuals can earn the highest marks. If, although he does his best, a student finds that he is not at the top in school marks, there is no need for a galling feeling of inferiority. There are many fields of human endeavor other than schoolwork in which he can be superior.

Sometimes college freshmen develop excessive feelings of inferiority because they are no longer the "bright and shining lights" that they were in their local high schools. They may give up and leave college. Probably the trouble is not that they are actually inferior as students. Competition is keener in college than in high school because high school students with lower grades tend not to go to college. Students who fail to recognize this fact become emotionally disturbed in making the adjustment to the new demands and standards of college work. Poor mental health rather than lack of ability is responsible for their failure in college.

What are the symptoms of excessive feelings of inferiority? If we are able to recognize symptoms of excessive feelings of inferiority in ourselves, we can start to improve our outlook. If we recognize symptoms of excessive feelings of inferiority in our friends, we can do much to help them. The following are outstanding and common symptoms of excessive feelings of inferiority.

1. Seclusiveness and avoidance of social contacts
2. Envy of the social attainments and possessions of others

SOME EMOTIONAL PROBLEMS OF HIGH SCHOOL STUDENTS

3. Excessive sensitivity to criticism (may even apply general social criticism to himself)

4. The frequent use of the phrases "I never had a chance" or "Other people always get the breaks"

5. Frequent pointing out of real or imaginary faults of others

6. Resentment upon not winning in competitive games; charging unfairness on the part of opponent or officials

7. Over-responsiveness to flattery and compliments

8. Excessive self-consciousness if required to appear before a group

9. Fear of attempting any activity in which success is not certain

10. Bullying younger or smaller persons (an attempt to secure a temporary feeling of superiority)

11. Boasting about personal accomplishments (another attempt to secure a temporary feeling of superiority)

12. Talking in a loud and impressive tone of voice, to attract attention

13. Wearing "flashy" or odd clothing or extreme hair styles to attract attention

14. Awkwardness and lack of poise in social situations

15. Resentment at any expression of social authority on the part of others

16. Girl wishing she had been born a boy because girls never have a chance; boy wishing he had been born a girl because girls have all the chances

17. "Perfectionistic behavior"—doing a given bit of work over and over

One symptom of feelings of inferiority is to frequently point out to someone else his real or imaginary faults.

again, even after it has been done as well as possible; a vain striving after unattainable perfection

18. Excessive compensatory behavior, such as the student who studies excessively because he feels inferior in athletics or the athlete who trains excessively because he feels inferior in classroom work. However, compensatory behavior may be highly desirable. Much of the great literary and scientific progress of the world has been accomplished by individuals who were compensating for feelings of inferiority. If a person is happy in his work, such compensation shows a desirable adjustment to life.

THRILLS AND THRILL-SEEKING

Young persons often find life very thrilling. Older persons often wish that they could return to the thrilling days of youth. Since thrilling situations are notorious for arousing emotions, they are relevant to this chapter on emotional problems.

What makes a situation thrilling? The basic characteristic of a thrill is suspense. In a thrilling situation there is a possibility of danger or risk, but at the same time there is a chance of escape or winning—of coming out ahead. For the most part, suspense results in a rather sudden, intense, and pleasant emotional experience. We sometimes take deliberate chances in order to have the resulting pleasant emotional experience. A person may go to a race and be thrilled while watching a reckless driver because there is a chance

that the driver might be killed or injured, but there is also a chance that he might come through his reckless driving alive and uninjured. A person who knew with certainty that the driver was going to be killed would find the race horrifying, not thrilling.

What is meant by taking a chance? As used popularly, the word *chance* implies an agency of some kind which unpredictably governs the course of events. It is a kind of "fate." We have an automobile accident. We say that it was a matter of chance. If we had taken another road, or started five minutes earlier or later, the accident would not have occurred. Of course this is true, yet there is the possibility that if we had taken the other road or started earlier or later, we might have had a more serious accident. Often "chance" is used to rationalize carelessness or bad planning. Earlier we spoke of persons in poor mental health who let chance make their decisions.

"Chance" has another meaning. It is the theoretical probability of some occurrence, mathematically calculated in the light of related past experiences. It denotes a calculated risk. On the basis of carefully collected data, the actuary is able to compute just what the mathematical probability is that a given individual will live to a certain age. Life insurance rates are based on such "chance." Automobile accident insurance is based on calculated "chance." Insurance plays a very important role in our economy and social security, although it is not thrilling. Driving at excessively high speed may be thrilling for a driver or those watch-

SOME EMOTIONAL PROBLEMS OF HIGH SCHOOL STUDENTS

Surfing is an activity that provides many thrills. Part of the thrill comes from taking chances.

ing him, but to the automobile companies and the life insurance companies, he is just a cold statistic on which they have calculated. The event is not thrilling for them.

Why do people take chances? People take chances on events which they cannot control or do not try to control. Scientific experiments, including those in psychology, are very interesting, but the scientist would not ordinarily say that he is thrilled by his experiments. He takes every precaution to control as many factors as possible except the independent variable. As little as possible is left to chance. The child playing with his toy chemistry set is probably much more thrilled as he dumps the contents of one bottle into another than is the research chemist at work in his laboratory.

In many ordinary events of life, there are so many factors we do not know how to control that outcomes are often thought of as chance events. Young people are often willing to take chances in such life situations. Perhaps you feel that if you make a mistake, you have plenty of time to try again, at which time you will control factors you did not control the first time. This is often true, although there are cases in which the taking of a chance proves to be a fatal error. Perhaps you take a chance because you have not yet had enough experience to realize the possible and even probable outcomes of certain factors involved in a risk. Perhaps, as we saw in the previous section of this chapter, you take chances because you have been made to feel inferior. If you take a chance and win, you can feel superior.

Slow, steady progress is made by persons who calculate the risk as carefully as possible and plan accordingly. It must be admitted, however, that sometimes progress is furthered by those who are willing to take a chance involving quite a number of uncertain factors. Early in the morning on May 20, 1927, a young man started out to fly across the Atlantic. He had prepared for the trip, but, nevertheless, he knew there were chances of failure. Although he had studied weather conditions, sometimes storms developed unexpectedly. Other pilots at the same field were not willing to take the chance that day. This particular young pilot had a good engine, which had been carefully tested, yet sometimes even the best of engines "conk out." He was a well-trained pilot, but he had with him no copilot to take over in case of personal emergency. This young pilot might have gone down in mid-ocean, but Charles Lindbergh took a chance and won, and the civilized world was thrilled. He won, and aviation advanced.

On the morning of February 20, 1962, Colonel John Glenn took a chance on orbiting the earth. It is true that every known scientific precaution had been taken, yet something could have gone wrong. People all over the world were in suspense for several hours. Colonel Glenn won, the public was thrilled, and space exploration advanced.

The person who never experiences thrilling situations is not enjoying good mental health. Life involves taking chances. Some of the chances can be calculated or estimated in advance. Some situations involve so many variables that we speak of "luck." If we are lucky and win, we are pleasantly thrilled. A person should do what he can to control as many variables in his life as possible, but he should not worry about losing or be too depressed if he does lose. If he has controlled as many variables as possible, he can enjoy the thrills which accompany successes.

Now we shall consider a form of chance-taking, a means of securing a thrill, in which many young persons, and older ones, too, engage. We shall discuss gambling.

Why do people gamble? If asked why they gamble, most persons would probably say that they gamble in the hope of winning money or other prizes — that is, in the hope of increasing their incomes. Gambling may take the form of trying to get something expensive at a low price.

Young persons often feel the need for more income than they have so that they can expand their social activities or obtain much-desired possessions. Gambling looks to them like an easy solution to the problem. The young person may not know how to manage such income as he has and may waste much of his money. In the hope of recovering his losses, he may resort to gambling.

Gambling is partly a matter of thrill. No one gambles on an event if the outcome is absolutely certain. No one would put a nickel in a slot machine if he knew for sure that he would lose it (although the chances of doing so are always great). In case he does hit the jackpot, he is thrilled (and probably puts the money right back in the machine and loses it).

You would not buy a "gold brick" for a small sum if you were sure that it was only an ordinary brick covered with gold paint. You do not buy "bargains" if you are sure that the quality is poor, but you will be quite thrilled if you do succeed in buying at a low cost something which may have a much higher value. We all tend to feel that there is a chance we may be lucky.

In one experiment, 344 students were given four tests in different subject-matter fields. A gambling score was computed by permitting each student to ask for 2, 3, or 4 points for each question answered correctly. Twice the number asked was deducted if the question was answered incorrectly.

Boys consistently had higher gambling scores than girls. But both sexes tended to gamble more on unfamiliar than on familiar material, hoping for an improbable lucky guess.

Gambling may give a person a temporary feeling of superiority. When others watch him play, he hopes that they are admiring his "bravery." In case he wins, he enjoys the admiration and envy of his companions. The purchase of a "bargain" gives the buyer an opportunity to feel superior. He feels that he is a clever buyer.

Psychologically, gambling may contribute to a socially undesirable attitude toward money. The individual may come to look at money as something that may be obtained without effort and at the expense of the other fellow instead of as earned compensation for his own labor. (Certain giveaway television programs probably have the same undesirable psychological effect.)

How do swindlers take advantage of the desire to gamble? "There's a sucker born every minute." Those who wish to swindle others never have to worry about the scarcity of victims. At one time a psychologist asked managers of 45 Better Business Bureaus to rate various swindling appeals. The three most powerful appeals reported were these: (1) appeal to the desire for easy money (shortcuts to high profits or large savings), (2) appeal to vanity (building up the person's self-importance), (3) the confidence appeal (playing on the trustfulness or ignorance of the person). It was found that persons who had been swindled once made the

easiest victims for the next swindler.

From their experience these Better Business Bureau managers reported that swindlers tended to be well-dressed, pompous persons. They tended to use much advertising and publicity. They paid their personal bills and kept a good credit rating so as to allay suspicion. They lived in luxury (easy come — easy go). The swindlers told the truth but not the whole truth. They tended to talk rapidly so as not to give their victims a chance to ask questions or to object.

What mathematical chance does a gambler have? Pure gambling is the betting of money or something else of value upon an outcome governed purely by chance. Betting on the throw of a pair of dice may be pure gambling. We know from the mathematics of chance that certain combinations can be expected to appear a given percentage of the time in a large number of throws of the dice.

At one time a high school class was asked to shoot craps. All together 3,000 throws of dice were made. The theoretical mathematical chance and the experimental data secured by the class are shown on the following page. The rolling of the dice closely approximated mathematical chance. Had the number of throws been greater, the relationship between experimental data and pure chance would have been closer.

Much gambling involves both chance and intellectual cleverness or manual skill. Some people bet on basketball games. Elements of chance or "luck" are involved, but they are also betting

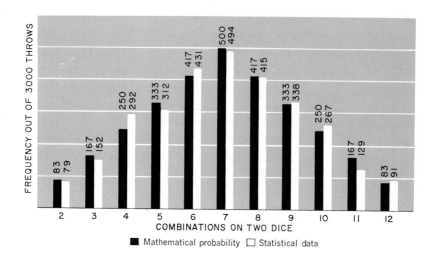

COMBINATION ON TWO DICE	THEORETICAL CHANCE	EXPERIMENTAL DATA
2	83	79
3	167	152
4	250	292
5	333	312
6	417	431
7	500	494
8	417	415
9	333	338
10	250	267
11	167	129
12	83	91

on their cleverness in observing the abilities shown by the two teams in past games. An individual may bet on his skill in playing such a game as billiards, or he may bet on the outcome of a game of cards. In the card game his chances of winning depend in part upon the chance of the deal and in part upon his cleverness in playing the cards—assuming that the cards are not "fixed" in some way. The winner is thrilled and feels superior. He may have increased his income temporarily.

Why is it impossible to beat professional gambling? A person who bets his money on pure gambling schemes as suggested in the section on the mathematics of gambling will neither lose nor win money in the long run.

Some gambling establishments—for example, the casino at Monte Carlo—are operated on a mathematical basis. In such places, the management knows exactly its mathematical advantage and how much it will earn in the long run. Records are kept so that

SOME EMOTIONAL PROBLEMS OF HIGH SCHOOL STUDENTS

if there is a deviation from the expectancy of chance, the odds set by the casino can be corrected. If a player cares to do so, he can calculate his chances of losing.

Many players try to devise a system to beat the percentage that gambling houses win. One individual even succeeded in doing so with a card game called "blackjack," or "twenty-one." By using a computer to figure out the chances of drawing specific cards, he developed a formula for the order in which most cards would appear. In fact, he published a book on the subject. However, his system relied upon the dealer not reshuffling the deck of cards from which he was dealing after each play. The gambling houses soon caught on to his system and made it unworkable by having their dealers continually reshuffle the unused deck. Gambling establishments can generally readjust their rules to insure their percentage if the percentage seems to be in any danger.

As gambling is actually practiced in many gambling houses, the player doesn't even have the mathematical chance that he has at a place such as Monte Carlo. For example, a gambling house may not use honest dice all the time. Dice can be loaded and changed in other ways so that the simple mathematics of chance will not apply.

A catalogue of a company manufacturing gambling devices contains some enlightening information. The owner of a punch-board is told before he purchases the board what he can expect in the way of profit; for example, "Takes in $160.00, pays out $70.00." Slot machines can be set to give varying percentages of profit to the owner. The description of a raffle wheel says, "It is simple in appearance, looks homemade, and can pass the most careful inspection. . . . The arrow is under control at all times, and no experience is needed to operate it." One marble game is described in the catalogue by this interesting statement: ". . . and can also be set fair."

Even in gambling that seems to be based on skill, the operators of "practical" gambling establishments make sure that they will win. Sometimes a customer is given an opportunity to demonstrate his skill at hitting various objects by throwing balls. One of the catalogues referred to above described a game as follows:

Some individuals find it difficult to resist the thrill of gambling, despite the odds against winning in professional casinos.

The bottles are placed on a board in a pyramid; the player tries to knock all the bottles off the board with three baseballs. This would appear very simple, but due to the special construction of the bottles can only be accomplished when allowed by the operator.

Another game involves tossing rings over pegs. A description of the game includes the following statement, "With this peg it is possible to load your stand with watches, guns, stag-handled knives, etc., with no danger of losing any."

Is there much thrill involved in gambling where the player is sure to lose in the long run?

DAYDREAMING

Excessive feelings of inferiority may be followed by daydreaming, although not all daydreaming is a way of compensating or an escape from reality. Some attention was given to daydreaming and whether it is desirable when we discussed thinking processes in Chapter 5 (page 118). Now we shall examine some forms which daydreaming may take.

How common is daydreaming? A psychologist questioned a group of college students about their habits of daydreaming. He found that only about 2 percent reported no recent daydreams. Approximately half the group reported that within the past month they had had repeated daydreams. Another psychologist asked college students whether or not they daydreamed frequently. Sixty-nine percent responded in the affirmative. In still another case a psychologist questioned 1,475 persons, ranging in age from seven to twenty-one and beyond. All but two or three of this large group reported daydreaming.

Often it is difficult to say whether a given bit of daydreaming is constructive or merely wishful. Perhaps it is in part constructive and in part wishful. Adolescence is a time for daydreaming, but an individual should take care not to spend too much time in daydreaming. He should see to it that daydreaming does not become an end in itself rather than an incentive to work.

When does daydreaming become undesirable? Imagination may be very constructive and helpful to a young person, but sometimes imagination takes nonconstructive forms, becoming mere wishful thinking. The wishful-thinking kind of daydream is often a reaction to feelings of frustration. Instead of leading to action, such daydreams become ends in themselves. The individual is so satisfied with daydreaming that he is a major-league baseball player that he does not bother to go out for his high school baseball team. Content with imagining that he is a great movie actor, he does not care for the work of taking part in his high school class play. He daydreams that he is very popular and has dozens and dozens of friends. His visions are so satisfying that he does not feel it necessary to develop a pleasing personality in order to win and hold real friends.

We shall give special attention to two forms which daydreaming often takes, to help enable you to evaluate your own daydreams.

What is the "conquering hero" daydream? Psychologists give the name "conquering hero" to a very common form of daydreaming. In this form the individual imagines himself performing great deeds while an appreciative audience applauds. A boy wishes to become a great musician. One day his music teacher criticizes his playing technique. Instead of going to the work of practicing in order to correct the error, he indulges in a wishful daydream.

He imagines himself practicing his music lesson. A world-famous musician happens to be in town, and while strolling down the street this great musician hears the sweet strains of our hero's music practice. Recognizing talent immediately, he rushes to the door and asks to see the budding musical genius. The great musician is so charmed by the technique, that he arranges to give free lessons.

In a short time our hero finds himself on the concert stage. An audience is held spellbound by his playing. He studies under other great masters, and becomes famous all over America and throughout the world.

Finally he decides to give his home town a "break." He returns home for a visit. The whole town is waiting at the airport to greet him. The high school band is playing as the plane rolls to a stop. He steps off the plane while photographic bulbs flash and newsreel cameras grind. He glances over the applauding crowd and notes his former music teacher, the one who had had the "nerve" to criticize his technique. He generously bestows a forced smile on this amateur musician. The "conquering hero" has come home.

His beautiful daydream is so satisfying that our hero feels it unnecessary to practice his music. As a result, at the next lesson his technique is poorer than before. Instead of practicing, he indulges in the daydream again and again. Finally he ceases taking music lessons. He drops out of the high school band. His musical career is ended, except in his daydreams, where he imagines the musician he wishes he might be — and never will be.

As another example, daydreaming may bring visions of great achievements in athletics, without accompanying participation in high school athletics. As still another, the dream may take the form of the "hero" graduating from college with all honors, although his present studies are being neglected. Or the daydreamer may see herself walking down the aisle of a great church while the organ plays a wedding march. She has "conquered" in matters of love. Such a dream may be so pleasant that the dreamer does not bother to make social contacts which might eventually lead to a happy marriage.

What is the "suffering hero" daydream? All daydream "heroes" are not conquering heroes. Sometimes they are "suffering heroes." The daydream takes the form of self-pity, from which the "sufferer" derives considerable satisfaction.

A high school girl once related the following daydream. In the elementary school that she had attended, the teacher made pupils stand on their desks as punishment for misconduct. The other children were permitted to laugh at the child being punished. (The teacher who used this form of punishment certainly did not know very much about principles of mental hygiene.)

Evidently our heroine was not a model pupil from the teacher's point of view, for frequently she had to undergo the humiliating and tiresome experience of standing on her desk. She came to think of herself as a martyr suffering under the tyranny of the teacher. In her daydreams the desk on which she was standing suddenly broke. She fell to the floor. Her leg was broken. (In some way the pain involved was of a rather pleasant nature.) The teacher cried, "Oh, you poor little thing!" Then our heroine was picked up tenderly and taken home. A physician set the leg (still without pain) and "bawled out" the teacher for making children stand on their desks. Each day for weeks the teacher brought our painlessly suffering heroine candy and flowers. The other school children sent her presents. Everyone showered her with sympathy.

Perhaps a young man has had a misunderstanding with his girl friend. Of course this is a very unpleasant experience. In his daydream he sees her crossing a street. A speeding car is bearing down on her, but she does not see it. Our hero dashes into the street and shoves her to one side just in time, but alas, too late for himself! The car strikes him. An ambulance comes. He sees the girl wringing her hands in agony as he is gently placed in the ambulance and rushed to the hospital. Hours later he is in a hospital room filled with flowers (most of them from the girl friend), but he is not long for this world. Our "suffering hero" has given his all for a girl who did not appreciate him until it was too late. The daydream is so painfully pleasant that he does not bother either to correct the misunderstanding or to find a new girl friend.

In the illustrations used, the daydreamers took the trouble to invent their own dreams. Some persons do not bother to invent dreams of their own but use ready-made daydreams. They take a story from a thrilling movie, novel, or love-story magazine. They identify themselves with the hero or heroine of the romantic tale.

Why are "suffering heroes" and "conquering heroes" not true heroes? Probably everyone has enjoyed being a "suffering hero" at some time in his life, but such daydreaming is to be discouraged. It is not constructive, it becomes an end in itself, and it sometimes leads to disastrous results. Some persons derive so much enjoyment from being "suffering heroes" in their daydreams that they go on to actual suffering, although not as heroes. Young persons have been known to inflict injury on themselves and even to commit suicide in order to arouse sympathy. When such a thing does happen, the individual does not receive the sympathy he expected and craved. Friends realize that he has made a poor adjustment to life, that he is in poor mental health. Instead of becoming a hero, he is more likely to arouse pity.

From the point of view of mental hygiene, the "conquering hero" daydream is more wholesome than the "suffering hero" daydream. However, the "conquering hero" must continually check on himself by asking, "Is this daydreaming an end in itself, or is it leading me to action that will make me the successful person I dream of being?"

DATING

In America, dating is an accepted social institution. Some young people begin dating while still in elementary school or junior high school. The practice becomes more common in high school and in the years immediately following high school. Then marriage

Although dating may involve some difficult and uncomfortable moments, it also provides many pleasant and enjoyable ones.

follows for most people. According to the love stories in many popular magazines, books of fiction, movies, and television programs, dating is practiced by all young people. According to popular fiction, there are amusing and sometimes confusing incidents, but, on the whole, everyone is having a marvelous time. There is factual evidence to the contrary, however.

In Chapter 16 we shall consider some problems of marriage and the family. For the present, attention will be concentrated on some of the disturbing emotional problems involved in dating.

How is dating related to prestige? Presumably dating is designed to provide young people with pleasant social experiences which may eventually lead to marriage. Yet prestige often plays an important part in dating. A boy may seek a date with a certain girl simply because she is considered one of the prettiest girls in school. To be seen with her will improve his social standing. A girl may want a date with a certain boy because he is an athletic hero or is the wealthiest boy in school. Her prestige will rise just because she has had a date with this desirable catch. Often young people do not seem to ask themselves, "Do I care for this person?" but rather, "Does this date help make me a social success?"

The girl who is seldom asked for a date may feel that she is not well liked. The boy who is turned down when he asks for a date may feel that his prestige in the group is thereby lowered, especially if it becomes generally known that he has been turned down.

Percentages of High School Students Answering "Yes" and "No" to Some Questions Concerning Social Poise

QUESTION	BOYS		GIRLS	
	YES	NO	YES	NO
Do you feel at ease in introducing people?	57	41	69	29
In general, is it difficult for you to carry on a conversation with the opposite sex?	39	58	37	61
Are you afraid of making a mistake at a social affair?	51	45	55	43
Are there some members of your class whose competency and fearlessness in social affairs makes you feel inferior and inadequate?	43	50	51	43

Although dating should involve more than prestige, prestige-seeking does complicate our American customs of dating.

Do you feel at ease on a date? If you do not feel at ease on a date, you are not abnormal or peculiar. In fact, there is evidence that about half of all high school boys and girls have feelings of social inadequacy and insecurity. In one study, high school students were asked to answer certain questions concerning social poise. Most questions were answered "Yes" or "No," but for each question there were some students who found the answers so difficult to give that they did not respond. Some of the questions asked and percentages of responses given by boys and girls are indicated in the table above.

In addition to the questions indicated in the table, the boys were asked, "Do you feel at ease in asking a girl to attend a social affair with you?" Forty-five percent answered in the affirmative, but 47 percent answered in the negative and 8 percent did not answer the question. Another question asked of boys was, "Does it bother you much to walk across the floor and ask a girl for the next dance?" Thirty-four percent said "Yes," 41 percent said "No," and 25 percent declined to answer.

The girls were asked, "Have you ever wanted to ask a boy to take you to a dance, but didn't do it?" Forty-two percent of the girls admitted that they had wished to ask a boy but could not get up enough courage, 50 percent answered in the negative, and 8 percent did not answer at all. Another question asked of girls was, "Does it bother you if boys don't 'cut in' on you at a dance?" The responses were: "Yes," 16 percent; "No," 71 percent; the remainder gave no answer.

If you are not at ease in some social situations, you have plenty of company. You may wish to ask the above questions of some group in your school, making certain that the responses are kept anonymous.

Why aren't school dances better attended? Most schools provide various

SOME EMOTIONAL PROBLEMS OF HIGH SCHOOL STUDENTS

Percentages of High School Boys and Girls Giving Various Reasons for Not Attending School Dances

REASONS	BOYS	GIRLS
I don't know how to dance.	74	39
I would only sit or stand around and not have a good time.	36	30
I did not have the money.	25	18
Only those who are paired off with a member of the opposite sex really have a good time.	16	26
I would be out late at night, and my parents disapprove of that.	11	21
I felt that my clothing was not good enough.	8	12
Feelings of inferiority, inadequacy, of not belonging.	6	18
I do not approve of dancing.	11	6
Parents object to my dancing.	6	10

kinds of social events, but in many schools dances are the main social affairs. In many schools the young person who cannot dance reasonably well is seriously handicapped socially. Surveys have indicated that more than 90 percent of freshmen entering college know how to dance. Again, popular fiction, motion pictures, and television programs tend to suggest that everyone goes to high school dances. The fact is that high school dances are often poorly attended, considering the ratio of students at the dances to the total student enrollment. In one survey, 694 tenth- and twelfth-grade boys and 676 tenth- and twelfth-grade girls in ten high schools gave their reasons for not attending school dances. The principal reasons given are indicated in the table above. Do you think that some of the "reasons" indicated may actually have been rationalizations? How do you account for sex differences in the percentages?

Boys had some special problems in connection with going to dances.

Thirty-six percent of the boys not attending school dances gave as their reason that they had no good way of getting the girl to and from the dances. The girls didn't wish to walk when they were all dressed up and wearing high heels, which is understandable. Twenty-five percent of the boys admitted that they just lacked the nerve to ask the girls to go with them. "I did not have a special girl that I wished to take" was given by 30 percent of the boys as their reason for not going to dances. On the other side of the ledger, it is of interest to note that 42 percent of the girls said that they didn't go to the dances because they didn't have a special boyfriend to escort them. Could anything be done to work out a mutually happy solution for these boys and girls who didn't go to dances because of lack of a special friend? Would a dating bureau operated by some club in the school be an acceptable solution, or would there be too much social prejudice against such a bureau? What could be done to assist students with other emotional problems that kept them from attending school dances?

How do social relationships become easier? Many emotional problems are solved, or at least lessened, through experience in dealing with the problems. Emotional problems involved in dating are no exception. At one time, 750 high school students were asked to indicate what experiences or methods they had found helpful in acquiring social ease. They listed a total of 828 experiences or methods, of which 25 percent implied the value of practice. As one student said, "The more dances you go to, the more at ease you feel. Your first dance is usually your worst." A boy said, "After you ask a girl to a dance several times, it's a lot easier."

Quite a number of students said they just had to work up their courage. As one boy said, "I decided one night to 'do or die.' Went up to a girl and asked her." Still more of the students said they had to steel themselves against embarrassment. One said, "Acquire the feeling of 'What's the difference if I do make a mistake?'" Another said, "My motto is 'If you do your best, you can't do any better.'"

There were other suggestions for acquiring social ease. Some said that the example of a boy or girl friend helped. Some learned social graces by watching some of their teachers or other older persons whose social skills they admired. Books on etiquette and articles on manners answered many questions that would otherwise have remained as emotional problems. The classroom offered some help, for example, classes which included instruction on and practice in making introductions and asking for dates. Clubs, such as Home Economics and Charm clubs, gave members an opportunity to have social experiences under conditions which were not emotionally charged. Of course, parents helped, although they didn't always realize their help was needed until they were asked.

Percentages of High School Seniors Discussing Certain Topics

TOPIC	OFTEN OR VERY OFTEN		SELDOM OR NEVER	
	BOYS	GIRLS	BOYS	GIRLS
Ball games, outdoor sports	71	43	5	22
Jokes	64	52	9	16
Motion pictures	44	40	11	7
Having dates	41	61	26	12
Government, politics, etc.	36	17	30	53
Parties	33	61	23	9
Teachers	32	37	24	19
Machines, engines, etc.	30	5	32	88
Inventions, airplanes, etc.	27	2	35	73
Books	21	49	36	18
Movie stars	18	37	40	20
Arts, painting, etc.	10	18	73	51

SOME EMOTIONAL PROBLEMS OF HIGH SCHOOL STUDENTS

What is there to talk about on a date?
Conversation, or the lack of it, can result in very emotional situations. The weather doesn't last very long as an interesting topic of conversation. In one study, the topics of conversation of high school seniors were recorded as indicated in the table on page 389.

The girl who is afraid that she will run out of something to talk about with the average boy could study sports, machines, inventions, and so on. The boy who doesn't want to run out of conversation with the average girl can well afford to know the current topics concerning dates and parties, books, movie stars, and so on. Of course, if a particular boy or girl is involved embarrassing lulls in the conversation can be prevented by being familiar with his or her special interests. Silence does not have to be regarded as uncomfortable, either. At times it can be relaxing and enjoyable.

Dating during high school years is a social custom which brings pleasant emotional experiences to many students, but dating also brings unpleasant and disturbing emotional experiences to many other students and probably to all students at some time.

ASSUMING THE ROLES OF MEN AND WOMEN

As we go through life we assume many roles. The word *role* refers to the kind of behavior which society expects of an individual in a particular social situation. The doctor acts more or less as other doctors do, the housewife acts as she thinks most housewives do, the student tries to behave as he thinks typical students behave. Under a variety of circumstances, we each assume roles which we believe appropriate to our particular sex.

What determines the male and female roles in a society? The roles which men and women in a society are expected to assume are determined in part by biological differences and in part by the culture. In the course of social development, men have tended to do work requiring muscular strength, and women have tended to do work related to the home and the care of children. This division of roles reflects biological differences.

Cultural influences are very important in determining the roles of each of the sexes. For example, although the woman is traditionally the homemaker, the man has traditionally assumed the more dominant role in the home. In our culture, man tends to dominate in other social situations as well; for example, in the job world men often get better positions and better pay than do equally competent women.

From early in life into adult years, there is a tendency for individuals in our society to prefer activities that are considered masculine. By the time children are in kindergarten and for the next few grades, boys show a much stronger preference for masculine than for feminine things. Furthermore, most girls show a greater preference for masculine than for feminine things. For example, in one study it was found that between 60 and 70 percent of the girls in the first four grades of school said that they would rather work with building tools than with cooking and baking utensils. When adults were asked such questions as "Have you sometimes wished you were of the opposite sex?" only $2\frac{1}{2}$ to 4 percent of the men indicated that they could recall having had this wish, but 20 to 31 percent of women indicated that they could recall having the desire to be men.

Girls and women can enter masculine roles more easily than boys and men can enter feminine roles. Girls and women may wear shirts and trousers, but boys and men cannot wear skirts or dresses. Society does not object to girls playing with trucks, guns, and other masculine toys, but little boys are not supposed to play with dolls and other toys associated with the traditional interests of girls. Without much social disapproval, women can enter what are considered masculine vocations; there are women bus drivers, barbers, and doctors. Yet men who enter what has traditionally been considered a feminine field, such as work as a registered nurse or in a beauty parlor, are subject to considerable social disapproval and may be looked down upon by other men.

In spite of what has been said about the traditional roles of men and women, there is evidence that within the past generation many changes have taken place in what is considered masculine and what is considered feminine. The roles of the two sexes are tending to converge. Some schools now offer courses in cooking and child care for boys, and courses in home repairs for girls. Husbands often help with such household duties as dishwashing and housecleaning, especially if their wives hold jobs outside the home.

Traditionally a woman's role has been in the home. Today, however, many women hold part-time or full-time jobs outside the home.

Do women ever act inferior or submissive in order to please men? In modern colleges men and women compete equally for scholastic honors and for leadership in many student activities, but on dates or other paired relationships with men, do women adopt the traditional feminine role of acting somewhat inferior and submissive? In one study, 163 college women were asked some specific questions concerning whether or not they pretended to be inferior to men. Data are indicated in the table on the following page. (For the first two questions, some girls did not answer, so percentages do not total 100.)

SOME EMOTIONAL PROBLEMS OF HIGH SCHOOL STUDENTS

Percentages Showing How College Women Answered Questions Concerning Pretended Inferiority to Men

QUESTION	FREQUENCY			
	VERY OFTEN OR OFTEN	SEVERAL TIMES	ONCE OR TWICE	NEVER
When on dates, how often have you pretended to be inferior in artistic knowledge or taste (in music, art, literature, and so forth)?	8.1	15.6	23.2	51.9
How often have you pretended to be intellectually inferior to the man?	14.3	16.9	26.3	41.9
How often have you "played dumb" on dates because you thought the man preferred you that way?	7.5	11.2	22.6	58.7
How often have you pretended to be athletically inferior when participating in some sport with a man?	6.9	8.1	29.4	55.6

Another question was "In your opinion, to what extent is it damaging to a girl's chances for dates if she is known to be outstanding in academic work?" Of these college women, 2.5 percent expressed the opinion that to be known for outstanding academic work was very much of a handicap as far as getting dates was concerned, 24.5 percent thought it was somewhat of a handicap, 37.6 percent thought it a slight handicap, and 35.4 percent considered it no handicap.

Further study of the data in this survey revealed that most college women who sometimes simulated inferiority to boys were not disturbed by the contradiction between their conceptions of themselves as the equal of men and the inferior roles which they played. The inferiority role was just part of the "line" which was appropriate for dating situations. When a woman's association with a man developed into a serious love relationship, the dating role with its "line" of inferiority was no longer called for and she could assume an equal role.

Just because one sex may tend to dominate in many situations does not necessarily mean that one sex is deriving more satisfaction from life than is the other sex. As an individual learns to play his or her expected role, he or she may derive a great deal of satisfaction and happiness from it. The individual who feels that he must fight his or her role is likely to experience a great deal of dissatisfaction and unhappiness.

Hopefully blood pressures have not risen and feelings of hostility between the sexes have not developed as a result of this discussion of male and female roles in our society. The discussion should instead lead to a better understanding of your own role and the roles of the opposite sex. Perhaps as a result of the discussion, you may wish to help promote attitudes favorable to equality of the sexes.

FAMILY CONFLICTS

Since there are dangers of conflict in any social situation, it is not surprising to find some conflicts developing within home circles. Nevertheless, most young people seem to get along fairly well with their parents, brothers, and sisters. In one study in which about 2,000 high school students were asked to express themselves concerning their parents, more than two-thirds of the boys and three-fifths of the girls offered no criticisms of their parents. Most of the comments indicated a sincere devotion to parents.

On what subjects do adolescents and their parents disagree? A number of studies have been made of the sources of conflict between high school students and their parents. Since most of the studies are in rather close agreement, only one will be mentioned in detail.

A group of 730 adolescents, 348 boys and 382 girls, was asked to indicate the ways in which they disagreed with their parents. Some of the data are indicated in the table below. Are some of these problems similar to yours? Are there other problems that you would like to add to the list? How do you account for the differences in percentages for boys and girls? Don't overlook the fact that for none of the circumstances mentioned did as many as half of the boys and girls come into conflict with their parents.

Sources of Disagreement Between Adolescent Boys and Girls and Their Parents

SOURCE OF DISAGREEMENT	PERCENT OF BOYS	PERCENT OF GIRLS
Number of times you go out on school nights	45.1	47.6
Hours you get in at night	45.4	42.7
Grades at school	40.2	31.2
Your spending money	37.4	28.8
Use of automobile	35.6	29.6
The boys or girls you choose as friends	25.0	27.0
Home duties (raking leaves, cooking, etc.)	19.0	26.4
Going to unchaperoned parties	15.8	27.5
The way you dress	14.4	24.6
Attendance at religious services	19.0	18.6
Religious observance other than attendance at religious services	15.2	13.9
Clubs and societies you belong to	5.5	10.5

SOME EMOTIONAL PROBLEMS OF HIGH SCHOOL STUDENTS

Why do adolescents and their parents disagree? It is easy for young people to say of their parents, "They just don't understand me!" It is easy for parents to say, "He (or she) doesn't realize what is good for him (or her)!" Psychologically, are there more basic reasons?

You are the most precious possession your parents have. No wonder they wish to take good care of you. You may be disgusted with some of your parents' attitudes sometimes, but suppose they weren't interested in you?

You were a small child for a long time, and your parents had to make many decisions for you: what you would eat, what time you would be put to bed, what you would wear, where you would go, and so on. They established habits of caring for you. It may be difficult for them to realize that today you have enough insight into your own problems to make many wise decisions for yourself.

Parents aren't the only ones who have difficulty in adjusting to your changing status. So do you! You know that today you are capable of doing many things that you were unable to do even a few years ago. For example, you may be able to drive a car quite well. Why can't your parents realize this? Furthermore, since you buy some gas once in a while, it does not cost them anything for you to drive the car. But what about the over-all picture of auto repairs, depreciation, and insurance? You are biologically mature enough to drive, but are you economically mature enough to pay doctor and hospital bills in case you have an accident? Can you stand the financial burden of a lawsuit in case you injure someone or do extensive property damage? (Insurance doesn't always take care of this even if you pay the insurance bill.) Even though you are quite mature in some ways, you are still probably dependent on your parents in many ways: for housing, for food, for medical care, for all or part of the cost of clothing.

Social conflicts usually involve adjustments by those on both sides of a given question. Perhaps your parents do need to make a better adjustment to the fact that you are rapidly becoming an adult. Perhaps you need to take a more balanced view of your present status. Probably you have already taken on some adult responsibilities and privileges, and you will be constantly assuming others. At the same time you are probably not ready (or eager) to assume all the responsibilities of adulthood, so that you cannot yet take advantage of all its privileges.

Do your parents sometimes feel inferior to you? From your study of psychology, you know that no one likes to be made to feel inferior. As you grow older, you realize that you are becoming more and more adequate in meeting the problems of life. It is quite a jolt to your parents to realize that you can now do some things better than they can. You make them feel inferior, although they may not like to admit it. Furthermore, having sons and daughters your age makes them realize that they no longer enjoy the classification of "young married people." They have to realize that they are becoming middle-aged, which may be a difficult adjustment for them to make. They need your help rather than your opposition.

Why do adolescents "fight" with their brothers and sisters? If you have brothers and sisters, you have probably had some "spats" with them. Perhaps you have felt guilty following such emotional upsets. You know that, basically, you loved them, but ... As with other human relations, your adjustment with your brothers and sisters will be helped if you stop to consider some of the psychological factors that may be involved.

Psychologists use the term *sibling rivalry* to refer to the inability of one child to share affection with his or her brothers and sisters. There is competition between a given child and his siblings (that is, the other children in the home) for material things, such as toys. More important, there is competition for the time, praise, and attention of the parents, as well as for the love of the parents and other relatives. Probably the child is not aware of this competition as such, but once in a while a direct conflict flares up. There is a "fight."

What is it like to be the oldest child in the family? Suppose that you are the oldest child in the family. For a very important year or more, you were the only child in the family. Your parents and other relatives thought that you were just about the most wonderful baby or small child that ever existed. You were showered with presents. Your mother devoted practically all of her time to caring for you, and your father hurried home from work to do his share of lavishing attention on you. Then, in the course of events, a new baby came into the family.

Probably you were delighted with the new arrival just as you had been delighted with any new plaything. In a very short time, however, the novelty wore off. You wanted your mother or father to do something for you, as they had in the past, but by word or action your parents said: "I'm sorry, I just can't now. I'm tending to the baby." You didn't feel as secure as you had before. In fact, you may have felt quite rejected although, actually, your parents weren't rejecting you. Relatives and friends came to see the new baby and didn't pay as much attention to you as they had on visits before there was a baby brother or sister. Soon the brother or sister began to get into your toys and perhaps broke some of them. You tried to defend your possessions by giving the brother or sister a vigorous shove—or worse. There was a howl, and you were scolded or otherwise punished. You had a rival. Although that was years ago, attitudes developed. You don't fight over toys today and you are able to take care of yourself; yet there is probably still some feeling that your younger sibling gets all the breaks.

What is it like to be the youngest child in the family? Suppose that you are the youngest child in the family. As you grew up, there was at least one child (and maybe more) in the home who was bigger and stronger than you. He or she could run faster and hit harder than you could. Everyone talked about how grown-up he or she was get-

SOME EMOTIONAL PROBLEMS OF HIGH SCHOOL STUDENTS

ting to be. Your brother or sister had such marvelous toys and could go places that you couldn't go. You may have felt inferior, and that feeling of inferiority may have become deeply rooted. Today, in an attempt to feel superior, you point out to your brother or sister how accomplished you are. Now his or her superiority is threatened, and you hear, "Oh, that's nothing. Anybody can do that." A family "spat" starts.

What is it like to have both older and younger siblings? Of course, you may have one or more older siblings and one or more younger siblings. As a child you had to compete with an older brother or sister who had certain advantages just because of greater age. You had competition from the other direction, too. Your baby brother or sister demanded much time and attention. Is it any wonder that even today there are rivalries and emotional incidents between you and your brothers and sisters?

What is it like to be the only child in the family? Although the only child does not have the problem of sibling rivalry, he also does not have the advantages of brothers and sisters. Popularly, it is said that an only child is of necessity spoiled and has an undesirable personality. As a result of their study of this question, however, most psychologists believe that being an only child is less important than is generally supposed. It is true that if a child is an only child because the parents quarrel and do not wish to have more children or have separated, the home influences may have an undesirable effect on the personality development of the child. On the other hand, some parents are biologically unable to have more than one child even though they may wish to have several. Or the parents may decide to have no more than one child for financial reasons. In these cases, there is probably no quarrel or separation to produce undesirable effects on the personality development of their child.

Parental attitudes toward a child in the home are very important to the child's personality development. That is, parents who are understanding and affectionate can bring up a child in a desirable way whether he is an only child or one of six.

What effect does the order of his birth in the family have upon a child? Psychological studies of the personalities of children in various *ordinal positions* (that is, the order in which the children were born) have failed to indicate that birth order establishes a biological effect on the kind of personality that a child develops. A child's ordinal position in a family does, however, alter the circumstances under which he is reared. For example, the first-born child is an only child for some period of time, while the second-born child is reared from birth with another sibling. Such differing circumstances do contribute to differing personality patterns. One study has indicated that the older child in a two-child family tends to be serious, shy, and oriented toward adults, while the younger child tends to be cheerful, easy-going, and less studious than his older sibling.

Other studies have consistently shown a relationship between birth order in a family and certain other variables. For example, eminent individuals are more likely to have been first-born, or the eldest, child. Also, an over-proportionate number of first-born children are likely to go to college, and an even larger percentage will go on to graduate school. Both male and female first-born have been found to be more socially conforming than later-born children; and first-born females, when fearful, desire the company of others more strongly than do later-born females. Additional studies have attempted to establish a relationship, if any, between birth order and such variables as alcoholism, schizophrenia, identification, and delinquency, but the results of different studies have been inconsistent up to the present time.

How can brothers and sisters help you in making social adjustments? Life is full of compensations. Having brothers and sisters in the home raises problems. On the other hand, there is the compensation that learning to live with your brothers and sisters gives you practice in the art of living amicably with others near your own age. Living with them may provide experiences that

The playfulness and affection of an older brother can provide experiences which help his sister to make social adjustments outside the family.

SOME EMOTIONAL PROBLEMS OF HIGH SCHOOL STUDENTS

will be of incalculable value to you when the time comes for you to learn the social adjustments involved in marriage. The other children in the family bring their friends into the home and so widen each child's circle of friends. A girl can be instrumental in getting dates for her brother, and vice versa.

Will I get along better with my brothers and sisters as I grow older? If you have occasional "fights" with your brothers and sisters, you need not be unduly concerned about these unpleasant situations, although you should strive to prevent as many disagreements as possible. Basically, there is probably a very deep love between you and your siblings. Such love often comes to the surface very clearly in times of crisis, even though it may not be apparent at other times.

Just now, you are trying to establish your place in life as an adult. Because you may feel insecure at this time, rivalry with your siblings may be keener than it was earlier. It is comforting to know that as you grow older, there will probably be less conflict with your brothers and sisters and more open affection for them. At one time a group of college students was asked, "Do you have any conflicts with a brother or sister now?" Less than a third of them said, "Yes." Don't you think far more than a third had such conflicts when they were younger? Don't you think even fewer of them will have conflicts as they become still older and establish homes of their own?

Is your consideration of some basic psychological reasons for sibling rivalry helping you in making a desirable social adjustment with your own brothers and sisters?

BREAKING FAMILY TIES

Adolescents have to face the problem of breaking at least some of their home ties. They may go away to college, they may find work in a place at some distance from their homes, they may be called to military service, they may marry and establish homes of their own. Even if they work in their home towns and continue to live at home, there will be a difference in the home relationships. The young people will be wage earners and therefore will no longer be entirely dependent upon the home for financial support. This time is a difficult one for both parents and children. It is important to consider how principles of mental hygiene can be applied to help parents and children make the necessary adjustments.

The breaking of home ties is a gradual process of separation. Both parents and their adolescent sons and daughters should recognize that this is not something which happens suddenly and is then over forever. In America, the process of attaining adult status tends to be more abrupt and difficult than in some other countries, where the authority of the parents is relinquished more gradually. In fact, in some countries the authority of the parent continues until his death. In such countries, the end of adolescence does not mean that there is a marked change in parental authority, even though the young person gets a job and marries.

Psychologists use the term *emancipation* to refer to the process of separation from one's family and the attaining of freedom from family control, especially from the control of parents. Emancipation is normally achieved in late adolescence. It involves independence in thought as well as in overt behavior. The emancipated person exhibits self-reliance.

In infancy the time comes when the baby must be weaned from the mother for its own good, although it is still very dependent upon the mother. Later the child goes to school. Contacts with teachers and other adults make him less psychologically dependent upon his parents. Although the adolescent is usually still quite dependent upon the home for care and advice, to some extent he is becoming able to provide his own food, shelter, clothing, and recreation. The adolescent's readiness for emancipation is based, at least to a large degree, on the feeling of personal security which he or she has developed through the affectionate relationships in the home.

What problems arise when home ties are broken? In the weaning that takes place in infancy, adjustments must be made by both the baby and the mother. In the emancipation that takes place in adolescence, adjustments must be made by both the young persons and their parents. Sometimes young persons are so interested in their own adjustments to more mature living that they forget the other side of the picture — that their parents are having to adjust their lives to the fact that their children have grown up.

Emancipation does not mean a lessening of the love between parents and their children. The mother who weans her baby does not do so because she is beginning to love him less than before. She is simply facing the fact that the baby is growing and changing. He cannot continue to develop as he should and still be dependent upon the mother for food. He needs a broader diet for his further development. As the mother furnishes this broader diet, the baby learns to love her more and more. When parents send their children to kindergarten or the first grade, they do so because they love the children enough to want them to grow toward self-reliance. In fact, their love for and pride in their children increases as they see them developing, just as does the children's appreciation of and love for the parents.

The parents who urge their children to go away from home to attend college or to make business connections do not do so because they are beginning to love them less than before. They are simply facing the fact that the children are growing and changing. The children cannot continue to develop as they should and still be dependent upon the parents for all their food, shelter, clothing, education, and recreation. The young people need a broader and more independent social life for their further development. They must begin to depend more upon themselves. As the parents help them to secure this broader and more mature social life, a new tie of mature friendliness comes into existence.

Unfortunately, conflicts may develop in the process of emancipation. The young person may find that the social and religious practices in his new en-

SOME EMOTIONAL PROBLEMS OF HIGH SCHOOL STUDENTS

vironment are somewhat different from those to which he has been accustomed. He wishes to enter into the life of his new environment. At the same time he wishes to stick to the customs and practices of his childhood days. College and university students often experience such conflict.

Sometimes the parents misunderstand or misinterpret the young person's changing attitudes. On the other hand, young people may fail to appreciate that the attitudes of their parents are based on a broad background of experience. Such conflicts must be analyzed and studied by both adolescents and their parents if they are to maintain good mental health. Often a frank and unemotional discussion of the problem reveals the basic cause of the conflict. The problem can be solved in this way without too much difficulty.

What happens if emancipation is too long delayed? Unfortunately, the process of emancipation does not always take place in adolescence. Sometimes people reach full adulthood and middle life without achieving independence and self-reliance.

One psychologist reports a case of two sisters who are nearly forty years of age. They are unmarried and live with their mother. The mother insists upon supervising their social contacts. When they go out for the evening, they are told at just what time they must be back. The mother no longer punishes them with a whip, but she gives them tongue-lashings if they disobey her wishes. The sisters have passed up chances of being happily married because of the mother's disapproval.

Although old enough to have adolescent children of their own, these sisters are not emancipated. They are unhappy and in poor mental health.

Individuals may not succeed in business or in their professions because they have never learned to make their own decisions. They disappoint the very parents they are striving to please. They may never marry, because they are unable to accomplish the necessary breaking of home ties. If they do marry, they may not be happy. Whenever there is the least disagreement or misunderstanding in the new home, they run back to their childhood home for consolation. Mother-in-law stories based on such situations are supposed to be funny, but in reality they are tragic. They are indicative of incomplete emancipation. Individuals who do not achieve emancipation are refusing to recognize that someday, in the course of nature, the parents will leave them. Then the adjustment will be doubly difficult.

Is homesickness a serious problem? The process of emancipation often includes a going away from the home environment, at least for some time. The young person finds himself in new surroundings among strangers. An adjustment must be made to the new circumstances, and sometimes this adjustment is difficult. While making the adjustment the individual may experience homesickness, or nostalgia. Those who are left at home, as well as the one who leaves, may experience it. When living away from home for the first time, a person must try, in his letters and visits, to help the people he has left at home, as they should try to help him.

Homesickness is sometimes considered a joke by individuals who have never been homesick or who are not homesick at the time. To the one who is homesick the experience is certainly not a joke. It is a most unpleasant experience. Psychologists recognize that homesickness is a serious matter. They try to help homesick individuals in making the necessary adjustments to the new environment. The person who is very homesick is far from enjoying good mental health.

There are no characteristic symptoms that exist in every case of homesickness, but at least some of the following symptoms are found frequently: "a lump in the throat," an empty feeling in the stomach, loss of sleep, loss of appetite, listlessness, loneliness, weeping, a feeling of hopelessness, a "sensation" of a heavy weight in the abdomen, fear that something terrible is happening at home, loss of ambition, inability to think of anything except home.

What are some means for relieving homesickness? Just as there are many and varied symptoms of homesickness, so there are many and varied forms of treatment. Basically, the homesick individual must strive to make a happy adjustment to the new environment. He must face the present rather than live in the past. He must attend social functions such as get-acquainted dances and church parties. Going to a social gathering may be difficult for the person who is homesick. He may feel that it will only make him more homesick

Young people may feel homesick when they are away from home for the first time and have to adjust to new surroundings.

to be among strangers, but he must go. Of course he must go with the idea of making new friends. Often he will find others who are homesick and wish to make new friends; they can be of mutual help to each other.

If he attends a social affair and spends the evening in a corner feeling sorry for himself, he will be more homesick than before. If his evening's recreation is to be nothing more than going to a movie, he should try to find a friend with whom to share the experience. Alone at a movie, he may find himself very homesick indeed.

Work is splendid treatment for homesickness. The young person away from home who throws himself into his business or college work with interest

401

and enthusiasm is not only laying the basis for success in his field of endeavor; he is also doing much to counteract homesickness.

Every effort should be made to keep the body in good working condition. Emotional states involve physiological processes. Homesickness is an emotional experience. Anything that will help produce normal physiological functioning will help prevent homesickness. A nostalgic person may feel that he is too homesick to eat. Yet he must eat, and the food must be substantial body-building food rather than tidbits. He should try to get plenty of sleep and plenty of exercise, for these are necessary to the proper functioning of the body. The boy or girl who is striving to overcome homesickness may well join an organization which offers facilities for athletic work. By taking physical training under such auspices, the individual will be helping to keep his body in good working condition. At the same time he will be making friends.

Do visits home help to relieve homesickness? Some people recommend visits home as treatment for homesickness. This may or may not be good advice. An occasional visit is often helpful, but when a person makes the visit, he must make it with the determination to enjoy the entire visit, including the time of return at the end of the visit. A visit home often makes a person realize that, although he hasn't been aware of it, he has made considerable adjustment to his new environment. He is glad to see the old friends back home. But his circle of friends has broadened, and he is content to return to the work and social life of the new environment.

On the other hand, instead of relieving homesickness, visits home may actually make the trouble more severe. Sometimes young people who are away from home seek to relieve their homesickness by going home every weekend. The visits may give temporary relief, just as some drugs may temporarily relieve a pain. The drug covers up the pain for a time, but it does not effect a cure of the basic disorder. Of necessity, most social activities in college and business life take place during the weekends. The young person who goes home every weekend is missing the very social opportunities he needs for the permanent curing of his homesickness. If homesick during a weekend, he may find a long-distance telephone call a reasonably satisfying substitute for a visit. The telephone call will largely satisfy his desire for a visit home. At the same time, he will be able to remain in the new environment and make friends there.

How can homesickness be prevented? The young person who is not yet faced with the problem of leaving home can prepare for the time of his departure. Thus, when the time comes, the experience will not be unpleasant. He should make occasional overnight visits away from home. The visit may be with a school friend or a relative. The place visited may be in the young person's home town or at some distance from home. The details are not important. The important thing is that everyone should have some experience in being away from the home circle. Overnight trips with an athletic team, band, or debating team afford the high school student opportunities for being away from home under pleasant circumstances. A week or two in a summer camp is not only enjoyable in itself but also helps prepare for the ultimate launching out from the home environment. Short visits away from the home and family circle should begin in childhood.

The study and practice of accepted forms of etiquette will make it easier for a person to take his place later on in new social groups. Anyone who has developed a pleasing personality before leaving home will find adjustment to social life in a new environment relatively easy. The young person who develops the habit of entering into his work with interest and enthusiasm will avoid some unpleasant nostalgic experiences later in life.

Terms to Add to Your Vocabulary

chance	gambling	role
"conquering hero" daydream	homesickness	sibling rivalry
emancipation	ordinal position	"suffering hero" daydream
feelings of inferiority	prestige	thrill

Suggestions for Activities

1. How do your problems compare with those of other young people? There are checklists or inventories which will assist you in answering this question. The following are recommended:

   Billett-Starr Youth Problems Inventory (Senior Level). Harcourt, Brace & World.

   Elias, Gabriel, *The Family Adjustment Test*. Psychometric Affiliates, Box 1625, Chicago, Ill. 60690.

   Mooney Problem Check List (Level H is for senior high school). The Psychological Corporation, 304 East 45th Street, New York, N.Y. 10017.

   Have your teacher order, as publishers do not sell directly to students.

2. Make a three-column table. In the first column, jot down circumstances under which you feel inferior or ill at ease. In the second column, indicate as frankly as you can why you feel inferior under each of these circumstances. In the third column, indicate what you can do to overcome the feeling of inferiority in each case. If there is a handicap that cannot be overcome, indicate how you can compensate by superior achievement under other circumstances.

3. How thrilling is gambling? If you have an opportunity to observe someone gambling, note his reactions. Does he seem to be thrilled if he is lucky? Does he put in more money than he takes out? Does he say anything to indicate that he is having a thrilling experience? It is not recommended that you waste your money trying to experience a thrill.

SOME EMOTIONAL PROBLEMS OF HIGH SCHOOL STUDENTS

4. Perform an experiment on the throwing of dice, as described on pages 380–81. In your *Record of Activities and Experiments* an experiment on pitching pennies is suggested. You will find such experiments very interesting, but are they "thrilling"?

5. What is your pet daydream? Is it a "conquering hero" or a "suffering hero" daydream? Is it in part based on a movie, television, or printed story? Perhaps some individuals who will not be embarrassed will tell their daydreams to the class. Each member may profit by finding that his own daydreams are not as unusual as he may have thought.

6. On the basis of material in this chapter and other material brought out in class discussion, make up a list of complaints students have concerning family conflicts. Each member of the class will indicate on an unsigned slip which statements apply to him or her ($\sqrt{}$), do not apply (X), or possibly do not apply (?). You may wish to have the lists mimeographed in order to make a survey of the entire school. Each sheet should have a place for the respondent to indicate the sex and class (freshman, soph-

omore, junior, senior). The data so obtained can serve as a basis for class discussion and as a help in individual problem solving.

7. Assign a few students to participate in a role-playing situation concerned with some emotional problem common to many high school students, for example, the problem of where a girl should go on a date and what time she should be home. There might be four actors assigned to the roles of daughter, boyfriend, father, mother. Each actor will express himself as he would if he were actually in the situation and will react to the others not as actors, but as real-life characters in the situation. For example, the girl will try to think of the other actors as my father, my mother, my boyfriend. As the drama unfolds without script or practice, are frustrations and conflicts brought into the open and frankly discussed? Are helpful suggestions made?

Some or all of the remainder of the class can make an interaction diagram for further study. In the example suggested, make four squares on a sheet of paper and label each with one of the roles. Every time one of the actors

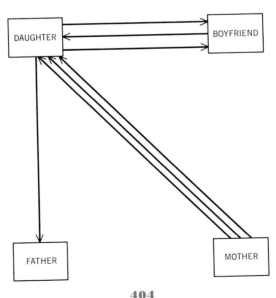

speaks to another actor, draw a line between the appropriate squares and indicate by an arrowhead the direction of the remark. For instance, in the illustration on page 404 the daughter addressed her remarks to her boyfriend twice, and he spoke to her once. She spoke to her father once, and her mother spoke to her three times. If you repeat the drama using four different actors, you will be able to make some very interesting comparisons.

8. Make a survey in order to determine how many of the students in your school, or class, fall in each of the following categories: only child, oldest child, youngest child, intermediate child. Also, you may wish to ask how many brothers and sisters each one has. What percentage of the students fall in each of the four ordinal-position categories? What is the average-sized family in your school or class? What are the psychological implications?

Suggestions for Further Reading

Coleman, James, *Personality Dynamics and Effective Behavior,* Scott, Foresman. Part III, "Resources for Effective Living," discusses various problems of emotional behavior, including constructive ways to express feelings and maintain a sense of humor. Also, you may wish to read about the question of tranquilizers and psychotherapy. The Prologue suggests how modern psychology can help people answer three basic questions: Who am I? Where am I going? Why?

Daniel, Robert S., ed., *Contemporary Readings in General Psychology,* 2nd ed., Houghton Mifflin. Pages 140–42, "Are the Sexes Really Equal?"

Hilgard, Ernest R., and Richard C. Atkinson, *Introduction to Psychology,* 4th ed., Harcourt, Brace & World. Chapter 4, "Adolescence and Adulthood."

Jenkins, Gladys G., and Joy Neuman, *How to Live with Parents,* Science Research Associates.

Leuba, Clarence, *Man: A General Psychology,* Holt, Rinehart & Winston. Pages 538–45, "Masculine and Feminine Characteristics."

Lindgren, Henry C., Donn Byrne, and Lewis F. Petrinovich, *Psychology: An Introduction to a Behavioral Science,* 2nd ed., John Wiley. Chapter 3, "Adolescence and Adulthood." This chapter is especially pertinent to problems of high school students.

McKeachie, Wilbert J., and Charlotte L. Doyle, *Psychology,* Addison-Wesley. Pages 470–77, "Adolescence."

Mahoney, Harold J., and T. L. Engle, *Points for Decision,* rev. ed., Harcourt, Brace & World. Chapter 1, "What's Your Problem?"; Chapter 4, "Relations at Home"; Chapter 9, "Facing Some Personal Problems."

Munn, Norman L., *Psychology,* 5th ed., Houghton Mifflin. Pages 236–41, "Fantasy"; pages 260–61, "The Only Child and Birth Order."

Remmers, H. H., and C. G. Hackett, *What Are Your Problems?* Science Research Associates.

Ruch, Floyd L., *Psychology and Life,* 7th ed., Scott, Foresman. Pages 101–03, "Developmental Tasks."

Seidman, Jerome M., ed., *The Adolescent: A Book of Readings,* rev. ed., Holt, Rinehart & Winston. Pages 321–32, "The Status of Adolescents in American Society: A Problem in Social Identity"; pages 524–28, "Clothing and Appearance."

Stevenson, G. S., *Tensions—And How to Master Them,* New York (Public Affairs Pamphlet). A condensation of *Master Your Tensions and Enjoy Living Again,* Prentice-Hall.

Ullmann, Frances, *Getting Along with Brothers and Sisters,* Science Research Associates.

SOME EMOTIONAL PROBLEMS OF HIGH SCHOOL STUDENTS

CHAPTER 15

Mental illness

The term "mental illness" is a broad one. Many different kinds of mental disorders of different origins are often labeled as mental illnesses. Although it is difficult to draw a sharp line, psychologists sometimes speak of two kinds of mental disorders: organic and functional. *Organic disorders* are those which can be attributed to known physiological causes, such as disease or injury to the nervous system, malfunctioning of glands, or toxic conditions in the body. *Functional disorders* are those for which there are no clearly defined physiological causes. (There is, however, increasing evidence that chemical imbalances in the body may be involved in what had previously been thought of as functional disorders.) The so-called functional disorders are generally said to account for at least 95 percent of all mental illness cases.

MENTAL ILLNESS AS A SOCIAL PROBLEM

On page 320 we discussed what we mean by good mental health. Obviously, many persons do not achieve this lifetime goal.

Am I mentally ill? In newspapers, in popular magazines, or in radio and television programs and in our religious institutions, we learn of the great frequency of mental illness. The statistics they quote may sound quite alarming. These sources of public education are striving to awaken public interest in the problem of mental health. The individuals and organizations calling our attention to the extent of mental illness are to be commended for the work they are doing. However, a word of caution is in order.

Did you ever open a popular book on medicine, or even a book from a doctor's library, and discover that you had some of the symptoms of whatever disease was described on that page? Although the chances were very remote that you had that disease, you may have become unnecessarily concerned about your symptoms. Only your physician is in a position to determine whether or not you have the symptoms of a given illness. There is danger that as you read the symptoms of mental illness in this book and elsewhere, and as you learn of statistics on mental illness, you will become unnecessarily and falsely alarmed. Don't try to diagnose yourself on the subject of mental illness! If you really believe that you are not in good mental health, go to a person trained to diagnose and treat such illness. You might well decide to consult your family physician. If you really are not in good mental health, he may diagnose and treat your difficulty, or he may suggest that you go to a psychiatrist or clinical psychologist.

What are some statistics on mental illness? It is difficult to determine the exact number of mentally ill persons in the United States, but it is estimated that at least one person in every ten, or about 20 million in all, has some form of mental disorder that requires psychiatric treatment. There are about 1,800,000 mentally ill persons in our hospitals, about 750,000 of them in mental hospitals. At least 50 percent of all general medical and surgical cases treated by private physicians and hospitals have a mental illness complication.

There would be far more patients in mental hospitals except that the facilities of such hospitals are already being used to the limit and, in some instances, even beyond the limit. New hospitals cannot be built fast enough to keep up with the need for admissions. Furthermore, many mentally ill persons are cared for, often inadequately, in prisons, infirmaries, nursing homes, their own homes, the homes of relatives, and various other institutions not called mental hospitals. Approximately 19 percent of all general hospitals, or over 1,000 such hospitals, admit psy-

chiatric patients. There are 1,500 governmental and nongovernmental outpatient clinics in the United States, many of them operating on only a parttime basis. The number of outpatient clinics is increasing, but at least 4,000 full-time clinics are needed to provide one clinic for every 50,000 Americans. There is some indication, however, of a recent decrease in the number of patients in mental hospitals, at least partially because of better techniques of treatment, such as the use of new drugs.

Mental illness occurs at all ages. Each year our hospitals admit about 2,800 children under fifteen years of age and about 14,500 adolescents and young adults between the ages of fifteen and twenty-four. During World War II, one out of every eight men examined for the draft was not admitted to military service because of personality problems, that is, because he was not in sufficiently good mental health to do military service. Even after such screening, many men who were unable to adjust to military life were admitted to the services. About half of all separations from the services were due to more or less severe maladjustment, in other words, to lack of sufficiently good mental health.

No doubt you will wish to look up statistics on mental illness in your state. You may wish to secure more detailed statistics on mental illness in the United States. Do not be disturbed if the figures you uncover do not always agree. Conditions are changing, and statistics which were correct a few years ago may not be correct today. Also, statistics may differ from one source to another, depending on just what is meant by "mental illness."

What has been done to attack the problem of mental illness? With so many persons not enjoying good mental health, the need to remedy the social and personal problems of mental illness has become increasingly evident. Here we will look briefly at what some individuals and groups have done and are continuing to do to solve these serious problems.

As we have seen, modern mental hospitals are often overcrowded. Treatment is often not as adequate as it should be. Nevertheless, there has been a great improvement. In the earlier days of our country, conditions in "insane asylums" were very bad. Pioneer work in improving conditions was done between 1840 and 1881 by a schoolteacher, Dorothea Dix. She visited jails, asylums, and poorhouses and taught a Sunday-school class in a women's prison. Shocked at the deplorable conditions she found, she determined to campaign for improvement. Through her efforts, public interest was aroused and millions of dollars were raised to build suitable hospitals. A resolution presented by Congress in 1901 described her as "among the noblest examples of humanity in all history."

Another important figure was Clifford Beers, a man who experienced mental illness himself. Upon recovery, he determined to help others. In a famous book, *A Mind That Found Itself*, he described his own mental illness and the undesirable treatment he received in three typical institutions of that day. Beers succeeded in arousing the interest and assistance of many public-spirited citizens, including some professional men.

In 1909 Clifford Beers founded the National Committee for Mental Hygiene, an organization which has done much to promote mental health in the United States and even in other countries. It has now merged with other organizations to form the National Association for Mental Health. The purpose of this association is "to bring some few central truths of mental health to the attention of every person in the country; to see that psychiatric services are available at whatever level needed.— mental hospitals, clinics, psychiatrically oriented teachers; to facilitate research on the whole problem of improving emotional health."*

Other organizations such as the American Psychological Association, the American Psychiatric Association, the American Social Science Association, and the American Psychoanalytic Association are attacking the problem of mental illness on a national level. There are state and local organizations for laymen and for professional workers that strive for the improvement of mental health.

Interest in mental hygiene and realization of the need for it have become so great that the United States Government has accepted responsibility for combating mental illness in the nation. In 1946 the National Mental Health Act was passed, the purpose of which is to reduce the amount of mental ill-

* Oren Root, Basic Aims of the National Association for Mental Health. *Mental Hygiene,* Vol. 1 (1951), pp. 1–4.

ness and to give every citizen an opportunity to enjoy the best possible mental health. The United States Public Health Service, in carrying out the provisions of the National Mental Health Act, is assisting the various states with their programs of mental hygiene. Moreover, through research, the Public Health Service is striving to find out more about the basic problems of mental illness. It is assisting in the training of professional workers in the field of mental health.

Interest in mental health is international. Although much needs to be done to improve mental health and care for the mentally ill in America, some other countries with vast populations (for example, India and China) have far fewer facilities than we have for caring for their mentally ill. A number of international organizations are working toward the improvement of mental health throughout the world. The World Federation for Mental Health is a group of nongovernment organizations concerned with problems of mental health. As stated in its Articles of Association, the purpose of this federation is "To promote among all peoples and nations the highest possible level of mental health (which term wherever used in these Articles shall be deemed to include mental health in its broadest biological, medical, educational, and social aspects)."*

Although there are many organizations attacking the problem of mental health, organizations are composed of and work through individuals. Much

* World Federation for Mental Health, *Annual Report,* London, 1948–49, p. 84.

Even in the twentieth century some mental hospitals are overcrowded, understaffed, and in need of building repairs.

as hospital and clinic buildings are needed, there is far greater need for trained individuals to work in such places. Our state and county hospitals care for about 90 percent of all hospitalized mental patients, but they have a great shortage of trained personnel. Although our voluntary short-term hospitals have an average of 218 doctors, nurses, and other workers per 100 patients, our state and county mental hospitals have only 32 such persons per 100 patients. These state and county hospitals need psychiatric aides to provide care and companionship for patients, recreational therapists to teach patients how to enjoy life through play, and occupational therapists to teach patients how to make and create something of their own and so to relieve restlessness and discouragement. There is a great need for both men and women psychiatric nurses and psychiatric social workers. Obviously, many clinical psychologists and psychiatrists are also needed.

Some of you may want to attack the problem of mental illness by serving as unpaid, volunteer, part-time workers in our hospitals and clinics; others may want to serve as salaried, full-time workers. Some state hospitals will hire high school or college students for part-time work with mental patients. The basic need in attacking the problem of mental illness is for experimentation and research. For those of you with the ability and desire to be scientists, it is a great field of opportunity. Each of such professions as psychology, sociology, medicine, and pharmacology has highly trained men and women doing research in an attempt to bring about a better understanding of mental illness. As more and more research is done and brought together, great forward strides in diagnosis and therapy should result.

NEUROTIC BEHAVIOR

Before turning to a study of those so severely ill that they must be treated in mental hospitals, we shall consider neurotic behavior. A neurotic person is one who is suffering from a mild form of mental disorder. (In recent years there has been a growing tendency to avoid speaking of neurotic behavior as a form of mental illness; nevertheless, we shall discuss such behavior in this chapter.) It has been estimated that there are about ten million neurotic persons in the United States, although that figure is very rough and depends upon just what is meant by "neurotic." Ordinarily, neurotic persons do not find it necessary to enter mental hospitals for treatment, although often they need the help of a psychiatrist or clinical psychologist.

What is meant by neurosis? The term *neurosis* (nŏŏ·rō′sis) is used to describe certain kinds of maladjusted behavior most commonly characterized by anxiety and tension. The neurotic individual is restless and uneasy; he anticipates the future with considerable fear. Anxiety and tension may be acute for many persons; that is, it may build up rather suddenly and last but a short time. Popularly, acute anxiety is referred to as "nervousness." The term "neurosis" is reserved for the case in which the anxiety and tension is chronic, that is, long-lasting.

Sometimes the term "psychoneurosis" is used instead of "neurosis," but psychologists generally prefer the shorter term.

The words "neurosis" and "nervousness" may suggest to you some damage to or malfunctioning of the nerves, but such is not the case. Neurotic behavior is generally believed to be based on faulty emotional habits and attitudes rather than on organic disturbances; it is a problem of inadequate adjustment. In other words, a neurosis is a functional disorder.

What are the symptoms of neurosis?
Some neurotic people cannot seem to sit still; they fidget. They may show spasmodic twitchings of the face or other parts of the body, known as *tics*. For example, they may grimace or blink the eyelids more frequently and rapidly than necessary. They may bite their nails, drum on the table with their fingers, tap on the floor with their feet, rub their hands together, or twist part of their clothing. At any sharp noise they are likely to jump violently; they are extremely annoyed by a continuous noise, such as that of a running motor. They go around "with a chip on their shoulders" and make cutting remarks. If another driver puts a slight dent in the fender of such a person's car, the latter becomes emotionally upset and may cry or fume.

The neurotic person worries a great deal and lives in some dread of the future. He may be easily moved to tears. He may have unreasonable fears, called *phobias* (fō′bē·əs); for example, he may be very much afraid of cats. Often he does not get a normal amount of sleep. The term *obsessive-compulsive* refers to the behavior of neurotic persons beset by morbid, fixed, haunting ideas, such as the repeated memory of a near drowning, or the recurring urge to wash their hands.

The neurotic person often shows an exaggerated anxiety about his health and delights in telling friends about his pains. He complains of being tired much of the time, even when he has done practically no work. He may complain of stomach trouble and express a dislike for many foods. An individual who is preoccupied with bodily ailments and who exaggerates every trifling symptom is known as a *hypochondriac*. During World War II a study was made to find what foods were disliked by 79 neurotic soldiers. This experimental group was compared with a control group of 254 normal soldiers. Out of a list of 20 foods, the neurotic soldiers expressed a dislike for an average of 5.14 foods. The control group expressed a dislike for an average of only 1.23 foods.

Often the neurotic person doubts his own ability and finds it difficult to make decisions. For example, there is a record of a high school boy who had much difficulty with his schoolwork. He constantly felt uncertain about whether he understood what he read. If he came across a word and was not absolutely certain of the exact meaning, he looked it up in the dictionary. Then he would look up definitions of words within that definition — and then definitions of words within those definitions. At times it took him a half-hour to read one page. Of course, careful reading is a mark of a good student, and he should look up in a dictionary words with which he is not familiar. The point is that this boy doubted his own ability and could not decide what he really knew and what he did not know.

Although neurotics have symptoms which vary widely, and not all neurotic symptoms are found in any one case, neurotic persons do have some common symptoms. The *"neurotic nucleus"* is characteristic of the individual feeling inadequate, tense, irritable, self-centered, and generally dissatisfied with his role in life, of being rigid in his thinking, of having somatic symptoms, of not realizing the inadequacy of his own nonintegrative behavior, and of being unable to withstand too much stress without becoming emotionally disturbed.

Such inadequate ways of behaving may lead to physical symptoms, such as high blood pressure. These physical symptoms may then cause the individual to worry, which could cause the physical symptoms to become more pronounced, thereby causing more worry, and so on; this situation is sometimes called a "vicious circle." If the symptoms release the individual from some unpleasant task, such as housework, a job, or schoolwork, they may promote the development of a neurotic illness still further.

What is a "nervous breakdown"? "Nervous breakdown" is a popular, not a scientific term. Persons who have the erroneous impression that mental illness is a disgrace may say that a friend or a relative has had a nervous breakdown instead of saying that he has a severe mental disorder. Sometimes the layman uses the term to refer to any condition of excessive anxiety and tenseness, a condition psychologists call a neurosis.

The term "nervous breakdown" is used by some students in another way. Each year about Thanksgiving time, some students drop their college work and go home. They tell their friends and relatives that they have studied so hard that they have had a nervous breakdown. These nervous breakdowns usually occur suddenly, just after the listing of those students who have done such poor work that they are to be dismissed from college. Hard study never caused a nervous breakdown, but too many social activities with resulting loss of sleep, improper food and irregular habits of eating, lack of wholesome exercise and recreation, and too much worrying may so reduce a person's health that he is unable to stand the work of studying.

What are the causes of neuroses? Although neuroses have been described as functional disorders, physiological factors may contribute to the development of a neurosis. This statement does not mean that the nerves are weak or destroyed. The human body is a very complicated organism, and all its parts interact. Sometimes one or more of the glands do not function properly, which may result in the development of neurotic patterns. The thyroid gland especially seems to be related to neurotic behavior.

If a person has some chronic physical disorder, such as arthritis, appendicitis, gallstones, or an abscessed tooth, he may show many of the symptoms that have been described. Have you noticed how easily you become irritated when you have a cinder in your eye? Anything that disturbs the smooth and orderly functioning of the body tends to produce anxiety and tension. A physician should make a careful check of the neurotic person and do what he can to correct any physical defects he may find.

Many times no physiological disturbance can be found in a neurotic person. His trouble probably has its basis in undesirable habits of thought rather than in physical defects. He worries

A neurotic child can be helped by play therapy, in which he uses the toys to act out his problems and release his pent-up emotions.

about things that cannot be helped. He is overconcerned with unimportant details. He tries to realize his ambitions in too short a time. He may even worry about the possibility of developing a severe mental disorder. Actually, neurotics seldom grow so much worse that they become severely ill.

How can you help a neurotic person? The neurotic, because of his anxieties, his tensions, his indecisiveness, may become very irritable and difficult to get along with. As students of psychology, we have some appreciation of his difficulty. We must try to help him rather than become angry with him.

We can help a neurotic individual by mixing sympathy with understanding. The neurotic needs help in over-coming his undesirable habits of thought. We must try not to irritate him. At the same time we should not shield him from the hard facts of life.

Prevention is always better than cure. One of the greatest obligations of parents is to help their children to develop desirable habits of thought and emotional attitudes.

What is conversion reaction? Although seldom observed in present-day clinics, an especially interesting form of neurotic behavior is *conversion reaction.* It is so called because the individual's psychological disturbances are "converted" into bodily disturbances. Formerly the condition was spoken of as hysteria or conversion hysteria. It was thought that only women, and especially unmarried women, displayed this form of unusual behavior.

Now it is known that men as well as women may show conversion reaction. In one large-scale war some soldiers became "paralyzed" in their right hands. Of course, being paralyzed, they could not shoot a gun. Hence, they had to leave the battlefront. When they were out of danger, the "paralysis" rapidly disappeared. Had these soldiers pretended to be paralyzed? In most cases, probably not. They were faced with a tremendous conflict: they wished to be brave soldiers, but at the same time they did not wish to die in battle. A soldier who is paralyzed cannot go into battle, nor can he be considered a coward. They were paralyzed because they thought they were paralyzed, rather than because there was any physical disturbance.

Did you ever know a child who had such a bad headache that he could not go to school? He did not wish to be considered a truant. At the same time he did not wish to take a test for which he was unprepared. Sick children are not expected to go to school, and they are not playing truant if they have a bad headache and stay home. Although unaware of this line of reasoning, the child solved his conflict by being sick. After it was too late to go to school, did the headache disappear rather suddenly? It was no longer needed; it had served its purpose.

Conversion reaction may take almost any form: jerking of various parts of the body, blindness, pains in various places, loss of sensitivity in various parts of the body, loss of speech, and so on.

Conversion reaction is probably learned behavior. Perhaps at some time an individual was faced with an unpleasant task and happened to develop a stomach ache, thus evading the task. Having a stomach ache was rewarded by getting out of something unpleasant. This may have happened several times. Soon the individual developed a functional stomach ache whenever he was faced with an unpleasant task, although he was not aware that the learning process had taken place.

As was said at the beginning of this discussion, conversion reaction is not observed so commonly today as earlier in the century. Perhaps our schools and other educational agencies have so increased popular knowledge about organic ailments that today most individuals are not likely to confuse functional and organic disorders. We do know that today conversion reactions are most commonly found among children and among adults of limited intellectual ability and education.

What are dissociative reactions? A *dissociative reaction* is one in which the individual views parts of his activities as separate from his own personality. It represents an extreme form of repression. Only three dissociative reactions will be discussed, although there are others, such as stupors and dream states.

One dissociative reaction is *amnesia* (am·nē′zhə, -zhē·ə), or loss of memory. In general, such memory lapses occur in the area of the personal aspects of an individual's life. An individual may forget that he is married, has children, owns a home, and has a job, but he usually does not forget how to use a knife and fork, make change for a dollar, or correctly identify colors. In brain-damage cases, amnesia may represent actual permanent loss of memory.

A second dissociative reaction, *fugue* (fyōōg), is found when the individual not only has amnesia but also engages in actual flight away from his usual geographical location. This condition applies to the individual who suddenly "wakes up" in a strange place, not knowing who he is or how he came to be there. Usually the person does not remember what has happened during his fugue, or flight away from home.

The third dissociative reaction, *multiple personality,* involves the development of two or more usually independent and separate personalities within the same person. It occurs rarely; the most famous recent case is the one on which the movie *Three Faces of Eve* was based. The multiple-personality reaction attempts to satisfy opposite desires by developing two separate personalities which possibly enable the person to avoid the guilt and confusion that would be present if only one personality existed. At some time we all have an impulse to act contrary to our usual behavior, but the neurotic develops inappropriate ways of handling such impulses.

What are psychosomatic disorders? In some cases individuals develop organic ailments attributed to emotional and other psychological causes. Such ailments often include actual damage to body tissue. These disorders are described as *psychosomatic.* Emotional factors, such as worry and anxiety, are known to be related to such ailments as high blood pressure, migraine headaches, ulcers, some skin diseases, asthma, and obesity (excessive overweight). Any treatment which helps to relieve emotional tensions also helps to relieve the organic damage, and, conversely, treatment which improves organic damage also improves emotional stress.

There is evidence from the laboratory as well as from clinical cases that emotional stress and peptic ulcers are related. In one experiment, rats were kept in a cage for thirty days under stressful conditions. Food and water were available, but the floor around the food and water was kept constantly charged with electricity, except every forty-eighth hour, when the current was turned off. A rat could satisfy its hunger and thirst only by enduring shock, except for the one hour in forty-eight. The rat was faced with the conflict between desire for food and water and the desire to escape shock. Six of the nine rats subjected to this experimental procedure developed peptic ulcers. Of course, there was a control group of rats. Food and water were available to these rats for only one hour in forty-eight, but they were not subjected to shock at any time, that is, they faced no conflict. They developed no ulcers.

In another experiment, monkeys were used as subjects. One monkey was designated as an "executive" monkey—he was responsible for what happened to another monkey. Both monkeys were placed in an apparatus where they could be given electric shocks every twenty seconds. How-

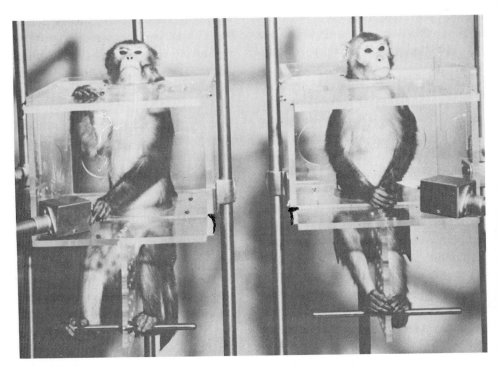

In this experiment only the "executive" monkey, on the left, has the authority to press a lever and prevent a shock to both animals.

ever, both monkeys could avoid the shock if the "executive" monkey pressed a lever when a red warning light flashed. After twenty-three days of the experiment, the "executive" monkey died, although he seemed to have been in good health at the beginning of the experiment. A post-mortem examination revealed that he had a large ulcer. The other monkey remained in good health. In a second experiment, the "executive" monkey did not die, but he did develop ulcers while his nonexecutive partner did not.

It has been estimated that approximately half of all patients under a physician's care have illnesses precipitated by emotional stress, that is, psychosomatic illnesses.

PSYCHOSIS

Having examined very briefly mild mental disorders known as neuroses, we shall now move on to more severe mental disorders.

What is a psychosis? Psychologists use the word *psychosis* (sī·kō′sis) for any severe mental disorder. A person suffering from psychosis is a *psychotic* patient. A psychosis may be either functional or organic, although the incidence of functional psychosis far outnumbers that of organic psychosis.

Sometimes psychotic persons are referred to popularly as "lunatics." If you have studied Latin, you will recognize that this word is derived from the

Latin word *luna,* meaning moon. Psychotic persons were formerly supposed to act in an unusually strange manner at the time of full moon. However, the words "lunatic," "crazy," and "maniac" are not used in modern psychological literature.

In legal circles the word "insanity" is used to refer to "any form of mental disorder which renders the individual incompetent to act in accordance with the legal and conventional standards of his social environment." A person is legally insane if he has been so declared by the courts. "Insanity" and "insane," therefore, are legal terms, not psychological ones.

What are some common misconceptions about psychosis? A psychotic person is often considered an object of amusement by the uninformed. The uninformed may also consider him sinful. Many years ago, psychotic persons were spoken of as being "possessed with evil spirits." Some primitive people practice trepanning (boring a hole in the skull) in order to permit the "evil spirits" to escape from the heads of these citizens. They believe that this process brings about a cure.

Probably because of the popular association of psychosis with evil spirits and sin, many persons still consider it a disgrace if anyone in the family is or ever has been psychotic.

At one time a psychologist overheard two women talking about another woman in the community who had just died. He was surprised to hear one of the women say that it was very fortunate that their neighbor had died. Then in a whisper (a true gossip's "whisper," which is loud enough to be heard through the wooden partition between a barbershop and a beauty parlor) she said, "Oh, it would have been such a disgrace to her family if she had lived. It wasn't generally known but I was told in strict confidence—I just must tell you—that she was off her head! The members of the family were afraid that they would have to put her in an insane asylum if she lived. It is so fortunate for the family that they have been mercifully spared that awful disgrace."

Is it a disgrace if one of our friends develops cancer, tuberculosis, or any other disease and has to be sent to a hospital for treatment? Quite the contrary. We are sorry for him and do everything we can to cheer him and help his family in their time of difficulty. If we see someone suffering from blood poisoning or heart trouble, do we consider the whole matter a big joke? From the psychological point of view, the person suffering from the form of abnormal personality development called psychosis is just as much in need of skillful, painstaking care as the person who is suffering from cancer.

Another common misconception about psychotic persons is that they are dangerous. As a matter of fact, the great majority of psychotic individuals are not dangerous. One may walk through most mental hospital wards in perfect safety.

One further misconception about mental illness is that it cannot be cured. If their illness is caught in time, however, between 70 and 80 percent of all mental patients can be released and can make a satisfactory adjustment to life. In some disorders, the recovery rate is higher than 90 percent.

On what basis is a person judged psychotic? There is no simple criterion that can be used to determine whether or not a given individual has a psychosis. Of course, the technical problems of diagnosis must be left to the clinical psychologist or psychiatrist. We may note, however, that it is often necessary to study an individual in terms of his social environment.

An individual who is not considered to have a psychosis in one environment might be considered to have one in another environment. One actual case is that of a woman who has been a patient in a mental hospital for a number of years. She will evidently have to spend the rest of her life in that hospital. Her girlhood home had been in a simple mountain community, where everyone in the community knew everyone else. It was essentially like a large family group. If the behavior of someone in the community was unusual, he might be considered a bit odd. Nevertheless, he was accepted as a normal member of the community.

One summer a man from a large city spent his vacation near this simple community. He met, fell in love with, and married a girl of the community. The neighbors said that she and her family were "a bit odd" but "good, honest, hard-working people." The girl was physically attractive, and the man thought of this more than of her "oddness." He took his bride back to the city with him, and they established their new home. All was well for a short time, but soon the neighbors began talking about the odd behavior of the bride. Since they did not know her as well as her neighbors back in the mountains had known her, they could not understand her somewhat unusual behavior. Not understanding her, they began to be afraid of her. Before long her behavior was considered so unusual that she was declared legally insane and placed in a mental hospital.

A social worker visited her mountain home. He reported that this "insane" woman was no more odd than her brothers, sisters, and parents who were living a "sane" life in the simple mountain environment. If she could have returned to her girlhood home, she probably would have been considered a normal member of the community. Unfortunately, this return was impossible. The city to which she moved after her marriage was in a different state from that of her girlhood home. She had been declared legally insane in the state to which she moved. The law did not permit that state to send an insane patient over the state line.

Ordinarily, if an individual talks about how much he hates certain other persons and how he would like to kill them, he is considered psychotic. His behavior is abnormal, and he is placed in a mental hospital for treatment. But suppose that war is declared. The great majority of persons begin talking about how much they hate the people who live in the enemy country. They are anxious to kill those people. If they are unusually successful in doing so, they are known as heroes and are decorated with medals. Are they psychotic? We do not speak of them as being psychotic, for they are doing the "normal" thing. That is, they are doing what is socially accepted at the time. If, after the war, some of these persons continue to hate and kill, we place them either in mental hospitals or in prisons. The behavior that was considered normal during the war is now abnormal.

In summary, diagnosis of a mental disorder is based on medical, psychological, and sociological factors. Not only are medical and psychological factors important, but also the family and community setting where the disorder may have originated. In recent years attention has been given to the possibilities of diagnosis by computers. A complex process still in the beginning stages, such diagnosis basically consists of collecting an enormous amount of data on symptoms of disorders and electronically feeding this information into a computer, where it is stored. Data are then collected on a given patient, including his symptoms, possible history of any previous disorder, and laboratory tests. This information is fed into the computer, which compares the symptoms of the patient with the extensive data already in its storage unit and comes out with a report on the disorder. Such procedures are being used with some of the major organic diseases, but how valuable these procedures will be in the diagnosis of psychotic disorders remains to be seen.

FUNCTIONAL PSYCHOSES

It has already been pointed out that there are many more cases of functional psychoses than of organic psy-choses. Although in a functional psychosis organic factors are usually, if not always, involved, the basic difficulty seems to be an unsatisfactory adjustment to the environment. In this section we shall examine these severe mental disorders, which include manic-depressive behavior, schizophrenia, and paranoid reactions.

Does the turmoil of modern life bring on functional psychosis? Inheritance has often been suggested as the cause of severe mental disorders, but in most cases there is no conclusive evidence to support the suggestion. Some authorities believe that the pace of our modern life is responsible for a tremendous amount of psychosis. They believe that our constant rushing to catch buses, trains, and airplanes, our high-speed automobile driving, our honking horns, our blaring television sets, and our shrieking sirens all tend to produce functional psychosis. We are occasionally advised to return to a primitive state, where everything is supposed to be peaceful and quiet.

There is evidence, however, of psychosis among primitive peoples. In fact, primitive peoples have many causes for worry and dread which we do not have. Since they know nothing of modern medicine, they are constantly in dread of sudden sickness and death. There is ever present the fear of offending evil spirits or of being a victim of black magic. Conditions of modern life cannot be held as the cause of all functional psychosis, although, we might possibly reduce the number of persons who become psychotic by lessening some of the strain of modern life while at the same time retaining its benefits.

What are some other suggested causes? Popularly, it is believed that disappointment in love, a death in the family, a great financial loss, or family discord will cause functional psychosis. At some time in their lives, most persons go through such periods of emotional stress without having to be committed to mental hospitals. An emotional situation might help to bring on psychosis in the case of a poorly adjusted person, but the emotional situation does not, in itself, cause the functional psychosis.

What do psychologists think are the causes of functional psychosis? Psychologists find that roots of functional psychosis often go back to childhood. The child (or adult) who learns to pout and have temper tantrums may be more likely to become a manic-depressive patient than the individual who learns to face life more calmly. The child who never has an opportunity to play with other children, or who is never permitted to make decisions for himself, or who is always protected from the hard realities of life is in danger of developing an abnormal personality pattern. He may become so abnormal as to be classed as schizophrenic. The case of the individual who develops the habit of sidestepping the conflicts and problems of life by drifting into a world of daydreaming may someday be diagnosed as having paranoid reactions (see pages 423–24).

Behavior sometimes called "insane" is behavior that does not fit the way of life of a particular area. That is, to some extent mental illness is relative to the social environment. The United States is becoming an urbanized nation. Nowadays we have less opportunity to know our neighbors than did the residents of small towns, villages, and farms. Not knowing our neighbors, we do not understand their peculiarities. Hence, any unusual behavior is more likely to be judged as indicative of mental illness than was the case in the early days of our country.

Since so many of us live crowded together in our modern towns and cities, unusual behavior on the part of an individual is likely to result in destruction of property or in personal injury. Some individuals who injure others or destroy property may be judged legally insane.

Furthermore, social offenders who would formerly have been sent to prisons are today often committed to mental hospitals for treatment. This change in legal point of view accounts in part for the seeming increase in the amount of legal insanity.

Now that we are coming to consider psychosis an illness and not a disgrace, many persons are admitted to mental hospitals at their own request or at the request of relatives. Formerly, most of these persons would have been cared for in their own homes. Thus, they would not have been included in statistics on psychosis.

It is possible that the incidence of psychosis is on the increase. We must be careful, however, not to jump to this conclusion merely because of certain statistics. Many of the statistics prove only that more cases of psychosis are now being recognized and given treatment. Formerly these cases might have been ignored or hushed up.

What are the characteristics of manic-depressive behavior? The term *manic-depressive* is applied to a form of functional psychosis which is characterized by periods of excitement and periods of depression. "Manic" refers to the excited and excessively active periods. "Depressive" refers to the periods of unpleasant thoughts and inactivity.

At one time the patient will show manic behavior. For example, he may sing, shout, or move about rapidly. He may talk almost continuously. Sometimes he becomes so excited and active that he may destroy furniture or injure his fellow patients unless care is taken to prevent such destruction and injury. This phase of behavior will pass, and his behavior may be quite normal for a while. Then he may become depressed. During this phase of his behavior he becomes quite sad and dejected. He feels that he is just about the most miserable person on earth. He may refuse food because he feels that he is too unworthy to live. He may even attempt suicide.

In time he will become quite normal again. Later he may have another manic phase and still later another depressive phase. These periods may continue to alternate, although not necessarily at regular intervals nor following the same pattern. Actually, only 15 to 25 percent of manic-depressives show definite cycles of manic and depressive behavior. Most so-called manic-depressives are either manic or depressive.

Persons who often show these extreme forms of excitement or depression, or who alternate between the two, are unusual, that is, abnormal. Do persons who are not patients in mental hospitals ever show similar behavior? We all have times when we feel full of pep and enthusiasm and other times when we have the blues. Some persons seem to have more pep than others, some seem to be more subject to the blues, and some alternate between these moods. Of course, having occasional spells of the blues or of excitement does not mean that a person is psychotic. There is, however, reason to believe that both the cycles of the manic-depressive patient and the "pep-blues" cycles of all of us are related to physiological cycles.

This drawing of a swan was done by a manic-depressive patient when he was in a period of elation.

Manic-depressive persons constitute about 2 percent of first admissions into mental hospitals, which seems to indicate a decrease in such patients as compared with first admissions in earlier years. The decrease may exist, however, because more manic-depressive patients may be going to private clinics or hospitals. Their chances of being discharged from the hospital and returning to normal home and community life are quite good. With modern treatment the recovery rate of manic-depressives is higher than 90 percent, although three out of four patients will have recurring attacks.

What are the characteristics of schizophrenia? The term *schizophrenia* (skit′sō·frē′nē·ə) literally means "split mind." The layman often speaks of "split personality" in referring to the form of mental illness known to psychologists and psychiatrists as schizophrenia. Formerly this form of illness was referred to as "dementia praecox" (di·men′shə prē′koks), a term literally meaning "mental deterioration in youth." This term, now obsolete, was inaccurate, because most cases of schizophrenia develop during adulthood rather than during childhood or adolescence.

Approximately half of all patients in hospitals for the permanent care of the mentally ill have schizophrenia, which is characterized by seclusiveness and withdrawal from the realities of life. These patients often seem to live in a dream world, ignoring life as it goes on around them. Sometimes they sit in a curled-up position all day. Apparently they are unaware of the presence of the other patients or of nurses. If placed in a certain position, some of these patients may stay in that position for a considerable period of time. Sometimes schizophrenic patients exhibit behavior which can be described by the word "silly," although that, of course, is not a technical term. They will say things wholly inconsistent with the conversation going on around them. They show peculiar little mannerisms, such as grimacing. Still other patients show their withdrawal from the realities of life by building up delusions. They may think that they are great persons. Sometimes they believe that they are being persecuted.

Another characteristic of many schizophrenic patients is that they are disoriented; that is, they are unable to relate themselves to their surroundings or to time. Upon questioning they may not be able to tell where they are or what day of the week or month it is or even what year it is. They may fail to eat their meals. They may not be able to give their own names. Obviously, persons who are so disoriented must be cared for in hospitals.

We do not know whether or not schizophrenia is inheritable. Statistics do indicate that schizophrenia tends to "run in families," but this is not sufficient evidence for saying that it is inheritable. The child living in a home where either of the parents is developing a schizophrenic psychosis is living in an environment likely to result in his own withdrawal from reality and his own disorientation. A higher frequency of abnormal electroencephalogram (EEG) patterns have been found in adult schizophrenia. Remember, though, that this is a correlated, not a causative, relationship.

Although schizophrenia is classified as a functional disorder, there is increasing evidence that there is, at least in some cases, a physiological basis for schizophrenia. In one study a substance called *taraxein* was found in the blood of schizophrenic patients. This substance was injected into non-psychotic volunteers, who developed temporary symptoms similar to schizophrenia. At present, however, it is not known which occurs first, taraxein or schizophrenia. Even if taraxein were found in every schizophrenic individual, yielding a perfect correlation between the two factors, causation could not be inferred. Other factors could be causing both of these variables. Further scientific evidence is needed before definite conclusions can be drawn regarding a more specific relationship between taraxein and schizophrenia.

The chances of recovery from this form of psychosis are not so good as for manic-depressive psychosis. Figures from mental hospitals differ, depending upon the treatments used and the conditions under which patients are discharged. With modern treatment, however, more than one-half of first-admission schizophrenics are discharged in less than six months after admission, and nearly all are discharged within the first year.

What are paranoid reactions? Psychotic persons who suffer from persistent, systematized delusions are said to show *paranoid reactions*. We have just seen that such delusions are characteristic of some schizophrenic patients; in fact, most hospital patients displaying paranoid reactions are classified as schizophrenics. Cases of pure paranoia are extremely rare, and many persons displaying some paranoid reactions are never hospitalized.

The delusions which characterize paranoid reactions may take the form of delusions of grandeur. The individual may believe that he is a great author, a multimillionaire, a world-famous physician, a great inventor, a member of a royal family, and so on. Accompanying the delusions of grandeur there are often delusions of persecution. The patient talks about how his enemies are plotting against him, how scheming persons are trying to steal his money, how others have copied his ideas for inventions. He often insists that his enemies have succeeded in having him unjustly confined in the hospital. Frequently there are delusions of reference. Even the most trivial incidents take on a personal reference. Whenever he sees two persons talking, he is sure that they are talking about him. A nurse or doctor may happen to make some slight gesture, but the patient insists that this hand movement is a signal to his enemies. If his place at the table in the hospital is changed, he thinks that it has been changed because the food being served to the new place is poisoned.

A brief review of a case history will serve to illustrate a paranoid reaction. A patient in a mental hospital believes that he is a general in the army—although in actuality he never rose above the rank of private first class. Each

morning he writes out the orders of the day for the army. Parts of these orders are in code so that enemy agents cannot read them. The patient is a college graduate, keeps up on current events, and talks in an interesting manner. He gives very logical-sounding explanations. The cottage in which he lives is his office, the other patients in the cottage are members of his military staff, the entire hospital is an army post, and all the patients are soldiers or nurses. He reports that the President of the United States makes frequent reference to him in press releases, although not by name.

ORGANIC PSYCHOSES

The psychoses we shall discuss in this section—paresis, senile psychosis, and alcoholic psychosis—are organic because they result from damage to the central nervous system. You may read of other ways of classifying the psychoses mentioned in this section. Instead of being classified as functional or organic, psychoses are sometimes categorized as either acute or chronic. *Acute* brain disorders include temporary and reversible brain-tissue impairment, such as is found in drug, poison, and alcohol intoxication and in certain circulatory disturbances. Acute psychosis usually has a fairly rapid onset and lasts a comparatively short amount of time. *Chronic* brain disorders are those psychoses which involve relatively fixed brain-tissue dam-

This schizophrenic artist's withdrawal from reality is shown by the deterioration of structure in his cat portraits.

age, such as those caused by the process of aging or by permanent head injury. Chronic psychosis is usually of lengthy duration and uncertain recovery.

What is paresis? *Paresis* (pə·rē′sis or par′ə·sis) is the name given to the form of psychosis caused by syphilitic infection of the brain. The term "paresis" is the one most frequently used in psychological literature. This form of psychosis is sometimes, however, referred to as "general paralysis of the insane," "dementia paralytica," "softening of the brain," or "progressive general paralysis." Do not assume that "paralysis" and "paresis" are synonymous, though. Many persons have paralysis who are not suffering from paresis.

Not everyone who has syphilis becomes a paretic. In fact, of all those who contract syphilis, only about 5 percent become paretics. Syphilis may destroy any part of the body, but if the brain is the part destroyed, paresis results. When the brains of paretics are examined after death, the destruction of brain tissue can be plainly seen. About 1 percent of all first admissions to mental hospitals are persons suffering from paresis.

Paretics often show paranoid reactions. They may display a false sense of well-being. They tend to look at the world through rose-colored glasses. For example, they might make the most rash and foolhardy investments because they feel sure that everything will turn out perfectly.

The paretic walks with a characteristic shuffling gait. His speech is disturbed. He mixes up his words and syllables. He has a faulty memory. He becomes indifferent to social proprieties, with a resulting vulgarity.

Within the past thirty years, medical science has made great strides in the effective treatment of syphilis. If the patient is treated by modern methods, he has a very good chance of recovery.

What is senile psychosis? An organic psychosis which sometimes affects old people is called *senile psychosis*. The term "senility" is applied to the general deterioration that often accompanies old age. Old persons often show a breakdown in the functioning of their bodies; they have many pains and discomforts. The brain, as well as other parts of the body, does not always function as efficiently as in earlier days. There may be cerebral arteriosclerosis, that is, a thickening and hardening of the wall of the arteries resulting in a decreased circulation of blood in the brain.

If a large blood vessel bursts in the brain, the elderly person is said to have had a "stroke." Following this bursting of the blood vessel, he may be paralyzed or he may become unconscious. In severe cases death may follow. If only a tiny capillary in the brain bursts, the brain is not damaged to a great extent, but the old person may show confusion in his thinking. He may not be able to recall recent past experiences; he may become angry easily. Often his behavior is childish, and it is said that he is in his "second childhood."

Such paranoid reactions as delusions of persecution may develop. The elderly person may believe that his relatives and friends are mistreating him, that they are whispering unpleasant things about him. He may even believe that they are trying to kill him to get his money. Of course, the very ones he believes are plotting against him may be the ones who love him most and who would do everything in their power to help him.

Senile psychosis accounts for about 8 percent of first admissions to mental hospitals.

Why is old age often a personal problem for young people? Many young people are faced with the problem of having grandparents or other older persons in their homes. This may or may not cause difficulty in family adjustments. The older people may do much to help in the work of the home. On the other hand, they may cause conflicts. In one study of 193 men and women with a median age of seventy-four years, it was found that one-third expected their grown, married children to obey them. Thirty percent believed that they should interfere in the training of their grandchildren. The grandchildren were placed in the difficult position of wishing to please their parents and their grandparents. The parents were placed in the difficult position of wishing to please their parents and their children. Such difficulties often result in emotional disturbances.

The older person in the home may present financial problems. The family budget may have to be stretched to include food, clothing, and medical care for the older members. This means less money for the younger members of the family, which may become a source of tension.

How can you assist the older person? What can you do to help old people? In the first place, you must not make fun of them or blame them for their delusions, for their childish behavior, for their inability to remember, for their irritability, or for their confused thinking. Such forms of behavior are merely symptoms of the general deterioration that is taking place. Fortunately, some old persons do not show marked signs of deterioration.

It is very important to make older persons feel wanted and useful. In the study referred to in the previous section, two-thirds of the old people indicated that they felt unwanted and in the way. As a child, if you ever felt unwanted and in the way, you have some idea of how these older people feel. Old people do not wish to sit around and do nothing but rest. They can and should do useful work even though they can't do it with your speed and accuracy. You will be helping the grandparents in your home when you say, "I have a lot of studying to do tonight, I would appreciate it a lot if you will help me with the dishes," or "I'm going on a date this evening. Will you help trim the flowers while I cut the grass so I can get ready in time?" Remind them of what they can do rather than of what they cannot do.

Older people have had many experiences in life which you cannot have had at your age. Ask them for advice, even though you can't always follow it. Ask them about events when they were young. You may learn some history in a firsthand and interesting way, and they will enjoy recalling these incidents for you.

Basically, the greatest thing you can do for older persons is to show them your love and approval. Most of your adventures are still to come; most of theirs are behind them.

Why is old age a social problem? Since the percentage of old persons in our population is increasing, the social problem of old age is becoming more and more challenging. Medical science and improved living conditions make it possible for people to live longer nowadays. Accordingly, psychologists are becoming increasingly interested in the problems of old age. The American Psychological Association now has a Division on Maturity and Old Age. Old age further complicates our already enormous problem of crowded mental hospitals. Many private and public institutions are needed to care for senile and other old persons. Old persons may also cause society an economic problem.

How can society help the older person? Socially there is much to be done in the way of helping persons in the later years of life. Old people yearn to be of use in society, but they are often forced to become useless, and thus unhappy. Monotony is deadly — no one wishes to rust away. By our present-day systems of pensions, old-age assistance, and Medicare, we attempt to relieve the financial strain of idleness in old age. We do not, however, relieve all of the psychological strain. In fact, all too often we discourage and even prohibit the older person from doing useful work. If the unpleasant aspects of senility are to be prevented, business, industry, and the professions must permit healthy older persons to work for pay. Not so much can be expected of them as of younger workers, but

Elderly persons can still perform many functions and activities, and can do them with an amount of experience that younger persons lack.

neither need the pay be as high. Older persons seldom have to bear the financial responsibilities of rearing children. Unfortunately, labor unions and business policy often will not permit this reduced but adequate pay for such work as older persons can do.

Can anything be done to prevent an undesirable old age? Of necessity, we all shall grow old in years, but perhaps we need not show the behavior sometimes found in old persons. If you wish to be happy in old age, you must prepare for that period of life while you are still young. A severely exhausting life may tend to bring on the symptoms of senility. There is some evidence that the excessive use of alcohol while one is young leads to early and unhappy old age. In general, anything that you can do to keep a strong, healthy body is a step in preventing the unpleasant effects of old age.

To guard against idleness in later years, young persons must think far ahead, even beyond the period of active business life. The young person who develops interests in hobbies, recreational reading, and social problems and who learns how to make friends can look forward to a happy old age. He will never have to complain of having nothing to do. What you will be like in old age depends to a great extent upon your present mental health.

Modern medicine is doing much to prevent or reduce the undesirable aspects of old age. By the administration of certain hormones and vitamins, the physician can do much to keep the body, including the central nervous system, of the old person in relatively good condition.

What is alcoholic psychosis? In Chapter 10 (page 269) we considered the effects of alcohol on efficiency. In addition, we should note that with the use of alcohol the individual becomes less inhibited. Activities which would have seemed wrong before drinking seem all right following the drinking. Many drinkers have a false sense of relaxation and security. They feel quite sociable. Everything is just fine. There is some escape from unpleasant realities. With the taking of more alcohol, the individual's speech, motor coordination, and vision become disturbed. His thinking becomes confused. Still later, the user enters a stuporous state and finally "passes out." There is complete escape.

To determine whether or not an individual is drunk, generally the amount of alcohol consumed is not as important as the concentration of alcohol in the blood stream. Fortunately most individuals "pass out" before they consume enough alcohol to kill them. Individuals usually pass out when the concentration of alcohol reaches a 0.50 percent concentration level; a concentration level higher than 0.55 percent is considered lethal.

Just how an individual will respond to alcohol cannot be determined simply by how much alcohol he takes. Many people become happy under the influence of alcohol, but some become sad and some become irritable and pugnacious. Alcoholism is only a symptom of a deep-seated personality maladjustment.

The person who uses excessive amounts of alcohol over a long period of time is likely to show general physiological deterioration. Alcoholic psychosis is likely to occur in persons who have been chronic alcoholics for a number of years. Unfortunately, alcoholic psychosis seems to be increasing: 15 percent of all first admissions to mental hospitals are cases of alcoholic psychosis, a higher percentage than in recent years. Here are some mental illnesses which are fundamentally alcoholic in origin.

1. *Delirium tremens.* Delirium tremens is found in a small percentage of those who have engaged in heavy drinking for a long period of time. Trembling of the hands and other parts of the body is apparent. The individual is apprehensive, confused about time and place, restless, and irritable. He often suffers from insomnia. He has vivid hallucinations: "pink elephants" or other large animals, snakes, rats, bugs of all kinds.

2. *Acute hallucinosis.* This alcoholic illness resembles delirium tremens in many ways but is characterized by auditory hallucinations. The patient hears "voices" talking about him, calling him names, and accusing him of all kinds of crimes. The voices threaten him with horrible punishment. He may become terror-stricken and scream for help. He may arm himself for a fight, or he may attempt suicide.

3. *Korsakoff's psychosis.* This mental illness occurs in older alcoholics, often after approximately twenty-five years of chronic alcoholism. The outstanding symptom is inability to remember previous experiences, espe-

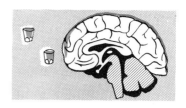
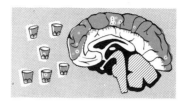
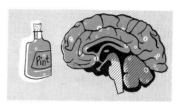

After two drinks of whisky, the alcohol affects the cerebral cortex of the brain and causes a person to become less inhibited. If he takes as many as six ordinary-sized drinks, the individual will have trouble with muscular coordination. His speech and gestures will be less controlled, and he may "see double." If he drinks as much as a pint, he may "pass out."

cially recent ones. The patient is unable to recall eating a meal even though he has just left the table. He may have just talked to someone but doesn't remember the person at all a minute after the individual has left the room. The patient often fills in the gaps in his recall with fanciful tales which may sound quite plausible until the facts are checked.

4. *Pathological intoxication.* Unlike the previous forms of alcoholic illness, pathological intoxication may follow the consumption of only a very

MENTAL ILLNESS

small quantity of alcohol. It is especially likely to occur if the user is very tired or emotionally upset. The patient may become violently angry and brutal. He may kill, rob, burn, or commit other crimes. He may commit suicide.

What can be done to help the alcoholic?
Alcoholism is one of the most serious health problems facing us today, yet there is no generally accepted technique for treating it. We have almost no special hospitals for the treatment of alcoholics. General hospitals usually offer treatment for severe cases only, and their treatment is of short duration. In most communities, the alcoholic goes to jail instead of to a hospital. In many jails, half of the inmates are alcoholics, yet jails have neither the equipment nor the professional staff to care for alcoholics. The "drunk" is sobered up, but he is not treated.

As we have said before, alcoholism is generally a symptom of a basic personality maladjustment. Alcoholism is a result rather than a cause of the individual's difficulties. When we treat just the alcoholism, we are treating the symptom rather than the illness. The alcoholic is cured only when he learns to meet life's responsibilities and difficulties by attacking them rather than running away from them through the use of alcohol.

Mention will be made of only one well-known form of treatment, the services of Alcoholics Anonymous. This organization was started by two men who had helped themselves and each other to recover from alcoholism. They decided that they wanted to assist others who have a problem with alcohol. If you live in a city, look in your telephone book and you will probably find this organization listed. Your daily newspaper may have the name listed under "Personal." These notices indicate that the organization is ready to serve at any time. Although individual help is given, Alcoholics Anonymous essentially conducts a form of group therapy. Meetings are held in which individuals can have social life and entertainment without going to a bar. Also, at these meetings problems of the alcoholic are discussed; persons who have been "through the mill" tell of their experiences and of how they have been helped. The alcoholic is made to feel that he is not alone with his problems, that he is a member of an important group, that he will be more successful if he attacks his problems than if he runs away from them. Reports indicate that treatment by Alcoholics Anonymous is effective, sooner or later, in about three fourths of the cases that come for help. It works only when the individual is willing to admit that he has been escaping his problems by means of alcohol and desires to be helped. An individual must avoid alcoholic beverages completely once he has been treated, because taking even one drink is likely to cause alcoholism to recur.

Although progress is being made, more research on alcoholism is needed. The alcoholic needs help rather than condemnation. Some large business concerns have psychiatric programs designed to help their alcoholic employees. In alcoholism, as elsewhere, prevention is better than cure. The individual in good mental health need not worry about becoming an alcoholic.

CONVULSIVE DISORDERS

Psychologists use the term *convulsive disorders* to refer to those disorders popularly spoken of as "epilepsy."

What are convulsive disorders? For practical purposes, convulsive disorders are usually described under one of four classifications, although these terms are sometimes replaced with others which denote the area of the brain most involved. Convulsive disorders account for less than 2 percent of first admissions to mental hospitals.

1. *Grand mal* (grän mȧl′) [great illness]. The symptoms of the grand mal are very pronounced, and more than one-half of all convulsive disorders exist in this form. Historically, this form of seizure has been known as the "falling sickness." The person loses consciousness and falls, usually with a cry or a moan. His muscles become stiff, and he may bite his tongue or cheek as the muscles stiffen. At first he may be pale, and then his face will become flushed; the pupils of his eyes dilate. The skin may become blue or slightly purple. This stage usually lasts about half a minute. Then the individual begins a violent jerking of his arms, head, jaws, and trunk. Many times there is a frothing at the mouth, which is caused simply by air being forced through the saliva. The patient may cough and grunt. Sometimes he loses control of the bowels and bladder. This stage may last for only part of a minute, or it may last as long as from five to ten minutes.

After this phase the individual goes into a stuporous sleep lasting for several hours. Upon awakening, he may feel fatigued and complain of a headache, but he does not remember anything about his behavior or thoughts during the seizure. In fact, upon regaining consciousness, he may resume a conversation at the exact point where it was interrupted by the seizure.

2. *Petit mal* (pə·tē′ mȧl′) [little illness]. The symptoms of the petit mal are much more mild. The individual may become dizzy. He may lose consciousness for a few seconds. There may be a slight trembling. Sometimes the eyes appear to be staring vacantly. He seldom falls. In fact, his friends may not be aware that he has had a seizure. They may note only that he paused in his conversation or that he stopped in his work for a second or two.

3. *Jacksonian.* The form of convulsive disorder known as Jacksonian is much like the grand mal form except that the attack begins in one part of the body as muscle twitching, or with a feeling of numbness or tingling, and then spreads over the entire side of the body. The patient often does not lose consciousness until the attack spreads to a considerable part of the body.

4. *Psychomotor.* In the psychomotor form of convulsive disorder, the person loses consciousness but continues with the activity in which he has been engaged and appears to be conscious. The attacks usually do not last more than a few minutes, yet they can last for several days. Patients have been known to harm themselves or to

commit vicious crimes while having a psychomotor attack, but later they remembered nothing of the incident, with the possible exception of a vague feeling that they had done something terrible. A person having a psychomotor attack should not be forcibly restrained unless absolutely necessary for safety, because to do so may increase the severity of the seizure.

Convulsive seizures are sometimes preceded by sensations of light, sounds, tastes, or smells. These sensations are imaginary in that no stimuli for them exist outside the person. Such a hallucination at the beginning of an attack is spoken of as an *aura*.

What causes convulsive disorders? The causes of the convulsive disorders just described are not known definitely. There are evidences of various physiological disturbances; however, we shall not go into this medical problem. As we saw in Chapter 10 (page 259), the brain-wave patterns of persons having convulsive disorders are distinctive. We are not sure to what extent heredity is a factor in convulsive disorders, but in many cases it probably only predisposes a person toward the illness. Brain injuries occurring before, during, or after birth, or an infection following such diseases as measles or encephalitis may be factors in producing convulsive seizures. With adequate modern medical and social care, 80 percent of persons with convulsive seizures can probably lead relatively normal and happy lives.

Who are the persons with convulsive disorders? Psychological studies of people with convulsive disorders have shown that there is no typical personality picture which characterizes them. Most persons with convulsive disorders have normal intellectual ability, and some famous persons have been included in this group — Julius Caesar, Lord Byron, Alexander the Great, Guy de Maupassant, Paganini, and Van Gogh. In one study of 95 college students with convulsive disorders, it was found that 70 percent of them were capable of doing creditable college work. It is true, however, that in some cases persons with convulsive disorders do show deterioration and come to function at a retarded level.

We do not know just how many persons in the United States suffer from convulsive disorders. Estimates have placed the figure at anywhere from 500,000 to 1,000,000 people. In World War II about six draftees in a thousand showed some form of convulsive behavior. Both men and women are subject to the various convulsive disorders. Probably fewer than 10 percent of those who have convulsive disorders are in institutions for the special care of such persons. At least 70 percent of persons suffering from some form of convulsive disorder display their first symptoms before they are twenty years of age. Electroencephalogram (EEG) patterns are used in helping to determine whether patients who have not had a seizure in several years should continue treatment.

How can you help a person displaying convulsive behavior? You should always treat such persons with genuine sympathy. They may be irritable, stubborn, inconsiderate of others, and conceited. You must recognize such behavior as a symptom of a disorder, and you should not consider their acts as personal offenses. Because of their condition, such persons may have difficulty in their school and college studies.

Adults subject to convulsive seizures often have difficulty in finding jobs because of popular prejudice against them. Generally they cannot drive cars safely, although on the approval of a physician and under certain medical conditions, some persons having convulsive disorders can obtain a driver's license. There are, however, many jobs that they can do as well as, and as safely as, anyone else.

Basically, you can help individuals with convulsive disorders by thinking of them and treating them as normal people but as people who have a special problem of adjustment.

TREATMENT
FOR THE MENTALLY ILL

What conditions are found in mental hospitals? Some persons still use the term "insane asylum" to refer to an institution for the care of the mentally ill. For many persons this term signifies some kind of dark, damp, crowded place, with heavy iron bars at all doors and windows and a great deal of confusion and uproar. In the past, mentally ill persons were indeed kept in such places. Our word "bedlam" comes from the popular name of a centuries-old asylum in London, St. Mary's of Bethlehem. The inmates of an asylum were supposed to be under affliction because of their sins, or the "sins of their fathers." The keepers were likely to be favored politicians.

"Asylum" means a place of refuge or security. It is true that public attitudes are such that psychotic persons often need a place of refuge. Today, however, we try to give them more than a place of security; we try to cure them. With this change in point of view has come a change in name. Today we speak of "mental hospitals," or just use the word "hospitals," rather than "insane asylums."

Although most mental hospitals are organized for long-term treatment of patients, there are some to which mentally ill persons can go without legal formality, just as other ill persons go to general hospitals. The mental illness of such persons is usually of relatively short duration, so that treatment often can be brief but effective. In just a few weeks or months the patient is able to return to his home, work, and social life. Some mental hospitals have outpatient clinics where mentally ill persons can go for diagnosis and therapy without ever having to remain in the hospital for care.

The officials in charge of many mental hospitals are psychiatrists and psychologists of the highest order. They are well trained for their work. They are keenly interested in the well-being of those placed in their care. The buildings are properly ventilated and heated; there are pictures on the walls and curtains at the windows. Schoolwork, vocational training, and play are on the daily programs. The food is nourishing and well cooked. Special as well as general medical care is given when needed.

Many mental hospitals now have modern facilities, up-to-date equipment, and well-trained staff members to diagnose and treat patients.

Nevertheless, old-fashioned "insane asylums" still exist in some parts of our country. Reports have appeared of overcrowding, unsanitary conditions and neglect or even ill-treatment of patients. Where these shocking conditions exist, the basic need is usually for more public interest and more money. It will require an investment of the taxpayers' time and money to provide new buildings and well-qualified staff members.

How are patients treated in up-to-date hospitals? In modern, well-run mental hospitals, those being cared for are spoken of as patients. This idea of patients in a hospital is quite different

from the popular notion of "nuts" in a "nut house." A mental hospital, like any other hospital, is a place where patients are sent for careful diagnosis and treatment. Just as in other hospitals, the aim of the mental hospital is to cure patients and return them to their homes, community life, and work.

Hospitals hold parties and dances and provide movies, games, and bus rides in an attempt to get patients to renew their interests in social life. Patients are given work to do. A hospital staff is not interested in the amount of work done for its own sake but is very much interested in the attention that the patients give to the work. If a patient has definite work to do for which he is responsible, he is less likely to remain lost in his dream world.

In our older mental hospitals you may see bars at the windows. Some persons think these bars are for the same purpose as bars on prison windows. As a matter of fact, in most cases they are used for the protection of the patients. Sometimes patients, when very excited or depressed, might commit suicide by jumping from an upper story of a hospital. In modern mental hospitals, the bars are so built into the structure of the windows that they cannot be recognized, and the patients do not have the feeling of being confined behind bars. If the hospital is built on a one-floor plan, bars are not necessary for many patients. If a patient jumps out the window, he gets nothing more than a bump.

It has been found that a tub bath or pool bath in water kept at about body temperature is helpful for calming excited patients. Sometimes they are wrapped in cold wet sheets for the same purpose. In either case the treatment is known as *hydrotherapy*. Massage may be used. *Electrotherapy* provides the application of heat by means of infrared lamps and high-frequency currents. These are only a few of the many different types of therapy.

Perhaps you have heard of the use of strait jackets in mental hospitals. A *strait jacket* is merely a jacket made of strong cloth, opening down the back instead of the front. The sleeves are much longer than the patient's arms, and they are closed at the ends. The patient is simply placed in the jacket with his arms folded across his chest and the long sleeves tied together at the back. The jacket is applied in periods of great excitement or depression, to keep the patient from using his hands to destroy furniture or injure other patients or himself. Such jackets do not help cure patients, however, and are very rarely used now in the better mental hospitals.

Persons not familiar with mental hospitals imagine padded cells as horrible places. Some hospitals do have rooms with padded walls or no furniture, so that a patient who is extremely excited or extremely depressed cannot injure himself. Such rooms are not used for most patients. In fact, with the use of modern drugs, a patient may be in a padded cell only long enough for a psychiatrist or other trained individual to administer a drug to him. Upon receiving the drug, the patient can usually return to the ward, work, or recreational activity in a matter of minutes.

What are some other therapeutic treatments used in mental hospitals? There are a number of drugs that are helpful in treating mental patients. For example, tranquilizing (ataractic) drugs help to relieve the fears and anxieties of disturbed patients. Although drug therapy treats symptoms, not causes, of disorders, the alleviation of symptoms sometimes breaks the vicious circle of mental illness and may result in improved behavior. The husband who no longer feels as much anxiety may begin to treat his wife better, who in turn begins to show more love and affection toward her husband. When used judiciously, such drugs are of definite therapeutic value.

In an informal atmosphere, the members of this group therapy session discuss their own and each other's problems.

A new type of drug called Indoklon (in·dok′lon) has been studied and found to have about the same results as electric shock. *Electric shock treatment* consists of sending a mild electric current through certain areas of the brain. In electric shock treatment, the length and severity of the current can be controlled so that the patient feels no pain from the shock, but he usually awakens with a headache and becomes apprehensive when approached for additional electric shock treatments. In *Indoklon therapy* the patients are not usually as apprehensive about treat-

ment and do not have as severe headaches. In treating some disorders of extremely depressed individuals with electric shock or Indoklon, recovery is higher than 90 percent. Such treatment has shortened the recovery time for neurotic and psychotic depressive disorders from several years to a few months.

Group therapy is another form of treatment for the mentally ill. In this technique, patients meet together to talk over their problems. Each learns that others have problems, too, and together they work out solutions. (Remember our discussion of this type of therapy as used by Alcoholics Anonymous.)

Sometimes patients are encouraged to act out on a stage situations in their lives which trouble them. The term *psychodrama* is used for this technique of treatment.

A new type of therapy, which has some experimental evidence to substantiate it, is called *behavior therapy*. Its procedures are based on the theory that maladjustive or inappropriate behavior is learned and therefore can be unlearned through the use of conditioning techniques (see Chapter 3). Behavior therapy has been used with both neurotic and psychotic patients. In one study, schizophrenic patients who had refused to eat without help were taught to eat by being given a specified time limit within which they had to eat or the dining-room doors were closed. Under such imposed restrictions, most individuals will more readily eat supper. Although this method is not universally accepted by psychologists and requires more experimental evidence, behavior therapy does open up new avenues of research for the treatment of mental illness.

Whatever the therapeutic technique, the objective of mental hospitals is to enable as many patients as possible to return to their home communities and to their places in society.

What happens to patients who are cured and return home? Sometimes former patients in mental hospitals have difficulty finding acceptance in communities to which they return. They often have difficulty in finding work. Social groups will not accept them as members. There is still much prejudice against those who have been mentally ill. Would we hesitate to accept into the community social life a person who had been cured of pneumonia in a hospital? Would we be afraid to give him a job? Then why should we not permit the person cured in a mental hospital to take his place in society and lead a happy, normal life? Both have been sick; both have been cured. Some individuals state that anyone who has been in a mental hospital and has been cured may become disturbed again and have to return to the mental hospital. In some cases, this is true, but when you go to the doctor with a sore throat and he cures it, does he guarantee that you will never have a sore throat again? Of course not. The doctor cures your sore throat and prescribes certain preventive measures to enable you to better avoid having another sore throat. It is the same with mental illness. We cannot guarantee that the individual will not become emotionally disturbed again any more than your medical doctor can guarantee that you will never have a sore throat again.

Much can now be done to cure, or at least improve, mentally ill persons. In the future, as research leads the way, more and better treatments will be possible. The best treatment, however, is still prevention. Are you striving to maintain good mental health?

Terms to Add to Your Vocabulary

acute hallucinosis
acute psychosis
amnesia
aura
behavior therapy
chronic psychosis
conversion reaction
convulsive disorders
delirium tremens
dissociative reaction
electric shock treatment
electrotherapy
fugue
functional disorders
grand mal

group therapy
hydrotherapy
hypochondriac
Indoklon therapy
insanity
Jacksonian convulsive
 disorder
Korsakoff's psychosis
manic-depressive
multiple personality
neurosis
"neurotic nucleus"
obsessive-compulsive
organic disorders
paranoid reactions

paresis
paretic
pathological intoxication
petit mal
phobia
psychodrama
psychomotor
psychosis
psychosomatic
psychotic
schizophrenia
senile psychosis
strait jacket
taraxein
tic

Suggestions for Activities

1. There seem to be many common expressions which suggest that some of our organic processes are related to emotional and other psychological causes. For example, when we become irritated or angry with someone, we say, "You give me a pain in the neck!" If we have a very frightening experience, we say, "I was so scared that my flesh fairly crawled!" For a few days note and jot down such expressions as you hear them. Bring your notes to class and make up a list of "psychosomatic" expressions. (Classes report that they can gather lists of twenty or more such expressions without much difficulty.)

2. Visit a drugstore in order to look over the "nerve" and sleep-inducing preparations available without prescription. If you have studied chemistry, you will be interested in reading the labels. Are such preparations a satisfactory answer to the problems of the nervous person?

3. Write a theme on the behavior of some well-known person in history whose reactions were so unusual that he might be called psychotic. You might consider such figures as Caligula, Ivan the Terrible (a Czar of Russia), Napoleon, and Hitler. Some famous literary men have shown psychotic symptoms.

4. Have an elderly man and woman speak to your class, telling about historical events of which they have personal knowledge, the kinds of social events they enjoyed when they were your age, the schools they attended. If such a project is not feasible, perhaps you can at least talk with your grandparents. What will you be like when you are their age?

5. Check the telephone directory or look under "Personal" in the classified advertisements of your newspaper to find out if the services of Alcoholics Anonymous are available in your community. A member of this organization might be willing and glad to speak to your class.

6. You cannot have the experience of being a patient in a mental hospital as an "activity" for your psychology class. You can, however, have a vicarious experience. In the "Suggestions for Further Reading" on the next page you will find a number of informative autobiographies of persons who have been patients in mental hospitals.

7. If it can be arranged, visit a mental hospital to see how patients are cared for. Although in most cases you will not be able to tell by looking at patients, a doctor or a psychiatric aide may be able to point out one psychosis or another.

8. If mental hospitals and institutions for the care of persons with convulsive disorders are too distant for a visit, you may be able to visit a county infirmary. No doubt some persons will show psychotic symptoms; some will be senile.

9. Look in your local telephone directory for the address of a mental health organization in your area. If you find such an organization, make contact and ask about the organization's activities. For instance, they may have volunteer groups that visit patients in mental hospitals. You might report on their activities to the class. Quite often volunteer groups take small gifts to patients. Maybe you could organize some activity in your school (with permission) to help this group raise money to purchase small gifts or items that patients need. (These gifts are usually nothing more than a bar of soap, colorful ribbon, a tie, and so on.) You might even be able to help start a patient on the road to recovery by your activities.

Suggestions for Further Reading

Atkinson, Donald T., *Magic, Myth and Medicine*, Fawcett Publications. A brief history of medicine.

Beers, Clifford W., *A Mind That Found Itself*, rev. ed., Doubleday. The autobiography of a man who was mentally ill and who set out to improve conditions in mental hospitals. This book created widespread interest in mental hygiene.

Chappell, Matthew N., *Worry and Its Control*, rev. ed. (previous title, *In the Name of Common Sense*), Collier Books. By a psychologist who wants to help people find happier and more creative lives.

Coleman, James, *Personality Dynamics and Effective Behavior*, Scott, Foresman. Part II, "The Dynamics of Individual and Group Behavior," discusses neurotic disorders and functional psychotic disorders as well as disorders associated with brain damage, addiction to alcohol or drugs, and psychosomatic disorders. Part IV, "Problems of Older People," contains an annotated bibliography.

Daniel, Robert S., ed., *Contemporary Readings in General Psychology*, 2nd ed., Houghton Mifflin. In the second edition, Part VI contains nine articles on "Behavior Is Dynamic," of which the following articles are recommended: pages 221–24, "The Pathology of Boredom"; pages 224–28, "What People Dream About"; pages 242–44, "What's a Nervous Breakdown, Anyhow?"

Drake, Raleigh, *Abnormal Psychology*, Littlefield, Adams.

Green, Hannah, *I Never Promised You a Rose Garden*, New American Library. The story of an adolescent psychotic patient in a mental institution.

Hilgard, Ernest R., and Richard C. Atkinson, *Introduction to Psychology*, 4th ed., Harcourt, Brace & World. Chapter 21, "Mental Health and the Behavior Disorders"; Chapter 22, "Psychotherapy and Related Techniques."

Josselyn, Irene M., *Emotional Problems of Illness*, Science Research Associates.

Kafka, Franz, *The Trial*, Knopf. The story of a paranoid patient's inability to grasp reality and his tendency to interpret all events as persecution.

Kalish, Richard A., *The Psychology of Human Behavior*, Wadsworth. Chapter 14, "The Troubled Personality."

Leuba, Clarence, *Man: A General Psychology*, Holt, Rinehart & Winston. Chapter 21, "Abnormal Personalities and Personality Disorders" (especially pages 570–91); pages 516–17, "Advantages and Disadvantages of Age" and "New Roles with Age."

Lindgren, Henry C., Donn Byrne, and Lewis F. Petrinovich, *Psychology: An Introduction to a Behavioral Science*, 2nd ed., John Wiley. Chapter 12, "Personal Adjustment and Mental Hygiene."

McKeachie, Wilbert J., and Charlotte L. Doyle, *Psychology*, Addison-Wesley. Chapter 14, "Maladjustment."

Morgan, Clifford T., and Richard A. King, *Introduction to Psychology*, 3rd ed., McGraw-Hill. Chapter 14, "Behavior Disorders."

Munn, Norman L., *Psychology*, 5th ed., Houghton Mifflin. Chapter 9, "Personality," pages 277–89, "Psychoneurotic Personalities," "Psychotherapy of the Neuroses," and "Psychotic Personalities."

Piersall, Jim, with Al Hirschberg, *Fear Strikes Out: The Jim Piersall Story*, Little, Brown. The story of a player for the Boston Red Sox who entered a mental hospital for treatment and later returned to his job as a big-league baseball player.

Ruch, Floyd L., *Psychology and Life*, 7th ed., Scott, Foresman. Chapter 13, "Reactions to Frustration," pages 475–85, "Neurotic Reactions," and "Psychotic Reactions"; Chapter 14, "Mental Health and Therapy."

Sanford, Fillmore H., *Psychology: A Scientific Study of Man*, 2nd ed., Wadsworth. Chapter 17, "Neurosis, Psychosis, and Psychotherapy."

UNIT **6**

THE FAMILY AND OTHER SMALL GROUPS

16

The family group

You are spending, and will spend, much of your life as a member of small groups. For most persons the family is the small group within which much of their behavior is centered. When they are children, their lives usually revolve around their parental homes. Later, if they become parents, their lives usually center around their own families.

Between the time of living in the parental home as a child and establishing a home of one's own, there is a period of dating, courtship, and engagement culminating in marriage. We shall briefly examine this period leading up to a family before we consider the family group itself.

ROMANTIC LOVE
BEFORE MARRIAGE

Although biological factors are one foundation upon which romantic love is built, the behavior involved in romantic love is best explained by the learning process. Two individuals of opposite sexes mutually reinforce each other's behavior. They "fall in love." Learning to love is basic to part of romantic love.

What are some dating customs in which individuals learn to love? So common is unchaperoned dating in the United States, Canada, and some European countries that we sometimes think it is the only way in which a young man and woman can learn to love each other. Yet in some parts of the world, such as in many Latin American countries, chaperoned dating is still the accepted custom. A parent, some other older relative of the girl, or a trusted friend of the family usually accompanies the couple whenever they go out together. Within these dating customs, as in unchaperoned dating, young people learn to love each other, to marry, and to raise a family.

There is a reason behind customs that put restrictions on dating. For quite a few years parents have first made decisions affecting the behavior of their children and then assisted their children in making their own decisions. Most parents believe that such assistance should not suddenly come to an end when their sons and daughters begin dating, even though their adolescent offspring often do not appreciate this assistance when it comes in the form of restrictions.

Customs of dating have changed greatly in the United States during the past century, especially in the past half-century. You might ask your parents, grandparents, or other older married persons what dating was like when they were your age. If views that seemed modern to them seem dated to you, remember that someday your adolescent children will probably resist your attempts to assist them and will consider you old-fashioned.

What are some characteristics of romantic love? How does a person know he is in love? Although there is no simple answer, a person romantically in love usually displays most of the following characteristics.

1. There is a strong physical attraction.

2. Every effort is made to present the best appearance. The boy displays his physical strength and skill. He is gallant and protective. The girl dresses her loveliest and tries to be very sweet.

3. The individual believes that this love is forever; it is the "real thing" at last.

4. Marriage is looked forward to as a period of continuous bliss. (Unfortunately, such practical considerations as earning enough money to raise a family or coping with the difficulties of maintaining a home are sometimes overlooked.)

5. Blissful daydreaming about the loved one is common.

6. The individual is willing to make any sacrifice in order to win the love of the beloved. He or she is willing to reform, to turn over a new leaf. (Many times such reforms do not last very long after the wedding ceremony.)

7. The beloved is idealized. He or she is thought to be incapable of any but the most noble thoughts and deeds. There tends to be a complete glossing over of any faults or deficiencies which the beloved may have. (Awareness of the faults generally comes later on.)

8. Jealousy is often present. In one study of adolescents in love, 34 percent of the sources of their conflicts were found to be matters of jealousy or possessiveness.

9. Separation or anything else that interferes with the romance is very painful to the lovers.

10. There may be some quarreling. If lovers learn to quarrel, they will probably continue to do so after marriage. An occasional "spat," however, should not be taken too seriously.

11. In our culture, the boy tends to dominate the courting situation, while the girl displays a certain amount of coyness and shyness. There are indications, however, that girls are beginning to play a more active role in courtship, and in some cases even take the initiative.

Does platonic love ever become romantic love? Many times a man and a woman begin dating because there are very few other eligible individuals in the community. Perhaps they will agree at first that there is to be no romantic love— that this is to be a "mere friendship," or platonic love (named after Plato, who wrote about friendship and non-romantic love). After they have gone together awhile, each finds that the other has many desirable qualities. They come to enjoy each other's com-

Two people romantically in love often experience tenderness, physical attraction, and exhilaration in each other's presence.

pany. After their engagement and marriage, some may say that the couple were drawn together by an irresistible force or were fated for each other, but psychologists believe that they had learned to love each other.

Although the view of learned love at first may not sound as thrilling as the irresistible-force view, isn't it more thrilling to have enough admirable qualities to cause someone to learn to love you?

How much time is needed for learning to love? A study made of happily and unhappily married couples shows the importance of learning to love. The authors of this research studied 374 unhappily married and 436 happily married couples. They found how long each couple had been acquainted before becoming engaged, and the length of time between engagement and marriage. The results are indicated in the table on the opposite page.

Of course, this study must not be taken as proof that a long friendship or a long engagement can guarantee happiness in marriage. Nevertheless, it is evidence that hasty marriages, entered into by people who are not well acquainted, are less likely to be happy than marriages between men and women who have learned to know each other.

Another study covered 526 married couples. It was found that the marital adjustment of 39.3 percent of the couples who dated each other less than three months before marriage was poor. Of those couples who dated each other less than three months, only 32.1 percent reported good adjustment, the remaining couples reporting fair adjustment. On the other hand, only 12.6 percent of the couples who dated each other for three to five years before marriage reported poor marital adjustment, and 56.8 percent of them reported good adjustment.

Of the couples who had been engaged less than three months before marriage, 50.0 percent reported poor marital ad-

Average Period of Acquaintanceship and Engagement for 374 Unhappily Married and 436 Happily Married Couples

	AVERAGE ACQUAINTANCE IN MONTHS BEFORE ENGAGEMENT	AVERAGE NUMBER OF MONTHS BETWEEN ENGAGEMENT AND MARRIAGE
Unhappy marriage	20.15	7.51
Happy marriage	28.30	12.46

justment. Only 25.7 percent reported good adjustment. On the other hand, only 11.0 percent of the couples engaged two years or more reported poor marital adjustment; 62.6 percent reported good adjustment.

Although many factors enter into a happy marriage, these figures are evidence that the chances for a happy marriage are increased when there is an opportunity for learning to love before marrying.

That many couples do not really learn to love each other is shown by our divorce rate. No doubt, the great majority of the couples who later became divorced thought that they loved each other before marriage. Evidently, though, sufficient learning did not take place, either before or after marriage.

Is love at first sight psychologically possible? Love at first sight, in which a man and a woman meet and immediately fall in love through an irresistible force that miraculously brings them together, does not seem to agree with the view of love as a learning process. Yet occasionally a man and a woman do seem to "fall in love" the first time they meet or after a very short acquaintanceship. How can such behavior be explained psychologically?

Probably most adults have had several experiences of falling in love at first sight. Each of us builds up ideals in connection with love, and when we meet someone of the other sex, we measure that person in terms of our ideals. If this first rough measure shows that the person does not meet our ideals, we do not continue our relationship with him or her. Thus, the process of learning to love does not go on with that person. If the person continues to hold some attraction, we may learn to love him or her. When two people learn to love each other and get married, they may look back on the beginning of their relationship as love at first sight.

We shall now turn to a discussion of some characteristics and problems of marriage.

ROMANTIC LOVE IN MARRIAGE

Following the marriage ceremony, romantic love should not cease although, as the years pass, it may change in form and intensity. We shall consider some studies made by psychologists and sociologists.

What are some of the problems between married people? Marriage is not a

The Ten Most Serious Grievances of Some Married Persons

HUSBANDS' COMPLAINTS REGARDING WIVES	RANK FOR SERIOUSNESS	WIVES' COMPLAINTS REGARDING HUSBANDS
Nags me	1	Selfish and inconsiderate
Not affectionate	2	Unsuccessful in business
Selfish and inconsiderate	3	Untruthful
Complains too much	4	Complains too much
Interferes with my hobbies	5	Does not show his affection
Slovenly in appearance	6	Does not talk things over
Quick-tempered	7	Harsh with children
Interferes with my discipline	8	Touchy
Conceited	9	No interest in children
Insincere	10	Not interested in home

state of continuous bliss. There are joys in marriage, but there are duties and responsibilities as well. Sometimes there are financial problems; sooner or later there is bound to be sickness; there are sometimes disagreements. The marriage ceremony does not miraculously make two individuals with different heredities and environments into one personality. After the ceremony they still have their individual likes and dislikes.

At one time, some engaged men and women were measured on 38 aspects of personality. The records were kept, and twenty years later the measurements were repeated for 116 of the couples who had married and continued to live together as husband and wife. In general, there had been little tendency, with the passing of the years, for the husbands to become more like their wives or for the wives to become more like their husbands. In fact, for 21 of the 38 aspects of personality, coefficients of correlation were slightly lower after twenty years than they had been at the time of the original measurements. Yet these marriages had not ended in divorce.

It is not necessarily undesirable for married persons to disagree. In fact, disagreement on some topics seems to be necessary if there is to be a high degree of marital happiness. Disagreement is dangerous only when it results in quarreling or in the giving up by one person of any attempt to understand the other's point of view.

Unfortunately, marriage sometimes results in unhappiness instead of happiness. Is there any basic cause for unhappy marriages (besides the factor of too sudden marriages just mentioned)? Many factors enter into the problem, but let us consider the results of a study made by one psychologist. He asked a group of men to indicate the things they disliked about their wives. The wives were given an opportunity to indicate what they did not like about their husbands. The ten principal grievances, arranged in order of seriousness, are indicated in the table above. You will note that "selfish and inconsiderate" stands high on both lists and that selfishness and inconsiderateness exist in most of the other grievances listed. Men and women cannot be very selfish and also be happy in marriage. Selfishness is characteristic of children's love, but, as we have seen, the scope of love should expand as a person matures.

Does having friends contribute to happiness in marriage? Romantic love is closely related to friendship. Married persons should be romantically in love with only one person. There is evidence, however, that those who learn to have pleasant social relationships with members of both sexes are the same ones who learn how to make their marriages successful. For example, one study of 526 married couples produced these findings: Of the husbands who reported that they had few or almost no men friends, 40.0 percent had made a poor marital adjustment, 29.2 percent had made a fair adjustment, and only 30.8 percent had made a good adjustment. On the other hand, the men who reported having several men friends were more successful in their marital adjustment. The percentages for poor, fair, and good adjustments were 21.2, 31.8, and 47.0, respectively. Husbands who reported that they had almost no women friends were found to have marital adjustments rated as follows: poor, 48.2 percent; fair, 18.5 percent; good, 33.3 percent. On the other hand, those men reporting that they had several women friends (these were friendships, not romantic loves) had marital adjustments rated as follows: poor, 22.0 percent; fair, 26.2 percent; good, 51.8 percent.

Similarly, wives who had almost no friends of either sex were less well-adjusted than wives who had more friendships.

There was some indication, however, that having many friends is less related to good marital adjustment than having a small number of friends. Possibly, if a person has too many friends, he may spend much of his time with them instead of devoting himself to learning how to make the most successful home adjustment.

What are some characteristics of a happy marriage? What factors tend to contribute to a happy marriage and successful home adjustment? In one study, 450 persons over sixty-five years of age were interviewed and asked to tell which period in their lives they thought had been the happiest. Fifty percent said that they had been happiest between the ages of twenty-five and forty-five. Twenty percent said that they had been happiest between the ages of fifteen and twenty-five. These ages are the ones in which marriage, starting a family, and guiding children's lives usually take place. For these 450 persons, the chief determining factor in happiness appeared to be marriage and family life. For those who married and had families, the happiest period of their lives was when they were working hardest and bringing up a family.

Happiness in marriage is related to the desire for children and having children. The previously mentioned investigation of 526 married couples included examining the relationship between marital adjustment and the

THE FAMILY GROUP

desire for children. The individuals were asked whether or not they desired children. It was already known whether they had children and, if so, how many. The relationships between desire for children, having children, and marital adjustment are indicated in the table below.

Notice that desire for children is very directly related to success in marital adjustment. Perhaps you will be surprised to note that couples who desired children but did not have any were better adjusted than couples who both desired children and had them. Children bring many problems into the home. Later in this chapter we shall discuss some of these problems and the suggestions of psychologists concerning them. Perhaps couples who desired children and who had them would be better adjusted if they knew more about solving the problems of child guidance.

Friendships, unselfishness, and the desire for children are important to marital happiness. The list in the next column presents some other factors related to marital happiness.

Cooperative attitude

Respect for each other's individuality

Self-confidence

Health

Economic sufficiency (not necessarily wealth)

Happy childhood in the lives of the couple

Having lived as a child in a home with happily married parents

Wholesome sex education in childhood and absence of degrading sex attitudes

Wholesome sex harmony between husband and wife

Common interests and friends

Lack of conflict with the mother or father

Attachment to the parents and to brothers and sisters

Firm but not harsh discipline in childhood

Parental approval of the marriage, both on the side of the wife and the side of the husband

Similarity of religious belief, ethnic background, amount of formal edu-

Relationships Between Desire for Children, Having Children, and Marital Adjustment

CHILDREN AND DESIRE FOR THEM	MARITAL ADJUSTMENT (PERCENT)		
	POOR	FAIR	GOOD
None, but desired	9.4	26.9	63.7
One or more, and desired	20.4	32.8	46.8
None and not desired by husband, wife, or both	55.0	24.3	20.7
One or more but not desired by husband, wife, or both	66.7	22.2	11.1

THE FAMILY AND OTHER SMALL GROUPS

cation, intellectual ability, and socio-economic class

One more research study will be mentioned. A psychologist secured the cooperation of 300 engaged couples and gave them a battery of psychological tests. After nearly twenty years, he was able to contact all 600 of these persons and repeat his measurements. Of the original 300 engaged couples, 278 (92.7 percent) had married. Of these 278 marriages, 12 (4.3 percent) had been terminated by death and 39 (14.0 percent) had been terminated by divorce. What were the characteristics of the couples whose marriages had lasted?

One characteristic of these couples was that they had not married while they were in their teens. For the persons tested after approximately twenty years, the average age of the men at the time of the original testing was 26.7 years and of the women 24.7 years. Nearly 90 percent of these men and women were between twenty-one and thirty when first tested. The couples were not of low intellectual ability or limited schooling. A group test at the time of original testing indicated an average IQ of 115 for the men and 112 for the women. Of the men, 75 percent had attended college for at least one year, and approximately two out of three of the women had attended college for at least some time. Furthermore, these men and women had agreed to and did take part in a long-term scientific research project, a fact which in itself indicated intellectual and educational superiority. One other characteristic was that many of the couples had religious affiliations; 82 percent of the men and 89 percent of the women indicated membership in some church.

It is of interest to note that of the 22 broken engagements (out of the 300 total engagements), only 5 of the 44 individuals involved did not later marry someone else.

From your supplementary reading, and possibly from your own observations, can you suggest other factors which might be related to happiness in marriage?

With so many variables involved, the goal of making a happy marriage may seem difficult, indeed. Further research, including the vast possibilities of more detailed analysis through the use of computers, may some day provide psychologists with more specific answers to the question "What factors tend to contribute to a happy marriage?" Meanwhile, young persons must be sure to check that not too many unfavorable factors exist before the marriage, and they should resolve to do their best to solve their problems after marriage.

LOVE BETWEEN CHILDREN AND PARENTS

Is love between children and parents "natural" or learned? Is *filial love* — the love of children for their parents — "natural" or learned? You may say, "Of course, children naturally love their parents." By "naturally" you would probably mean that there is some kind of inherited force that makes children love those who gave them birth. It is true that the great ma-

Parents who give their children love and include them in activities are also giving them an important basic security.

jority of children do love their parents more than they love any other adults in the world. But does this love exist because the parents gave them birth or because the children have learned to love their parents?

From our previous discussion of love, the answer to the above question can only be that one learns to love his parents. We have seen that baby monkeys may even learn to love surrogate mothers made of wire and cloth (pages 348–49). Because it is learned, filial love is a finer thing than if it were merely the result of some mysterious, compelling force. The human baby comes into the world a very helpless creature. He can take food if it is presented to him, but he cannot go about seeking his food. He needs to be kept warm. Who usually supplies the infant with food, clothing, and shelter? Of course, the parents are usually the ones who take care of the baby. This care goes on for years, during which time the child learns to love his parents.

Do children learn to love foster parents? Could a child love foster parents as "naturally" and as much as he could love his biological parents? Suppose that very soon after birth an infant is adopted by strangers who care for the child as if he were their own. Would he love them as much as he would his biological parents? In terms of love as learned, the only answer is yes.

Take the case of a girl who had been adopted as an infant. For years she did not know that she was an adopted child. The foster parents did not tell her, because of the mistaken fear that she would not love them if she knew. Then one day some neighbors felt it their duty to tell the girl that she was "merely" an adopted child. The girl did not believe them and ran to the house to ask her foster parents whether or not she was an adopted child. Although they feared that she would no longer love them, the foster parents told her the truth. She immediately made this significant statement, "Oh, I love you more than ever now, because you have done so much for me and have loved me even though I was not your own child." Actually, psychologically speaking, she *was* their own child.

Is parental love a learning process? The love of parents for their children is spoken of as *parental love*. In the normal home, parents look forward to the coming of an infant. During the months of waiting for its birth, they are learning to love it. They are overjoyed when it finally arrives. If they have not seen other newborn infants, the parents may be disappointed at first in the appearance of their newborn child. But a newborn baby loses his wrinkles and red face fairly soon after birth. And as they care for him, they learn to love him more and more.

Sometimes people speak of "mother love" as though it were something a mother experiences merely because she is a mother. The great majority of mothers certainly do love their children, but they learn to love them. The mother plays a very important role in the life of the child both before and after birth. It is during this long period that she normally learns to love the child. There is no reason, however, to think that the mother has any more "natural" love for the children in the home than the father has — except insofar as the mother may have more opportunity to care for, and so learn to love, the children.

A psychologist reports that at one time he was on the witness stand in a divorce case. Because the intellectual ability of the child involved was thought to be unusual, the child's intelligence became a factor in determining whether the mother or the father should receive custody of the child. Therefore, the psychologist had been asked to administer an intelligence test and to interpret the results. Following the psychologist's technical report, the lawyer for the mother asked, "In your opinion as a psychologist, isn't it true that a mother naturally has more love for a child to whom she has given birth than does the father?" Through this question the lawyer assumed he would increase his client's chances of receiving the care of her child. He quickly dismissed the psychologist as a witness when the psychologist stated that in his opinion the mere physiological processes of motherhood would not in themselves cause the mother to have any more love than the father had for the child, since love was fundamentally a matter of learning.

Psychologists cannot accept the popular belief that parents "naturally" love their children. Parental love as a matter of learning is a more simple and scientifically accurate explanation and so is more acceptable to psychologists.

Do parents always love their children? Occasionally, married persons do not want children in the home. They may think that children are a source of annoyance or a financial burden. Their love for any children born to them is quite limited. Their attitudes toward children prevent them from learning to love children.

To give another example of unlearned parental love, the father and mother of an illegitimate child are biologically its parents, but often they do not want to learn to love the child born

THE FAMILY GROUP

to them. In fact, they may abandon the child or put him up for adoption as soon as possible.

In the section on filial love, you saw that children learn to love foster parents just as they learn to love their biological parents. Suppose that in a hospital each of two babies were given to the parents of the other. (Hospitals are very careful, however, to prevent this kind of accident.) Would not the two sets of parents learn to love the children who were not biologically their own? A man and a wife who are unable to have offspring often find parental happiness in learning to love adopted children. As in other forms of love, parental love becomes even more wonderful when we remember that it comes from learning rather than from mere blind force.

THE FAMILY'S MENTAL HEALTH

In the unit on mental health, we made the point that prevention is better than cure in problems of mental health. We shall now consider the area in which the most effective preventive work can be done—the training of children.

Most of you will marry and have children. If you are to be good parents, you must be prepared to apply principles of mental hygiene in the training of your children. Probably at present you have many opportunities to be with children in your home, in your friends' homes, and in other social situations. Possibly you take care of children while their parents are away. What better time than now to learn how to

guide children so that they will grow into well-adjusted and happy adults?

Some parents look for a book or books that will tell them just what to do whenever a problem arises with their children. In your study of psychology, you have learned something about the complexness of human behavior. It is quite obvious that there are no simple solutions to many of the problems of child guidance. It is far better to understand basic principles of psychology and then to apply these principles to specific problems as they arise.

What are some symptoms of poor mental health in children? The following list describes some symptoms of a child who is having difficulties in his adjustment to life.

1. The child who is not reasonably satisfied with his own particular life situation is probably not enjoying good mental health. Most children desire toys they do not have, but there is something basically wrong when the child is never satisfied with his toys. The child who never likes his playmates, or who constantly wishes that he or she had been born the opposite sex, is not facing life in a desirable way.

2. Most children often enjoy being the center of attention, but the child who constantly demands the attention of other children and adults is indicating a basic feeling of inferiority and insecurity.

3. Children should learn to take responsibility. The child who is overconcerned about almost everything, however, is probably striving toward impossible perfection.

4. Children must be taught about germs and the need for cleanliness, but the child who is unduly concerned about his health and cleanliness may become an adult with poor mental health.

5. Baby talk and other babyish mannerisms are cute in babies. The older child who clings to such babyish habits too long is resisting learning to achieve social satisfaction in a more mature manner.

6. Certain habits suggest that a child is in need of help rather than punishment if he is to develop good mental health. Habits such as crying too easily, chewing on parts of his clothing, having his feelings hurt easily, wishing to eat all the time even when not hungry, having temper tantrums, and so on are all observed rather commonly in children. Nevertheless, such habits need attention.

7. It must not be thought, however, that all emotional behavior on the part of a child is indicative of poor mental health. It is quite normal for a child to jump up and down when very pleased, to clap his hands, shout, be enthusiastic, to sing as he plays. In fact, the child who does not display such emotional behavior may lack good mental health.

Do children need guidance in social problems? An adult is likely to think that the child has no social problems, that he lives in a world in which everyone is kind to him. It is true that children's social problems are not identical to those of adults. Nevertheless, children do have difficulty in adjusting their lives to the lives of adults and of other children in their environment. One psy-

Children should be encouraged to express their exuberance. A lack of emotional behavior indicates poor mental health.

chologist asked a group of 275 second- and third-grade children some questions about their social problems. Nearly half the children said that other children and adults were mean to them. Boys, more frequently than girls, reported that both adults and other children were mean to them. City children were subject to more meanness than were rural children.

Twenty percent of the boys in this study and nearly as high a percentage of the girls felt that no one at home loved them. Approximately 40 percent of the boys and 35 percent of the girls said that someone at home was so mean to them that they often became angry.

One way to help a child achieve increasing independence is to give her a responsibility, such as feeding her dog.

media, he develops attitudes favorable toward war and unfavorable toward peace, he may come to believe that war is glorious but that peace is disgraceful. If he is taught to consider peoples of other nations or ethnic groups necessarily wrong just because they do not agree with the opinions of his own group, he is destined to have a narrow basis by which to understand others. Training for world social participation must include not only national patriotism but understanding of other nations as well. Heroes of peace must be honored as well as those who were heroes in war.

How can the child be guided in ways of freedom and responsibility? Good mental health on the part of the parents is necessary for the development of good mental health in the child. Parents must be able to love their children wisely, for unwise parental love can do harm to a child. "Mother love" has been appropriately termed "smother love" in those cases where the mother so smothered the development of the child that he does not mature emotionally and socially. For the best interests of the child, he must have increasing amounts of freedom.

Probably in the great majority of the homes, the parents and brothers and sisters did love these children. The important point is that so many children felt that they were not loved. Feelings of insecurity had developed. A child is not enjoying good mental health when he feels that he is living in a hostile environment. Such a child is not being prepared for community, state, national, and international citizenship.

A child should receive guidance to prepare him for participation in the social problems of his country and of the world. If, through parades, movies, television programs, and other mass

In one study a psychologist asked fathers and mothers to answer a questionnaire concerning their attitudes toward freedom and responsibility for a child as contrasted with strict control. The behavior of the children of these parents was rated by the nursery school teachers of the children. It was found that parents who expressed approval of freedom and responsibility for children had children whose behavior was judged to be considerably more favorable than unfavorable. On the other hand, parents who expressed approval of strict parental control had children whose behavior was judged to be more unfavorable than favorable.

It is much easier to direct, interfere, criticize, and tell a child just what to do and what not to do than it is to guide him toward freedom and responsibility. Yet it is the latter path that wise parents try to follow. Of course, guiding children in the development of freedom and responsibility does not mean teaching them to disregard the rights and welfare of others. Society demands that the individual accept responsibilities as well as enjoy personal freedom.

What are some specific problems in child guidance? We shall continue our consideration of child guidance within the home. Although there are many areas in which a greater knowledge of how to guide a child's behavior can be helpful, we shall discuss only six topics: discipline, lying, cheating, fears, fairy tales, and television.

THE PROBLEM OF DISCIPLINE

What is the psychological meaning of discipline? The problem of discipline must be faced by everyone who is responsible for guiding a child's behavior. Many persons use the words "discipline" and "punishment" interchangeably. We shall use *discipline* to mean the entire program of adapting the child to social life. Punishment may occasionally be necessary in this program, but it plays only a minor and an emergency role.

Prevention of socially undesirable behavior is easier and more effective than the attempted correction of such behavior after it has developed. It is much better to place dishes on high shelves than it is to punish the child who breaks dishes easily reached on low shelves. Providing little sticks to play with is much better than punishing the child for playing with matches.

The ultimate goal of discipline is the achievement of self-control or self-discipline. A well-adjusted adult does not have to be told what to do and when to do it. He disciplines himself. The child can learn self-discipline only through experience with self-discipline. If an adult controls a child's behavior by telling him exactly what to do on all occasions, the adult may secure what seems at the time to be faultless behavior from the child. Yet that child is not learning self-control. Discipline should be a matter of guidance, or leadership, and should rely on example rather than coercion.

We may think that a child should pick up his playthings. We could achieve this result by commanding the child to pick up his toys and then rewarding him with candy for doing so — or spanking him if he does not comply. But if we always use such methods, how will the child learn self-regulation? On the other hand, we can suggest to the child that he is old enough now to take care of his own possessions. We could mention how much neater the room will be after he picks up his toys. We might suggest that he take the responsibility for putting his toys away each evening now that he is so grown-up. The child who is disciplined by being trained to accept his little responsibilities is being prepared for a responsible adulthood.

Why must discipline be consistent? One fundamental principle of discipline is that treatment of the child be consistent. If one day we permit him to scatter his toys all over the floor and the next day we forbid him to do so, how can we expect him to know what is desirable behavior?

When told not to take his toys out of the toy chest, the child will probably ask, "Why?" This is a perfectly reasonable question. Yet many children receive the answer, "Never mind why. Do as you are told!" The adult has a reason for telling the child not to scatter his toys around on a particular day. Perhaps friends are coming, and the house should be neat and orderly. Why not take time to explain this reason to the child? The explanation may take just a little more time than the command "Do as you are told!" but it will help to prepare the child for a responsible adulthood.

When two or more adults share the responsibility of training a child, they must be careful to keep this joint training consistent. If the father says, "You may ride your tricycle around the block," and the mother says, "Don't ride your tricycle around the block," how can the child be expected to know what is socially desirable behavior? The child will soon learn to take advantage of such disagreement. Adults engaged jointly in the serious business of training children must have frequent conferences and agree on fundamental principles of discipline.

Should a child be given extrinsic rewards? An *extrinsic reward* is an artificial one, not directly or logically associated with the behavior being rewarded. Should extrinsic rewards be used in child training? Should we promise to give Johnny a penny if he will eat his spinach? Or promise Betty a new doll if she will hang up her clothes every day? Such artificial rewards must be used sparingly. Any reward loses its value if given frequently and for too little achievement.

It is true that artificial rewards produce temporarily desirable behavior. Johnny eats his spinach and Betty hangs up her clothes. In the long run, however, the results of using rewards of this kind may be quite undesirable. The giving of paper stars, buttons, and merit cards is a less objectionable form of rewarding children than that of bribing them with pennies or presents. The star, button, or card has value only insofar as it is related to desirable behavior; it may help the child to recognize the value of social approval. A child who does not feel the need for learning the alphabet may learn it in order to have a star placed after his name on a school chart. Along with the alphabet, the child learns that even though a task may be unpleasant, it can be satisfying if it brings the approval of his parents, teacher, and classmates.

Social leaders find that adults as well as children appreciate artificial rewards. The Red Cross, community chests, and other philanthropic organizations give buttons and window stickers to those who contribute to their causes. The buttons and stickers give recipients the satisfaction of feeling part of an

THE FAMILY AND OTHER SMALL GROUPS

important social group, which approves of them.

When artificial rewards are given to children, the adult dispensing them should strive to help the children understand the social value of the behavior being rewarded. The adult should distinguish between the social value and the actual worth of the artificial rewards by themselves.

When should intrinsic rewards be used?
An *intrinsic reward* is logically associated with the behavior being rewarded. It is better to train a child to work for intrinsic rewards than for extrinsic rewards and, whenever possible, intrinsic rewards should be substituted for artificial ones. Johnny is interested in growing up to be a big, strong man like his father—or maybe like his favorite television hero. If we explain to Johnny that eating a good breakfast will help him to achieve this goal and if we weigh and measure him frequently, with appropriate comments on his growing muscles, the penny or the paper star becomes unnecessary or at most supplementary. Betty is interested in being a woman just like Mother. If we explain to her that Mother puts her own clothes away and if occasionally we comment on how grown-up Betty is getting to be, a new doll or an award button will not be necessary.

Should artificial punishment be used?
Closely related to the question of rewards is the question of punishment. Should Johnny be spanked if he does not eat his spinach? Should Betty be slapped if she does not hang up her clothes? For many adults, the answer to these questions seems to be, "Yes, it works." Or they quote, "Spare the rod and spoil the child." Yet when we discussed punishment in connection with operant conditioning in Chapter 3, we learned that the effectiveness of artificial punishment is uncertain. Artificial punishment only sometimes extinguishes behavior, while reward usually reinforces behavior.

Since artificial punishments are not always very effective, why are they used so frequently? Perhaps the answer is to be understood in terms of the effect that punishment has upon parents or other adults, rather than in terms of the permanent effects of punishment upon children. When a child does something of which the adult does not approve and is punished immediately, the child ceases his undesirable behavior for the time being. That is, the adult's action is immediately reinforced by the cessation of the child's annoying behavior. This kind of child punishment–adult reinforcement occurs a few times. The adult quickly learns that he can operate on the environment to bring about a desired result by punishing the child. (See pages 52–60 for a review of operant conditioning.)

Although it is doubtful that artificial punishment will be eliminated in child training, the effects of punishment should lead us to be cautious about its use. It seems clear that punishment merely suppresses behavior but does not result in the desired unlearning.

For evidence that punishment suppresses but does not change the total picture of undesired behavior, we have the results of animal experiments. In one experiment two groups of rats learned to press a bar in order to obtain food. Then this response of both groups was extinguished by not providing them with food when they pressed the bar. In addition to withholding their food, one group received electric shocks during the first few times that they pressed the bar. Then no more shocks were given. It is true that the group punished with electric shocks temporarily made fewer bar pressings during the first stage of extinction than did the group that simply had food withheld. By the end of the experiment, however, the punished group had made as many bar pressings as the group that was not punished. In other words, the punishment did not weaken the bar-pressing behavior over any period of time. As soon as the punishment ceased, the response reoccurred at full strength. Since punishment fails to impress upon the child what he should do, it does not have a lasting effect, although it may repress undesired behavior temporarily. (To review reward and punishment, see pages 59–60.)

If punishment is to be administered, ordinarily we would expect that it should be administered every time the undesirable behavior takes place. Yet there is some experimental evidence that intermittent punishment may be more effective than punishment administered every time the undesirable behavior occurs. (Partial reinforcement is discussed on pages 50, 56–57.)

On what occasions is artificial punishment unavoidable? Although punishment is not the soundest way of dealing with undesirable behavior, it sometimes seems unavoidable. Some adults seem to require artificial punishment to maintain some semblance of socially approved behavior. Such adults are not socially well-adjusted. Possibly they had too much artificial punishment when they were children and cannot understand any other kind. Our aim is to guide children so that as adults they will not have to be controlled by police and prisons.

There are some occasions when artificial punishment must be used with children. Corporal punishments such as spanking are artificial because they are not the logical consequences of undesirable behavior. Although punishment should be the logical consequence of the undesirable act, logical punishment can hardly be arranged in many cases. And at times the intrinsic punishment itself is undesirable. For example, the logical consequence of playing in the street is injury or death in traffic, a very undesirable punishment. It may be necessary to use some form of artificial punishment temporarily as a deterrent, especially with very young children.

How should corporal punishment be administered? If corporal punishment must be used, it should not be administered while the adult is angry. Punishment should be only for the purpose of producing socially desirable behavior on the part of the child. Punishment administered in anger is usually more severe than is necessary for learning purposes. When we are angry, we do not realize our own strength.

Another guideline is that punishment should be administered immediately following the undesirable behavior. This is simply an application of the principle of conditioning, studied in the chapter on learning. Nevertheless, it is better not to punish immediately if the adult cannot control his anger.

An even better rule is that a child should be punished at the beginning of undesired behavior rather than after the behavior has been completed. Many children like to poke wires or other metal objects into electric outlets. Why not? They see their parents plug in lamps, the vacuum cleaner, and the television. Yet poking a wire into an outlet can be dangerous to the child. It is better psychologically, as well as for his safety, to punish the child as he prepares to poke the wire into the outlet rather than after he has done so.

If corporal punishment for undesirable behavior seems necessary, the punishment can be made more effective if, as soon as possible, some similar but desirable behavior can be reinforced. If we punish a child for putting a wire into an electric outlet, it would be more effective if he then began putting pegs into his pegboard, for which he would immediately get a pat on the back or some other reinforcement.

Can physical punishment cause problems in the child's mental health? As we have seen, punishment usually fails to impress upon the child what he should do. In addition, punishment may cause the child to become emotionally upset, especially if the punishment is very severe. One study of 376 children examined the relationship between feeding problems and the extent to which children were punished. Seventeen percent of the mothers who rarely or never used physical punishment reported feeding problems with their children. Twenty percent of the mothers who used physical punishment occasionally to fairly often reported feeding problems. Of those mothers who regularly used physical punishment, however, 36 percent reported feeding problems. Evidently, frequent use of physical punishment upsets some children enough to cause problems in areas unrelated to the punishment, such as feeding.

Sometimes parents say they never punish their children by using corporal punishment. The implication is that they have done nothing to injure their children's mental health. This may be true. On the other hand, remember that such scolding statements as "I'm ashamed of you," "I won't love you anymore if you ever do that again," or "Nice children don't behave like that" are a form of punishment that can also be psychologically harmful to a child.

What is some experimental evidence about reward vs. punishment? If it is necessary to use reward or punishment, it is usually better to use reward rather than punishment. We shall mention one further experiment that bears out this principle. A psychologist had four groups of school children work on a series of tests in arithmetic addition for five consecutive days. The groups, designated as first, second, third, and fourth, were equal in ability at the

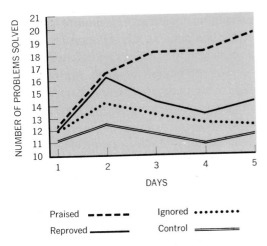

The relative effects of reward, punishment, and indifference on efficiency

ignored group, they seem to have profited slightly by hearing others praised or reproved.

Does the personality of the child affect the use of praise and blame? Although psychologists generally consider praise superior to blame, there are times when this is not always true. In one case, 124 fifth-grade pupils were given a simple work test. The teacher praised them by placing a G (good) or blamed them by placing a P (poor) on the test papers, regardless of the work accomplished.

The children in this study had all been given a personality inventory. Although the children did not know it, they had been divided into two groups. Those in one group were basically introverted; those in the other group were basically extroverted. It was found that praise, if repeated often enough, increased the work output of introverted children, while blame increased the work output of extroverted children. Such a study as this suggests that both praise and blame may be used effectively as techniques of discipline. In using one or the other, it is necessary to take into consideration individual differences in personality.

THE PROBLEM OF LYING

Although most people agree that children should be guided so that they will tell the truth and be honest, studies show that many children and adults do not tell the truth.

What is lying? Dictionaries usually define *lying* as telling falsehoods with

beginning of the experiment. Each day the first group was called to the front of the room, and the members were publicly praised for their work. The second group was called to the front of the room each day and the members were publicly reprimanded for poor work. To all four groups of school children praise was a form of reward and a reprimand was a form of punishment. The third group was ignored, although the members were in the same room and could hear the others being praised or reproved. The fourth group served as a control. They were in another room and could hear neither the praise nor the reproof. The results of the experiment are indicated graphically above.

You will note in the figure at the top of the page that, at first, reward and punishment were equally effective in producing desired school activity. After the first session, however, punishment lost its effect, whereas reward continued to be effective. As for the

the intent to deceive. Children often define lying simply as saying something for which they will be punished. Unfortunately, children are often punished for lying when they are not lying according to the adult definition. The child may tell something he believes is true which is untrue. At this early stage of learning, he may be confusing fact with that which is not fact. Perhaps he confuses a fairy tale with truth. He may tell an imaginative story which adults interpret as a lie—although they would not condemn an equally imaginative story told by an adult fiction writer. As a general rule, we can say that up to around the age of four, the "untruths" of children are not lies; that is, their tales do not involve deliberate intent to deceive.

Even adults are not always truthful. We do not frown strongly upon a lie that is told to protect a friend. Many of us may tell "cultural" lies. For example, a girl may say that she is going to be busy on a certain evening rather than tell a boy the truth—that she does not wish to have a date with him. Adults must appreciate the difficulty children experience in learning to distinguish between truthfulness and untruthfulness. They must not overlook children's lies in the sense of pretending not to notice them. On the other hand, they must look for the basic causes for any lies their children may tell. A lie may be a consequence of the social immaturity of a child, or it may be a symptom of a basic problem of poor mental health.

Why do children tell lies? The child may tell a tall tale, which is obviously untruthful, to attract attention to himself. Such a lie should be regarded as a symptom of feelings of inferiority. Instead of being punished, the child should be helped to find other ways of satisfying his desire for approval and recognition.

The child may lie because an adult suggests the lie to him. The mother may say, "You did well on that test at school today, didn't you? Because if you didn't . . .!" The child may have made a poor grade on the test, but how can he answer the question truthfully when it is phrased in such a way? Sometimes children lie because adults force them to give an immediate answer, whereas the children might give truthful answers if they had enough time to think them out.

The child may purposefully tell an untruth in self-defense. The child who has accidentally broken a dish is asked whether or not he did so. He may know from past experience that he will be punished for breaking the dish if he tells the truth; therefore, he lies. In such a case the fault is more with the parents' methods of child guidance than with the child.

Selfishness is often the basic motive for lying. The child may lie to protect himself at the expense of others. He may say that a brother or sister broke the dish that he actually had broken. Possibly his lie is an attempt to get revenge on the brother or sister for something displeasing they may have done to him.

Among young children there is a tendency to escape from a very unpleasant situation by denying that it ever existed. They lie about an event, trying to make it not so by saying it is not so. Sometimes adults show similar behavior upon receiving very bad news. They may say, "Oh, no! it can't be true."

When under emotional stress, the child may even convince himself, at least for the moment, that his statement is true, although adults call it a lie. Often, however, when adults make similar untrue statements they call it rationalizing, not lying.

THE PROBLEM OF CHEATING

Cheating among children is not unusual. In Chapter 6 you learned some basic causes for cheating and some ways in which psychologists measure cheating. Instances were given of children cheating in schoolwork and in party games. Sometimes, children cheat as a kind of thrilling sport. "Getting away with it" is a game. If they win, the other children will look up to them as being clever.

Do children learn to cheat? Most children are not specifically and directly taught to cheat. In fact, most children are probably taught that cheating is wrong. But psychologists have found that there is often little relationship between moral knowledge and moral conduct. Unfortunately, the child may readily learn to cheat from the example of adults and other children. A psychologist asked 376 children in the primary grades, "Do the boys and girls often try to cheat you?" Of the boys, 42 percent replied in the affirmative. Of the girls, 33 percent replied in the affirmative. Then the children were

asked, "Is it all right to cheat if no one sees you?" Nine percent of the boys and 12 percent of the girls answered yes. In other words, one child out of ten thought that it was all right to cheat if no one observed that he was cheating. Obviously, ways must be found for children to develop attitudes that are favorable toward honesty and unfavorable toward dishonesty. Situations must be provided that will give children an opportunity to feel secure and successful without having to resort to dishonesty in an effort to achieve their goals.

What is cheating like in schools? Cheating does not disappear with the passing of childhood. You may know of instances of cheating in high school. It should be noted, however, that students who admitted to cheating in surveys had poorer final marks than noncheaters, in spite of their cheating.

If we see someone stealing, offering a bribe, or using his social position to secure some special privilege, we are likely to become infuriated. If we know that a small child cheats in school, we are quick to condemn him. Yet if we see someone cheating on a high school test or know that a student hands in another student's report as though it were his own, we hesitate to report the incident or even to reprimand the cheater. Indirectly we are offering our approval of cheating even though we do not cheat ourselves.

In some high schools a teacher who has several sections of the same course will give an examination in each of the classes on the same day. The students in the ten o'clock class ask the students in the previous class what questions were asked. The same thing happens for subsequent classes. This gives the students in later classes some advantage, even though the teacher may not ask exactly the same questions in all classes. Isn't this a form of cheating?

What is cheating like in colleges? Surveys have indicated that nearly half of the college students tested admitted to cheating at some point during their college life. And there may be other students who cheated but did not admit to it.

In one college, the professors in a certain department agreed to give an objective departmental examination, using the same question for all classes. Before the day of the examination, the professors announced that the same questions would be asked in all classes. It was discovered that students in nine o'clock classes scored better than the students in eight o'clock classes. Students in ten o'clock classes scored better than students in nine o'clock classes and much better than students in eight o'clock classes. Throughout the day, mean scores increased. When they returned the scored examination to the students, the professors announced that marks for all students in the department would be made up in terms of the normal frequency distribution. Students in the eight o'clock classes received many D's and F's, whereas students in late afternoon classes received mostly A's and B's.

At the time of the next departmental examination, it was announced that the same policy would be followed. But

Exchanging answers with someone else in an exam is detrimental both to the individuals involved and to the class, yet students sometimes condone such cheating.

this time scores for the eight o'clock classes fell into a normal frequency distribution without skewing. Even the scores in the late afternoon classes fell into a normal frequency distribution and had the same range and median as the scores in the early morning classes. This change in class scores occurred because students in early classes had not told the questions to students in later classes, since to do so would only lower their own marks. Cheating seems to take place among at least some college students when circumstances permit it but not when the students giving away the information are going to be penalized for doing so.

What can be done about cheating? Most students cheat to raise their marks. Yet even if there is no cheating, marks, as they are given in many schools today, may be inaccurate measurements of actual student accomplishment. In time various mechanical aids and new teaching methods may free teachers from having to spend so much of their time teaching facts and then basing students' marks on the acquisition of these facts. Teachers may eventually be free to guide students mainly in the areas of creative thinking and the development of social values. Under these conditions students could compete with their own previous records rather than with the records of other students. (In some schools, traditional marks have already disappeared.) Relieved of the pressure of competitive marks, isn't it possible that someday students may no longer cheat in school?

Probably in a relatively few years you will be parents and will have children in school. How will you react to any known cases of cheating by your children?

THE PROBLEM OF FEAR

Children are afraid more often than adults realize. A psychologist questioned some children in primary grades and found that 31 percent of the boys and 49 percent of the girls admitted that they were often afraid of things. Probably even more of the children than would admit it were frequently afraid.

Are fears learned? Is it "just natural" for children to be afraid of the dark, of dead animals, of white rats, or of a policeman? To the contrary, the evidence indicates that such fears are not inborn. Children learn these fears.

The snake, in particular, has earned a reputation as an object of people's fears. Do children have an unlearned fear of snakes? Do they show signs of fear the very first time they see a snake? We have laboratory evidence that even adult chimpanzees fear snakes the first time they see one. The chimpanzees tested had been raised from birth in a laboratory, where it was known that they had never seen a snake before. Human children often show fear of a snake the first time they see one, too.

However, not all babies fear snakes on first exposure. An infant chimpanzee that is frequently exposed to snake-like objects from birth does not show fear the first time it sees an actual snake. Children whose parents are fond of snakes and keep them as pets throughout the life of the child do not show fear of snakes. Perhaps it is the strangeness and the sudden slithering movements of the snake that make some human and chimpanzee babies afraid of them, not the fact that the organism is a snake. Since fear of snakes does not usually develop until a child is two or three years of age, the child by then has had many opportunities to learn to be afraid of similar strange objects and creatures.

What are some other things that children fear? Death is a concept that a child finds almost impossible to comprehend. Therefore, he easily learns to fear death. By the age of five, many children have a fear of dying. Perhaps a

THE FAMILY AND OTHER SMALL GROUPS

grandparent, other relative, or playmate died following an illness or an accident. To soften the fact of death, the parents may tell the child that the deceased is asleep. The child soon realizes, however, that the person who meant so much to him is not around anymore. Is it any wonder that some children become terrified at the thought of going to bed at night if sleeping means death to them? Is it any wonder that some children want a light left on in their bedroom so that if they awaken they can be sure at once that they are not "asleep"?

Children can learn to be afraid of fear itself. Especially in the case of boys, the child who is experiencing fear is told, "Don't be afraid. Be brave. Be a little man." Since he is very anxious to become a man, being afraid means to him that he is not masculine and so he fears being afraid. Unfortunately, he does not know that brave soldiers in combat are often quite afraid, show their fear, and are willing to admit that they are afraid.

Fear of a specific object or situation that becomes very intense, exaggerated, and apparently unreasonable is known as a *phobia*. Prefixes can be added to the word "phobia" to designate the nature of the fear. For example, *acrophobia* is a fear of high places; *claustrophobia* is a fear of closed or confined places. Many phobias have their origin in childhood experiences, although an adult often does not remember the situation that produced the phobia.

There are certain situations that a child must learn to fear for his own safety. A child must learn to be careful

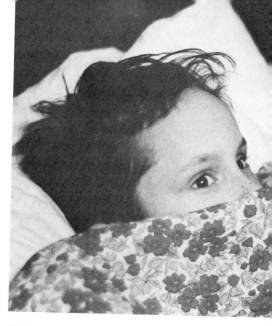

Sights and sounds that are familiar to a child by day may seem strange, unfamiliar, and arouse fear at night.

close up paw

of moving cars. He must learn that under some circumstances fire is dangerous. He must learn that some substances are unsafe to eat. He must have wholesome fears of those dangers everyone must face. This does not mean, of course, that he ought to be terrified by every situation.

What causes fear in children? One source of fear in children is the sensation of falling. Sudden removal of bodily support produces an emotional reaction in very young infants which is usually interpreted as fear. If an infant is accidentally dropped he will show a fear reaction even though he lands quite safely on a nice soft mattress. An infant held in an elevator that begins a very rapid descent will probably cry in fear.

A loud noise will also cause a fear reaction in infants. An infant may be

THE FAMILY GROUP

This little girl shows no fear in a situation that would frighten many children. She has not learned to be afraid around horses.

quite happy in his crib, he may even be asleep, but if he hears a pan drop or some other loud noise, he will probably start crying.

The suddenness with which a child is stimulated seems to be related to fear. In fact, the suddenness of a noise seems to be more important than the loudness of the noise in causing fear.

Another source of fear is the strangeness of a situation, especially if the situation occurs rather suddenly. Many a carefully planned Christmas festivity for a child has been spoiled by the sudden appearance of a strange man with a strange white beard, wearing a red suit and shouting a strange "Ho! Ho! Ho!"

The older a child becomes, the better he is able to differentiate between the familiar and the strange. As he comes to recognize what is strange to him, the child becomes more likely to react to strangeness by crying or some other expression of fear. The sudden appearance of a stranger will cause panic among chimpanzees who have been accustomed to seeing only a few men who regularly feed them. It has been demonstrated that chimpanzees will show fear even when their regular keepers appear in unfamiliar clothing. Human beings often fear strange people or people dressed in unusual costumes.

If there is any great discrepancy between what a person expects and what actually happens, fear is likely to occur. A child expectantly waiting for his mother to walk through the door sees

THE FAMILY AND OTHER SMALL GROUPS

a dog come running out instead. Although the child is not ordinarily afraid of dogs, there may well be a fear reaction.

Of course, the most common source of human fears seems to depend upon learned expectancies of distress or pain, which begin developing in childhood.

What happens when fear is induced experimentally in rats? We can learn something about the production of fear by examining a laboratory experiment in which fear was produced in rats by means of an electric shock. The apparatus for the experiment consisted of a box that had two compartments, one painted black and the other painted white. Rats were placed in the white compartment and given several brief electric shocks. In the first part of the experiment there was no way for the rat to escape from the white compartment. They jumped and squealed. They were afraid. Thereafter, the rats jumped and squealed whenever they were placed in the white compartment, although they received no more electric shocks. A learned, or conditioned, fear had developed.

The next step in the experiment was to provide a door so that the rats could escape from the white compartment to the black compartment. They quickly learned to open the door and escape. No shock was given in the black compartment, and no shock was ever given in the white compartment after the means of escape was provided. Nevertheless, whenever they were placed in the white compartment, the rats promptly "escaped" into the safe black compartment. They were escaping not from pain, since there was no pain, but from the fear-producing situation.

The child may acquire intense fear of some situation, just as the rats acquired a fear of the white-box situation. As we have seen, if these exaggerated fears persist, the individual has developed a phobia.

How can adults counteract the unfortunate fear experiences of children? Adults cannot prevent every unfortunate experience from taking place, but they can help a child to face fearful experiences as part of life. Some children are afraid because of a personal fear-producing experience. For example, the child who has been hurt in an automobile accident may generalize his fear and become afraid of cars. When a child has a fear experience, adults should not exclaim "Oh!" and "Ah!" and "Poor little thing!" They should remove the danger, care for the child if he has been injured, and assure him that he is safe.

In counteracting unfortunate fear experiences, adults should apply their knowledge of conditioning. If the child has been burned on the stove, he should then have pleasant experiences with the stove—possibly he could watch his mother cook something that he especially likes. If he has learned to be afraid of dogs, an adult may help by playing with a puppy in his presence and encouraging him to pat the puppy. The child who has learned to be afraid of automobiles may be taken for a short ride under as pleasant circumstances as possible, probably in the company of other children who are not afraid.

One psychologist was faced with the problem of helping a child who was afraid of rabbits. To rid the child of this fear, the psychologist used the principle of conditioning. One situation that always brought the child pleasure was eating. While the child was eating, a rabbit was placed just inside the door of the room. The rabbit was safely caged. Day by day, when the child was eating, the rabbit was brought a little farther into the room. Finally the child would pet the rabbit. The fear response was gone. You will note that the psychologist worked slowly and carefully. Otherwise, the child might possibly have learned to be afraid of food instead of learning to enjoy the presence of rabbits.

The child should have opportunities to become acquainted with feared situations on his own, free from compulsion or enticement by adults. He should be able to approach and retreat from the fear-producing situation at his own will. In the case of the fear of rabbits just mentioned, the caged rabbit might have been placed in the child's playroom where the child could gradually come closer to it or retreat, whenever he desired. Experiments indicate that as the child gradually moves closer and closer to the fear-producing situation without showing fear, extinction of that fear is taking place.

A very basic way of dealing with children's fears is to help the children develop skills which will enable them to cope with possible fearful situations. Parents who teach or otherwise provide instruction in swimming and water safety may not only be counteracting unfortunate past experiences, but they are also preventing future unfortunate experiences in the water.

Do adults unintentionally teach or increase a child's fears? Most of the fears that children have are the result of teaching by adults and other children. Sometimes this teaching is not intended by the adult. Perhaps an adult is unreasonably afraid of snakes, even harmless little ones. If, while with a child, he sees a garter snake and shows fear, the child will learn to have the same unreasonable fear. Adults should strive not to show their unreasonable fears in the presence of children.

If we force a child to participate in a feared situation, we are forcing the child to practice an undesirable response that is likely to become even more undesirable. Sometimes well-meaning parents coax their two- or three-year-old children far into the surf. Sooner or later the children are knocked down by big waves and become terrified of the water. Wise parents let their children play along the beach where the water is only a few inches deep, for a whole day if necessary. Later, they will find their children plunging fearlessly into the surf.

As adults, we may be tempted to steer the child away from all experiences which have frightened the child in the past. This, however, would prevent the child from learning how to meet such situations when they reoccur. To steer the child away from all possible fear-producing situations or to shield him carefully from any mention of fearful situations assumes that he will forget his fears over a period of time. Yet studies have shown that the passing of time in itself does not necessarily insure forgetting. In fact, the fears may become intensified.

Why is fear an undesirable means of discipline? In far too many cases, the teaching of fears is intentional. If parents do not want a child to disturb things in a room, they may tell him that it is dark in the room and that a bogeyman will get him if he goes into it. The child may be told that a policeman will come and take him away if he does not behave or that a doctor will cut off the child's ears. Lies and threats may stop undesirable behavior, at least until the child recognizes them for what they are. But such a cure is worse than the disease.

Fear should never be used as a means of discipline. To instill unnecessary and unreasonable fears in a child is to prepare him for a maladjusted and unhappy adult life. We cannot expect a timid child to grow into a self-confident adult. It is true that by a long and careful period of training, many childhood fears can be overcome; but it is best to remember the principle that prevention is better than cure.

FAIRY TALES AND FOLK STORIES

Should children be told fairy tales and folk stories? It is customary to tell children various fairy tales and folk stories, some of which go far back in the history of literature. Unfortunately, at the time many of these stories developed, it was considered desirable to control children through fear. Some lesson-teaching fairy tales are filled with horror-producing incidents. Evil

Children love to be read to before going to bed. It is important for the child's well-being, however, that an appropriate story is selected.

witches and dragons roam the land, ready to capture children who do not obey their parents. We may tell the child that the events in these stories happened long ago, but to the small child "long ago" may mean not more than a few days ago. We may tell the child that the events happened far away, but to him "far away" may mean not more than a day's travel in the family car.

Folk stories may confuse a child who is in the early stages of learning the difference between fact and fiction. They often give fictitious answers to children's questions about the facts of nature, such as what makes the sun rise, or why chipmunks are striped.

Still other stories suggest to the child that a person does not need to work for the things he needs or desires. Perhaps a good fairy will come along and give him everything that he wants, requiring that he make no effort other than wishing. He may feel dissatisfied and unhappy because the normal life he must live is so inferior to the unlimited joys in the world pictured to him in the stories. He may drift into a dream world from which it will be difficult to escape.

Fairy tales and folk stories are part of our literary culture and should be accessible to children. Many psychologists believe, however, that it is better to withhold such stories until the child has a fairly good grasp of the facts of his environment. After the child feels secure in his knowledge of nature, he is ready for and should be told the classical fairy tales and folk stories of our culture. After he knows enough about his environment to recognize that evil witches and dragons exist only in sto-

ries, he may not be unduly disturbed by horror-producing tales. The child might still do well to miss some of the very gruesome or highly misleading fairy tales and folk stories. At any rate he needs to know what is true in the stories and what is make-believe.

TELEVISION WATCHING

One very important area of family behavior is that of watching television programs. Most of the activities in which children participate, such as school classes, school athletic events, Boy Scouts or Girl Scouts, and even many church activities, are not centered around the home. Other than mealtimes, watching television is often one of the few occasions when the family is together as a group.

How common is television watching? It has been estimated that more than 90 percent of American homes have television sets. In the average home the set is turned on about five hours a day seven days a week, and even more frequently during the winter months. The average American child spends approximately 17 percent of his waking hours watching television. Children and parents often look at the same programs for hours, although the parents sometimes think that children should not watch some of their programs.

At one time, psychologists were quite interested in studying the influence of movies, radio programs, and comic books on the behavior of children. Although still interested in these areas of entertainment, today psychologists are directing much of their attention toward studying the influence of television, since television has reduced considerably the amount of time spent on these other forms of entertainment.

How do teachers and parents regard television? Although some teachers and various other people have suggested that television is, or will be, the downfall of education, there is little evidence that television has affected scholastic attainment. The child who spends an excessive amount of time viewing television programs may do poorer work in school than those who spend less time with the set, but in many such cases the school difficulty was present before a television set was purchased. Excessive viewing is often a symptom of a deeper maladjustment rather than a basic cause of poor schoolwork. In fact, television has wonderful possibilities as a teaching device that enables the classroom teacher to expand the experiences of children. For example, few children would have an opportunity to see and hear a political convention, but with television they can learn about a convention first hand. Educational television provides programs to supplement the work of the classroom teacher.

Parents tend to feel that television has more advantages than disadvantages for their children. On occasion, parents may say, "I wish we had never bought that television set." Yet research studies have indicated that nineteen out of twenty parents would buy a set again if faced with the decision.

It is true that favorite television programs may necessitate some revision of meal and bedtime schedules, which may cause emotional upsets in the home. Some parents, however, have reported that children eat more slowly and are less "fussy" if they are watching television and that watching television helps children to relax before going to bed. Parents, as well as psychologists and educators, tend to be critical of the "horror and violence" kinds of programs, since these programs do not calm the child or provide him with constructive experiences.

What are some results of television watching on children? We know that the same program will have different effects on different children. For instance, children who have few friends tend to daydream more about a program after seeing it than do children who have a more adequate social life. Also, after watching a given program, boys tend to remember the fight scenes in which the male hero of the program participated, whereas girls tend to remember the romantic scenes involving the heroine of the program.

We shall now look more closely at two research studies on the influence of television on children. In one study, children were divided into two groups, those spending an unusually large amount of time watching television (heavy viewers) and those spending relatively little time watching television (light viewers). Also, the IQ's for all the children were secured and the children were divided into three groups: those having low IQ's, those having middle IQ's, and those having

	LOW IQ	MIDDLE IQ	HIGH IQ
Light viewers:			
6th grade	24	27	36
10th grade	33	49	70
Heavy viewers:			
6th grade	76	73	64
10th grade	67	51	30

high IQ's. A third variable in this study was that some of the children were in the sixth grade and some were in the tenth grade. The data are summarized in the table above.

You will note that the percentage of light viewers increases between the sixth and tenth grades, with the greatest increase in the high-IQ group, but that the percentage of heavy viewers decreases between the sixth and tenth grades, especially in the high-IQ group.

In a British study, a group of 78 children were divided into two matched subgroups: heavy television viewers and occasional television viewers. After all the children were given a personality inventory, those children having moderate-to-high scores on certain aspects of personality were then compared on the basis of whether they were heavy or occasional television viewers. The data are summarized in the table below.

As you can see, fewer children in the occasional television-viewing group had personal problems related to feelings of rejection, social insecurity, and

**Percentages of Children with Problems of Personal Adjustment
Considered as Heavy Television Viewers and Occasional Television Viewers**

MODERATE-TO-HIGH SCORES CONCERNING	HEAVY VIEWERS	OCCASIONAL VIEWERS
Feelings of rejection by other children (not being popular, feeling left out of things, and so on)	58	39
General feeling of social insecurity (feeling shy, feeling different from other children, and so on)	45	35
Anxiety about growing up (marrying, leaving school, finding a job, and so on)	48	37

anxiety than was the case for children in the heavy television-viewing group.

Now that we have considered behavior in a very basic small group, the family, including behavior leading up to the establishment of a home, behavior in the two-member group consisting of husband and wife, and some of the problems in the behavior of children likely to be born into the home, we shall examine, in the next chapter, some fundamental patterns of behavior in other small groups, such as the classroom.

Terms to Add to Your Vocabulary

acrophobia	filial love	phobia
claustrophobia	intrinsic reward	platonic love
discipline	lying	romantic love
extrinsic reward	parental love	

Suggestions for Activities

1. As a class, make a collection of valentines. Put these on a display board. Study each one in order to see whether it suggests love as a long-time matter of learning or as something which happens at first sight. Do the valentines suggest that there are problems as well as pleasures connected with love?

2. As a class, make a collection of cards such as are often sent to parents on Mother's Day and Father's Day. Do the verses on such cards tend to suggest love as a learning process to a greater extent than do the verses on valentines?

3. Make a survey in your school in order to determine to what extent going steady is practiced and how students feel about the practice. You might ask such questions as the following: Do you consider that you are going steady now? Have your parents objected to your going steady in the past? Do you favor high school students' going steady? Your questionnaire should provide a place for the respondent to indicate his or her sex and class. Of course, no names should be given.

4. Analyze some current popular love songs. If available, compare these songs with love songs written twenty to thirty or more years ago. Are the aspects of love emphasized then similar to those emphasized today? Do songs describe love as a learning process? Is the emphasis on physical attraction? Do the songs suggest basic characteristics necessary for a happy married life?

5. Note and record the kinds of disciplinary measures used by parents. These records can be compiled merely by observing parents with their children at social gatherings or in such public places as stores. Do parents suggest some fearful outcome if the child does not behave? Do they suggest that the child will not be loved if he does not do as the parents wish? Is ridicule used? Is there corporal punishment or threat of such punishment? Is there any indication that the children return to the forbidden behavior soon after such techniques are used? Which is a more common method of discipline—punishment or reward? Compare your findings with those of your classmates.

6. Arrange with a teacher in elementary school or a mother giving a party for her child to carry out an experiment on honesty in games. Probably four of you will need to work together as a committee. Place four pans containing beans or other small objects at one end of a room or playground. At the other end, place four empty goal pans. Have four children pick up one bean at a time, run to the other end, place it in the goal pan, run back for another bean, and so on. Set a time limit of two or three minutes for each group. A prize of some kind can be offered. Each member of the committee will count the number of trips made by the child assigned to him or her and the number of beans that the child places in the goal pan. Your committee will then compare the number of trips made with the number of beans placed in the pans by each contestant. The children must not know what you are doing. Are there any differences between number of trips made and number of beans in the goal pans? If so, can the teacher or mother suggest why certain children may have cheated in this instance? Do their explanations agree with what you have learned about cheating?

7. Make a list of fears you had when you were a small child. Do you know the circumstances under which at least some of these fears developed? What efforts did your parents make to counteract these fears? If you find that your children have such fears, how will you attempt to counteract them?

8. Modify several fairy tales from the point of view of mental hygiene. If you have a chance (say, baby-sitting), read your fairy tales to children and note their reactions. Also, ask them what "long ago" and "far away" mean.

9. Watch some of the television programs which are so popular with children. If possible, watch a program with a child so that you can note his reactions. A few days after watching the program, ask the child to tell you about it. Does he remember thrilling details more than a possible "moral" tacked on at the close of the program?

Suggestions for Further Reading

Burgess, Ernest W., et al., *Courtship, Engagement and Marriage,* Lippincott.

Hilgard, Ernest R., and Richard C. Atkinson, *Introduction to Psychology,* 4th ed., Harcourt, Brace & World. Chapter 3, "Infancy and Childhood," pages 75–88, "Personality Development in Early Childhood."

Himmelweit, Hilde, A. N. Oppenheim, and Pamela Vince, *Television and the Child,* Oxford University Press.

Kendler, Howard H., *Basic Psychology,* Appleton-Century-Crofts. Chapter 13, "Personality," pages 461–65, "Family Relations and Social Behavior."

McKeachie, Wilbert J., and Charlotte L. Doyle, *Psychology,* Addison-Wesley. Appendix II, "Psychology in Today's World," pages 631–33, "Changing Patterns of Family Organization."

Ruch, Floyd L., *Psychology and Life,* 7th ed., Scott, Foresman. Chapter 7, "The Management of Learning and Retention," pages 236–39, "Guidance as an Aid to Learning."

Schramm, Wilbur L., J. Lyle, and E. B. Parker, *Television in the Lives of Our Children,* Stanford University Press.

Sears, Robert R., E. E. Maccoby, and H. Levin, *Patterns of Child Rearing,* Harper & Row.

Whittaker, James O., et al., *Introduction to Psychology,* W. B. Saunders. Chapter 3, "The Development of Behavior," pages 77–81, "The Family and Socialization."

YOU AND SOCIETY

- CHAPTER **18**

  Social attitudes and social problems

- CHAPTER **19**

  You and the world of work

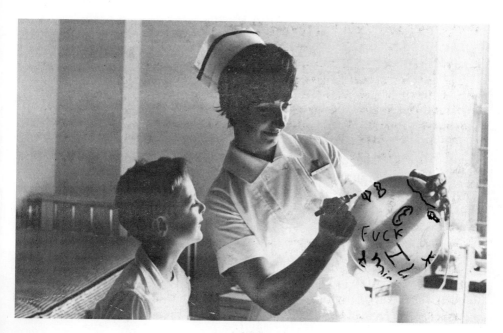

CHAPTER

18

Social attitudes and social problems

In other courses you have probably studied about such social problems as prejudice, propaganda, crime, and war. In this chapter, emphasis will be upon the psychological aspects of such problems rather than upon attempting to present the entire social problem. The chapter will include experimental evidence. Nevertheless, considerable supplementary reading in connection with some of its topics might be very useful.

SOCIAL ATTITUDES AND THEIR MEASUREMENT

An *attitude* may be defined as a readiness to respond favorably or unfavorably to a person, object, situation, or event. When a person expresses an opinion, he is revealing an attitude by verbalizing it. An attitude can be revealed in ways other than through an opinion; for example, the way a person treats the members of a minority group reveals his attitude toward them. People have attitudes toward everything from their pets to world problems. The attitudes which will be of primary concern to us in this chapter, however, are

those which relate to social situations, problems, and questions. We term these attitudes *social attitudes*.

Of necessity, the social attitudes of all of us are based on very limited experiences. We often fail to realize this fact. Thus, we may find our friends and ourselves lightly expressing opinions, if not convictions, on social questions of all degrees of importance.

When does an attitude become a prejudice? Sometimes we hear it said that all politicians are corrupt or that most of the Chinese smoke opium, or that all college professors are absent-minded and impractical. Such very general statements are often made quite emphatically and positively. How can it be held that all politicians are corrupt unless it has been proved definitely that every politician has been guilty of corruption? How can a whole people be characterized by those who have never visited or studied that nation?

At one time a questionnaire was given to 1,725 native-born educated Americans. They were given a list of national and ethnic groups (English, Chinese, French, etc.) and asked to rank them from most preferred to least preferred in a variety of social situations. Some of the situations were "Would admit to close kinship by marriage," "Would admit to my club as personal friends," "Would admit to my street as neighbors." For all the situations given, the Hindu group was at or near the bottom of the list. That is, an overwhelming majority of these 1,725 Americans were prejudiced against Hindus. How much do you think they knew about Hindu society? How many of them do you suppose had ever met or even seen a Hindu?

Any attitude, either for or against a given social question, which prevents us from considering and evaluating new evidence correctly is spoken of as *prejudice*. If we say that all politicans are corrupt because we know a few who are corrupt, we are merely expressing an attitude. Suppose we meet a politician who very evidently is not corrupt. If we refuse to recognize his honesty and do not change our statement concerning all politicians, our attitude is one of prejudice and is highly unjust.

An experiment was carried out with sixty students, thirty of whom were known to be favorably inclined to a particular minority group and thirty known to be unfavorably inclined to that minority group. Ten students from the favorably inclined section and ten from the unfavorably inclined section read once an 828-word article presenting data and opinions about differences between the minority group and a majority group. Then they wrote reports, as complete as possible, of what they had read. Ten more students from each

section followed the same procedure, this time reading the reports of the first ten members of their respective sections instead of reading the original article. The final ten students in each section read the second reports of their respective subsections and wrote down what they could remember.

There was a decrease of roughly 50 percent for both groups in number of facts and opinions correctly reproduced in the process of reporting. Because people do not retain all they read, this decrease was to be expected. It should be noted, however, that students in the section favorably disposed toward the minority group tended strongly to remember statements favorable to the minority group. Students in the section unfavorably disposed toward the minority group tended strongly to remember statements unfavorable to the minority group. May we not infer that we are much more likely to remember and repeat those statements which agree with our views, leaving out many of the opposing statements, and that this kind of prejudice enters into our daily conversation? Someone tells us what he heard, and we tell it to someone else. But do we remember and tell "the truth, the whole truth, and nothing but the truth"?

How are social attitudes measured? If we are to study social attitudes scientifically, we must have some means for measuring them. We cannot hope to measure all of an individual's attitudes; we must measure his attitudes on specific social questions.

One technique for measuring attitudes is to give an individual a sheet

SOCIAL ATTITUDES AND SOCIAL PROBLEMS

containing a number of specific statements on a given social problem. He is asked to indicate which statements he agrees with and which ones he disagrees with. For example, on one scale for measuring attitudes toward war, we find such statements as these: "War is ennobling, and stimulating of our highest and best qualities"; "There is no progress without war"; "He who refuses to fight is a true hero"; "It is the moral duty of the individual to refuse to participate in any way in any war, no matter what the cause."

A score value for each statement on the measuring scale is obtained. From these scores any individual can calculate just how his attitudes on specific social questions compare with the attitudes of a large number of other persons.

A somewhat similar technique consists of statements about a social problem. Instead of asking individuals simply whether or not they agree with each statement, this technique has persons indicate the degree to which they agree or disagree according to a definite rating scale.

Attitudes may also be measured by asking individuals to complete statements, for example, "If a Communist were to come to my home, I would . . ." or, "If a Communist were to come to their homes, most people would . . ."

In measuring public attitudes, trained interviewers often call on randomly selected individuals and ask each person to express his opinion concerning certain issues or questions. The replies resulting from a large number of such interviews are carefully tabulated and analyzed. In such *random sampling,* the sample group is selected in such a way that any individual in the given total population may be included in the sample group. For example, suppose that you wished to measure the attitudes of students in your high school toward law enforcement. It might be possible to get the opinion of every student in your school. If, however, your school is very large or if your time is limited, you might get a sample group by taking every other name or perhaps every tenth name from an alphabetically arranged list of all the students in your school.

Sometimes it is desirable to use *stratified sampling* rather than purely random sampling. In stratified sampling, the selection of individuals is done by dividing the total population into a number of nonoverlapping groups, the number in each group being proportional to the total population. Suppose that there are 500 students in your high school, composed of the four classes in the following numbers: freshmen, 200; sophomores, 150; juniors, 100; seniors, 50. You might wish to select, in a random way, 20 freshmen, 15 sophomores, 10 juniors, and 5 seniors and then measure their attitudes.

One psychologist selected a sampling of 3,000 high school students from all over the nation. He asked them to indicate how they felt about certain aspects of the great problem of social discrimination. Part of his data are presented in the table on the following page. You may wish to make a similar survey in your high school to measure social attitudes and then compare your results with those found in this earlier study. How to take such a survey is described in your *Record of Activities and Experiments*.

Might not a sampling from a limited area of the country have indicated attitudes that differ considerably from these attitudes expressed by a national sampling? Do you think that the attitudes of your parents might be different from your attitudes?

INFLUENCES IN THE DEVELOPMENT OF SOCIAL ATTITUDES

Does early infancy influence later social attitudes? Many of our social attitudes are developed during childhood in the environment of the home. There is evidence to suggest that even the experiences of early infancy may in-

Attitudes of 3,000 High School Students Toward Social Discrimination (Percentages Expressing Each Opinion)

	AGREE	UNDECIDED; PROBABLY AGREE	UNDECIDED; PROBABLY DISAGREE	DISAGREE
Pupils of all races and nationalities should attend school together everywhere in this country.	58	16	7	19
People of different races should not dance together.	23	15	19	43
There should be laws against marriage between persons of different races.	31	12	15	42
Swimming pools should admit people of all races and nationalities to swim in the same pool.	38	16	13	33
Public eating places should serve people of all races and nationalities, even at the same table if the customers want it that way.	65	9	6	20
All theaters should admit people of all races and nationalities and allow them to sit anywhere they want.	62	9	7	22
Hotels are right in refusing to admit people of certain races or nationalities.	21	12	17	50
People of different races and nationalities should be allowed to live in the same neighborhoods.	50	13	12	25
There are people of some races and nationalities who are by nature less capable of advancement.	53	13	9	25
All kinds of people—no matter what race or national origin—can become 100% Americans.	73	11	4	12

SOCIAL ATTITUDES AND SOCIAL PROBLEMS

fluence our later attitudes toward members of our families and toward members of the other sex. Some experiments with very young kittens are most thought-provoking. One group of kittens was kept in incubators away from their mothers and litter-mates during the first six days of life (before their eyes opened). Other kittens were isolated when they were five days of age and were kept in isolation for ten to thirteen days (the period just after their eyes opened). Still other kittens were not isolated until the eighteenth day following birth. In some of the experiments, the kittens were deprived of their mothers but not of their litter-mates. In other experiments, kittens were deprived of their litter-mates but not of their mothers. What kinds of behavior were shown later by these various groups of kittens?

The kittens that were isolated for the first six days of life never nursed properly and tended to sleep in corners by themselves rather than with the other kittens. Kittens isolated at five days of age took much longer to adjust to their families than did kittens reared with their mothers and litter-mates. Those kittens not isolated until they were eighteen days old had little or no difficulty in adjusting to their families. It was found that separation from the mother resulted in greater disturbance than did separation from litter-mates. Males separated from their mothers were later greatly disturbed in the presence of a female cat and never mated successfully.

We must be careful not to carry our analogy too far, but there is the suggestion in these experiments that ex-periences in infancy may account, to some extent, for the difficulty which some persons have in later adjustment to courtship and marriage. The experiments may suggest the value of "rooming-in" plans used in some modern maternity wards and hospitals. In this plan, the newborn infant is kept close to his mother rather than being isolated from her in a nursery.

Does the home influence social attitudes? There is often a great similarity between the attitudes of children and the attitudes of their parents on such matters as war, religion, politics, foreigners, and education. Using a measure of attitudes toward religion, some psychologists found a correlation of +.57 between the attitudes of mothers and sons. For mothers and daughters the correlation was +.69; for fathers and both sons and daughters the correlation was +.64.

Antisocial as well as socially favorable attitudes may result from the influences of the home. In one study it was found that 86.7 percent of a group of delinquents had relatives with delinquent or criminal records. Most of these relatives were members of the immediate family. In another case, 144 families were studied. From these families there was a total of 185 delinquent children. In every case in which there was a record of stealing or fraud on the part of one or both parents, there was also a record of stealing on the part of a child in the family.

Although it may seem incredible, a few parents and guardians actually teach their children to commit crimes. There is a record of one boy whose

YOU AND SOCIETY

stepmother definitely sent him to the railroad yard for the purpose of breaking into boxcars and stealing. After he had become proficient in this crime, he was sent to the market to steal vegetables for the family table. He learned some of the techniques of stealing from a stepbrother.

Children learn to respond to social problems in particular ways very largely as a result of home influences.

How do the mass media influence our attitudes? The newspapers that come into our homes play an important part in the development of attitudes on various social problems. On first thought you might assume that newspaper reports of current events are plain news. But if you compare two newspapers, you will realize that the same event may be reported in quite different terms and with different effect even in "factual" articles. The editorials are admitted attempts to develop specific attitudes on the part of the readers.

It is generally recognized that the press exerts a powerful influence in the development of social attitudes, but it is difficult to measure that influence. In one attempt at such measurement, university students took part in an experiment which they believed to be simply one on the psychology of reading. In actuality, the whole experiment was carefully designed for the purpose of learning to what extent newspaper editorials influenced social attitudes. Fifteen different issues of the university newspaper were printed in the usual way, except that in some copies there were editorials unfavorable to a particular ambassador. In other copies

Newspapers and magazines, which are purchased and widely read every day, exert a tremendous influence on public opinion.

there were editorials favorable to the same ambassador. The editorials were read in class, and the students were requested not to look at the papers outside class. Half of the students read the unfavorable editorials, half read the favorable ones. Neither group of students knew that the other group was reading different material.

Before the experiment was begun, a test revealed that neither group of students had ever heard of this particular ambassador. After these editorials had been read an attitude scale was given to the students in order to determine how favorable their attitudes were toward the ambassador. Ninety-eight percent of the students who had read the favorable editorials were biased in favor of the ambassador. Eighty-six percent of the students who had read the unfavorable editorials were biased against the ambassador. Also, there was evidence that fifteen editorials were more than the number required to produce such bias. Some students read only seven editorials and seemed to be as biased as those who had read fifteen.

What are some other factors that influence the change of attitudes? In one study the attitudes of subjects were determined for a variety of socially significant situations. These subjects were then hypnotized and given post-hypnotic suggestions that some of their attitudes and previously held beliefs would change. Some individuals who were originally against certain situations not only became in favor of them but began to develop ideas that were consistent with and supported their "new" attitudes.

Another study has shown that a direct intent to influence individuals was not as effective as an indirect attempt to produce attitude change. In this bit of research, the attitude changes of subjects who knew that they were trying to be influenced were compared with the attitude changes of subjects who were intentionally allowed to overhear a conversation. To express this finding in terms of an everyday situation, when you overhear gossip you were not supposed to hear, you might be more influenced than if someone told you directly what you had overheard.

What is propaganda? The word "propaganda" appears frequently in any psychological discussion of attitudes. For many persons this term has come to have an undesirable connotation. *Propaganda,* however, simply refers to any organized attempt to influence social attitudes. The word has been somewhat humorously defined as "the art of making up the other man's mind." Propaganda may even be highly desirable.

Propaganda is not a twentieth-century invention. Excavators found walls of the old city of Pompeii (buried in 79 A.D.) covered with election appeals. There had been an organized attempt in this Roman provincial town to influence citizens to vote in a particular way. Politicians in our day can use newspapers, radio, and television for propaganda as well as the ancient means of direct speech and signs.

Various labor, educational, professional, social-welfare, and religious groups use propaganda to further their causes. In recent years much propaganda has been directed toward developing a public attitude favorable to programs of mental hygiene. Commercial advertising is an excellent example of propaganda. Another example is the use of propaganda in connection with war. In wartime there are organized attempts to produce attitudes unfavorable to the enemy and favorable to the home country. Or, if a country is trying to maintain neutrality, it is likely to become the object of propaganda by each of the warring sides. Such propaganda is more dangerous the more its origin and true character are hidden from the people.

Also, in time of war propaganda is used to keep people from becoming too discontented with the hardships they must bear. As one psychologist has expressed it, "Properly organized propaganda, disseminated on a large enough scale, may serve over a term of years as a substitute for butter, and even as a substitute for bread."

How influential is propaganda? Something of the power of propaganda is to be seen in the data obtained from an experiment with three groups of college students. First of all, certain phonograph records were played to the three groups of students. No comment of any kind was made on the records. The students were asked to rate each record on a line 134 millimeters long, the left end of the line meaning "I dislike it very much," the right end meaning "I like it very much."

As the next step, the students of Group I were presented with some favorable comment about the records. For example, in connection with one record they were told, "Selection No. 2 is from the opera *The Twilight of the Gods*. In a previous opera, Siegfried has won Brünnhilde by braving a circle of fire in the middle of which she was sleeping. The present selection is known as 'Siegfried's Rhine Journey.' After bidding his bride a tender farewell and presenting her with the famous magical ring, he starts off on the journey. In this music we can, perhaps, catch the spirit of the fearless hero as he rides forth to his destiny, and the very intensity of the music brings to us a feeling of the vitality of this young world of gods and heroes."

No comment at all was made to the members of Group II, the control group. They were not even told the title of the composition.

Students of Group III were presented with some unfavorable material about the records. For example, in connection with the same record mentioned above, they were told, "Selection No. 2 is 'Siegfried's Rhine Journey' by Richard Wagner. In a series of four operas, Wagner glorified the pagan gods and warriors of the ancient Germans. It is an interesting fact that Adolf Hitler was passionately fond of Wagner's music, and many people think that Wagner expresses in this music the primitive brutality and the pagan anti-Christian tendencies which are a part of the Nazi philosophy. It was reported that before important diplomatic conferences, Hitler frequently ordered a performance of a

Changes in Ratings of Enjoyment of Music as Related to Favorable and Unfavorable Propaganda

GROUP	FIRST HEARING	COMMENT	SECOND HEARING	GAIN
I	356	Favorable	384	28
II	301	None	315	14
III	351	Unfavorable	355	4

Wagnerian opera at which he was the sole spectator, and it is supposed that he listened to the music in order to work himself up to such a frame of mind that he was able to crush his adversaries and bring them to their knees."

Finally, the records were played a second time. The students were asked to rate them once more. Data for all three groups on both hearings are presented in the table on page 517. These data are group averages for four records. Had all students rated each record at the extreme right end of the rating line, indicating that they liked the record very much, the score would have been 536 (that is, 4×134). Had they rated each record exactly halfway between "I dislike it very much" and "I like it very much," the score would have been 268 (134 divided by 2, then multiplied by 4). Observe that average scores in the table are all above 268. In other words, there was a generosity error, a tendency to overrate (see page 150).

Also, note that ratings of all groups increased on the second hearing of the records. We learn to appreciate and enjoy music in part by hearing it repeated. The group hearing unfavorable comment, however, increased their rating scores by very little as compared with the control group, which heard no comment on the records. On the other hand, the group hearing favorable comment had a gain slightly greater than twice that of the control group. If propaganda is a powerful force in a field such as music, wouldn't it be even more powerful when applied to controversial social issues?

In the laboratory, it has been demonstrated that subjects who have been in a room where they were isolated from the usual sights and sounds were so eager to have sensory contacts that they would listen to and, in many cases, accept statements contrary to their usual beliefs — even, for example, when such statements were ridiculous statements about ghosts. This is a technique of brainwashing. Also, during a crisis, such as in time of war, flood, or riots, most people are willing to accept almost any propaganda that urges some kind of forceful action.

It is usually said that primacy is extremely important in determining the effectiveness of propaganda. The advertiser who is first to call the attention of the public to his product is said to have a great advantage in the matter of sales. The nation which gets its propaganda into a neutral country before a rival nation can do so is said to have a great advantage in influencing the attitudes of the people in that country. In laboratory studies where propaganda on both sides of a question is presented systematically, however, primacy does not prove to be a very significant factor in influencing attitudes. Nevertheless, under the usual circumstances of social life, the side getting its propaganda before the public first has a great advantage because, having once been influenced by a given bit of propaganda, many individuals are no longer interested in and do not expose themselves to communications presenting another point of view.

Propaganda seems to be a necessary part of our social life. Certainly it is a force in national and international affairs. Our problem is to recognize it, to get the propaganda from both sides, and then and only then to make our own decisions.

How can propaganda be detected and analyzed? Can a citizen learn to recognize propaganda so that he will not be unduly influenced by it? In one experimental study a large number of persons, mostly high school students, were given a test. This test contained statements, taken from various propaganda sources, concerning the relations between the United States and various areas in the Pacific. The answers to the test revealed that the persons examined were influenced by the propaganda material.

Thereupon the persons examined were divided into two groups. One group was used as a control. The other group was given pamphlets to study which explained the methods and uses of propaganda. The control group was not given copies of the pamphlets. Later both groups were tested again, with material similar to that used in the first test. It was found that the group which had learned something of the techniques of propaganda was now less influenced by propaganda than was the other group. (In this study, the independent variable was the knowledge gained from reading the pamphlets on propaganda, and the dependent variable was the ability of the individuals to recognize propaganda so that they would not be unduly influenced by it.)

From 1937 until the period of World War II, there was an organization in this country known as the Institute for Propaganda Analysis. The object of

this organization was "to help the intelligent citizen detect and analyze propaganda." The Institute suggested that there are seven common techniques used in propaganda. These techniques are quoted here in the hope that you will use them to recognize and critically evaluate propaganda when you see or hear it. Do you think that these techniques apply as much today as they did when they were written?

1. *Name-calling,* giving an idea a bad label, is used to make us reject and condemn the idea without examining the evidence.

For example, there are the words "heretic," "Hun," "Red," "saboteur," "Communist," "demagogue," "economic royalist," "Tory," "appeaser," "agitator," "Copperhead," and "reactionary."

Unfortunately, in our society it seems to be true that groups are held together more firmly by common hates and bitterness than by common loyalties and brotherly love.

2. *Glittering generality,* associating something with a "virtue word," is used to make us accept and approve the thing without examination of evidence.

The glittering generality is essentially name-calling in reverse. The propagandist attempts to identify his program with some known good. He uses such virtue words as "civilization," "democracy," "the American way," "patriotism," "motherhood," "charity." There is evidence of a relation between the pleasantness of a proposition and the tendency to believe it. One psychologist asked university students to grade a series of religious, political, and ethical propositions for their pleasantness. Then he asked them to grade the same propositions as to willingness to accept them as true. The coefficient of correlation between the pleasantness of a proposition and the amount of belief in it was slightly over +.80. A person tends to accept as true those statements that are agreeable to him.

3. *Transfer* carries the authority, sanction, and prestige of something respected and revered over to something else, in order to make the latter acceptable; or it carries authority, sanction, and disapproval to cause us to reject and disapprove something the propagandist would have us reject and disapprove.

Cartoons of the respected and revered Uncle Sam are used in many advertisements to induce us to accept the product or service being advertised. It is hoped that we shall associate all the virtues of Uncle Sam with the advertised product or service.

4. *Testimonial* consists in having prominent people say that a given idea or program or product or person is good or bad.

Prominent athletes, musicians, and debutantes give their endorsements to patent medicines, cigarettes, breakfast foods, and so on—for a price.

5. *Plain folks* is the method by which a speaker attempts to convince his audience that he and his ideas are good because they are "of the people," the "plain folks."

Politicians, labor leaders, businessmen, and even ministers and educators win our confidence by appearing to be persons like ourselves—"just plain folks among the neighbors." In election years, candidates show their devotion to little children and the common, homey things of life. They have front-porch campaigns. For the benefit of newspapermen they raid the kitchen cupboard and find there some of the good wife's apple pie. They go to country picnics; they attend service at the old frame church; they pitch hay and go fishing; they show their devotion to home and mother.

6. *Card-stacking* involves the selection and use of facts or falsehoods, illustrations or distractions, and logical or illogical statements in order to present the best or the worst possible case for an idea, program, person, or product.

Perhaps the truth is told, but not the whole truth. Only such facts are given as will be favorable to the propagandist's own cause or unfavorable to the opponent's cause. Underemphasis and overemphasis are used to dodge issues and evade facts. If an embarrassing question is asked, the propagandist raises a new issue instead of answering.

7. *Bandwagon* has as its theme, "Everybody, at least all of *us,* is doing it"; with it, the propagandist attempts to convince us that all members of a group to which we belong are accepting his program and that we must therefore follow our crowd and "jump on the bandwagon."

An essential feature in any propagandist's program is a slogan. Because he wants us to follow the crowd in masses, he directs his appeal to groups already held together by ties of nationality, religion, race, sex, vocation. Thus propagandists campaigning for or against a program will appeal to people as Catholics, Protestants, or Jews; as members of the white race or as Negroes; as farmers or as schoolteachers; as housewives or as miners.*

Can attitudes of tolerance be developed by associating with diverse groups? We just saw on pages 513–19 how prejudices can develop. What about the other side of the picture? Can tolerance be developed? Sometimes the word "tolerance" has the unfortunate connotation of "putting up with." Some people say that they "tolerate" a minority group, by which they seem to mean that they put up with members of the group, although they do not approve of them. We shall use the word "tolerance" to denote the development of mutual understanding and the promotion of harmony among divergent groups.

It is easy to say that we believe in tolerance, but it is often difficult to practice it, because of our prejudices. There is the story of a student who wrote a term paper in which he gave numerous examples of intolerance and pointed out how unfair they were. Then he concluded with "If there is anything in the world I can't tolerate, it is people who are intolerant."

Tolerance, as we have defined it, can be furthered by the association of

* Alfred McClung Lee and Elizabeth Briant Lee, *The Fine Art of Propaganda* (New York: Institute for Propaganda Analysis and Harcourt, Brace and Co., 1939), pp. 23–24. Copyright 1939 and 1967. Reprinted by permission of the copyright owners, Alfred McClung Lee and Elizabeth Briant Lee.

divergent social groups, provided their association is a pleasant working together for common goals — winning a war or ridding a city of slum districts, for example. Prejudice, rather than tolerance, will develop if contacts with other groups are unpleasant, if the groups have no common goals toward which they are working.

THE PROBLEM OF DELINQUENCY AND CRIME

By *crime* we mean any act that at the time of its commission is forbidden and punishable by the laws of the social group to which the culprit or felon belongs. The word *delinquency* is used, especially by psychologists, to refer to crimes committed by those who are not legally of age. Perhaps you

This boy's first appearance before a judge can mark the beginning or the end of his criminal offenses.

are tired of hearing about delinquency. Newspapers, magazines, public speakers, clergymen, and teachers are constantly bringing delinquency up for consideration. As students of psychology, however, you cannot ignore the problem of delinquency. Since you are closer to the problem because of your age, we shall emphasize delinquency rather than adult criminality. The juvenile delinquent of today may well be the adult criminal of tomorrow, unless preventive measures are taken.

How serious a problem is delinquency?
There is no doubt that delinquency is an increasing social problem in the United States. Many social organizations and governmental agencies are concerned with the problem and are striving for a solution to it. However, to find data that give a true and complete picture of delinquency is impossible. Data from the various states are not always comparable because of differences in state laws and the organization of state courts. Furthermore, many communities have social agencies that adjust cases of delinquency without referring them to the juvenile courts. Nevertheless, it is of interest to note that the United States Department of Health, Education and Welfare reports 200,000 cases, including traffic cases, disposed of by juvenile courts in 1940. By 1950 the number had increased to 280,000 and by 1960 to 820,000. At the present time over one million juveniles each year find themselves in trouble with the law. It should be added, however, that about 80 percent of the young people in the United States lead responsible social lives and do not be-

come involved in delinquent activities. Unfortunately, some individuals tend to overgeneralize and condemn the majority of young people on the basis of the actions of the minority.

Although statistics cannot tell the whole story, they do give an impressive picture of the extent of crime. Students should look up current data. Useful sources are the *World Almanac and Book of Facts, Uniform Crime Reports* (by the Federal Bureau of Investigation), and the *Statistical Abstract of the United States.*

The following questions about crimes in the United States should be investigated:

1. How many crimes were committed in the latest year covered? How many arrests were made?

2. What was the cost of crime in terms of property lost?

3. How many criminals were under twenty-one years of age? How many were twenty-one to thirty? What proportion of the total population fell in these groups? What age group had the greatest number of arrests?

4. What was the ratio of men to women among criminals?

Delinquents are also a problem in the armed services. One study followed the military careers of 470 delinquents who had police records. It was found that half of them had unsatisfactory military records, such as dishonorable discharges, whereas only slightly over 10 percent of a control group had unsatisfactory military records. More than one-fifth of the delinquents did succeed in becoming noncommissioned officers or officers, but then over half of the control group also became officers.

How may we account for the fact that so many young persons, as well as older ones, do not live within the general social rules? We shall note a number of factors which are related to the development of delinquent behavior, after which we shall consider the more fundamental psychological bases for crime.

Is heredity the cause of delinquency? Some people think that an individual inherits his criminal tendencies. But psychologists cannot accept the statement that criminality is inherited.

At one time it was suggested that criminals could be distinguished from law-abiding citizens by certain physical characteristics, presumably inherited. It was said that the typical criminal had dark and thick hair, long and thick ears, overdeveloped canine teeth but no wisdom teeth, and so on. A scientific study of criminals failed to verify this theory. There is some evidence, however, that physical disabilities and deformities are found more frequently in criminals and other social-problem cases than in the general population. Only insofar as unfortunate physical appearance and bodily incapacities increase an individual's frustration can it be said that physical characteristics are even indirect causes of criminality. No one likes to be called "baby face," "runt," and so on. Some such unfortunate physical characteristics may be a product of heredity.

Although it is not certain, some individuals may inherit certain structural defects of the brain and so tend, under unfortunate environmental conditions, to become antisocial in their behavior.

There is evidence that brain damage resulting from certain illnesses such as sleeping sickness (epidemic encephalitis) and measles may be related to antisocial behavior, but this is an environmental rather than a hereditary influence.

In general, it is more profitable to look to sources other than heredity to understand the basic causes of delinquency and crime.

Is low intellectual ability a basic factor in delinquency? There was a time when delinquency was thought to be very closely related to mental retardation, and in turn, mental retardation was thought to be almost entirely a matter of heredity. Today, with improved intelligence tests and techniques of research, we are not so much inclined to think of mental retardation as a basic cause of delinquency. For example, in one study of 500 delinquent boys ranging in age from ten to eighteen years, it was found that only 2.4 percent could be diagnosed as truly mentally retarded. Of the boys considered not mentally retarded, 17.2 percent were above what is generally considered to be average intellectual ability.

Although the overall intelligence-test scores of delinquents are not greatly different from the overall intelligence-test scores of nondelinquents, scores on verbal factors of intellectual ability do tend to be lower for delinquents than for nondelinquents. Delinquents tend to be retarded in vocabulary development and in reading and writing ability. Their ideas tend to be concerned with the present rather than with the future.

It is true that sometimes persons of low intellectual ability do become involved in crimes because they are unable to understand our complicated social regulations, or because they are susceptible to suggestions made by persons of greater intellectual ability. For example, one mentally retarded adolescent girl knew that it was wrong to steal, but her friends suggested that she serve as lookout for them. They were breaking into lockers and posted this girl as a sentry to signal them if anyone in authority was sighted. The authorities came from an unexpected direction, and all the girls were caught. The mentally retarded girl could not understand why she was considered guilty as an accomplice. She had reasoned that since she would not actually be taking anything from the lockers, there was nothing wrong in being a lookout, and anyway, she wanted to be friendly with and help the other girls. Many persons of low intellectual ability are very honest, trustworthy citizens, especially if they are treated sympathetically by their associates. And the possession of high intellectual ability by no means precludes the possibility that an individual will become a criminal. In fact, considerable intellectual ability is required in order to carry out some crimes. One psychologist studied the relationship between intellectual ability as measured by intelligence tests and the kinds of crimes committed by 3,942 prisoners. He found that 52.9 percent of the prisoners convicted of fraud were of above average intellectual ability and only 22.0 percent were below average. The commission of fraud requires considerable intellectual ability. The victim must be deceived in such a clever way that he is induced to part with property or to surrender some legal right without adequate compensation.

Are social conditions in the home a factor in delinquency? We have already noted how children's social attitudes are developed in the home. In some cases, they develop attitudes favorable toward delinquency (pages 514–15).

Two investigators made a comparative study of a group of 500 delinquent boys and a group of 500 nondelinquent boys. The two groups were matched for age, intellectual ability, national origin, and residence in underprivileged neighborhoods. As contrasted to the nondelinquent boys, the delinquent boys tended to come from homes of little affection and understanding; from homes broken by divorce, desertion, separation, or death; from homes in which the parents were either too lax or too harsh in disciplinary measures. A higher percentage of the parents of the delinquents than of the nondelinquents had no more than an elementary school education at the time of marriage. The fact that they had not taken advantage of the opportunities for education is more fundamental than their mere lack of schooling. The parents of the delinquent boys tended to be unable to provide sufficient financial income or to manage what income there was. The fact that they had not adjusted to financial conditions is more important than the lack of money itself, but the feelings of frustration and inferiority that developed in their children, as a result of lack of sufficient money, no doubt accounted for some delinquent behavior.

In another study it was found that the majority of delinquent boys felt rejected by their fathers, with whom the typical boy identifies, and felt more loved by their mothers.

Do schools contribute to delinquency? Schools as much as any social agency — and often more than any other — prevent delinquency. Modern schools with their varied curricula, clubs, social events, and recreational facilities give young people opportunities for self-expression, for developing feelings of adequacy, and for wholesome recreation. Without these school programs, no doubt our problem of juvenile delinquency would be much greater than it is.

Nevertheless, sometimes school situations are very frustrating to young people. In those communities in which the schools are crowded and the teachers are burdened with unduly heavy class and extracurricular duties, there is very little opportunity for the teachers to give attention to the problems and needs of individual students. The student who needs help so that he can compete scholastically and socially, but is unable to secure such help, may turn to delinquent behavior by way of compensation, as a way to gain some feeling of achievement.

We can quote from a United States Senate committee on delinquency:

The subcommittee believes that the nation's first line of defense in preventing juvenile delinquency is the school. . . . One of the greatest steps which this nation can take to prevent juvenile delinquency is to embark at once upon a vigorous program to reduce the acute shortage in classroom space and the too-large size of classes. . . . Unless we pay out the money for better school facilities today, we shall have to pay out the money in the years to come for more police and more prisons.*

Are neighborhood conditions a factor in delinquency? Delinquency tends to be concentrated in the socially and economically poor sections of large cities. In studying the delinquency in areas of a city, it is customary to get a detailed map of the city and then place a colored pin in the map to indicate the home address of each delinquent or adult criminal. The pins tend to concentrate in three kinds of areas: (1) business districts or areas near business districts, (2) manufacturing areas with their adjacent slum or run-down areas, (3) districts in which the nature of the population is changing, that is, districts in which families of one race or nationality are moving out and being replaced by families of another race or nationality. The two groups probably differ in traditions, customs, and moral codes. Often neither the parents nor the children of the two groups get along well with each other.

At one time, the city of Chicago was divided into areas radiating out from the main business district toward the residential districts. The delinquency rate for each area was computed. In some areas near the main business district, one boy out of five had been arrested for some offense, and no doubt many who had committed offenses were not apprehended by the police. In

* "Congress Studies Juvenile Delinquency," *National Education Association Journal*, 1955, p. 304.

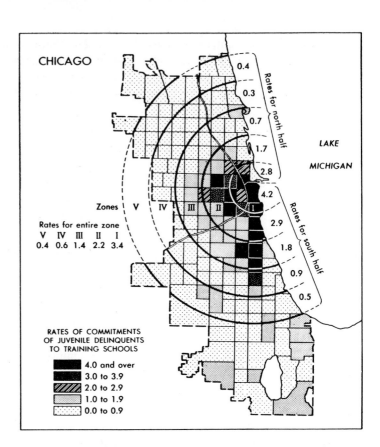

CHICAGO

LAKE

MICHIGAN

Rates for north half

0.4
0.3
0.7
1.7
2.8
4.2

Rates for south half

2.9
1.8
0.9
0.5

Zones V IV III II I

Rates for entire zone
V   IV   III   II   I
0.4 0.6 1.4 2.2 3.4

RATES OF COMMITMENTS
OF JUVENILE DELINQUENTS
TO TRAINING SCHOOLS

4.0 and over
3.0 to 3.9
2.0 to 2.9
1.0 to 1.9
0.0 to 0.9

This map, part of a study of delinquency in Chicago, indicates that the delinquency rate is highest at the city's core, which has a large slum area. The rate decreases as the city's outskirts are approached.

some of the more desirable residential districts, the figures showed that not even one boy out of one hundred had had any difficulty with the police. Not only juvenile records of crime but also adult records were seriously high in the undesirable districts near the business section of the city. Later studies, extending over a considerable period of years, revealed that the delinquency rate in the areas near the business district continued highest even though the national and racial origins of the population changed from time to time. A child or young person living in such areas was almost sure to know some criminals personally and to hear their bragging and their tales of battles with the police.

Although most delinquents come from neighborhoods where there is overcrowding, poverty, adult friction, and lack of wholesome recreational facilities, you will note that, in the above survey, some delinquents did come from the better and even the best socioeconomic districts. There is some delinquency in rural areas, which may increase as urban workers move into the country and as travel from urban to rural areas becomes easier and easier.

What are delinquent gangs like?
Crimes, especially those of the young, are often committed by groups or gangs. In the study indicated in the previous section, 89 percent of those

brought into court on charges of stealing had committed their offenses while with one or more companions. One former delinquent states in his own life account:

Whenever the boys got together, they talked about robbing and made more plans for stealing. I hardly knew any boys who did not go robbing. The little fellows went in for petty stealing, breaking into freight cars, and stealing junk. The older boys did big jobs like stick-up, burglary, and stealing autos. The little fellows admired the "big shots" and longed for the day when they could get into the big racket. Fellows who had "done time" were big shots and looked up to and gave the little fellows tips on how to get by and pull off big jobs.*

We tend to speak of such gangs as antisocial in their behavior. In a way, gangs are among the most social of all human groups, but their goals and activities are antisocial, or contrary to the welfare of the community. One investigator reports the following characteristics in juvenile gangs:

1. They are nonutilitarian. Members steal for "kicks" rather than because they need or even can use what they steal.

2. They are malicious. There is spite, contempt, and defiance in the behavior of the members.

3. They are negativistic. The gang considers right whatever is considered wrong by society at large, and vice versa.

4. They are versatile. They are quite "efficient" in many forms of crime: stealing, vandalism, trespassing, and so on.

* A. K. Cohen, *Delinquent Boys: The Culture of the Gang* (New York: Free Press, 1955).

5. They are characterized by impatience and impetuousness. The members are out for quick fun and excitement at a moment's notice.

6. They are very self-centered. The members have a social code for their gang, but as a rule the gang is hostile to other social groups — police, church, school, social workers, home, and even other gangs.

In summary, delinquents generally come from a broken home, are rejected by one or both parents, tend to drop out of school, which makes it more difficult for them to find jobs, and usually feel that society has neglected them. In delinquent gangs, they find others who feel the same way; they can gain some approval and recognition from other members of the gang while escaping from society. Such gangs tend to promote hostile feelings toward society. Members of the gang will violate the law quite often just to gain more approval from other gang members. Unfortunately there seems to be an increasing number of "girl gangs," whose purposes and functions are similar to those of "boy gangs."

How do high school students account for delinquency? A group of high school students were asked how they accounted for the fact that some young people from their age group, and even from their school, were involved in delinquent behavior. You may not agree with all of their explanations, or you may wish to add to them.

1. *As a joke.* It is quite a joke to walk out of a store with concealed merchandise, to enter a tavern when one is under the legal age, to "borrow" a car.

Sometimes antisocial gang activities result when teen-agers have too much leisure time and do not know how to spend it.

Why is such behavior considered a joke? If an individual feels inferior, he enjoys doing anything that will give him a temporary feeling of superiority by "putting it over" on someone.

2. *As a thrill.* We have already considered what is meant by a thrill (page 377). Such activities as leaving a store with stolen merchandise, running through stoplights, driving at illegal speeds, and entering taverns illegally are thrilling because they involve risk and danger. At the same time there is a possibility of getting away with it.

3. *To treat friends.* Persons of limited funds, especially if they feel inferior and rejected by others of their age, may steal so that they can treat companions. In this way they try to meet their needs for making friends. Of course, young people in good mental health can make friends in more desirable ways.

4. *To attract the other sex.* It is quite normal and desirable to wish to be attractive to the other sex. If a young man feels frustrated in making such social contacts, however, he may steal in order to buy expensive clothing for himself and expensive presents for the girl friend. Girls are especially likely to steal clothing to impress their boy friends with their appearance.

5. *Childhood experiences.* One girl in the group said that perhaps some adolescents steal because some of their needs in childhood were not satisfied. As children, they felt insecure. Perhaps they were made fun of by other children. As they grew older, such persons turned to delinquent behavior to even up things in this world.

6. *Don't know any better.* Many students disagreed with this explanation for delinquency. They were quite sure that adolescents know right from wrong. The boy who offered this explanation insisted, however, that some young people think it is quite all right to commit such antisocial acts as carving names or initials on soda-fountain tables or school desks, crowding into

528

buses without paying the fare, or stealing hotel towels.

What personality patterns are characteristic of delinquents?

Unfavorable home, school, and neighborhood conditions are related to the production of delinquent behavior, but no single factor can be indicated as the basis of delinquency. Delinquency is the product of the interplay of many factors. Delinquent behavior can be understood only by examining the personalities of individuals who commit the antisocial acts.

In our discussion of mental health, we have considered persons who are neurotic (pages 410–16). Such persons often meet their problems and frustrations by brooding and worrying. Psychologically, such behavior is undesirable, but it usually does not have a direct effect on the individual's fellowmen. On the other hand, the delinquent meets his problems and frustrations by striking back at society. He feels insecure and unacceptable. He tries to compensate by defying society.

After comparing 500 delinquents with 500 nondelinquents (pages 524–25), the investigators concluded that the delinquents could be characterized as being "hostile, defiant, resentful, suspicious, stubborn, socially assertive, adventurous, unconventional, nonsubmissive to authority."

The criminal is often childish in his emotional reactions. In one study of 316 delinquents, coefficients of correlation ranging from −.62 to −.77 were found between degree of delinquency and emotional maturity. That is, delinquents tend to be emotionally immature. The criminal is easily excited to anger and fear and tends to worry. He has temper tantrums on an adult scale. He may attempt to give the impression that he is big, tough, and superior, but actually he is afraid and feels inferior. He is willing to do almost anything that he feels is thrilling, so that he can feel superior.

Some additional personality characteristics of delinquents include impulsiveness, thinking less highly of themselves than nondelinquents think of themselves, having difficulty in interpreting consequences of behavior, and, in many cases, experiencing less reaction to fear-provoking situations than do most persons. One experiment which illustrated the last characteristic was conducted with criminals and noncriminals. Each group was given a choice, after the presentation of a visual stimulus, of receiving an immediate shock or a delayed shock. The noncriminals elected to be shocked immediately; that is, they preferred to get it over with rather than endure the short (ten-second) delay. The criminals, on the other hand, elected the delayed shock because, as they stated after the experiment was over, they had very little fear during the period of anticipating the shock.

In the chapter on mental illness, delusions of persecution and grandeur were described as paranoid reactions. Many criminals show a paranoid trend. They say that they have never had a chance in life, that the teacher had it in for them when they were at school, that the police have it in for them. Accompanying this feeling of persecution is a desire to feel superior in some way, which may be satisfied for a time by achieving some unusually bold crime.

What can be concluded about factors causing crime? There is no clear-cut general pattern of criminal personality, but one psychologist experienced in prison work characterizes the prison inmate by saying, "On the average, he is a young man, emotionally unstable, vocationally untrained, a product of an environment economically, socially, morally impoverished. He is usually . . . torn by conflicting values."

PREVENTION OF DELINQUENCY AND CRIME

What can be done to prevent or cure the social ills of delinquency and crime? It is a question worth trying to answer from the financial as well as from the social point of view. One estimate finds that each habitual criminal costs society $50,000. Each delinquent and adult criminal also costs society a vast amount of suffering and unhappiness. No such simple answers as slum clearance and better schools, valuable as they are, will magically change basic personality patterns which are responsible for delinquency and crime. Any steps which will lead to healthier personalities will lead toward the elimination of this social problem. Many delinquents and criminals have some desirable personality traits — loyalty and leadership, for example — that need redirection.

How effective is punishment in preventing delinquency and crime? If we believe that society should take revenge on a person who has disobeyed the laws, prisons are a simple answer to our problem of treatment. According to this view, the worse the prison, the better the punishment. We must be able to say that "justice" has been satisfied, regardless of the damage the punishment may do.

The theory of deterrent treatment is a more enlightened one. According to this theory, we may have to place an offender in prison, but the imprisonment will not be for the purpose of revenge. We place him in prison so that he will not be able to continue his stealing, so that he cannot murder more victims, so that he will know better than to commit another crime. The deterring effect of imprisonment may not be limited to the one who has committed the crime. His experience may serve as an example to others. The public whipping posts and stocks of colonial days were supposed to have a deterring influence on other possible offenders in the community. Hangings were formerly carried out in public so that any potential criminals among the spectators might learn a lesson.

No doubt there is some justification for the theory of deterrent treatment. Mounting crime rates suggest, however, that it has not been a notable success. Often we hear or read about fitting the punishment to the crime. A more basic question would be how to fit the punishment to the criminal so that he would no longer be a criminal. We should judge the criminal as well as the crime. Still more basic would be the question of how to guide personality development so that criminal behavior would not develop.

All too often punishment serves to increase criminality rather than to lessen it. Prisoners usually believe that they can expect only the worst from everyone they meet, especially law-enforcement officials. They tend to think that everyone is against them. They have been made to feel worthless and inferior. The deeper such feelings become established in the personality structure, the greater is the tendency toward compensation by way of crime.

Also, imprisoning individuals allows contacts with other persons who have criminal records. Often such contacts provide a means for the younger offender, who has less experience in crime, to "learn the ropes" from the ones who are more experienced at violating the laws.

Why should punishment be prompt and certain? To what extent punishment will be a deterrent is determined largely by the certainty and promptness with which it is administered. Unfortunately, in many American cases punishment for disobeying the law is neither certain nor prompt. Even a minor trial may be deferred for months.

Those in charge of law enforcement in America realize that there is need for more prompt and certain punishment. The chairman of a State Penal Code Commission has made the following significant statement:

I believe the greatest deterrent to crime is a quick trial and positive punishment, no matter what the amount of punishment would be. It is the one fact that criminals seem to know, that they can be arrested, enter bail, and have the date of their reckoning deferred indefinitely, which encourages them to continue their evil ways. The certainty that one would be tried and punished immediately, no matter whether he entered bail or not, in my judgment would help the cause of justice immensely.*

Can the lives of criminals be reformed? Promptness of trial is but one aspect of the problem of handling criminals. What is to be the treatment of a person who has been convicted? Punishment has been discussed. Today considerable emphasis is placed upon another form of treatment for those who have committed crimes, the treatment of reform. Literally the treatment consists in "re-forming" the lives of those who have committed offenses rather than in punishing them for past offenses. Some of our penal institutions are spoken of as reform schools. Certainly this idea of schools designed to reform lives is very different from the idea of prisons designed for the purpose of administering revenge.

There are psychologists on the staffs of some of our modern penal institutions. It is the first duty of these psychologists to study the personal histories and present attitudes of the prisoners. Then, on the basis of such studies, they prescribe individual treatment designed to help the offenders readjust to social life.

The report of a psychologist connected with the courts in a large city indicates that a psychologist is able to assist in reforming the lives of social offenders. Offenders were interviewed in order to learn about their early and recent experiences and thus determine

* A. T. Poffenberger, *Applied Psychology*, Appleton-Century-Crofts, 1928, p. 507 (from an unpublished M.A. thesis by J. S. Durham).

something of their basic personality patterns. An attempt was made to discover their attitudes toward crime and toward the future and to find out how much responsible behavior their records showed. Also, some psychological tests were administered. On the basis of such individual studies, the psychologist recommended for or against granting probation.

The courts did not always follow the recommendations of the psychologist; still, over a period of one year, 193 persons recommended by the psychologist were placed on probation. These persons were helped and studied over a period of six years while out on probation. In 69.9 percent of the cases, the prediction of the psychologist was confirmed—the individuals made good. In an additional 4.7 percent there was some question about the cases. If this much could be done by a single psychologist, how much more might have been done had the assistance of a psychiatrist and psychiatric social workers been available?

It is true that reformed criminals do not always make "perfect" citizens. Psychologists do not hope to perform miracles. Often only a slight redirection of behavior is sufficient to accomplish a great deal in the way of reforming the lives of both young and adult offenders.

What can be done to help prisoners reform their lives? In modern prisons we find the prisoners at work, usually making clothing or other supplies for use in the prison or other state institutions. Sometimes they are paid small amounts for their work. They may spend this money for candy, tobacco, and other luxuries within the prison, they may send it to their families, or they may save it for use when they are released from prison. Trades are taught in modern prisons. There are classes in reading, writing, and other elementary school subjects for those who are illiterate. There are other classes for those ready for advanced educational work. The teachers for these classes are usually selected from the prison population.

Not only are prisoners trained so that they can earn a respectable living after they leave prison, but they are also trained to enjoy leisure time in a socially approved manner. Many crimes are planned and committed during leisure time. Baseball, football, and other games help prisoners to learn how to enjoy leisure time both when in prison and after leaving prison.

As they readjust their lives, prisoners are given more and more responsibilities and privileges. Those that seem worthy of trust are spoken of as "trusties." Trusties may be permitted to work outside the prison walls. Sometimes they are even permitted to make short visits to their homes.

The process of reforming the lives of prisoners is not complete when the individual is released from the prison walls. A psychologist or other social worker visits the former prisoner frequently in order to help him become adjusted to nonprison life. The psychologist helps him in finding suitable work and a wholesome recreational life. The individual in many instances becomes a good citizen. There has been reform rather than revenge.

What can be done to prevent the development of delinquents and adult criminals? The old saying "An ounce of prevention is worth a pound of cure" is nowhere more true than in the field of crime. It is much more efficient to prevent the development of delinquents than it is to cure adult criminals. Parks, libraries, properly supervised youth organizations, and schools play important roles in crime prevention. Steps to eliminate poverty and social insecurity are also steps in the direction of crime prevention. Modern police systems stress that the officers, as they make their rounds, should try to understand the individual citizens and their problems. They are to serve as arbitrators in minor disputes and to give a helping hand whenever possible, as well as to make occasional needed arrests.

A group of high school students, discussing how to prevent delinquent behavior, suggested three steps which adults should take:

1. Provide more wholesome recreational facilities. They pointed out that vandalism at Halloween was formerly much greater than it is today because many communities now provide parties and other recreational events which are more fun than vandalism. (Ask your parents and grandparents about Halloween practices when they were young.)

2. Take care not to make delinquency easy. Adults are often careless about leaving ignition keys in parked cars. Such a practice is placing an unnecessary temptation before some young people. Stores are often careless about leaving valuable merchandise lying on counters where it can all too easily be taken without notice.

3. Parents should sympathize with their adolescent children who become involved in scrapes with the law. Too frequently they try to excuse themselves and to escape responsibility by placing all the blame on their children when, as a matter of fact, they have failed in some of their duties as parents. There should be cooperation between parents and their children rather than condemnation of children by parents. Children should work with their parents on the problem of delinquency. Perhaps other suggestions occur to you of what adults could do to help prevent delinquency.

Social reforms take place slowly. Yet, with the elimination of poverty and economic insecurity, the day may come when adolescents and adults will not commit crimes to secure the neces-

These inmates at a California prison are receiving vocational training to prepare them for their return to society.

sities and common pleasures of life. Better housing and better general economic conditions will mean fewer feelings of frustration for children. When adult "big shots" find socially approved methods for meeting their needs and pleasures, children will not have undesirable examples to imitate. A permanent program of crime prevention will have been established. Replacing slum districts with desirable residential districts, being sure that there is work for people to do, and providing recreational opportunities are all valuable, not only in themselves but as means of preventing crime. The basic preventive measure is insuring better mental health for all citizens.

MOBS AND CRIME

What is a mob? A *mob* is merely an incidentally (or accidentally) formed group of individuals acting under great emotional stress. The emotion involved is commonly one of anger. If the emotion is fear, the resulting behavior is usually spoken of as *panic*. A mob is similar to an ordinary crowd, except that in an ordinary crowd there is very little, if any, general emotional stress. When an individual forms part of a mob, he may do things that he would not be at all likely to do if he were acting independently. In a mob he may participate in murder, although he would abhor an act of killing at any other time.

How can we account for the behavior of mobs? How can we account for the fact that in a mob an individual will behave as he would not be apt to be-

have under any other circumstances? In a mob he has a feeling of power that he is not likely to experience apart from the mob. He feels that he has the approval and protection of the group and will not be punished for his behavior. The desire for the approval of our fellow men contributes to social order under most circumstances, but response to mob approval results in disorder and the weakening of the entire social structure.

The individuals in a mob hear the same general sounds; they see the same general happenings. There is a common stimulation. Thus, there is often a somewhat common response.

The compactness of any crowd has much to do with the behavior of the individuals comprising it. An audience that fills a small hall will laugh and applaud more than will an audience of the same number scattered over a large auditorium. There is more opportunity for one individual to stimulate another in the compact group. It is much more difficult for a speaker on radio or television to get enthusiastic support for his cause from the widely scattered members of his invisible audience than it is for a speaker standing before a compact visible audience. In the radio or television situation, the speaker must apply all stimulation, or most of it, himself. In the auditorium situation the speaker, if he does well, can depend upon the additional stimulation — for his audience and himself — of nods of approval and hand-clapping by members of the audience. In a mob, such social facilitation among members of the group is even greater than in an orderly audience.

How can the behavior of mobs be controlled? The persons in a mob, who may be under emotional stress because of the commission, or the alleged commission, of some major crime, are set for activity of some kind. They are unorganized, have no plan of action, and are very open to suggestion. They are extremely uncritical of what may be suggested. Their leader is usually some fellow who merely happens to be standing on a box or in a brightly lighted area or who is in some other situation where he may easily become the focus of attention. If he cries, "Chase him out of town!" the individuals comprising the mob will probably start chasing their victim; if the leader cries, "Hang him!" the individuals in the mob will probably attempt a hanging. The members of the mob seldom ask, "Who is this fellow and by what right does he command?"

Anyone wishing to prevent an act of violence on the part of a mob or to overcome panic in a crowd must first get into a position where he can be seen and heard. Then he must unhesitatingly give positive, clear commands or suggestions.

Once a mob was chasing a young man because a rumor had been started that he had committed an atrocious crime. The young man was well ahead of his pursuers when he turned a corner and ducked into a vacant building. A citizen standing on the corner saw the fugitive enter the building, saw the mob coming, and realized what was happening. He leaped to the top of a parked automobile, pointed down the street, and cried, "There he goes!" The mob ran down the street at full speed. Soon a few individuals dropped out of

Orderly individuals can become a mob when they are in a compact group that is reacting to emotional stimulation.

the mad race. Others quickly followed their example, and presently the mob dispersed. Later the young man was given a fair trial in court and was found to be innocent. A life had been saved, and a community had been spared lasting shame by a sensible man who knew how to deal with a mob.

What are some means for preventing mob behavior? Although a mob usually forms and carries out its activity in a very short while, the foundation for mob behavior frequently has been laid during a considerable period of time. For example, in time of war or fear of war, a citizen reads how the enemy has agents and sympathizers everywhere; he hears the same kind of thing at public lectures and over radio or television, sees motion pictures suggesting the menace of disloyal persons in our midst, and hears gossip on the subject.

Then one day someone notes that a man in a crowd has not removed his hat, although the band is playing "The Star-Spangled Banner." The crowd becomes a mob and maltreats the offender, who quite possibly was engrossed in thought and did not realize that the national anthem was being played. Had it not been for the long period of training in suspicion, someone would probably have touched the offending man on the shoulder and suggested that he remove his hat, and all would have been settled quietly. You can help to prevent mob violence if you refuse to gossip lightly on dangerous subjects and if you read newspapers and listen to speakers critically.

Police officers know that in times of excitement mob action can be prevented if they can keep a sizable crowd from forming. Therefore, they keep people moving on the streets and scatter all groups. It helps to prevent mob violence if you do not enter into a crowd that may become angry. Where the members of a community learn to respect and trust their law-enforcement officers, there can be little danger of mob violence or of panic.

Individuals who begin to form their own laws and claim that their laws are above and beyond the legal laws of society become a tremendous potential danger to the society. In a society such as ours, the existing laws must be obeyed. If a law is unjust, it can and should be changed by legal and peaceful means. There is no justifiable occasion for the overthrow of this law by force.

Many social agencies strive to teach people how to live in harmony. They do their best to promote social cooperation and to discourage social antagonism. Any training for good citizenship contributes to the prevention of mob violence and the preservation of public honor. In a community in which good mental health prevails, mob violence is not likely to appear.

THE CRIME OF WAR

The crimes of individuals against their social group constitute a major problem. There is a far greater social problem, the crime of nation against nation, the crime called war. In terms of our definition of crime, war may not always be a "crime." Yet, when it is carried on in defiance of international laws, war is legally a crime as well as a socially tragic blunder.

Figures on the total financial cost of war soon become so astronomical in size that no one can appreciate them. Each adult, however, realizes just a bit of the financial burden when he pays direct and indirect taxes for the support of recent and even long-past wars. The cost in human suffering is so great that people cannot comprehend it, although they have some understanding of it when injury or death affects their family or close circle of friends.

What are the causes of the crime of war? Where can we place the blame for war? To eliminate one idea, psy-

YOU AND SOCIETY

chologists do not believe that war can be attributed to instinct, as pointed out in Chapter 2. No evidence of anything resembling warfare has been found in excavations of the remains of early man. Primitive man was, and in many cases still is, a hunter. Wars for conquest are not found among such primitive peoples. It is only after man begins to settle on the land, to acquire and hoard, that wars develop. Today social attitudes developing out of economic rivalry are usually, if not always, the basic factors in bringing about war.

Sometimes it is said that war is beastlike, but such a statement is not fair to the beasts. It does not agree with the facts. War is an organized attack of one social group upon another social group. Such attacks are not made by the nonhuman animals. It is true that animals will prey upon other species in order to obtain food, but they do not "fight" in the way that man fights with his fellowmen. It is true that sometimes when very hungry, an animal will devour a member of its own species. An animal will attack a member of its own species for possession of a mate. In warfare, however, the human individual is not generally fighting for personal gain or satisfaction. In many cases he does not even want to go to war.

It is said that wars are nature's method of improving the human species, in that only the most fit survive and later reproduce their kind. A moment's thought about this statement will indicate its falsity. The military services reject those who are physically weak, mentally retarded, or emotionally

An inevitable product of war is destruction. These city buildings crumble under a bombing attack.

unstable. The best rather than the worst of the population is killed in time of war. Modern war acts as an agency of biological selection – but the selection is not in the best interests of the human species.

We must not place the blame for war on biological "nature." As one scientist expressed it,

War . . . is the most unnatural, the most artificial, of all animal activities, for it originates in artificial causes, is waged by highly artificial entities called states, is fought from artificial motives, with artificial weapons, for artificial ends.

What can be done to prevent war? Can man do anything to prevent the crime of war? Many groups are working frantically in the hopes of finding an affirmative answer before it is too late.

The Peace Corps is one effort to lessen the chances of war. It attempts to establish communication and improve social conditions in other countries.

During World War I, World War II, and more recent conflicts, psychologists have taken a very active part in many fields of military service and civilian war work. What do psychologists basically think about war? From their study of "human nature" (behavior), do they have any suggestions for securing peace in the world?

At one time some psychologists especially interested in social problems drew up a statement of psychological principles about war. This statement was submitted to members and associates of the American Psychological Association. These psychologists were asked to sign and return the statement if, in their opinion as psychologists, the principles were psychologically sound. Of the 2,038 psychologists who replied to the request, over 99 percent subscribed to the statement. Approximately 300 of these psychologists were in the armed services at the time.

Because the statement is psychologically so basic, parts of it are repeated here. The principles that referred specifically to World War II, which was in progress at the time the statement was sent out, have been omitted.

HUMAN NATURE AND THE PEACE

A STATEMENT BY PSYCHOLOGISTS

Humanity's demand for lasting peace leads us as students of human nature to assert ten pertinent and basic principles which should be considered in planning the peace. Neglect of them may breed new wars, no matter how well-intentioned our political leaders may be.

1. *War can be avoided. War is not born in men; it is built into men.*

No race, nation, or social group is inevitably warlike. The frustrations and conflicting interests which lie at the root of agressive wars can be reduced and redirected by social engineering. Men can realize their ambitions within the framework of human cooperation and can direct their aggressions against those natural obstacles that thwart them in the attainment of their goals.

2. *In planning for permanent peace, the coming generation should be the primary focus of attention.*

Children are plastic; they will readily accept symbols of unity and an international way of thinking in which imperialism, prejudice, insecurity, and ignorance are minimized. In appealing to older people, chief stress should be laid upon economic, political, and educational plans that are appropriate to a new generation, for older people, as a rule, desire above all else better conditions and opportunities for their children.

3. *Racial, national, and group hatreds can, to a considerable degree, be controlled.*

Through education and experience people can learn that their prejudiced ideas about the English, the Russians, the Japanese, Catholics, Jews, Negroes, are misleading or altogether false. They can learn that members of one racial, national, or cultural group are basically similar to those of other groups, and have similar problems, hopes, aspirations, and needs. Prejudice is a matter of attitudes, and attitudes are to a considerable extent a matter of training and information.

4. *Condescension toward "inferior" groups destroys our chance for a lasting peace.*

The white man must be freed of his concept of the "white man's burden." The English-speaking peoples are only a tenth of the world's population; those of white skin only a third. The great dark-skinned populations of Asia and Africa, which are already moving toward a greater independence in their own affairs, hold the ultimate key to a stable peace. The time has come for a more equal participation of all branches of the human family in a plan for collective security.

. . . .

8. *The root desires of the common people of all lands are the safest guide to framing a peace.*

Disrespect for the common man is characteristic of fascism and of all forms of tyranny. The man in the street does not claim to understand the complexities of economics and politics, but he is clear as to the general directions in which he wishes to progress. His will can be studied (by adaptations of the public-opinion poll). His expressed aspirations should even now be a major guide to policy.

9. *The trend of human relationships is toward ever wider units of collective security.*

From the cave man to the twentieth century, human beings have formed larger and larger working and living groups. Families merged into clans, clans into states, and states into nations. The United States are not [fifty] threats to each other's safety; they work together. At the present moment the majority of our people regard the time as ripe for regional and world organization, and believe that the initiative should be taken by the United States of America.

What efforts for peace can the behavioral sciences make? Can scientists in the fields of psychology, sociology, and social anthropology, commonly called the *behavioral* sciences, make a significant contribution to world peace? There is reason to believe that they can. Already psychologists, and other behavioral scientists, have amassed a great deal of knowledge which can be helpful in bringing about peaceful international relationships, and they are constantly searching for more knowledge.

Psychologists do not limit themselves to the study of individual behavior; more and more they are coming to study the behavior of groups. Scientists have done much work in the area of cross-cultural research. They know a great deal about the various peoples of the world, about their values and about how they adjust to threatening situations. Scientists have studied the attitudes which individuals in one country have toward the citizens of another country. They know a great deal about the causes and effects of frustration on individuals and on groups. They know something about the causes and aggressive expressions of hostility. They have learned that, under some conditions, hostility can be reduced by permitting people to express their feelings quite openly.

Scientists have learned the value of group discussion. They have learned that people are more likely to follow up on decisions which they make for themselves than they are to follow up on decisions which others impose on them. Psychologists and other behavioral scientists have made many studies of social attitudes and techniques of persuasion.

Through their studies on learning, psychologists know that reinforcing a given bit of behavior with expressed approval or other form of reward is generally more effective in bringing about desired results than is punishment for undesired behavior. A nation might do well to express approval of what it considers to be desirable behavior on the part of another nation, instead of merely expressing disapproval of what it considers undesirable behavior.

All of these findings are available to the policy-makers and to the diplomats of the world who must make and carry out the decisions which determine the nature of international relationships. Hopefully, the continuing research of the behavioral scientists will provide still more information which can be used to further the cause of easing international tensions and of developing international cooperation and understanding.

Terms to Add to Your Vocabulary

attitude	panic	social attitude
crime	prejudice	stratified sampling
delinquency	propaganda	tolerance
mob	random sampling	

Suggestions for Activities

1. Someone in the class should write a short dramatic story of two or three hundred words. Include in this story a number of specific facts, such as dates, names, and figures.

   Make a list of ten students. The writer should read his story to the person whose name appears first on the list. Ask this person to remember the story and repeat it to the second person on the list but not to do so until the following day. The writer of the story will keep the original and only written copy of it. Have the story passed by word of mouth from one person to another, day after day, until at the end of ten days the tenth person on the list hears it. Have him write what he heard.

   The original story and the retold version should now be read to the class. Were any facts forgotten, distorted, or perhaps added in the chain?

2. Bring to class for discussion editorials from newspapers differing radically in point of view on some social problem. Analyze the editorials in terms of techniques of propaganda.

3. Divide a bulletin board into two parts. On one side post newspaper and magazine articles which tell of juvenile delinquency. On the other side post clippings and articles which tell of desirable social activities of young people and organized youth groups. Which material is easier to find? Do most of the articles on delinquency refer to boys or to girls? Do most of them refer to young people who are in high school or to those who have dropped out of school? Consider the same questions for the articles on desirable social activities.

4. Do you know of any delinquent behavior? Have a locked box in which students can drop unsigned notes telling of stealing, unlawful automobile driving, and other illegal acts which they have seen being performed by teen-agers. A committee can work over the notes in order to prepare material for class discussion.

5. For a week, watch and report on television programs depicting crime. Are the plays realistic? Is the offender depicted as a hero? Are law-enforcement officers depicted as heroes? Are crime techniques demonstrated? Are the offenders young, middle-aged, or old persons? Are the offenders men or women? What suggestions are made for preventing crime, other than punishment? You may wish to make similar studies for motion pictures, pulp magazine crime stories, and comic books or strips.

6. Make a list of statements designating attitudes toward the law. Some of the statements should be favorable toward the law, some unfavorable. For example, one such published scale contains such statements as the following: "The law is the true embodiment of eternal justice." "No man can violate the law and be my friend." "The law is fundamentally sound in spite of mistakes by Congress and courts." "Since law is made by man, it may be either good or bad." "The law is rotten to the core." "All law should be overthrown." Present your list of statements to various groups in your school. Ask the individuals to check the statements with which they agree, place a cross beside those with which they disagree, and indicate by a question mark those about which they are uncertain. What percentage of students agree with each statement? disagree? are uncertain? Are there sex differences? age differences?

In the same way, you may wish to measure attitudes toward such social problems as war, treatment of criminals, use of alcoholic beverages, and compulsory education. If you are using *Record of Activities and Experiments,* you will find there further suggestions for measuring attitudes.

7. Have a police officer, judge, or social worker speak to your class on delinquency and crime. If this person can remain long enough, have a buzz session, breaking up the class into groups of five or six so that each group can come up with two or three important questions for the speaker. If the speaker cannot devote this much time to your class, have your buzz session before he comes and thus have some questions ready for him in advance.

8. If asked whether or not they respect and strive to obey the traffic laws, most persons will say, "Yes." Measurement of actual driving behavior may give a more realistic measurement of attitudes toward traffic laws. Select a fairly busy intersection with clear visibility and a stop sign but no traffic light or officer supervision. Place yourself in some inconspicuous position and keep a record of driver behavior under four headings: (1) driver brings car to complete stop, (2) driver slows down almost to a full stop, (3) driver slows down slightly,

(4) driver does not slow down at all. Present your findings to the class preparatory to a discussion of the public's obedience to laws.

9. Have as a speaker someone trained and experienced in military life. Ask him to speak on war from his point of view. Have as another speaker someone who is frankly opposed to war. How do you account for the differences in attitudes of these two people? Do they have some attitudes in common? What is your attitude after hearing both speakers? Have you modified your attitude as a result of what the speakers have said?

Suggestions for Further Reading

Abelson, Herbert, *Persuasion — How Opinions and Attitudes Are Changed,* Springer. This book discusses over one hundred published experiments on persuasion.

Allport, Gordon W., *The Nature of Prejudice,* Doubleday.

Alpenfels, Ethel J., *Sense and Nonsense About Race,* Friendship Press. This book discusses common misconceptions about races. It is written from the point of view of anthropology.

Coleman, James, *Personality Dynamics and Effective Behavior,* Scott, Foresman. Part II, "The Dynamics of Individual and Group Behavior," considers how groups develop and are structured, how a group influences an individual, and the influence of the individual on the group.

Daniel, Robert S. ed., *Contemporary Readings in General Psychology,* 2nd ed., Houghton Mifflin. Pages 232–35, "The Psychology of Toleration"; pages 351–56, "A Case for Graduated Unilateral Disengagement"; pages 375–80, "Implications of Recent Advances in Prediction and Control of Behavior"; pages 380–86, "Behavior Control and Social Responsibility"; pages 393–99, "Psychology and the Space Frontier."

Hilgard, Ernest R., and Richard C. Atkinson, *Introduction to Psychology,* 4th ed., Harcourt, Brace & World. Chapter 23, "Social Psychology," pages 583–98, "Attitudes and Opinions."

Kalish, Richard A., *The Psychology of Human Behavior,* Wadsworth. Chapter 17, "The Importance of Values."

Kinkead, Eugene, *In Every War But One,* Norton. A popular and well-done treatment of brainwashing.

Leuba, Clarence, *Man: A General Psychology,* Holt, Rinehart & Winston. Pages 563–69, "Delinquents and Criminals"; pages 616–20, "Crowd Phenomena"; Chapter 23, "Producing Social Change."

McKeachie, Wilbert J., and Charlotte L. Doyle, *Psychology,* Addison-Wesley. Chapter 16, "The Person and Society."

Mahoney, Harold J., and T. L. Engle, *Points for Decision,* rev. ed., Harcourt, Brace & World. Chapter 10, "Why Do Some of Us Go Wrong?"

Packard, Vance, *The Hidden Persuaders,* McKay. A study of how Americans are persuaded to buy and vote as they do.

Paton, Alan, *Cry, the Beloved Country,* Scribner. A novel dealing with race relations and crime, emphasizing environmental background. The setting is South Africa.

Ruch, Floyd L., *Psychology and Life,* 7th ed., Scott, Foresman. Chapter 15, "The Individual and Society," pages 571–82, "Illegal Behavior"; and Chapter 16, "Communication and Persuasion."

Slavson, S. R., *Re-educating the Delinquent Through Group and Community Participation,* Collier Books. An interesting firsthand account of one person's experience in restoring disturbed young people to purposeful, normal living.

Strang, Ruth, *Facts About Juvenile Delinquency,* Science Research Associates.

19

You and the world of work

Throughout your study of psychology, you have been learning how you can make efficient adjustments to the problems of life. In this last chapter, attention will be given to problems of vocational adjustment. First, how can psychology help you to choose a life vocation in which you will be happy and useful? Second, what have psychologists learned from their studies of work, both in the laboratory and in industry? Finally, in the event that you are interested, how can you become a psychologist?

CHOOSING YOUR VOCATION

Sometimes after graduating from high school or college, young people drift into any jobs that happen to be available. After a year or two a young man may find that he is not suited to the job he has taken; he then hunts for another job which, at least for the time being, seems attractive to him. After a few years he may drift to still another job. Eventually he settles into some kind of work and stays with it during the remaining years of his active vocational life. The job eventually selected may be one in which he can be happy and efficient. On the other hand, some people seem to drift through life without ever finding work suitable to their abilities and interests. In many cases it seems that the vocation a person follows is determined simply by the nature of the first job from which he is not fired.

Certainly every young man or woman needs to give very careful consideration to the selection of a lifetime occupation. Since individuals are not born into the world to do only one particular kind of work, they can sometimes spend a good deal of time at various jobs before discovering what work best suits them. One psychologist questioned 700 adults and found that 45 percent of them said they would choose a different vocation if they could start again at the age of eighteen. Of course, many of them might have been dissatisfied with this second choice, had they been able to start over again. Industrial psychologists have reported that approximately 60 percent of all job dissatisfactions are traceable to emotional maladjustments rather than to lack of aptitude or skill.

Either to spend years hunting a suitable vocation or to go through life without ever doing work for which you are particularly suited is inefficient. Although there are no surefire schemes for helping people find suitable vocations, psychologists are able to assist young people in the very serious business of selecting fields of work.

Your school guidance department will help you with your plans for the future, but here you can learn about some of the ways in which psychology contributes to vocational guidance.

What factors contribute to job satisfaction? Labor union agreements tend to emphasize that desirable "wages, hours, and working conditions" contribute to an individual's satisfaction with his job. If asked what they want from a job, most people would probably say "money" on first thought. In one nationwide survey, however, employed men were asked, "If by some chance you inherited enough money to live comfortably without working, do you think you would work anyway?" Only 20 percent said that they would not work. Although in our society some money is obviously a necessity, there are other factors that influence job satisfaction even more. A job contributes a great deal to an individual's self-respect, and a job serves as an indicator of an individual's social status.

In general, individuals in the professions and other white-collar jobs are more likely to be satisfied with their work than are people in the unskilled, semiskilled, and even skilled trades. Probably the difference in job satisfaction is to be understood in terms of the extent to which one is involved in his work. In professional and administrative work one is likely to be job-oriented in many of his interests. His social life as well as his business life may be centered around his job. On the other hand, the social life of those individuals in jobs requiring less training and skill is likely to be centered elsewhere than around the job.

One indication of the difference in job satisfaction between professional and executive workers and workers in routine jobs is their attitude toward the passage of time while they work. The professional and executive worker looks at the clock occasionally and wonders where the time has gone, since there is so much that he wanted to do and so little time left to do it in. The routine worker looks at the clock frequently and wishes that time would pass more quickly, since it seems as if the workday will never end.

For the professions, and many times for the higher administrative positions, a college education is required. Studies have indicated that college graduates are more likely to achieve vocational satisfaction than are individuals with less formal schooling.

What are some sources of dissatisfaction with jobs? In many cases the individual working for a very large organization has very little independence or opportunity to display initiative. He is governed by numerous rules and regulations. If he aspires to the higher positions within the organization, he is likely to become dissatisfied when he experiences conflict between his vocational role and his family role. For example, the worker may have promised to take his family on a picnic, an occasion to which they are looking forward. At the last minute he finds that he must attend an important meeting connected with his job. He must choose between fulfilling his job obligations and satisfying his family obligations.

In many large organizations a man can advance in terms of position and salary only if he moves from one city to another at fairly frequent intervals. Such moving makes school adjustment difficult for his children and social adjustment difficult for his whole family.

Women have some special problems in finding job satisfaction. In our society, a woman is expected to play the role of homemaker, yet she may also have a job outside the home. With two jobs making demands on her time and energies, she may not be able to do either one well enough to satisfy herself.

How important is intelligence in determining choice of a vocation? From the chapter on intelligence, you learned that there is some relationship between vocational success and intelligence as measured by tests. You should remember, however, that all work is honorable if it is done well. Unfortunately some persons have the undemocratic idea that white-collar and "clean-hands" jobs are more honorable, and possibly easier, than jobs in which the workman needs to wear overalls and get his hands dirty. Anyone who is happy and efficient in his work is successful, no matter what the nature of that work may be.

If a person does not do well in his high school or early college work, even though he tries his best, and if scores on intelligence tests indicate that he is not above the average, he might do well to drop plans for a professional career. On the other hand, if a student does well in high school or early college work and his scores on intelligence tests indicate that he is above the average, he may well consider preparation for some kind of professional work — such work as that of a physician, lawyer, psychologist, high school teacher, or engineer. The professional field would offer a challenge to his abilities throughout life, and he would probably be happy in his work. If he drifted into some kind of routine work, he would not be motivated to special effort; hence, he would not be happy in his work. If, however, everyone of above-average intellectual ability were to enter the professions, these fields would soon be overcrowded. There is a great need for individuals of high intellectual ability who can bring something of professional attitudes and skills to nonprofessional work.

From the chapter on intelligence, you also learned that knowledge of the factors of intelligence can be valuable in choosing a vocation. If a person knows how he measures up in various mental abilities, he will have some clues about vocations he may choose. For example, a person who scores high in verbal fluency might think about becoming a writer. If an individual has ability with numbers, he may choose to become an accountant.

A person's general intelligence and ability in various factors of intelligence, as measured by intelligence tests and as indicated by schoolwork, can help him determine both the level on which he can work and the kind of work he can do. He can also learn about his abilities from aptitude tests.

What are aptitude tests? Psychologists have developed tests, known as *aptitude tests,* that will help a young person, before he takes specific training in a particular kind of work, to judge whether or not he would be likely to succeed in that work. Aptitude tests do not provide a magic score which in itself will tell a person just what kind of work he should train for, but they often give him information which may help him to arrive at such a decision.

Your primary concern is with the possibility of using aptitude tests as part of your vocational planning. Sometimes business organizations use aptitude tests to assist them in selecting people who will be likely to profit from their training programs. For example, the president of a large company reported that the use of aptitude and other psychological tests had enabled his employment office to weed out 85 percent of untrainable men who applied for work. The industrial psychologist is often called upon to develop aptitude tests for the various jobs to be filled in his particular factory or office. The use by industrial and other business personnel departments of the results of tests, especially aptitude tests, in the selection of individuals for job placement is called *vocational selection.*

After an individual has taken an aptitude test, his score can be compared with the scores of others who have taken the same test and have gone on to training or work experience in the given field. For example, at one time 200 girls applied for admission to a hospital school of nursing and were given a nursing aptitude test. Of the 200 applicants, 93 were admitted to training—a very select group. Of the 93 girls, 21 dropped out of training for reasons other than failure: marriage, poor health, lack of interest, family problems, and so on. Scholastic records were kept for the remaining 72 girls. Upon the completion of the three years of training, the records were divided into two categories: (1) girls who had failed scholastically or who had graduated with grade-point averages placing them in the lower one-third of their class, (2) girls who graduated with a grade-point average placing them in the upper two-thirds of their class. Data are presented graphically on page 547. Obviously, the scores presented at the left are not percentages.

You will note that all girls who made a score of 130 or above on this aptitude test graduated in the upper two-thirds of their class, whereas no girl with a raw score below 80 graduated in the upper two-thirds of the class. Conversely, no girl with an aptitude test score of 130 and above failed scholastically or graduated in the lower third of the class, whereas all girls with scores below 80 either failed or graduated in the lower third of their class. A study of this graph reveals that this particular aptitude test is a very good, although not perfect, indicator of a girl's likelihood of succeeding in nurses' training. Any girl considering entering nurses' training could feel that her score on this test would be a very important factor to consider in making a final vocational choice. Any hospitals considering applicants for training could feel that scores on this test were important factors to consider in making their decisions.

If possible, you should take some aptitude tests. Taking such tests will help you to learn something of your own aptitudes, although you must be careful not to jump to conclusions, not to place more faith in a few scores than is warranted. Aptitude tests are available in many fields — art, clerical work, mechanical work, music, sales, science, stenography, teaching, and so on. The procedure, conducted by such trained individuals as guidance counselors, of using the results of tests to aid an individual in determining for which occupation he would probably be best suited, is known as *vocational guidance.* In case you are unable to take such tests, you should be familiar with a few illustrations.

The person taking a mechanical aptitude test may be asked to do a bit of matching. In one column there may be pictures of a hammer, a wrench, and a saw; in a second column, pictures of a board, a nail, and a nut. We can at least imagine someone who knows so little about mechanical work that he would think a hammer should be used on a nut, a saw on a nail, and a wrench on a board. Instead of pictures, some mechanical aptitude tests use actual tools. One mechanical aptitude test contains a series of pictures of pulleys with belts connecting them. The pulleys are of different sizes, and some of the belts are crossed while others are not. The person taking the test is asked to indicate whether the second pulley would turn in the same direction as the first of two pulleys or whether it would turn in the opposite direction, and whether the second pulley would turn faster, slower, or at the same speed as the first pulley.

Among other things, a stenographer must be able to write and transcribe

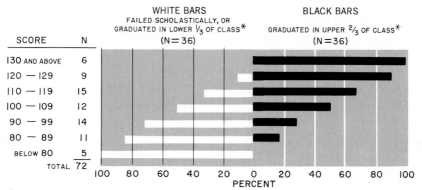

Success in nurses' training, related to scores on a nursing aptitude test (data from The Psychological Corporation, New York City)

YOU AND THE WORLD OF WORK

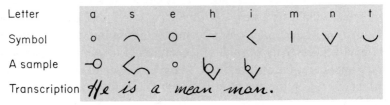

Letter	a	s	e	h	i	m	n	t
Symbol	o	⌢	O	–	<	I	∨	∪
A sample								
Transcription	*He is a mean man.*							

symbols other than the usual letters. In one shorthand aptitude test and as one part of that test, the individual is asked to transcribe a page written in special symbols that look something like, but are not, regular shorthand. The above is a sample.

You will note that here, as in true shorthand, letters which are not pronounced are not written. "Mean" is written "m-e-n" because the "a" is not pronounced. How would you transcribe the following?

Is personality a factor in choosing a vocation? In the discussion of personality, you learned that individuals differ greatly in their personality patterns. A very introverted person would not be likely to enjoy the work of the salesman or the politician. Even though he were to devote much time and energy to such work, he would probably never be as effective a salesman or politician as an individual who was very extroverted in his personality pattern. On the other hand, the very extroverted individual would probably be unhappy and inefficient in research or clerical work. The very introverted individual might well be successful in either of these fields.

Suppose there are two individuals,

one predominantly introverted and the other predominantly extroverted. And suppose that both individuals are interested in mechanical production. The extroverted individual would probably be most efficient and happy as a foreman or other leader of workmen. The introverted individual would probably be most efficient and happy as a skilled mechanic working on delicate and intricate machines.

The girl who is very extroverted is more likely to be efficient and happy in such occupations as selling and social welfare work. The girl who is very introverted is more likely to be efficient and happy in such occupations as bookkeeping and stenography. The high school or college student considering the choice of a life occupation should give serious consideration to his predominant personality traits as measured by personality inventories and by the ratings of teachers and others who know him.

Personality is important for vocational success even in machine-tending jobs and heavy manual work. Such jobs require faithfulness in attendance. The person who is easily disturbed emotionally and who is unable to get along well with his fellow workers is likely to be absent from his work more frequently than the well-adjusted workman. There is evidence that personality factors have an effect upon the amount and quality of output of workmen.

Is interest a major factor? A person may have the general intelligence and the aptitude required to carry on a given kind of work, and his general personality pattern may indicate possible success in that work. Even so, he will probably be unhappy and not highly successful unless he is vitally interested in the work.

A case in point is that of a dentist who was neither very happy nor very successful in his profession. When he was in high school he was very interested in music and wished to become a professional musician. His parents were determined, however, that he should become a dentist. They refused to provide money for a musical education but offered to pay all expenses connected with dental training. The young man went to a university and succeeded in passing the necessary courses in the school of dentistry, but he spent as much time as possible in university musical activities. After graduation he opened an office, and his friends patronized him when they needed dental work. Nevertheless, his practice did not grow as it should have. He spent his evenings directing an orchestra. When the orchestra played for dances, he would be up until the small hours and often fail to meet his dental appointments the next morning. His interests were in music rather than in dentistry. If he had prepared for a musical career, he would probably have been successful in that field. As things actually turned out, he was neither an efficient dentist nor a really good musician.

Interest is an important factor in selecting a vocation, and therefore the interest must be a genuine one. Young people often think that they would be interested in a specific kind of work. Yet after some training or experience in the field, they find that their original interest was based on a superficial knowledge of the vocation.

Many high schools today have files containing *occupational briefs,* which are usually short pamphlets or brochures containing pertinent information on specific occupations such as dentistry, engineering, psychology, and social work. From these briefs you can learn a good deal about different jobs. Often the better briefs will contain information such as (1) academic work or experience generally required; (2) personality, interests, and aptitudes best suited for the job; (3) general salary ranges; (4) working conditions; (5) demand for applicants; and (6) future outlook. Many additional points may also be covered in occupational briefs. An individual interested in finding out more about a specific occupation can benefit from reading briefs on that vocation.

A girl may have a rather vague idea that she would be interested in teaching as a vocation. She has been in school and has seen something of the work of the teachers. But the essential point is whether or not her likes and dislikes really are similar to the likes and dislikes of most teachers. Unless they are, she would probably not be happy and efficient in the career of a teacher.

The uniform of a nurse may be very appealing to a young girl, and the girl may plan to enter nursing as a vocation. She is not likely to be a success in nursing, however, unless her interests are similar to those of most nurses. A boy may think that he would like to be an officer in one of the branches of military service. Perhaps he thinks the uniforms are attractive or that he would like to give orders. Such aspects of military life are very superficial. Unless a boy has the basic interests of most officers, he is not likely to succeed as an officer.

How do psychologists measure vocational interests? Psychologists have developed *vocational interest inventories* that help the individual to determine whether or not his interests are similar to those of persons engaged in a specific occupation. There is a definite relationship between success in a given kind of work and interests that are commonly associated with that kind of work. Furthermore, there is evidence that as a rule, things best liked by an individual when he is young will be liked more and more with increasing age. Also, those things disliked by an individual when he is young tend to be disliked more and more as he grows older.

One widely used interest inventory of this kind — and one often used in high schools — requires about 45 minutes for administration.* For each item, the individual is asked to indicate which one of three activities he likes most and which one he likes least. For example, he might be asked to make

these decisions for the following three activities:

> Collect autographs
> Collect coins
> Collect butterflies

The measuring device can then be scored to indicate the strength of an individual's interests in each of ten vocational areas: outdoor work, mechanical work, computation, science, persuasion, art, literary work, music, social service, clerical work. The individual can then determine how his interests compare with the interests of others in a certain area or combination of areas.

Another interest-measuring device by the same psychologist measures an individual's preferences for personal and social activities.† It can be scored to indicate whether a person's interests are primarily those involving working with ideas, being active in groups, avoiding conflicts, directing others, or being in familiar and stable situations. Certainly these interests, as well as those mentioned in the previous paragraph, are important in planning one's school and job future.

Still another test developed by the same psychologist relates an individual's interests to specific jobs, for example, the jobs of the accountant, the architect, the chemist, the dentist, various types of engineers, the farmer, the lawyer, the auto mechanic, the minister, the psychologist, the department store salesman, the high school mathe-

---

* *Kuder Preference Record — Vocational.* Science Research Associates.

† *Kuder Preference Record—Personal.* Science Research Associates.

matics or science teacher, the long-distance truck driver.*

One other widely used instrument to measure interests is the *Strong Vocational Interest Blank*. For this test, the patterns of scores of individuals successfully engaged in specific occupations were analyzed, and their interests were associated with their occupational group. The result is that individuals who answer items on the *Strong Vocational Interest Blank* are comparing their interests with the interests of persons who have been successful in particular occupational groups. For example, an individual giving answers similar to those given by psychologists would have interests which are similar to successfully engaged psychologists. If you are considering entering the field of psychology, where you would work with other psychologists, and you have interests vastly different from other psychologists, then you will probably be less happy in this field than in another field where your interests are more similar. Remember, however, that a lack of similar interests is not an absolute guarantee that you would be unhappy, nor does great interest absolutely guarantee that you will be successful in that field. Success and happiness in a specific occupation also depend upon many other factors.

In one study of the interests of psychologists, using the *Strong Vocational Interest Blank,* it was found that psychologists in general have interests which are similar to those of artists, physicians, dentists, and architects.

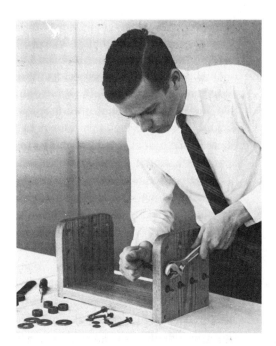

This test in using mechanics' tools will help an individual predict his success at servicing various machines.

The implication is that psychologists are interested in an appreciation of beauty and in systematic investigation to promote the welfare of human beings. A large number of psychologists were also, however, found to have interests similar to those of persons in the quantitative sciences, such as engineering, mathematics, and physics. As a general rule, psychologists do not score as high in fields such as teaching, social science, school superintendent, and YMCA secretarial work. Psychology is both a science and a profession. Six areas of psychological work will be discussed later on in this chapter.

What are some other points to remember about interests? One point to remember is that interests may develop

* *Kuder Preference Record—Occupational.* Science Research Associates.

through experience. Young persons often think that they would not be at all interested in some occupations. Yet after they have learned something about these occupations, they may find that they are very much interested in them. Our schools try to develop many interests in students which will put students in a better position to choose their life occupations. A person should not wait too long in deciding on an occupation; neither should he jump to a decision before he learns something about the field of choice.

Sometimes students take a vocational interest inventory and are dissatisfied with the resulting scores. They say that the inventory is not valid, because it does not agree with their personal opinions of what they think they would like to do as a life vocation. Psychologists have found that interest inventory scores may not correlate to any significant degree with short-time interests and achievement. Inventory scores may, however, correlate significantly when interests and achievement are measured over a considerable period of time. A point to remember is that scores on an interest inventory are arrived at by more scientific and standardized procedures than are opinions about interests and in the long run are usually more accurate.

The question is often raised as to whether or not the individual can bias the results of an interest inventory toward or away from specific areas. Actually, you can bias the results of some inventories but at the expense of working against your own future. If you wish, for example, to score high in social service to "prove" to others and perhaps yourself that you are interested in other human beings and that you should enter this occupation, you can intentionally give answers that do not truly indicate your interests. Later on, however, you may find that you have led yourself into an unsatisfactory job. The person administering the inventory is concerned with gaining as much valid and reliable information about you as possible to help you. Intentionally giving false information about yourself only hurts you.

What does industry look for in college graduates? One university made a survey in order to learn what industry looked for in college graduates. Replies from executives in about seventy major companies indicated that, in general, industry looked for three things: (1) an effective personality, (2) participation in campus activities, (3) high marks. They were anxious to have employees who would know how to work cooperatively with their fellows, who had the knack of meeting and talking to people easily, and who were attractive in appearance and dress. Seventy percent of the executives said that they preferred graduates who had worked at part-time jobs while in college. One executive said, "We find that they have been willing to work harder. They realize the value of money, have taken their education more seriously, have developed greater qualities of initiative and responsibility." Students should be careful, however, not to devote so much time to part-time jobs that they do poor, and even failing, college work.

Although the business executives

pointed out that some students overdid extracurricular activities, they preferred graduates with extracurricular experience. They found that such persons cooperated and at the same time would not permit themselves to be left in routine positions. They tended to become the leaders and junior executives in industry. Only one-fifth of the executives indicated that high marks in college were essential for success in most of the positions in their businesses. In fact, one executive declared, "Frankly, we are scared of a person who has nothing but marks to offer." It should be added, however, that for technical and scientific jobs, the executives were interested in and required high marks in the records of those they employed.

SCIENTIFIC STUDIES OF WORK

Activity of any kind may be spoken of as work. This section is especially concerned with work as it can be measured in the psychology laboratory and with studies of *vocational work,* that is, work done regularly in order to earn a living. Looking at work from the scientific point of view requires speaking in terms of measurements and specific facts.

How is muscular work measured in a psychology laboratory? Work can be measured by asking a person to lift an object. By knowing the weight of the object and how high it is lifted, we can easily calculate the amount of work done. If the person is asked to lift the object repeatedly, it is found that as he becomes fatigued, the height

to which he is able to lift the object gradually decreases. A work graph can be made, showing on one axis the amount of work done at each trial and on the other axis the number of successive trials. From such a graph we can learn some basic principles of vocational efficiency.

To simplify the experiment, the subject's arm may be strapped to a horizontal board so that he cannot use his whole arm. All but one finger may be strapped to the board, so that he can use only the muscles that move his free finger. Next the experimenter can put a string on the free finger, run the string over a pulley, and attach an object of known weight to the end of the string. Such an instrument is known as an *ergograph* (*erg* means "work"). The subject is told to lift the weight as high as he can with his free finger and to do so repeatedly. A metronome is set in motion, and the subject is told to lift the weight on one tick, let it drop on the next tick, lift it again on the third tick, drop it on the fourth tick, and so on. The height of each lift is recorded on a revolving drum called a *kymograph.*

A record obtained from such an experiment is shown at the top of page 554. There are some slight irregularities in the heights to which the object was lifted on successive trials, but there is one outstanding characteristic of the graph. There is a *general decrement,* or decrease in amount of work done, on successive trials. This general decrement is characteristic of all work graphs in which the work has been of such difficulty as to produce muscle fatigue and in which the work has continued for some time.

A kymograph record of work done in continual lifting of a weight without knowledge of results or incentive.

How does motivation affect a work graph? In making the record shown above, a screen was placed so that the subject could not see the recording instrument. He had no way of knowing how much work was being accomplished at each trial. He was working blindly, without any incentive except that of getting some routine work done. On another day, after the subject had rested from the first experiment, he was asked to lift the same object in the same way. This time, however, he was permitted to see the work record as it was being made. As he worked, he could compare the results of each trial with the results of previous trials. Furthermore, before the experiment was begun, a horizontal line was drawn across the top of the graph. The subject was told to see if he could make the recording line touch this line. This horizontal line gave him a goal toward which to work. The graph obtained in this experiment is shown below. You will note that again there is general decrement and some irregularity in the work graph.

Now compare the second graph on this page with the one at the top. Both records are based on the work of the same individual, and the weight of the object being lifted was the same in both cases. But owing to motivation caused by the introduction of a goal and knowledge of results, decidedly more work was accomplished when the second graph was made than when the first was made.

Sometimes motivation will be so great that there will actually be a *work increment,* that is, an increase in the amount of work done over a period of time.

What are some characteristics of work graphs? Although general decrement is the outstanding characteristic of the work graph, sometimes other features are found. The person doing the work may begin with a great deal of enthusiasm. For a short time there is little decrement. Then the enthusiasm wears off, and the subject begins to get bored with the work and to realize that he cannot keep up his starting pace. At

A kymograph record of work done in continual lifting of a weight with knowledge of results and with incentive of a goal.

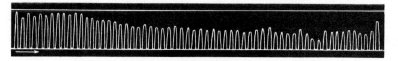

this point there is often a rather sharp drop in the work graph. Then the characteristic decrement occurs. When we find such a burst of work at the beginning of a task and then a rather sudden drop to more normal production, we say that there is an "initial spurt."

Sometimes a subject does not do so much work at the beginning of an experiment as he does a short time later. There is a "warming-up period" before the maximum work per trial is attained. Following this maximum production, general decrement sets in.

If near the close of the experiment the subject is told, "You have only one more minute to work" or "Only five more trials now," there is usually an increase in amount of work done per trial. Seemingly, the subject has been lifting the weight as high as he possibly could. Yet under the incentive of knowing that the end is near, he may show what is called an "end spurt," as in the graph at the bottom of page 554.

After the subject has been working awhile, he may be told, "Stop! Relax and rest." Following a period of rest, he goes on with his weight lifting. It is found that he is able to lift the weight higher than he had been lifting it just before the rest period; there is a "spurt following rest."

What has been learned by studying production records in industry? Psychologists who work in industry measure and study work production so that efficiency can be increased. In the case of work which involves considerable muscular activity but which is not overly monotonous, their studies usually show that there is a warming-up period in the morning while workmen get out their tools and settle down to work. Production decrement commonly begins about the middle of the morning. The noon rest eliminates some of this decrement, but it appears again toward the middle of the afternoon. The peak of production is usually lower in the afternoon than in the morning, and decrement is commonly more pronounced in the afternoon than in the morning. Individual records show considerable fluctuations in output, and general production records differ somewhat from one industry to another. The top graph on page 556 is, however, typical of industrial work-production graphs.

For work that is very monotonous and boring, individual work graphs tend to be very irregular, since individuals differ greatly in the way they react to monotonous work. However, the bottom graph on page 556 is probably typical of work graphs for monotonous work over a half-day. Following a warming-up period, there is a very marked decrement, but as the relief from the work approaches, production may return to almost maximum for the work period.

It should be added that many weekly work-production records show a warming-up period for Monday and Tuesday, with maximum production being achieved on Wednesday. This maximum production is followed by a decreasing daily production.

What can be done to increase industrial production? Scientific industrial studies show that the introduction of occasional short rest periods during the workday tends to improve total

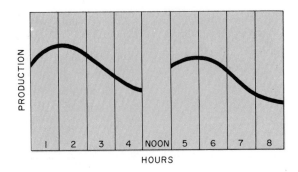

A typical industrial-production graph for work that is not highly monotonous (period of one full day)

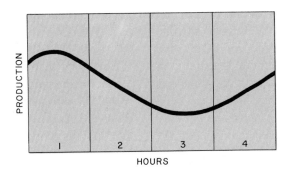

A typical industrial-production graph for highly monotonous work (period of one half-day)

production by from 5 to 20 percent. For example, in one industry production was increased from 16 to 18 articles an hour by introducing a plan of having men work 25 minutes and then rest 5 minutes rather than working steadily. Even in clerical work, there is evidence that workers tend to pause and rest about 3 minutes out of an hour. The employer who not only permits but requires frequent rest periods, such as "coffee breaks," actually gets more work done for his money.

Pay is often used to provide motiva-tion in industrial work. Workmen may be paid a fixed amount per hour or per day, regardless of the amount of work done. This system of pay is known as a *time-rate* system. These workmen may then be offered a bonus for all work done in excess of the usual amount. Or a *piece-rate* system of pay may be used, in which a fixed amount is paid for each piece produced. The bonus and piece-rate systems were intro-duced into industry to provide goals and simple methods for measuring progress.

Studies show that under some circumstances the piece-rate system results in more efficient work than does the bonus system. Under other circumstances the bonus system proves to be more effective. Whatever the scheme used, motivation results in an increase in the amount of work done per unit of time. Of course, there is a limit beyond which workmen cannot improve.

Workmen sometimes report that they find it a strain to work under a piece-rate system and that they are not so happy in their work as they are under a time-rate system of pay. Factory superintendents often report that work done under a piece-rate system of pay is carelessly done and that there is greater waste of material than when men work on a time-rate system.

Inefficient production may be a result of boredom rather than of actual fatigue. Modern industry is so organized that a workman may perform the same operation over and over, hour after hour, day after day, month after month. He may not even know the use of the part he is making. Certain evidence indicates that persons of high intellectual ability and very extroverted persons are especially likely to be bored by simple repetitive work, but the great majority of industrial workers experience at least some boredom.

There are a number of individuals, often called "time study personnel," or "efficiency experts," who investigate the procedures by which men in industry operate machines for the purpose of finding easier and quicker ways of operation. To discover the best operating procedures, these individuals investigate the movements and procedures of each job separately. Sometimes they film the workers' actions and study them in detail, looking for a way to eliminate unnecessary movements. One of their basic aims is to discover the most efficient behavior patterns of performing various types of jobs. What may work best for one person may not work as well for another person. They may find, however, by analyzing work procedures in experimental studies, that some behavior patterns are the most efficient for everyone involved. Books on industrial psychology deal with the efficiency of work operations in detail.

Another way to increase production in industry is to discover the most efficient methods and conditions under which the individual learns various tasks. If the best learning conditions for various tasks can be found and foremen of shops or other supervisory personnel can be taught to use them, production can be increased and the morale of employees kept higher. One example of industry adopting efficient learning methods which psychologists had developed is the case of programed materials, which some industries use for teaching their employees basic facts about new jobs or new equipment. Efficient learning methods benefit both industry and the individual.

What can be done to relieve monotony? Rest periods are helpful in overcoming boredom. Rotation of routine tasks so that a given workman does not stay on a particular task too long has been found to relieve boredom. The workman who is intensely interested in a hobby at home or who participates in some kind of interesting recreation after work hours is less likely to be bored by his job than the workman whose interests are more limited. Modern industries provide various social and recreational activities and encourage outside interests for their employees. If workmen are permitted to talk to each other as they work, they may relieve the monotony of their jobs. Music played during working hours sometimes helps to relieve monotony and increase production.

A man may work on a very small but necessary part of a very complicated machine and never realize the importance of his work. He may not know what his fellow workers are doing in other parts of the factory. It is not surprising that he becomes bored. In some industries men are given an opportunity to visit other departments. Thus they can see something of the intricate workings of the plant. They are permitted to inspect and observe in operation the large finished product for which they have been making one tiny part.

Is daydreaming a safe way out of monotony? The individual workman may find relief from the monotony of his work by drifting into daydreams as he works. One psychologist tells of a woman whose job consisted of wrapping electric-light bulbs in tissue paper and putting them into a carton. She had performed this operation approximately 13,000 times daily for twelve years. Nevertheless, when interviewed she reported that she found her work interesting and pleasant. She daydreamed of where the lamps were going and imagined seeing them in hotels, theaters, restaurants, homes, and so on.

You will recognize that such daydreaming may become very undesirable from the point of view of mental health. When it helps the worker to escape boredom on a monotonous job, it may be justified, but there is the danger that the dreamer will develop the habit of sidestepping the unpleasant realities of life and will use daydreams when unnecessary and undesirable.

It is entirely possible that much industrial unrest is a consequence of the monotony of modern factory work rather than of dissatisfaction with wages. As compared with the monotony of tending the same machine week after week, a strike might well be a very thrilling event in the life of a workman.

THINKING AS WORK

How much work is involved in thinking? In the laboratory and industrial studies we have been discussing, the kinds of work involved require rather strenuous muscular activity. Now we shall consider the milder physical work of thinking. Many persons in industry and in the professions make their primary contribution to the work of the world through thinking processes. Even those whose primary work is that of thinking do some muscular work in connection with their vocations. The accountant writes and operates calculating machines. The surgeon uses his arm and hand muscles in performing operations. The chemist handles test tubes and beakers. In vocations based primarily on thinking activity, however, the muscular activity is seldom great enough to produce such marked decrement as we noted in the preceding section.

What do experimental studies show? At one time a university student set herself the task of making a scientific study of the work involved in thinking. For example, she practiced doing such four-place multiplication problems as these:

$$2645 \qquad 7954$$
$$\underline{5784} \qquad \underline{3528}$$

With practice she was able to do all of the multiplications without having the original problems in sight and without writing down any intermediate products. She did all the work "in her head" and wrote down the final product. (If you think such a task did not require much thinking, try it. You might try beginning with two-place numbers.)

After practice in this arduous thinking work, she set herself the task of solving such problems on four successive days from about 11 A.M. to about 11 P.M., without any time out for meals. Each day she solved 67 problems. The first day of the four-day experiment it took her, on the average, 9.47 minutes to solve each problem, the second day the average time was 9.13 minutes, the third day it was 7.55 minutes, and on the last day only 7.45 minutes. With the passing of the experimental days, she actually increased in speed efficiency.

It is true that she made slightly more errors in her work as the experiment progressed from day to day. The first day she made an average of 1.5 errors per problem, the second and third days an average of 1.9 errors per problem, and on the last day 2.3 errors per problem. A record was kept of the length of time required to solve each successive problem on each day. These data did indicate that, with the passing of the hours of each day, there was a tendency for more and more time to be required for each successive solution. For example, on the fourth day of the experiment the average time required for solving each problem was 4.45 minutes near the beginning of the day and 8.54 minutes near the close of the day. Also, there was a slight increase in number of errors, from 2.0 near the beginning of the fourth day to 3.1 near the close of the day. At various times during the day, however, she made fewer errors than she made at the beginning of the day.

In this well-known early experiment, only one person was involved. A more recent repetition of the experiment, however, with more persons participating, confirmed the general findings of the earlier experiment. Another psychologist found that over a period of five hours of intense mental work (solving addition problems), there was only a reduction of 20 percent in output.

Do we become "too tired to think any more"? The above experiments did indicate some decrement in work efficiency with the passing of time. The significant point, however, is that individuals are able to do difficult mental work over considerable periods of time. After two or three hours of hard thinking work, most of us feel that we are

The World of Work

There are many interesting and stimulating occupations open to young people. Jobs vary considerably in the amount of skill and training they require, in the salary they pay, in where they are performed — whether in an office, shop, or outdoors — and in status. These factors, and how they relate to your abilities, interests, and personality, should be considered in selecting an occupation.

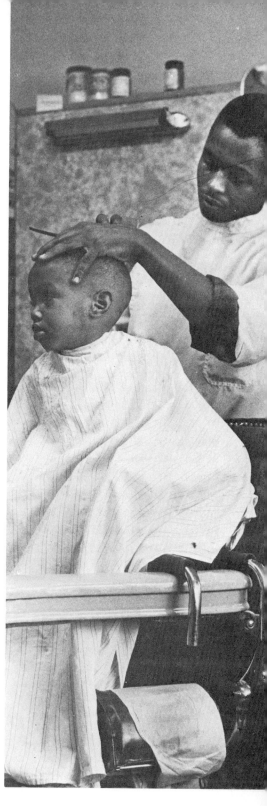

just too fatigued to think any longer. It is true that a person doing very heavy muscular work would be so fatigued that he might be unable to do any work long before a twelve-hour work period was completed. In work that is primarily a matter of hard thinking, however, the point of complete exhaustion would probably not be reached for much more than twelve hours.

Experimental studies suggest that our complaints of being "too tired from thinking to think any more" are not justified in terms of actual fatigue. There must be some other explanation.

In one experiment, subjects were asked to grade English compositions for a period of four hours. At intervals they were asked to estimate how much they were enjoying the work. Efficiency of the work was also measured. Results are indicated in the graph below. The two top lines show that, on the basis of initial efficiency, the

percentage of drop in both speed and accuracy was slight. The lowest line plainly shows that there was a distinct and steady drop in the satisfaction or enjoyment that the work gave.

In general, the evidence seems to indicate that what is usually considered to be fatigue in the work of thinking is really boredom. The work may be continuing at a high rate of efficiency, even though the worker no longer enjoys it and says that he is fatigued. In the work of thinking, feelings are a poor indication of efficiency. Many times, the efficient worker can and must continue with his work, even though he believes himself to be too tired to work.

PSYCHOLOGY AS A VOCATION

You are nearing the close of your present course in psychology. A few of you may wish to go on with your training and become professional psychologists. All of you should have some idea of and appreciation for both the areas in which psychologists work and the training required to become a psychologist. The fields in which psychologists specialize can be divided broadly into six major groupings.*

1. Experimental and physiological psychologists. In their laboratories, experimental psychologists study not only overt behavior but also physiological processes—the functions of

PERCENT (y-axis: 30, 40, 50, 60, 70, 80, 90, 100)
TIME IN MINUTES (x-axis: 0, 40, 80, 120, 160, 200, 240)

——— Accuracy —·—· Speed - - - Satisfaction

* Based on a pamphlet, *Career Opportunities in Psychology,* by Dr. William F. Soskin and published by the American Psychological Association. Also, see Elizabeth Ogg's *Psychologists in Action* (Public Affairs Pamphlet No. 229).

the glands and nervous system, for example. Many experimental and physiological psychologists are employed in university and college departments of psychology. Some psychologists work as research scientists in laboratories maintained by private industries, governmental agencies, hospitals, and philanthropic foundations.

Sometimes psychological work is classified as either basic or applied, although there need be no sharp line drawn between the two. Experimental psychologists often engage in research aimed at discovering fundamental principles or laws—*basic* psychology. For example, such psychologists may strive to understand and explain basic principles and laws of color vision. Other psychologists take the basic principles and laws and apply them to current practical situations and problems—*applied* psychology. On the basis of basic principles of color vision, an applied psychologist might develop a new test of color blindness. The psychologists in the remaining five classifications are concerned primarily with applied psychology.

2. Industrial and consulting psychologists. As the name implies, industrial psychologists work with industry. They develop programs for selecting, training, and promoting employees. They strive to improve morale; that is, they try to bring about good relations between groups of workers, and between workers and management, and to inspire job satisfaction.

Sometimes businesses call upon psychologists to assess consumer preferences and the relative appeal of various kinds of advertising. For example, a psychologist may survey a careful sampling of housewives to learn what kind of articles they prefer in magazines written primarily for women readers. He is measuring consumer preference. A psychologist may be asked to investigate whether people prefer advertisements containing large illustrations and relatively little reading matter, or vice versa. In this case, he is measuring advertising appeal.

Human engineering psychologists work at designing machines that can be operated efficiently. They help design dials, gauges, and various instruments so that they can be read and operated with a minimum of error. Similar tasks are performed by military psychologists. They assist in selecting personnel for special military duties and devise ways for training them. They study such phenomena as the psychological effect of modern high-speed flight and the fear reactions of soldiers in combat. Some industrial psychologists form consulting firms used by business organizations.

3. Social psychologists. These psychologists, often working with sociologists, study the behavior of individuals as members of groups. They conduct research concerned with such problems as leadership, segregation, prejudice, and the effects of disaster (floods, for example) on human behavior. They may specialize in public opinion surveys. In time of war, they may study the morale of defense workers, the influences of propaganda, the spread of rumors, and the attitude of the public toward the war effort.

4. Educational and school psychologists. Both educational and school psychologists are concerned with the problems of young people; no sharp line exists between the two fields of work. However, educational psychologists are most likely to be concerned with basic problems of teaching, learning, and the personality development of children. Educational psychologists often work in university departments of psychology or education.

As the name implies, school psychologists work in school systems. They advise students about their educational and job plans. They help students with their personal, oftentimes highly emotional, problems. They strive to bring about happy working conditions between students, teachers, and parents. They are often called upon to discover why certain students are having difficulty with their schoolwork and how such students can be helped. They work with crippled children and with children who have speech or reading difficulties. They often administer, or are responsible for the administration of, psychological tests—intelligence tests, aptitude tests, vocational interest inventories, school achievement tests, and measures of personality. Some school psychologists devote part of their time to teaching psychology courses in the high schools of their school system.

5. Clinical psychologists. Clinical psychologists devote their time to counseling and otherwise helping persons who have disturbing personal problems. Their primary concern is with problems of mental health and individual adjust-

ment. Their job is to help individuals to help themselves. Their work is not confined to clinics, for they may work in mental hospitals, in child guidance centers, in prisons, in connection with the work of juvenile and other courts, in social welfare agencies, and in college and even in some elementary and high school counseling centers. Some clinical psychologists establish offices to which anyone needing their help can come. In a hospital or clinic setting, they are likely to work as members of a team, along with psychiatrists, social workers, and other specialists. They may carry on psychotherapy, that is, provide treatment for individuals with emotional or personality disturbances. Many clinical psychologists carry on or direct research programs in order to learn more about basic problems and treatment of disturbed individuals. Research is not limited to experimental psychology.

6. Counseling and guidance psychologists. The work of counseling and guidance psychologists is closely related to and at some points may overlap the work of both school psychologists and clinical psychologists. Whereas school psychologists work with children, counseling psychologists are more likely to work with individuals in the late adolescent years or with adults. They may specialize in assisting young persons to select a lifework, though they also deal with other personal problems. They are often employed in vocational guidance centers, in marriage clinics, and in student counseling centers in school systems and colleges and universities.

A student who is interested in becomi..g a psychologist can gather worth-while experience and preparation by working with children.

In recent years psychologists have begun to play a more important role than they had previously in the area of space travel. Before manned space flight began, chimpanzees were trained prior to flights to perform specific tasks while in space flight. Such measures were important to determine the feasibility of sending human beings on these flights. It was necessary to determine what effects, if any, such factors as weightlessness and isolation in space would have on the physiological and psychological condition of human beings. As man explores everything from the frontiers of outer space to the lower depths of the oceans, psychologists will play increasingly important roles to aid man to better understand man, the environments in which he lives, and his relationships to these different environments.

What training is necessary to become a psychologist? There is no short or easy road to becoming a psychologist. It is, however, an interesting road, and it leads to a rewarding, worthwhile destination.

Even in high school you can begin general preparation for becoming a psychologist. Basically, you must take your school's college preparatory course, including one or two foreign languages, as many mathematics and science courses as possible, and courses in social studies, composition, and literature. You can broaden your background by participating in science fairs, junior academies of science, and other science activities. You may be able to visit a university department of psychology, tour its laboratories, observe some research in progress, and talk with members of the faculty and graduate students. A college or university near you may have special programs for high school students, such as a High School Science Day or a High School Career Day. You might even have an opportunity to participate in a high school science institute, spending part of a summer vacation visiting various university laboratories and then working as an assistant in some particular laboratory (possibly a psychology laboratory).

As you have learned throughout your course in psychology and as we have just noted in the previous section, psychologists do many different kinds of work. College preparation for such varied work must be broad. Later specialization will be built on this broad foundation. You will need to take such college courses as history, philosophy, political science, and literature. You will also need thorough training in English composition. As a background for later specialization in the science of psychology, you will need to take basic college courses in physiology, biology, physics, mathematics, sociology, and anthropology.

Of course, in addition to a broad background in related fields, you will need to take undergraduate courses in psychology. This training should include courses in general psychology, something like the course which you are just completing but at the more difficult college level. You must take courses especially devoted to experimental theories and techniques. You will wish to get some training along such lines as physiological psychology, learning theories, abnormal psychology, social psychology, theories and practices of testing, statistical techniques, and developmental psychology. The college or university you choose will guide you in your selection of suitable courses.

The psychologist-in-training in a college or university, and even the high school student considering psychology as a vocation, can often gain valuable experience through summer or part-time nonprofessional work in mental hospitals, factories, or children's camps.

Following college graduation with a bachelor's degree, the future psychologist must go on to graduate training leading to the Doctor of Philosophy (Ph.D) degree, or possibly to some other doctoral degree. Training for this degree requires a minimum of three years, although generally at least four years of graduate work are necessary. More often, the time required is six or seven years, and not infrequently the student spends ten to fifteen years in preparation. It should be added that for much of this time, he is earning a living with part-time teaching, working under a research grant, or doing some other kind of work in his field. The median age for a recipient of the Ph.D. in psychology is about thirty-one years.

The Ph.D. degree is not granted simply upon the completion of a certain number of advanced courses. The candidate for the degree must be able to demonstrate that he has a broad as well as a specialized knowledge of psychology, that he can do and has already done research work, that he is ready to assume responsibility for carrying on and advancing psychology as a science and as a profession.

Even after such extensive training,

he may need further specialized training, just as a physician may specialize after receiving his M.D. degree. The psychologist may gain experience working as an intern (under supervision) in his field of specialization, for example, in a mental hygiene clinic, a mental hospital, a factory or office, a child guidance center, a social welfare agency, or a school. Many psychologists take advantage of financial grants for doing post-doctoral research in order to gain further experience in scientific methodology and techniques.

Perhaps this seems like a long training program. It is, but it is no longer than that in many other professional fields. Perhaps you feel that you do not have sufficient money to enable you to spend seven or more years in a university. Such a program does require money, but do not become too concerned about finances. Colleges and universities have various programs for providing financial assistance to worthy undergraduate students. For the graduate student who has demonstrated his competence, there are governmental and private funds available.

In planning his training, the psychology student should prepare to meet the licensing or certification requirements of the state in which he plans to work in case the state has a law regulating the practice of psychology. If he is planning to enter industrial, clinical, or counseling psychology, he should prepare to take the examinations given by the American Board of Examiners in Professional Psychology.

Are there different levels of psychological work? There are some op-portunities for doing work of a limited psychological nature without the long and strenuous training just indicated. Strictly speaking, however, a person doing such work cannot be called a psychologist.

Two-year college programs are being designed to train subprofessional personnel for work of a psychological nature in mental hospitals, schools for the retarded, child guidance clinics, and so on. Or possibly you are thinking of discontinuing your training after you have received a college bachelor's degree with a major in psychology. Will there be vocational opportunities for you with this amount of training? To answer this question, two psychologists sent a questionnaire to leaders in business and industry, schools and universities, governmental agencies, and social service organizations, asking about job opportunities for college majors in psychology. Almost all employers emphasized the importance of a broad liberal arts background rather than the particular major field of study. They said they were seeking individuals who had not only excelled in schoolwork but who, in addition, had participated in extracurricular activities, had shown initiative, and had taken responsibility. The survey did reveal, however, that psychology majors would probably find their greatest opportunities in such areas as personnel administration, management training, and to some extent in sales, advertising, and production, although a college major in psychology was not a prerequisite for such jobs. In addition, there were opportunities for the college psychology major in educational, governmental, and social service areas. The employers stressed the importance of training in statistics and in English grammar, composition, and report writing. It was pointed out that most large organizations have their own in-training programs for providing the specialized preparation and experience needed for their jobs.

There are opportunities for psychological work for those who go on to a master's degree in psychology (usually awarded for one or two years' advanced study beyond the bachelor's degree). For example, such persons do work in connection with the problems presented by children having scholastic and behavior difficulties, including administration of various kinds of tests. They may do testing and other work in psychological clinics, although they do not have responsibility for final diagnosis and treatment. They may teach psychology in the increasing number of high schools that offer the course. In addition to their training in psychology, would-be teachers must take the courses necessary to get a teaching license and should prepare to teach in one or two other fields as well.

It must be recognized that, although work of a psychological nature can be done by those with less than doctoral training, the salaries are lower than for those individuals with the more complete training. It must be admitted that male psychologists receive higher salaries than female psychologists with the same amount of training and experience, but there are many opportunities for women in psychology, especially in child guidance clinics and as school psychologists.

LOOKING AHEAD

When you began your study of psychology, you probably did not even have a clear idea of the nature of the material to be discussed in the course. (Reread the section of your *Record of Activities and Experiments* in which you gave your ideas about psychology. Take the "test" again and compare your "before-and-after" scores as directed in the *Record.*) On page 2 of this textbook, psychology was defined as the science that studies the behavior of organisms. This definition should mean much more to you now than at the beginning of the course.

You have learned to distinguish between the work of well-trained psychologists and the work of untrained quacks in the field. You have developed some appreciation of how psychologists study personality and of how the principles of psychology may help men and women to develop socially effective personalities. You now know something about the development of behavior. IQ's are no longer a mystery to you. You have faced the social problems of caring for both the mentally retarded and the mentally ill.

You have considered the problem of the influences of heredity and environment on the development of the individual. You have learned how your body operates in keeping you in touch with your environment. You are a more efficient student as a consequence of your scientific study of learning, and you have learned a great deal about how to keep in good mental health. You have studied about behavior in small groups, and about applications of prin-

YOU AND SOCIETY

ciples of psychology in meeting the problems of marriage and parenthood. You have seen how principles of psychology can be applied to social problems and to vocational problems.

You are nearing the end of this course in psychology. Some of you will take courses in psychology at college, some of you may major in this field, and a few of you will take the training necessary to reach the top levels of psychology. For many of you, your present course will be your only formal study of psychology, although in the years to come you will read about it in magazines and books, and hear about it from many other sources. No doubt some of these future contacts will be with questionable psychology and even pseudo-psychology, as well as with psychologically sound material. As a result of your present course, you should always try to distinguish between what is called "psychology" but is not, and what is true, scientific, and professional psychology.

Terms to Add to Your Vocabulary

applied psychology	kymograph	vocational selection
aptitude test	occupational brief	vocational interest inventory
basic psychology	piece-rate pay	vocational work
ergograph	time-rate pay	work increment
general decrement	vocational guidance	

Suggestions for Activities

1. If it can be arranged, take a mechanical aptitude test, or an aptitude test in the fields of art, clerical skill, nursing, and so on. One test available is the *Turse Shorthand Aptitude Test,* published by Harcourt, Brace & World. This test illustrates what is meant by aptitude as contrasted with ability. Results of any such tests you may take will be of interest and value to you. But remember that they must not be used as a sole basis for selecting a life vocation.

2. Most industrial tests are not suitable for classroom use. However, if it can be arranged, take the *Survey of Working Speed and Accuracy* test by Floyd L. Ruch, published by the California Test Bureau. It is designed for use in the "selection, placement, upgrading, and transfer of workers performing routine operations calling for speed and accuracy."

3. A number of measuring devices are available which measure interests rather than aptitudes. In connection with the work of the guidance department or in connection with your class in psychology, you may wish to take the *Kuder Preference Record* (published by Science Research Associates). The Kuder record has three forms: Vocational, Personal, and Occupational.

4. In concluding your course in psychology, ask some psychologist to speak to the class about his or her work. Your school system may have a full- or part-time psychologist. Local industries may employ psychologists. There will be one or more psychologists on the staff of any

child guidance clinic. Institutions for the care of the mentally retarded, the mentally ill, and people who have broken the law will have psychologists who might be willing to discuss their work.

5. Write a report on "How my ideas of psychology and psychologists have changed during my study of psychology" or "Why I think I might wish to become a psychologist."

Suggestions for Further Reading

Daniel, Robert S., ed., *Contemporary Readings in General Psychology,* 2nd ed., Houghton Mifflin. Pages 90–95, "Research on Skills"; pages 386–92, "The Psychologist's Services in Solving Daily Problems"; and pages 400–03, "Aptitude Tests: Can They Steer You to Success?"

Hilgard, Ernest R., and Richard C. Atkinson, *Introduction to Psychology,* 4th ed., Harcourt, Brace & World. Chapter 24, "Psychology as a Profession." This is an especially fascinating chapter for those of you who are considering psychology as a future occupation.

Jobs in Psychology, Job Family Series, Science Research Associates.

Journal of School Psychology. Read a few articles in recent issues of this periodical, which should be in your school or public library.

Kalish, Richard A., *The Psychology of Human Behavior,* Wadsworth. Chapter 9, "The Student at College"; and Chapter 15, "Career Planning and the World of Work." Also, Appendix I, "College Orientation."

Leuba, Clarence, *Man: A General Psychology,* Holt, Rinehart & Winston. Pages 500–01, "Tests for Special Aptitudes."

Lindgren, Henry C., Donn Byrne, and Lewis F. Petrinovich, *Psychology: An Introduction to a Behavioral Science,* 2nd ed., John Wiley. Chapter 17, "Psychology Applied to Problems of Educational and Occupational Choice"; Chapter 18, "Psychology Applied to Problems in Business and Industry"; and Chapter 19, "Psychology Applied to Problems of International Behavior."

McKeachie, Wilbert J., and Charlotte L. Doyle, *Psychology,* Addison-Wesley. Appendix II, "Psychology in Today's World."

Mahoney, Harold J., and T. L. Engle, *Points for Decision,* rev. ed., Harcourt, Brace & World. Chapter 6, "Choosing a Vocation"; Chapter 7, "Learning About Jobs"; Chapter 12, "Getting and Holding a Job"; Chapter 13, "Continuing Education after High School"; Chapter 14, "Entering the Service."

Munn, Norman L., *Psychology,* 5th ed., Houghton Mifflin. Chapter 18, "Working Efficiently."

Ogg, Elizabeth, *Psychologists in Action,* New York (Public Affairs Pamphlet, No. 229). If you have not read this booklet in connection with Chapter 1, you may wish to do so now.

—— *Psychotherapy—A Helping Process,* New York (Public Affairs Pamphlet No. 329).

Ross, Sherman, and Robert F. Lockman, *A Career in Psychology,* American Psychological Association.

Ruch, Floyd L., *Psychology and Life,* 7th ed., Scott, Foresman. Section B, "Frontiers In Psychology." This section contains some of the most recent work in a variety of areas within the field of psychology. It provides interesting and thought-provoking ideas.

Sanford, Fillmore H., *Psychology: A Scientific Study of Man,* 2nd ed., Wadsworth. Pages 141–44 deal with tests of specific abilities, aptitudes, and interests.

Seidman, Jerome M., ed., *The Adolescent: A Book of Readings,* rev. ed., Holt, Rinehart & Winston. Pages 456–68, "Looking at Occupations."

Appendix

In connection with your study of psychology, you may find a need for some additional knowledge of statistics. If you take an intelligence test, personality inventory, aptitude test, or any other standardized measuring instrument, you will encounter certain technical terms used to describe the construction of the instrument or to interpret the scores. A number of these terms are explained in this Appendix. Also, to more fully understand the results of some psychological studies, it is helpful to be acquainted with certain statistical tools that psychologists use in measuring behavior. Those of you who are interested in mathematics can learn more about statistics by consulting the readings suggested at the end of this Appendix.

Statistics may be defined as the mathematical procedures for selecting, organizing, and interpreting data to determine relationships or degree of significance. Although many individuals believe that statistics involves complex mathematical relationships and procedures, elementary statistics actually requires only addition, subtraction, multiplication, and division. The mathematical procedures involved can be performed by an average ninth-grade student. The difficult part of statistics comes in understanding what the end product means, not in the computational procedures.

ORGANIZING DATA

Frequency distribution. Suppose that fifty scores of tenth-grade students on a biology quiz appeared as follows:

10	8	9	6	8	5	9	7	5	9
6	8	6	10	6	9	7	8	10	7
8	9	8	6	10	7	8	8	9	7
7	9	8	6	9	6	8	7	10	8
6	9	7	8	8	8	10	7	8	9

These scores can be compared and interpreted but only on a superficial basis. They would be somewhat more meaningful if arranged in the following order, from the highest to the lowest:

10	10	10	10	10	10	9	9	9
9	9	9	9	9	9	9	8	8
8	8	8	8	8	8	8	8	8
8	8	8	8	7	7	7	7	7
7	7	7	7	6	6	6	6	6
6	6	6	5	5				

However, compare the above arrangement of scores with the following frequency distribution:

SCORE	TALLY	FREQUENCY
10	卌 /	6
9	卌 卌	10
8	卌 卌 卌	15
7	卌 ////	9
6	卌 ///	8
5	//	2
		$N = 50$

It is now possible to tell exactly how many times a score occurred. Such a system is known as a *frequency distribution,* which is a means of arranging data to obtain the frequency with which a certain score, or other data, occurs. To group the scores in this manner, simply tally the number of times each score occurred and add the tally marks as illustrated in the example. This method of organizing data is used constantly in psychology and is even more necessary if further statistics will be required at a later date.

Sometimes it becomes impractical to tally each individual score. This happens when both N, which is the number of scores or cases, and the *range,* which is the numerical difference between the lowest and highest scores, are large. It then becomes necessary to employ *class intervals,* that is, to group the data according to specific numerical intervals rather than tallying individual scores. For example, if you wished to make a distribution of college entrance examination scores that ranged from 260 to 770, instead of tallying each score within the range, you could make a frequency distribution in terms of class intervals of 25, which would look like the following:

CLASS INTERVAL	TALLY	FREQUENCY
750–774	𝍓 ////	9
725–749	𝍓 𝍓 /	11
700–724	𝍓 𝍓 𝍓	15
.		
.		
.		
275–299	𝍓 ///	8
250–274*	𝍓 ///	8

Although there is no universal agreement on the number of class intervals to have in a frequency distribution, the most generally accepted number is from 10 to 15 intervals. To obtain the size of the class interval, decide how many intervals you wish to have and divide this into the range of scores. Class intervals are usually in units of 5, 10, 15, 25, 50, or 100. Remember

*Although it appears as if the range of each interval is only "24" (250–274), the range of each interval is computed on the basis of the *lower* and *upper limits* of each interval, which is 249.5 to 274.5. Theoretically, 250 represents any score from 249.5 to 250.49999.

that if you use too many intervals, it becomes troublesome to tally scores, and if you use too few, the individual scores lose their value. After selecting the number and size of intervals, determine the midpoint of each interval, which is found by adding the lowest number of the interval to the highest and dividing by 2. The midpoint of each interval then represents all scores within the interval.

CLASS INTERVAL	MIDPOINT	f	cf	$c\%$
50–54	52	6	185	100
45–49	47	9	179	97
40–44	42	14	170	92
35–39	37	22	156	84
30–34	32	25	134	72
25–29	27	30	109	59
20–24	22	26	79	43
15–19	17	23	53	29
10–14	12	17	30	16
5–9	7	8	13	7
0–4	2	5	5	3

$$N = 185$$

There is one additional step that can be used to increase the value of the frequency distribution. This step is accomplished by cumulating the frequencies from the bottom to the top (see table above). Notice that the 0–4 class interval has a frequency of 5 and the 5–9 class interval a frequency of 8, making a total of 13. The frequency of each succeeding class interval is added until the highest interval of 50–54 is reached with a total of 185, which can be checked against the total N of 185. The cumulative percent ($c\%$) is obtained by dividing the cumulative frequency (cf) by N. Now it is possible to state not only how many scores were obtained at a specific point but also what percent. For example, we can tell at a glance that 109, or approximately 59 percent, of the scores are 29 or lower. Conversely, we can state that 41 percent (100 − 59 percent) are scores of 30 or higher.

As you can see, only adding, subtracting, multiplying, and dividing have been used in our statistical computations. Perhaps you have begun to realize that organizing data does have a definite place in psychology and that the procedures used are relatively simple.

Frequency polygon. This graphical method of presenting data is probably already familiar to you. A *frequency polygon* is a pictorial representation of the frequencies of scores, which are plotted as dots on a graph and connected by a continuous line to form a curve.

Curves may take several shapes, depending upon the distribution. They may be relatively symmetrical and bell-shaped, indicating that the majority of measurements fall into the middle, or average, range, with a small number quite evenly distributed at the extremes to either side. Other curves are skewed to the right (positively skewed), extending downward more gradually on the right side, or skewed to the left (negatively skewed), with a longer tail on the left side, indicating an uneven distribution. A curve is *skewed,* or asymmetrical, because the scores have piled up at one end instead of being grouped in the middle. When scores are positively skewed, they tend to pile up on the left-hand side of the curve, whereas when they are negatively skewed, they tend to pile up on the right-hand side of the curve. There are also bimodal curves, which are discussed on page 577 of this Appendix.

It should be noted that when data are plotted, the lower left-hand corner of the graph is nearly always the "zero" point. The numerical value of the variables increases going up the vertical axis (also known as the *ordinate,* or *Y* axis) and going from left to right across the horizontal axis (*abscissa,* or *X* axis). When single scores are used, they are plotted individually; when class intervals are plotted, the midpoints of each are used.

Histogram. Another way of presenting a frequency distribution graphically is in the form of a *histogram* (sometimes called a *column diagram*), which indicates frequencies with bars

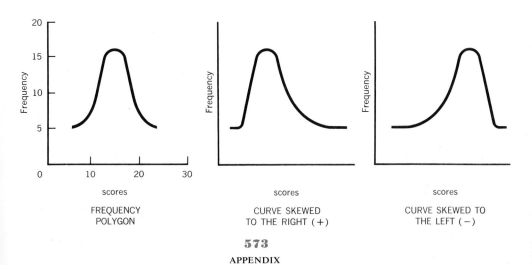

FREQUENCY POLYGON

CURVE SKEWED TO THE RIGHT (+)

CURVE SKEWED TO THE LEFT (−)

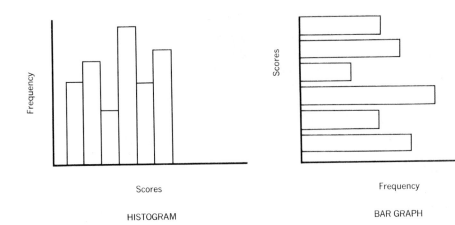

Frequency | Scores

HISTOGRAM

Scores | Frequency

BAR GRAPH

rather than lines. A histogram is plotted by placing the base of each rectangle, or bar, on the horizontal axis for the distance of one class interval and raising the height of the rectangle to a level appropriate to the frequency plotted on the vertical axis.

If a histogram is turned sideways, so that the columns actually look like bars protruding from left to right, the histogram is then called a *bar graph*. You will notice that in a bar graph the frequency is plotted on the horizontal axis and the scores, or other data, on the vertical axis. Also, you will notice that a bar graph has space between the bars (found in some histograms, too).

THE NORMAL DISTRIBUTION

The bell-shaped curve mentioned previously, indicating relatively symmetrical distribution, approximates one of the most useful concepts in the field of statistics. This is a theoretical concept known as the *normal curve,* which is an idealized, perfectly symmetrical curve representing an idealized normal frequency distribution. A normal curve has the following

characteristics: (1) It has one high point, from which the line slopes downward smoothly on both sides. (2) It is bilaterally symmetrical, that is, one side is exactly like the other, only in reverse. (3) It is bell-shaped. (4) The sloping lines on either side never touch the base line. (5) The mean, median, and mode are numerically the same (see pages 576–77).

Observe in the illustration of a normal curve distribution on page 575 the percentage of cases that fall in each equal section on either side of the curve's highest point. These percentages apply to any data that follow a normal curve pattern.

Most psychological measurements and test scores, as well as physical traits like height and weight, follow a normal curve pattern when N is large. Since a normal curve is a theoretical construct, however, it can be found only when N becomes infinitely large. If, for example, you plotted standardized test scores for everyone in your state in a frequency polygon, the curve would be very close to a normal curve. If you plotted scores for everyone in the nation, the scores would come closer to a normal distribution pattern

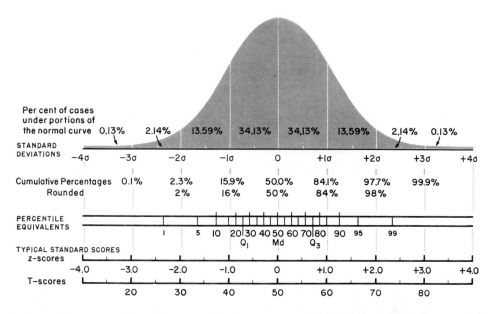

Per cent of cases under portions of the normal curve 0.13% 2.14% 13.59% 34.13% 34.13% 13.59% 2.14% 0.13%

STANDARD DEVIATIONS −4σ −3σ −2σ −1σ 0 +1σ +2σ +3σ +4σ

Cumulative Percentages 0.1% 2.3% 15.9% 50.0% 84.1% 97.7% 99.9%
Rounded 2% 16% 50% 84% 98%

PERCENTILE EQUIVALENTS 1 5 10 20 30 40 50 60 70 80 90 95 99
Q₁ Md Q₃

TYPICAL STANDARD SCORES
z-scores −4.0 −3.0 −2.0 −1.0 0 +1.0 +2.0 +3.0 +4.0
T-scores 20 30 40 50 60 70 80

but probably would not be a perfect normal curve. Scores that have been plotted for over a million individuals in the armed forces look very much like a normal curve.

PERCENTILES, DECILES, QUARTILES

The student who takes a test may wish to know how his score compares with others who have taken the same test. His score can be compared in terms of percentiles (sometimes called centiles), deciles, or quartiles.

Norms, or standards used for comparing scores, are determined by giving the test to a large number of representative persons and arranging their scores in order from highest to lowest. The scores can then be divided into 100 groups called *percentiles* (or centiles), into 10 groups called *deciles,* or into 4 groups called *quartiles*. When someone new takes the test, he can interpret his score in terms of these norms. Highest

scores are located in the ninety-ninth percentile, the tenth decile, or the fourth quartile. Lowest scores are located in the first percentile, first decile, or first quartile.

A percentile is a point on a 100-point scale which indicates the percent of individuals receiving scores that fall below that particular percentile. A student who finds that his score falls at the sixty-ninth percentile point knows that his score equaled or exceeded the scores made by 69 percent of the students on whom the test was standardized. A student whose score falls at the fifth percentile point knows that his score equaled or exceeded the scores made by only 5 percent of the students on whom the test was standardized.

It should be emphasized that any objective psychological test can have more than one set of norms. For example, suppose that a biology test is standardized on ninth-, tenth-, and eleventh-grade students. A student taking biology in the tenth grade would use the tenth-grade norms to compare his score.

MEASURES OF CENTRAL TENDENCY

A *measure of central tendency* is an average, that is, a typical or representative value for a group of measures; it is the central point of the distribution around which other scores tend to group. The most commonly used averages are the mean, median, and mode.

Mean. In statistical writing the word *mean* is used to designate the value popularly spoken of as the "average." It is calculated by dividing the sum of all the values in a series by the number of cases in the series. The mean for the eleven test scores in the left column of the following example is 79.09 or, to the nearest first decimal place, 79.1.

65	100		100
95	95		95
60	95		95
100	90		90
85	85		85
95	80	Median	80 ⎫
65	70		70 ⎬ Median = 75
90	65 ⎫		65 ⎫
65	65 ⎬ Mode		65 ⎬ Mode
80	65 ⎭		65 ⎭
70	60		60
11)870			50

79.09 = Mean

We usually compute means in order to compare the scores made by a group at different times or to compare one group with another group. Suppose there are two classes in your school taking psychology and both classes are given the same examination. You find that the mean score for one class is 5 points higher than the mean score for the other class. Does this difference signify that one class is really better than the other, or can the difference be accounted for in terms of chance?

Possibly if another test were given to both classes, the means might be equal, or the mean of the former poorer class might even be higher than the mean of the former better class. In general, the greater the number of students in each class, the more confidence can be placed in the difference between means.

Although we cannot go into the computation here, there are statistical procedures for determining how much confidence can be placed in a difference between means. Perhaps we can be virtually certain that one class is superior to the other. We may have to say that the difference in means is significant at the "1 percent level of significance"; that is, 99 times out of 100 we would be correct in assuming that there is a true difference between the two classes. We might have to say that the difference in means is significant at the "5 percent level of significance"; that is, 95 times out of 100 we would be correct in assuming that there is a true difference between the two classes.

If you are especially interested in this area of statistics, pursue some of the suggestions for further reading given on page 582.

Median. Another measure of central tendency is the median. The *median* is the middle score when the scores are arranged in order from highest to lowest. The center column of test scores given on this page is arranged in order with the highest at the top. The median is the sixth score from the top (or bottom)—that is, 80.

When the number of scores is even, the median is a score halfway between the two middle scores. Suppose that in addition to the scores indicated in the center column there had been a twelfth score of 50, as indicated in the column of figures at the right. In that case the median would have been 75.

Mode. A third measure of central tendency is the mode. The *mode* is the value that occurs most frequently in a distribution. In both the eleven-score and the twelve-score examples given on page 576, the mode is 65. There are more scores of 65 than any other single score. If the score of 90 had been 95, there would have been two most common values, 65 and 95. In that case the distribution would be termed *bimodal,* or having two modes.

Which should you use, the mean, the median, or the mode? The best procedure is to use all three measures of central tendency. If for some reason you would like to have extremely deviate scores affect the measure of central tendency, use the mean. If you do not wish to have extremely deviate scores affect the measure of central tendency, use the median. Sometimes individuals choose to report whichever measure will give them the best showing. For example, an employer wishing to indicate that his employees receive high salaries might report the mean salary. If he includes his own salary of $15,000 and has two other employees with salaries of $3,000 each, the mean of all salaries is $7,000. If he reported both mean and median salaries, however, you would know that something was wrong, since the two measures differ considerably, the median being only $3,000.

MEASURES OF VARIABILITY

In addition to measures of central tendency there are measures of variability, which represent the dispersion of a distribution. One such measure is the *range,* which is the numerical difference between the highest and the lowest scores in the distribution and shows the spread of the distribution. Another is the *standard deviation,* which measures the degree to which scores vary from the mean. For a discussion of standard deviation, see the Appendix in the *Record of Activities and Experiments.*

CORRELATION

The scatter diagram. Some explanation of the meaning of coefficients of correlation was given in Chapter 6. Further understanding of the meaning of correlation can be secured by studying a special kind of graph called a *scatter diagram.* In such a graph, scores on one test or measuring device are indicated on one axis. Scores on another test or measuring device are indicated on the other axis. Consider the following example: Eleven students take algebra and biology tests. The question is: What correlation is there between the scores on the two tests? To what extent do those who did well on the algebra test also do well on the biology test?

Suppose that pupil A made a score of 100 on the algebra test and a score of 100 on the biology test. On the left-hand scatter diagram on page 578 this pupil's score on *both* tests is represented by the uppermost dot. Suppose that pupil B made a score of 90 in algebra and 90 in biology. His score on both tests is represented by the next highest dot. In this hypothetical problem we shall suppose that each pupil made exactly the same score in

A scatter diagram, illustrating correlation

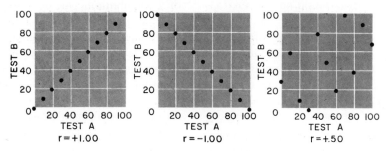

biology that he made in algebra: 80 and 80, 70 and 70, and so on down to pupil K, who made zero on both tests. The dots on the scatter diagram would line up as shown. In this case there is perfect *positive correlation* ($r = +1.00$) between scores on the two tests.

Now suppose that these same students take another test in algebra and another test in biology. This time assume that the higher each pupil scored in algebra the lower he scored in biology. Pupil A made a score of 0 in algebra and 100 in biology; pupil B, 10 in algebra and 90 in biology; and so on to pupil K, who made 100 in algebra and 0 in biology. The dots on the scatter diagram would line up as shown in the middle graph. In this case there is perfect *negative correlation* ($r = -1.00$) between the scores on the two tests.

In actual practice such a perfect relationship is not found. It might happen, for example, that pupil A made 70 in algebra and 100 in biology; pupil B made 80 in algebra and 40 in biology; C made 40 in algebra and 80 in biology; D made 50 in each; and so on. These scores and others are indicated by dots in the graph to the right in the figure above. Degrees of correlation between $+1.00$ and -1.00 are expressed by numbers such as $+.50$, $+.83$, $.00$, $-.50$, $-.04$. In the right-hand graph, the dots tend to line up in a positive direction. That is, they tend to slant upward from left to right, although not in a straight line. You cannot compute the coefficient of correlation from the scatter diagram, but if you worked it out by means of a statistical formula, you would find that the coefficient of correlation is $+.50$ ($r = +.50$). Had the dots tended to line up in the opposite direction— that is, slanting downward from left to right—the coefficient of correlation would have been negative.

Computing a coefficient of correlation by the rank-difference method. In computing coefficients of correlation, psychologists usually employ an accurate procedure called the *product-moment* method. This procedure takes account both of the size of the scores and of their positions in the series. We need not consider it here. An easier procedure called the *rank-difference* method will probably serve your purpose quite satisfactorily if you wish to compute the correlation between any two measures for a small group like a school class. In the rank-difference method, account is taken only of the position of scores in a series and not of their absolute values.

Coefficients of correlation computed by the product-moment method are designated by the letter r, while correlations computed by the rank-difference method are usually designated by the Greek form of the same letter, ρ (rho).

An illustration of computation of ρ, as shown in the discussion below, will serve to explain the technique. Suppose that your class takes two examinations, one in algebra and one in physics. The question is: How much relationship is there between the scores made by the same individuals in algebra and in physics? The steps to be taken in computing ρ by the rank-difference method are as follows:

Step 1. Record in a column the names of all individuals taking both tests. In the first column in our illustration below, the letters stand for names.

Step 2. In a second column, record the scores made by each individual on the algebra test. In our illustration pupil A made 83 in algebra, B made 65, and so on. (It makes no difference whether we put the algebra scores in the second or in the third column.)

Step 3. In a third column, record the scores made by each individual on the physics test. In our illustration A made 75, B made 60, and so on.

Step 4. In a fourth column, indicate the rank order of each individual's score in algebra. Pupil C made the highest score on the algebra test, so he is given rank 1; pupil G made the next highest score in algebra, so he is given rank 2; pupil I was third; and so on.

Computation of Correlation by the Rank-Difference Method

(1) PUPIL	(2) SCORES IN ALGEBRA	(3) SCORES IN PHYSICS	(4) RANK IN ALGEBRA	(5) RANK IN PHYSICS	(6) DIFFER-ENCES IN RANKS (D)	(7) DIFFER-ENCES IN RANKS SQUARED (D^2)
A	83	75	6	7.5	1.5	2.25
B	65	60	12	11.5	.5	.25
C	100	98	1	2	1.0	1.00
D	75	90	9	4	5.0	25.00
E	77	80	8	6	2.0	4.00
F	85	70	5	9	4.0	16.00
G	95	100	2	1	1.0	1.00
H	73	60	10	11.5	1.5	2.25
I	90	85	3	5	2.0	4.00
J	80	75	7	7.5	.5	.25
K	87	93	4	3	1.0	1.00
L	70	65	11	10	1.0	1.00
						58.00

$$\rho = 1 - \frac{6 \times (\text{sum of } D^2)}{N(N^2 - 1)} = 1 - \frac{6 \times (58.00)}{12(144 - 1)} = 1 - \frac{348}{1716} = 1 - .20 = .80$$

Values of ρ tend to be between .01 and .02 less than values of r.

Step 5. In a fifth column, indicate the rank order of each individual's score in physics. Pupil G made the highest score in physics, so he is given rank 1; and so on. The score of 80 made by pupil E is sixth in rank, but you will note that two pupils, A and J, made scores of 75. If the scores of A and J were not equal, we would give one a rank of 7 and the other a rank of 8. Since they are equal, we designate both by the rank of 7.5 (mean of 7 and 8) and then give pupil F with a score of 70 a rank of 9. If the scores of three pupils had been the same, each would have been given the middle rank (the mean) of the next three ranks.

Step 6. In a sixth column, indicate the difference between the ranks in algebra and physics for each pupil; that is, find the numerical difference between the values in columns 4 and 5. Pupil A ranked 6 in algebra and 7.5 in physics, a difference of 1.5; pupil B ranked 12 in algebra and 11.5 in physics, a difference of 0.5; for pupil C there was a difference of 1; for pupil D there was a difference of 5; and so on.

Step 7. In a seventh column, indicate the square of each of the differences shown in column 6. For pupil A we find a difference of 1.5 in column 6, so this number is squared $(1.5 \times 1.5 = 2.25)$. For pupil B the difference in column 6 is 0.5, and this number squared equals .25; and so on.

Step 8. Add the figures in column 7. The sum in the illustration is 58.00.

Step 9. Substitute known values in the following formula:

$$\rho = 1 - \frac{6 \times (\text{sum of } D^2)}{N(N^2 - 1)}$$

In our illustration the sum of the differences in ranks squared, column (D^2), is 58.00. N in the formula represents the number of individuals whose scores are being correlated, 12 in our illustration.

Step 10. Perform the arithmetical computation indicated in the formula in order to find the degree of correlation between the two sets of scores. In our illustration ρ equals $+.80$.

Percents and coefficients. The significance of a particular coefficient of correlation can be somewhat better understood if we note the percent of cases in which individuals are "in agreement" in two traits in the sense of being above average in both traits, below average in both, or above average in one and below in the other.

The percents for different coefficients are given in the table below. The table shows, for example, that when .50 is the coefficient, $66\frac{2}{3}$ percent of persons are either above average in both traits or below average in both traits and that $33\frac{1}{3}$ percent of persons are above average in one trait and below average in the other.

COEFFICIENT OF CORRELATION	PERCENT OF CASES	
	IN AGREEMENT	IN DISAGREEMENT
.00	50	50
.10	53	47
.20	57	43
.30	60	40
.40	63	37
.50	$66\frac{2}{3}$	$33\frac{1}{3}$
.60	70	30
.70	75	25
.80	80	20
.90	86	14
.95	90	10
1.00	100	00

Correlation and causation. One of the most frequent misinterpretations of correlation is that it shows causation between variables. Actually, a correlation between intelligence and an individual's grade point average does *not* mean that one causes the other. Consider the following two examples: Someone once ran a correlation between the rise and fall of the Nile River and the rise and fall of grade-point averages at a well-known girls' college and found a significant relationship between the two. Another person ran a correlation between the increase in the number of miles of paved roads in the United States and the increase in lung cancer and obtained a significant correlation. Would you claim that one variable is the cause of the other in these examples? A correlation indicates that two factors vary together, but it does not provide a causal explanation.

Correlation and prediction. The most valuable usage of correlation is prediction. Knowing that two variables correlate allows us to predict the value of one variable when we know the value of the other. For example, if we had a high correlation between college grade-point averages and high school grades or between college entrance examination scores and college grades, we could use these variables to predict how well an individual would do in college. If the correlation were perfect, we could predict precisely what grades the student would get in college. However, perfect correlations are not found in actual educational or psychological measurements.

VALIDITY AND RELIABILITY

Validity. Authors of standardized tests are careful to explain why their tests are valid. By the *validity* of a test is meant the accuracy with which

it measures that which it is intended to measure. Suppose that your teacher of psychology reads and speaks German fluently. Absent-mindedly he writes your psychology examination in German and sends it to class on a day when he cannot be present. Such a test would not give a valid measure of your knowledge of psychology. Only those students who could read German would have their knowledge of psychology measured. All others would probably fail on the examination, regardless of how much they knew about psychology.

Correlation is often used in determining and expressing the degree of validity of a test. Scores on the test are correlated with some other measure of what the test is intended to measure. For example, suppose that some students are given a prognosis test in algebra—a test given at the beginning of an algebra course to determine the probable degree of success of the students in the course. The validity of the test could be measured by correlating these test scores with scores obtained later on a final examination covering the work of the course. The extent to which those who made high scores on the prognosis test tended to make high scores on the final examination and those who made low scores on the prognosis test tended to make low scores on the final examination would be a measure of the validity of the prognosis test.

Reliability. The *reliability* of a test means the self-consistency of the test. On some tests reliability may be measured by correlating the scores on one half of a test with scores on the other half of the same test. For example, scores on the odd-numbered questions may be correlated with scores on the even-numbered questions. Also, the reliability of a test may be measured by correlating scores made on the test with scores made on the same test by the same students upon repeating the test. Some standardized tests are published in two equivalent forms. If the same students take both forms, correlation between the two sets of scores is a measure of reliability. The higher the coefficient of correlation found by any of these methods, the greater is the reliability of the test.

Conclusion. Although this Appendix may seem to provide long and detailed information, it is only a very brief introduction to the field of statistics. There are many procedures and ideas left unmentioned.

One of the major disadvantages in presenting such a brief introduction to statistics is that individuals may believe that they are experts in the field. Remember that to be able to make an adequate interpretation of statistical procedures and results requires a great deal more study. Before you draw any conclusions from the results of statistical studies, especially of measurements that you may conduct, it is best to check with someone who has a solid background in the field.

Suggestions for Further Reading

Blommers, Paul J., and E. F. Lindquist, *Elementary Statistical Methods in Psychology and Education,* Houghton Mifflin.

Edwards, Allen L., *Statistical Analysis,* rev. ed., Holt, Rinehart & Winston.

Garrett, H. E., *Elementary Statistics,* 2nd ed., Van Rees.

Hilgard, Ernest R., and Richard C. Atkinson, *Introduction to Psychology,* 4th ed., Harcourt, Brace & World. Chapter 15, "Statistical Methods and Measurement"; pages 418–20. "Reliability and Validity."

Huff, Darrell, and Irving Geis, *How to Lie with Statistics,* W. W. Norton. An interesting and often amusing discussion of the misuses of statistics.

Moroney, M. J., *Facts from Figures,* Penguin Books. A general introduction to statistics for the person who is not a mathematics major.

Munn, Norman L., *Psychology,* 5th ed., Houghton Mifflin. Pages 68–86, "The Scientific Study of Individual Differences," "Statistical Analysis of Individual Differences," "The Distribution of Individual Differences," "The Status of the Individual," "Correlation," and "Statistical Supplement."

Ruch, Floyd L., *Psychology and Life,* 7th ed., Scott, Foresman. Pages 137–45, a discussion of validity and reliability, normal distribution, measures of central tendency, measures of deviation, and correlation.

Sanford, Fillmore H., *Psychology: A Scientific Study of Man,* 2nd ed., Wadsworth. Pages 157–63, "Describing Distributions"; pages 169–74, "Correlation."

Spence, J. T., *et al., Elementary Statistics,* Appleton-Century-Crofts.

Wallis, Wilson Allen, and H. V. Roberts, *Statistics: A New Approach,* Free Press.

Glossary

abnormal Away from the normal. In psychology, *abnormal* is usually used to refer to undesirable deviations in behavior or deficiencies in intellectual ability.

absolute pitch Ability to name correctly a particular tone that is sung or played, without directly comparing it with any heard tone, or the ability to sing a required tone without a reference tone being given.

acute hallucinosis A condition, often of alcoholic origin, characterized by hallucinations, especially auditory hallucinations.

adolescence The period between childhood and adulthood; roughly from ages twelve to twenty-one for girls and from thirteen to twenty-two for boys.

adrenal glands A pair of endocrine glands located over the kidneys.

aggression Hostile or angry activity in which there is attack on other persons: physical injury, destruction or taking of their property, or ridicule.

all-or-nothing thinking A form of uncritical thinking.

alpha wave (or **rhythm**) An electrical brain wave which maintains a steady rhythm of fluctuations during normal waking periods.

ambiversion A term which may be used to describe personality that is balanced between the extremes of introversion and extroversion.

anthropomorphism The attribution of human characteristics to beings other than man, as in fairy stories when animals talk to each other or to human beings.

anxiety A state of generalized fear and dread, which usually seems unattached to a specific object or event, and is often related to the future.

aptitude The ability to acquire or the likelihood of acquiring, with training, some knowledge or skill. An **aptitude test** measures what an individual is likely to be able to accomplish with training rather than what he has accomplished already.

ataractic drugs Tranquilizing medicines to reduce worry and anxiety.

atmospheric perspective The difference in clarity between objects close by and objects far away. Objects which appear to be hazy are perceived as being distant; well-defined objects are perceived as being near.

attitude A persisting readiness to respond to a situation in a given evaluative way. **Social attitude** is the readiness to respond in a definite way to either general or specific social stimuli.

aura A sensationlike experience preceding or marking the onset of an epileptic seizure.

autistic thinking Wishful thinking in which the individual imagines his world as being more like the world in which he would like to live than is justified by the facts of reality.

autokinetic illusion The apparent motion of a small, fixed dot of light located in a dark room.

autonomic nervous system A functional classification for those parts of the central and peripheral nervous systems which govern involuntary behavior.

behavior The activity of an organism, including muscular, glandular, and thinking activity.

behavior sampling A method of measuring certain specific traits of personality by means of an actual sampling of behavior.

behavioral sciences The sciences most concerned with human and animal behavior. The principal ones are psychology, sociology, and social anthropology, but certain areas of economics, history, political science, and zoology are also included.

brainstorming A method of creative thinking in which all ideas that seem to have any bearing on a problem are noted but are not critically evaluated until some later time.

brainwashing A popular term for the process of social pressure, and often physical torture, through which an individual is induced to change his behavior and attitudes to conform with the standards of his captors. Sensory deprivation is one technique of brainwashing.

branching program A form of instruction which progresses step by step but also provides alternative, or branching, supplementary information if the subject makes incorrect responses.

brightness The quality of light as determined by the amplitude or intensity of the stimulating light waves. A dimension of a color in terms of its nearness in brilliance to white as contrasted with black.

central nervous system A structural classification for the part of the nervous system composed of the brain and spinal cord.

chromosomes Small rodlike bodies in the cell nucleus. A human cell nor- mally has 46 chromosomes, arranged in 23 pairs. (See **genes.**)

chronological age (CA) The number of years and months a person has lived from birth to the present.

clairvoyance The perception of an external object without the use of known sense organs.

classical (or **Pavlovian**) **conditioning** The repeated pairing of an unconditioned stimulus, which originally elicited a given response, with another stimulus until this conditioned stimulus elicits the given response.

coding The process involved in the transferring of information from short-term memory to long-term memory. Also, the patterning of sensory impulses traveling along the same nerve fibers but remaining differentiated at higher levels of the central nervous system.

coefficient of correlation A number to express the degree of relationship between paired measures. Usually designated by the letter r.

color blindness (color weakness) Inability to discriminate certain hues. In the most common form, red and green are seen as alike and are confused with a faded yellow.

communication The process of transmitting or exchanging symbols, such as words or gestures, which are understood by the two or more organisms engaged in the interaction.

compensation A defense mechanism in which an individual makes up for or disguises an undesirable trait by exaggerating a desirable trait.

complementary colors Colors whose light waves when mixed in proper proportions are seen as gray.

concept The meaning, expressed in words or other symbols, which an individual attaches to the common property of a variety of objects or situations.

conditioned response (CR) The new or acquired response elicited by a stimulus not originally capable of arousing it.

conditioned stimulus (CS) The new stimulus, in a conditioning process, that was originally ineffective in eliciting a given response but has become capable of doing so.

conditioning The learning of some particular response to a stimulus.

conflict The state of tension or stress involved when an individual is faced simultaneously with either opposing or mutually exclusive impulses, tendencies, or desires.

consciousness Awareness at the present moment, with resulting ability to react to the environment.

control group A comparison group of subjects in an experiment usually matched to an experimental group but with whom the independent variable (condition being studied) is not present or is controlled.

conversion reaction A neurotic reaction in which an individual's psychological disturbances are changed or converted into bodily disturbances, such as paralysis of an arm or inability to recall past experiences. This term is replacing the older terms *hysteria* and *conversion hysteria*.

convulsive disorders Diseases often characterized by varying degrees of convulsive behavior and unconsciousness.

correlation The tendency of certain paired measures to vary in relationship to each other. (See **coefficient of correlation**.)

counter-conditioning Replacing one conditioned response to a stimulus with another (usually incompatible) response. The process is often used to eliminate undesirable behavior.

creative thinking Nonroutine directed thinking in which the individual seeks new solutions to problems or new forms of artistic expression; the thinking is along new lines for the individual, although others may have done similar thinking.

cretinism A condition of arrested mental and physical development resulting from insufficient thyroid secretion in early childhood.

crime An act or the performance of an act which, at the time of its commission, is forbidden and punishable by the laws of the social group to which the individual commiting the act belongs and which is subject to social condemnation.

cross-sectional method A means of studying human behavior by observing individuals of different age levels simultaneously.

data The mass of measured, factual materials collected and recorded for large groups. (*Data* is plural; the singular is *datum*.)

daydream Imaginative thinking engaged in by an individual while awake and usually involving fulfillment of wishes in some form. In the **conquering-hero daydream** the individual imagines himself performing great and heroic deeds while an appreciative audience applauds. The **suffering-hero daydream** is based on self-pity. Although the dreamer's imaginary suffering is painless or pleasantly painful, it elicits sympathy from others.

decile Any of the even tenth percentiles.

deductive reasoning The process of reasoning from general principles or rules to particular cases or consequences.

delinquency Socially nonconforming behavior, or crimes, committed by those who are not legally of age.

delusion An extremely false belief which persists in spite of evidence or proof to the contrary.

deoxyribonucleic acid (DNA) A chemical substance in the cell nucleus that is largely responsible for genetic inheritance.

dependent variable The factor the changed condition of which is considered to be a consequence of, to correspond to, or to depend upon the independent variable in an experiment; it is often a response to a definite, measured stimulus.

discipline The entire program of adapting the child to social life; the learning of the rules by which we live. Also, a branch of learning arranged for systematic study.

discrimination The tendency to respond to certain stimuli of a given kind in one way and to respond to somewhat different stimuli in another way, as when an animal or person makes one response to a reinforced stimulus and another response to a stimulus that is not reinforced.

dominant characteristic A characteristic which appears in all individuals of the first generation of descendants. A characteristic which prevents the appearance of the corresponding recessive characteristic.

dream A train of thoughts and images which usually makes a rather incoherent story and which ordinarily occurs during sleep.

drive A physiological condition that impels an organism to activity. The activity is usually directed toward some appropriate goal; for example, the hunger drive impels an animal or person to food-seeking activity.

duct gland A gland that discharges its secretion through an outlet onto an external or internal surface of the body.

ductless gland A gland having no duct (outlet). Sometimes used synonymously with *endocrine gland,* although some ductless glands do not function as endocrine glands.

ego A psychoanalytic term referring to the rational aspect of the personality. The part of the personality that tries to balance the demands of the id and superego. Also, the individual's conception of himself.

eidetic image An exceedingly vivid image (usually visual) which may be as clear as a perception but is generally recognized as subjective. Much more common in children than in adults. Popularly spoken of as a "photographic mind."

electroconvulsive therapy (ECT) A form of shock therapy in which a high voltage is passed through the head for a very brief period of time, producing temporary loss of awareness. It is used in the treatment of mental illness.

electroencephalogram (EEG) A record of the minute electrical oscillations, or brain waves, which accompany the activity of the brain. The record made by an electroencephalograph when it is connected with electrodes placed on the scalp over the brain.

emancipation The process of separation from one's family and the attaining of freedom from family control, especially during adolescence.

emotion A stirred-up state of an individual. An acute disturbance of the individual involving widespread physiological changes, which are either pleasant or unpleasant.

emotional maturity The displaying of emotional behavior such as is usual and expected of grownup persons.

empathy Inner mimicry; the ability to understand another person's attitudes, especially those that are emotionally toned.

endocrine gland A ductless gland whose secretions, or hormones, are absorbed by the lymph or blood.

environment The external forces, conditions, and influences that surround an organism's life and affect its activities.

epilepsy (See **convulsive disorders.**)

ergograph An instrument for recording the amount of continuous work done with a certain set of muscles.

eugenics The science of heredity, especially as it is concerned with measures for improving the human species by attention to breeding.

euthenics A branch of applied science that aims at improving the human species by regulating environment.

exclusive group A group whose members place restrictions and limitations upon the opportunity for others to participate.

experimental group A group of subjects in an experimental situation on whom the independent variable, or condition being studied, is varied.

explicit behavior Behavior which is easily observed and measured. Sometimes referred to as *overt* behavior.

extinction The dying out of an established conditioned response as a consequence of presenting the conditioned stimulus without the usual reinforcement.

extrasensory perception (ESP) Becoming aware of objects without the use of sense organs.

extrinsic reward An artificial reward, not inherently associated with the behavior being reinforced.

extroversion A general term indicating the tendency for an individual to center his interests in his external environment and in social life. Also spelled *extraversion*.

fantasy Imaginative thinking or daydreaming which is usually pleasant and provides the individual with some temporary relief from his frustrations.

fatigue Decreased ability of an organism, or part of it, as in the case of a muscle, to perform further work.

feedback (See **psychological feedback.**)

feelings Experiences of pleasantness or unpleasantness, including passions, desires, cravings, interests, likings, and dislikings. Also, *feeling* may refer to the sense of touch.

figure-ground relationship A situation perceived as divided into two parts—the part that is focused on is the figure, and the remaining part is the background.

filial love The love of children for their parents.

foster home A home other than that of the biological parents.

frame The single unit displayed at each step in programed learning.

fraternal twins Twins developing from two ova (eggs) fertilized by two sperms. They may be of the same sex or different sexes.

friendship A social relationship between two persons in which there is mutual attraction, cooperation, trust, and reinforcement. The term is usually applied to relationships in which attraction for a person of the other sex is not present or is not emphasized. Friendship implies more than a casual acquaintanceship.

frustration The thwarting or blocking of motivated behavior so that a prompt and effective adjustment cannot be made. **Frustration tolerance** is the ability of an individual to withstand frustration without developing undesirable modes of response such as becoming emotionally upset or neurotic.

functional disorder A mental illness with no demonstrable organic basis (although there may be such a basis). A mental illness depending upon previous experiences in the person's life rather than upon bodily defects.

galvanic skin response (GSR) The change in electrical resistance of the skin, especially as such change accompanies an emotional state.

gambling The betting of money, or something else of value, upon an outcome governed by chance. In pure gambling the chances of winning or losing are governed by the mathematical laws of chance; but as usually practiced, gambling involves much trickery and even flagrant dishonesty.

generalization In conditioning—after a conditioned response has been established to a certain stimulus, other similar stimuli will also result in that response. Also, the reaching of a general conclusion or judgment based upon specific facts or observations.

generosity error A tendency, when rating some situation or person, to overrate.

genes Factors in a cell which determine the transmission and development of hereditary characteristics. Tiny parts within chromosomes.

genetics The branch of biology concerned with heredity.

genius An individual of very superior intellectual ability. Formerly, an individual with an IQ of 140 or higher was often spoken of as a genius, but today there is a tendency to limit the use of the term to individuals with IQ's of 180 or higher.

genotype The sum of all the biological characteristics that an individual is capable of transmitting to his offspring, or a single such characteristic.

gerontology The scientific investigation of the characteristics of old age.

gifted Used to describe persons with exceptional or special abilities or persons of high intellectual ability (IQ's about 140 to about 180) but not quite so high as represented by the term *genius*.

gonads Sex glands that provide the sperm and egg cells for reproduction, and produce hormones which determine secondary sex characteristics and influence sexual behavior.

group dynamics The study of the foundation and functioning of groups, and the interpersonal relationships that develop between the members.

group therapy A psychotherapeutic treatment in which a small group of people meet to discuss their problems and to interact.

hallucination A misinterpretation of ideas as perceptions. A senselike perception for which there is no appropriate external stimulus, as in the case of a psychotic person who hears voices speaking to him although there are no voices or other sounds which might be interpeted as voices.

halo effect A tendency, when one person is rating another, to be influenced by an estimate of some other trait or by a general impression of the individual being rated; the general impression may be either favorable or unfavorable.

heredity The sum of the characteristics transmitted from parent to child by the germ plasm.

heuristic concept A formulation that originates in order to explain something; it is an approximation, unprovable, having no existence on its own.

hormones Chemical substances produced by endocrine glands.

hue A technical term for "color" (red, green, blue, yellow, etc.). The characteristic of a visual impression as determined by the wavelength of the light stimulus.

hydrotherapy Any of many forms of treatment of disease by means of water, including showers and wrapping the patient in wet sheets.

hyper- (as a prefix) Unusually great or excessive. When prefixed to the name of a gland, it designates overactivity of that gland.

hypnosis An artificially induced state characterized chiefly by extreme suggestibility. Usually, though not always, resembling sleep but physiologically different from it.

hypo- (as a prefix) Under, below. When prefixed to the name of a gland, it designates underactivity of that gland.

hypothalamus A part of the brain-stem which serves as a center for the autonomic nervous system and influences emotional behavior.

hypothesis An assumption adopted as a tentative explanation of observed facts and as the basis for further reasoning or investigation.

hysteria (See **conversion reaction**.)

id A psychoanalytic term referring to the unconscious primitive urges, mainly sexual and aggressive in nature, that underlie behavior.

identical twins Twins developing from a single fertilized ovum (egg), thus having the same heredity. Always of the same sex.

identification A defense mechanism in which an individual identifies himself with some individual or organization which he believes to be successful or distinguished.

illusion A false perception.

imagination The reproduction and reorganization of past experiences into a present ideational experience.

implicit behavior Behavior not easily observable by another person without the aid of special, sensitive measuring instruments; for example, implicit speech consists of inaudible, tiny muscular movements of the speech apparatus during thinking, which can be detected only by use of very delicate instruments. Sometimes implicit behavior is referred to as *covert* behavior.

imprinting A special kind of very rapid learning that occurs in some animals, notably birds, at a certain early stage in their development. It is relatively insusceptible to forgetting or extinction.

inclusive group A group whose members strive to expand their activities and include more people.

incubation A stage in creative thinking characterized by absence of active thinking about a given problem. A period in which no obvious progress in problem-solving occurs.

independent variable The factor the

effects of which are being examined in an experiment. It is selected and then manipulated by the experimenter in some systematic and predetermined manner while all, or as many as possible, other variables are held constant. The independent variable is often a stimulus, the response to which is the dependent variable.

Indoklon therapy A therapeutic technique used to alleviate the symptoms of neurotic and psychotic patients.

inductive reasoning The process of reasoning from particular facts or cases to general conclusions.

insanity A legal term for any mental illness in which an individual is judged to be incapable of assuming normal responsibility for his acts. (See **psychosis**.)

insight An apparently rather sudden grasp of the relationships involved in problem solving.

inspiration A step in creative thinking which follows preparation and incubation and in which there is a rather sudden solution of the problem under consideration.

instinct (See **species-specific behavior**.)

intelligence The ability of a complex organism to adapt itself adequately to its environment. Now thought to include a number of specific factors.

intelligence quotient (IQ) The ratio of mental age to chronological age times 100. $IQ = (MA/CA) \times 100$. (The actual chronological age of an adult is not used. Modern tests of intellectual ability compute a standard score which corresponds roughly to the traditional IQ.)

interaction-oriented group A group whose primary purpose is to establish social contacts and to interact with others.

interest A set or preparation which motivates a person in a certain direction.

interposition A cue to depth perception which indicates that when one object partially blocks the view of another, the object blocking the view is closer than the object behind it. Such a cue may be monocular.

interviewing A method of judging a person in a relatively short time by means of a standardized (or an informal) conversational situation.

intrinsic reward A reward that is logically associated with, and an integral part of, the behavior being reinforced.

introversion A general term indicating the tendency for an individual to center his interests in himself and in his own experiences.

inventory, personality A standardized questionnaire or self-rating scale in which an individual gives information about his attitudes and overt behavior, which can then be evaluated in terms of norms. Usually a paper-and-pencil questionnaire, answered by selecting "Yes," "No," "?", or some other given answers.

kymograph An instrument for recording changes in activity over a period of time. The recording is usually made on a revolving drum.

laissez-faire A French term meaning "allow to do." A laissez-faire leader exercises little, if any, control, guidance, or assistance to his group.

latent learning Learning which takes place in the absence of reinforcement but is utilized when reinforcement is given. Learning that becomes evident only when it is being used.

Law of Intermediates A law stating that when hues not opposite each other on the color circle are mixed together, the resulting color will be intermediate between the two hues, and the saturation of that color will be closest to the hue which has the greater proportion in the mixture.

leader The individual in a group who exerts the greatest influence upon the members of the group. He or she guides the thinking of the group and initiates, directs, or organizes the activity of the group.

learning Acquiring the ability to respond adequately to a situation. The modification of behavior through experience.

linear perspective The perception of objects as smaller and closer together the more distant they are from the observer.

linear program A form of instruction which contains a series of statements arranged in a step-by-step progression to which the subject responds and then learns immediately whether or not his answer is correct.

long-term memory The storage and retention of information that has been situated briefly in the short-term memory.

longitudinal method A means of studying human behavior by observing the development of the same individual or group over a considerable period of time.

loudness The intensity of a sound, determined primarily by the amplitude of the sound waves.

love A feeling of attachment toward some person based on mutual reinforcement. The word often, but not necessarily, suggests attraction for someone of the other sex.

lying Communication, usually verbal, with intent to deceive. The "lying" of children is often to be understood as a mere confusion in thinking, as attention seeking, or as self-defense.

manic-depressive A psychosis which usually includes periods of excitement with overactivity and periods of melancholy with underactivity.

marital love The love between married persons.

mass media Instruments of communication which present a common message to a large number of people at the same time, or nearly the same time: books, the press, radio, television, films, and so on.

maturation Bodily growth or development and the accompanying behavioral changes.

maze A learning device consisting of a correct pathway and blind alleys; it can be used in both animal and human learning experiments.

mean The arithmetic average in a series of values.

median The middle score in a distribution when the scores are arranged in order from lowest to highest.

memory trace The assumed changes that occur in the nervous system between the time learning takes place and the time it is recalled. It is hypothesized that these changes explain the process of retention.

mental age (MA) A measure of mental development in terms of the ability of average individuals of various ages, especially children.

mental deficiency A term used to refer to the condition of individuals of subnormal intellectual ability. Some psychologists reserve this term for those whose lack of ability is a result of brain damage or other organic defect. (See **mental retardation**.)

mental health A way of living such that a person is well adjusted to his social environment, both from his own point of view and from the point of view of others.

mental hospital A hospital for the care and treatment of persons suffering from various psychoses or, possibly, psychoneuroses. The term is displacing the older term *insane asylum* and in turn is being displaced by the simple term *hospital.*

mental hygiene The investigation and practice of ways of living that tend to prevent or remedy maladjustments, especially those of an emotional nature.

mental maturity The condition of complete general mental development. In terms of intelligence testing, mental maturity is attained at the time when a person ceases to improve his score on a general intelligence test as he grows older. Also, may be called *intellectual maturity.*

mental retardation A term used to refer to the condition of individuals of subnormal intellectual ability. Some psychologists reserve this term for those who have undue difficulty in learning but with no evident organic basis for the difficulty.

mesmerism An early term for hypnotism.

mind The organization of behavior. (The word is seldom used in psychological writings.)

mnemonic device An artificial aid to learning; a catchword or formula employed to facilitate recall. Usually of very limited and temporary value.

mob An incidentally, or accidentally, formed group of individuals acting under great emotional stress, often in an attempt to control the behavior of those who oppose them or to accomplish some illegal act.

mode The most common value in a series of values. If there are two most common values, the distribution is said to be *bimodal.*

mood A mild emotional state that lingers for some time, but not permanently, after the emotion-producing situation has passed.

morale The prevailing attitude of the individuals in a group, or of the group as a whole, marked by confidence, loyalty, and desire to work toward group goals.

motivation A general term referring to regulation of behavior in such a way as to satisfy the individual's needs and enable him to work toward his goals. Aspirations, attitudes, and interests are involved.

negative correlation A statistical relationship which shows that as one variable increases in value, the other variable decreases.

nerve impulse The current or disturbance that travels along a nerve fiber following stimulation.

neurosis (plural, *neuroses*) A milder form of mental difficulty than a true psychosis. A neurotic person needs medical and psychological care, although usually he does not have to enter a mental hospital for treatment.

noise An undesired and unpleasant sound, usually produced by an unsteady medley of vibrations.

nonsense syllable A meaningless syllable which can be pronounced but which does not represent a meaningful word. For example, *lar, bic, ral.*

norm A standard or representative value for a group.

normal curve A bilaterally symmetrical, bell-shaped curve on a graph, which indicates a normal frequency distribution.

normal frequency distribution A distribution such that most of the cases fall midway between the two extremes, with fewer and fewer cases as either extreme is approached.

nostalgia Homesickness.

observation A method used in psychology to gather data; usually done by someone trained in the procedure.

obsessive-compulsive Describes psychoneurotic behavior characterized by preoccupation with unwanted ideas and persistent impulses to repeat certain acts over and over.

operant conditioning The strengthening of a given response by immediately presenting a reinforcing stimulus if (and only if) the response occurs.

ophthalmograph An instrument used to record the eye movements of an individual as he reads.

opinion The verbal expression of an attitude. A conclusion or judgment based on grounds admittedly insufficient to produce certainty.

ordinal position The place of an individual in the family as determined by birth order: first child, second child, and so on.

organic disorder A mental disorder which can be attributed to damage to or disease in the body, especially the nervous system.

organism Any living thing capable of maintaining its existence by itself. Organisms may be divided into two classes, plants and animals. In psychology the term almost always refers to animals.

overlearning Learning in which practice goes beyond the point of bare, required mastery.

panic A rather sudden, highly emotional reaction of fear.

paradoxical sleep The first stage of sleep, in which an individual is only slightly asleep according to EEG records and yet is difficult to arouse when having rapid eye movements (REM).

paranoid reactions Reactions characterized by persistent, systematized delusions of grandeur, persecution, and reference (the individual believes, without justification, that people are talking about him or doing things to him).

parapsychology A branch of study concerned with phenomena that are generally considered very unusual, fantastic, and even allegedly supranormal: trances, telepathy, clairvoyance, apparitions, mediumistic phenomena, and so on.

parasympathetic nervous system A division of the autonomic system concerned with maintaining ordinary body functions. It usually works in opposition to the sympathetic nervous system.

parental love The love of parents for their children.

paresis, general An organic psychosis resulting from syphilitic infection of the brain. A person suffering from paresis is spoken of as a *paretic*.

peer A person considered to be one's equal, or a companion or associate of about the same age or ability.

percentile The position of a score or other measure in a distribution on the basis of percentages. The point or value in a distribution below which lies the percentage of the group indicated by that number.

perception Sensation plus meaning. The process of getting to know the environment by means of the senses.

performance test A specialized test in which verbal directions play a minimum role.

peripheral nervous system A structural classification for the nerves which branch out from the spinal cord and brain.

personality The unique or individual pattern of a person's life; the fundamental organization of an individual's characteristic adjustment to his environment; that which sets a person apart from other individuals and determines how they respond to him.

phenomenon (plural, *phenomena*) Any observable fact or event.

phenotype The actual, observable characteristic which makes its appearance or is manifested in an individual.

phi phenomenon An illusion in which there is apparent visual movement.

phobia A strong, unreasonable, persistent fear.

pitch The highness or lowness of a sound as determined chiefly by the vibration frequency.

pituitary gland An endocrine gland, located on the underside of the brain, secreting several hormones which influence growth, sex development, and metabolism.

placebo Any preparation that contains no medicine but is given to an individual who believes that he is receiving a medicine.

plateau In a learning graph, an intermediate period of little or no apparent progress preceded and followed by periods of measurable progress.

platonic love (or **friendship**) A social relationship between a man and a woman that does not involve romantic affection, although in time it may come to do so.

popularity The state of being pleasing to, admired by, or esteemed by many persons.

positive correlation A statistical relationship which shows that as one variable increases in value, the other variable also increases.

precognition The "perception" of a future event through extrasensory means and without rational inference.

preconscious A psychoanalytic term referring to past events of which the individual can become aware when desired.

prejudice An attitude, either for or against a given social question, which prevents one from evaluating new evidence dispassionately.

prestige The attribute of being very favorably regarded by one's associates so that one is influential. Often implies glamour to adolescents.

proactive inhibition The tendency for present learning to interfere with the recall of later learned material. (See **retroactive inhibition.**)

procrastination An escape or withdrawal mechanism which gives an individual temporary relief from a distressful situation by postponing his attack on a task.

programed book A teaching device, combining modern principles of learning with traditional teaching methods, in which material to be learned is broken up into a series of prearranged simple steps. Such a book is so arranged that correct responses are reinforced immediately.

programed learning Learning from material arranged in a series of sequential steps which enable the learner to proceed with a minimum of error and with a maximum of reinforcement.

projection A defense mechanism in which an individual attributes to others his own unethical motives or thoughts, or places the blame for his difficulties upon others.

projective technique A method of evaluating personality in which an individual externalizes his ideas, emotional states, and motives by attributing them in a free and unrestricted manner to other individuals or objects in the environment, for instance, telling what he "sees" in ink blots or in a given picture.

propaganda Any organized attempt to influence attitudes—that is, to spread particular ideas or beliefs. Advertising is a very common example of propaganda.

pseudo- (as a prefix) False, pretended.

pseudogroup effect Falsely attributing certain results to group influence when no group communication has occurred.

psychiatry A division of the body of medical knowledge pertaining to the diagnosis, care, and treatment of persons suffering from both mild and severe mental disorders. A *psychiatrist* is a physician specializing in the study and treatment of mental disorders.

psychoanalysis A system of psychological theory and treatment devised by Sigmund Freud.

psychodrama A spontaneous play in which individuals act out situations relevant to their personal problems.

psychokinesis The subdivision of parapsychology in which it is said that the thoughts of an individual influence the activity of some physical object or the outcome of some event.

psychological feedback Knowledge of results. The process of providing the individual with information as to the correctness of previous responses so that he can make adjustments in his behavior. (Also, *feed-back* is used to indicate the return of impulses to a control center of the nervous system.)

psychology The science that studies the behavior of organisms.

psychoneurosis (See **neurosis**.)

psychophysics The study of the relationships between the physical qualities of stimuli and their consequent sensory experiences.

psychosis A serious prolonged mental disorder. Popularly spoken of as insanity, although this term should be reserved for legal usage. The individual having a psychosis is said to be *psychotic*.

psychosomatic disorder An illness in which physical disturbances, such as ulcers and allergies, are attributable to or aggravated by prolonged emotional disturbances.

psychotherapy The treatment of disorders by psychological methods.

punishment Any form of unpleasant or painful stimulation applied to an experimental subject for nonperformance of a response which the experimenter has chosen as the correct response. Popularly, it is any penalty inflicted upon a person or animal for wrongdoing.

pupillometrics A method of studying emotional reactions to pleasant and unpleasant stimuli by measuring the size of the pupil of the subject's eye when stimuli are presented. A pleasant stimulus causes the pupil to enlarge; an unpleasant stimulus results in contraction.

quartile One of the points in a distribution by which the distribution is divided into fourths. The 75th, 50th, and 25th percentiles. Sometimes used to denote the quarter—that is, the interval.

rapid eye movements (REM) The movements of an individual's eyes which occur when he is asleep and usually indicate that he is dreaming.

rapport A comfortable, unconstrained, and cooperative relationship between individuals, as in an interviewing or testing situation.

rating The assigning of a rank or score to an individual. Also, an individual's position in a scale of values. A **rating scale** provides a uniform method of securing judgments of an individual's personality traits.

rationalization The process of justifying conduct or opinions by inventing socially acceptable reasons. The rationalizer may not realize that he is explaining his behavior in terms of socially approved and high-sounding reasons instead of real reasons.

reaction formation A defense mechanism in which an individual's expressed attitudes and his behavior are in the opposite direction from his basic, socially disapproved motives.

reaction time The interval of time between the beginning of a stimulus and the beginning of a voluntary response to it.

reasoning A form of thinking in which one attempts to solve a present problem on the basis of general principles derived from elements in two or more previous experiences. A form of thinking in which experiences are organized in such a way that conclusions can be reached which are consistent with all known relevant facts.

recessive characteristic A characteristic that is latent and does not appear in the first generation of descendants, although it may appear in subsequent generations. A characteristic that does not appear in the presence of the corresponding dominant characteristic.

reflex A relatively simple, unlearned, involuntary response to a stimulus.

regression A defense mechanism in which a frustrated individual retreats to a less mature, and usually less adequate, way of meeting his problems.

reinforcement In classical or Pavlovian conditioning, presentation of the unconditioned stimulus immediately following the conditioned stimulus, such as giving an animal an electric shock immediately following the sounding of a bell. In operant or instrumental conditioning, the strengthening of a response when it leads to satisfaction, typically a reward of some kind. If the reinforcement does not directly satisfy a need but had previously been associated with such satisfaction, the term *secondary reinforcement* is used. Reinforcement is said to be *positive* if its presentation strengthens a response and *negative* if its removal strengthens a response.

reliability (as used in statistics) The self-consistency of a test or other measuring device.

repression A defense mechanism by means of which an individual selectively "forgets" unpleasant or undesirable situations that, remembered, would result in feelings of shame, pain, or guilt.

research Any systematic, careful, firsthand observation of phenomena in order to understand better the constitution or operation of the environment.

response Any organic process involving activity of a muscle or gland and resulting from stimulation. A reaction.

retarded individuals Persons of limited intellectual ability, usually classified under three headings: (1) *Mildly retarded.* Individuals who can take care of their personal needs and can often make a fairly satisfactory adjustment in the community, especially if given some social guidance. Formerly referred to as *morons,* they have IQ's that range from about 50 to 70, and they are educable. (2) *Moderately retarded.* Individuals who can learn to take care of themselves to a limited extent and can do some useful work but need constant supervision. Formerly referred to as *imbeciles,* their IQ ranges from about 35 to 49, and most are educable. (3) *Severely retarded.* Individuals who are of such low intellectual ability that they are unable to care for their personal needs or make any kind of adequate social adjustment. Formerly referred to as *idiots,* their IQ's range from about 34 down to as low as can be measured, and they are trainable. The most extreme cases (IQ's 20 and below) are known as *profoundly retarded.*

retention Persistent aftereffect of an experience, which may result in modified subsequent experience; a holding onto what has been learned.

retinal disparity The difference in the two images projected onto the retinas of the right and left eyes. This slight difference in the viewing angle of the two eyes contributes to depth perception.

retroactive inhibition The tendency of later learned material to interfere with the recall of previously learned material. (See **proactive inhibition.**)

ribonucleic acid (RNA) A chemical substance, manufactured by DNA, which helps to implement cellular development and is thought to be important in memory.

role The kind of behavior expected of an individual in a particular group situation. **Role playing** is a technique for teaching principles of interpersonal relationships by having individuals act out parts in a spontaneous play. For example, one student-teacher may play the role of a teacher while the other student-teachers play the roles of children in a school-like situation.

Rorschach test A projective technique for evaluating personality. Ten ink blots as standardized by Hermann Rorschach are presented to the individual under study.

sampling The selection for study of a set of individuals or measurements from the total population or group. In **random sampling** the selection is made solely by chance and in such a way that every individual or measurement has an equal and independent chance of being included in the sample. In **stratified sampling** the total number of individuals or measurements in the population is first divided into a number of nonoverlapping groups and then a random sampling is taken within each group. The number of cases in each group is proportional to that group's representation in the total population.

saturation The degree to which any "color" differs from a gray of the same brightness. Pure colors are highly saturated; such colors as maroon and pink are low in saturation.

scapegoat An individual (or group) that bears the blame for the misdeeds or mistakes of others.

schizophrenia A psychosis characterized by seclusiveness and extreme withdrawal from the realities of life, peculiar mannerisms, emotional blunting, delusions, and disorientation as to time and place. Formerly, this psychosis was referred to as **dementia praecox.**

science Organized or systematic knowledge. Usually applied to some specific field of knowledge.

secondary reinforcement When, as a result of being associated with a primary reinforcement, some object or event becomes itself a reinforcer.

self concept The view that an individual has of himself. In Freudian terms, his ego.

senility Mental and physiological damage or injury incident to old age.

sensation The physiological arousal of a sense organ by a stimulus. Sensation does not involve organization, meaning, or association.

sensory deprivation Making it physiologically impossible for an organism to use one or more of its senses or placing it in an environment where there is practically no sensory stimulation.

serial learning Learning responses in a prescribed sequence; verbatim learning of poetry or prose or a list of words or syllables; learning motor activities in a prescribed order.

short-term memory The process of initial and brief storage of sensory information, which is accessible to immediate recall.

sibling rivalry A child's feelings of hostility and jealousy resulting from his inability to share parental affection and recognition with a brother or sister, regardless of respective ages.

siblings Offspring of the same parents, regardless of age or sex of such offspring.

size constancy The tendency of a known object to appear to be the same size regardless of how close or far away it is.

sociodrama A spontaneously acted short play in which the members of a group act out the roles of the characters in the play, thus helping the group to study some problem of interpersonal behavior.

socioeconomic A term used in referring to an individual's environment with respect to the very closely related factors of social relationships and general financial status.

sociometry The study of the interpersonal relations of a group by having each member express an opinion about every other member. A diagram of the interaction among group members is called a *sociogram.*

sour-grapes rationalization A form of rationalization in which a person says that he does not want that which he cannot have or achieve.

species-specific behavior Behavior characteristic of the great majority of the members of a given species acting under the same or highly similar circumstances. This term is coming to replace the term *instinctive behavior.*

spontaneous recovery The reappearance of a conditioned response after a rest period following extinction but without further reinforcement.

statistics The mathematical procedures for gathering, analyzing, and interpreting data. Statistical procedures are often used in the design of experiments. Also, used to refer to classified facts or data.

status An individual's position and degree of acceptance in a group.

stereoscope An optical instrument which blends two flat pictures taken from slightly different angles so that a solid object is perceived in relief.

stereotype A preconceived idea of the appearance or behavior of individuals of a given group; racial, political occupational, etc. *Stereotyped behavior* is behavior which is not altered by circumstances.

stimulus An energy or energy change acting on a receptor (sense organ) and exciting it. A situation or event inside or outside an organism which results in activity of some kind.

stimulus generalization A situation in which an organism associates one stimulus with a similar stimulus and because of the similarity responds to the second stimulus in the same way that he responds to the original.

subject The person or animal exposed to any kind of experimental treatment and whose behavior is then observed and measured. The responses of the subject are the dependent variable of the experiment.

sublimation The transfer or redirection of emotionally aroused energy, especially sexual energy, into more socially approved forms of creative or social expression.

subliminal Below the threshold. Subliminal stimuli are so weak that the individual is not aware of their influence on his behavior. *Subliminal perception* is perception of stimulus cues of which the individual is not conscious.

superego A psychoanalytic term for that which is commonly called "conscience" and which criticizes the ego. The ethical or moral aspects of personality.

surrogate An organism (or object) which serves as a substitute for some other organism in the life of an animal or human being.

sweet-lemons rationalization A form of rationalization in which a person says that what he has is just what he wants.

sympathetic nervous system A division of the autonomic system which becomes active in emergency or emotional situations and which usually functions in opposition to the parasympathetic system.

tact The ability to say or do what is best or most suitable under delicate or difficult circumstances. The ability to adjust socially to others so as to promote friendly relations and avoid antagonizing situations.

task-oriented group A group whose primary purpose is to perform a specific job or task.

teaching machine A somewhat mechanical auto-instructional device in which the learner indicates his answer to a question or his solution of a problem and then is reinforced immediately. The material presented for learning may be determined by the learner's performance. (See **programed book** for a device based on the same principles but in book form.)

telepathy The alleged communication of thought from one person to another by other than the usual means of sensory stimulation.

theory A logically organized principle, based on considerable data, proposed as an explanation for what is observed. A theory is based on more evidence than is an hypothesis.

therapy Treatment.

thinking Implicit activity by means of which a person or animal manipulates past experiences (not physically present to the senses) through the use of symbols. Much thinking is subvocal or covert speech behavior.

thrill A sudden, intense, and usually pleasant emotional experience involving suspense. In the experience there is a possible danger or risk, but at the same time there is the chance of escape or of winning.

thyroid gland A very important endocrine gland, located in the front of the neck close to the larynx (in the upper part of the windpipe), which influences metabolism and growth. The hormone secreted by this gland is thyroxin, largely iodine in content.

tic A twitch of a muscle or muscle group, especially in the face. It is not subject to voluntary control.

timbre The quality of a sound as determined by the complexity of the sound waves, that is, by the pattern of overtones.

tolerance Mutual understanding and harmony among divergent groups. A willingness to bear with and appreciate those whose views differ from one's own views.

tone A sound whose stimulus consists of a regular wave.

trait A relatively constant pattern or dimension of behavior. The characteristics which indicate similarities between people. Those traits which are characteristic of most persons are spoken of as *primary traits*.

transfer, transfer of training, transfer of learning The effect of prior learning on later learning. If the prior learning facilitates the later learning, there is said to be *positive transfer*. If the prior learning interferes with the later learning, there is said to be *negative transfer*.

type A class of persons alleged to have a particular trait. Psychologists seldom use the word.

unconditioned response (UCR) The response elicited by the original (unconditioned) stimulus at the beginning of a conditioning process.

unconditioned stimulus (UCS) The original stimulus that elicits the desired response before the conditioning process begins.

unconscious The absence of an awareness of some desires, experiences, concepts, and information which, under ordinary circumstances, are not generally available on the conscious level.

validity (as used in statistics) The extent to which a test or other measuring device measures that which it is supposed to measure.

visible spectrum Hues that are visible to the eye arranged according to wavelengths, with violet being a short wavelength and red a long wavelength.

worry Persistent nonadjustive thinking about the past, present, and future. A chronic subacute form of fear.

Index

Emancipation, 398–99, 586. *See also* Adolescent, Maturity, Parents.

Emotion, 180–82, 345, 586–87; conflicts, 12; control, 330–33, 358; development, 177; disturbance, 22, 273; effect on digestion, 276–77; facial expression, 277; helpful reactions, 329–30; immaturity, 529; innate, 178–79; laboratory production, 274; maturity, 333; measurement, 274–75, 277–80, 282; problems, 372–404; response to stress, 277–78; study, 5; unpleasant, 345

Emotional behavior, 330–33, 358, 453

Emotional maturity, 587

Empathy, 491, 587

Endocrine gland, 263, 587. *See also* Ductless gland.

Endomorph, 145

Environment, 248, 587; euthenics, 249; influence, 248; intellectual stimulation, 221; Intelligence Quotient and, 234–36; learning, 284–305; pre-birth, 231; social, 242. *See also* Heredity, Sensory deprivation.

Epilepsy, 259. *See also* Convulsive disorders.

Equilibrium, 308

Ergograph, 553, 587

Etiquette, 360

Eugenics, 234, 248–49, 587

Euthenics, 248–49, 587

Examinations, 126–30; psychological study, 9–10; recall and recognition, 93–94; stress and, 209; techniques, 126–30. *See also* Learning, Study.

Exclusive group, 477–78, 587. *See also* Small groups.

Executives, 365–66

Experiment, 9–15; control group, 10; hypothesis, 9, 11; importance, 14; laboratory, 15; method, 10; procedures, 9–11; selective breeding, 231–32; thinking as work, 559; use of animals, 11–14; use of evidence from, 14

Experimental group, 10, 587

Experimental psychologists, 562–63

Explicit (overt) behavior, 587

Extinction, 48–49, 56, 587. *See also* Learning, Response.

Extrasensory perception (ESP), 29, 32, 587

Extrinsic reward, 456–57, 587

Extroversion, 146, 587; blame and work activity, 460

Eye movements, 286–87

Eye muscles, 309

Fairy tales, 469–70. *See also* Fear.

Family, 442–78; changing roles in, 489; child's ordinal position, 405

Family conflict, 393–98, 403; grandparents, 426. *See also* Adolescent, Sibling rivalry.

Family history, 232–33, 250. *See also* Environment, Heredity.

Fantasy, 117, 587

Fear, 180–82, 331–32, 474; adult imparting, 468; causes of children's, 465–66; counteracting child's, 467–68; death, 464–65; discipline and, 469, 471; experimental induction, 467; learning, 464. *See also* Conditioning, Emotion.

Feeble-mindedness *see* Mental retardation

Feedback *see* Psychological feedback

Feelings, 587. *See also* Emotion.

Figure-ground relationship, 478, 587. *See also* Small groups.

Filial love, 449, 587. *See also* Family.

Follower, 368–69. *See also* Leader.

Foreconscious, 21

Forgetting, 96–99. *See also* Extinction, Learning, Repression.

Foster parents, 450–51

Frame, 587; defined, 60

Fraternal twins, 237–38, 587

Fraternities, 483. *See also* Small groups.

Frequency distribution, 140, 571–74

Frequency polygon, 573

Freud, Sigmund, 21, 187

Friendship, 109, 328–29, 370, 447, 587–88; animal experiments, 348; defined, 347; development, 351–52; human infant experiments, 349–50; sex differences, 351–52. *See also* Love.

Frustrating situations, 321–22

Frustration, 174, 534, 588; defined, 320; delinquency, 523; emotional response, 328–33; experiments, 320–21; overcoming, 325–28; responses, 325–44; tolerance, 322

Fugue, 415

Functional disorder, 406, 588; among primitives, 419; causes, 420–21; manic-depressive, 420–22; neurotic behavior, 410; paranoid reactions, 420. *See also* Neurosis, Psychosis.

Functional psychosis, 418–24

Galton, Sir Francis, 219

Galvanic skin response (GSR), 275–76, 588

Galvanometer, 276

Gambling, 379–83, 403–04, 588

Gangs, 526–27; characteristics, 527. *See also* Delinquency.

Generalization, 52, 588; definition, 50
Generosity error, 150
Genes, 228–29, 588; inheritance, 230
Genetics, 228, 588
Genius, 206, 218, 588. *See also* Intelligence quotient.
Genotype, 228, 234, 588. *See also* Heredity, Phenotype.
Gerontology, 588
Gesell, Arnold, 168, 169
Giantism, 264
Gifted, 588; children, 218–20
Glamor, 274. *See also* Popularity.
Glands, 262–67, 273
"Glittering generality," 519
Goiter, 264
Gonads, 266, 588
Gordon Personal Profile and Personal Inventory, 163
Grades *see* Examinations, Motivation
Grand mal, 431
Graphic rating scale, 149
Graphs, 191; changes in, 190–91; common emotions (worry), 181; developmental, 167; emotional development, 179; extinction and spontaneous recovery, 49; frequency distribution, 141, 142; frequency polygon, 573; histogram, 573–74; industrial production, 556; intelligence scores, 190; kymograph, 554; learning, 81, 83, 88, 89, 91, 95; normal distribution, 574–75; scatter diagram, 577–78
Group *see* Leader, Small group
Group cohesiveness, 486–87
Group dynamics, 475, 588
Group influences, 502–05. *See also* Conformity.
Group pressure, 503
Group therapy, 436, 588. *See also* Alcoholics Anonymous.
Growth, 264
Guidance counselor, 7, 547

Habit, 453; defined, 57; faulty emotional, 410; intermittent reinforcement, 57; thought, 412
Hallucination, 297–98, 313, 588
Halo effect, 150–51, 589
Handicap, 192, 373–74; deafness, 305–06; response, to physical, 334
Hearing, 300–01
Height-weight patterns, 170–71
Heredity, 226–41, 252, 589; controlling, 233–34; mental ability, 240–41; mental retardation, 217; schizophrenia, 422; studies, 231–34
Heuristic, 23, 589; defined, 4

Histogram, 573–74
Hitler, Adolf, 517, 518
Hobby, 335, 558
Home influence, 514–15
Homesickness, 400–03
Hormones, 263, 265, 589
Hue, 287, 589. *See also* Color.
Hydrotherapy, 435, 589
Hyper- (prefix), 589
Hypnosis, 21, 23–29, 98, 259, 516, 589; in animals, 28; anesthesia, 27–28; behavior, 25–26; definition, 23–24; fallacies, 25; inducing, 24; subjects, 25; uses, 27–28
Hypo- (prefix), 589
Hypochondriac, 411
Hypothalamus, 273, 589. *See also* Emotion.
Hypothesis, 589; defined, 9. *See also* Experiment.
Hysteria *see* Conversion reaction

Id, 21, 22, 23, 187, 589
Identical twins, 169, 192, 237–41, 589; reared in different environments, 239–40
Identification, 336, 346, 483, 589
Idiot, 216, 597
Illusion, 297, 589; experiment, 315–16; practical applications, 298–300
Imagination, 589, defined, 117
Imbecile, 216, 597. *See also* Mental retardation.
Implicit (covert) behavior, 66–67, 103, 589. *See also* Thinking.
Imprinting, 244–45, 251, 589
Imprisonment, 530; effect, 531. *See also* Crime.
Inattention, 96–97
Incentive, 554. *See also* Motivation.
Inclusive group, 477, 589. *See also* Small groups.
Incubation, 111–12, 589
Independence, 173–74
Independent variable, 9, 10, 89, 589–90
Indoklon therapy, 436, 590
Inductive reasoning, 196, 590
Inferiority feelings, 372–77, 403; delinquency, 524, 528; lying, 461; symptoms, 375–76
Ink-blot (Rorschach) technique, 160, 597
Insane asylum *see* Mental hospitals
Insanity, 590. *See also* Psychosis.
Insight, 590; animal experiments, 65; causes, 66–68; character, 66; defined, 65; human, 65–66
Inspiration, 112, 590. *See also* Creativity.
Instinct *see* Species-specific behavior
Institute for Propaganda Analysis, 519
Institutionalization, 350–51

Mannerisms, 361, 371

Marital love, 591

Marriage, 109, 186, 329, 386; courtship, 442–45; desire for children and stability, 448; factors for happiness in, 444–45, 449; problems, 445–47; romantic love in, 445–49; stable, 110; teen-age, 449

Masculine role, 390, 391

Mass media, 515, 591

Massed practice, 82; nonserial learning, 84

Maturation, 166, 591; defined, 242; emotional, 333; friendly behavior, 348; human learning, 245–46; institutional rearing of infants, 349; social, 184. *See also* Behavior, Development.

Maturity, 394; emotional, 333; mental, 205–06

Maze learning, 43–45, 591

Mean (average), 78, 141, 576, 591

Meaningfulness, 80–81. *See also* Learning efficiency.

Measurement, 8, 576–77; cheating, 157–59; group cohesiveness, 486–87; intelligence, 194–202; intelligence tests, 198–212; learning, 88–91; mental abilities, 189; methods, 8; muscular work, 553–55; normal frequency distribution, 140–42; personality, 148–62; retention, 92, 95, 98; sampling, 512–13; variability, 577; vocational interest, 550–52. *See also* Statistics, Tests.

Median, 141, 576–77, 591; defined, 199

Medicare, 427

Memorizing, 84, 86, 95, 196

Memory, 414; amnesia, 415; auditory, 201; biochemical analysis, 98–99; types, 99

Memory factor, 196

Memory trace, 98–99, 591

Mendel, Gregor, 226–27

Mendel's laws, 226–27

Mental abilities, 195–97.

Mental age (MA), 199, 203, 204, 591. *See also* Intelligence Quotient.

Mental deficiency, 591. *See also* Mental retardation.

Mental development, 187; problems in study, 187

Mental fatigue, 559, 562

Mental health, 4, 198, 319, 373, 400, 406, 437–38, 558, 591–92; child rearing, 452–72; defined, 320; delinquents, 523, 528–30; fairy tales, 474; frustration, 320–22; mob violence and, 536; old age, 425–28; symptoms of children's difficulties, 452–53. *See also* Child guidance, Punishment.

Mental hospitals, 407, 409–10, 433–37, 564, 592

Mental hygiene, 516, 592. *See also* Mental health.

Mental illness, 25, 529, 406–39; age incidence, 407; curability, 417–18; draft rejections, 407; hypnosis in, 28; need for research, 410; social environment, 420; as social problem, 406–10; statistics, 407–08; treatment, 408–09, 433–37; types, 406; use of drugs in, 435. *See also* Neurosis, Psychosis.

Mental retardation, 222, 523–24, 592; causes, 217–18; family-tree studies, 232–33; mild, 214–16; moderate, 213–14; severe, 213

Mesmer, Franz Anton, 24

Mesmerism, 24, 592. *See also* Hypnosis.

Mesomorph, 145

Midpoint, 572. *See also* Class interval.

Migratory birds, 35, 36, 37, 38

Mind, 3, 4, 17, 21, 592

Mind That Found Itself, A, 408

Mnemonic devices, 86–87, 101, 592

Mob, 534–36, 592

Mode, 141, 577, 592

Mongoloid, 228

Monotony, 557–58. *See also* Boredom.

Mood, 358, 592

Morale, 563, 592; democratic groups, 488; group, 487

Moron, 216, 597

Mother, 451; monkey surrogate, 348–49, 450

Motivation, 75, 241–44, 592; achievement, 220–21; boredom, 90; competition, 78; defined, 76; interest, 77–78, 549; IQ and, 220–21, 205; knowledge of result as, 60–64, 76, 80–82; payment systems, 557; rivalry, 78–79. *See also* Emotion, Learning, Psychoanalysis.

Motor development, 173–77; sequence, 176–77

Multiple personality, 415

Music, 302

"Name-calling," 519. *See also* Propaganda.

National Association for Mental Health, 408

National Committee for Mental Hygiene, 408

National Mental Health Act *(1946),* 408–09

Nature and nurture *see* Heredity, Environment

Negative correlation, 147, 578, 592

Nerve impulse, 592

"Nervous breakdown," 412. *See also* Neurosis.

Rationalization, 341–44, 388, 596; group, 343–44
Reaction formation, 596
Reaction time, 260–62, 596
Reading, 285–87; eye movements, 286–87; maturation, 246
Reasoning, 119–22, 596; children's, 119–20; college students', 120–21; deductive, 121–22; group vs. individual, 122; inductive, 121
Reasoning factor, 196
Recall, 93. *See also* Memory.
Recessive characteristics, 227, 596
Recognition, 93–94. *See also* Memory.
Reflex, 35, 43, 176, 596; defined, 33. *See also* Classical conditioning, Nervous system.
Reformation, 531–32. *See also* Imprisonment, Punishment.
Regression, 338, 596
Reinforcement, 52, 53, 54, 56–58, 62, 88, 459, 596; defined, 49–50; group feedback, 492. *See also* Learning, Operant conditioning.
Relearning, 92–93
Reliability, 581–82, 596
Remembering, 92–96; methods, 93–94. *See also* Forgetting, Memorizing.
Repression, 98, 337, 596
Research, 596; cross-cultural, 539–40; defined, 3. *See also* Behavior, Environment, Heredity, Intelligence, Learning, Measurement, Personality measurement, Psychology, Vocation, Work.
Response, 9, 45–47, 596; development, 166; extinguished, 56; frustration, 345; learned, 56. *See also* Conditioning, Reinforcement, Stimulus.
Responsibility in children, 454–55
Retarded individuals, 212–18, 597
Retention, 92, 94, 100, 597; general ideas, 95; sleep and, 95–96, 100; understanding 124. *See also* Learning efficiency, Memory.
Retinal (binocular) disparity, 310, 597. *See also* Perception.
Retirement, 177, 186
Retroactive inhibition, 97, 597
Revised Stanford-Binet, 219
Reward, 456–57; extrinsic, 456–57; intrinsic, 457; vs. punishment, 459–60. *See also* Reinforcement.
Ribonucleic acid (RNA), 98–99, 229, 597
Risk, 377, 378
Role, 488, 597; purposes in assuming, 489–90
Role playing, 367, 404, 597; leader, 367; psychodrama, 436; small groups, 488–90. *See also* Leadership.
Romantic love, 347, 442–45; characteristics, 443, 444. *See also* Marriage.
Rorschach, Hermann, 160; ink-blot test, 597
Rote learning, 84, 86, 95, 196

Salivation *see* Classical conditioning
Sampling, 152, 597; random, 512, 597; stratified, 512, 597
Saturation, 288, 597
Scapegoat, 343, 597. *See also* Propaganda.
Scatter diagram, 577–78
Schizophrenia, 422–23, 598; physiological factor, 423
School dances, 388
Science, 4, 5, 539, 598; defined, 2–3
Secondary reinforcement, 57–58, 598
Security, 539; parental love and, 450; small groups and, 483. *See also* War.
Self-concept, 22, 173, 187, 598; body development, 170; learned, 188; motor development, 174–76. *See also* Ego.
Self-respect, 358–60
Selfishness, 461; and unhappy marriage, 446–47
Senile psychosis, 425–26
Senility, 425, 598
Sensation, 598; defined, 285; perception and, 284–85
Sensory adaptation, 285
Sensory cues, 30, 32
Sensory deprivation, 311–14; 598; effects, 312–14. *See also* Brainwashing.
Serial learning, 598
Sex roles, 390–93. *See also* Courtship.
Sheldon, W. H., 145. *See also* Personality.
Short-term memory (STM), 99, 598
Shorthand, 548
Sibling rivalry, 395–98, 598. *See also* Family conflict.
Siblings, 238, 598
Simon, Théodore, 198
Sincerity, 357
Size constancy, 310, 598
Skewed curve, 573
Skin senses, 307–08
Skinner, B. F., 53–54
Skinner box, 53. *See also* Learning, Operant conditioning.
Sleep, 24, 271–73; experiment, 9, 11, 100; learning in, 95–96. *See also* Dreams, Rapid eye movements.
Slogan, 520–21
Small groups, 486–88; atmosphere, 488;